Accounting

Walter B. Meigs, Ph.D., C.P.A.

Professor of Accounting
University of Southern California

Charles E. Johnson, Ph.D., C.P.A.

Late Professor of Accounting
University of Oregon

A. N. Mosich, Ph.D., C.P.A.

Professor of Accounting
University of Southern California

Financial Accounting

Library of Congress Catalog Card Number 71-112840

07-041350-9

56789 KPKP 75432

This book was set in News Gothic by York Graphic Services, Inc., and printed on permanent paper and bound by Kingsport Press. The designer was Merrill Haber. The editors were Richard F. Dojny, Michael Elia, and Sonia Sheldon. William P. Weiss supervised the production.

Preface

This short text is intended as a one-semester introduction to accounting. It is suitable for courses of 3 to 4 semester-hours' credit or, for schools on the quarter system, courses of 4 to 6 quarter-hours' credit. To shorten the course still further, if necessary, Chapters 6, 14, and 17 may be omitted, without loss of continuity.

The reduction in length from the conventional introductory accounting text has been accomplished by minimizing procedural details and by concentrating on financial accounting as a unified body of knowledge. We have placed primary emphasis on the responsibility of the modern corporation to do an adequate job of financial reporting to investors and others outside the corporate entity. However, management's use of accounting data is by no means neglected.

We believe this approach will have relevance for nearly every college student, regardless of whether he elects to take additional courses in accounting. The business administration student *not* majoring in accounting will gain a well-rounded knowledge of financial accounting in preparation for a second, terminal course devoted to managerial accounting. The non-business student (especially from such fields as economics and public administration) will find that this short book will help him to understand the accounting concepts in today's economic environment. In some schools the tightening of curricula has led faculty members to feel that it is no longer feasible for accounting majors to devote a full year to introductory accounting. These schools may prefer that accounting majors complete this short one-semester book and then move into courses in intermediate accounting and cost accounting.

Many graduate schools of business administration offer streamlined introductory courses in accounting for students whose undergraduate work has been in other fields. This text has sufficient theoretical depth to interest the mature student, and also offers a wide range of difficulty in problem material so that the instructor can shape the course to meet the needs of classes of different degrees of maturity and ability.

Among the special features of this book are the use of the corporate form of organization as the basic model in illustrations and problems and the inclusion of a *demonstration problem* at the end of nearly every chapter. A complete solution to each demonstration problem appears in the back of the textbook. By studying the demonstration problems and their solutions, the student will strengthen his ability to apply theoretical concepts to other problem situations.

An abundance of questions, exercises, and problems will be found at the end of each chapter. This material has been class-tested; it illustrates the application of accounting principles to realistic business situations, with a minimum of time-consuming, repetitive, drill-type problems.

Supplementary materials

A full assortment of supplementary materials accompanies this text. These materials include:

1. A set of six *Achievement Tests* and a *Comprehensive Examination.* Each test covers two or three chapters; the *Comprehensive Examination* covers the entire text and may be used as a final examination.

2. A *Self-study Guide.* Written by the authors of the textbook, this *Self-study Guide* enables the student to measure his progress by immediate feedback. The *Self-study Guide* includes an outline of the most important points in each chapter, an abundance of objective questions, and several short exercises for each chapter. In the back of the *Self-study Guide* are answers to questions and solutions to exercises to help the student evaluate his understanding of the subject. The *Self-study Guide* will also be useful in classroom discussions and for review by students before examinations.

3. Working Papers. A package of *partially-filled-in working papers* for the problem material is published separately from the text. On these work sheets, the problem headings and some preliminary data have been entered to save students much of the mechanical pencil-pushing inherent in problem assignments. Also available is a package of specially designed *blank accounting forms* with a number of sheets of each type appropriate for a typical semester's assignments.

4. Practice Set. A practice set, in which the model firm is a corporation, is designed for use after covering the first six chapters of the book.

5. Check List of Key Figures for Problems. This list is available in quantity to instructors who wish to distribute key figures to students. The purpose of the check list is to aid students in verifying their problem solutions and in discovering their own errors.

6. Transparencies of Problem Solutions. A visual aid prepared by the publisher for the instructor who wishes to display in a classroom the complete solutions to most problems.

In the development of problem material for this book, special attention has been given to the inclusion of problems of varying length and difficulty. By referring to the time estimates, difficulty ratings, and problem descriptions in the *Solutions Manual,* the instructor can choose problems that best fit the level, scope, and emphasis of the course he is offering.

Walter B. Meigs
Charles E. Johnson
A. N. Mosich

Contents

The General Journal. Showing the Source of Postings in Ledger Accounts. The Running Balance Form of Account. Ledger Accounts. Proving the Ledgers. Variations in Special Journals. Direct Posting From Invoices.

Mechanical Data Processing

Unit Record for Each Transaction. Use of Office Equipment in a Manual Data Processing System. Simultaneous Preparation of Documents, Journals, and Ledgers. Accounting Machines. Punched Cards and Tabulating Equipment. Automated Data Processing.

Electronic Data Processing

EDP in the Field of Business. Elements of an EDP System. Input Devices. Output Devices. Processing Operations in the Computer. Differences between Mechanical and Electronic Data-processing Systems. Dependability of EDP Equipment. Accounting Applications of the Computer. Do Computers Make Decisions? EDP Advantages Other Than Speed.

Questions
Exercises
Problems

Single Proprietorships

Owner's Equity Accounts for a Single Proprietorship. Closing the Books. Financial Statements and Work Sheet for Single Proprietorship.

Partnerships

Features of a Partnership. Advantages and Disadvantages of a Partnership. Partnership Accounting. Opening the Books. Additional Investments. Withdrawals by Partners. Closing the Books of a Partnership. Income Statement and Income Distribution for a Partnership. Statement of Partners' Capitals. Other Aspects of Partnership Accounting.

Corporations

Advantages of the Corporate Form of Organization. Disadvantages of the Corporate Form of Organization. Formation of a Corporation. Sources of Corporate Capital.

Authorization and Issuance of Capital Stock

Capital Stock Outstanding. Preferred and Common Stock. Par Value. Issuance of Capital Stock. The Underwriting of Stock Issues. Market Price of Common Stock. Stock Issued for Assets Other Than Cash. Par Value and No-par Value Stock. Subscriptions to Capital Stock. Special Records of Corporations.

Demonstration Problem
Questions
Exercises
Problems

Financial Accounting

1

Accounting: The basis for business decisions

Accounting has often been called the "language of business" because people in the business world—owners, managers, bankers, brokers, attorneys, engineers, investors—use accounting terms and concepts to describe the events that make up the existence of businesses of every kind. It is usually true that as a person gains familiarity with a language he begins to understand better the country in which that language is spoken and the customs and actions of people who speak it. Similarly, as you gain a knowledge of accounting you will increase your understanding of the way businesses operate and the way in which business decisions are made. Finally, a language is a man-made means of communication; languages change gradually to meet the changing needs of society. Accounting, too, is a man-made art, one in which changes and improvements are continually being made in the process of communicating business information.

THE PURPOSE AND NATURE OF ACCOUNTING

The underlying purpose of accounting is to provide financial information about any economic entity, usually a business enterprise. This information is needed by a business manager to help him plan and control the activities of his organization. It is also needed by outsiders—owners, creditors, investors, and the public—who have supplied money to the business or who have some other interest that will be served by information about its financial position and operating results.

To supply this much-needed financial information, it is necessary to create a systematic record of business transactions, in terms of money. In essence, a business is a collection of economic resources devoted to a particular purpose or goal. An orderly description of these resources, their source, and the way in which they are employed to promote a growth in value is a natural starting point. Goods and services are purchased and sold, credit is extended to customers, debts are incurred and repaid, cash is received and expended—these are typical of the events to be recorded. Of course, not all business events can be measured and described in monetary terms. Therefore, we do not show in the accounting records the appointment of a new chief executive or the signing of a labor contract, except as these happenings in turn affect future business transactions.

In addition to compiling a narrative record of events as they occur, we shall also classify various transactions and events into related groups or categories. Classification enables us to reduce a mass of detail into compact and usable form. For example, grouping all transactions in which cash is received or paid out is a logical step in developing useful information about the cash position of the company.

In order to be helpful to anyone, the information we have recorded and classified must be summarized in the form of a report or statement, that is, a concise picture of the significant findings gleaned from the detailed records. We want to show where the business stands financially at the time of our report, and the process by which it has arrived at this position.

These three rather natural and logical steps—*recording, classifying,* and *summarizing*—form the basic process by which accounting information is created. Accounting as we know it today has evolved over a period of several hundred years. During this time certain rules, conventions, and procedures have become accepted as standard. Some of these rules are simply traditional and, like driving on the right side of the road, operate to reduce confusion. Others follow logically from the objectives which accounting is designed to attain. Knowing the rules of accounting construction is a prerequisite to understanding the way accounting information is developed and what it means.

Accounting extends beyond the process of *creating* information. The ultimate objective of accounting is the *use* of this information, its analysis and interpretation. A good accountant is always concerned with the significance of the figures he has produced. He looks for meaningful relationships between events and financial results; he studies the effect of various alternatives; and he searches for significant trends that will throw some light on what will happen in the future.

Interpretation and analysis are not the sole province of the accountant. If managers, investors, and creditors are to make effective use of accounting information, they too must have some understanding of how the figures were put together and what they mean. Strangely enough, an important part of this understanding is to recognize clearly the limitations of accounting reports. A business manager, an investor, or a creditor who lacks training in accounting may fail to appreciate the extent to which accounting information is based upon estimates rather than upon precisely accurate measurements.

Persons with little knowledge of accounting may also fail to understand the difference between accounting and bookkeeping. **Bookkeeping** means the recording of transactions, the record-making phase of accounting. The recording of transactions tends to be mechanical and repetitive; it is only a small part of the field of accounting and probably the simplest part. A person might become a reasonably proficient bookkeeper in a few weeks or months; to become a professional accountant, however, requires several years of study and experience.

The work of accountants

In terms of career opportunities, the field of accounting may be divided into three areas:

1. Private businesses employ accountants to perform accounting functions ranging all the way from bookkeeping to designing accounting systems, preparing various reports and statements, and interpreting the results. The chief accounting officer of a private business of any size is usually called the *controller,* in recognition of the fact that one of the primary uses of accounting data is to aid in controlling business operations. The controller manages the work of the accounting staff. He is also a part of the management team charged with the task of running the business, setting its objectives, and seeing that these objectives are met.

2. Certified public accountants are independent professional persons, comparable to physicians or lawyers, who offer accounting services to clients for a fee. The CPA certificate is a license to practice granted by the state on the basis of a rigorous examination and evidence of practical experience. Although the CPA performs a wide variety of accounting-related services, his principal function is to review the accounting records of a business concern and issue a report in which he expresses his professional opinion as to the fairness of the financial statements. Persons outside the business, who rely upon financial statements for information, attach considerable importance to the CPA's report because they know that it represents the conclusions of an independent expert who has made a thorough review of the accounting records.

The public accounting profession is relatively young; it began in England and dates in the United States from about 1896 when the first CPAs were licensed by the State of New York. In recent years the profession has expanded tremendously because of the increasing demand for accounting services. In addition to auditing, the CPA renders many other services to his clients. He is often called upon to prepare or assist in the preparation of income tax returns, and to design and install accounting systems. He also acts as a consultant on a wide variety of financial and business problems. Among the factors responsible for the spectacular growth of professional accounting have been the increasing size and complexity of business corporations, the growing interest of the general public in stock ownership, the increasing complexity of income and other forms of taxation, and the broadening of governmental regulation of business activity.

3. A third field of accounting is *governmental and institutional accounting.* The officers and elected representatives of the federal, state, and local governments rely on financial information to help them direct the affairs of their agencies just as do the executives of private corporations. Many of the taxes levied by government are based upon accounting results, and governmental units find it advisable to employ accountants to verify tax information submitted by individuals and businesses.

Many governmental accounting problems are similar to those applicable to private industry. In other respects, however, accounting for governmental affairs requires a somewhat different approach because the objective of earning a profit is absent from public affairs. Universities, hospitals, churches, and other nonprofit institutions also follow a pattern of accounting that is similar to governmental accounting.

The work of an accountant employed by a governmental unit or nonprofit enterprise is similar in nature to that performed by both the controller and the public accountant. Many CPAs are in fact employed in this field. Government auditors review the accounting records of various departments and subdivisions and of private businesses which hold government contracts, in much the same way as do independent public accountants. Internal revenue agents perform auditing functions in examining income tax returns and the accounting data on which they are based. Accountants are employed by the Securities and Exchange Commission to aid in a critical review of the financial statements of corporations which offer securities for sale to the public.

Specialized phases of accounting

All business concerns, large and small, in every kind of industry, find it necessary to record transactions and prepare periodic financial statements from accounting records. Within this area of general accounting, or in addition to it, a number of specialized phases of accounting have developed. Among the more important of these are:

Design of accounting systems. Although the same basic accounting principles are applicable to all types of businesses, each enterprise requires an individually tailored set of accounting forms, records, and reports to fit its particular needs. Designing an accounting system and putting it into operation is thus a specialized phase of accounting. With the advent of various accounting machines and electronic data-processing equipment, the problems that arise in creating an effective accounting system have become increasingly complex. On the other hand, once the system is devised and working, machines take much of the drudgery out of the bookkeeping process. Electronic data processing also makes it possible to compile data that would be too costly to gather by hand methods, and increases materially the speed with which reports can be made available to management and to outsiders.

Cost accounting. Knowing the cost of a particular product, a manufacturing process, or any business operation is vital to the efficient management of that business. The phase of accounting particularly concerned with collecting and interpreting cost data has come to be known as *cost accounting.* Determining the cost of anything is not as simple as it appears at first glance, because the term *cost* has many meanings and different kinds of costs are useful for different purposes.

Budgeting. A budget is a plan of financial operations for some future period, expressed in accounting terms. By using a budget, management is able to make comparisons between planned operations and the actual results achieved. A budget is thus an attempt to preview operating results before the actual transactions have taken place. A budget is a particularly valuable tool because it provides each element of the business with a specific goal, and because it gives management a means of measuring the efficiency of performance throughout the company.

Tax accounting. The primary source of revenue for the federal government, and an important source for many state governments, is a tax on the income of individuals and businesses. The computation of taxable income is closely related to the problem of measuring the operating income of a business. As income tax rates have gone up and the determination of taxable income has become more complex, both private and public accountants have devoted more time to the problems of taxation. Tax accounting includes planning business operations in order to minimize the impact of taxes, as well as preparing tax returns.

Auditing. All large corporations, and a great many small companies as well, are audited each year by a CPA firm. This annual audit consists of a systematic investigation of the financial statements and of the underlying accounting records for the purpose of determining whether these financial statements give a fair and dependable picture of financial position and the results of operations.

In addition to retaining CPA firms to make independent annual audits, most large corporations also maintain *internal auditing* departments. The internal auditor, unlike the CPA, is an employee of the company. His responsibility is solely to the management of his company rather than to creditors, stockholders, and other outsiders. The goal of the internal auditor is to aid management by investigating and reporting on accounting, financial, and other operations of the company. It is his job to determine whether the various divisions of the organization are complying with company policies, and whether internal controls designed to protect assets and to prevent fraud are working properly.

Two primary business objectives

The management of every business must keep foremost in its thinking two primary objectives. The first is to earn a profit. The second is to have on hand sufficient funds to pay debts as they fall due.

A business is a collection of resources committed by an individual or group of individuals, who hope that the investment will increase in value. Investment in any given business, however, is only one of a number of alternative investments available. If a concern does not earn as great a profit as might be obtained from alternative investments, its owners will be well advised to sell or terminate the business and invest elsewhere. A firm that continually operates at a loss will quickly exhaust its resources and be forced out of existence. Therefore, in order to operate successfully and to survive, the owners or managers of an enterprise must direct the business in such a way that it will earn a reasonable profit.

Business concerns that have sufficient funds to pay their debts promptly are said to be *solvent.* In contrast, a firm that finds itself unable to meet its obligations as they fall due is called *insolvent.* Solvency must also be ranked as a primary objective of any enterprise, since a firm that is insolvent will be forced by its creditors to close its doors.

Profits and solvency are of course not the only objectives of businessmen. There are many others, such as providing jobs for people, creating new and improved products, providing more goods and services at a lower cost. It is clear, however, that a business cannot hope to accomplish these things unless it meets the two basic tests of survival—operating profitably and staying solvent.

Accounting as the basis for management decisions

How does a business executive know whether his company is earning profits or incurring losses? How does he know whether the company is solvent or insolvent, and whether it will probably be solvent, say, a month from today? The answer to both these questions in one word is *accounting.* Not only is accounting the process by which the profitability and solvency of a firm can be measured, but it provides information needed as a basis for making business decisions that will enable management to guide the firm on a profitable and solvent course.

Stated simply, managing a business is a matter of deciding what should be done, seeing to it that the means are available, and getting people employed in the business to do it. At every step in this process management is faced with alternatives, and every decision to do something or to refrain from doing something involves a choice. Successful managers must make the right choice in at least a majority of situations. In most cases the probability that a good decision will be made depends on the amount and validity of the information that the manager has about the alternatives and their consequences. It is seldom true that all the information needed is either available or obtainable. Often a crystal ball in good working order would be helpful. As a practical matter, however, information which flows from the accounting records, or which can be developed by special analysis of accounting data, constitutes the basis on which a wide variety of business decisions should be made.

What prices should the firm set on its products? If production is increased, what effect will this have on product costs? Will it be necessary to borrow from the bank? How much will costs increase if a pension plan is established for employees? Is it more profitable to produce and sell product A or product B? Shall a given part be made or be bought from suppliers? Should an investment be made in new equipment? All these are examples of decisions that should depend, in part at least, upon accounting information. It might be reasonable to turn the question around and ask: What business decisions could be intelligently made without the use of accounting information? Examples would be hard to find.

It is safe to say that business on almost any scale could scarcely exist without accounting records. In large-scale business undertakings such as the manufacture of automobiles or the operation of nationwide chains of retail stores, and even in enterprises much smaller than these, the top executives cannot possibly have close physical contact with and knowledge of the details of operations. Consequently, these executives must depend to an even greater extent than the small businessman upon information provided by the accounting system. Furthermore, taxing and regulatory authorities require that accounting records be maintained to make possible the determination of taxes and the enforcement of regulations.

Forms of business organization

A business enterprise may be organized as a single proprietorship, a partnership, or a corporation. The single proprietorship and partnership forms of organization are common for small retail stores and shops, for farms, and for professional practices in law, medicine, and public accounting. Nearly all large businesses and many small ones are corporations. The dominant role of the corporation in our economy is based on such advantages as the ease of gathering large amounts of money, transferability of shares in ownership, limited liability, and continuity of existence.

Accounting principles apply to all three forms of business organization, but are most carefully defined to aid corporations in making satisfactory financial reports to public investors. In this book we shall use the corporate form of organization as our basic model, along with some specific references to single proprietorships and partnerships.

For an individual to start a small business of which he is the sole owner requires no legal formalities. The organization of a partnership requires only an agreement (written or oral) among the persons joining together as partners, (A written agreement is highly desirable in order to lessen the chance of misunderstanding and disputes.) The formation of a corporation, however, does entail some legal formalities. Application must be filed with state officials for a *corporate charter.* The application for a charter is often referred to as the *articles of incorporation.* After payment of an incorporation fee to the state and approval of the articles of incorporation by the designated state official, the corporation comes into existence. A charter, which may be merely the approved application, is issued as evidence of the company's corporate status. The incorporators (who have subscribed for capital stock and therefore are now stockholders) hold a meeting to elect directors and to pass bylaws as a guide to the conduct of the company's affairs. The directors in turn hold a meeting at which officers of the corporation are appointed to serve as active managers of the business; capital stock certificates are issued to the subscribers; and the formation of the corporation is complete.

FINANCIAL STATEMENTS: THE STARTING POINT
IN THE STUDY OF ACCOUNTING

The preparation of financial statements is not the first step in the accounting process, but it is a convenient point to begin the study of accounting. The financial statements are the means of conveying to management and to interested outsiders a concise picture of the profitability and financial condition of the business. Since these statements are in a sense the end product of the accounting process, the student who acquires a clear understanding of the content and meaning of financial statements will be in an excellent position to appreciate the purpose of the earlier steps of recording and classifying business transactions.

There are two major financial statements, the balance sheet and the income statement. Together, these two statements (each a page or less in length) summarize all the information contained in the hundreds or thousands of pages comprising the detailed accounting records. In this introductory chapter and in Chapter 2, we shall explore the nature of the balance sheet, or statement of financial condition, as it is sometimes called. Once we have become familiar with the form and arrangement of the balance sheet and with the meaning of technical terms such as assets, liabilities, and owners' equity, it will be as easy to read and understand a report on the financial condition of a business as it is for an architect to read the blueprint of a proposed building.

After we have gained some skill in reading (and preparing) a balance sheet, we shall round out our introduction to financial statements in Chapter 3 by a similar study of the income statement, which tells the story of profits or losses experienced by the firm. Then, having acquired a speaking acquaintance with financial statements, we shall in the next few chapters examine the recording procedures and other accounting processes which make possible the preparation of financial statements.

The balance sheet

The purpose of a balance sheet is to show the financial condition of a business as of a particular date. Every business prepares a balance sheet at the end of the year, and many concerns prepare one at the end of each month. A balance sheet consists of a listing of the assets and liabilities of a business and of the owners' equity. The balance sheet on page 9 portrays the financial condition of the Wilson Travel Company at December 31.

Note that the balance sheet sets forth in its heading three items: (1) the name of the business, (2) the name of the statement "Balance Sheet," and (3) the date of the balance sheet. Below the heading is the body of the balance sheet, which consists of three distinct sections: assets, liabilities, and the stockholders' equity. The remainder of this chapter is largely devoted to making clear the nature of these three sections.

We can tell from the illustrated balance sheet that Wilson Travel

Balance
Sheet
Shows
Financial
Condition
at a
Specific
Date

WILSON TRAVEL COMPANY
Balance Sheet
December 31, 19___

Assets		Liabilities & Stockholders' Equity		
Cash	$22,500	*Liabilities:*		
Accounts receivable	4,500	*Accounts payable*		$23,200
Land	15,000	*Stockholders' equity:*		
Building	36,000	*Capital stock* . .	$50,000	
Office equipment	5,400	*Retained*		
		earnings . . .	10,200	60,200
	$83,400			$83,400

Company is a corporation, because the ownership section is listed as *stockholders' equity* and shows that capital stock of $50,000 has been issued. A corporation is the only form of business organization which issues capital stock, or in which the owners are called stockholders.

Assets. In general, assets are economic resources which are owned by a business. Assets may have definite physical character, such as buildings, machinery, or merchandise. On the other hand, some assets exist not in physical or tangible form, but in the form of valuable legal claims or rights; examples are amounts due from customers, government bonds, and patent rights.

One of the most basic, and at the same time most controversial, problems in accounting is the assignment of dollar values to the assets of a business. Two kinds of assets cause little difficulty. Cash and amounts due from customers represent funds that either are available for expenditure or will be in the near future (when the customers pay their accounts). The amount of cash on hand is a clear statement of the dollars that are available for expenditure. The amount that customers owe the business (after taking into account that some receivables may prove uncollectible) represents the dollars that will be received in the near future.

Other assets such as land, buildings, merchandise, and equipment represent economic resources that will be used in producing income for the business. The prevailing accounting view is that such assets should be accounted for on the basis of the dollars that have been invested in these resources, that is, the cost incurred in acquiring such property or property rights. In accounting terms, therefore, the "value" or "valuation" of an asset ordinarily means the *cost* of that asset.

For example, let us assume that a business buys a tract of land for use as a building site, paying $40,000 in cash. The amount to be entered in the accounting records as the value of the asset will be the cost of $40,000. If we assume a booming real estate market, a fair estimate of the sales value of the land 10 years later might be $100,000. Although the market price or economic value of the land has risen greatly, the accounting value as shown by the accounting records and by the annual balance sheet would continue unchanged at the cost of $40,000.

In reading a balance sheet, it is important to bear in mind that the dollar amounts listed do not indicate the prices at which the assets could be sold, nor the prices at which they could be replaced. One useful generalization to be drawn from this discussion is that a balance sheet does not show "how much a business is worth."

It is appropriate to ask *why* accountants do not change the recorded values of assets to correspond with changing market prices for these properties. One reason is that the land and building used to house the business are acquired for use and not for resale; in fact, these assets cannot be sold without disrupting the business. The balance sheet of a business is prepared on the assumption that the business is a continuing enterprise, a "going concern." Consequently, the present estimated prices at which the land and buildings could be sold are not of particular importance since these properties are not intended for sale.

Another reason for using cost rather than market values in accounting for assets is the need for a definite, factual basis. The cost of land, buildings, and many other assets purchased for cash can be rather definitely determined. Estimated market values, on the other hand, for assets such as land and buildings are not factual and definite; market values are constantly changing and are largely a matter of personal opinion. Of course at the date of acquisition of an asset, cost and value are ordinarily the same because the buyer would not pay more than the asset was worth and the seller would not take less than current market value. The bargaining process which results in a sale serves to establish both the current market value of the property and the cost to the buyer. With the passage of time, however, the current market value of assets is likely to differ considerably from the cost recorded in the owner's accounting records.

Although the cost of many assets can be determined in a definite manner as the result of a cash purchase, the measurement of cost in some cases may be rather difficult. For example, when a factory machine is purchased, a question arises as to whether the cost basis of the machine should include (1) the charges for transporting, installing, and testing it, and (2) the salary paid the purchasing agent and engineering employees, who may have devoted considerable time to making a choice among various competing machines on the market. Another common example is that of a manufacturing concern which constructs a building for its own use. Identifying and measuring all the costs to be included in the total cost of the building will require many borderline decisions.

The wide changes in the purchasing power of the dollar in recent years have raised serious doubts as to the adequacy of the conventional cost basis in accounting for assets. Proposals for adjusting recorded dollar amounts to reflect changes in the value of the dollar are receiving increasing attention, and are discussed in Chapter 15. Accounting concepts are not as exact and unchanging as many persons assume; to serve the needs of a fast-changing economy, accounting concepts and methods must also undergo continuous evolutionary change.

The problem of valuation of assets is one of the most complex in the entire field of accounting. It is merely being introduced at this point; in later chapters we shall explore carefully some of the valuation principles applicable to the major types of assets.

Liabilities. Liabilities are debts. All business concerns have liabilities; even the largest and most successful corporations find it convenient to purchase merchandise and supplies on credit rather than to pay cash at the time of each purchase. The liability arising from the purchase of goods or services on credit (on time) is called an *account payable,* and the person or company to whom the account payable is owed is called a *creditor.* These terms are applicable to the personal affairs of individuals as well as to business concerns. For example, when a college student opens a charge account at the Campus Clothing Store and buys a new suit on credit, he is thereby incurring a liability, an account payable. He could properly refer to the Campus Clothing Store as a creditor and to himself as a debtor. Among the more common types of liabilities that may be owed by a business are accounts payable, notes payable, and taxes payable.

Business concerns frequently find it desirable to borrow money as a means of supplementing the funds invested by owners, thus enabling the business to expand more rapidly. The borrowed funds may, for example, be used to buy merchandise which can be sold at a profit to the firm's customers. Or, the borrowed money might be used to buy new and more efficient machinery, thus enabling the company to turn out a larger volume of products at lower cost. When a business borrows money for any reason, a liability is incurred and the lender becomes a creditor of the business. The form of the liability when money is borrowed is usually a *note payable,* a formal written promise to pay a certain amount of money, usually with interest, at a definite future time. An account payable, as contrasted with a note payable, does not involve the issuance of a formal written promise to the creditor. When a business has both notes payable and accounts payable, the two types of liabilities are shown separately in the balance sheet. The sequence in which these two liabilities are listed is not important. A figure showing the total of the liabilities should also be inserted, as shown by the illustration on page 12.

The creditors have claims against the assets of the business, usually not against any particular asset but against the assets in general. The claims of the creditors are liabilities of the business and have priority over the claims of owners. Creditors are entitled to be paid in full even if such payment should exhaust the assets of the business, leaving nothing for the owners. The issue of valuation, which poses so many difficulties in accounting for assets, is a much smaller problem in the case of liabilities, because the amounts of most liabilities are definitely stated.

*One of
Key
Figures
on
Balance
Sheet Is
Total
Liabilities*

WESTSIDE CLEANING COMPANY
*Balance Sheet
December 31, 19____*

Assets		*Liabilities & Stockholders' Equity*		
Cash	*$ 1,500*	*Liabilities:*		
Accounts receivable	*3,000*	*Notes payable*		*$ 6,000*
Land	*7,000*	*Accounts payable*		*4,000*
Building	*15,000*	*Total liabilities*		*$10,000*
Office equipment	*1,000*	*Stockholders' equity:*		
Delivery equipment	*2,500*	*Capital stock*	*$15,000*	
		Retained		
		earnings	*5,000*	*20,000*
	$30,000			*$30,000*

Owners' equity. The owners' equity in a business is equal to the total assets minus the liabilities. The equity of the owners is a residual claim; as the owners of the business they are entitled to whatever remains after the claims of the creditors are fully satisfied. For example:

The Westside Cleaning Company has total assets of	*$30,000*
And total liabilities amounting to	*10,000*
Therefore, the owners' equity must equal	*$20,000*

Suppose that the Westside Cleaning Company borrows $1,000 from a bank. After recording the additional asset of $1,000 in cash and recording the new liability of $1,000 owed to the bank, we would have the following:

The Westside Cleaning Company now has total assets of	*$31,000*
And total liabilities are now	*11,000*
Therefore, the owners' equity still is equal to	*$20,000*

It is apparent that the total assets of the business were increased by the act of borrowing money from a bank, but the increase in total assets was exactly offset by an increase in liabilities, and the owners' equity remained unchanged. The owners' equity in a business is not increased by the incurring of liabilities of any kind.

The owners' equity in a corporation usually comes from two sources:

1. Investments by persons who receive in exchange shares of the corporation's capital stock and are therefore called stockholders

2. Earnings from profitable operation of the business

Only the first of these two sources of owners' equity is considered in this chapter. The second source, an increase in owners' equity through earnings of the business, will be discussed in Chapter 3.

The balance sheet equation. One of the fundamental characteristics of every balance sheet is that the total figure for assets always equals the total figure for liabilities and owners' equity. This agreement or balance of total assets with total equities is one reason for calling this statement of financial condition a *balance sheet.* But *why* do total assets equal total equities? The answer can be given in one short paragraph, as follows:

The dollar totals on the two sides of the balance sheet are always equal because these two sides of the statement are merely two views of the same business property. The listing of assets shows us what things the business owns; the listing of liabilities and owners' equity tells us who supplied these resources to the business and how much each group supplied. Everything that a business owns has been supplied to it by the creditors or by the owners. Therefore, the total claims of the creditors plus the claims of the owners equal the total assets of the business.

The equality of assets on the one hand and of the claims of the creditors and the owners on the other hand is expressed in the equation:

Balance Sheet Equation	*Assets = liabilities + owners' equity* $30,000 = $10,000 + $20,000

The amounts listed in the equation were taken from the balance sheet of the Westside Cleaning Company illustrated on page 12. A balance sheet is nothing more than a detailed statement of this equation.

Regardless of whether a business grows or contracts, this equality between the assets and the claims against the assets is always maintained. Any increase in the amount of total assets is necessarily accompanied by an equal increase on the other side of the equation, that is, by an increase in either the liabilities or the owners' equity. Any decrease in total assets is necessarily accompanied by a corresponding decrease in liabilities or owners' equity. The continuing equality of the two sides of the balance sheet can best be illustrated by taking a brand-new business as an example and observing the effects of various transactions upon the balance sheet.

Effects of business transactions upon the balance sheet

Assume that John Green, Susan Green, and R. J. Hill organized a corporation called Greenhill Real Estate Company. A charter was obtained from the state authorizing the new corporation to issue 2,000 shares of capital stock with a par value of $10 a share.[1] John and Susan Green each invested $8,000 cash and R. J. Hill invested $4,000. The entire authorized capital stock of $20,000 was therefore issued as follows: 800 shares to John Green; 800 shares to Susan Green; and 400 shares to R. J. Hill.

Each of the three stockholders received a stock certificate as evidence of his equity in the corporation. The certificate for 800 shares issued to John Green is illustrated below:

Capital
Stock
Certificate

Certificate No._____ -1-_____   _____ -800- ____*Shares*

GREENHILL REAL ESTATE COMPANY

Incorporated under the laws of the State of California

*This is to certify that*____ John Green ____

is the owner of _____ — 800 — _____ *fully paid and*

nonassessable shares of the capital stock of $10 par value per

share of Greenhill Real Estate Company transferable on the

books of the corporation by the holder hereof in person or by

duly authorized attorney, upon surrender of this certificate

properly endorsed. Witness the seal of the corporation and the

signatures of its duly authorized officers on this ____ *1ST* ____

day of ____ September, 19 ____.

Susan Green   John Green
Secretary   **SEAL**   *President*

The planned operations of the new business called for obtaining listings of houses and commercial property being offered for sale by owners, ad-

---

[1]Par value is the amount assigned to each share of stock in accordance with legal requirements. The concept of par value is fully explained in Chap. 7.

vertising these properties, and showing them to prospective buyers. The listing agreement signed with each owner provides that Greenhill Real Estate Company shall receive at the time of sale a commission equal to 6% of the sales price.

The new business was begun on September 1 with the deposit of $20,000 in a bank account in the name of the business, Greenhill Real Estate Company. The initial balance sheet of the new business then appeared as follows:

Beginning Balance Sheet of a New Business

GREENHILL REAL ESTATE COMPANY
Balance Sheet
September 1, 19___

Assets		Stockholders' Equity	
Cash	$20,000	Capital stock...........	$20,000

Purchase of an asset for cash. The next transaction entered into by Greenhill Real Estate Company was the purchase of land suitable as a site for an office. The price for the land was $7,000 and payment was made in cash on September 3. The effect of this transaction on the balance sheet was twofold: first, cash was decreased by the amount paid out; and second, a new asset, Land, was acquired. After this exchange of cash for land, the balance sheet appeared as follows:

Balance Sheet Totals Unchanged by Purchase of Land for Cash

GREENHILL REAL ESTATE COMPANY
Balance Sheet
September 3, 19___

Assets		Stockholders' Equity	
Cash	$13,000	Capital stock..........	$20,000
Land	7,000		
	$20,000		$20,000

Purchase of an asset and incurring of a liability. On September 5 an opportunity arose to buy a complete office building which had to be moved to permit the construction of a freeway. A price of $12,000 was agreed upon, which included the cost of moving the building and installing it upon Greenhill Real Estate's lot. As the building was in excellent condition and would have cost approximately $20,000 to build, It was considered as a very fortunate purchase.

The terms provided for an immediate cash payment of $5,000 and payment of the balance of $7,000 within 90 days. Cash was decreased $5,000, but a new asset, Building, was recorded at cost in the amount of $12,000. Total assets were thus increased by $7,000 but the total of liabilities and owners' equity was also increased as a result of recording the $7,000 account payable as a liability. After this transaction had been recorded, the balance sheet appeared as follows:

Totals Increased Equally by Purchase on Credit

GREENHILL REAL ESTATE COMPANY
Balance Sheet
September 5, 19___

Assets		Liabilities & Stockholders' Equity	
Cash	$ 8,000	Liabilities:	
Land	7,000	Accounts payable......	$ 7,000
Building.............	12,000	Stockholders' equity:	
		Capital stock	20,000
	$27,000		$27,000

Note that the building appears in the balance sheet at $12,000, its cost to Greenhill Real Estate Company. The estimate of $20,000 as the probable cost to construct such a building is irrelevant. Even if someone should offer to buy the building from Greenhill Real Estate Company for $20,000 or more, this offer, if refused, would have no bearing on the balance sheet. Accounting records are intended to provide a historical record of *costs* actually incurred; therefore, the $12,000 price at which the building was purchased is the amount to be recorded.

Sale of an asset. After the office building had been moved to Greenhill Real Estate Company's lot, Green decided that the lot was much larger than was needed. The adjoining business, Carter's Drugstore, wanted more room for a parking area so, on September 10, Greenhill Real Estate Company sold the unused part of the lot to Carter's Drugstore for a price of $2,000. Since the sales price was computed at the same amount per foot as the corporation had paid for the land, there was neither a profit nor a loss on the sale. No down payment was required but it was agreed that the full price would be paid within three months. By this transaction a new asset in the form of an account receivable was acquired, but the asset Land was decreased by the same amount; consequently, there was no change in the amount of total assets. After this transaction, the balance sheet appeared as shown at the top of page 17.

In the illustration thus far, Greenhill Real Estate Company has an account receivable from only one debtor, and an account payable to only one creditor. As the business grows, the number of debtors and creditors will increase, but the Accounts Receivable and Accounts Payable accounts will

*No Change
in Totals
by Sale
of Land
at Cost*

GREENHILL REAL ESTATE COMPANY
Balance Sheet
September 10, 19___

Assets		*Liabilities & Stockholders' Equity*	
Cash	$ 8,000	Liabilities:	
Accounts receivable......	2,000	Accounts payable......	$ 7,000
Land	5,000	Stockholders' equity:	
Building..............	12,000	Capital stock	20,000
	$27,000		$27,000

continue to be used. The additional records necessary to show the amount receivable from each debtor and the amount owing to each creditor will be explained in Chapter 6.

Purchase of an asset on credit. A complete set of office furniture and equipment was purchased on credit from General Equipment, Inc., on September 14. The amount of the transaction was $1,800, and it was agreed that payment should be made later. As the result of this transaction the business owned a new asset, Office Equipment, but it had also incurred a new liability. The increase in total assets was exactly offset by the increase in liabilities. After this transaction the balance sheet appeared as follows:

*Totals
Increased
by
Acquiring
Asset on
Credit*

GREENHILL REAL ESTATE COMPANY
Balance Sheet
September 14, 19___

Assets		*Liabilities & Stockholders' Equity*	
Cash	$ 8,000	Liabilities:	
Accounts receivable......	2,000	Accounts payable......	$ 8,800
Land	5,000	Stockholders' equity:	
Building..............	12,000	Capital stock	20,000
Office equipment	1,800		
	$28,800		$28,800

Collection of an account receivable. On September 20, cash in the amount of $500 was received as partial settlement of the account receivable from Carter's Drugstore. This transaction caused cash to increase and the accounts receivable to decrease by an equal amount. In essence, this transaction was merely the exchange of one asset for another of equal value. Consequently, there was no change in the amount of total assets. After this transaction was completed the balance sheet appeared as shown at the top of page 18.

Totals
Unchanged
by
Collection
of a
Receivable

GREENHILL REAL ESTATE COMPANY
Balance Sheet
September 20, 19___

Assets		Liabilities & Stockholders' Equity	
Cash	$ 8,500	Liabilities:	
Accounts receivable......	1,500	Accounts payable......	$ 8,800
Land	5,000	Stockholders' equity:	
Building..............	12,000	Capital stock	20,000
Office equipment	1,800		
	$28,800		$28,800

Payment of a liability. On September 30 Greenhill paid $1,000 in cash to General Equipment, Inc. This payment caused a decrease in cash and an equal decrease in liabilities. Therefore the totals of assets and equities were still in balance. After this transaction, the balance sheet appeared as follows:

Totals
Decreased
by Paying
a Liability

GREENHILL REAL ESTATE COMPANY
Balance Sheet
September 30, 19___

Assets		Liabilities & Stockholders' Equity	
Cash	$ 7,500	Liabilities:	
Accounts receivable......	1,500	Accounts payable......	$ 7,800
Land	5,000	Stockholders' equity:	
Building..............	12,000	Capital stock	20,000
Office equipment........	1,800		
	$27,800		$27,800

The transactions which have been illustrated for the month of September were merely preliminary to the formal opening for business of Greenhill Real Estate Company on October 1. During September no sales were arranged by the company and no commissions were earned. Since we have assumed that the business had no revenues and no expenses during September, the stockholders' equity at September 30 is shown in the above balance sheet at $20,000, unchanged from the original investment on September 1. September was a month devoted exclusively to organizing the business and not to regular operations. In succeeding chapters we shall continue the example of Greenhill Real Estate Company by illustrating operating transactions and considering how the net income of the business can be determined.

CORPORATIONS, PARTNERSHIPS, AND SINGLE PROPRIETORSHIPS

The form of business organization used for illustration in this chapter is a corporation, Greenhill Real Estate Company. A corporation is a separate legal entity or "artificial being" chartered by the state, and the owners' equity section of the balance sheet is called Stockholders' Equity. If the business were a partnership of two or more persons, we would use the caption Partners' Equity instead of Stockholders' Equity, and would list under that caption the amount of each partner's equity. If the form of the business were a single proprietorship, the owner's equity section would consist of only one item, the equity of the proprietor. These three methods of showing the ownership equity on the balance sheet may be illustrated as follows:

Equity of Stockholders, of Partners, and of a Single Proprietor

For a Corporation

Stockholders' equity:		
Capital stock	$1,000,000	
Retained earnings	278,000	
Total stockholders' equity		$1,278,000

For a Partnership

Partners' equity:		
William Abbott, capital	$25,000	
Raymond Barnes, capital	40,000	
Total partners' equity		$ 65,000

For a Single Proprietorship

Owner's equity:		
John Smith, capital		$ 30,000

The preceding illustration of the ownership equity of a corporation shows that $1 million of capital was invested in the corporation by stockholders, and that through profitable operation of the business an additional $278,000 of earned capital has been accumulated. The corporation has chosen to retain this $278,000 in the business rather than to distribute these earnings to the stockholders as dividends. The total earnings of the corporation may have been considerably more than $278,000, because any earnings which were paid to stockholders as dividends would not appear on the balance sheet. The term *retained earnings* describes only the earnings which were *not* paid out in the form of dividends.

Corporations are required by state laws to maintain a distinction between capital stock and retained earnings. In a single proprietorship, capital earned through profitable operations and retained in the business is merely added to the amount of the original invested capital and a single figure is shown for the owner's equity. A similar procedure is followed in a partnership, each partner's capital being increased by his share of the net income. There is no theoretical reason why the balance sheet for a single proprietorship or a partnership should not show each owner's equity divided into two portions: the amount originally invested, and the earnings retained in the business, but customarily this separation is not made for an unincorporated business.

USE OF FINANCIAL STATEMENTS BY OUTSIDERS

Another function of accounting is to provide annual or quarterly reports to outsiders who have an interest in the affairs of the business. The balance sheet is one of the financial statements prepared at regular intervals for management and owners and also distributed to bankers, creditors, credit agencies, investors, government agencies, and other outsiders. In large corporations quarterly and annual balance sheets and income statements are designed especially for use by outsiders; more frequent and detailed internal reports are prepared for use by management.

Through careful study of the balance sheet, it is possible for the outsider with training in accounting to obtain a fairly complete understanding of the financial condition of the business and to become aware of significant changes in financial condition that have occurred since the date of the preceding balance sheet. Bear in mind, however, that financial statements have limitations. As stated earlier, only those factors which can be reduced to monetary terms appear in the balance sheet. Let us consider for a moment some important business factors which are not set forth in the balance sheet. Some companies have a record of good relations with labor unions, freedom from strikes, and mutual respect between management and employees. Other companies have been plagued by frequent and bitter labor disputes. The relationship between a company and a union of its employees is certainly an important factor in the successful operation of the business, but it is not mentioned in the balance sheet. Perhaps a new competing store had just opened for business across the street; the prospect of intensified competition in the future will not be described in the balance sheet.

Bankers

Bankers who have loaned money to a business concern or who are considering making such a loan will be vitally interested in the financial statements of the business. By studying the amount and kinds of assets in relation to the amount and payment dates of the liabilities, a banker can form an opinion as to the ability of the concern to pay its debts promptly. The banker gives particular attention to the amount of cash and of other assets (such as accounts receivable, which will soon be converted into cash; he compares the amount of these assets with the amount of liabilities falling due in the near future. The banker is also interested in the amount of the owners' equity, as this ownership capital serves as a protecting buffer between the banker and any losses which may befall the business. Bankers are seldom, if ever, willing to make a loan unless the financial statements and other information concerning the prospective borrower offer reasonable assurance that the loan can be repaid promptly at the maturity date.

Other creditors

Another important group making constant use of balance sheets consists of the credit managers of manufacturing and wholesaling firms, who must decide whether prospective customers are to be allowed to buy merchandise on credit. The credit manager, like the banker, studies the balance sheets of his customers for the purpose of appraising their debt-paying ability. Credit agencies such as Dun & Bradstreet, Inc. make a business of obtaining financial statements from virtually all business concerns and appraising their debt-paying ability. The conclusions reached by these credit agencies are available to businessmen willing to pay for credit reports about prospective customers.

Owners

The financial statements of corporations listed on the stock exchanges are eagerly awaited by millions of stockholders. A favorable set of financial statements may cause the market price of the company's stock to rise dramatically; an unfavorable set of financial statements may cause the "bottom to fall out" of the market price. Current dependable financial statements are one of the essential ingredients for successful investment in securities. Of course, financial statements are equally important in single proprietorships and partnerships. The financial statements tell the proprietor just how successful his business has been and summarize in concise form its present financial position.

Others interested in financial statements

In addition to owners, managers, bankers, and merchandise creditors, other groups making use of financial statements include governmental agencies, employees, financial analysts, and writers for business periodicals. Some very large corporations have more than a half million stockholders; these giant concerns send copies of their annual financial statements to each of these many owners. In recent years there has been a definite trend toward wider distribution of financial statements to all interested persons, in contrast to the attitude of a generation or more ago when many companies regarded their financial statements as confidential information.

The purpose of this recital is to show the student the extent to which a modern industrial society depends upon accounting. Even more important, however, is a clear understanding at the outset of your study of this subject that accounting does not exist just for the sake of keeping a record, or in order to fill out social security records, income tax returns, and various other reports required by government agencies. These are but auxiliary functions. The prime and vital purpose of accounting, and the function which makes it a part of the fascination of business, is to aid in the choice among alternatives that faces everyone who plays a part in the business world.

DEMONSTRATION PROBLEM*

The accounting data (listed alphabetically) for the Crown Auto Wash as of August 31, 19___, are shown below. The figure for Cash is not given but it can be determined when all the available information is assembled in the form of a balance sheet.

Accounts payable	$ 9,000
Accounts receivable	800
Buildings	60,000
Cash	?
Capital stock	50,000
Land	40,000
Machinery & equipment	85,000
Notes payable	32,000
Retained earnings	99,400
Supplies	400

On September 1, the following transactions occurred:

(1) Additional capital stock was issued for $15,000 cash.
(2) The accounts payable of $9,000 were paid in full. (No payment was made on the notes payable.)
(3) One-quarter of the land was sold at cost. The buyer gave his promissory note for $10,000. (Interest applicable to the note may be ignored.)
(4) Washing supplies were purchased at a cost of $2,000, to be paid for within 10 days. Washing supplies were also purchased for $600 cash from another car-washing concern which was going out of business. These supplies would have cost $1,000 if purchased through regular channels.

Instructions
a. Prepare a balance sheet as of August 31, 19___.
b. Prepare a balance sheet as of September 1, 19___.

QUESTIONS

1. In broad general terms, what is the purpose of accounting?

2. Not all the significant happenings in the life of a business can be expressed in monetary terms and entered in the accounting records. List two examples of significant events affecting a business which could not be satisfactorily entered in its accounting records.

3. Distinguish between *bookkeeping* and *accounting.*

° *Note to student: Solutions to the Demonstration Problems will be found in the back of this book. We recommend that you prepare a complete solution to the problem before making comparisons with the solution in the book.*

4. What is the principal function of a certified public accountant?

5. Cost accounting may be regarded as a specialized phase of accounting utilized by virtually every kind of industry. List four other specialized phases of accounting of comparable importance.

6. Information available from the accounting records provides a basis for making many business decisions. List five examples of business decisions requiring the use of accounting data.

7. Define *assets.* List five examples.

8. Mint Corporation was offered $500,000 cash for the land and buildings occupied by the business. These assets had been acquired five years ago at a price of $300,000. Mint Corporation refused the offer, but is inclined to increase the land and buildings to a total valuation of $500,000 in the balance sheet in order to show more accurately "how much the business is worth." Do you agree? Explain.

9. State precisely what information is contained in the heading of a balance sheet.

10. State the balance sheet equation. Can it be stated in another way?

11. Explain which of the three forms of business organization discussed in this chapter you would consider most appropriate for
    a. A manufacturer of farm machinery and earth-moving equipment
    b. A CPA firm
    c. A midwestern farm of 320 acres
    d. A small beauty shop

12. What are the two major financial statements? State briefly the purpose of each.

EXERCISES

1. a. If the assets of a corporation total $150,000 and the stockholders' equity totals $65,000, the liabilities must total $_____.
    b. The balance sheet of Ray Corporation shows retained earnings of $25,000. The assets amount to $120,000 and are twice as large as the liabilities. The amount of capital stock must be $_____.
    c. In the partnership of Jones & Brown, the asset total is 50% larger than the total of the liabilities. The ownership equity of partner Jones is only half as much as that of Brown. If the total assets amount to $90,000, the amount of Brown's ownership equity must be $_____.

2. Indicate the effect of each of the following transactions upon the total assets of a business by use of the appropriate phrase: "increase total assets," "decrease total assets," "no change in total assets."

    a. Purchase of office equipment for cash
    b. Payment of a liability
    c. Borrowing money from a bank
    d. Investment of cash by owner
    e. Purchase of a delivery truck at a price of $2,500, terms $500 cash and the balance payable in 20 equal monthly installments

    f.   Sale of land for cash at a price equal to its cost

    g. Sale of land on account (on credit) at a price equal to its cost

    h. Sale of land for cash at a price in excess of its cost

    i.   Sale of land for cash at a price below its cost

    j.   Collection of an account receivable

3.   The total assets of the Universal Corporation amount to $1.5 million and its total liabilities to $600,000. During the five years of its existence, the corporation has been quite successful and has earned total profits equal to exactly one-half of the original capital invested by stockholders. Of the profits earned, one-half has been distributed as dividends to stockholders; the other half has been retained in the business. Prepare the stockholders' equity section of the balance sheet, including dollar amounts. Explain how you determined the amounts.

4.   On December 31, 1970, the assets of the Mill Corporation amounted to $240,000. One year later the assets had increased to $300,000 and the stockholders' equity was $192,000. Liabilities were $68,000 greater on December 31, 1971, than they had been at December 31, 1970. What was the amount of the stockholders' equity at December 31, 1970? Explain the basis for your answer.

5.   Prepare a balance sheet for the Harding Corporation as of June 30, 19___, from the following information:

Accounts payable	$ 9,675
Accounts receivable	7,650
Buildings	60,000
Land	30,000
Cash	11,220
Office equipment	3,150
Notes payable	30,000
Delivery truck	?
Capital stock	60,000
Retained earnings	17,220

6.   The following balance sheet of Granite Corporation is incorrect because of improper headings and the misplacement of several accounts. Prepare a corrected balance sheet.

GRANITE CORPORATION
March 31, 19___

Assets		*Owner's Equity*	
Capital stock	$ 55,000	*Accounts receivable*	$ 37,100
Cash	11,400	*Accounts payable*	13,100
Building	48,500	*Supplies*	1,200
Office equipment	12,900	*Automobiles*	16,700
		Retained earnings	59,700
	$127,800		$127,800

PROBLEMS

1-1 Use the following information to prepare a balance sheet for the McGraw Corporation as of March 31, 19___.

Accounts payable	$ 63,200
Accounts receivable	84,600
Automobiles	19,600
Buildings	170,000
Capital stock	200,000
Cash	?
Land	60,000
Notes payable	70,000
Office equipment	16,400
Retained earnings	62,400

1-2 Prepare a balance sheet for the Parkman Company as of December 31 of the current year, making use of the following information:

Capital stock	$40,000
Retained earnings	21,800
Office equipment	2,200
Office supplies	1,300
Accounts receivable	14,400
Accounts payable	7,100
Cash	6,800
Land	15,500
Buildings	32,500
Delivery equipment	3,400
Notes payable	?

1-3 Show the effect of each of the following five business transactions by preparing a new balance sheet after each one.

(1) On May 6, Mountain TV Repair Company was organized and $15,000 of par value capital stock was issued for cash.

(2) On May 8, land and a building were purchased for cash at a cost of $8,000 for the land and $3,000 for the building.

(3) On May 13, tools and equipment were purchased for a down payment of $200 and a final payment of $900 payable in 30 days.

(4) On May 15, a delivery truck was acquired at a cost of $2,500. A cash down payment of $1,000 was made, with the balance to be paid within 60 days.

(5) On June 10, the account payable incurred by the purchase of tools and equipment on May 13 was paid in full.

1-4 *Instructions*

Prepare a balance sheet as of November 1 based on the data in (1). Prepare a new balance sheet after transactions for each of the following days have been completed.

(1) The balance sheet data (listed alphabetically) for National Business Service as of November 1, 19___, were:

Accounts payable		$ 34,000
Accounts receivable		3,900
Buildings		90,000
Business machines		105,000
Cash		25,000
Land		?
Notes payable		83,000
Notes receivable		15,000
Supplies		8,000
Capital stock		164,000

(2) On November 2, additional capital stock was issued for $28,000 in cash. A cash payment of $25,000 was made to the holders of the notes payable, reducing the amount of these obligations to $58,000.

(3) On November 3, the note receivable for $15,000 was collected.

(4) On November 4, a $10,000 cash payment was made in partial settlement of the accounts payable.

(5) On November 5, supplies costing $1,000 were purchased on credit, payment to be made within 30 days. Additional business machines were purchased for cash in the amount of $9,000.

1-5 By close study of the series of balance sheets shown below, you can determine what transactions have taken place. Prepare a list of these transactions by date of occurrence. (For example, the transactions leading to the balance sheet of September 1, 19___, could be described as follows: "On September 1, 19___, Bayside Corporation issued $76,000 par value of capital stock for cash.")

(1)

BAYSIDE CORPORATION
Balance Sheet
September 1, 19___

Assets		Stockholders' Equity	
Cash	$76,000	Capital stock	$76,000

(2)

BAYSIDE CORPORATION
Balance Sheet
September 5, 19___

Assets		Liabilities & Stockholders' Equity	
Cash	$ 50,000	Liabilities:	
Land	66,000	Accounts payable	$ 40,000
		Stockholders' equity:	
		Capital stock	76,000
	$116,000		$116,000

(3)

BAYSIDE CORPORATION
Balance Sheet
September 8, 19___

Assets		Liabilities & Stockholders' Equity	
Cash.....................	$ 30,000	Liabilities:	
Supplies.................	6,000	Accounts payable........	$ 40,000
Land	66,000	Stockholders' equity:	
Equipment..............	14,000	Capital stock...........	76,000
	$116,000		$116,000

(4)

BAYSIDE CORPORATION
Balance Sheet
September 10, 19___

Assets		Liabilities & Stockholders' Equity	
Cash.....................	$ 20,000		
Supplies.................	8,000	Liabilities:	
Land	66,000	Accounts payable........	$ 33,000
Equipment..............	15,000	Stockholders' equity:	
	$109,000	Capital stock...........	76,000
			$109,000

(5)

BAYSIDE CORPORATION
Balance Sheet
October 4, 19___

Assets		Liabilities & Stockholders' Equity	
Cash.....................	$ 17,000	Liabilities:	
Supplies.................	8,000	Accounts payable........	$ 30,000
Land	66,000	Stockholders' equity:	
Equipment..............	15,000	Capital stock...........	76,000
	$106,000		$106,000

1-6 Use the information given below to prepare a balance sheet for the Fairfield Corporation as of December 31, 19___.

Accounts receivable	$ 65,200
Accounts payable.........................	87,350
Buildings	106,100
Capital stock............................	100,000
Cash	?
Delivery trucks	28,600
Land....................................	60,000
Notes payable	70,000
Office equipment	15,000
Retained earnings	41,600

1-7 Prepare a balance sheet as of June 1, 1971, for Royal Real Estate Company. Also prepare a separate balance sheet after each of the three transactions. Each balance sheet should reflect all transactions to date.

Accounts payable	$ *15,000*
Buildings	*96,250*
Office equipment	*26,500*
Office supplies	*?*
Capital stock	*100,000*
Retained earnings	*84,000*
Cash	*9,000*
Land	*62,000*

June 2   One-half of the land was sold to a contractor at a price of $31,000. A down payment of $5,000 in cash was received and the buyer agreed to pay the balance within 10 days.

June 3   A cash payment of $2,500 was made on an account payable.

June 10   Cash in the amount of $26,000 was received from the buyer of the land in final settlement of the June 2 transaction.

2 Recording changes in financial condition

Many business concerns have several hundred or even several thousand business transactions each day. It would obviously be impracticable to prepare a balance sheet after each transaction, and it is quite unnecessary to do so. Instead, the many individual transactions are recorded in the accounting records, and, at the end of the month or other accounting period, a balance sheet is prepared from these records.

The use of accounts for recording transactions

The accounting records include a separate page for each item that appears in the balance sheet. For example, a separate record is kept for the asset Cash, showing all the increases and decreases in cash which result from the many transactions in which cash is received or paid. A similar record is kept for every other asset, for every liability, and for each component of the ownership equity. The form of record used to record increases and decreases in a single balance sheet item is called an *account,* or sometimes a *ledger account.* All these separate accounts are usually kept in a loose-leaf binder, and the entire group of accounts is called a *ledger.*

Today many businesses use computers for maintaining accounting records, and data may be stored on magnetic tapes rather than in ledgers. However, an understanding of accounting concepts is most easily acquired by study of a manual accounting system. The knowledge gained by working with manual accounting records is readily transferable to any type of automated accounting system. For these reasons, we shall use standard written accounting forms such as ledger accounts as the model for our study of basic accounting concepts. These standard forms continue to be used by a great many businesses.

THE LEDGER

Ledger accounts are a means of accumulating information needed by management in directing the business. For example, by maintaining a Cash account, management can keep track of the amount of cash available for meeting payrolls and for making current purchases of merchandise. This record of cash is also useful in planning future operations, and in advance planning of applications for bank loans. The development of the annual budget requires estimating in advance the expected receipts and payments of cash; these estimates of cash flow are naturally based to some extent on the ledger accounts showing past receipts and payments.

In its simplest form, an account has only three elements: (1) a title, consisting of the name of the particular asset, liability, or owners' equity; (2) a left side, which is called the *debit* side; and (3) a right side, which is called the *credit* side. This form of account, illustrated below, is called a T account because of its resemblance to the letter T. More complete forms of accounts will be illustrated later.

T Account:
A Ledger
Account in
Simplified
Form

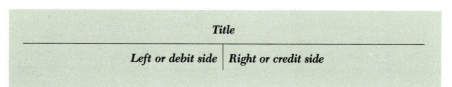

Title	
Left or debit side	*Right or credit side*

Debit and credit entries

An amount recorded on the left or debit side of an account is called a *debit,* or a *debit entry;* an amount entered on the right or credit side is called a *credit,* or a *credit entry.* Accountants also use the words debit and credit as verbs. The act of recording a debit in an account is called *debiting* the account; the recording of a credit is called *crediting* the account. A debit to an account is also sometimes called a *charge* to the account; an account is debited or *charged* when an amount is entered on the left side of the account.

Students beginning a course in accounting often have preconceived but erroneous notions about the meanings of the terms debit and credit. For example, to some people unacquainted with accounting, the word credit may carry a more favorable connotation than does the word debit. Such connotations have no validity in the field of accounting. Accountants use *debit* to mean an entry on the left-hand side of an account, and *credit* to mean an entry on the right-hand side. The student should therefore regard debit and credit as simple equivalents of left and right, without any hidden or subtle implications.

To illustrate the recording of debits and credits in an account, let us go back to the cash transactions of the Greenhill Real Estate Company. When the various receipts and payments of cash in this business during September are recorded in an account, the receipts are listed in vertical order on the debit side of the account and the payments are listed on the credit side. The dates of the transactions may also be listed, as shown in the illustration on page 31.

Note that the total of the cash receipts, $20,500, is in small-size figures so that it will not be mistaken for a debit entry. The total of the cash payments

Cash Trans-actions Entered in Ledger Account	Cash			
	9/1		20,000	9/3	7,000
	9/20	7,500	500	9/5	5,000
			20,500	9/30	1,000
					13,000

(credits), amounting to $13,000, is also in small-size figures to distinguish it from the credit entries. These *footings,* or memorandum totals, are merely a convenient step in determining the amount of cash on hand at the end of the month. The difference in dollars between the total debits and the total credits in an account is called the *balance.* If the debits exceed the credits the account has a *debit balance;* if the credits exceed the debits the account has a *credit balance.* In the illustrated Cash account, the debit total of $20,500 is larger than the credit total of $13,000; therefore, the account has a debit balance. By subtracting the credits from the debits ($20,500–$13,000), we determine that the balance of the Cash account is $7,500. This debit balance is noted on the debit (left) side of the account. The balance of the Cash account represents the amount of cash owned by the business on September 30; in a balance sheet prepared at this date, Cash in the amount of $7,500 would be listed as an asset.

Debit balances in asset accounts. In the preceding illustration of a cash account, increases were recorded on the left or debit side of the account and decreases were recorded on the right or credit side. The increases were greater than the decreases and the result was a debit balance in the account.

All asset accounts normally have debit balances; as a matter of fact, the ownership by a business of cash, land, or any other asset indicates that the increases (debits) to that asset have been greater than the decreases (credits). It is hard to imagine an account for an asset such as land having a credit balance, as this would indicate that the business had disposed of more land than it had acquired and had reached the impossible position of having a negative amount of land.

The balance sheets previously illustrated in Chapter 1 showed all the assets on the left side of the balance sheet. The fact that assets are located on the left side of the balance sheet is a convenient means of remembering the rule that an increase in an asset is recorded on the *left* (debit) side of the account, and also that an asset account normally has a debit (*left-hand*) balance.

Asset Accounts Normally Have Debit Balances	Any Asset Account	
	(Debit) *Increase*	*(Credit)* *Decrease*

Credit balances in liability and owners' equity accounts. Next we must consider the method of recording increases and decreases in the amounts that comprise the right-hand side of the balance sheet, that is, the liabilities and the owners' equity. Increases in liability and owners' equity accounts are recorded by credit entries and decreases in the accounts are recorded by debits.

The relationship between entries in these accounts and their position on the balance sheet may be summed up as follows: (1) liabilities and owners' equity belong on the *right* side of the balance sheet; (2) an increase in a liability or an owners' equity account is recorded on the *right* side of the account; and (3) liability and owners' equity accounts normally have credit (*right-hand*) balances.

Liability Accounts and Owners' Equity Accounts Normally Have Credit Balances

Any Liability Account
or Owners' Equity Account

| (Debit) Decrease | (Credit) Increase |

The diagram on page 33 emphasizes again the relationship between the position of an account in the balance sheet and the method of recording an increase or decrease in the account. The accounts used are those previously shown in the balance sheet (page 18) prepared for the Greenhill Real Estate Company.

Concise statement of the rules of debit and credit. The rules of debit and credit, which have been explained and illustrated in the preceding sections, may be concisely summarized as follows:

Mechanics of Debit and Credit

Asset Accounts	Liability & Owners' Equity Accounts
Increases are recorded by debits Decreases are recorded by credits	Increases are recorded by credits Decreases are recorded by debits

Equality of debits and credits. Every business transaction affects two or more accounts. *Double-entry bookkeeping*, which is the system in almost universal use, takes its name from the fact that equal debit and credit entries are made for every transaction. If only two accounts are affected (as in the

Diagram of Balance Sheet Accounts

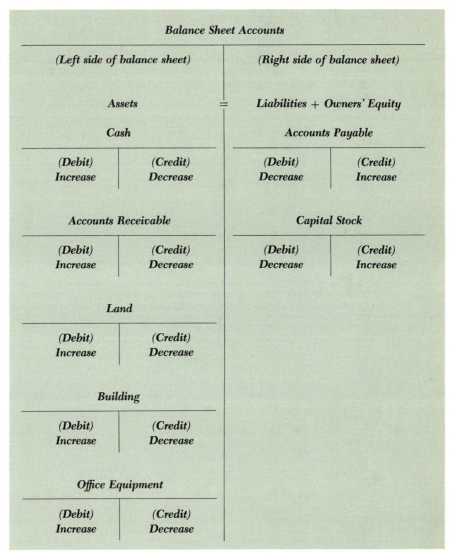

Balance Sheet Accounts

| *(Left side of balance sheet)* | *(Right side of balance sheet)* |

Assets = **Liabilities + Owners' Equity**

Cash

| *(Debit)* Increase | *(Credit)* Decrease |

Accounts Payable

| *(Debit)* Decrease | *(Credit)* Increase |

Accounts Receivable

| *(Debit)* Increase | *(Credit)* Decrease |

Capital Stock

| *(Debit)* Decrease | *(Credit)* Increase |

Land

| *(Debit)* Increase | *(Credit)* Decrease |

Building

| *(Debit)* Increase | *(Credit)* Decrease |

Office Equipment

| *(Debit)* Increase | *(Credit)* Decrease |

purchase of land for cash) one account, Land, is debited, and the other account, Cash, is credited for the same amount. If more than two accounts are affected by a transaction, the sum of the debit entries must be equal to the sum of the credit entries. This situation was illustrated when the Greenhill Real Estate Company purchased a building for a price of $12,000. The $12,000 debit to the asset account, Building, was exactly equal to the total of the $5,000 credit to the Cash account plus the $7,000 credit to the liability account, Accounts Payable. Since every transaction results in an equal amount of debits and credits in the ledger, it follows that the total of all debit entries in the ledger is equal to the total of all the credit entries.

Recording transactions in ledger accounts: illustration

The procedure for recording transactions in ledger accounts will be illustrated by using the September transactions of Greenhill Real Estate Company. Each transaction will first be analyzed in terms of increases and decreases in assets, liabilities, and stockholders' equity. Then we shall follow the rules of debit and credit in entering these increases and decreases in T accounts. Asset accounts will be shown on the left side of the page; liability and stockholders' equity accounts on the right side. For convenience in following the transactions into the ledger accounts, the letter used to identify a given transaction will also appear opposite the debit and credit entries for that transaction. This use of identifying letters is for illustrative purposes only and is not used in actual accounting practice.

Transaction (a). The sum of $20,000 cash was invested in the business on September 1, and 2,000 shares of capital stock were issued.

Recording an Investment in the Business

Analysis	*Rule*	*Entry*
The asset Cash was increased	*Increases in assets are recorded by debits*	*Debit: Cash, $20,000*
The stockholders' equity was increased	*Increases in stockholders' equity are recorded by credits*	*Credit: Capital Stock, $20,000*

Cash	*Capital Stock*
9/1 (a) 20,000	9/1 (a) 20,000

Transaction (b). On September 3, Greenhill Real Estate Company purchased land for cash in the amount of $7,000.

Purchase of Land for Cash

Analysis	*Rule*	*Entry*
The asset Land was increased	*Increases in assets are recorded by debits*	*Debit: Land $7,000*
The asset Cash was decreased	*Decreases in assets are recorded by credits*	*Credit: Cash, $7,000*

Cash	
9/1 20,000	9/3 (b) 7,000

Land	
9/3 (b) 7,000	

Transaction (c). On September 5, the Greenhill Real Estate Company purchased a building from X Company at a total price of $12,000. The terms of the purchase required a cash payment of $5,000 with the remainder of $7,000 payable within 90 days.

Purchase of an Asset, with Partial Payment

Analysis	Rule	Entry
A new asset, Building, was acquired	Increases in assets are recorded by debits	Debit: Building, $12,000
The asset Cash was decreased	Decreases in assets are recorded by credits	Credit: Cash, $5,000
A new liability, Accounts Payable, was incurred	Increases in liabilities are recorded by credits	Credit: Accounts Payable, $7,000

Cash				Accounts Payable	
9/1	20,000	9/3	7,000		9/5 (c) 7,000
		9/5 (c) 5,000			

Building	
9/5 (c) 12,000	

Transaction (d). On September 10, the Greenhill Real Estate Company sold a portion of its land on credit to Carter's Drugstore for a price of $2,000. The land was sold at its cost, so there was no gain or loss on the transaction.

Sale of Land on Credit

Analysis	Rule	Entry
A new asset, Accounts Receivable, was acquired	Increases in assets are recorded by debits	Debit: Accounts Receivable, $2,000
The asset Land was decreased	Decreases in assets are recorded by credits	Credit: Land, $2,000

Accounts Receivable	
9/10 (d) 2,000	

Land			
9/3	7,000	9/10 (d) 2,000	

Transaction (e). On September 14, the Greenhill Real Estate Company purchased office equipment on credit from General Equipment, Inc., in the amount of $1,800.

	Analysis	Rule	Entry
Purchase of an Asset on Credit	*A new asset, Office Equipment, was acquired*	*Increases in assets are recorded by debits*	*Debit: Office Equipment, $1,800*
	A new liability, Accounts Payable, was incurred	*Increases in liabilities are recorded by credits*	*Credit: Accounts Payable, $1,800*

Office Equipment		Accounts Payable	
9/14 (e) 1,800		*9/5 7,000*	
		9/14 (e) 1,800	

Transaction (f). On September 20, cash of $500 was received as partial collection of the account receivable from Carter's Drugstore.

	Analysis	Rule	Entry
Collection of an Account Receivable	*The asset Cash was increased*	*Increases in assets are recorded by debits*	*Debit: Cash, $500*
	The asset Accounts Receivable was decreased	*Decreases in assets are recorded by credits*	*Credit: Accounts Receivable, $500*

Cash			
9/1 20,000	*9/3 7,000*		
9/20 (f) 500	*9/5 5,000*		

Accounts Receivable			
9/10 2,000	*9/20 (f) 500*		

Transaction (g). A cash payment of $1,000 was made on September 30 in partial settlement of the amount owing to General Equipment, Inc.

Payment of a Liability

Analysis	Rule	Entry
The liability Accounts Payable was decreased	Decreases in liabilities are recorded by debits	Debit: Accounts Payable, $1,000
The asset Cash was decreased	Decreases in assets are recorded by credits	Credit: Cash, $1,000

Cash				Accounts Payable		
9/1	20,000	9/3	7,000	9/30 (g) 1,000	9/5	7,000
9/20	500	9/5	5,000		9/14	1,800
		9/30	(g) 1,000			

Standard form of the ledger account

The standard form of ledger account provides for more information than the T accounts used in preceding illustrations. The only change from the T account to a formal ledger account is the addition of special rulings, as shown by the following illustration:

Standard Form of Ledger Account

				Title of Account			Account No. ( )	
Date	Explanation	Ref	Amount	Date	Explanation	Ref	Amount

Note that each side of the account has identical columns as follows:

Date column. The date of the transaction is listed here.

Explanation column. This column is needed only for unusual items, and in most companies is seldom used.

Ref (Reference) column. The page number of the journal on which the transaction is recorded is listed in this column, thus making it possible to trace ledger entries back to their source. The use of a *journal* is explained later in this chapter.

Amount column. The amount of the entry is entered here.

The headings for these columns are usually not printed on ledger paper, although paper with column headings is also available. Since T accounts provide the basic elements of a ledger account, they are used in this text in preference to the standard form of account to achieve simplicity in illustrating accounting principles and procedures.

Numbering of ledger accounts

Accounts are generally arranged in the ledger in the same order as they appear in the balance sheet, and an identification number is assigned to each account. In the following list of accounts, certain numbers have not been assigned; these numbers are held in reserve so that additional accounts can be inserted in a loose-leaf ledger in balance sheet sequence whenever such new accounts become necessary. In this illustration, the numbers from 1 to 29 are used exclusively for asset accounts; numbers from 30 to 49 are reserved for liabilities; and numbers in the 50s signify stockholders' equity accounts.

System for Numbering Ledger Accounts

Account Title	Account Number
Assets:	
Cash	1
Accounts receivable	2
Land	20
Building	22
Office equipment	25
Liabilities:	
Accounts payable	30
Stockholders' equity:	
Capital stock	50

In large businesses with many more accounts, a more elaborate numbering system would be needed. Some companies use a four-digit number for each account; each of the four digits carries special significance as to the classification of the account.

THE JOURNAL

In our description of accounting procedures thus far, emphasis has been placed on the analysis of transactions in terms of debits and credits to ledger accounts. Although transactions could be entered directly in ledger accounts in a very small business, it is much more convenient and efficient in all businesses, large or small, to record transactions first in a journal, and later to transfer the debits and credits to ledger accounts. The *journal,* or *book of original entry,* is a chronological record, showing for each day the debits and credits from transactions; it also may include explanatory information concerning transactions. At convenient intervals the debits and credits in the journal are transferred to the accounts in the ledger; as we have already seen, the ledger accounts serve as the basis from which the balance sheet and other accounting reports are prepared.

The term transaction was explained and illustrated in Chapter 1, but a concise definition at this point may be a helpful reminder. A transaction is an event which is recorded in the accounting records. Common examples are the payment or collection of cash, a purchase or sale on credit, and the payment of dividends to the owners. Note that a transaction has an accounting value and has an influence on financial statements. Events such as the opening of a competing business or the retirement of an employee, although possibly of importance to the business, are not entered in the accounts and are not considered to be transactions.

The unit of organization for the journal is the transaction, whereas the unit of organization for the ledger is the account. By making use of both a journal and a ledger, we can achieve several advantages which are not possible if transactions are recorded directly in ledger accounts:

1. The journal shows all information about a transaction in one place and also provides an explanation of the transaction. In a journal entry, the debits and credits for a given transaction are recorded together, but when the transaction is recorded in the ledger, the debits and credits are entered in different accounts. Since a ledger may contain hundreds of accounts, it would be very difficult to locate all the facts about a particular transaction by looking in the ledger. The journal is the record which shows the complete story of a transaction in one entry.

2. The journal provides a chronological record of all the events in the life of a business. If we want to look up the facts about a transaction of some months or years back, all we need is the date of the transaction in order to locate it in the journal.

3. The use of a journal helps to prevent errors. If transactions were recorded directly in the ledger, it would be very easy to make errors such as omitting the debit or the credit, or entering the debit twice or the credit twice. Such errors are not likely to be made in the journal, since the offsetting debits and credits appear together for each transaction. It is of course possible to forget to transfer a debit or credit from the journal to a ledger account, but such an error can be detected by tracing the entries in the ledger accounts back to the journal.

The general journal: illustration of entries

Many businesses maintain several types of journals. The nature of operations and the volume of transactions in the particular business determine the number and type of journals needed. The simplest type of journal, and the one with which we are concerned in this chapter, is called a *general journal.* It has only two money columns, one for debits and the other for credits; it may be used for all types of transactions.

The process of recording a transaction in a journal is called *journalizing* the transaction. To illustrate the use of the general journal, we shall now journalize the transactions of the Greenhill Real Estate Company which have previously been discussed.

Efficient use of a general journal requires two things: (1) ability to analyze the effect of a transaction upon assets, liabilities, and owners' equity; and (2) familiarity with the standard form and arrangement of journal entries.

September Journal Entries for Greenhill Real Estate Company

Ledger Posting

		General Journal			(Page 1)
Date		Account Titles and Explanation	LP	Debit	Credit
19___					
Sept.	1	Cash...............................	1	20,000	
		Capital Stock.............	50		20,000
		Issued 2,000 shares of capital stock in ex-change for cash invested in the business.			
	3	Land............................	20	7,000	
		Cash....................	1		7,000
		Purchased land for office site.			
	5	Building.......................	22	12,000	
		Cash....................	1		5,000
		Accounts Payable..........	30		7,000
		Purchased building to be moved to our lot. Paid part cash; balance payable within 90 days to X Company.			
	10	Accounts Receivable..............	2	2,000	
		Land....................	20		2,000
		Sold the unused part of our lot at cost to Carter's Drugstore. Due within three months.			
	14	Office Equipment.................	25	1,800	
		Accounts Payable..........	30		1,800
		Purchased office equipment on credit from General Equipment, Inc.			
	20	Cash............................	1	500	
		Accounts Receivable........	2		500
		Collected part of receivable from Carter's Drugstore.			
	30	Accounts Payable.................	30	1,000	
		Cash....................	1		1,000
		Made partial payment of the liability to General Equipment, Inc.			

Our primary interest is in the analytical phase of journalizing; the procedural steps can be learned quickly by observing the following points in the illustrations of journal entries shown above.

1. The year, month, and day of the first entry on the page are written in the date column. The year and month need not be repeated for subsequent entries until a new page or a new month is begun.

2. The name of the account to be debited is written on the first line of the entry and is customarily placed at the extreme left next to the date column. The amount of the debit is entered on the same line in the left-hand money column.

3. The name of the account to be credited is entered on the line below the debit entry and is indented, that is, placed about 1 inch to the right of the date column. The amount credited is entered on the same line in the right-hand money column.

4. A brief explanation of the transaction is usually begun on the line immediately below the title of the account. The explanation need not be indented.

5. A blank line is usually left after each entry. This spacing causes each journal entry to stand out clearly as a separate unit and makes the journal easier to read.

6. An entry which includes more than one debit or more than one credit (such as the entry on September 5) is called a *compound journal entry.* Regardless of how many debts or credits are contained in a compound journal entry, all the debits are customarily entered before any credits are listed.

7. The LP (ledger page) column just to the left of the debit money column is left blank at the time of making the journal entry. When the debits and credits are later transferred to ledger accounts, the numbers of the ledger accounts are listed in this column to provide a convenient cross reference with the ledger.

Posting

The process of transferring the debits and credits from the journal to the proper ledger accounts is called *posting.* Each amount listed in the debit column of the journal is posted by entering it on the debit side of an account in the ledger, and each amount listed in the credit column of the journal is posted to the credit side of a ledger account.

The mechanics of posting may vary somewhat with the preferences of the individual bookkeeper. For example, the debits and credits may be posted in the sequence shown in the journal, or all the debits on a journal page may be posted first. The following sequence is commonly used:

1. Locate in the ledger the first account named in the journal entry.

2. Enter in the debit column of the ledger account the amount of the debit as shown in the journal.

3. Enter the date of the transaction in the ledger account.

4. Enter in the Reference column of the ledger account the number of the journal page from which the entry is being posted.

5. The recording of the debit in the ledger account is now complete; as evidence of this fact, return to the journal and enter in the LP (ledger page) column the number of the ledger account or page to which the debit was posted.

6. Repeat the posting process described in the preceding five steps for the credit side of the journal entry.

Entering the journal page number in the ledger account and listing the ledger page in the journal provide a cross reference between these two records. The audit of accounting records always requires looking up some journal entries to obtain more information about the amounts listed in ledger accounts. A cross reference between the ledger and journal is therefore essential to efficient audit of the records. Another advantage gained from entering in the journal the number of the account to which a posting has been made is to provide evidence throughout the posting work as to which items have been posted. Otherwise, any interruption in the posting might leave the bookkeeper uncertain as to what had been posted.

Illustration. The journal entry for the first transaction of the Greenhill Real Estate Company is repeated at this point to illustrate the posting process. Note especially that the numbers of the ledger accounts are entered in the reference column of the journal.

Note the Posting References in the Journal

		Journal			*(Page 1)*
19___					
Sept.	*1*	*Cash*	*1*	*20,000*	
		Capital Stock	*50*		*20,000*
		Issued 2,000 shares of capital stock in exchange for cash invested in the business.			

The two ledger accounts affected by this entry appear as follows after the posting has been completed; note that the reference column of each account contains the number 1, indicating that the posting was made from page 1 of the journal.

Note the Posting References in the Ledger

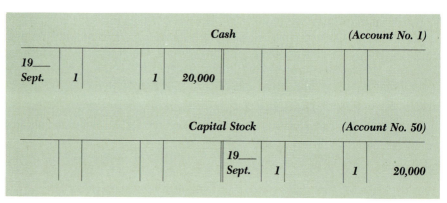

				Cash				*(Account No. 1)*
19___								
Sept.	*1*		*1*	*20,000*				

				Capital Stock				*(Account No. 50)*
				19___				
				Sept.	*1*		*1*	*20,000*

Ledger accounts after posting

After all the September transactions have been posted, the ledger of the Greenhill Real Estate Company appears as shown on page 43. The accounts are arranged in the ledger in balance sheet order, that is, assets first, followed by liabilities and stockholders' equity.

Ledger
Showing
September
Trans-
actions

Cash (Account No. 1)

19—					19—				
Sept.	1		1	20,000	Sept.	3		1	7,000
	20	7,500	1	500		5		1	5,000
				20,500		30		1	1,000
									13,000

Accounts Receivable (Account No. 2)

19—					19—				
Sept.	10	1,500	1	2,000	Sept.	20		1	500

Land (Account No. 20)

19—					19—				
Sept.	3	5,000	1	7,000	Sept.	10		1	2,000

Building (Account No. 22)

19—									
Sept.	5		1	12,000					

Office Equipment (Account No. 25)

19—									
Sept.	14		1	1,800					

Accounts Payable (Account No. 30)

19—					19—				
Sept.	30		1	1,000	Sept.	5		1	7,000
						14	7,800	1	1,800
									8,800

Capital Stock (Account No. 50)

					19—				
					Sept.	1		1	20,000

Computing balances of ledger accounts

The computation of the balance of the Cash account was illustrated earlier in this chapter, but a concise statement of a commonly used procedure for computing the balance of an account containing several entries may be useful at this point.

1. Add the debits in the account and insert the total in small figures just below the last entry in the debit column.

2. Add the credits in the account and insert the total in small figures just below the last entry in the credit column.

3. Compute the difference between the debit total and the credit total. If the account has a debit balance, enter this amount as a small figure to the left of the last debit entry; if the account has a credit balance, enter this amount to the left of the last credit entry.

THE TRIAL BALANCE

Since equal dollar amounts of debits and credits are entered in the accounts for every transaction recorded, the sum of all the debits in the ledger must be equal to the sum of all the credits. If the computation of account balances has been accurate, it follows that the total of the accounts with debit balances must be equal to the total of the accounts with credit balances.

Before using the account balances to prepare a balance sheet, it is desirable to *prove* that the total of accounts with debit balances is in fact equal to the total of accounts with credit balances. This proof of the equality of debit and credit balances is called a *trial balance.* A trial balance is a two-column schedule listing the names and balances of all the accounts in the order in which they appear in the ledger; the debit balances are listed in the left-hand column and the credit balances in the right-hand column. The totals of the two columns should agree. A trial balance taken from the ledger of the Greenhill Real Estate Company appears below:

Trial Balance at Month-end Proves Ledger is in Balance

GREENHILL REAL ESTATE COMPANY
Trial Balance
September 30, 19___

Cash	$ 7,500	
Accounts receivable	1,500	
Land	5,000	
Building	12,000	
Office equipment	1,800	
Accounts payable		$ 7,800
Capital stock		20,000
	$27,800	$27,800

Dollar signs are not used in journals or ledgers. Some accountants use dollar signs in trial balances; some do not. In this book, dollar signs are used in trial balances. Dollar signs should always be used in the balance sheet, the income statement, and other formal financial reports. In the balance sheet, for example, a dollar sign is placed by the first amount in each column and also by each amount listed below an underlining.

Uses and limitations of the trial balance

The trial balance provides proof that the ledger is in balance. The agreement of the debit and credit totals of the trial balance gives assurance that:

1. Equal debits and credits have been recorded for all transactions.

2. The debit or credit balance of each account has been correctly computed.

3. The addition of the account balances in the trial balance has been correctly performed.

Suppose that the debit and credit totals of the trial balance do not agree. This situation indicates that one or more errors have been made. Typical of such errors are: (1) the entering of a debit as a credit, or vice versa; (2) arithmetic mistakes in balancing accounts; (3) clerical errors in copying account balances into the trial balance; (4) listing a debit balance in the credit column of the trial balance, or vice versa; and (5) errors in addition of the trial balance.

The preparation of a trial balance does not prove that transactions have been correctly analyzed and recorded in the proper accounts. If, for example, a receipt of cash were erroneously recorded by debiting the Land account instead of the Cash account, the trial balance would still balance. Also, if a transaction were completely omitted from the ledger, the error would not be disclosed by the trial balance. In brief, the trial balance proves only one aspect of the ledger, and that is the equality of debits and credits.

Despite these limitations, the trial balance is a useful device. It not only provides assurance that the ledger is in balance, but it also serves as a convenient steppingstone for the preparation of financial statements. As explained in Chapter 1, the balance sheet is a formal statement showing the financial condition of the business, intended for distribution to managers, owners, bankers, and various outsiders. The trial balance, on the other hand, is merely a working paper, useful to the accountant but not intended for distribution to others. The balance sheet and other financial statements can be prepared more conveniently from the trial balance than directly from the ledger, especially if there are a great many ledger accounts.

DEMONSTRATION PROBLEM

a. Auto Parks, Inc., was organized on October 1 and carried out several transactions prior to opening for business on November 1. The partially filled in journal for this organizational period appears below. You are to determine the titles of the accounts to be debited and credited in these journal entries.

			Journal			*(Page 1)*
19__						
Oct.	1	Debit CASH		90,000		
		cREDit Capital Stock				90,000
		Issued 9,000 shares of $10 par value capital stock for cash.				
	2	Debit LAND		24,000		
		CREDit CASH				4,000
		C D Notes Payable				20,000
		Purchased land. Paid part cash and issued note payable for balance.				
	3	D BUILDing		3,600		
		C CASH				3,600
		Purchased a small portable building for cash.				
	4	D - Equip		1,600		
		C ACC PAYABLE				1,600
		Purchased cash register from Bar & Co. on account.				
	24	Debit - ACCt PAY		700		
		CREDit - CASH				700
		Paid part of account payable to Bar & Co.				

b. Post the preceding journal entries to the proper ledger accounts. Insert the ledger account number in the LP column of the journal as each item is posted.

Cash (1)

Land (21)

Building   (23)

Office Equipment   (25)

Accounts Payable   (43)

Notes Payable   (45)

Capital Stock   (50)

c. Complete the following trial balance as of October 31, 19____.

AUTO PARKS, INC.
Trial Balance
October 31, 19___

Cash . . . . $

Land . . . .

Building . . . .

Office equipment . . . .

Accounts payable . . . . $

Notes payable . . . .

Capital stock . . . .
                                                          $ $

QUESTIONS

1. Explain precisely what is meant by each of the phrases listed below. Whenever appropriate, indicate whether the left or right side of an account is affected and whether an increase or decrease is indicated.
   a. A debit of $200 to the Cash account
   b. Credit balance
   c. Credit side of an account
   d. A debit of $600 to Accounts Payable
   e. Debit balance
   f. A credit of $50 to Accounts Receivable
   g. A debit to the Land account

2. What relationship exists between the position of an account on the balance sheet and the rules for recording increases in that account?

3. Certain accounts normally have *debit balances* and other types of accounts normally have *credit balances.* State a rule indicating the position on the balance sheet of each such group of accounts.

4. For each of the following transactions, indicate whether the account in parentheses should be debited or credited, and give the reason for your answer.
   a. Purchased a typewriter on credit, promising to make payment in full within 30 days. (Accounts Payable)
   b. Purchased land for cash. (Cash)
   c. Sold an old, unneeded typewriter on 30-day credit. (Office Equipment)
   d. Obtained a loan of $5,000 from a bank. (Cash)
   e. Issued 1,000 shares of $25 par value capital stock for cash of $25,000. (Capital Stock)

5. What is a T account? How does it differ from a ledger account?

6. Compare and contrast a journal and a ledger.

7. During the first week of an accounting course, one student expressed the opinion that a great deal of time could be saved if a business would record transactions directly in ledger accounts rather than entering transactions first in a journal and then posting the debit and credit amounts from the journal to the ledger. Student B agreed with this view but added that such a system should not be called double-entry bookkeeping since each transaction would be entered only once. Student C disagreed with both A and B. He argued that the use of a journal and a ledger was more efficient than entering transactions directly in ledger accounts. Furthermore, he argued that the meaning of double-entry bookkeeping did not refer to the practice of maintaining both a journal and ledger. Evaluate the statements made by all three students.

8. Which step in the recording of transactions requires greater understanding of accounting principles?
   a. The entering of transactions in the journal
   b. The posting of entries to ledger accounts

9. What purposes are served by the preparation of a trial balance?

10. What is the difference between an *account* and a *ledger?*

11. Criticize the following statement. "Nearly all business enterprises use the double-entry method of bookkeeping. Under this system the number of accounts with debit balances must agree with the number of accounts with credit balances. This equality of accounts causes the books to be in balance."

12. A student beginning the study of accounting prepared a trial balance in which two unusual features appeared. The Buildings account showed a credit balance of $20,000, and the Accounts Payable account a debit balance of $100. Considering each of these two abnormal balances separately, state whether the condition was the result of an error in the records or could have resulted from proper recording of an unusual transaction.

EXERCISES

1. The following accounts show the first seven transactions of Daylight Corporation. Write a one-sentence explanation of each transaction.

Cash				Accounts Payable			
May 1	90,000	May 12	10,000	June 20	500	May 20	500
		May 31	4,000				
		June 20	500				

Land				Notes Payable			
May 12	40,000					May 12	30,000
						May 31	18,500

Building	
May 31	22,500

Office Equipment	
May 20	500

Capital Stock	
May 1 (9,000 shares)	90,000

2. Henry Riley, accountant for the Mason Company, prepared a trial balance of the ledger at December 31, but found that it did not balance. In searching for the cause, he discovered that a transaction for the purchase of a copying machine had been recorded by a debit of $1,275 to the Office Equipment account and a debit of $1,275 to Accounts Payable. The credit column of the incorrect trial balance had a total of $144,900. How much was the total of the debit column of the trial balance before correction of the error? Explain.

3. Blake Corporation was organized on January 1 by Henry Blake and four of his friends. During the year the following events occurred.

a. The corporation issued 100,000 shares of $1 par value capital stock in exchange for $100,000 cash invested by Blake and his friends.

b. Land and a building were purchased at a cost of $40,000. The amount of $5,000 was paid in cash and a note payable issued for the balance of $35,000. (Interest is to be ignored.)

c. An additional 35,000 shares of capital stock were issued in exchange for the $35,000 note payable previously issued by the corporation in **b** above.

d. Office equipment was purchased on account at a cost of $6,500.

e. A partial payment of $2,000 was made on the account payable incurred in **d** above.

f. James Hilton, one of the original stockholders and owner of 10,000 shares, sold his entire holdings to his brother-in-law for $15,000 cash and a boat valued at $4,000.

g. One item of office equipment which had cost $350 was found to be defective and was returned to the supplier, who allowed full credit for the item.

For each of the above seven events, indicate the net effect on the total assets, the total liabilities, and the total owners' equity. As an illustration of the form to be used in tabulating your answer, the first event would be described as follows:

	Assets	*Liabilities*	*Owners' Equity*
a.	Issued capital stock + $100,000	–0–	+ $100,000

4. Analyze separately each of the following transactions.

a. On June 1, the Wilbur Company was organized and issued 2,500 shares of $10 par value capital stock in exchange for $25,000 cash.

b. On June 2, land was acquired for $12,000 cash.

c. On June 3, a prefabricated building was purchased from Ez-Built Supply Company at a cost of $8,000. A cash payment of $6,000 was made. The balance was to be paid within 30 days.

d. On June 4, office equipment was purchased from Modern Office Equipment Company at a cost of $4,000. A down payment of $1,000 was made in cash. A note payable was issued for the balance.

e. On July 3, the balance due Ez-Built Supply Company was paid.

Note: The type of analysis to be made is illustrated by the following example, using item **a** above.

a. (1) The asset Cash was increased. Increases in assets are recorded by debits. Debit Cash, $25,000.

 (2) The stockholders' equity was increased. Increases in stockholders' equity are recorded by credits. Credit Capital Stock, $25,000.

PROBLEMS

2-1 Research Corporation was organized to gather information on consumer behavior on behalf of its clients. The following alphabetical list shows the account balances at February 28, 19___:

Accounts payable.	$ 4,809.36
Accounts receivable	1,045.80
Automobiles	7,800.00
Capital stock.	40,000.00
Cash	6,200.00
Furniture & fixtures	?
Garage building.	3,100.00
Land	20,000.00
Notes payable	52,500.00
Notes receivable.	13,000.00
Office building	44,000.00
Office machines	3,550.00
Office supplies.	265.30
Retained earnings	8,287.10
Taxes payable	587.50
United States government bonds	5,000.00

Instructions

a. Rearrange the above data and prepare a trial balance.

b. Prepare a balance sheet.

2-2 Car Rental Corporation was organized on January 1. The following account titles and numbers were established for immediate use by the corporation; it was expected that additional accounts would be required before long.

Cash	10
Accounts receivable	11
Land	16
Building.	17
Automobiles	20
Office equipment	22
Accounts payable.	31
Notes payable	32
Capital stock.	40

The transactions by the corporation during January, 19——, including the initial investment by the stockholders, were as follows:

Jan. 1   Issued 20,000 shares of $10 par value capital stock in exchange for $200,000 cash.

Jan. 2   The corporation purchased land for $25,000 and a building on the lot for $16,000. A cash payment of $20,000 was made and a promissory note issued for the balance.

Jan. 4   Purchased 50 new automobiles at $2,500 each from Fleet Motor Company. Paid $30,000 cash, the balance to be paid in 30 days.

Jan. 5   Sold an automobile to one of the stockholders at cost. The stockholder paid $500 in cash and agreed to pay the balance within 30 days.

Jan. 7 One automobile proved to be defective and was returned to Fleet Motor Company. The amount due the creditor was reduced by $2,500.

Jan. 9 Purchased a cash register and office desks at a cost of $2,300 cash.

Jan. 28 Paid $12,500 cash to Fleet Motor Company.

Instructions

a. Prepare journal entries for the month of January.

b. Post to ledger accounts, and determine their balances.

c. Prepare a trial balance.

2-3 The Stenographic Service Company started business in September, 19____. The business is located in a suburban office building and provides typing, duplicating, and other stenographic services to the tenants of the building and to other clients. As of September 30, 19____, the ledger accounts contained entries as follows:

Cash			
Sept. 1	50,000	Sept. 2	4,440
16	550	25	1,250
		28	300

Delivery Equipment	
Sept. 2	6,200

Accounts Receivable			
Sept. 6	1,100	Sept. 16	550

Notes Payable			
Sept. 25	1,000	Sept. 2	15,000

Office Supplies			
Sept. 17	1,500	Sept. 26	20
20	250		

Accounts Payable			
Sept. 25	250	Sept. 17	1,500
26	20	20	250
28	300		

Office Equipment			
Sept. 2	13,240	Sept. 6	1,100

Capital Stock, $10 par			
		Sept. 1	50,000

Instructions

a. Reconstruct the journal entries as they were probably made by the company's bookkeeper, giving a full explanation for each transaction.

b. Determine account balances and prepare a trial balance as of September 30, 19____.

c. Prepare a balance sheet as of September 30, 19____.

2-4 Account numbers and balances for the Monroe Express Co. at April 30, 1971, were as follows:

Account Number		Account Balance
11	Cash	$10,690
13	U.S. government bonds.............................	4,000

Account Number		Account Balance
16	Accounts receivable.	$ 3,640
20	Land	25,000
23	Building	40,000
24	Delivery trucks	32,000
26	Office equipment	1,500
30	Notes payable	37,000
32	Accounts payable	5,380
34	Property taxes payable	1,500
40	Capital stock	50,000
41	Retained earnings	22,950

The transactions for May, 1971, were as follows:

May 1   Paid $1,500 for property taxes due this day.

May 2   Paid $2,250 in partial settlement of accounts payable.

May 4   Purchased a postage meter for $300 cash.

May 6   Collected $800 from Main Street Department Store (applicable to Accounts Receivable).

May 7   Purchased a new truck at a cost of $2,900 from Pacific Motor Company. A cash down payment of $1,000 was made. A promissory note was issued for the balance, to be paid in monthly installments of $200 beginning June 7 (with a final payment of $100).

May 8   Collected an account receivable of $1,000 from Grant Furniture Company.

May 16   Sold U.S. government bonds for cash, $4,000.

May 23   Sold half the land to Main Street Department Store as their new site for a warehouse, selling price $12,500. Main Street Department Store agreed to pay within 30 days.

Instructions

a.   Transfer the April 30 balances to ledger accounts.

b.   Prepare journal entries (page 30 of general journal) for the month of May.

c.   Post to ledger accounts.

d.   Prepare a trial balance as of May 31, 1971.

e.   Prepare a balance sheet as of May 31, 1971.

2-5   The account titles and numbers used by Educational TV, Inc., are listed below:

Cash	11
Accounts receivable	15
Supplies	19
Land	21
Building	22
Transmitter	23
Telecasting equipment	24
Film library	25
Notes payable	31
Accounts payable	32
Capital stock	51

The transactions for March, 19___, were as follows:

Mar. 1   A charter was granted to Joseph Blair for the organization of Educational TV, Inc. Blair invested $182,500 cash and received 25,000 shares of stock in exchange.

Mar. 3   Purchased land at a cost of $25,000 from Inland Development Company, making a cash down payment of $3,000 and signing a promissory note for the balance.

Mar. 5   Purchased a transmitter at a cost of $100,000 from AC Mfg. Co., making a cash down payment of $40,000. The balance, in the form of an account payable, was to be paid in monthly installments of $1,500, beginning March 15.

Mar. 6   Erected a telecasting and office building at a cost of $50,000, paying cash.

Mar. 8   Purchased telecasting equipment at a cost of $46,000 from Telequip Corp., paying cash.

Mar. 9   Purchased a film library at a cost of $51,995 from Modern Film Productions, making a down payment of $14,000 cash, with the balance payable in 30 days.

Mar. 12   Sold part of the film library to City College; cost was $10,000, and selling price also was $10,000. City College agreed to pay the full amount in 30 days.

Mar. 15   Paid $1,500 cash to AC Mfg. Co. as the first monthly payment on the account payable created on March 5.

Mar. 25   Bought supplies costing $1,750, paying cash.

Instructions
a.   Prepare journal entries.
b.   Post to ledger accounts.
c.   Prepare a trial balance as of March 31, 19___.
d.   Prepare a balance sheet.

2-6   John Adams and Warner Heller have operated as independent real estate agents in Atlanta, Georgia, for many years. Early in 19___, they agree to combine their separate businesses into a corporation. The balance sheets for Adams and Heller before they combine their businesses follow:

	Adams	Heller
Cash	$ 1,500	$ 2,500
Accounts receivable	12,500	15,000
Land	40,000	50,000
Buildings	30,000	60,000
Office equipment	16,000	11,500
	$100,000	$139,000
Accounts payable	$ 10,000	$ 15,000
Notes payable	20,000	19,000
Owners' capital	70,000	105,000
	$100,000	$139,000

The A & H Realty Corporation was organized on January 20, 19___, issuing 10,000 shares of no-par stock with an assigned value of $175,000. Asset values stated on the records of each realtor are to be retained by the corporation. Heller's books will be used to record all transactions of the corporation. Accordingly, Adams' assets and liabilities are transferred to the corporation; Heller's capital account is closed out; and capital stock is issued to Adams and Heller in proportion to the capital invested (assets less liabilities).

During the remainder of January, 19___, the following transactions are completed by the A & H Realty Corporation:

Jan. 21 Collected $7,500 on accounts receivable.

Jan. 23 Paid $5,000 on accounts payable and $4,000 on notes payable.

Jan. 26 Issued an additional 1,000 shares of stock to employees for a total consideration of $20,000 in cash. (Credit Capital Stock, $20,000.)

Jan. 29 Sold surplus office equipment on account for $2,800. The equipment is carried on the books at $2,800.

Jan. 31 Purchased a vacant lot for $10,500. Paid $1,250 down; balance is due on February 28, 19___.

Instructions

a. Prepare journal entries to record the issuance of capital stock to Adams and Heller on Heller's books (which are retained by the corporation).

b. Prepare journal entries to record the transactions after the corporation is organized.

c. Determine account balances after all transactions have been posted to ledger accounts of the corporation and prepare a balance sheet as of January 31, 19___. Account numbers need not be assigned to the ledger accounts.

3 Measuring business income

The earning of net income or profits is the chief goal of most business concerns. The individuals who organize a corporation and invest in its capital stock do so with the hope and expectation that the business will operate at a profit, thereby increasing their ownership equity in the business. In other words, *profit is an increase* in owners' equity resulting from successful operation. From the standpoint of the individual firm, profitable operation is essential if the firm is to succeed or even to survive.

Profits may be retained in the business to finance expansion, or may be distributed to the owners. Some of the largest corporations have become large by retaining their profits in the business and using these profits for purposes of growth.[1] Retained profits may be used, for example, to acquire new plant and equipment, to carry on research leading to new and better products, and to extend sales operations into new territories. A satisfactory rate of business profits is generally associated with high employment, an improving standard of living, and a strong, expanding national economy.

Since the drive for profits underlies the very existence of business concerns, it follows that a most important function of an accounting system is to provide information about the profitability of the business. Before we can measure the profits of a business, we need to establish a sharp, clear meaning for *profits*. The word is used in somewhat different senses by economists, lawyers, and the general public. Perhaps for this reason, accountants prefer to use the alternative term *net income*, and to define this term very carefully. At this point, we shall adopt the technical accounting term "net income" in preference to the less precise term "profits."

In Chapter 1, accounting was referred to as the "language of business," and some of the key words of this language such as *assets, liabilities,* and *owners' equity,* were introduced. In the present chapter we want to establish clear working definitions for *revenue, expenses,* and *net income.* Very concisely stated, *revenue minus expenses equals net income.* To understand why this is true and how the measurements are made, let us begin with the meaning of revenue.

[1] A recent balance sheet of General Motors Corporation, for example, shows total stockholders' equity of about $10 billion, of which more than $8 billion is in the form of retained earnings.

Revenue *total income received*

When a business renders services to its customers or delivers merchandise to them, it either receives immediate payment in cash or acquires an account receivable which will be collected and thereby become cash within a short time. The revenue for a given period consists of the inflow of cash and receivables from sales made in that period. For any single transaction, the amount of revenue is a measurement of the asset values received from the customer. Another means of earning revenue is through investment, for example, the interest earned on a bank savings account or on a government bond, and the dividends received through ownership of capital stock.

Not all receipts of cash represent revenue. As shown in Chapter 1, a business may obtain cash by borrowing from a bank. This increase in cash is offset by an increase in liabilities in the form of a note payable to the bank. The owners' equity is not changed by the borrowing transaction. Collection of an account receivable is another example of a cash receipt that does not represent revenue. The act of collection causes an increase in the asset, cash, and a corresponding decrease in another asset, accounts receivable. The amount of total assets remains unchanged, and, of course, there is no change in liabilities or owners' equity.

As another example of the distinction between revenue and cash receipts, let us assume that a business begins operations in March and makes sales of merchandise or services to its customers in that month as follows: sales for cash, $25,000; sales on credit (payable in April), $15,000. The revenue for March is $40,000, the total amount of cash received or to be received from the month's sales. When the accounts receivable of $15,000 are collected during April, they must not be counted as revenue a second time.

Revenue causes an increase in owners' equity. The inflow of cash and receivables from customers increases the total assets of the company; on the other side of the accounting equation, the liabilities do not change, but the owners' equity is increased to match the increase in total assets. Bear in mind, however, that not every increase in owners' equity comes from revenue. As illustrated in Chapter 1, the owners' equity is also increased by the investment of assets in the business by the owners.

Expenses

Expenses represent the cost of the goods and services used up or consumed in the process of obtaining revenue. Examples include salaries paid employees, charges for newspaper advertising and for telephone service, and the wearing out (depreciation) of the building and office equipment. All these items are necessary to attract and serve customers and thereby to obtain revenue. Expenses are sometimes referred to as the "cost of doing business," that is, the cost of the various activities necessary to carry on a business.

Expenses cause the owners' equity to decrease. Revenue may be regarded as the positive factor in creating net income, expenses as the negative factor. The relationship between expenses and revenue is a significant one; the expenses of a given month or other period are incurred in order to generate revenue in that same period. The salaries earned by sales employees waiting on customers during July are applicable to July revenues and should be treated as July expenses, even though these salaries may not actually be paid to the employees until sometime in August.

As previously explained, revenues and cash receipts are not one and the same thing; similarly, expenses and cash payments are not identical. Examples of cash payments which are not expenses of the current period include the purchase of an office building for cash, the purchase of merchandise for later sale to customers, the repayment of a bank loan, and the distribution of cash dividends by the business to the stockholders. In deciding whether a given item should be regarded as an expense of the current period, it is often helpful to pose the following questions:

1. Was the alleged "expense" incurred in order to produce revenue of the current period?
2. Does the item in question reduce the owners' equity?

Dividends ~Not An expense!~

A dividend is a distribution of assets (usually cash) by a corporation to its stockholders. Although the payment of a dividend reduces the owners' equity in the corporation, a dividend is not an expense. Unlike payments for advertising, rent, and salaries, the payment of dividends does not serve to generate revenues.

Although withdrawals by the owner of an unincorporated business are somewhat similar to dividends paid by a corporation, significant differences exist. Dividends are paid only when the corporation's board of directors takes formal action to declare a dividend, and dividend payments ordinarily cannot be greater than the retained earnings. The dividend is always a specific amount, such as $1 per share.

Since the declaration and payment of a dividend reduces the stockholders' equity, it could be recorded by debiting the Retained Earnings account. A better procedure is to debit an account called Dividends, which is then closed into the Retained Earnings account at the end of the year.

Relating revenue and expenses to time periods

A balance sheet shows the financial position of the business at a given date. An income statement, on the other hand, shows the results of operations over *a period of time.* In fact, the concept of income is meaningless unless it is related to a period of time. For example, if a businessman says, "My business produces net income of $5,000," the meaning is not at all clear; it could be made clear, however, by relating the income to a time period, such as "$5,000 a week," "$5,000 a month," or "$5,000 a year."

The accounting period. Every business concern prepares a yearly income statement, and most businesses prepare quarterly and monthly income statements as well. Management needs to know from month to month whether revenues are rising or falling, whether expenses are being held to the level anticipated, and how net income compares with the net income of the preceding month and with the net income of the corresponding month of the preceding year. The term *accounting period* means the span of time covered by an income statement. It may consist of a month, a quarter of a year, a half year, or a year.

Many income statements cover the calendar year ended December 31, but an increasing number of concerns are adopting an annual accounting period ending with a month other than December. Generally a business finds it more convenient to end its annual accounting period during a slack season rather than during a time of peak activity. Any 12-month accounting period adopted by a business is called its *fiscal year.* A fiscal year ending at the annual low point of seasonal activity is said to be a *natural business year.* The fiscal year selected by the federal government for its accounting purposes begins on July 1 and ends 12 months later on June 30.

Transactions affecting two or more accounting periods. The operation of a business entails an endless stream of transactions, many of which begin in one accounting period but affect several succeeding periods. Fire insurance policies, for example, are commonly issued to cover a period of three years. In this case, the apportionment of the cost of the policy by months is an easy matter. If the policy covers three years (36 months) and costs, for example, $360, the expense each month of maintaining insurance is $10.

Not all transactions can be so precisely divided by accounting periods. The purchase of a building, furniture and fixtures, machinery, a typewriter, or an automobile provides benefits to the business over all the years in which such an asset is used. No one can determine in advance exactly how many years of service will be received from such long-lived assets. Nevertheless, in measuring the net income of a business for a period of one year or less, the accountant must estimate what portion of the cost of the building and similar long-lived assets is applicable to the current year. Since the apportionments for these and many other transactions which overlap two or more accounting periods are in the nature of estimates rather than precise measurements, it follows that income statements should be regarded as useful approximations of annual income rather than as absolutely accurate determinations.

The only time period for which the measurement of net income can be absolutely accurate is the entire life span of the business. When a business concern sells all its assets, pays its debts, and ends its existence, it would then theoretically be possible to determine with precision the net income for the time period from the date of organization to the date of dissolution. Such a theoretically precise measurement of net income would, however, be too late to be of much use to the owners or managers of the business. The practical needs of business enterprise are well served by income statements of reasonable accuracy that tell managers and owners each month, each quarter, and each year the results of business operation.

Rules of debit and credit for revenue and expenses

Our approach to revenue and expenses has stressed the fact that revenue increases the owners' equity, and expenses decrease the owners' equity. The rules of debit and credit for recording revenue and expenses follow this relationship, and therefore the recording of revenue and expenses in ledger accounts requires only a slight extension of the rules of debit and credit presented in Chapter 2. The rule previously stated for recording increases and decreases in owners' equity was as follows:

Increases in owners' equity are recorded by credits.
Decreases in owners' equity are recorded by debits.

This rule is now extended to cover revenue and expense accounts:

Revenue increases owners' equity; therefore revenue is recorded by a credit.

Expenses decrease owners' equity; therefore expenses are recorded by debits.

Ledger accounts for revenue and expenses

During the course of an accounting period, a great many revenue and expense transactions occur in the average business. To classify and summarize these numerous transactions, a separate ledger account is maintained for each major type of revenue and expense. For example, almost every business maintains accounts for Advertising Expense, Telephone Expense, and Salaries Expense. At the end of the period, all the advertising expenses appear as debits in the Advertising Expense account. The debit balance of this account represents the total advertising expense of the period and is listed as one of the expense items in the income statement.

Revenue accounts are usually much less numerous than expense accounts. A small business such as the Greenhill Real Estate Company in our continuing illustration may have only one or two types of revenue, such as commissions earned from arranging sales of real estate, and commissions earned from the rental of properties in behalf of clients. In a business of this type, the revenue accounts might be called Sales Commissions Earned and Rental Commissions Earned. For physicians and attorneys conducting a professional practice, the revenue account is often called Fees. Businesses which sell merchandise of any kind rather than services generally use the term Sales for the revenue account.

Recording revenue and expense transactions: illustration. The organization of the Greenhill Real Estate Company during September has already been described in Chapters 1 and 2. The illustration is now continued for October, during which month the company earned commissions by selling several residences for its clients. Bear in mind that the company does not own any residential property; it merely acts as a broker or agent for clients wishing to sell their houses. A commission of 6% of the sales price of the house is charged for this service. During October the company not only earned commissions but also incurred a number of expenses.

Note that each illustrated transaction which affects an income statement account also affects a balance sheet account. This pattern is consistent with our previous discussion of revenue and expenses. In recording revenue transactions, we shall debit the assets received and credit a revenue account. In recording expense transactions, we shall debit an expense account and credit the asset Cash, or perhaps a liability account if payment is to be made later. The transactions for October were as follows:

Oct. 1   Paid $120 for publication of newspaper advertising describing various houses offered for sale.

	Analysis	Rule	Entry
Advertising Expense Incurred and Paid	The cost of advertising is an expense	Expenses decrease the owners' equity and are recorded by debits	Debit: Advertising Expense, $120
	The asset Cash was decreased	Decreases in assets are recorded by credits	Credit: Cash, $120

Oct. 6   Earned and collected a commission of $2,750 by selling a residence previously listed by a client.

	Analysis	Rule	Entry
Revenue Earned and Collected	The asset Cash was increased	Increases in assets are recorded by debits	Debit: Cash, $2,750
	Revenue was earned	Revenue increases the owners' equity and is recorded by a credit	Credit: Sales Commissions Earned, $2,750

Oct. 16   Newspaper advertising was ordered at a price of $90, payment to be made within 30 days.

	Analysis	Rule	Entry
Advertising Expense Incurred but Not Paid	The cost of advertising is an expense	Expenses decrease the owners' equity and are recorded by debits	Debit: Advertising Expense, $90
	An account payable, a liability, was incurred	Increases in liabilities are recorded by credits	Credit: Accounts Payable, $90

Oct. 20   A commission of $1,130 was earned by selling a client's residence. The sales agreement provided that the commission would be paid in 60 days.

	Analysis	Rule	Entry
Revenue Earned, to Be Collected Later	An asset in the form of an account receivable was acquired	Increases in assets are recorded by debits	Debit: Accounts Receivable, $1,130
	Revenue was earned	Revenue increases the owners' equity and is recorded by a credit	Credit: Sales Commissions Earned, $1,130

Oct. 30   Paid salaries of $1,700 to office employees for services rendered during October.

	Analysis	Rule	Entry
Salaries Expense Incurred and Paid	Salaries of employees are an expense	Expenses decrease the owners' equity and are recorded by debits	Debit: Office Salaries Expense, $1,700
	The asset Cash was decreased	Decreases in assets are recorded by credits	Credit: Cash, $1,700

Oct. 30   A telephone bill for October amounting to $48 was received. Payment was required by November 10.

	Analysis	Rule	Entry
Telephone Expense Incurred, to Be Paid Later	The cost of telephone service is an expense	Expenses decrease the owners' equity and are recorded by debits	Debit: Telephone Expense, $48
	An account payable, a liability, was incurred	Increases in liabilities are recorded by credits	Credit: Accounts Payable, $48

Oct. 30   A dividend of 30 cents per share, or a total of $600, was declared and paid.

	Analysis	Rule	Entry
Payment of a Dividend	Payment of a dividend decreases the owners' equity	Decreases in owners' equity are recorded by debits	Debit: Dividends, $600
	The asset Cash was decreased	Decreases in assets are recorded by credits	Credit: Cash, $600

Entries for declaration and later payment of a dividend. A small corporation with only a few stockholders may choose to declare and pay a dividend on the same day. In large corporations with thousands of stockholders and constant transfers of shares, an interval of a month or more will separate the date of declaration from the later date of payment.

Assume for example that on April 1 the board of directors of Universal Corporation declares the regular quarterly dividend of $1 per share on the 1 million shares of outstanding capital stock. The board's resolution specifies that the dividend will be payable on May 10 to stockholders of record on April 25. To be eligible to receive the dividend, an individual must be listed on the corporation's books as a stockholder on April 25, the date of record. Two entries are required: one on April 1 for the declaration of the dividend, and one on May 10 for its payment, as shown below.

Dividends Declared and . . .

Apr. 1	Dividends 1,000,000	
	Dividends Payable	1,000,000
	Declared dividend of $1 per share payable May 10 to stockholders of record April 25.	

. . . Dividends Paid

May 10	Dividends Payable 1,000,000	
	Cash	1,000,000
	Paid the dividend declared on April 1.	

The Dividends Payable account is a liability which comes into existence when the dividend is declared and is discharged when the dividend is paid.

Now returning to our continuing illustration of Greenhill Real Estate, the journal entries to record the October transactions are as follows:

October Journal Entries for Greenhill Real Estate Company

Journal					(Page 2)	
19__						
Oct.	1	Advertising Expense	70	120		
		Cash	1		120	
		Paid for newspaper advertising.				

October Journal Entries for Greenhill Real Estate Company (Continued)	6	Cash......................... Sales Commissions Earned..... Earned and collected commission by selling residence for client.	1 61	2,750	2,750
	16	Advertising Expense............... Accounts Payable .... Ordered newspaper advertising; payable in 30 days.	70 30	90	90
	20	Accounts Receivable............... Sales Commissions Earned..... Earned commission by selling residence for client; commission to be received in 60 days.	2 61	1,130	1,130
	30	Office Salaries Expense............. Cash.................... Paid office salaries for October.	72 1	1,700	1,700
	30	Telephone Expense................. Accounts Payable .... To record liability for October telephone service.	74 30	48	48
	30	Dividends .... Cash.................... Paid dividend to stockholders (2,000 shares at 30 cents per share).	52 1	600	600

The ledger of the Greenhill Real Estate Company after the October transactions have been posted is now illustrated. For all accounts with more than one entry, the totals and month-end balances are noted in handwritten figures. The accounts appear in the ledger in financial statement order as follows:

Balance sheet accounts
   Assets
   Liabilities
   Owners' equity
Income statement accounts
   Revenue
   Expenses

To conserve space in this illustration, several ledger accounts appear on a single page. In actual practice, however, each account occupies a separate page in the ledger.

*Posting
October
Trans-
actions to
Ledger
Accounts*

Cash (1)

19__					19__				
Sept.	1		1	20,000	Sept.	3		1	7,000
	20	7,500	1	500		5		1	5,000
				20,500		30		1	1,000
Oct.	6	7,830	2	2,750					13,000
				23,250	Oct.	1		2	120
						30		2	1,700
						30		2	600
									15,420

Accounts Receivable (2)

19__					19__				
Sept.	10	1,500	1	2,000	Sept.	20		1	500
Oct.	20	2,630	2	1,130					
				3,130					

Land (20)

19__					19__				
Sept.	3	5,000	1	7,000	Sept.	10		1	2,000

Building (22)

19__									
Sept.	5		1	12,000					

Office Equipment (25)

19__									
Sept.	14		1	1,800					

Accounts Payable (30)

19__					19__				
Sept.	30		1	1,000	Sept.	5		1	7,000
						14	7,800	1	1,800
									8,800
					Oct.	16		2	90
						30	7,938	2	48
									8,938

Posting
October
Trans-
actions to
Ledger
Accounts
(Continued)

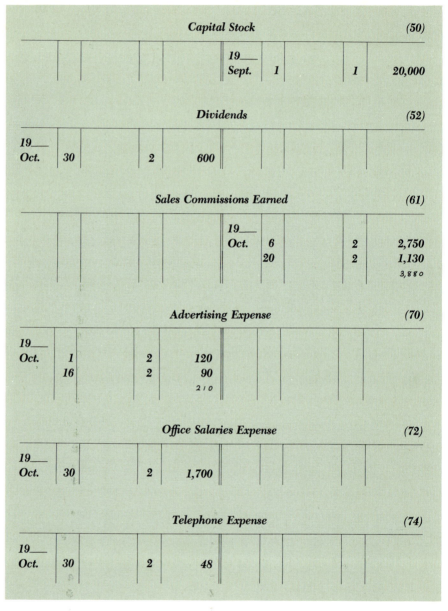

Capital Stock (50)

			19—				
			Sept.	1		1	20,000

Dividends (52)

19—							
Oct.	30		2	600			

Sales Commissions Earned (61)

			19—			
			Oct.	6	2	2,750
				20	2	1,130
						3,880

Advertising Expense (70)

19—					
Oct.	1	2	120		
	16	2	90		
			210		

Office Salaries Expense (72)

19—					
Oct.	30	2	1,700		

Telephone Expense (74)

19—					
Oct.	30	2	48		

Trial balance

The trial balance on page 67 was prepared from the preceding ledger accounts.

Recording depreciation at the end of the period

This trial balance includes all the October expenses requiring cash payments such as salaries, advertising, and telephone service, but it does not include any depreciation expense. Although depreciation expense does not require

<table>
<tr><td>*Proving*
the
Equality
of Debits
and
Credits</td><td colspan="3">

GREENHILL REAL ESTATE COMPANY
Trial Balance
October 31, 19___

</td></tr>
</table>

Cash	$ 7,830	
Accounts receivable	2,630	
Land	5,000	
Building	12,000	
Office equipment	1,800	
Accounts payable		$ 7,938
Capital stock		20,000
Dividends	600	
Sales commissions earned		3,880
Advertising expense	210	
Office salaries expense	1,700	
Telephone expense	48	
	$31,818	$31,818

a monthly cash outlay, it is nevertheless an inevitable and continuing expense. Failure to make an entry for depreciation expense would result in understating the total expenses of the period and consequently in overstating the net income.

Building. The office building purchased by the Greenhill Real Estate Company at a cost of $12,000 is estimated to have a useful life of 20 years. The purpose of the $12,000 expenditure was to provide a place in which to carry on the business and thereby to obtain revenue. After 20 years of use the building will be worthless and the original cost of $12,000 will have been entirely consumed. In effect, the company has purchased 20 years of "housing services" at a total cost of $12,000. A portion of this cost expires during each year of use of the building. If we assume that each year's operations should bear an equal share of the total cost (straight-line depreciation), the annual depreciation expense will amount to $\frac{1}{20}$ of $12,000, or $600. On a monthly basis, depreciation expense is $50 ($12,000 cost ÷ 240 months). There are alternative methods of spreading the cost of a depreciable asset over its useful life, some of which will be considered in Chapter 13.

The journal entry to record depreciation of the building during October follows:

| *Recording*
Deprecia-
tion of
Building | 19___
Oct. | 31 | *Depreciation Expense: Building*
    Accumulated Depreciation: Building
To record depreciation for October. | 76
23 | 50 | 50 |

The Depreciation Expense account will appear in the income statement for October along with the other expenses of salaries, advertising, and telephone expense. The Accumulated Depreciation: Building account will appear in the balance sheet as a deduction from the Building account.

Office equipment. Depreciation on the office equipment of the Greenhill Real Estate Company must also be recorded at the end of October. This equipment cost $1,800 and is assumed to have a useful life of 10 years. Monthly depreciation expense on the straight-line basis is, therefore, $15, computed by dividing the cost of $1,800 by the useful life of 120 months. The journal entry is as follows:

Recording
Deprecia-
tion of
Office
Equip-
ment

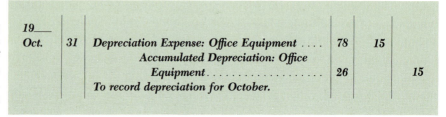

19__				
Oct.	31	*Depreciation Expense: Office Equipment*	78	15
		Accumulated Depreciation: Office		
		Equipment.................	26	15
		To record depreciation for October.		

No depreciation was recorded on the building and office equipment for September, the month in which these assets were acquired, because regular operations did not begin until October. Generally, depreciation is not recognized until the business begins active operation and the assets are placed in use. Accountants often use the expression "matching costs and benefits" to convey the idea of writing off the cost of an asset to expense during the time periods in which the business enjoys the use of the property.

The journal entry by which depreciation is brought on the books at the end of the month is called an *adjusting entry.* The adjustment of certain asset accounts and related expense accounts is a necessary step at the end of each accounting period so that the information presented in the financial statements will be as accurate and complete as possible. In the next chapter, adjusting entries will be shown for some other matters in addition to depreciation.

The adjusted trial balance

After all the necessary adjusting entries have been made at the end of the period, an adjusted trial balance is prepared to prove that the ledger is still in balance. The adjusted trial balance on page 69 differs from the trial balance shown on page 67 because it includes accounts for depreciation expense and accumulated depreciation.

FINANCIAL STATEMENTS

The income statement

When we measure the net income earned by a business we are measuring its economic performance—its success or failure as a business enterprise.

Adjusted
Trial
Balance

GREENHILL REAL ESTATE COMPANY
Adjusted Trial Balance
October 31, 19___

Cash	$ 7,830	
Accounts receivable	2,630	
Land	5,000	
Building	12,000	
Accumulated depreciation: building		$ 50
Office equipment	1,800	
Accumulated depreciation: office equipment		15
Accounts payable		7,938
Capital stock		20,000
Dividends	600	
Sales commissions earned		3,880
Advertising expense	210	
Office salaries expense	1,700	
Telephone expense	48	
Depreciation expense: building	50	
Depreciation expense: office equipment	15	
	$31,883	$31,883

Stockholders, prospective investors, managers, and bankers are anxious to see the latest available income statement and thereby to judge how well the company is doing. The October income statement for Greenhill Real Estate Company appears as follows:

Income
Statement
for
October

GREENHILL REAL ESTATE COMPANY
Income Statement
For the Month Ended October 31, 19___

Sales commissions earned		$3,880
Expenses:		
Advertising expense	$ 210	
Office salaries expense	1,700	
Telephone expense	48	
Depreciation expense: building	50	
Depreciation expense: office equipment	15	2,023
Net income		$1,857

This income statement shows that the revenue during October exceeded the expenses of the month, thus producing a net income of $1,857. Bear in mind, however, that our measurement of net income is not absolutely accurate or precise, because of the assumptions and estimates involved in the accounting process. We have recorded only those economic events which are evidenced by accounting transactions. Perhaps during October the Greenhill Real Estate Company has developed a strong interest on the part of many clients who are on the verge of buying or selling homes. This accumulation of client interest is an important step toward profitable operation, but is not reflected in the October 31 income statement because it is not subject to objective measurement. Remember also that in determining the amount of depreciation expense we had to estimate the useful life of the building and office equipment. Any error in our estimates is reflected in the net income reported for October. Despite these limitations, the income statement is of vital importance, and indicates that the new business has operated profitably during the first month of its existence.

Retained earnings statement

Retained earnings is that portion of the stockholders' equity created by earning and retaining net income. The *statement of retained earnings,* which covers the same time period as the related income statement, shows the sources of increase and decrease in retained earnings for that period.

Retained Earnings Statement for October

GREENHILL REAL ESTATE COMPANY	
Statement of Retained Earnings	
For the Month Ended October 31, 19___	
Net income for the month	$1,857
Less: Dividends	600
Retained earnings, October 31, 19___	$1,257

In this example the company had no retained earnings at the beginning of the period. The statement for the following month would show a beginning balance of $1,257.

Balance sheet

The following balance sheet was prepared from data in the adjusted trial balance and the statement of retained earnings. Previous illustrations of balance sheets have been arranged in the *account form,* that is, with the assets on the left side of the page and the liabilities and owners' equity on the right side. This illustrated balance sheet is shown in *report form,* that is, with the liabilities and owners' equity sections listed below rather than to the right of the asset section. Both the account form and the report form are widely used. Note that this balance sheet includes two columns of figures in both the asset portion and in the section for liabilities and stockholders' equity. One or more additional columns are used whenever two or more related items are to be combined or offset in computing the summary figures for the right-hand column.

Balance Sheet at October 31: Report Form

GREENHILL REAL ESTATE COMPANY
Balance Sheet
October 31, 19___

Assets

Cash		$ 7,830
Accounts receivable....................................		2,630
Land		5,000
Building..	$12,000	
Less: Accumulated depreciation	50	11,950
Office equipment..	$ 1,800	
Less: Accumulated depreciation	15	1,785
		$29,195

Liabilities and Stockholders' Equity

Liabilities:		
Accounts payable		$ 7,938
Stockholders' equity:		
Capital stock..	$20,000	
Retained earnings	1,257	21,257
		$29,195

The relationship between the income statement, the retained earnings statement, and the balance sheet is shown in the stockholders' equity section of the balance sheet. The stockholders' original capital investment of $20,000 appears unchanged under the caption of Capital Stock. The Retained Earnings account had a zero balance at October 1, but as explained in the retained earnings statement, it was increased by the $1,857 of net income earned during October and decreased by the $600 dividend paid, leaving a balance of $1,257. The amount of the Retained Earnings account at any balance sheet date represents the accumulated earnings of the company since the date of incorporation, minus any losses and minus all dividends distributed to stockholders. One reason for maintaining a distinction between capital stock and retained earnings is that a corporation usually cannot legally pay dividends greater than the amount of retained earnings. The separation of these two elements of ownership may also be enlightening because it shows how much of the total owners' equity resulted from the investment of funds by stockholders and how much was derived from earning and retaining net income.

In the Greenhill Real Estate Company illustration, we have shown the two common ways in which the owners' equity in a business may be increased: (1) investment of cash or other assets by the owners, and (2) operating the business at a profit. There are also two common ways in which the owners' equity may be decreased: (1) payment of dividends, and (2) operating the business at a loss.

CLOSING THE BOOKS

Revenue and expense accounts are closed at the end of each accounting period by transferring their balances to a summary account called Income Summary. When the credit balances of the revenue accounts and the debit balances of the expense accounts have been transferred into one summary account, the balance of this Income Summary will be the net income or net loss for the period. If the revenues (credit balances) exceed the expenses (debit balances), the Income Summary account will have a credit balance representing net income. Conversely, if expenses exceed revenues, the Income Summary will have a debit balance representing net loss.

Revenues Minus Expenses Equal Net Income

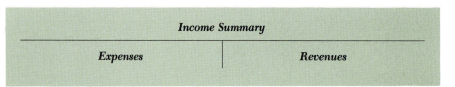

As previously explained, all debits and credits in the ledger are posted from the journal; therefore, the closing of revenue and expense accounts requires the making of journal entries and the posting of these journal entries to ledger accounts. A journal entry made for the purpose of closing a revenue or expense by transferring its balance to the Income Summary account is called a *closing entry*. This term is also applied to the journal entries (to be explained later) used in closing the Income Summary account and the Dividends account into the Retained Earnings account.

A principal purpose of the year-end process of closing the revenue and expense accounts is to reduce their balances to zero. Since the revenue and expense accounts provide the information for the income statement of *a given accounting period,* it is essential that these accounts have zero balances at the beginning of each new period. The closing of the books has the effect of wiping the slate clean and preparing the accounts for the recording of revenues and expenses during the succeeding accounting period.

It is common practice to close the books only once a year, but for illustration, we shall now demonstrate the closing of the books of the Greenhill Real Estate Company at October 31 after one month's operation.

Closing entries for revenue accounts. Revenue accounts have credit balances. Closing a revenue account, therefore, means transferring its credit balance to the Income Summary account. This transfer is accomplished by a journal entry debiting the revenue account in an amount equal to its credit balance, with an offsetting credit to the Income Summary account. The only revenue account of the Greenhill Real Estate Company is Sales Commissions

Earned, which had a credit balance of $3,880 at October 31. The journal entry necessary to close this account is as follows:

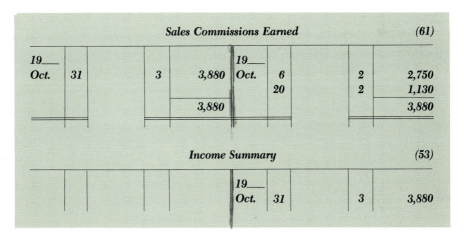

Closing a
Revenue
Account

			Journal			(Page 3)
19__						
Oct.	31	Sales Commissions Earned	61	3,880		
		Income Summary	53		3,880	
		To close the Sales Commissions Earned account.				

After this closing entry has been posted, the two accounts affected will appear as follows:

Sales Commissions Earned (61)

19__					19__				
Oct.	31		3	3,880	Oct.	6		2	2,750
						20		2	1,130
				3,880					3,880

Income Summary (53)

					19__				
					Oct.	31		3	3,880

The Sales Commissions Earned account is now closed and has a zero balance. The equal totals on both sides of the account and the ruling of the account (double lines under the totals) show that it has no balance. When account balances were computed for use in preparing a trial balance, small figures were placed in the ledger account to show the totals and balances. After an account has been ruled as shown in this illustration, there is no longer any need for these small figures and they may be erased.

Closing entries for expense accounts. Expense accounts have debit balances. Closing an expense account means transferring its debit balance to the Income Summary account. The journal entry to close an expense account, therefore, consists of a credit to the expense account in an amount equal to its debit balance, with an offsetting debit to the Income Summary account.

There are five expense accounts in the ledger of the Greenhill Real Estate Company. Five separate journal entries could be made to close these five expense accounts, but the use of one compound journal entry is an easier, more efficient, timesaving method of closing all five expense accounts.

<table>
<tr><td rowspan="10">*Closing Various Expense Accounts*</td><td>*19___*</td><td></td><td></td><td></td><td></td></tr>
<tr><td>*Oct.*</td><td>*31*</td><td>*Income Summary* . . . .</td><td>*53*</td><td>*2,023*</td></tr>
<tr><td></td><td></td><td>*Advertising Expense* . . . .</td><td>*70*</td><td>*210*</td></tr>
<tr><td></td><td></td><td>*Office Salaries Expense* . . . .</td><td>*72*</td><td>*1,700*</td></tr>
<tr><td></td><td></td><td>*Telephone Expense* . . . .</td><td>*74*</td><td>*48*</td></tr>
<tr><td></td><td></td><td>*Depreciation Expense: Building* . .</td><td>*76*</td><td>*50*</td></tr>
<tr><td></td><td></td><td>*Depreciation Expense:*</td><td></td><td></td></tr>
<tr><td></td><td></td><td>*Office Equipment* . . . .</td><td>*78*</td><td>*15*</td></tr>
<tr><td></td><td></td><td>*To close the expense accounts.*</td><td></td><td></td></tr>
</table>

After this closing entry has been posted, the Income Summary account and the five expense accounts will appear as follows:

Income Summary *(53)*

19___					*19___*				
Oct.	*31*		*3*	*2,023*	*Oct.*	*31*		*3*	*3,880*

Advertising Expense *(70)*

19___					*19___*				
Oct.	*2*		*2*	*120*	*Oct.*	*31*		*3*	*210*
	16		*2*	*90*					
				210					*210*

Office Salaries Expense *(72)*

19___					*19___*				
Oct.	*30*		*2*	*1,700*	*Oct.*	*31*		*3*	*1,700*

Telephone Expense *(74)*

19___					*19___*				
Oct.	*30*		*2*	*48*	*Oct.*	*31*		*3*	*48*

Depreciation Expense: Building (76)

| 19__ | | | | 2 | | 50 | 19__ | | | | 3 | | 50 |
| Oct. | 31 | | | | | | Oct. | 31 | | | | | |

Depreciation Expense: Office Equipment (78)

| 19__ | | | | 2 | | 15 | 19__ | | | | 3 | | 15 |
| Oct. | 31 | | | | | | Oct. | 31 | | | | | |

Ruling closed accounts. The ruling of the closed accounts should be studied closely. The ruling process was similar for the Sales Commissions Earned account (page 73) and the Advertising Expense account because both these accounts contained more than one entry on a side. A single ruling was placed on the same line across the debit and credit money columns. The totals were entered just below this single ruling and a double ruling was drawn below the totals. The double ruling was also placed across the date columns and the reference columns in order to establish a clear separation between the transactions of the period just ended and the entries to be made in the following period. All the expense accounts except Advertising Expense contained only one debit entry: In ruling an account with only one debit and one credit, it is not necessary to enter totals; the double lines may be placed just below the debit and credit entries.

Closing the Income Summary account. The five expense accounts have now been closed and the total amount formerly contained in these accounts appears on the debit side of the Income Summary account. The commissions earned during October appear on the credit side of the Income Summary account. Since the credit entry of $3,880 representing October revenue is larger than the debit of $2,023 representing October expenses, the account has a credit balance of $1,857—the net income for October.

The net income of $1,857 earned during October causes the stockholders' equity to increase. The credit balance of the Income Summary account is, therefore, transferred to the Retained Earnings account by the following closing entry:

| Net Income Earned Increases Stockholders' Equity | 19__ Oct. | 31 | Income Summary . . . . Retained Earnings . . . . To close the Income Summary account for October by transferring the net income to the Retained Earnings account. | 53 51 | 1,857 | 1,857 |

After this closing entry has been posted, the Income Summary account has a zero balance, and the net income earned during October appears in the Retained Earnings account as shown below:

						Income Summary				(53)
19___						*19___*				
Oct.	*31*		*3*	2,023	*Oct.*	*31*		*3*	3,880	
	31		*3*	1,857						
				3,880					3,880	

						Retained Earnings				(51)
					19___					
					Oct.	*31*		*3*	1,857	

In our illustration the business has operated profitably with revenues in excess of expenses. Not every business is so fortunate; if the expenses of a business are larger than its revenue, the Income Summary account will have a debit balance. In this case, the closing of the Income Summary account would require a debit to the Retained Earnings account and an offsetting credit to the Income Summary account. A debit balance in the Retained Earnings account is referred to as a *deficit;* it would be shown as a deduction from Capital Stock in the balance sheet.

Note that the Income Summary account is used only at the end of the period when the books are being closed. The account has no entries and no balance except during the process of closing the books at the end of the accounting period.

Closing the Dividends account. As explained earlier in this chapter, the payment of dividends to the owners is not considered as an expense of the business and, therefore, is not taken into account in determining the net income for the period. Since dividends do not constitute an expense, the Dividends account is closed not into the Income Summary account but directly to the Retained Earnings account, as shown by the following entry:

Dividends Account Is Closed to Retained Earnings Account

19___					
Oct.	*31*	Retained Earnings.....................	*51*	600	
		Dividends..................	*52*		600
		To close the Dividends account.			

After this closing entry has been posted, the Dividends account will have a zero balance, and the dividends distributed during October will appear as a deduction or debit entry in the Retained Earnings account, as shown on page 77.

					Dividends				*(52)*
19___					19___				
Oct.	30		2	600	Oct.	31		3	600

					Retained Earnings				*(51)*
19___					19___				
Oct.	31		3	600	Oct.	31		3	1,857

Summary of closing procedure. The closing of the books may be illustrated graphically as follows:

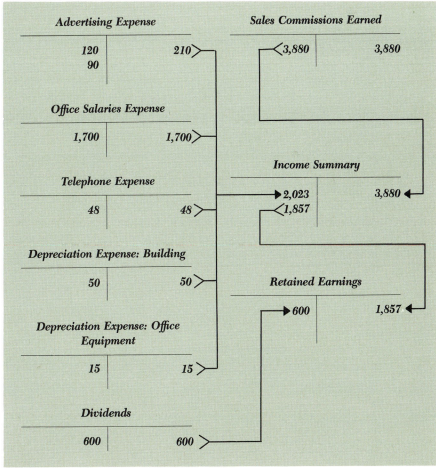

Diagram Showing Closing of the Books

Let us now summarize briefly the procedure of closing the books.

1. Close the various revenue and expense accounts by transferring their balances into the Income Summary account.

2. Compute the balance of the Income Summary account. (If revenues exceed expenses, the account will have a credit balance, indicating the business has earned net income. If expenses exceed revenues, the account will have a debit balance, indicating the business has operated at a net loss.)

3. Close the Income Summary account by transferring its balance into the Retained Earnings account.

4. Close the Dividends account into the Retained Earnings account.

After-closing trial balance

After the revenue and expense accounts have been closed, it is desirable to take an *after-closing trial balance,* which of course will consist solely of balance sheet accounts. There is always the possibility that an error in posting the closing entries may have upset the equality of debits and credits in the ledger. The after-closing trial balance, or *post-closing trial balance,* is prepared from the ledger. It gives assurance that the books are in balance and ready for the recording of the transactions of the next accounting period.

	GREENHILL REAL ESTATE COMPANY		
Only	*After-closing Trial Balance*		
Balance	*October 31, 19___*		
Sheet			
Accounts			
Remain	Cash	$ 7,830	
Open	Accounts receivable	2,630	
after	Land	5,000	
Closing	Building	12,000	
Entries	Accumulated depreciation: building		$ 50
Are	Office equipment	1,800	
Posted	Accumulated depreciation: office equipment		15
	Accounts payable		7,938
	Capital stock		20,000
	Retained earnings		1,257
		$29,260	$29,260

Sequence of accounting procedures

The accounting procedures described to this point may be summarized in eight steps, as follows:

1. Journalize transactions. Enter all transactions in the journal, thus creating a chronological record of events.

2. Post to ledger accounts. Post debits and credits from the journal to the proper ledger accounts, thus creating a record classified by accounts.

3. *Prepare a trial balance.* Prove the equality of debits and credits in the ledger.

4. *Make end-of-period adjustments.* Draft adjusting entries in the journal, and post to ledger accounts.

5. *Prepare an adjusted trial balance.* Prove again the equality of debits and credits in the ledger.

6. *Prepare financial statements.* An income statement is needed to show the results of operation for the period. A statement of retained earnings is needed to show the changes in retained earnings during the period and the closing balance. A balance sheet is needed to show the financial condition of the business at the end of the period.

7. *Journalize and post closing entries.* The closing entries clear the revenue, expense, and dividend accounts, making them ready for recording the events of the next accounting period, and also bring the Retained Earnings account up-to-date.

8. *Prepare an after-closing trial balance.* This step ensures that the ledger remains in balance after posting of the closing entries.

DEMONSTRATION PROBLEM

The trial balance for Rex Insurance Agency, Inc., at November 30, 19___, and data for adjustments are presented below. The business was organized on September 1; the books have been closed and financial statements prepared each month.

Cash	$ 3,750	
Accounts receivable	1,210	
Office equipment	4,800	
Accumulated depreciation: office equipment		$ 80
Accounts payable		1,640
Capital stock		6,000
Retained earnings		1,490
Dividends	500	
Commissions earned		4,720
Advertising expense	800	
Salaries expense	2,600	
Rent expense	270	
	$13,930	$13,930

The useful life of the office equipment was estimated at 10 years.

Instructions
a. Prepare the adjusting journal entry needed at November 30.
b. Prepare an adjusted trial balance.
c. For the month ended November 30, prepare an income statement, a statement of retained earnings, and a balance sheet in report form.

QUESTIONS

1. Does a well-prepared income statement provide an exact and precise measurement of net income for the period or does it represent merely an approximation of net income? Explain.

2. For each of the following financial statements, indicate whether the statement relates to a single date or to a period of time:
   a. Balance sheet
   b. Income statement
   c. Statement of retained earnings

3. What is the meaning of the term *revenue?* Does the receipt of cash by a business always indicate that revenue has been earned? Explain.

4. What is the meaning of the term *expenses?* Does the payment of cash by a business always indicate that an expense has been incurred? Explain.

5. Explain the rules of debit and credit with respect to transactions recorded in revenue and expense accounts.

6. Supply the appropriate term (debit or credit) to complete the following statements.
   a. The Capital Stock account, Retained Earnings account, and revenue accounts are increased by _____ entries.
   b. Asset accounts and expense accounts are increased by _____ entries.
   c. Liability accounts and owners' equity accounts are decreased by _____ entries.

7. Supply the appropriate term (debit or credit) to complete the following statements.
   a. When a business is operating profitably, the journal entry to close the Income Summary account will consist of a _____ to that account and a _____ to Retained Earnings.
   b. When a business is operating at a loss, the journal entry to close the Income Summary account will consist of a _____ to that account and a _____ to Retained Earnings.
   c. The journal entry to close the Dividends account consists of a _____ to that account and a _____ to Retained Earnings.

8. Jensen Corporation, a firm of real estate brokers, had the following transactions during June. Which of these transactions represented revenue to the firm during the month of June? Explain.
   a. Arranged a sale of an apartment building owned by a client, James Robbins. The commission for making the sale was $2,000, but this amount would not be received until July 20.
   b. Collected cash of $1,500 from an account receivable. The receivable originated in April from services rendered to a client.
   c. Borrowed $4,000 from the National Bank, to be repaid in three months.
   d. Collected $150 from a dentist to whom Jensen Corporation rented part of its building. This amount represented rent for the month of June.
   e. Issued additional capital stock of $2,000 par value for cash of $2,000.

9. A business had the following transactions, among others, during January. Which of these transactions represented expenses for January? Explain.
    a. Paid $300 salary to a salesman for time worked during January.
    b. Paid $60 for gasoline purchases for the delivery truck during January.
    c. Purchased a typewriter for $300 cash.
    d. Paid $2,000 in settlement of a bank loan obtained three months earlier.
    e. Paid a dividend of $500.
    f. Paid a garage $200 for automobile repair work performed in November.

10. How does depreciation expense differ from other operating expenses?

11. Assume that a business acquires a delivery truck at a cost of $3,600. Estimated life of the truck is four years. State the amount of depreciation expense per year and per month. Give the adjusting entry to record depreciation on the truck at the end of the first month, and explain where the accounts involved would appear in the financial statements.

EXERCISES

1. Supply the missing figures in the following independent cases:

    a.   *Capital stock (no change during year)* . . . . $ 60,000
           Dividends for the year   6,000
           Retained earnings at beginning of year   24,000
           Net income for the year   18,000
           Total stockholders' equity at end of year . . . .   _____

    b.   *Retained earnings at end of year* . . . . $ 83,700
           Dividends for the year   16,400
           Net income for the year   31,200
           Retained earnings at beginning of year . . . .   _____

    c.   *Net income for the year* . . . . $_____
           Retained earnings at end of year   48,200
           Retained earnings at beginning of year   42,600
           Dividends for the year   12,400

    d.   *Dividends for the year* . . . . $_____
           Retained earnings at end of year   102,700
           Net income for the year   28,500
           Retained earnings at beginning of year   91,200

    e.   *Total stockholders' equity at beginning of year* . . . . $ 71,300
           Total stockholders' equity at end of year   89,400
           Amount received from additional capital stock issued
             during year   6,500
           Net income for the year . . . .   _____
           Dividends for the year   7,600

2. Label each of the following statements as true or false. Explain the reasoning underlying your answer and give an example of a transaction which supports your position.
    a. Every transaction that affects an expense account also affects a revenue account.

b. Every transaction that affects a revenue account also affects a liability account.

c. Every transaction that affects a balance sheet account also affects an income statement account.

d. Every transaction that affects an income statement account also affects a balance sheet account.

e. Every transaction that affects an expense account also affects an asset account.

f. Every transaction that affects a revenue account also affects another income statement account.

3. Barton Corporation's income statement showed net income of $22,610 for the month of October. In recording October transactions, however, certain transactions were incorrectly recorded. Study the following list of selected October transactions; identify any which were incorrectly recorded. Also give the journal entry as it should have been made, and compute the correct amount of net income for October.

a. Earned a commission of $2,500 by selling a residence for a client. Commission to be received in 60 days. Recorded by debiting Commissions Earned and crediting Accounts Receivable.

b. A payment of $250 for newspaper advertising was recorded by debiting Advertising Expense and crediting Accounts Receivable.

c. Received but did not pay a bill of $285 for October telephone service. Recorded by debiting Telephone Expense and crediting Commissions Earned.

d. Made an error in computing depreciation on the building for October. Recorded as $25. Should have been $250.

e. Recorded the payment of a $2,000 dividend by debiting Salaries Expense and crediting Cash.

4. Sable Corporation's balance sheets at the beginning and end of the year showed the following summary figures:

	Beginning of Year	End of Year
Assets	$140,000	$185,000
Liabilities	90,000	100,000

Compute the net income or net loss from operations for the year in each of the following independent cases:

a. No dividends were declared or paid during the year and no additional capital stock was issued.

b. No dividends were declared or paid during the year, but additional capital stock was issued at par in the amount of $50,000.

c. Dividends of $15,000 were declared and paid during the year. No change occurred in capital stock.

d. Dividends of $8,000 were declared and paid during the year, and additional capital stock was issued at par in the amount of $18,000.

PROBLEMS

3-1 The May transactions of the World Travel Corp. are listed as follows:

(1) On May 1, World Travel Corp. arranged a round-the-world trip for Mr. and Mrs. John Peterson. A commission of $575 cash was collected from the steamship company.

(2) On May 4, World Travel Corp. paid $425 cash for an advertisement in the travel section of the *New York Times*.

(3) On May 5, arranged fly-now, pay-later European trips for several clients. Italia Airlines agreed to pay World Travel Corp. a commission of $1,500 for services rendered, payment to be made as soon as travel agreements were confirmed.

(4) On May 10, placed another advertisement in the *New York Times* for $495, payment to be made in 30 days.

(5) On May 12, collected cash in the amount of $1,500 from Italia Airlines.

(6) On May 30, received a bill for telephone expense during May for $1,121, payable June 10.

(7) On May 30, purchased office equipment for $310 in cash.

(8) On May 31, declared a cash dividend of $15,000, payable on June 30.

Instructions

Analyze each transaction, then prepare the necessary journal entry. The following will illustrate an analysis of a transaction, using (1) above as an example:

(1) **a.** The asset Cash was increased. Increases in assets are recorded by debits. Debit Cash, $575.

    b. Revenue was earned. Revenue increases the owners' equity and is recorded by a credit. Credit Commissions Earned, $575.

3-2 Olympic Auto Repair, Inc., was organized on July 1, 19___. The company follows a policy of preparing financial statements and closing its books each month. On September 30, 19___, the following adjusted trial balance was prepared.

OLYMPIC AUTO REPAIRS, INC.
Adjusted Trial Balance
September 30, 19___

Cash	$ 1,790	
Accounts receivable	450	
Land.	21,000	
Building.	6,000	
Accumulated depreciation: building		$ 75
Equipment	3,600	
Accumulated depreciation: equipment.		90
Accounts payable.		2,576
Capital stock.		25,000
Retained earnings, Sept. 1, 19___		4,464
Dividends.	1,000	
Repair service revenue		5,920
Advertising expense	125	

Depreciation expense: building	25	
Depreciation expense: equipment	30	
Repair parts expense	900	
Utilities expense	60	
Wages expense	3,145	
	$38,125	$38,125

Instructions

a. Prepare financial statements (income statement, statement of retained earnings, and a balance sheet in report form).

b. What were the estimated lives of the building and the equipment as assumed by the company in setting the depreciation rates?

3-3 Mountain Airlines, Inc., was organized on May 1, 19___ for the purpose of carrying passengers to and from remote fishing and hunting lodges. The following transactions were completed during May.

May 1   Issued 10,000 shares of $10 par value capital stock for cash of $100,000.

May 2   Purchased a helicopter for $40,200 and spare parts for $4,000, paying cash.

May 3   Paid $600 cash to rent a building for May.

May 15   Cash receipts from passengers for the first half of May amounted to $2,900.

May 16   Paid $2,250 to employees for services rendered during the first half of May.

May 16   Placed advertising in local newspapers for publication during May. The agreed price of $125 was payable within ten days after the end of the month.

May 28   Paid $480 to United Motors for maintenance and repair service during May.

May 29   Received a gasoline bill from Western Oil Co. amounting to $610 and payable by June 10.

May 31   Paid $2,250 to employees for services rendered during the last half of May.

May 31   Cash receipts from passengers during the last half of May amounted to $3,860.

The useful life of the helicopter for depreciation purposes was estimated to be ten years. The account titles and account numbers used by the company included the following:

Cash 11		Fees earned .51	
Spare parts 14		Advertising expense 61	
Helicopter 21		Depreciation expense: helicopter 63	
Accumulated depreciation: helicopter . .23		Gasoline expense 65	
Accounts payable 31		Rent expense 67	
Capital stock 41		Repair & maintenance expense 69	
		Salaries expense 71	

Instructions

a. Prepare journal entries for the operating transactions in May and also for the month-end adjusting entry for depreciation of the helicopter.
b. Post to ledger accounts.
c. Prepare an adjusted trial balance as of May 31, 19____.

3-4 The Olive Corporation provides public relations services to clients in the entertainment industry. Its offices are rented from a life insurance company on a 10-year lease which expires in three years.

Condensed balance sheet data for the corporation at the end of the last two calendar years are presented below:

	Year 1	Year 2
Cash	$ 25,000	$ 15,000
Receivables from clients	100,000	140,000
Supplies	1,000	1,000
Office equipment	17,500	32,500
Less: Accumulated depreciation	(3,000)	(5,750)
Total assets	$140,500	$182,750
Accounts payable	$ 10,000	$ 10,000
Capital stock	50,000	75,000
Retained earnings	80,500	97,750
Total liabilities & stockholders' equity	$140,500	$182,750

In order to be in a position to carry the expanded amount of receivables from clients and to acquire badly needed office equipment, the owners of the Olive Corporation invested additional cash in the business early in Year 2. At the end of Year 2, the corporation declared and paid a cash dividend. The net income for the corporation for the Year 2 follows:

Fees billed to clients		$125,000
Expenses (excluding depreciation)	$75,000	
Depreciation expense: office equipment	2,750	77,750
Net income		$ 47,250

Instructions

a. Prepare a statement of retained earnings for Year 2.
b. Prepare closing entries required at the end of Year 2.
c. The owners are concerned over the fact that cash decreased by $10,000 during Year 2 despite a handsome profit of $47,250. Prepare a schedule of cash receipts and disbursements to explain the reasons for the decrease in cash.

3-5 Listed below in alphabetical order are the accounts comprising the adjusted trial balance of North Insurance Agency, Incorporated, at December 31, 19____.

Accounts payable	$ 732
Accounts receivable	1,568
Accumulated depreciation: building	400

Accumulated depreciation: office equipment	$ 200
Advertising expense	360
Buildings	43,000
Capital stock	50,000
Cash	9,800
Commissions earned	8,676
Depreciation expense: building	200
Depreciation expense: office equipment	100
Dividends	1,000
Land	24,000
Lighting expense	328
Notes payable	19,000
Office equipment	9,000
Retained earnings, Dec. 1, 19___	15,336
Salaries expense	4,800
Telephone expense	188

Instructions

a. Prepare an adjusted trial balance with the accounts arranged in the customary sequence of ledger accounts.

b. Prepare financial statements (income statement, statement of retained earnings, and a balance sheet in report form).

3-6 Given below are the balance sheet accounts on June 1, 1972, and the adjusted trial balance as of June 30, 1972, for Betty's Beauty Salon, Incorporated:

	June 1		June 30	
Cash	$14,500		$15,850	
Fees receivable	32,350		28,000	
Beauty supplies on hand	1,650		1,450	
Fixtures	16,300		20,000	
Accumulated depreciation: fixtures		$ 3,500		$ 3,650
Payable to suppliers		1,250		550
Note payable to bank		15,000		3,500
Capital stock		25,000		25,000
Retained earnings		20,050		20,050
Dividends			10,000	
Fees earned				45,000
Operating expenses			22,200	
Depreciation			150	
Interest expense			100	
	$64,800	$64,800	$97,750	$97,750

All fees are recorded in Fees Receivable. Beauty supplies were purchased during the month for $300 and were recorded in the Operating Expenses account.

Instructions
a. Prepare all entries (in aggregate form) that were recorded during the month of June.
b. Prepare an after-closing trial balance as of June 30, 1972.

3-7 Otis Healy & Co., Inc., offers investment counseling and brokerage services to its clients and earns revenue in the form of commissions, dividends on securities owned, and interest on loans made to customers for the purchase of securities. The adjusted trial balance of the corporation was as follows at December 31, 19____.

OTIS HEALY & CO., INC.
Adjusted Trial Balance
December 31, 19____

Cash	$ 95,100	
Marketable securities	310,500	
Customer debit balances	180,000	
Land	30,000	
Building	80,000	
Accumulated depreciation: building		$ 12,200
Furniture & equipment	120,000	
Accumulated depreciation: furniture & equipment . . .		31,500
Loans payable		304,850
Miscellaneous payables		21,400
Capital stock		250,000
Retained earnings, Jan. 1		225,600
Dividends declared	10,000	
Commissions earned		195,000
Dividends earned		12,000
Interest earned		15,250
Advertising expense	22,250	
Office expense	45,100	
Interest expense	25,900	
Depreciation expense	18,250	
Salaries and bonuses	120,500	
Miscellaneous expense	10,200	
	$1,067,800	$1,067,800

Instructions
From the trial balance and supplementary data given, prepare the following as of December 31:
a. Closing entries
b. After-closing trial balance
c. Income statement for year 19____
d. Balance sheet as of December 31, 19____
e. Statement of retained earnings for 19____

3-8   The Sherer Trucking Co. was organized on February 1, 19___, by Peter Sherer to haul goods throughout the western United States. During February the following transactions occurred:

Feb. 2   Peter Sherer deposited $200,000 cash in a bank account in the name of the business, the Sherer Trucking Co., in exchange for 200,000 shares of $1 par value stock.

Feb. 2   Purchased land for $25,000 and building for $54,000, paying $24,000 in cash and signing a $55,000 mortgage payable bearing interest at 6%.

Feb. 3   Purchased 10 trucks from Hevi Motors Co. at a cost of $15,000 each. A cash down payment of $30,000 was made, the balance to be paid by April 1.

Feb. 7   Billed customers for $2,500 for services to date. Collected $500 in cash; balance to be paid within 30 days (credit Sales).

Feb. 10   Purchased office equipment for cash, $6,000.

Feb. 14   Billed customers, $7,200; collected $3,100 in cash; balance to be paid within 30 days.

Feb. 16   Paid salaries to drivers for the first half of the month, $4,150.

Feb. 21   Transported large shipment of grapes and other fruit for a grower and collected the entire fee of $6,500.

Feb. 28   Paid salaries for the second half of the month, $4,380.

Feb. 28   Received a gasoline bill for the month of February from Lerner Oil Company in the amount of $3,440, payable by March 10.

Feb. 28   Received bills of $1,650 for repair work on trucks during February.

Feb. 28   Paid $1,000 to holder of mortgage payable ($275 interest expense and a $725 reduction in the liability).

Feb. 28   Billed customers $4,050 for hauling during last week of February. The amount is due on March 31, 19___.

Sherer estimated the useful life of the building at 20 years, of trucks at 4 years, and of equipment at 10 years. Depreciation is computed to the nearest month.

Instructions

a.   Prepare journal entries. (Number journal pages to permit cross reference to ledger.)

b.   Post to ledger accounts. (Number ledger accounts to permit cross reference to journal.)

c.   Prepare a trial balance as of February 28, 19___.

d.   Prepare adjusting entries and post to ledger accounts.

e.   Prepare an adjusted trial balance.

f.   Prepare an income statement for February, and a balance sheet as of February 28, 19___.

g.   Prepare closing entries and post to ledger accounts.

h.   Prepare an after-closing trial balance.

Chapter
4 End-of-period adjustments

To serve the needs of management, investors, bankers, and other groups, financial statements must be as complete and accurate as possible. The balance sheet must contain all the assets and liabilities at the close of business on the last day of the period. The income statement must contain all the revenue and expenses applicable to the period covered but must not contain any revenue or expenses relating to the following period. In other words, a precise cutoff of transactions at the end of the period is essential to the preparation of accurate financial statements.

APPORTIONING TRANSACTIONS BETWEEN ACCOUNTING PERIODS

Some business transactions are begun and completed within a single accounting period, but many other transactions are begun in one accounting period and concluded in a later period. For example, a building purchased this year may last for 25 years; during each of those 25 years a fair share of the cost of the building should be recognized as expense. The making of adjusting entries to record the depreciation expense applicable to a given accounting period was illustrated in the preceding chapter. Let us now consider some other transactions which overlap two or more accounting periods and therefore require adjusting entries.

PRINCIPAL TYPES OF TRANSACTIONS REQUIRING ADJUSTING ENTRIES

The various kinds of transactions requiring adjusting entries at the end of the period may be classified into the following four groups:

1. Recorded costs which must be apportioned between two or more accounting periods. Example: the cost of a building.

2. Recorded revenue which must be apportioned between two or more accounting periods. Example: commissions collected in advance for services to be rendered in future periods. *Subscriptions*

3. Unrecorded expenses. Example: wages earned by employees after the last payday in an accounting period.

89

✶   *4.* Unrecorded revenue. Example: commissions earned but not yet collected or billed to customers.

To demonstrate these various types of adjusting entries, the illustration
of the Greenhill Real Estate Company will be continued for November. We
shall consider in detail those November transactions relating to adjusting
entries. The routine operating transactions during November such as the
earning of sales commissions and payment of expenses are not considered
individually, but their overall effect is shown in the November 30 trial
balance included in the work sheet on page 98.

Recorded costs apportioned between accounting periods

When a business concern makes an expenditure that will benefit more than
one period, the amount is usually debited to an asset account. At the end
of each period which benefits from the expenditure, an appropriate portion
of the cost is transferred from the asset account to an expense account.

Insurance. On November 1, the Greenhill Real Estate Company paid $180
for a three-year fire insurance policy covering the building. This expenditure
was debited to an asset account by the following journal entry:

<table>
<tr><td rowspan="5">*Expendi-
ture for
Insurance
Policy
Recorded
as Asset*</td><td colspan="2">Prepaid insurance</td></tr>
<tr><td>*Unexpired Insurance* ....</td><td>*180*</td></tr>
<tr><td>   *Cash* ....</td><td>*180*</td></tr>
<tr><td colspan="2">*Purchased three-year fire insurance policy.*</td></tr>
</table>

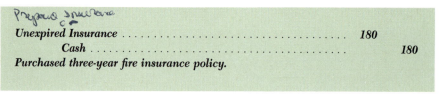

Since this expenditure of $180 will protect the company against fire loss
for three years, the cost of protection each year is ⅓ of $180, or $60. The
insurance expense applicable to each month's operations is $\frac{1}{12}$ of the annual
expense, or $5. In order that the accounting records for November show
insurance expense of $5, the following adjusting entry is required at Novem-
ber 30:

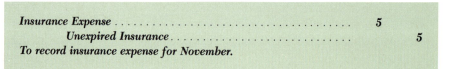

<table>
<tr><td rowspan="4">*Portion
of Asset
Expires
(Becomes
Expense)*</td><td>*Insurance Expense* ....</td><td>*5*</td></tr>
<tr><td>   *Unexpired Insurance* ....</td><td>*5*</td></tr>
<tr><td colspan="2">*To record insurance expense for November.*</td></tr>
</table>

This adjusting entry serves two purposes: (1) it apportions the proper
amount of insurance expense to November operations, and (2) it reduces
the asset account so that the correct amount of unexpired insurance will
appear in the balance sheet at November 30.

Office supplies. On November 2, the Greenhill Real Estate Company
purchased a sufficient quantity of stationery and other office supplies to last
for several months. The cost of the supplies was $240, and this amount was
debited to an asset account by the following journal entry.

Expendi-
ture for
Office
Supplies
Recorded
as Asset

Office Supplies	240
Cash	240
Purchased office supplies.	

No entries were made during November to record the day-to-day usage of office supplies, but on November 30 a careful count was made of the supplies still on hand. This count showed unused supplies with a cost of $200. It is apparent, therefore, that supplies costing $40 were used during November. An adjusting entry is made on the basis of the November 30 count, debiting an expense account $40 (the cost of supplies consumed during November), and reducing the asset account by $40 to show that only $200 worth of office supplies remained on hand at November 30.

Portion of
Supplies
Used
Represents
Expense

Office Supplies Expense	40
Office Supplies	40
To record consumption of office supplies in November.	

Depreciation of building. The November 30 journal entry to record depreciation of the building used by the Greenhill Real Estate Company is exactly the same as the October 31 entry explained in Chapter 3.

Cost of
Building Is
Gradually
Converted
to Expense

Depreciation Expense: Building	50
Accumulated Depreciation: Building	50
To record depreciation for November.	

This allocation of depreciation expense to November operations is based on the following facts: the building cost $12,000 and is estimated to have a useful life of 20 years (240 months). Using the straight-line method of depreciation, the portion of the original cost which expires each month is $1/_{240}$ of $12,000, or $50.

The Accumulated Depreciation: Building account now has a credit balance of $100 as a result of the October and November credits of $50 each. The book value of the building is $11,900, that is, the original cost of $12,000 minus the accumulated depreciation of $100. The term *book value* means the net amount at which an asset is shown in the accounting records, as distinguished from its market value. *Carrying value* is an alternative term, with the same meaning as book value.

Depreciation of office equipment. The November 30 adjusting entry to record depreciation of the office equipment is the same as the entry for depreciation a month earlier, as shown in Chapter 3.

Cost of Office Equipment Is Gradually Converted to Expense

Depreciation Expense: Office Equipment *15*
          Accumulated Depreciation: Office Equipment *15*
To record depreciation for November.

Original cost of the office equipment was $1,800, and the estimated useful life was 10 years (120 months). Depreciation each month under the straight-line method is therefore $\frac{1}{120}$ of $1,800, or $15.

What is the book value of the office equipment at this point? Original cost of $1,800 minus accumulated depreciation of $30 leaves a book value of $1,770.

What would be the effect on the financial statements if the adjusting entries for depreciation of the building and office equipment were omitted at November 30? In the income statement the expenses would be understated by $65 ($50 depreciation of building and $15 depreciation of office equipment), and net income for the month would be overstated by $65. In the balance sheet the assets would be overstated by $65; the owners' equity would be overstated the same amount because of the $65 overstatement of the net income added to retained earnings. If depreciation had not been recorded in either October or November, the overstatement in the balance sheet at November 30 would, of course, amount to $130 with respect both to assets and to owners' equity.

Recorded revenue apportioned between accounting periods

On November 1, James Fortune, a client of the Greenhill Real Estate Company, asked the company to manage a considerable amount of rental properties. The duties consisted of keeping the buildings rented, arranging for repairs, and collecting rents which were to be deposited in Fortune's bank account. It was agreed that $100 a month would be a reasonable fee to the Greenhill Real Estate Company for its services. Since Fortune was leaving the country on an extended trip, he paid the company for six months' service in advance at the time of signing the agreement. The journal entry to record the transaction on November 1 was as follows:

Commission Collected but Not Yet Earned

Cash *600*
          Unearned Rental Commissions *600*
Collected in advance six months' commissions for management of Fortune properties.

Note that no service had been performed for the customer at the time the $600 was received. As emphasized in Chapter 3, not every receipt of cash represents revenue. In this case the receipt of cash represented an advance payment by the customer which obligated the Greenhill Real Estate Company to render services in the future. Revenue is earned only by the *rendering* of services to a customer, or the *delivering* of goods to him. A portion of the agreed services ($\frac{1}{6}$, to be exact) will be rendered during November, but it would be unreasonable to regard the entire $600 as revenue in that month. The commission is earned gradually over a period of six months as the Greenhill Real Estate Company performs the required services. The $600 collected in advance is therefore credited to an **unearned revenue** account at the time of its receipt. Some accountants prefer the alternative term *deferred revenue.* At the end of each month, an amount of $100 will be transferred from unearned revenue to an earned revenue account by means of an adjusting entry. The first in this series of transfers will be made at November 30 as follows:

Entry to Recognize Earning of a Part of Commission	*Unearned Rental Commissions* **100**	
	Rental Commissions Earned	**100**
	Commission earned from Fortune property management in November.	

The $500 credit balance remaining in the Unearned Rental Commissions account represents an obligation to render $500 worth of services in future months; therefore, it belongs on the balance sheet in the liability section. An unearned revenue account differs from other liabilities since it will ordinarily be settled by the rendering of services rather than by making a cash payment, but it is nevertheless a liability. The Rental Commissions Earned account is shown in the income statement as revenue for the month.

Unrecorded expenses

Adjusting entries are necessary at the end of each accounting period to record any expenses which have been incurred but not recognized in the accounts. Salaries of employees and interest on borrowed money are common examples of expenses which accumulate day by day but which may not be recorded until the end of the period. These expenses are said to *accrue,* that is, to grow or accumulate.

Accrual of interest. On November 1, the Greenhill Real Estate Company borrowed the sum of $1,000 from a bank. Banks required every borrower to sign a *promissory note,* that is, a formal, written promise to repay the amount borrowed plus interest at an agreed future date. (Various forms of notes in common use and the accounting problems involved will be discussed more fully in Chapter 12.) The note signed in this case, with certain details omitted, is shown on page 94.

Note
Payable
Issued to
Bank

> $1,000   Los Angeles, California   November 1, 19--
>
> Three months .... after date ....I............ promise to pay
>
> to the order of .... American National Bank
>
> ————One thousand and no/100———— .... dollars
>
> for value received, with interest at .... 6 per cent
>
> Greenhill Real Estate Company
>
> By .... *John Green* ....
>
> President

The note payable is a liability of the Greenhill Real Estate Company, similar to an account payable but different in that a formal written promise to pay is required and interest is charged on the amount borrowed. A Notes Payable account is credited when the note is issued; the Notes Payable account will be debited three months later when the note is paid. Interest accrues throughout the life of the note payable, but it is not payable until the note matures on February 1. To the bank making the loan, the note signed by Greenhill is an asset, a note receivable. The revenues earned by banks consist largely of interest charged borrowers.

The journal entry made on November 1 to record the borrowing of $1,000 from the bank was as follows:

When
Bank
Loan Is
Obtained

Cash	*1,000*	
Notes Payable		*1,000*
Obtained three-month, 6% loan from bank.		

No *payment* of interest was made during November, but one month's interest expense, or $5 ($1,000 × 6% × $\frac{1}{12}$), was *incurred* during the month. The following adjusting entry is made at November 30 to charge November operations with one month's interest expense and also to record the amount of interest owed to the bank at the end of November.

Interest
Expense
Incurred
in
November

Interest Expense	*5*	
Interest Payable		*5*
To record interest expense applicable to November.		

The debit balance in the Interest Expense account will appear in the November income statement; the credit balances in the Interest Payable and Notes Payable accounts will be shown in the balance sheet as liabilities. These two liability accounts will remain on the books until the maturity date on the loan, at which time a cash payment to the bank will eliminate both the Notes Payable account and the Interest Payable account.

Accrual of salary. On November 20, Greenhill hired a part-time salesman whose duties were to work afternoons calling on property owners to secure listings of property for sale or rent. The agreed salary was $75 a week for a five-day week, payable each Friday; payment for the first week was made on Friday, November 24.

Assume that the last day of the accounting period, November 30, fell on Thursday. The salesman had worked four days since being paid the preceding Friday and therefore had earned $60 ($^4/_5$ × $75). In order that this $60 of November salary expense be reflected in the accounts before the financial statements are prepared, an adjusting entry is necessary at November 30.

Salaries Expense Incurred but Unpaid at November 30	*Sales Salaries Expense*	*60*	
	Sales Salaries Payable		*60*
	To record salary expense and related liability to salesman for last four days' work in November.		

The debit balance in the Sales Salaries Expense account will appear as an expense in the November income statement; the credit balance in the Sales Salaries Payable account is the amount owing to the salesman for work performed during the last four days of November and will appear among the liabilities on the balance sheet at November 30.

The next regular payday for the salesman will be Friday, December 1, which is the first day of the new accounting period. Since the books were adjusted and closed on November 30, all the revenue and expense accounts have zero balances at the beginning of business on December 1. The payment of a week's salary to the salesman will be recorded by the following entry on December 1:

Payment of Salaries Incurred in Two Accounting Periods	*Sales Salaries Payable*	*60*	
	Sales Salaries Expense	*15*	
	Cash		*75*
	Paid weekly salary to salesman, $60 of which was previously recorded as Sales Salaries Payable.		

Note that the net result of the November 30 accrual entry has been to split the salesman's weekly salary expense between November and December. Four days of the work week fell in November, so four days' pay, or $60, was recognized as November expense. One day of the work week fell in December so $15 was recorded as December expense.

No accrual entry is necessary for office salaries in the Greenhill Real Estate Company because the office employees are paid on the last working day of the month.

Unrecorded revenue

The treatment of unrecorded revenue is similar to that of unrecorded expenses. Any revenue which has been earned but not recorded during the accounting period should be recognized in the accounts by means of an adjusting entry, debiting an asset account and crediting a revenue account.

On November 16, the Greenhill Real Estate Company entered into a management agreement with Henry Clayton, the owner of several office buildings. The company agreed to manage the Clayton properties for a commission of $80 a month, payable on the fifteenth of each month. No entry is made in the accounting records at the time of signing the contract, because no services have yet been rendered and no change has occurred in assets or liabilities. The managerial duties were to begin immediately, but the first monthly commission would not be received until December 15. The following adjusting entry is therefore necessary at November 30:

Commis-	*Rental Commissions Receivable*	*40*	
sions	*Rental Commissions Earned*		*40*
Earned	*To record revenue accrued from services rendered Henry Clayton*		
but Uncol-	*during November.*		
lected			

The debit balance in the Rental Commissions Receivable account will be shown in the balance sheet as an asset. The credit balance of the Rental Commissions Earned account, including earnings from both the Fortune and Clayton contracts, will appear in the November income statement.

The collection of the first monthly commission from Clayton will occur in the next accounting period (December 15, to be exact). Of this $80 cash receipt, half represents collection of the asset account, Rental Commissions Receivable, created at November 30 by the adjusting entry. The other half of the $80 cash receipt represents revenue earned during December; this should be credited to the December revenue account for Rental Commissions Earned. The entry on December 15 appears at the top of page 97.

The net result of the November 30 accrual entry has been to divide the revenue from managing the Clayton properties between November and December in accordance with the timing of the services rendered.

Collection
of
Commis-
sion
Applicable
to Two
Account-
ing
Periods

Cash *80*	
Rental Commissions Receivable	*40*
Rental Commissions Earned	*40*
Collected commission for month ended December 15. One-half	
of the commission had previously been recorded as	
Rental Commissions Receivable.	

THE WORK SHEET

The work necessary at the end of an accounting period includes construction of a trial balance, journalizing and posting of adjusting entries, preparation of financial statements, and journalizing and posting of closing entries. So many details are involved in these end-of-period procedures that it is easy to make errors. If these errors are recorded in the journal and the ledger accounts, considerable time and effort can be wasted in correcting them. Both the journal and the ledger are formal, permanent records. They may be prepared manually in ink, produced on bookkeeping machines, or created by a computer in a company utilizing electronic data-processing equipment. One way of avoiding errors in the permanent accounting records and also of simplifying the work to be done at the end of the period is to use a *work sheet.*

A work sheet is a large columnar sheet of paper, especially designed to arrange in a convenient systematic form all the accounting data required at the end of the period. The work sheet is not a part of the permanent accounting records; it is prepared in pencil by the accountant for his own convenience. If an error is made on the work sheet, it may be erased and corrected much more easily than an error in the formal accounting records. Furthermore, the work sheet is so designed as to minimize errors by auto-matically bringing to light many types of discrepancies which might otherwise be entered in the journal and posted to the ledger accounts.

The work sheet may be thought of as a testing ground on which the ledger accounts are adjusted, balanced, and arranged in the general form of financial statements. The satisfactory completion of a work sheet provides considerable assurance that all the details of the end-of-period accounting procedures have been properly brought together. After this point has been established, the work sheet then serves as the source from which the formal financial statements are prepared and the adjusting and closing entries are made in the journal.

Preparing the work sheet

A commonly used form of work sheet with the appropriate headings for the Greenhill Real Estate Company is illustrated on page 98. Note that the

Enter Ledger Account Balances before Adjustments in Trial Balance Columns on Work Sheet

GREENHILL REAL ESTATE COMPANY
Work Sheet
For the Month Ended November 30, 19____

	Trial Balance		Adjustments		Adjusted Trial Balance		Income Statement		Retained Earnings Statement		Balance Sheet	
Cash	9,600											
Accounts receivable	2,330											
Unexpired insurance	180											
Office supplies	240											
Land	5,000											
Building	12,000											
Accumulated depreciation: bldg.		50										
Office equipment	1,800											
Accumulated depreciation: off. equip.		15										
Notes payable		1,000										
Accounts payable		7,865										
Unearned rental commissions		600										
Capital stock		20,000										
Retained earnings, Nov. 1, 19___		1,257										
Dividends	500											
Sales commissions earned		3,128										
Advertising expense	425											
Office salaries expense	1,700											
Sales salaries expense	75											
Telephone expense	65											
	33,915	33,915										

heading of the work sheet contains six pairs of money columns, each pair consisting of a debit and a credit column. The procedures to be followed in preparing a work sheet will now be illustrated in six simple steps.

1. Enter the ledger account balances in the Trial Balance columns. The titles and balances of the ledger accounts at November 30 are copied into the Trial Balance columns of the work sheet, as illustrated on page 98. It would be a duplication of work to prepare a trial balance as a separate schedule and then to copy this information into the work sheet. As soon as the account balances have been listed on the work sheet, these two columns should be added and the totals entered.

2. Enter the adjustments in the Adjustments columns. The required adjustments for the Greenhill Real Estate Company have been explained earlier in this chapter; these same adjustments are now entered in the Adjustments columns of the work sheet. (See page 100.) As a cross reference, the debit and credit parts of each adjustment are keyed together by placing a key figure to the left of each amount. For example, the adjustment debiting Insurance Expense and crediting Unexpired Insurance is identified by the key figure (1). The use of the key figures makes it easy to match a debit entry in the Adjustments columns with its related credit. The identifying figures also key the debit and credit entries in the Adjustments columns to the brief explanations which appear at the bottom of the work sheet.

The titles of any accounts debited or credited in the adjusting entries but not listed in the trial balance are written on the work sheet below the trial balance. For example, Insurance Expense does not appear in the trial balance; it is written on the first available line below the trial balance totals. After all the adjustments have been entered in the Adjustments columns, this pair of columns must be totaled. Proving the equality of debit and credit totals tends to prevent arithmetic errors from being carried over into other columns of the work sheet.

3. Enter the account balances as adjusted in the Adjusted Trial Balance columns. The work sheet as it appears after completion of the Adjusted Trial Balance columns is illustrated on page 101. Each account balance in the first pair of columns is combined with the adjustment, if any, in the second pair of columns, and the combined amount is entered in the Adjusted Trial Balance columns. This process of combining the items on each line throughout the first four columns of the work sheet requires horizontal addition or subtraction. It is called *cross footing,* in contrast to the addition of items in a vertical column, which is called *footing* the column.

For example, the Office Supplies account is seen to have a debit balance of $240 in the Trial Balance columns. This $240 debit amount is combined with the $40 credit appearing on the same line in the Adjustments column; the combination of a $240 debit with a $40 credit produces an adjusted debit amount of $200 in the Adjusted Trial Balance debit column. As another example, consider the Office Supplies Expense account. This account had no balance in the Trial Balance columns but shows a $40 debit in the Adjust-

Enter Required Adjustments in Adjustments Columns and Key Them to Explanatory Footnotes

GREENHILL REAL ESTATE COMPANY
Work Sheet
For the Month Ended November 30, 19___

	Trial Balance		Adjustments*		Adjusted Trial Balance		Income Statement		Retained Earnings Statement		Balance Sheet	
Cash	9,600											
Accounts receivable	2,330											
Unexpired insurance	180			(1) 5								
Office supplies	240			(2) 40								
Land	5,000											
Building	12,000											
Accumulated depreciation: bldg.		50		(3) 50								
Office equipment	1,800											
Accumulated depreciation: off. equip.		15		(4) 15								
Notes payable		1,000										
Accounts payable		7,865										
Unearned rental commissions		600	(5) 100									
Capital stock		20,000										
Retained earnings, Nov. 1, 19___		1,257										
Dividends	500											
Sales commissions earned		3,128										
Advertising expense	425											
Office salaries expense	1,700											
Sales salaries expense	75											
Telephone expense	65		(7) 60									
	33,915	33,915										
Insurance expense			(1) 5									
Office supplies expense			(2) 40									
Depreciation expense: bldg.			(3) 50									
Depreciation expense: off. equip.			(4) 15									
Rental commissions earned				(5) 100								
				(8) 40								
Interest expense			(6) 5									
Interest payable				(6) 5								
Sales salaries payable				(7) 60								
Rental commissions receivable			(8) 40									
			315	315								

* Adjustments:
(1) Portion of insurance cost which expired during November
(2) Office supplies used
(3) Depreciation of building during November
(4) Depreciation of office equipment during November
(5) Earned ¼ of commission collected in advance on the Fortune properties
(6) Interest expense accrued during November on note payable
(7) Salesman's salary for last four days of November
(8) Rental commission accrued on Clayton contract in November

Enter Adjusted Amounts in Adjusted Trial Balance Columns of Work Sheet

GREENHILL REAL ESTATE COMPANY
Work Sheet
For the Month Ended November 30, 19____

Account	Trial Balance Dr	Trial Balance Cr	Adjustments* Dr	Adjustments* Cr	Adjusted Trial Balance Dr	Adjusted Trial Balance Cr	Income Statement	Retained Earnings Statement	Balance Sheet
Cash	9,600				9,600				
Accounts receivable	2,330				2,330				
Unexpired insurance	180			(1) 5	175				
Office supplies	240			(2) 40	200				
Land	5,000				5,000				
Building	12,000				12,000				
Accumulated depreciation: bldg.		50		(3) 50		100			
Office equipment	1,800				1,800				
Accumulated depreciation: off. equip.		15		(4) 15		30			
Notes payable		1,000				1,000			
Accounts payable		7,865				7,865			
Unearned rental commissions		600	(5) 100			500			
Capital stock		20,000				20,000			
Retained earnings, Nov. 1, 19____		1,257				1,257			
Dividends	500				500				
Sales commissions earned		3,128				3,128			
Advertising expense	425				425				
Office salaries expense	1,700				1,700				
Sales salaries expense	75		(7) 60		135				
Telephone expense	65				65				
	33,915	33,915							
Insurance expense			(1) 5		5				
Office supplies expense			(2) 40		40				
Depreciation expense: bldg.			(3) 50		50				
Depreciation expense: off. equip.			(4) 15		15				
Rental commissions earned				(5) 100 (8) 40		140			
Interest expense			(6) 5		5				
Interest payable				(6) 5		5			
Sales salaries payable				(7) 60		60			
Rental commissions receivable			(8) 40		40				
			315	315	34,085	34,085			

* Explanatory notes relating to adjustments are the same as on page 100.

ments debit column. The combination of a zero starting balance and $40 debit adjustment produces a $40 debit amount in the Adjusted Trial Balance.

Many of the accounts in the trial balance are not affected by the adjustments made at the end of the month; the balances of these accounts (such as Cash, Land, Building, or Notes Payable in the illustrated work sheet) are entered in the Adjusted Trial Balance columns in exactly the same amounts as shown in the Trial Balance columns. After all the accounts have been extended into the Adjusted Trial Balance columns, this pair of columns is totaled to prove that no arithmetic errors have been made up to this point.

4. Extend each amount in the Adjusted Trial Balance columns horizontally across the work sheet into one of the six remaining columns. Revenue and expense accounts are extended into the Income Statement columns. The amounts in the Retained Earnings account and the Dividends account are entered in the Retained Earnings Statement columns. Assets and liabilities are entered in the Balance Sheet columns.

The process of extending amounts horizontally across the work sheet should begin with the account at the top of the work sheet, which is usually Cash. The cash figure is extended to the Balance Sheet debit column. Then the accountant goes down the work sheet line by line, extending each account balance to the appropriate column. The work sheet as it appears after completion of this sorting process is illustrated on page 103. Note that each amount in the Adjusted Trial Balance columns is extended to one *and only one* of the six remaining columns.

5. Total the Income Statement columns. The difference of $828 represents the net income and is entered as a balancing figure in the Income Statement debit column. Since net income causes an increase in retained earnings, the $828 figure is also entered in the Retained Earnings Statement credit column. Final totals are now computed for the Income Statement columns. The work sheet as it appears after this step is shown on page 104.

As indicated above, the net income or net loss for the period is determined by computing the difference between the two Income Statement columns. In the illustrated work sheet, the credit column total is the larger and the excess of $828 represents net income. Note on the work sheet that the net income of $828 is identified by writing the caption "Net income" in the space provided for account titles.

Let us assume for a moment that the month's operations had produced a loss rather than a profit. In that case the Income Statement debit column would exceed the credit column. The excess of the debits (expenses) over the credits (revenues) would have to be entered in the credit column in order to bring the two Income Statement columns into balance. The incurring of a loss would decrease the retained earnings; therefore, the loss would be entered in the Retained Earnings Statement debit column.

6. Compute the amount of retained earnings at the end of the month; enter this amount of $1,585 as a balancing figure in the Retained Earnings Statement debit column and also in the Balance Sheet credit column. Total both pairs of columns. The completed work sheet appears on page 105.

GREENHILL REAL ESTATE COMPANY
Work Sheet
For the Month Ended November 30, 19___

Extend Each Adjusted Amount to Columns for Income Statement, Retained Earnings Statement, or Balance Sheet

Account	Trial Balance Dr	Trial Balance Cr	Adjustments Dr	Adjustments Cr	Adjusted Trial Balance Dr	Adjusted Trial Balance Cr	Income Statement Dr	Income Statement Cr	Retained Earnings Statement Dr	Retained Earnings Statement Cr	Balance Sheet Dr	Balance Sheet Cr
Cash	9,600				9,600						9,600	
Accounts receivable	2,330				2,330						2,330	
Unexpired insurance	180			(1) 5	175						175	
Office supplies	240			(2) 40	200						200	
Land	5,000				5,000						5,000	
Building	12,000				12,000						12,000	
Accumulated depreciation: bldg.		50		(3) 50		100						100
Office equipment	1,800				1,800						1,800	
Accumulated depreciation: off. equip.		15		(4) 15		30						30
Notes payable		1,000				1,000						1,000
Accounts payable		7,865				7,865						7,865
Unearned rental commissions		600	(5) 100			500						500
Capital stock		20,000				20,000						20,000
Retained earnings, Nov. 1, 19___		1,257				1,257				1,257		
Dividends	500				500				500			
Sales commissions earned		3,128				3,128		3,128				
Advertising expense	425				425		425					
Office salaries expense	1,700				1,700		1,700					
Sales salaries expense	75		(7) 60		135		135					
Telephone expense	65				65		65					
	33,915	33,915										
Insurance expense			(1) 5		5		5					
Office supplies expense			(2) 40		40		40					
Depreciation expense: bldg.			(3) 50		50		50					
Depreciation expense: off. equip.			(4) 15		15		15					
Rental commissions earned				(5) 100 (8) 40		140		140				
Interest expense			(6) 5		5		5					
Interest payable				(6) 5		5						5
Sales salaries payable				(7) 60		60						60
Rental commissions receivable			(8) 40		40						40	
			315	315	34,085	34,085						

* Explanatory notes relating to adjustments are the same as on page 100.

Total Income Statement Columns and Enter Net Income as a Balancing Figure

GREENHILL REAL ESTATE COMPANY
Work Sheet
For the Month Ended November 30, 19____

Account	Trial Balance Dr	Trial Balance Cr	Adjustments Dr	Adjustments Cr	Adjusted Trial Balance Dr	Adjusted Trial Balance Cr	Income Statement Dr	Income Statement Cr	Retained Earnings Statement Dr	Retained Earnings Statement Cr	Balance Sheet Dr	Balance Sheet Cr
Cash	9,600				9,600						9,600	
Accounts receivable	2,330				2,330						2,330	
Unexpired insurance	180			(1) 5	175						175	
Office supplies	240			(2) 40	200						200	
Land	5,000				5,000						5,000	
Building	12,000				12,000						12,000	
Accumulated depreciation: bldg.		50		(3) 50		100						100
Office equipment	1,800				1,800						1,800	
Accumulated depreciation: off. equip.		15		(4) 15		30						30
Notes payable		1,000				1,000						1,000
Accounts payable		7,865				7,865						7,865
Unearned rental commissions		600	(5) 100			500						500
Capital stock		20,000				20,000						20,000
Retained earnings, Nov. 1, 19____		1,257				1,257				1,257		
Dividends	500				500				500			
Sales commissions earned		3,128				3,128		3,128				
Advertising expense	425				425		425					
Office salaries expense	1,700				1,700		1,700					
Sales salaries expense	75		(7) 60		135		135					
Telephone expense	65				65		65					
	33,915	33,915										
Insurance expense			(1) 5		5		5					
Office supplies expense			(2) 40		40		40					
Depreciation expense: bldg.			(3) 50		50		50					
Depreciation expense: off. equip.			(4) 15		15		15					
Rental commissions earned				(5) 100 / (8) 40		140		140				
Interest expense			(6) 5		5		5					
Interest payable				(6) 5		5						5
Sales salaries payable				(7) 60		60						60
Rental commissions receivable			(8) 40		40						40	
			315	315	34,085	34,085	2,440	3,268				
Net income							828			828		
							3,268	3,268				

* Explanatory notes relating to adjustments are the same as on page 100.

GREENHILL REAL ESTATE COMPANY

Work Sheet
For the Month Ended November 30, 19____

* Explanatory notes relating to adjustments are the same as on page 100.

Account	Trial Balance Dr	Trial Balance Cr	Adjustments* Dr	Adjustments* Cr	Adjusted Trial Balance Dr	Adjusted Trial Balance Cr	Income Statement Dr	Income Statement Cr	Retained Earnings Statement Dr	Retained Earnings Statement Cr	Balance Sheet Dr	Balance Sheet Cr
Cash	9,600				9,600						9,600	
Accounts receivable	2,330				2,330						2,330	
Unexpired insurance	180			(1) 5	175						175	
Office supplies	240			(2) 40	200						200	
Land	5,000				5,000						5,000	
Building	12,000				12,000						12,000	
Accumulated depreciation: bldg.		50		(3) 50		100						100
Office equipment	1,800				1,800						1,800	
Accumulated depreciation: off. equip.		15		(4) 15		30						30
Notes payable		1,000				1,000						1,000
Accounts payable		7,865				7,865						7,865
Unearned rental commissions		600	(5) 100			500						500
Capital stock		20,000				20,000						20,000
Retained earnings, Nov. 1, 19____		1,257				1,257				1,257		
Dividends	500				500				500			
Sales commissions earned		3,128				3,128		3,128				
Advertising expense	425				425		425					
Office salaries expense	1,700				1,700		1,700					
Sales salaries expense	75		(7) 60		135		135					
Telephone expense	65				65		65					
	33,915	33,915										
Insurance expense			(1) 5		5		5					
Office supplies expense			(2) 40		40		40					
Depreciation expense: bldg.			(3) 50		50		50					
Depreciation expense: off. equip.			(4) 15		15		15					
Rental commissions earned				(5) 100 / (8) 40		140		140				
Interest expense			(6) 5		5		5					
Interest payable				(6) 5		5						5
Sales salaries payable				(7) 60		60						60
Rental commissions receivable			(8) 40		40						40	
			315	315	34,085	34,085	2,440	3,268				
Net income							828			828		
							3,268	3,268	500	2,085		
Retained earnings, Nov. 30, 19____									1,585			1,585
									2,085	2,085	31,145	31,145

Complete Work Sheet By Entering New Balance of Retained Earnings in Debit Column of Retained Earnings Statement and Credit Column of Balance Sheet

The Balance Sheet columns now prove the familiar proposition that assets are equal to the total of liabilities and stockholders' equity. Any lack of agreement in the totals of the Balance Sheet columns would indicate an error in the work sheet.

Preparing financial statements from the work sheet

Preparing the formal financial statements from the work sheet is an easy step. All the information needed for the income statement, the statement of retained earnings, and the balance sheet has already been sorted and arranged in convenient form in the work sheet.

Income statement. The income statement shown below contains the amounts listed in the Income Statement columns of the work sheet on page 105.

Data Taken from Income Statement Columns of Work Sheet	**GREENHILL REAL ESTATE COMPANY** *Income Statement* *For the Month Ended November 30, 19___*

Revenue:

Sales commissions earned		*$3,128*
Rental commissions earned		*140*
Total revenue		*$3,268*

Expenses:

Advertising	*$ 425*	
Office salaries	*1,700*	
Sales salaries	*135*	
Telephone	*65*	
Insurance	*5*	
Office supplies	*40*	
Depreciation: building	*50*	
Depreciation: office equipment	*15*	
Interest	*5*	
Total expenses		*2,440*
Net income		*$ 828*

At this point we are purposely ignoring corporate income taxes, which are introduced in Chapter 7 and considered more fully in Chapter 17.

Statement of retained earnings. The statement of retained earnings for the month of November (page 107) shows the amounts listed in the Retained Earnings Statement columns of the work sheet.

Balance sheet. The balance sheet on page 107 contains the amounts listed in the Balance Sheet columns of the work sheet.

Recording adjusting entries in the accounting records. After the financial statements have been prepared from the work sheet at the end of the period,

Data
Taken
from
Retained
Earnings
Statement
Columns
of Work
Sheet

GREENHiLL REAL ESTATE COMPANY
Statement of Retained Earnings
For the Month Ended November 30, 19___

Retained earnings, November 1, 19___	$1,257
Net income for the month (per income statement).................	828
	$2,085
Dividends......................................	500
Retained earnings, November 30, 19___	$1,585

the ledger accounts are adjusted to bring them into agreement with the statements. This is an easy step because the adjustments have already been computed on the work sheet. The amounts appearing in the Adjustments columns of the work sheet and the related explanations at the bottom of

Data
Taken
from
Balance
Sheet
Columns
of Work
Sheet

GREENHILL REAL ESTATE COMPANY
Balance Sheet
November 30, 19___

Assets

Cash		$ 9,600
Accounts receivable		2,330
Rental commissions receivable.................		40
Unexpired insurance..........................		175
Office supplies		200
Land..		5,000
Building.....................................	$12,000	
Less: Accumulated depreciation	100	11,900
Office equipment.............................	$ 1,800	
Less: Accumulated depreciation	30	1,770
		$31,015

Liabilities & Stockholders' Equity

Liabilities:		
Notes payable		$ 1,000
Accounts payable		7,865
Sales salaries payable..................		60
Interest payable.......................		5
Unearned rental commissions		500
Total liabilities....................		$ 9,430
Stockholders' equity:		
Capital stock	$20,000	
Retained earnings	1,585	21,585
		$31,015

the work sheet provide all the necessary information for the adjusting entries, as shown below, which are first entered in the journal and then posted to the ledger accounts.

Adjust-ments on Work Sheet Are Entered in Journal

		Journal		(Page 5)
19___ Nov.	30	Insurance Expense......................	5	
		Unexpired Insurance............		5
		Insurance expense for November.		
	30	Office Supplies Expense.................	40	
		Office Supplies		40
		Office supplies used during November.		
	30	Depreciation Expense: Building...........	50	
		Accumulated Depreciation: Building		50
		Depreciation for November.		
	30	Depreciation Expense: Office Equipment ...	15	
		Accumulated Depreciation: Office Equipment.................		15
		Depreciation for November.		
	30	Unearned Rental Commissions	100	
		Rental Commissions Earned......		100
		Earned ⅙ of commission collected in advance for management of the properties owned by James Fortune.		
	30	Interest Expense.......................	5	
		Interest Payable		5
		Interest expense accrued during November on note payable.		
	30	Sales Salaries Expense..................	60	
		Sales Salaries Payable...........		60
		To record expense and related liability to sales-man for last four days' work in November.		
	30	Rental Commissions Receivable	40	
		Rental Commissions Earned........		40
		To record the receivable and related revenue earned for managing properties owned by Henry Clayton.		

Recording closing entries. When the financial statements have been prepared from the work sheet, the revenue and expense accounts have served their purpose for the current period and should be closed. These accounts will then have zero balances and will be ready for the recording of revenue and expenses during the next fiscal period.

The journalizing and posting of closing entries were illustrated in Chapter 3. The point to be emphasized now is that the completed work sheet provides in convenient form all the information needed to make the closing entries. The preparation of closing entries from the work sheet may be summarized as follows:

1. To close the accounts listed in the Income Statement credit column, debit the revenue accounts and credit Income Summary.

2. To close the accounts listed in the Income Statement debit column, debit Income Summary and credit the expense accounts.

3. To close the Income Summary account, transfer the balancing figure in the Income Statement columns of the work sheet ($828 in the illustration) to the Retained Earnings account. A profit is transferred by debiting Income Summary and crediting the Retained Earnings account; a loss is transferred by debiting the Retained Earnings account and crediting Income Summary.

4. To close the Dividends account, debit the Retained Earnings account and credit the Dividends account.

The closing entries at November 30 are shown on page 110.

Sequence of accounting procedures when work sheet is used

In any business which maintains a considerable number of accounts or makes numerous adjusting entries, the use of a work sheet will save much time and labor. Since the work sheet includes a trial balance, adjusting entries in preliminary form, and an adjusted trial balance, the use of the work sheet will modify the sequence of accounting procedures given in Chapter 3 as follows:

1. Record all transactions in the journal as they occur.

2. Post debits and credits from the journal entries to the proper ledger accounts.

3. Prepare the work sheet. (The work sheet includes a trial balance of the ledger and all necessary adjustments.)

4. Prepare financial statements, consisting of an income statement, a statement of retained earnings, and a balance sheet.

5. Using the information shown on the work sheet as a guide, enter the adjusting and closing entries in the journal. Post these entries to ledger accounts.

6. Prepare an after-closing trial balance to prove that the ledger is still in balance.

Note that the first two procedures, consisting of the journalizing and posting of transactions during the period, are the same regardless of whether a work sheet is to be used at the end of the period.

Closing Entries Derived from Work Sheet

			Journal		*(Page 6)*
19__					
Nov.	30		Sales Commissions Earned	3,128	
			Rental Commissions Earned	140	
			Income Summary		3,268
			To close the revenue accounts.		
	30		Income Summary	2,440	
			Advertising Expense		425
			Office Salaries Expense		1,700
			Sales Salaries Expense		135
			Telephone Expense		65
			Insurance Expense		5
			Office Supplies Expense		40
			Depreciation Expense: Building . . .		50
			Depreciation Expense: Office Equipment		15
			Interest Expense		5
			To close the expense accounts.		
	30		Income Summary	828	
			Retained Earnings		828
			To close the Income Summary account.		
	30		Retained Earnings	500	
			Dividends		500
			To close the Dividends account.		

The accounting cycle

The above sequence of accounting procedures constitutes a complete accounting process, which is repeated in the same order in each accounting period. The regular repetition of this standardized set of procedures is often referred to as the *accounting cycle.*

In most business concerns the books are closed only once a year; for these companies the accounting cycle is one year in length. For purposes of illustration in a textbook, it is convenient to assume that the entire accounting cycle is performed within the time period of one month. The completion of the accounting cycle is always the occasion for closing the revenue and expense accounts and preparing financial statements.

Preparing monthly financial statements without closing the books

Many companies which close their books only once a year nevertheless prepare *monthly* financial statements for managerial use. These monthly statements are prepared from work sheets, but the adjustments indicated on the work sheets are not entered in the accounting records and no closing entries are made. Under this plan, the time-consuming operation of journalizing and posting adjustments and closing entries is performed only at the end of the fiscal year, but the company has the advantage of monthly financial statements.

DEMONSTRATION PROBLEM

The after-closing trial balance for the Creative Art & Design Company as of December 31, 1971, is shown below:

CREATIVE ART & DESIGN COMPANY
After-closing Trial Balance
December 31, 1971

Cash	$ 20,450	
Accounts receivable	18,750	
Art supplies	3,800	
Equipment	60,000	
Accumulated depreciation: equipment		$ 10,000
Accounts payable		1,250
Salaries payable		1,950
Capital stock		50,000
Retained earnings		39,800
	$103,000	$103,000

Following is a summary of transactions completed during January, 1972:

(1) Paid $700 rent covering the two-month period of January and February (debit Prepaid Rent).
(2) Purchased equipment costing $1,500 for cash.
(3) Declared a cash dividend of $5,000 payable February 26, 1972.
(4) Billed customers for $20,800 for art and design work performed or to be performed (credit Fees Earned).
(5) Collected $24,100 from customers.
(6) Paid salaries of $11,200, including $1,950 which was accrued on December 31, 1971.
(7) Purchased art supplies on credit, $2,900.
(8) Made payments to creditors, $3,300.
(9) Paid miscellaneous expenses of $1,200 in cash.

Adjustments required at the end of January are:

(1) Art supplies on hand amount to $3,000.
(2) Salaries earned by employees not paid as of January 31 are $600.
(3) Depreciation on the equipment for the month of January is estimated at $450.
(4) Work performed for customers which has not been billed amounts to $2,200.

(5) Of the billings to clients during January ($20,800), 5% was for work to be completed in February and March.

(6) Prepaid rent applicable to February amounts to $350.

Instructions

a. Prepare journal entries to record the transactions for the month of January and post to ledger accounts.

b. Prepare a trial balance using the first two columns of a 12-column work sheet. Complete the work sheet.

c. Prepare financial statements as of January 31, 1972.

d. Record the required adjusting and closing entries in the general journal. Post these entries in the ledger and rule the accounts.

e. Prepare an after-closing trial balance.

QUESTIONS

1. The Property Management Company manages office buildings and apartment buildings for various owners who wish to be relieved of this responsibility. The revenues earned for this service are credited to Management Fees Earned. On December 1, the company received a check for $1,800 from a client, James Thurston, who was leaving for a six-month stay abroad. This check represented payment in advance for management of Thurston's real estate properties during the six months of his absence. Explain how this transaction would be recorded, the adjustment, if any, to be made at December 31, and the presentation of this matter in the year-end financial statements.

2. At the end of 1972, the adjusted trial balance of the Black Company showed the following account balances, among others: Depreciation Expense: Building, $1,610; Building $32,200; Accumulated Depreciation: Building, $14,490. Assuming that straight-line depreciation has been used, what length of time do these facts suggest that the Black Company has owned the building?

3. The weekly payroll for salesmen of the Ryan Company amounts to $1,250. All salesmen are paid up to date at the close of business each Friday. If December 31 falls on Wednesday, what year-end adjusting entry is needed?

4. The Marvin Company purchased a three-year fire insurance policy on August 1 and debited the entire cost of $540 to Unexpired Insurance. The books were not adjusted or closed until the end of the year. Give the adjusting entry at December 31.

5. The net income reported by the Haskell Company for 1972 was $21,400, and the Retained Earnings account stood at $36,000. However, the company had failed to recognize that interest amounting to $375 had accrued on a note payable to the bank. State the corrected figures for net income and retained earnings. In what other respect was the balance sheet of the company in error?

6. Office supplies on hand in the Melville Company amounted to $642 at the beginning of the year. During the year additional office supplies were purchased at a cost of $1,561 and charged to Inventory of Office Supplies. At the end of the year a physical count showed that supplies on hand amounted to $812. Give the adjusting entry needed at December 31.

7. The X Company at December 31 recognized the existence of certain unexpired costs which would provide benefits to the company in future periods. Give examples of such unexpired costs and state where they would be shown in the financial statements.

8. In performing the regular end-of-period accounting procedures, does the preparation of the work sheet precede or follow the posting of adjusting entries to ledger accounts? Why?

9. Should the Adjusted Trial Balance columns be totaled before or after the adjusted amounts are carried to the Income Statement, Retained Earnings Statement, and Balance Sheet columns?

10. In extending adjusted account balances from the Adjusted Trial Balance columns to the remaining columns of the work sheet, is there any particular sequence to be followed in order to minimize the possibility of errors? Explain.

11. Do the totals of the balance sheet ordinarily agree with the totals of the Balance Sheet columns of the work sheet?

12. Is a work sheet ever prepared when there is no intention of closing the books? Explain.

EXERCISES

1. The following amounts are taken from consecutive balance sheets of the Frank Company:

	1/1/71	12/31/71
Unexpired insurance	$ 1,200	$1,880
Unearned rental revenue	1,250	600
Interest payable	200	875
Dividends receivable	300	120

The income statement for 1971 of the Frank Company shows the following items:

Insurance expense	$ 3,000
Rental revenue	12,000
Interest expense	1,000
Dividend revenue	500

Determine the following amounts of cash:

a. Paid during 1971 on insurance policies $_____
b. Received during 1971 as rental revenue $_____
c. Paid during 1971 for interest $_____
d. Received during 1971 as dividends $_____

2. For each of the items from **a** through **e** relating to Concerts, Inc., write first the journal entry (if one is required) to record the transaction and secondly, the adjusting entry, if any, required at October 31, the end of a fiscal period.
a. On October 1, paid rent for four months at $500 per month.
b. On October 2, sold season tickets to the Music Festival for a total of

$6,000. Four different programs were included in the festival, three in October and one in November (credit Unearned Admissions Revenue).

c. On October 3, an agreement was reached with John Adams, allowing him to sell refreshments in the theater. In return for this privilege, Adams agreed to pay 10% of his gross receipts to the management within three days after the conclusion of each program.

d. On October 4, four program notes, one for each of the four programs, were printed at a total cost of $360. Cash was paid.

e. On October 31, Adams reported that total refreshment sales at Program No. 3, which ended on October 30, amounted to $1,000. Adams had previously remitted appropriate amounts relating to Program Nos. 1 and 2.

3. From the information given below, prepare the adjusting entries required at November 30, the end of a fiscal period:

a. Accrued wages payable, $1,150.

b. Interest receivable on United States government bonds owned, $425.

c. A six-month bank loan in the amount of $25,000 has been obtained on October 1, at an annual interest rate of 6%. No interest expense had been recorded.

d. A tractor had been rented on November 11 at a daily rate of $10. No rental payment had yet been made. Continued use of the tractor was expected through the month of January.

e. On November 30, an agreement was signed to lease a truck for 12 months beginning December 1 at a rate of 15 cents a mile. Estimated usage is 1,500 miles per month.

4. The trial balances of Safety Insurance Agency, as of September 30, 1971, before and after the posting of adjusting entries, are shown below:

	Before Adjustments		After Adjustments	
Cash.	$ 3,090		$ 3,090	
Commissions receivable			100	
Inventory of office supplies	300		180	
Office equipment.	5,610		5,610	
Accumulated depreciation: office equipment		$ 2,150		$ 2,230
Accounts payable		775		775
Salaries payable.				200
Unearned commissions		200		140
John Safety, capital		4,925		4,925
Commissions earned		1,950		2,110
Salaries expense.	1,000		1,200	
Office supplies expense.			120	
Depreciation expense: office equipment			80	
	$10,000	$10,000	$10,380	$10,380

Prepare the adjusting entries in journal form.

PROBLEMS

4-1 Sky Basin Ski Resort, Inc., maintains its accounting records on the basis of a fiscal year ending March 31. The following information is available:

(1) A six-month bank loan in the amount of $100,000 had been obtained on February 1 at an annual interest rate of 6%. No interest expense has been recorded.

(2) Salaries earned by employees but unpaid amounted to $3,010.

(3) Depreciation on the ski lodge for the year ended March 31 was $14,200.

(4) Depreciation on a station wagon owned by the resort was based on a four-year life. The station wagon had been purchased new on December 1 at a cost of $4,800.

(5) A tractor had been leased from Lease-All, Inc., on March 17 at a daily rate of $10. Continued use of the tractor was expected through the month of April. No rental payment had yet been made.

(6) A portion of the land owned by the company was leased on January 1 to a service station operator at a yearly rental of $2,400. One year's rental had been collected in advance at the date of the lease and credited to Unearned Rental Revenue.

(7) Among the assets owned by the company were government bonds in the face amount of $10,000. Accrued interest receivable on the bonds at March 31 amounted to $200.

(8) On March 31, the company signed an agreement to lease a truck from Local Car Rentals, Inc., for a period of 12 months beginning April 1, at a rate of 15 cents a mile.

Instructions
a. From the information given above, draft the adjusting entries (including explanations) required at March 31.
b. Assume that all necessary adjusting entries at March 31 have been recorded and that net income for the year is determined to be $100,000. How much net income would have been indicated by the accounting records if the company had failed to make the above adjusting entries? Show computations.

4-2 The four-column schedule presented on page 116 represents the first four columns of a 12-column work sheet to be prepared for Consultants, Inc., for the month ended April 30, 19____. (The completed adjustment columns have been included to minimize the detail work involved.) These adjustments were derived from the following information available at April 30:

(1) Monthly rent expense, $400.

(2) Insurance expense for the month, $40.

(3) Advertising expense for the month, $150.

(4) Cost of supplies on hand, based on physical count on April 30, $760.

(5) Depreciation expense on equipment, $300 per month.

(6) Accrued interest expenses on notes payable, $50.

(7) Salaries earned by employees but not yet paid, $750.

(8) Services amounting to $500 were rendered during April for customers who had paid in advance. This portion of the Unearned Revenue account should be regarded as earned as of April 30.

	Trial Balance		Adjustments	
Cash..............................	$12,200			
Prepaid rent........................	1,200			(1) $ 400
Unexpired insurance.................	400			(2) 40
Prepaid advertising..................	1,500			(3) 150
Inventory of supplies................	1,000			(4) 240
Equipment..........................	30,000			
Accumulated depreciation: equipment...		$ 4,500		(5) 300
Notes payable, 8%..................		7,500		
Unearned revenue...................		1,200	(8) $ 500	
Capital stock.......................		10,000		
Retained earnings...................		20,200		
Dividends	1,000			
Revenue from services...............		10,100		(8) 500
Salaries expense	6,200		(7) 750	
	$53,500	$53,500		
Rent expense........................			(1) 400	
Insurance expense....................			(2) 40	
Advertising expense			(3) 150	
Supplies expense.....................			(4) 240	
Depreciation expense: equipment.......			(5) 300	
Interest expense.....................			(6) 50	
Interest payable				(6) 50
Salaries payable.....................				(7) 750
			$2,430	$2,430

Instructions

Prepare a 12-column work sheet utilizing the trial balance and adjusting data provided. Include at the bottom of the work sheet a brief explanation keyed to each adjusting entry.

4-3 The Morrison Corporation started business in late March of 1971 and is engaged in the remodeling of homes in the greater Los Angeles area. The capital stock of $60,000 in the corporation is owned by Donald Morrison and his wife, Jane, who has been keeping the accounting records on a somewhat "hit and miss" basis. Early in 1972, Mrs. Morrison prepared the financial statements shown below, which Mr. Morrison presented to the Builders National Bank in support of a $25,000 line of credit.

MORRISON CORPORATION
Balance Sheet
December 31, 1971

Cash......................	$ 2,250	Accounts payable...........	$13,250
Receivables................	26,800	Capital....................	62,500
Inventory of building supplies	6,700		
Equipment.................	40,000		
	$75,750		$75,750

MORRISON CORPORATION
Income Statement
Period: March–December 1971

Contract fees.		$86,400
Expenses:		
Building supplies used.	$45,000	
Dividends paid.	7,500	
Labor.	23,500	
Rent	3,500	
Other.	4,400	83,900
Net income.		$ 2,500

After reviewing the financial statements of the Morrison Corporation, the banker instructed Morrison "to restate the financial statements in conformity with generally accepted accounting principles." The banker specifically mentioned the need (1) to record depreciation for nine months; (2) to recognize expenses of 1971 which were not paid as of December 31, 1971; (3) to report the amount of retained earnings on the balance sheet; and (4) to correct the expense total as reported on the income statement.

Mrs. Morrison comes to you for assistance, and with her help, you ascertain the following:

(1) The equipment was acquired on March 31, 1971, and has an estimated useful life of eight years.
(2) Salaries payable on December 31, 1971, are estimated at $700.
(3) Building supplies costing $3,000 were erroneously reported as an expense on the income statement. This amount is still in storage and should be reported as an asset.
(4) Other expenses as reported consist of oil and gas, $1,100; advertising, $1,500; and office expense, $1,800.

Instructions
a. Prepare revised financial statements for the Morrison Corporation, including a statement of retained earnings.
b. Reconcile the corrected net income with the net income of $2,500 as determined by Mrs. Morrison.

4-4 The Reed Geophysical Company closes its books at the end of the calendar year.

REED GEOPHYSICAL COMPANY
Trial Balance
December 31, 1972

Cash	$12,540
Prepaid office rent	8,400
Prepaid dues and subscriptions	960
Inventory of supplies	1,300
Equipment	20,000
Accumulated depreciation: equipment.	1,200

Notes payable		$ 5,000
Unearned consulting fees		35,650
Capital stock		10,000
Retained earnings, 1/1/72		12,950
Dividends	$ 7,000	
Consulting fees earned		15,200
Salaries expense	26,900	
Telephone and telegraph expense	550	
Miscellaneous expenses	2,350	
	$80,000	$80,000

Other data

(1) On January 1, 1972, the Prepaid Office Rent account had a balance of $2,400, representing the prepaid rent for the months January to June, 1972, inclusive. On July 1, 1972, the lease was renewed and office rent for one year at $500 per month was paid in advance.

(2) Dues and subscriptions expired during the year in the total amount of $710.

(3) A count of supplies on hand was made at December 31; the cost of the unused supplies was $450.

(4) The useful life of the equipment has been estimated at 10 years from date of acquisition.

(5) Accrued interest on notes payable amounted to $100 at year-end. Set up a separate Interest Expense account.

(6) Consulting services valued at $32,550 were rendered during the year for clients who had made payment in advance.

(7) It is the custom of the firm to bill clients only when consulting work is completed, or, in the case of prolonged engagement, at six-month intervals. At December 31, engineering services valued at $3,000 had been rendered to clients but not yet billed. No advance payments had been received from these clients.

(8) Salaries earned by staff engineers but not yet paid amounted to $200 at December 31.

Instructions

a. Prepare a work sheet for the year ended December 31, 1972.

b. Prepare an income statement, a balance sheet, and a statement of retained earnings.

4-5 Holiday Airlines, Inc., was organized on June 1, 1971, to provide air service for visitors to a famous island resort. Assume that the company closes its books monthly. At December 31, 1971, the following trial balance was prepared from the ledger:

Cash	$125,160
Prepaid rental expense	36,000
Unexpired insurance	31,200
Prepaid maintenance expense	15,000

Spare parts	$ 38,000	
Aircraft	540,000	
Accumulated depreciation: aircraft		$ 51,300
Unearned passenger revenue		40,000
Capital stock, $10 par		500,000
Retained earnings		150,000
Dividends	8,000	
Passenger revenue		122,660
Fuel expense	9,200	
Salaries expense	57,800	
Advertising expense	3,600	
	$863,960	$863,960

Other data

(1) Monthly rent amounted to $2,000.

(2) Insurance expense for December was $2,600.

(3) All necessary maintenance work was provided by Ryan Air Services at a fixed charge of $5,000 a month. Service for three months had been paid for in advance on December 1.

(4) Spare parts used in connection with maintenance work amounted to $2,500 during the month.

(5) At the time of purchase the remaining useful life of the airplanes, which were several years old, was estimated at 5,000 hours of flying time. During December, total flying time amounted to 160 hours.

(6) The Chamber of Commerce purchased 2,000 special tickets for $40,000. Each ticket allowed the holder one flight normally priced at $25. During the month 400 tickets had been tendered.

(7) Salaries earned by employees but not paid amounted to $2,200 at December 31.

Instructions

a. Prepare a work sheet for the month ended December 31, 1971.

b. Prepare an income statement, a statement of retained earnings, and a balance sheet.

c. Prepare adjusting and closing journal entries.

4-6 Given below are the financial statements for Abner Promotions, Inc., at the end of its fiscal year July 31, 19___.

ABNER PROMOTIONS, INC.
Income Statement
For the Year Ended July 31, 19___

Fees earned		$60,000
Expenses:		
Office salaries expense	$22,820	
Rent expense	4,500	
Insurance expense	800	

Promotional supplies expense	$13,280
Depreciation expense: office & automotive equipment	3,000
Interest expense	600
Total expenses	$45,000
Net income	$15,000

ABNER PROMOTIONS, INC.
Balance Sheet
July 31, 19____

Assets

Cash		$14,275
Fees receivable		15,000
Prepaid rent		375
Unexpired insurance		400
Inventory of promotional supplies		4,100
Office & automotive equipment	$44,000	
Less: Accumulated depreciation	18,150	25,850
		$60,000

Liabilities & Stockholders' Equity

Liabilities:		
Notes payable	$20,000	
Accounts payable	1,000	
Interest payable	100	
Office salaries payable	650	
Unearned fees	8,450	
Total liabilities		$30,200
Stockholders' equity:		
Capital stock	$20,000	
Retained earnings	9,800	29,800
		$60,000

Selected accounts taken from the unadjusted trial balance on July 31, 19____, follow:

Prepaid rent	$ 750
Unexpired insurance	1,200
Inventory of promotional supplies	3,100
Accumulated depreciation: office & automotive equipment	15,150
Unearned fees	6,450
Fees earned	47,000
Office salaries expense	22,170

Dividends of $10,000 were paid in June of the current year.

Instructions

a. Prepare the adjusting journal entries that apparently were made by the accountant, and number the adjusting entries.

b. Reproduce the complete work sheet as it was prepared by the accountant. (*Suggestion:* Write in all the account titles as a first step, following the usual sequence of assets, liabilities, stockholders' equity, revenue and expenses. Next, fill in the amounts in the last six columns, using figures shown in the financial statements. Then, fill in the adjustments columns using the data developed in part **a** of the solution. Finally, by a "squeezing" process, you can determine the amounts for the adjusted trial balance columns and for the trial balance columns.)

Chapter

5 Accounting for purchases and sales of merchandise

The preceding four chapters have illustrated step by step the complete accounting cycle for a business rendering personal services. In contrast to the service-type business, there are a great many companies whose principal activity is buying and selling merchandise. These merchandising companies may be engaged in either the retail or wholesale distribution of goods. The accounting concepts and methods we have studied for a service-type business are also applicable to a merchandising concern; however, some additional accounts and techniques are needed in accounting for the purchase and sale of merchandise.

Income statement for a merchandising business
An income statement for a retail sporting goods store is illustrated on page 123 to show how net income is determined in a business which derives its entire revenue from selling merchandise. We shall assume that the business of the Campus Sports Shop consists of buying sports equipment from manufacturers and selling this merchandise to college students. To keep the illustration reasonably short, we shall use a smaller number of expense accounts than would generally be employed.

    Analyzing the income statement. How does this income statement compare in form and content with the income statement of the service-type business presented in the preceding chapters? The most important change is the inclusion of the section entitled Cost of Goods Sold. Note how large the cost of goods sold is in comparison with the other figures on the statement. The cost of the merchandise sold during the month amounts to $6,000, or 60% of the month's sales of $10,000. Another way of looking at this relationship is to say that for each dollar the store receives by selling goods to customers, the sum of 60 cents represents a recovery of the cost of the merchandise. This leaves a gross profit of 40 cents from each sales dollar, out of which the store must pay its operating expenses. In our illustration the operating expenses for the month were $2,800, that is, 28% of the sales figure of $10,000. Therefore, the gross profit of 40 cents contained in each dollar of sales was enough to cover the operating expenses of 28 cents and leave a net income of 12 cents.

*Note
Distinction
between
Cost of
Goods
Sold and
Operating
Expenses*

CAMPUS SPORTS SHOP
*Income Statement
For the Month Ended September 30, 19___*

Sales...		$10,000
Cost of goods sold:		
Inventory, Sept. 1...............................	$ 4,400	
Purchases..	9,100	
Cost of goods available for sale...............	$13,500	
Less: Inventory, Sept. 30........................	7,500	
Cost of goods sold........................		6,000
Gross profit on sales..		$ 4,000
Operating expenses:		
Salaries...	$ 2,230	
Advertising..	450	
Telephone...	60	
Depreciation..	40	
Insurance..	20	
Total operating expenses.................		2,800
Net income...		$ 1,200

Of course the percentage relationship between sales and cost of sales will vary from one type of business to another, but, in all types of merchandising concerns, the cost of goods sold is one of the largest elements in the income statement. Accountants, bankers, and businessmen in general have the habit of mentally computing percentage relationships when they look at financial statements. Formation of this habit will be helpful throughout the study of accounting, as well as in many business situations.

In analyzing an income statement, it is customary to compare each item in the statement with the amount of sales. These comparisons are easier to make if we express the data in percentages as well as in dollar amounts. If the figure for sales is regarded as 100%, then every other item or subtotal on the statement can conveniently be expressed as a percentage of sales. The cost of goods sold in most types of business will be between 60 and 80% of sales. Conversely, the gross profit on sales (excess of sales over cost of goods sold) will usually vary between an upper limit of 40% and a lower limit of 20% of sales. Numerous exceptions may be found to such a sweeping generalization, but it is sufficiently valid to be helpful in visualizing customary relationships on the income statement.

Accounting for sales of merchandise

If merchandising concerns are to succeed or even to survive, they must, of course, sell their goods at prices higher than they pay to the vendors or suppliers from whom they buy. The selling prices charged by a retail store must cover three things: (1) the cost of the merchandise to the store; (2) the operating expenses of the business such as advertising, store rent, and salaries of salesmen; and (3) a net income to the business.

The sale of merchandise, like the sale of services, is recorded by debiting Cash or Accounts Receivable and crediting a revenue account. The title for this revenue account is Sales, and it appears as the first item on the income statement.

Revenue from the sale of merchandise is usually considered as earned in the period in which the merchandise is delivered to the customer, even though payment in cash is not received for a month or more after the sale. Consequently, the revenue earned in a given accounting period may differ considerably from the cash receipts of that period.

The amount and trend of sales are watched very closely by management, investors, and others interested in the progress of a company. A rising volume of sales is evidence of growth and suggests the probability of an increase in earnings. A declining trend in sales, on the other hand, is often the first signal of reduced earnings and of financial difficulties ahead. The amount of sales for each year is compared with the sales of the preceding year; the sales of each month may be compared with the sales of the preceding month and also with the corresponding month of the preceding year. These comparisons bring to light significant trends in the volume of sales. The financial pages of newspapers regularly report on the volume and trend of sales for corporations with publicly owned stock.

Inventory of merchandise and cost of goods sold
In the income statement illustrated on page 123, the inventory of merchandise and the cost of goods sold are important new concepts which require careful attention. An inventory of merchandise consists of the goods on hand and available for sale to customers. In the Campus Sports Shop, the inventory consists of golf clubs, tennis rackets, and skiing equipment; in a pet shop the inventory might include puppies, fish, and parakeets. Inventories are acquired through the purchase of goods from wholesalers, manufacturers, or other suppliers. A company's inventory is increased by the purchase of goods from suppliers and decreased by the sale of goods to customers. The cost of the merchandise sold during the month appears in the income statement as a deduction from the sales of the month. The merchandise which is *not sold* during the month constitutes the inventory of merchandise on hand at the end of the accounting period and is included in the balance sheet as an asset. The ending inventory of one accounting period is, of course, the beginning inventory of the following period.

There are two alternative approaches to the determination of inventory and of cost of goods sold, namely, the *periodic inventory method* and the *perpetual inventory method.* Business concerns which sell merchandise of high unit value, such as automobiles or television sets, generally use a perpetual inventory system. This system requires the keeping of records showing the cost of each article in stock. Units added to inventory and units sold are recorded on a daily basis. At the end of the accounting period, the total cost of goods sold is easily determined by adding the costs recorded from day to day for the units sold.

The periodic inventory method. The majority of businesses, however, do not maintain perpetual inventory records; they rely instead upon a periodic inventory (a count of merchandise on hand) to determine the inventory at the end of the accounting period and the cost of goods sold during the period. The periodic inventory system may be concisely summarized as follows:

1. A physical count of merchandise on hand is made at the end of each accounting period.

2. The cost value of this inventory is computed by multiplying the quantity of each item by an appropriate unit cost. A total cost figure for the entire inventory is then determined by adding the costs of all the various types of merchandise.

3. The *cost of goods available for sale* during the period is determined by adding the amount of the inventory at the beginning of the period to the amount of the purchases during the period.

4. The *cost of goods sold* is computed by subtracting the inventory at the end of the period from the cost of goods available for sale. In other words, the difference between the cost of goods available for sale and the amount of goods remaining unsold at the end of the period is presumed to have been sold.

A simple illustration of the above procedures for determining the cost of goods sold follows:

Using the Periodic Inventory Method	*Beginning inventory (determined by count)*	*$1,000*
	Add: Purchases	*1,800*
	Cost of goods available for sale	*$2,800*
	Less: Ending inventory (determined by count)	*1,200*
	Cost of goods sold	*$1,600*

The periodic inventory system is the method we shall be working with throughout most of this book. Because of the importance of the process for determining inventory and cost of goods sold, we shall now consider in more detail the essential steps in using the periodic inventory system.

Taking a physical inventory. When the periodic inventory system is in use, there is no day-to-day record of the cost of goods sold. Neither is there any day-to-day record of the amount of goods unsold and still on hand. At the end of the accounting period, however, it is necessary to determine the cost of goods sold during the period and also the amount of unsold goods on hand. The figure for cost of goods sold is used in determining the profit or loss for the period, and the value of the merchandise on hand at the end of the period is included in the balance sheet as an asset.

To determine the cost of the merchandise on hand, a physical inventory is taken. The count of merchandise should be made if possible after the close of business on the last day of the accounting period. It is difficult to make an accurate count during business hours while sales are taking place; consequently, the physical inventory is often taken in the evening or on Sunday. After all goods have been counted, the proper cost price must be assigned to each article. The assignment of a cost price to each item of merchandise in stock is often described as *pricing the inventory.* Inventories of merchandise are usually valued at cost for accounting purposes, although some alternative bases will be discussed in Chapter 11, as well as alternative methods of determining cost.

Computing the cost of goods sold. The taking of a physical inventory at the end of the accounting period is a major step toward computing the cost of goods sold during the period. Let us illustrate the computation of cost of goods sold by considering the first year of operation for a new business. We can reasonably assume that there was no beginning inventory of merchandise at the inception of the enterprise. During the first year, the purchases of merchandise totaled $50,000. These purchases constituted the goods available for sale. A physical count of merchandise was made on December 31; the quantities shown as on hand were multiplied by unit cost prices, and a total cost for the inventory was computed as $10,000. If goods costing $50,000 were available for sale during the year and goods costing $10,000 remained unsold at year-end, then the cost of goods sold must have been $40,000, as summarized below:

Computing Cost of Goods Sold in First Year	*Inventory at beginning of period*	$ 000
	Purchases	50,000
	Cost of goods available for sale	$50,000
	Less: Inventory at end of period	10,000
	Cost of goods sold	$40,000

The merchandise on hand at the close of business December 31 of the first year is, of course, still on hand on January 1 of the second year. As previously stated, the *ending* inventory of one year is the *beginning* inventory of the following year. To continue our example, let us assume that in the second year of operation purchases amounted to $75,000 and the inventory of goods on hand at the end of the second year was determined by the taking of a physical inventory that amounted to $25,000. The cost of goods sold during the second year would be computed as shown at the top of page 127.

Dependability of the periodic inventory method. In computing the cost of goods sold by the periodic inventory method, we are making a somewhat

Computing	*Inventory at beginning of second year*	*$10,000*
Cost of	*Purchases*	*75,000*
Goods	*Cost of goods available for sale*	*$85,000*
Sold in	*Less: Inventory at end of second year*	*25,000*
Second	*Cost of goods sold*	*$60,000*
Year		

dangerous assumption that all goods not sold during the year will be on hand at the end of the year.

Referring to the above example, let us assume that, during the second year of operations, shoplifters stole $1,000 worth of merchandise from the store without being detected. The cost of goods available for sale is still $85,000, and the final inventory is still $25,000, but the cost of goods sold is not actually $60,000. The $60,000 difference between goods available for sale and goods in final inventory is composed of two distinct elements: cost of goods sold, $59,000, and cost of goods stolen, $1,000. However, under the periodic inventory method, the loss of goods by theft would not be apparent, and the cost of goods sold would erroneously be shown in the income statement as $60,000. A method of disclosing inventory shortages of this type is explained in Chapter 11.

Accounting for merchandise purchases

The purchase of merchandise for resale to customers is recorded by debiting an account called Purchases. The Purchases account is used *only* for merchandise acquired for resale. Assets acquired for use in the business (such as a delivery truck, a typewriter, or office supplies) are recorded by debiting the appropriate asset account, not the Purchases account. Only merchandise acquired for resale is entered in the Purchases account because this account is used in computing the cost of goods sold. The journal entry to record a purchase of merchandise is illustrated as follows:

Journal		
Entry for	*Purchases* 1,000	
Purchase	*Accounts Payable (or Cash)*	*1,000*
of Mer-	*Purchased merchandise from ABC Supply Co.*	
chandise		

At the end of the accounting period, the balance accumulated in the Purchases account represents the total cost of merchandise purchased during the period. This amount is used in preparing the income statement. The Purchases account has then served its purpose and it is closed to the Income Summary account. Since the Purchases account is closed at the end of each period, it has a zero balance at the beginning of each succeeding period.

Transportation-in. The cost of merchandise acquired for resale logically includes any transportation charges necessary to place the goods in the purchaser's place of business.

A separate ledger account is used to accumulate transportation charges on merchandise purchased. The journal entry to record the payment of transportation charges on inbound shipments of merchandise is as follows:

> *Transportation-in* *169.50*
>   *Cash (or Accounts Payable)* *169.50*
> *Air freight charges on merchandise purchased from Miller
> Brothers, Kansas City.*

Since transportation charges are part of the **delivered cost** of merchandise purchased, the Transportation-in account is combined with the Purchases account in the income statement to determine the cost of goods available for sale.

Purchase returns and allowances. When merchandise purchased from suppliers is found to be unsatisfactory, the goods may be returned to the seller, or a request may be made for an allowance on the price. A return of goods to the vendor is recorded as follows:

> *Accounts Payable* *1,200*
>   *Purchase Returns and Allowances* *1,200*
> *To charge Marvel Supply Co. for the cost of goods returned.*

Sometimes when the purchaser of merchandise finds the goods not entirely satisfactory, he may agree to keep the goods in consideration for a reduction or allowance on the original price. The entry to record such an allowance is essentially the same as that for a return.

The use of a Purchase Returns and Allowances account rather than the recording of returns by direct credits to the Purchases account is advisable because the books then show both the total amount of the purchases and the amount of purchases which required adjustment or return. Management is interested in the percentage relationship between goods returned and goods purchased, because the returning of merchandise for credit is a time-consuming, costly process. Excessive returns suggest that the purchasing department should look for more dependable sources of supply.

Illustration of accounting cycle using periodic inventory method

The October transactions of the Campus Sports Shop will now be used to illustrate the accounting cycle for a business using the periodic inventory system of accounting for merchandise.

Recording sales of merchandise. Sales of sports equipment during October amounted to $10,025. All sales were for cash, and each sales transaction was rung up on a cash register. At the close of each day's business, the total sales for the day were computed by pressing the total key on the cash register. As soon as each day's sales were computed, a journal entry was prepared and posted to the Cash account and the Sales account in the ledger. The daily entering of cash sales in the journal is desirable in order to minimize the opportunity for errors or dishonesty by employees in handling the cash receipts. In Chapter 6 a procedure will be described which provides a daily record of sales and cash receipts yet avoids the making of an excessive number of entries in the Cash and Sales accounts.

Recording sales returns and allowances. On October 27 a customer returned some unsatisfactory merchandise and was given a refund of $46. Another customer complained on October 28 of a slight defect in an article he had recently purchased and was given a refund of $10, representing half of the original price. The journal entries to record these returns and allowances were as follows:

Journal	Oct. 27	*Sales Returns and Allowances*	*46*	
Entries		*Cash*		*46*
for		*Made refund for merchandise returned by customer.*		
Returns				
and Allow-	Oct. 28	*Sales Returns and Allowances*	*10*	
ances		*Cash*		*10*
		Allowance to customer for defect in merchandise.		

Work sheet for a merchandising business. After the October transactions of the Campus Sports Shop had been posted to ledger accounts, the work sheet illustrated on page 130 was prepared. The first step in the preparation of the work sheet was, of course, the listing of the balances of the ledger accounts in the Trial Balance columns. In studying this work sheet, note that the Inventory account in the Trial Balance debit column still shows a balance of $7,500, the cost of merchandise on hand at the end of September. No entries were made in the Inventory account during October despite the various purchases and sales of merchandise. The significance of the Inventory account in the trial balance is that it shows the amount of merchandise with which the Campus Sports Shop began operations for the month of October.

Omission of Adjusted Trial Balance columns. In the work sheet previously illustrated in Chapter 4, page 105, the amounts in the Trial Balance columns were combined with the amounts listed in the Adjustments columns and then extended into the Adjusted Trial Balance columns. When there are only a few adjusting entries, many accountants prefer to omit the Adjusted Trial Balance columns and to extend the trial balance figures (as adjusted by the amounts in the Adjustments columns) directly to the Income Statement, Retained Earnings Statement, or Balance Sheet columns. This procedure is used in the work sheet for the Campus Sports Shop.

Recording the ending inventory on the work sheet. The key points to be observed in this work sheet are (1) the method of recording the ending

CAMPUS SPORTS SHOP
Work Sheet
For the Month Ended October 31, 19____

	Trial Balance		Adjustments*		Income Statement		Retained Earnings Statement		Balance Sheet	
Cash	6,569								6,569	
Inventory, Sept. 30	7,500				7,500					
Unexpired insurance	200			(2) 20					180	
Land	3,000								3,000	
Building	10,000								10,000	
Accumulated depreciation: building		960		(1) 40						1,000
Accounts payable		6,700								6,700
Capital stock		15,000								15,000
Retained earnings		4,940						4,940		
Dividends	300						300			
Sales		10,025				10,025				
Sales returns and allowances	56				56					
Purchases	8,100				8,100					
Purchase returns and allowances		600				600				
Transportation-in	200				200					
Advertising expense	250				250					
Salaries expense	2,000				2,000					
Telephone expense	50				50					
	38,225	38,225								
Depreciation expense: building			(1) 40		40					
Insurance expense			(2) 20		20					
			60	60						
Inventory, Oct. 31						9,000			9,000	
					18,216	19,625				
Net income					1,409			1,409		
					19,625	19,625	300	6,349		
Retained earnings, Oct. 31, 19____							6,049			6,049
							6,349	6,349	28,749	28,749

* Adjustments
(1) Depreciation of building during October
(2) Insurance premium expired during October

inventory and (2) the method of handling the various accounts making up the costs of goods sold.

After the close of business on October 31, a physical inventory was taken of all merchandise in the store. The cost of the entire stock of goods was determined to be $9,000. This ending inventory, dated October 31, does not appear in the trial balance; it is therefore written on the first available line below the other account titles. The amount of $9,000 is listed in the Income Statement credit column and also in the Balance Sheet debit column. By entering the ending inventory in the Income Statement *credit* column, we are in effect deducting it from the total of the beginning inventory, the purchases, and the transportation-in, all of which are extended from the trial balance to the Income Statement *debit* column.

One of the functions of the Income Statement columns is to bring together all the accounts involved in determining the cost of goods sold. The accounts with debit balances are the beginning inventory, the purchases, and the transportation-in; these accounts total $15,800. Against this total, the two credit items of purchase returns, $600, and ending inventory, $9,000, are offset. The three merchandising accounts with debit balances exceed in total the two with credit balances by an amount of $6,200; this amount is the cost of goods sold and appears in the income statement.

The ending inventory is also entered in the Balance Sheet debit column, because this inventory of merchandise on October 31 will appear as an asset in the balance sheet bearing this date.

Financial statements. The work to be done at the end of the period is much the same for a merchandising business as for a service-type firm. First, the work sheet is completed; then, financial statements are prepared from the data in the work sheet; next, the adjusting and closing entries are entered in the journal and posted to the ledger accounts; and finally, a post-closing trial balance is prepared. This completes the periodic accounting cycle.

The income statement for a merchandising business may be regarded as consisting of three sections: (1) the sales revenue section, (2) the cost of goods sold section, and (3) the operating expense section. The income statement on page 132 was prepared from the work sheet on page 130. The related statement of retained earnings and balance sheet are not shown since they do not differ significantly from previous illustrations. Note particularly the arrangement of items in the cost of goods sold section of the income statement; this portion of the income statement shows in summary form most of the essential accounting concepts covered in this chapter.

Closing entries. The entries used in closing revenue and expense accounts have been explained in preceding chapters. The only new elements in this illustration of closing entries for a trading business are the entries showing the elimination of the beginning inventory and the recording of the ending inventory. The beginning inventory is cleared out of the Inventory account by a debit to Income Summary and a credit to Inventory. A separate entry could be made for this purpose, but we can save time by making one compound entry which will debit the Income Summary account with the balance of the beginning inventory and with the balances of all temporary

CAMPUS SPORTS SHOP
Income Statement
For the Month Ended October 31, 19___

Revenue from sales:			
Sales		$10,025	
Less: Sales returns and allowances		56	
Net sales			$9,969
Cost of goods sold:			
Merchandise inventory, Sept. 30		$ 7,500	
Purchases	$8,100		
Less: Purchase returns and allowances	600	7,500	
Transportation-in		200	
Cost of goods available for sale		$15,200	
Less: Merchandise inventory, Oct. 31		9,000	
Cost of goods sold			6,200
Gross profit on sales			$3,769
Operating expenses:			
Salaries		$ 2,000	
Advertising		250	
Telephone		50	
Depreciation		40	
Insurance		20	
Total operating expenses			2,360
Net income			$1,409

proprietorship accounts having debit balances. The ***temporary proprietorship accounts*** are those which appear in the income statement. As the name suggests, the temporary proprietorship accounts are used during the period to accumulate temporarily the increases and decreases in the owners' equity resulting from operation of the business.

Closing	Oct. 31	Income Summary	18,216	
Temporary		Inventory (beginning)		7,500
Proprietor-		Purchases		8,100
ship		Sales Returns and Allowances		56
Accounts		Transportation-in		200
with Debit		Advertising Expense		250
Balances		Salaries Expense		2,000
		Telephone Expense		50
		Depreciation Expense		40
		Insurance Expense		20
		To close out the beginning inventory and the temporary proprietorship accounts having debit balances.		

Note that the above entry closes all the operating expense accounts as well as the accounts used to accumulate the cost of merchandise sold, and also the Sales Returns and Allowances account. Although the Sales Returns and Allowances account has a debit balance, it is not an expense account. In terms of account classification, it belongs in the revenue group of accounts because it serves as an offset to the Sales account and appears in the income statement as a deduction from Sales.

To bring the ending inventory on the books after the stocktaking on October 31, we could make a separate entry debiting Inventory and crediting the Income Summary account. It is more convenient, however, to combine this step with the closing of the Sales account and any other temporary proprietorship accounts having credit balances, as illustrated in the following closing entry.

Closing Temporary Proprietorship Accounts with Credit Balances

Oct. 31	Inventory (ending)	9,000	
	Sales	10,025	
	Purchase Returns and Allowances	600	
	Income Summary		19,625
	To record the ending inventory and to close all temporary proprietorship accounts having credit balances.		

The remaining closing entries serve to transfer the balance of the Income Summary account to the Retained Earnings account, and to close the Dividends account, as follows:

Closing Income Summary Account and Dividends Account

Oct. 31	Income Summary	1,409	
	Retained Earnings		1,409
	To close the Income Summary account.		
Oct. 31	Retained Earnings	300	
	Dividends		300
	To close the Dividends account.		

Summary of merchandising transactions and related accounting entries

The transactions regularly encountered in merchandising operations and the related accounting entries are concisely summarized at the top of page 134.

Internal control concepts

Our discussion of a merchandising business has emphasized the steps of the accounting cycle, especially the determination of cost of goods sold and the preparation of a work sheet and financial statements. Now we need to round out this discussion by considering methods by which management maintains control over purchases and sales transactions. These methods place particular emphasis upon the subdivision of duties within the company so that no one person or department handles a transaction completely from beginning to end. When duties are divided in this manner, the work of one

Customary Journal Entries Relating to Merchandise

Transactions during the Period	*Related Accounting Entries*	
	Debit	*Credit*
Purchase merchandise for resale	Purchases	Cash or Accounts Payable
Incur transportation charges on merchandise purchased for resale	Transportation-in	Cash or Accounts Payable
Return unsatisfactory merchandise to supplier, or obtain a reduction from original price	Cash or Accounts Payable	Purchase Returns & Allowances
Sell merchandise to customers	Cash or Accounts Receivable	Sales
Permit customers to return merchandise, or grant them a reduction from original price	Sales Returns & Allowances	Cash or Accounts Receivable
Inventory procedures at end of period		
Transfer the balance of the beginning inventory to the Income Summary account	Income Summary	Inventory
Take a physical inventory of goods on hand at the end of the period, and price these goods at cost	Inventory	Income Summary

employee serves to verify that of another and any errors which occur tend to be detected promptly.

To illustrate the development of internal control through subdivision of duties, let us review the procedures for a sale of merchandise on account by a wholesaler. The sales department of the company is responsible for securing the order from the customer; the credit department must approve the customer's credit before the order is filled; the stock room assembles the goods ordered; the shipping department packs and ships the goods; and the accounting department records the transaction. Each department receives written evidence of the action of the other departments and reviews the documents describing the transaction to see that the actions taken correspond in all details. The shipping department, for instance, does not release the merchandise until after the credit department has approved the customer as a credit risk. The accounting department does not record the sale until it has received documentary evidence that (1) the goods were ordered, (2) the extension of credit was approved, and (3) the merchandise has been shipped to the customer.

Assume for a moment, as a contrast to this procedure, that a single employee were permitted to secure the customer's order, approve the credit terms, get the merchandise from the stock room, deliver the goods to the customer, prepare the invoice, enter the transaction in the accounting records, and perhaps even collect the account receivable. If this employee made errors, such as selling to poor credit risks, forgetting to enter the sale in the accounting records, or perhaps delivering more merchandise to the customer than he was charged for, no one would know the difference. By the time such errors came to light, substantial losses would have been incurred.

If one employee is permitted to handle all aspects of a transaction, the danger of fraud is also increased. Studies of fraud cases suggest that many individuals may be tempted into dishonest acts if given complete control of company property. Most of these persons, however, would not engage in fraud if doing so required collaboration with another employee. Losses through employee dishonesty occur in a variety of ways: merchandise may disappear; payments by customers may be withheld; suppliers may be overpaid with a view to kickbacks to employees; and lower prices may be allowed to favored customers. The opportunities for fraud are almost endless if all aspects of a sale or purchase transaction are concentrated in the hands of one employee.

Because internal control rests so largely upon the participation of several employees in each transaction, it is apparent that strong internal control is more easily achieved in large organizations than in small ones. In a small business with only one or two office employees, such duties as the issuance of purchase orders, approval of credit, and maintenance of accounting records may necessarily have to be performed by the same employee. In later chapters numerous suggestions will be made for strengthening internal control in small organizations.

Another method of achieving internal control, in addition to the subdivision of duties, consists of having the printer include serial numbers on such documents as purchase orders, sales invoices, and checks. The use of serial numbers makes it possible to account for all documents. In other words, if a sales invoice is misplaced or concealed, the break in the sequence of numbers will call attention to the discrepancy.

A description of internal control solely in terms of the prevention of fraud and the detection of errors represents too narrow a concept of this managerial technique. The building of a strong system of internal control is an accepted means of increasing operational efficiency. Broadly defined, internal control includes the plan of organization and all measures taken by a business to safeguard assets, to ensure reliability in accounting data, to promote operational efficiency, and to encourage compliance with company policies.

In appraising the merits of various internal control procedures, the question of their cost cannot be ignored. Too elaborate a system of internal control may entail greater operating costs than are justified by the protection gained. For this reason among others, the system of internal control must be tailored to meet the requirements of the individual business. In most organizations, however, proper subdivision of duties and careful design of accounting procedures will provide a basis for adequate internal control and at the same time will contribute to economical and efficient operation.

Business papers

Carefully designed business papers and procedures for using them are necessary to ensure that all transactions are properly authorized and recorded. To illustrate this point in a somewhat exaggerated manner, let us assume that every employee in a large department store was authorized to purchase merchandise for the store and that no standard forms or procedures had been provided to keep track of these purchases. The result would undoubtedly be many unwise purchases, confusion as to what had been ordered and received, shortages of some types of merchandise, and an oversupply of other types. The opportunity for fraud by dishonest employees, as well as for accidental errors, would be unlimited under such a haphazard method of operation.

Each step in ordering, receiving, and making payment for merchandise purchases should be controlled and recorded. A similar approach is necessary to establish control over the sales function.

Purchase orders. A purchase order issued by Zenith Company to Adams Manufacturing Company is illustrated below.

Serially Numbered Order for Merchandise

PURCHASE ORDER

ZENITH COMPANY
10 Fairway Avenue
San Francisco, California

Order No.

999

To: Adams Manufacturing Company

Date Nov. 10, 1971

19 Union Street

Ship via Jones Truck Co.

Kansas City, Missouri

Terms: 2/10, n/30

Please enter our order for the following:

Quantity	Description	Price	Total
15 sets	Model S irons	$60.00	$900.00
50 dozen	X3Y Shur-Par golf balls	7.00	350.00

Zenith Company

By *D. D. McCarthy*

In large companies in which the functions of placing orders, receiving merchandise, and making payment are lodged in separate departments, several copies of the purchase order are usually prepared, each on a different color paper. The original is sent to the supplier; this purchase order is his authorization to deliver the merchandise and to submit a bill based on the prices listed. In a departmentalized business, carbon copies of the purchase order are usually routed to the purchasing department, accounting department, receiving department, and finance department.

The issuance of a purchase order does not call for any debit or credit entries in the accounting records of either the prospective buyer or seller. The company which receives an order does not consider for accounting purposes that a sale has been made until the merchandise is delivered. At that point ownership of the goods changes, and both buyer and seller should make accounting entries to record the transaction.

Invoices. The supplier (vendor) mails an invoice to the purchaser at the time of shipping the merchandise. An invoice contains a description of the goods being sold, the quantities, prices, credit terms, and method of shipment. The illustration below shows an invoice issued by Adams Manufacturing Company in response to the previously illustrated purchase order from Zenith Company.

Invoice Is Basis for Accounting Entry

ADAMS MANUFACTURING COMPANY
19 Union Street
Kansas City, Missouri

Sold to Zenith Company   Invoice No. 777

　　　　10 Fairway Avenue   Invoice date Nov. 15, 1971

　　　　San Francisco, Calif.   Your Order No. 999

Shipped to Same   Date shipped Nov. 15, 1971

Terms 2/10, n/30   Shipped by Jones Truck Co.

Quantity	Description	Price	Amount
15 sets	Model S irons	$60.00	$900.00
50 dozen	X3Y Shur-Par golf balls	7.00	350.00
			$1,250.00

From the viewpoint of the seller, an invoice is a *sales invoice;* from the buyer's viewpoint it is a *purchase invoice.* The invoice is the basis for an entry in the accounting records of both the seller and the buyer because it evidences the transfer of ownership of goods. At the time of issuing the invoice, the seller makes an entry debiting Accounts Receivable and crediting Sales. The buyer, however, does not record the invoice as a liability until he has made a careful verification of the transaction, as indicated in the following section.

Verification of invoice by purchaser. Upon receipt of an invoice, the purchaser should verify the following aspects of the transaction:

1. The invoice agrees with the purchase order as to prices, quantities, and other provisions.

2. The invoice is arithmetically correct in all extensions of price times quantity and in the addition of amounts.

3. The goods covered by the invoice have been received and are in satisfactory condition.

Evidence that the merchandise has been received in good condition must be obtained from the receiving department. It is the function of the receiving department to receive all incoming goods, to inspect them as to quality and condition, and to determine the quantities received by counting, measuring, or weighing. The purchasing department should prepare a separate receiving report for each shipment received; this report is sent to the accounting department for use in verifying the invoice.

The verification of the invoice in the accounting department is accomplished by comparing the purchase order, the invoice, and the receiving report. Comparison of these documents establishes that the goods described in the invoice were actually ordered, have been received in good condition, and were billed at the prices specified in the purchase order.

Debit and credit memoranda. If merchandise purchased on account is unsatisfactory and is to be returned to the supplier (or if a price reduction is agreed upon), a *debit memorandum* may be prepared by the purchasing company and sent to the supplier. The debit memorandum informs the supplier that his account is being debited (reduced) on the books of the buyer and explains the circumstances.

The supplier upon being informed of the return of damaged merchandise (or having agreed to a reduction in price), will issue a *credit memorandum* as evidence that the account receivable from the purchaser is being credited (reduced).

Trade discounts. Manufacturers and wholesalers in many lines of industry publish annual catalogs in which their products are listed at retail prices. Substantial reductions from the *list prices* shown in the catalog are offered to dealers and other large-scale purchasers. These reductions from the list prices (often as much as 30 or 40%) are called *trade discounts.* The entire schedule of discounts may be revised as price levels and market conditions fluctuate. To publish a new catalog every time the price of one or more products changes would be an expensive practice; the issuance of a new schedule of trade discounts is much more convenient and serves just as well in revising actual selling prices.

Trade discounts are not recorded in the accounting records of either the seller or the buyer. A sale of merchandise is recorded at the actual selling price and the trade discount is merely a device for computing the actual sales price. From the viewpoint of the company purchasing goods, the significant price is not the list price but the amount which must be paid, and this amount is recorded as the cost of the merchandise.

To illustrate the use of a trade discount, assume that the Martin Manufacturing Company sells goods to Austin Auto Repair at a list price of $100 with a trade discount of 30%. Martin Manufacturing Company would record the sale by the following entry:

Neither Seller . . .

Accounts Receivable	*70*	
Sales		*70*

The entry by Austin Auto Repair to record the purchases would be:

. . . nor Buyer Records Trade Discounts

Purchases	*70*	
Accounts Payable		*70*

Because trade discounts are not recorded in the accounts, they should be clearly distinguished from the cash discounts discussed below.

Cash discounts. Manufacturers and wholesalers generally offer a cash discount to encourage their customers to pay invoices. For example, the credit terms may be "2% 10 days, net 30 days"; these terms mean that the authorized credit period is 30 days, but that the customer may deduct 2% of the amount of the invoice if he makes payment within 10 days. On the invoice these terms would appear in the abbreviated form "2/10, n/30"; this expression is read "2, 10, net 30." The selling company regards a cash discount as a *sales discount;* the buyer calls the discount a *purchase discount.*[1]

To illustrate the application of a cash discount, assume that Adams Manufacturing Company sells goods to the Zenith Company and issues a sales invoice for $1,000 dated November 3 and bearing the terms 2/10, n/30. If Zenith Company mails its check in payment on or before November 13, it is entitled to deduct 2% of $1,000, or $20, and settle the obligation for $980. If Zenith Company decides to forego the discount, it may postpone payment for an additional 20 days until December 3 but must then pay $1,000.

Reasons for cash discounts. From the viewpoint of the seller, the acceptance of $980 in cash as full settlement of a $1,000 account receivable represents a $20 reduction in the amount of revenue earned. By making this concession to induce prompt payment, the seller collects accounts re-

---

[1]Some companies issue invoices payable 10 days after the end of the month in which the sale occurs. Such invoices may bear the expression "10 e.o.m."

ceivable more quickly and is able to use the money collected to buy additional goods. A greater volume of business can be handled with a given amount of invested capital if this capital is not tied up in accounts receivable for long periods. There is also less danger of accounts receivable becoming uncollectible if they are collected promptly; in other words, the older an account receivable becomes, the greater the risk of nonpayment.

Is it to the advantage of the Zenith Company to settle the $1,000 invoice within the discount period and thereby save $20? The alternative is for Zenith to conserve cash by postponing payment for an additional 20 days. The question may therefore be stated as follows: Does the amount of $20 represent a reasonable charge for the use of $980 for a period of 20 days? Definitely not; this charge is the equivalent of an annual interest rate of about 36%. (A 20-day period is approximately $\frac{1}{18}$ of a year; 18 times 2% amounts to 36%.) Most businesses are able to borrow money from banks at an annual rate of 9% or less. Well-managed businesses, therefore, generally pay all invoices within the discount period even though this policy necessitates borrowing from banks in order to have the necessary cash available.

Recording sales discounts. Sales of merchandise are generally recorded at the full selling price without regard for the cash discount being offered. The discount is not reflected in the seller's accounting records until payment is received. Continuing our illustration of a sale of merchandise by Adams Manufacturing Company for $1,000 with terms of 2/10, n/30, the entry to record the sale on November 3 is as shown by the following:

Sale *Entered* *at Full* *Price*	*Nov. 3* **Accounts Receivable** . . . . *1,000* **Sales** . . . . *1,000* *To record sale to Zenith Company, terms 2/10, n/30.*

Assuming that payment is made by the Zenith Company on November 13, the last day of the discount period, the entry by Adams to record collection of the receivable is as follows:

Sales *Discounts* *Recorded* *at Time of* *Collection*	*Nov. 13* **Cash** . . . . *980* **Sales Discounts** . . . . *20* **Accounts Receivable** . . . . *1,000* *To record collection from Zenith Company of invoice of* *November 3 less 2% cash discount.*

As previously explained, the allowing of a cash discount reduces the amount received from sales. On the income statement, therefore, the sales discounts appear as a deduction from sales, as shown at the top of page 141.

Treatment of Sales Discounts on Income Statement

Partial Income Statement		
Sales		$189,788
Less: Sales returns and allowances	$4,462	
Sales discounts	3,024	7,486
Net sales		$182,302

Recording purchase discounts. On the books of the Zenith Company, the purchase of merchandise on November 3 was recorded at the gross amount of the invoice, as shown by the following entry:

Purchase Entered at Full Price

Purchases	1,000	
Accounts Payable		1,000
To record purchase from Adams Manufacturing Company, terms 2/10, n/30.		

When the invoice was paid on November 13, the last day of the discount period, the payment was recorded as follows:

Purchase Discount Recorded When Payment Made

Accounts Payable	1,000	
Purchase Discounts		20
Cash..		980
To record payment to Adams Manufacturing Company of invoice of November 3, less 2% cash discount.		

The effect of the discount was to reduce the cost of the merchandise to the Zenith Company. The credit balance of the Purchase Discounts account should therefore be deducted in the income statement from the debit balance of the Purchases account.

Since the Purchase Discounts account is deducted from Purchases in the income statement, a question naturally arises as to whether the Purchase Discounts account is really necessary. Why not reduce the amount of purchases at the time of taking a discount by crediting Purchases rather than crediting Purchases Discounts? The answer is that management needs to know the amount of discounts taken. The Purchase Discounts account supplies this information. Any decrease in the proportion of purchase discounts to purchases carries the suggestion that the accounts payable department is becoming inefficient. That department has the responsibility of paying all invoices within the discount period, and management should be informed of failure by any department to follow company policies consistently. If management is to direct the business effectively, it needs to receive from the accounting system information indicating the level of performance in every department.

Monthly statements to customers. In addition to sending an invoice to the customer for each separate sales transaction, some concerns send each customer a statement at the end of the month. The customer's statement is similar to a ledger account and is sometimes called a statement of account. It shows the balance receivable at the beginning of the month, the charges for sales during the month, the credits for payments received or goods returned, and the balance receivable from the customer at the end of the month.

Upon receipt of a monthly statement from a vendor, the customer should make a detailed comparison of the purchases and payments shown on the statement with the corresponding entries in his accounts payable records. Any differences in the invoiced amounts, payments, or balance owed should be promptly investigated. Frequently the balance shown on the statement will differ from the balance of the customer's accounts payable record because shipments of merchandise and letters containing payments are in transit at month-end. These in-transit items will have been recorded by the sender but will not yet appear on the other party's records.

Classified financial statements

The financial statements illustrated up to this point have been rather short and simple because of the limited number of transactions and accounts used in these introductory chapters. Now let us look briefly at a more comprehensive and realistic balance sheet for a merchandising business. A full understanding of all the items on this balance sheet may not be possible until our study of accounting has progressed further, but a bird's-eye view of a fairly complete balance sheet is nevertheless useful at this point.

In the balance sheet of the Graham Company illustrated on page 143, the assets are classified into three groups: (1) current assets, (2) plant and equipment, and (3) other assets. The liabilities are classified into two types: (1) current liabilities and (2) long-term liabilities. This classification of assets and liabilities, subject to minor variations in terminology, is virtually a standard one throughout American business. The inclusion of captions for the balance sheet totals is an optional step.

The purpose of balance sheet classification. The purpose underlying a standard classification of assets and liabilities is to aid management, owners, creditors, and other interested persons in understanding the financial condition of the business. The banker, for example, would have a difficult time in reading the balance sheets of all the companies which apply to him for loans, if each of these companies followed its own individual whims as to the sequence and arrangement of accounts comprising its balance sheet. Standard practices as to the order and arrangement of a balance sheet are an important means of saving the time of the reader and of giving him a fuller comprehension of the company's financial position. On the other hand, these standard practices are definitely not iron-clad rules; the form and

THE GRAHAM COMPANY
Balance Sheet
December 31, 19___

Assets

Current assets:

Cash		$24,500
U.S. government bonds		10,000
Notes receivable		2,400
Accounts receivable	$26,960	
Less: Allowance for uncollectible accounts	860	26,100
Inventory		35,200
Prepaid expenses		1,200
Total current assets		$ 99,400

Plant and equipment:

Land		$10,000
Building	$24,000	
Less: Accumulated depreciation	1,920	22,080
Store equipment	$ 9,400	
Less: Accumulated depreciation	1,880	7,520
Delivery equipment	$ 2,800	
Less: Accumulated depreciation	700	2,100
Total plant and equipment		41,700

Other assets:

Land (future building site)	16,500
Total assets	$157,600

Liabilities & Stockholders' Equity

Current liabilities:

Notes payable	$11,500	
Accounts payable	19,040	
Accrued expenses payable	1,410	
Deferred revenues	1,100	
Total current liabilities		$ 33,050

Long-term liabilities:

Mortgage payable (due in 10 years)		25,000
Total liabilities		$ 58,050

Stockholders' equity:

Capital stock	$60,000	
Retained earnings	39,550	99,550
Total liabilities & stockholders' equity		$157,600

Note: A new item introduced in this balance sheet is the Allowance for Uncollectible Accounts of $860, shown as a deduction from Accounts Receivable. This is an estimate of the uncollectible portion of the accounts receivable and serves to reduce the valuation of this asset to the net amount of $26,100 that is considered collectible.

content of a well-prepared balance sheet today are different in several respects from the balance sheet of 25 years ago. No two businesses are exactly alike and a degree of variation from the conventional type of balance sheet is appropriate for the individual business in devising the most meaningful presentation of its financial position. Standardization of the form and content of financial statements is a desirable goal; but if carried to an extreme, it might prevent the growth of new improved methods and the constructive changes necessary to reflect changes in business practices.

The analysis and interpretation of financial statements is the subject of Chapter 16. At this point our objective is merely to emphasize that classification of the items on a balance sheet aids the reader greatly in appraising the financial condition of the business. Some of the major balance sheet classifications are discussed briefly in the following section.

Current assets. Current assets include cash, government bonds and other marketable securities, receivables, inventories, and prepaid expenses. To qualify for inclusion in the current asset category, an asset must be capable of being converted into cash within a relatively short period without interfering with the normal operation of the business. The period is usually one year, but it may be longer for those businesses having an operating cycle in excess of one year. The sequence in which current assets are listed depends upon their liquidity; the closer an asset is to becoming cash the higher is its liquidity. The total amount of a company's current assets and the relative amount of each type give some indication of the company's short-run, debt-paying ability.

The term *operating cycle* is often used in establishing the limits of the current asset classification. Operating cycle means the average time period between the purchase of merchandise and the conversion of this merchandise back into cash. The series of transactions comprising a complete cycle often runs as follows: (1) purchase of merchandise, (2) sale of the merchandise on credit, (3) collection of the account receivable from the customer. The word *cycle* suggests the circular flow of capital from cash to inventory to receivables to cash again.

In a business handling fast-moving merchandise (a supermarket, for example) the operating cycle may be completed in a few weeks; for most merchandising businesses the operating cycle requires several months but less than a year. In a manufacturing business the materials purchased must be processed before they are offered for sale; consequently, the operating cycle tends to be longer. For some aircraft manufacturers the period of time from the purchase of sheet aluminum until this material is converted into cash through sale of the completed airplane is about 27 months. The inventories of aluminum are nevertheless classified as current assets, because they will be converted into cash within the operating cycle of this particular industry.

Current liabilities. Liabilities that must be paid within the operating cycle or one year (whichever is longer) are called *current liabilities.* Current liabili-

THE GRAHAM COMPANY
Income Statement
For the Year Ended December 31, 19___

Gross sales			$310,890
Sales returns and allowances		$ 3,820	
Sales discounts		4,830	8,650
Net sales			$302,240

Cost of goods sold:

Inventory, Jan. 1			$ 30,040
Purchases	$212,400		
Transportation-in	8,300		
Delivered cost of purchases	$220,700		
Less: Pur. ret. and allow.	$2,400		
Purchase discounts	5,100	7,500	
Net purchases		213,200	
Cost of goods available for sale		$243,240	
Less: Inventory, Dec. 31		35,200	
Cost of goods sold			208,040
Gross profit on sales			$ 94,200

Operating expenses:

Selling expenses:

Sales salaries	$ 38,410		
Advertising	10,190		
Depreciation: building	840		
Depreciation: store equipment	940		
Depreciation: delivery equipment	700		
Insurance	1,100		
Miscellaneous	820		
Total selling expenses		$ 53,000	

General and administrative expenses:

Office salaries	$ 19,200		
Uncollectible accounts expense	750		
Depreciation: building	120		
Insurance expense	100		
Miscellaneous	930		
Total general and administrative expenses		21,100	
Total operating expenses			74,100
Income from operations			$ 20,100
Interest earned on investments			300
Net income			$ 20,400

ties are paid out of current assets, and a comparison of the amount of current assets with the amount of current liabilities is an important step in appraising the ability of a company to pay its debts in the near future.

Current ratio. Many bankers and other users of financial statements believe that for a business to qualify as a good credit risk, the total current assets should be at least twice as large as the total current liabilities. In studying a balance sheet, a banker or other creditor will compute the *current ratio* by dividing total current assets by total current liabilities. In the illustrated balance sheet of the Graham Company, the current assets of $99,400 are approximately three times as great as the current liabilities of $33,050; the current ratio is therefore 3 to 1, which would generally be regarded as a strong current position.

The excess of current assets over current liabilities is called *working capital;* the relative amount of working capital is another indication of short-term financial strength.

Classification in the income statement. A new feature to be noted in the illustrated income statement of the Graham Company (page 145) is the division of the operating expenses into the two categories of selling expenses and general and administrative expenses. This classification aids management in controlling expenses by emphasizing that certain expenses are the responsibility of the executive in charge of sales, and that other types of expense relate to the business as a whole. Some expenses, such as depreciation of the building, may be divided between the two classifications according to the portion utilized by each functional division of the business. The item of Uncollectible Accounts Expense listed under the heading of General and Administrative Expenses is an expense of estimated amount. It will be discussed fully in Chapter 10.

Another feature to note in the income statement of the Graham Company is that interest earned on investments is placed after the figure showing income from operations. Other examples of such nonoperating revenues are dividends on shares of stock owned, and rent earned by leasing property not presently needed in the operation of the business. Any items of expense not related to selling or administrative functions may also be placed at the bottom of the income statement after the income from operations. Separate group headings of Nonoperating Revenue and Nonoperating Expenses are sometimes used.

Condensed income statement. In the published annual reports of most corporations, the income statement is usually greatly condensed because the public is presumably not interested in the details of operations. A condensed income statement usually begins with *net* sales. The details involved in computing the cost of goods are also often omitted and only summary figures are given for selling expenses and general and administrative expenses. A condensed income statement for The Graham Company appears on page 147.

The statement of retained earnings for The Graham Company would not differ significantly from the form shown in previous illustrations.

<table>
<tr><td rowspan="11">A
Con-
densed
Income
State-
ment</td><td colspan="3" align="center">*THE GRAHAM COMPANY*
Income Statement
For the Year Ended December 31, 19___</td></tr>
</table>

Net sales		$302,240
Cost of goods sold		208,040
Gross profit on sales		$ 94,200
Expenses:		
Selling	$53,000	
General and administrative	21,100	74,100
Income from operations		$ 20,100
Interest earned on investments		300
Net income		$ 20,400

DEMONSTRATION PROBLEM

The financial statements of N. B. Trading Company for the year ended December 31, 19___, as prepared by the assistant bookkeeper when the bookkeeper suddenly resigned without notice, are shown below:

N. B. TRADING COMPANY
Profit & Loss Statement

Revenues:		
Sales	$380,100	
Purchase discounts	1,470	
Purchase returns & allowances	1,940	
Total		$383,510
Less: Costs & expenses:		
Purchases	$232,775	
Decrease in inventory	15,935	
Transportation-in	6,465	
Sales returns & allowances	1,860	
Sales discounts	630	
Office salaries	5,520	
Salesmen's salaries	39,650	
Advertising expense	7,245	
Miscellaneous selling expense	1,480	
Miscellaneous general expense	835	
Depreciation expense: store equipment	600	
Office supplies expense	840	
Uncollectible accounts expense	1,170	
Insurance expense	765	
Interest expense	4,500	
Total		$320,270
Net income		$ 63,240

N. B. TRADING COMPANY
Balance Sheet

Assets:

Cash	$ 15,655
Accounts receivable	21,170
Dividends paid	22,500
Land	74,000
Building	90,000
Inventory	54,930
Store equipment	15,400
Land held for future expansion	17,000
Total assets	$310,655

Liabilities:

Notes payable	$ 5,325
Accounts payable	19,260
Bank loans	19,600
6% first mortgage bonds payable	55,000
Allowance for uncollectible accounts	2,355
Accumulated depreciation: building	32,400
Accumulated depreciation: store equipment	6,400
Total liabilities	$140,340

Stockholders' equity:

Capital stock	$ 50,000
Retained earnings	118,045
Deferred revenue	2,270
Total stockholders' equity	170,315
Total liabilities & stockholders' equity	$310,655

Other data

(1) The building, one-quarter of which is used for sales activities, was acquired new 10 years ago at a cost of $90,000; estimated life was 25 years.
(2) Unexpired insurance as of December 31 amounted to $400.
(3) Unused office supplies on hand on December 31 amounted to $200.

Instructions

a. Prepare the necessary adjusting journal entries that should be recorded on the books of the N. B. Trading Company before correct financial statements can be prepared.
b. Prepare an income statement in good form for the year ended December 31, 19___.
c. Prepare a properly classified balance sheet as of December 31, 19___.
d. Prepare a statement of retained earnings for the year ended December 31, 19___.

QUESTIONS

1. In 1971, the Pacifica Import Company made all sales of merchandise at prices in excess of cost. Will the business necessarily report a net income for the year? Explain.

2. The Day Company made sales of merchandise on credit during July amounting to $122,000, of which $114,000 remained uncollected at July 31. Sales for cash during July amounted to $30,000 and an additional $99,000 was received from customers in payment for goods sold to them in prior months. Also during July, the Day Company borrowed $36,000 cash from the First Security Bank. What was the total revenue for July?

3. Compute the amount of cost of goods sold, given the following account balances: beginning inventory $22,000, purchases $84,000, purchase returns and allowances $4,500, transportation-in $500, and ending inventory $36,000.

4. During the current year, Davis Corporation purchased merchandise costing $200,000. State the cost of goods sold under each of the following alternative assumptions:
   a. No beginning inventory; ending inventory $40,000
   b. Beginning inventory $60,000; no ending inventory
   c. Beginning inventory $54,000; ending inventory $78,000
   d. Beginning inventory $90,000; ending inventory $75,000

5. During the taking of physical inventory at December 31, merchandise stored in a warehouse was overlooked and therefore omitted from the inventory. Assuming that the cost of the merchandise in the warehouse was $6,000, what were the effects of the error on the income statement and the balance sheet?

6. During the taking of physical inventory at December 31, 1972, certain merchandise which cost $2,500 was counted twice and the inventory was therefore overstated by $2,500. What was the effect of this error on the cost of goods sold? On net income for 1972?

7. Zenith Company uses the periodic inventory method and maintains its accounting records on a calendar-year basis. Does the beginning or the ending inventory figure appear in the trial balance prepared from the ledger on December 31?

8. State a general principle to be followed in assigning duties among employees if strong internal control is to be achieved.

9. For an invoice dated October 21, what is the last day of the credit period if the credit terms are
   a. 2/10, n/30?
   b. 10 e.o.m.?

10. Explain the terms *current asset, current liability,* and *current ratio.*

11. The Riblet Company has a current ratio of 3 to 1 and working capital of $60,000. What are the amounts of current assets and current liabilities?

12. What advantages do you see in reporting operating expenses in two categories: selling, and general and administrative?

13. Give an example of a nonoperating revenue item and an example of a nonoperating expense item.

14. Define a *condensed income statement* and indicate its advantages and possible shortcomings.

EXERCISES

1. Net income of the Amerada Asphalt Co. for 19___ amounts to 5% of net sales. Selling expenses are twice as large as net income but only one-half as large as general and administrative expenses, which amount to $40,000. Prepare a condensed income statement for the year ended on December 31, 19___.

2. Determine the amount of gross purchases for the period, given the following data:

Cost of goods sold	$130,500
Transportation-in	1,890
Beginning inventory	43,640
Purchase returns and allowances	2,150
Ending inventory	38,500
Sales	182,650

3. Give the accounting entry to be made, if any, for each of these events:
   a. Telephoned Benz Company and placed an order for $2,000 worth of merchandise.
   b. Issued a purchase order for $2,000 to the Benz Company in confirmation of yesterday's telephone order.
   c. Merchandise previously ordered from Benz Company was delivered today, and an invoice for $2,000 was received in the mail; credit terms 2/10, n/30.
   d. Mailed check for $1,960 to Benz Company in full settlement of account.

4. Given the following data, determine the amount of the beginning inventory.

Ending inventory	$38,450
Purchases	65,000
Cost of goods sold	41,900
Transportation-in	2,400
Purchase returns and allowances	4,600
Purchase discounts	1,100

5. Income statement data for the Carter Company for two years are shown below:

	Year 1	Year 2
Sales	$150,000	$200,000
Cost of goods sold	105,000	150,000
Selling expenses	15,000	25,000
General and administrative expenses	7,500	10,000

a.   The net income decreased from $_____ to $_____ from Year 1 to Year 2.

b.   The net income as a percentage of sales decreased by _____ percentage points during Year 2.

c.   The gross profit on sales decreased from 30% for Year 1 to _____% for Year 2.

d.   Selling expenses increased by _____% from Year 1 to Year 2 while sales increased by _____%.

6.   The following account balances appear on the statement of financial condition for the Dean Company:

Cash	*$ 80,000*
Accounts receivable	*50,000*
Inventory	*30,000*
Store equipment (net)	*100,000*
Other assets	*15,000*
Mortgage payable (due in 3 years)	*25,000*
Notes payable (due in 10 days)	*60,000*
Accounts payable	*20,000*
Retained earnings	*115,000*

a.   Total current assets for the Dean Company amount to $_____. Current liabilities amount to $_____.

b.   Working capital for the Dean Company amounts to $_____.

c.   Current ratio for the Dean Company is _____ to 1.

d.   Assuming that the Dean Company pays off the note, thus reducing cash to $20,000, the working capital would be $_____ and the current ratio would be _____ to 1.

PROBLEMS

5-1   Selected transactions of the Pacific Meat Distributors for the month of June are listed below:

June 4   Sold merchandise to Edward Bell on open account, $2,600.

June 5   Paid transportation charges on sale to Edward Bell, $125.

June 9   Edward Bell returned for credit $210 of the merchandise purchased on June 4 (no reduction in Transportation-out account).

June 12   Purchased office equipment from Candor Corporation for cash, $2,750.

June 19   Purchased merchandise for cash, $355.

June 24   Sold merchandise for cash, $2,150.

June 26   Refunded $130 to a customer who had made a cash purchase on June 24.

June 26   Purchased merchandise from Simpson & Company on open account, $1,120.

June 27   Paid by check transportation charges on merchandise purchased from Simpson & Company in the amount of $80.

June 29 Returned for credit of $150 merchandise purchased from Simpson & Company (no reduction of Transportation-in account).

June 30 Purchased stationery and other office supplies on account, $235.

Instructions

Prepare journal entries for the transactions listed above, assuming that the company uses the periodic inventory method.

5-2 Redwood Products Company records all purchase invoices before deducting purchase discounts. Merchandising transactions for the month of July are listed below:

July 1   Purchased merchandise from Newton Co. The list price was $25,000 with a trade discount of 20% and terms of 2/10, n/60.

July 1   Purchased merchandise from Ross Brothers for $11,000; terms 1/10, n/30.

July 5   Sold merchandise to K. R. Randall, $12,000; terms 2/10, n/30.

July 6   Returned to Newton Co. damaged merchandise having a cost after trade discount of $2,000.

July 11   Paid Newton Co. for invoice of July 1, less discount and returns.

July 15   Received cash in full settlement of K. R. Randall account.

July 22   Sold merchandise to May Co., $40,000; terms 2/10, n/30.

July 25   Purchased from Able Co. merchandise with list price of $18,000, subject to trade discount of 25% and credit terms of 1/10, n/30.

July 28   Returned for credit part of merchandise received from Able Co. Cost of the returned goods (after trade discount) was $400.

July 31   Paid Ross Brothers invoice of July 1.

Instructions

a.   Journalize these transactions, following the policy of recording purchase invoices at gross amount (after deducting trade discounts).

b.   Prepare a partial income statement, showing gross profit on sales. Assume the following inventories: June 30, $41,800; July 31, $53,100.

c.   Compute the balance of accounts payable.

d.   Compute the effective annual rate of interest Redwood Products Company would be paying if it failed to take advantage of discount terms on the Newton Co. invoice.

5-3 The controller of the Mini-Max Service Company was asked by the president whether the working capital position of the company appeared satisfactory in terms of the current ratio. The president also inquired as to the dollar balance of working capital. The following information taken from the accounts at December 31, 1972, includes the items to be used in developing answers to these questions:

Cash	*$18,180*
Interest payable	*300*
Advance payments from customers on sales orders	*2,500*
Allowance for uncollectible accounts	*1,000*
Notes payable	*30,000*
U.S. government bonds (temporary investment)	*12,000*
Accounts receivable	*61,900*

Accrued salaries payable	$ 1,400
Accounts payable	25,800
Interest receivable	320
Delivery equipment	8,800
Accumulated depreciation: delivery equipment	2,200
Inventory	88,600
Land	31,400
Retained earnings	41,000

Instructions

a. Compute the amount of working capital by arranging the appropriate items in the usual balance sheet sequence. You should list only those items which are necessary in determining working capital and the current ratio.

b. Compute the current ratio and explain why you regard the company as being in a strong or weak working capital position.

5-4 Listed below are the account balances for the Reese Corporation on December 31, 1972:

Cash	$ 28,600
Retained earnings	37,600
Accounts payable	10,780
Prepaid rent	900
Wages and salaries payable	2,350
Accumulated depreciation: buildings	14,300
Inventory	48,400
Delivery equipment	21,800
Stationery and office supplies	1,210
Capital stock	150,000
U.S. government bonds	10,000
Allowance for uncollectible accounts	1,400
Buildings	92,800
Accounts receivable	22,100
Store equipment	17,600
Land	35,000
Deferred revenues	300
Income tax payable	9,480
Bank loan (due Apr. 15, 1973)	30,000
Accumulated depreciation: store equipment	6,350
Mortgage note payable (due Apr. 1, 1976)	50,000
Notes receivable (due within six months)	7,500
Accrued interest payable	850
Unexpired insurance	600
Accumulated depreciation: delivery equipment	3,600
Investment in land (held as future building site)	30,500

Instructions

Prepare a classified balance sheet as of December 31, 1972, for the Reese Corporation. The various items of prepaid expenses may be combined into a single balance sheet amount.

5-5 The Southwest Corporation maintains its accounting records on the basis of a fiscal year ending April 30. After all necessary adjustments had been made at April 30, 1972, the adjusted trial balance appeared as follows:

SOUTHWEST CORPORATION
Adjusted Trial Balance
April 30, 1972

Cash	$ 23,265	
Accounts receivable	38,520	
Inventory (Apr. 30, 1971)	33,930	
Unexpired insurance	700	
Supplies	1,160	
Furniture and fixtures	49,700	
Accumulated depreciation: furniture and		
fixtures		$ 4,225
Accounts payable		13,300
Notes payable		7,000
Capital stock, $1 par value		50,000
Retained earnings		31,550
Sales		302,610
Sales returns & allowances	4,270	
Purchases	195,525	
Purchase returns & allowances		1,545
Transportation-in	9,850	
Salaries and wages expense	41,450	
Rent expense	8,400	
Depreciation expense: furniture and		
fixtures	1,255	
Supplies expense	1,415	
Insurance expense	790	
	$410,230	$410,230

The inventory on April 30, 1972, as determined by count, amounted to $38,750.

Instructions
a. Prepare an income statement for Southwest Corporation for the year ended April 30, 1972.
b. Prepare the necessary entries (in general journal form) to close the books on April 30, 1972.
c. Assume that the ending inventory of $38,750 was overstated $3,000 as a result of double counting part of the goods on hand at April 30, 1972. Prepare a three-column list of the items in the income statement developed in **a** above which are incorrect as a result of the $3,000 inventory overstatement. List in the second column the reported figures, and in the third column the corrected figures.

5-6 The trial balance of Bloomfield Corporation was prepared from the records of the firm on June 30, 19___, the close of its fiscal year.

BLOOMFIELD CORPORATION
Trial Balance
June 30, 19___

Cash	$ 20,700	
Accounts receivable	21,015	
Inventory, beginning.	37,240	
Unexpired insurance	720	
Office supplies.	505	
Land	30,440	
Buildings	68,000	
Accumulated depreciation: buildings		$ 19,120
Equipment	19,800	
Accumulated depreciation: equipment.		11,600
Accounts payable.		10,860
Capital stock		100,000
Retained earnings		26,570
Dividends.	10,000	
Sales		214,705
Sales returns & allowances	3,290	
Purchases	144,900	
Purchase returns & allowances		2,145
Transportation-in	2,965	
Salaries and wages expense	24,740	
Property taxes expense.	685	
	$385,000	$385,000

Other data
(1) The buildings are being depreciated over a 25-year useful life and the equipment over a 12-year useful life.
(2) Accrued salaries payable as of June 30 were $2,800.
(3) Examination of policies showed $450 unexpired insurance on June 30.
(4) Office supplies on hand at June 30 were estimated to amount to $210.
(5) Inventory of merchandise on June 30 was $30,000.

Instructions
a. Prepare a work sheet at June 30, 19___. You need not use the Adjusted Trial Balance columns.
b. Prepare an income statement for the year.
c. Prepare a classified balance sheet as of June 30, 19___.
d. Prepare a statement of retained earnings for the year.
e. Prepare closing journal entries.

5-7 The adjusted trial balance of Duncan Supply Company at December 31, 1972, is shown below. An inventory taken on December 31, 1972 amounted to $32,440. The following adjustments have been made to the original trial balance figures:

(1) Depreciation of buildings, $4,100; of delivery equipment, $1,500.
(2) Accrued salaries: office, $845; salesmen's, $950.
(3) Insurance expired, $250.
(4) Store supplies used, $1,000.

DUNCAN SUPPLY COMPANY
Adjusted Trial Balance
December 31, 1972

Cash	$ 9,310	
Accounts receivable	10,380	
Inventory, Jan. 1, 1972	28,650	
Store supplies	270	
Unexpired insurance	360	
Land	89,700	
Buildings	100,000	
Accumulated depreciation: buildings		$ 21,750
Delivery equipment	45,000	
Accumulated depreciation: delivery equipment		16,300
Accounts payable		22,450
Accrued salaries payable		1,795
Capital stock		200,000
Retained earnings, Jan. 1, 1972		85,165
Dividends	40,000	
Sales		171,220
Sales returns & allowances	2,430	
Purchases	138,900	
Purchase returns & allowances		1,820
Salesmen's salaries expense	26,000	
Delivery expense	2,800	
Depreciation expense: delivery equipment	1,500	
Office salaries expense	19,850	
Depreciation expense: buildings	4,100	
Insurance expense	250	
Store supplies used	1,000	
	$520,500	$520,500

Instructions

a. Prepare a work sheet, starting with the unadjusted trial balance. You need not use the Adjusted Trial Balance columns.
b. Prepare financial statements.
c. Prepare adjusting journal entries.
d. Prepare closing journal entries.

5-8 Because of the sudden illness of the full-charge bookkeeper of the Savannah Peach Company, the assistant bookkeeper, whose experience was quite limited, was asked to complete the year-end work. He prepared the financial statements listed below:

SAVANNAH PEACH COMPANY
Loss Statement
December 31, 19___

Sales	$510,000	
Purchase returns & allowances	3,800	
Purchase discounts	7,365	
Interest earned on investments	950	
Increase in inventory	5,130	$527,245
Purchases	$378,650	
Sales returns & allowances	8,980	
Sales discounts	4,640	
Transportation-in	23,735	
Interest expense	1,670	
Uncollectible accounts expense	2,120	
Depreciation expense: building	1,750	
Depreciation expense: store equipment	2,235	
Depreciation expense: delivery equipment	1,840	
Insurance expense	1,600	
Office salaries expense	15,500	
Executive salaries expense	41,000	
Sales salaries expense	60,875	
Miscellaneous selling expense	930	
Miscellaneous general expense	1,570	547,095
Net loss for year		$ 19,850

SAVANNAH PEACH COMPANY
Balance Sheet
December 31, 19___

Current assets:		
Notes receivable	$ 10,000	
Accounts receivable	25,500	
Cash	16,400	
Rent collected in advance	800	
Land	20,000	$ 72,700
Plant and equipment:		
Inventory	$ 53,505	
Store equipment	19,100	
Building	48,000	
Delivery equipment	14,500	135,105
Other assets:		
Marketable securities held as temporary investments . . .	$ 9,000	
Land held as future building site	12,500	21,500
Total assets		$229,305

Liabilities:

Accounts payable	$ 28,265	
Accrued salaries payable	2,185	
Prepaid expenses	800	
Notes payable	15,000	
First mortgage bonds payable	50,000	
Allowance for uncollectible accounts	1,640	
Accumulated depreciation: buildings	15,600	
Accumulated depreciation: store equipment	12,000	
Accumulated depreciation: delivery equipment	11,600	
Total liabilities		$137,090

Stockholders' equity:

Capital stock	$100,000	
Less: Deficit	7,785	92,215
Total liabilities & stockholders' equity		$229,305

Instructions

a. Prepare in acceptable form an income statement for the year ended December 31, 19____. (Allocate to selling expense 60% of building depreciation and $500 of insurance expense.)

b. Prepare a balance sheet as of December 31, 19____, properly classified.

c. What was the balance in the Retained Earnings account at the beginning of the current year?

Chapter

6

Data-processing systems: Manual, mechanical, and electronic

In the early chapters of an introductory accounting book, basic accounting principles can most conveniently be discussed in terms of a small business with only a few customers and suppliers. This simplified model of a business has been used in preceding chapters to demonstrate the analysis and recording of the more common types of business transactions.

The recording procedures illustrated thus far call for recording each transaction by an entry in the journal, and then posting each debit and credit from the journal to the proper account in the ledger. We must now face the practical problem of streamlining and speeding up this recording process so that the accounting department can keep pace with the rapid flow of transactions in a business of greater size.

MANUAL DATA PROCESSING

In a large business there may be hundreds or even thousands of transactions every day. It would be a physical impossibility for one bookkeeper to enter all these transactions in one journal and to post each transaction to the proper ledger accounts even though he worked 24 hours a day. If all the transactions were to be entered in one journal and posted to one ledger, it would not be possible to assign more employees to the job because only one person can work on a journal or ledger at a time.

To handle a large volume of transactions rapidly and efficiently, it is helpful to group the transactions into like classes and to use a specialized journal for each class. This will greatly reduce the amount of detailed recording work and will also permit a division of labor, since each special-purpose journal can be handled by a different employee. The great majority of transactions (perhaps as much as 80 or 90%) usually fall into four types. These four types and the four corresponding special journals are as follows:

Type of transaction	*Name of journal*
Sales of merchandise on credit	Sales journal
Purchases of merchandise on credit	Purchases journal
Receipts of cash	Cash receipts journal
Payments of cash	Cash payments journal

In addition to these four special journals, a *general journal* will be used for recording transactions which do not fit into any of the above four types. The general journal is the same book of original entry illustrated in preceding chapters; the adjective "general" is added merely to distinguish it from the special journals.

Sales journal

Illustrated below is a sales journal containing entries for all sales on account made during November by the Seaside Company. Whenever merchandise is sold on credit, several copies of a sales invoice are prepared. The information listed on a sales invoice usually includes the date of the sale, the serial number of the invoice, the customer's name, the amount of the sale, and the credit terms. One copy of the sales invoice is used by the seller as the basis for an entry in the sales journal.

Sales on Credit

	Date		Account Debited	Invoice No.	✔	Amount
Sales Journal						**(Page 1)**
19___						
Nov.	2	John Adams		301	✔	450
	4	Harold Black		302	✔	1,000
	5	Robert Cross		303	✔	975
	11	H. R. Davis		304	✔	620
	18	C. D. Early		305	✔	900
	23	John Frost		306	✔	400
	29	D. H. Gray		307	✔	1,850
						6,195
						(5) (41)

Note that the illustrated sales journal contains special columns for recording each of these aspects of the sales transaction, except the credit terms. If it is the practice of the business to offer different credit terms to different customers, a column may be inserted in the sales journal to show the terms of sale. In this illustration it is assumed that all sales are made on terms of 2/10, n/30; consequently, there is no need to write the credit terms as part of the journal entry. Only sales on credit are entered in the sales journal. When merchandise is sold for cash, the transaction is recorded in a cash receipts journal, which is illustrated later in this chapter.

Advantages of the sales journal. Note that each of the above seven sales transactions is recorded on a single line. Each entry consists of a debit to a customer's account; the offsetting credit to the Sales account is understood without being written, because sales on account are the only transactions recorded in this special journal.

An entry in a sales journal need not include an explanation; if more information about the transaction is desired it can be obtained by referring to the file copy of the sales invoice. The invoice number is listed in the sales journal as part of each entry. The one-line entry in the sales journal requires much less writing than would be required to record a sales transaction in the general journal. Since there may be several hundred or several thousand sales transactions each month, the time saved in recording transactions in this streamlined manner becomes quite important.

Every entry in the sales journal represents a debit to a customer's account. Charges to customers' accounts should be posted daily so that each customer's account will always be up-to-date and available for use in making decisions relating to collections and to the further extension of credit. A check mark ($\sqrt{}$) is placed in the sales journal opposite each amount posted to a customer's account, to indicate that the posting has been made.

Another advantage of the special journal for sales is the great saving of time in posting credits to the Sales account. In the illustrated sales journal above, there are seven transactions (and in practice there might be 700). Instead of posting a separate credit to the Sales account for each sales transaction, we can wait until the end of the month and make one posting to the Sales account for the total of the amounts recorded in the sales journal.

In the illustrated sales journal for November, the sales on account totaled $6,195. On November 30 this amount is posted as a debit to Accounts Receivable and as a credit to the Sales account. The ledger account number for Accounts Receivable (5) and for Sales (41) is entered under the total figure in the sales journal to show that the posting operation has been performed. To make clear the reason for this posting to Accounts Receivable, an explanation of the nature of controlling accounts and subsidiary ledgers is necessary.

Controlling accounts and subsidiary ledgers

In preceding chapters all transactions involving accounts receivable from customers have been posted to a single account entitled Accounts Receivable. Under this simplified procedure, however, it is not easy to look up the amount receivable from a given customer. In practice, nearly all businesses which sell goods on credit maintain a separate account receivable with each customer. If there are 400 customers this would require a ledger with 400 accounts receivable, in addition to the accounts for other assets, and for liabilities, owners' equity, revenue, and expense. Such a ledger would be cumbersome and unwieldy. Since only one person can work on a ledger at a time, it would be difficult for the posting of all these accounts to be kept up-to-date. Also, the trial balance prepared from such a large ledger would be a very long one. If the trial balance showed the ledger to be out of balance, the task of locating the error or errors would be most difficult. All these factors indicate that it is not desirable to have too many accounts in one ledger. Fortunately, a simple solution is available; this solution is to divide up the ledger into several separate ledgers.

In a business which has a large number of accounts with customers and creditors, it is customary to divide the ledger into three separate ledgers. All the accounts with *customers* are placed in alphabetical order in a separate ledger, called the *accounts receivable ledger.* All the accounts with *creditors* are arranged alphabetically in another ledger called the *accounts payable ledger.* Both of these ledgers are known as *subsidiary ledgers.*

After thus segregating the accounts receivable from customers in one subsidiary ledger and placing the accounts payable to creditors in a second subsidiary ledger, we have left in the original ledger all the revenue and expense accounts and also all the balance sheet accounts except those with customers and creditors. This ledger is called the *general ledger,* to distinguish it from the subsidiary ledgers.

When the numerous individual accounts with customers are placed in a subsidiary ledger, an account entitled Accounts Receivable continues to be maintained in the general ledger. This account shows the total amount due from all customers; in other words, this single controlling account in the general ledger takes the place of the numerous customers' accounts which have been removed to form a subsidiary ledger. The general ledger is still in balance because the controlling account, Accounts Receivable, has a balance equal to the total of the customers' accounts which were removed from the general ledger.

A controlling account entitled Accounts Payable is also kept in the general ledger in place of the numerous accounts with creditors which have been removed to form the accounts payable subsidiary ledger. Because these two controlling accounts represent the total amounts receivable from customers and payable to creditors, a trial balance can be prepared from the general ledger alone.

Posting to subsidiary ledgers and to control accounts. To illustrate the posting of subsidiary ledgers and of control accounts, let us refer again to the sales journal illustrated on page 160. Each debit to a customer's account is posted currently during the month from the sales journal to the customer's account in the accounts receivable ledger. The accounts in this subsidiary ledger are usually kept in alphabetical order and not numbered. When a posting is made to a customer's account, a check mark ($\sqrt{}$) is placed in the sales journal as evidence that the posting has been made to the subsidiary ledger.

At month-end the sales journal is totaled. The total sales for the month, $6,195, are posted as a credit to the Sales account and also as a debit to the controlling account, Accounts Receivable, in the general ledger. The controlling account will, therefore, equal the total of all the customers' accounts in the subsidiary ledger.

The diagram on page 163 shows the day-to-day posting of individual entries from the sales journal to the subsidiary ledger. The diagram also shows the month-end posting of the total of the sales journal to the two general ledger accounts affected, Accounts Receivable and Sales. Note that the amount of the monthly debit to the controlling account is equal to the sum of the several debits posted to the subsidiary ledger.

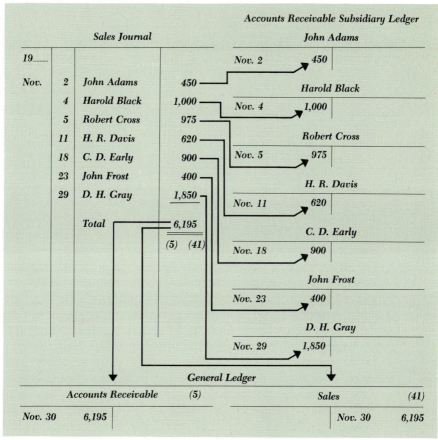

Purchases journal

The handling of purchase transactions when a purchases journal is used follows a pattern quite similar to the one described for the sales journal.

Assume that the purchases journal illustrated on page 164 contains all purchases of merchandise on credit during the month by the Seaside Company. The invoice date is shown in a separate column because the cash discount period begins on this date.

The five entries on page 164 are posted as they occur during the month as credits to the creditors' accounts in the subsidiary ledger for accounts payable. As each posting is completed a check mark (√) is placed in the purchases journal.

At the end of the month the purchases journal is totaled and ruled as shown in the illustration. The total figure, $7,250, is posted to two general ledger accounts as follows:

1. As a debit to the Purchases account
2. As a credit to the Accounts Payable controlling account

Purchases
on Credit

Purchases Journal					(Page 1)
Date	Account Credited		Invoice Date	✓	Amount
19____ Nov.	2 Alabama Supply Co.		19____ Nov. 2	✓	3,325
	4 Barker & Bright		4	✓	700
	10 Canning & Sons		9	✓	500
	17 Davis Co.		15	✓	900
	27 Excelsior, Inc.		25	✓	1,825
					7,250
					(50) (21)

The account numbers for Purchases (50) and for Accounts Payable (21) are then placed in parentheses below the column total of the purchases journal to show that the posting has been made.

Under the particular system being described, the only transactions recorded in the purchases journal are purchases of merchandise on credit. The term *merchandise* means goods acquired for resale to customers. If merchandise is purchased for cash rather than on credit, the transaction should be recorded in the cash payments journal, as illustrated on pages 170 and 171.

The diagram on page 165 shows the day-to-day posting of individual entries from the purchases journal to the accounts with creditors in the subsidiary ledger for accounts payable. The diagram also shows how the column total of the purchases journal is posted at the end of the month to the general ledger accounts, Purchases and Accounts Payable. One objective of this diagram is to emphasize that the amount of the monthly credit to the control account is equal to the sum of the several credits posted to the subsidiary ledger.

When assets other than merchandise are being acquired, as, for example, a delivery truck or an office desk for use in the business, the journal to be used depends upon whether a cash payment is made. If assets of this type are purchased for cash, the transaction should be entered in the cash payments journal; if the transaction is on credit, the general journal is used. The purchases journal is not used to record the acquisition of plant assets because the total of this journal is posted to the Purchases account.

Cash receipts journal

All transactions involving the receipt of cash are recorded in the cash receipts journal. One common example is the sale of merchandise for cash. As each cash sale is made, it is rung up on a cash register. At the end of the day the total of the cash sales is computed by striking the total key on the register. This total is entered in the cash receipts journal, which therefore contains

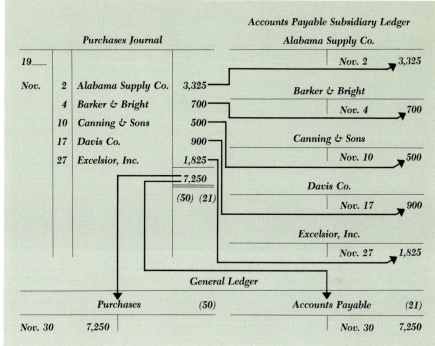

one entry for the total cash sales of the day. For other types of cash receipts, such as the collection of accounts receivable from customers, a separate journal entry may be made for each transaction. The cash receipts journal illustrated on the following two pages contains entries for selected November transactions, all of which include the receipt of cash.

Nov. 1   R. B. Jones organized the Seaside Company by investing $25,000 cash in exchange for 2,500 shares of capital stock of $10 par value.

Nov. 4   Sold merchandise for cash, $300.

Nov. 5   Sold merchandise for cash, $400.

Nov. 8   Collected from John Adams invoice of Nov. 2, $450 less 2% cash discount.

Nov. 10   Sold portion of land not needed in business for a total price of $7,000, consisting of cash of $1,000 and a note receivable for $6,000. The cost of the land sold was $5,000.

Nov. 12   Collected from Harold Black invoice of Nov. 4, $1,000 less 2% cash discount.

Nov. 20   Collected from C. D. Early invoice of Nov. 18, $900 less 2% cash discount.

Nov. 27   Sold merchandise for cash, $125.

Nov. 30   Obtained $4,000 loan from bank. Issued a note payable in that amount.

Note that the cash receipts journal illustrated below has three debit columns and three credit columns as follows:

Debits:

1. **Cash.** This column is used for every entry, because only those transactions which include the receipt of cash are entered in this special journal.

2. **Sales discounts.** This column is used to accumulate the sales discounts allowed during the month. Only one line of the cash receipts book is required to record a collection from a customer who takes advantage of a cash discount.

3. **Other accounts.** This third debit column is used for debits to any and all accounts other than Cash and Sales Discounts, and space is provided for writing in the name of the account. For example, the entry of November 10 in the illustrated cash receipts journal shows that cash and a note receivable were obtained when land was sold. The amount of cash received, $1,000, is entered in the Cash debit column, the account title Notes Receivable is written in the Other Accounts debit column and the amount of the debit to this account, $6,000. These two debits are offset by credit entries to Land,

Includes All Trans-actions Involving Receipt of Cash							

Cash Receipts Journ

						Debits			
							Other Accounts		
Date		*Explanation*	*Cash*	*Sales Discounts*		*Name*	*LP*	*Amount*
19___								
Nov.	*1*	*Investment by owner*	*25,000*					
	4	*Cash sales*	*300*					
	5	*Cash sales*	*400*					
	8	*Invoice Nov. 2, less 2%*	*441*	*9*				
	10	*Sale of land*	*1,000*			*Notes Receivable*	*3*	*6,000*
	12	*Invoice Nov. 4, less 2%*	*980*	*20*				
	20	*Invoice Nov. 18, less 2%*	*882*	*18*				
	27	*Cash sales*	*125*					
	30	*Obtained bank loan*	*4,000*					
			33,128	*47*				*6,000*
			(1)	*(43)*				*(X)*

$5,000, and to Gain on Sale of Land, $2,000, in the Other Accounts credit column.

Credits:

1. *Accounts receivable.* This column is used to list the credits to customers' accounts as receivables are collected. The name of the customer is written in the space entitled Account Credited to the left of the Accounts Receivable column.

2. *Sales.* The use of this column will save posting by permitting the accumulation of all sales for cash during the month and the posting of the column total at the end of the month as a credit to the Sales account (41).

3. *Other accounts.* This column is used for credits to any and all accounts other than Accounts Receivable and Sales. In some instances, a transaction may require credits to two accounts. Such cases are handled by using two lines of the special journal, as illustrated by the transaction of November 10, which required credits to both the Land account and to Gain on Sale of Land.

(Page 1)

			Credits		
Account Credited	Accounts Receivable		Sales	Other Accounts	
	✔	Amount		LP	Amount
ital Stock				30	25,000
			300		
			400		
₁ Adams	✔	450			
d				11	5,000
₁ on Sale of Land				40	2,000
old Black	✔	1,000			
). Early	✔	900			
			125		
es Payable				20	4,000
		2,350	825		36,000
		(5)	(41)		(X)

Posting the cash receipts journal. It is convenient to think of the posting of a cash receipts journal as being divided into two phases. The first phase consists of the daily posting of individual amounts throughout the month; the second phase consists of the posting of column totals at the end of the month.

Posting during the month. Daily posting of the Accounts Receivable credits column is desirable. Each amount is posted to an individual customer's account in the accounts receivable subsidiary ledger. A check mark ($\sqrt{}$) is placed in the cash receipts journal alongside each item posted to a customer's account to show that the posting operation has been performed. When debits and credits to customers' accounts are posted daily, the current status of each customer's account is available for use in making decisions as to further granting of credit and as a guide to collection efforts on past-due accounts.

The debits and credits in the Other Accounts sections of the cash receipts journal may be posted daily or at convenient intervals during the month. As the postings of individual items are made, the number of the ledger account debited or credited is entered in the LP (ledger page) column of the cash receipts journal opposite the item posted. Evidence is thus provided in the special journal as to which items have been posted.

Posting column totals at month-end. At the end of the month, the cash receipts journal is ruled as shown on pages 166 and 167. Before posting any of the column totals, it is first important to prove that *the sum of the debit column totals is equal to the sum of the credit column totals.*

After the totals of the cash receipts journal have been crossfooted, the following column totals are posted:

1. Cash debit column. Posted as a debit to the Cash account (1).

2. Sales discounts debit column. Posted as a debit to the Sales Discounts account (43).

3. Accounts receivable credit column. Posted as a credit to the controlling account, Accounts Receivable (5).

4. Sales credit column. Posted as a credit to the Sales account (41).

As each column total is posted to the appropriate account in the general ledger, the ledger account number is entered in parentheses just below the column total in the special journal. This notation shows that the column total has been posted and also indicates the account to which the posting was made. The totals of the Other Accounts columns in both the debit and credit sections of the special journal are not posted, because the amounts listed in these columns affect various general ledger accounts and have already been posted as individual items. The symbol X may be placed below the totals of these two columns to indicate that no posting is made.

Cash payments journal

Another widely used special journal is the cash payments journal, sometimes called the cash disbursements journal, in which all payments of cash are recorded. Among the more common of these transactions are payments of accounts payable to creditors, payment of operating expenses, and cash purchases of merchandise.

The cash payments journal illustrated on pages 170 and 171 contains entries for all November transactions of the Seaside Company which required the payment of cash.

Nov. 1	Paid rent on store building for November, $800.
Nov. 2	Purchased merchandise for cash, $500.
Nov. 8	Paid Barker & Bright for invoice of November 4, $700 less 2%.
Nov. 9	Bought land, $15,000, and building, $35,000, for future use in business. Paid cash of $20,000 and signed a promissory note for the balance of $30,000. (Land and building were acquired in a single transaction.)
Nov. 17	Paid salesmen's salaries, $600.
Nov. 26	Paid Davis Co. for invoice of November 17, $900 less 2%.
Nov. 27	Purchased merchandise for cash, $400.
Nov. 28	Purchased merchandise for cash, $650.
Nov. 29	Paid for newspaper advertising, $50.
Nov. 29	Paid for three-year insurance policy, $720.

Note in the illustrated cash payments journal that the three credit columns are located to the left of the three debit columns; any sequence of columns is satisfactory in a special journal as long as the column headings clearly distinguish debits from credits. The Cash column is often placed first in both the cash receipts journal and the cash payments journal because it is the column used in every transaction.

Good internal control over cash disbursements requires that all payments be made by check. The checks are serially numbered and as each transaction is entered in the cash payments journal, the check number is listed in a special column provided just to the right of the date column. An unbroken sequence of check numbers in this column gives assurance that every check issued has been recorded in the accounting records.

The use of the six money columns in the illustrated cash payments journal parallels the procedures described for the cash receipts journal.

Posting the cash payments journal. The posting of the cash payments journal falls into the same two phases already described for the cash receipts journal. The first phase consists of the daily posting of entries in the Accounts Payable debit column to the individual accounts of creditors in the accounts payable subsidiary ledger. Check marks ($\sqrt{}$) are entered opposite these items to show that the posting has been made. If a creditor telephones to inquire about any aspect of his account, information on all purchases and payments made to date is readily available in the accounts payable subsidiary ledger.

The individual debit and credit entries in the Other Accounts columns of the cash payments journal may be posted daily or at convenient intervals during the month. As the postings of these individual items are made, the

Includes
All Trans-
actions
Involving
Payment
of Cash

Cash Payments Journ

Date		Check No.	Explanation	Credits				
				Cash	Purchase Discounts	Other Accounts		
						Name	LP	Amou
19__								
Nov.	1	101	Paid Nov. rent	800				
	2	102	Purchased merchandise	500				
	8	103	Invoice Nov. 4, less 2%	686	14			
	9	104	Bought land and building	20,000		Notes Payable	20	30,00
	17	105	Paid salesmen	600				
	26	106	Invoice of Nov. 17, less 2%	882	18			
	27	107	Purchased merchandise	400				
	27	108	Purchased merchandise	650				
	29	109	Newspaper advertisement	50				
	29	110	Three-year ins. policy	720				
				25,288	32			30,00
				(1)	(52)			(X)

page number of the ledger account debited or credited is entered in the LP column of the cash payments journal opposite the item posted.

The second phase of posting the cash payments journal is performed at the end of the month. When all the transactions of the month have been journalized, the cash payments journal is ruled as shown on pages 170 and 171, and the six money columns are totaled. The equality of debits and credits is then proved before posting.

After the totals of the cash payments journal have been proved to be in balance, the totals of the columns for Cash, Purchase Discounts, Accounts Payable, and Purchases are posted to the corresponding accounts in the general ledger. The numbers of the accounts to which these postings are made are listed in parentheses just below the respective column totals in the cash payments journal. The totals of the Other Accounts columns in both the debit and credit section of this special journal are not to be posted, and the symbol X may be placed below the totals of these two columns to indicate that no posting is required.

(Page 1)

Account Debited	Debits				
	Accounts Payable		Purchases	Other Accounts	
	✓	Amount		LP	Amount
ore Rent Expense				54	800
urchases			500		
arker & Bright	✓	700			
and				11	15,000
uilding				12	35,000
les Salaries Expense				53	600
avis Co.	✓	900			
urchases			400		
urchases			650		
dvertising Expense				55	50
nexpired Insurance				6	720
		1,600	1,550		52,170
		(21)	(50)		(X)

The general journal

When all transactions involving cash or the purchase and sale of merchandise are recorded in special journals, only a few types of transactions remain to be entered in the general journal. Examples include the purchase or sale of plant and equipment on credit, the return of merchandise for credit to a supplier, and the return of merchandise by a customer for credit to his account. The general journal is also used for the recording of adjusting and closing entries at the end of the accounting period.

The following transactions of the Seaside Company during November could not conveniently be handled in any of the four special journals and were therefore entered in the general journal.

Nov. 25 A customer, John Frost, was permitted to return for credit $50 worth of merchandise that had been sold to him on November 23.

Nov. 28 The Seaside Company returned to a supplier, Excelsior, Inc., for credit $300 worth of the merchandise purchased on November 27.

Nov. 29   Purchased for use in the business office equipment costing $1,225. Agreed to make payment within 30 days to XYZ Equipment Co.

<table>
<tr><td colspan="6" align="center">*General Journal*   *(Page 1)*</td></tr>
<tr><td colspan="2">*Date*</td><td></td><td>*LP*</td><td>*Dr*</td><td>*Cr*</td></tr>
<tr><td>*19___*</td><td></td><td></td><td></td><td></td><td></td></tr>
<tr><td>*Nov.*</td><td>*25*</td><td>*Sales Returns and Allowances* . . . .</td><td>*42*</td><td>*50*</td><td></td></tr>
<tr><td></td><td></td><td>*Accounts Receivable, John Frost* . . .</td><td>*5/√*</td><td></td><td>*50*</td></tr>
<tr><td></td><td></td><td>*Allowed credit to customer for return of mer-*</td><td></td><td></td><td></td></tr>
<tr><td></td><td></td><td>*chandise from sale of Nov. 23.*</td><td></td><td></td><td></td></tr>
<tr><td></td><td>*28*</td><td>*Accounts Payable, Excelsior, Inc.* . . . .</td><td>*21/√*</td><td>*300*</td><td></td></tr>
<tr><td></td><td></td><td>*Purchase Returns and Allowances* . .</td><td>*51*</td><td></td><td>*300*</td></tr>
<tr><td></td><td></td><td>*Returned to supplier for credit a portion of*</td><td></td><td></td><td></td></tr>
<tr><td></td><td></td><td>*merchandise purchased on Nov. 27.*</td><td></td><td></td><td></td></tr>
<tr><td></td><td>*29*</td><td>*Office Equipment* . . . .</td><td>*14*</td><td>*1,225*</td><td></td></tr>
<tr><td></td><td></td><td>*Accounts Payable, XYZ Equipment*</td><td></td><td></td><td></td></tr>
<tr><td></td><td></td><td>*Co.* . . . .</td><td>*21/√*</td><td></td><td>*1,225*</td></tr>
<tr><td></td><td></td><td>*Purchased office equipment on 30-day credit.*</td><td></td><td></td><td></td></tr>
</table>

Operating Transactions Which Do Not Fit Any of the Four Illustrated Special Journals

Each of the above entries includes a debit or credit to a controlling account (Accounts Receivable or Accounts Payable); and also identifies by name a particular creditor or customer. When a controlling account is debited or credited by a *general journal entry,* the debit or credit must be posted twice: one posting to the controlling account in the general ledger and another posting to a customer's account or a creditor's account in a subsidiary ledger. This double posting is necessary to keep the controlling account in agreement with the subsidiary ledger.

For example, in the illustrated entry of November 25 for the return of merchandise by a customer, the credit part of the entry is posted twice:

1. To the Accounts Receivable controlling account in the general ledger; this posting is evidenced by listing the account number (5) in the LP column of the journal.

2. To the account of John Frost in the subsidiary ledger for accounts receivable; this posting is indicated by the check mark ($\sqrt{}$) placed in the LP column of the journal.

Showing the source of postings in ledger accounts

When a general journal and several special journals are in use, the ledger accounts should indicate the book of original entry from which each debit and credit was posted. An identifying symbol is placed opposite each entry in the reference column of the account. The symbols used in this text are as follows:

S1   meaning page 1 of the sales journal
P1   meaning page 1 of the purchases journal
CR1   meaning page 1 of the cash receipts journal
CP1   meaning page 1 of the cash payments journal
J1   meaning page 1 of the general journal

The running balance form of account

The form of account generally used in the subsidiary ledgers for accounts receivable and accounts payable has three money columns: Debit, Credit, and Balance, as illustrated below for an account receivable.

Subsidiary Ledger: Account Receivable

19__				Ref	Debit	Credit	Balance
Name of Customer							
July	1			S1	400		400
	20			S3	200		600
Aug.	4			CR7		400	200
	15			S6	120		320

The advantage of this three-column form of account is that it shows at a glance the present balance receivable from the customer or payable to a creditor. The current amount of a customer's account, for example, is often needed as a guide to collection activities, or as a basis for granting additional credit. In studying the above illustration note also that the Reference column shows the source of each debit and credit.

The three-column running balance form of account is used by many companies for accounts in the general ledger as well as for subsidiary ledgers.

Accounts appearing in the accounts receivable subsidiary ledger are assumed to have debit balances. If one of these customers' accounts should acquire a credit balance by overpayment or for any other reason, the word *credit* should be written after the amount in the Balance column.

Accounts in the accounts payable subsidiary ledger normally have credit balances. If by reason of payment in advance or accidental overpayment, one of these accounts should acquire a debit balance, the word *debit* should be written after the amount in the Balance column.

As previously stated, both the accounts receivable and accounts payable subsidiary ledgers are customarily arranged in alphabetical order and account numbers are not used. This arrangement permits unlimited expansion of the subsidiary ledgers, as accounts with new customers and creditors can be inserted in proper alphabetical sequence.

Ledger accounts

The general ledger. The general ledger accounts of the Seaside Company illustrated on pages 174–176 indicate the source of postings from the various books of original entry. The subsidiary ledger accounts appear on pages 177–178. To gain a clear understanding of the procedures for posting special journals, the student should trace each entry in the illustrated special journals into the general ledger accounts and also to the subsidiary ledger accounts where appropriate.

Note that the Cash account contains only one debit entry and one credit entry although there were many cash transactions during the month. The one debit, $33,128, represents the total cash received during the month and was posted from the cash receipts journal on November 30. Similarly, the one credit entry of $25,288 was posted on November 30 from the cash payments journal and represents the total of all cash payments made during the month.

General Ledger Accounts

Cash (1)

19__				19__			
Nov.	30	CR1	33,128	Nov.	30	CP1	25,288

Notes Receivable (3)

19__							
Nov.	10	CR1	6,000				

Accounts Receivable (5)

19__				19__			
Nov.	30	S1	6,195	Nov.	25	J1	50
					30	CR1	2,350

Unexpired Insurance (6)

19__							
Nov.	29	CP1	720				

Land (11)

19__				19__			
Nov.	9	CP1	15,000	Nov.	10	CR1	5,000

Building   (12)

19__									
Nov.	9		CP1	35,000					

Office Equipment   (14)

19__									
Nov.	29		J1	1,225					

Notes Payable   (20)

					19__				
					Nov.	9		CP1	30,000
						30		CR1	4,000

Accounts Payable   (21)

19__					19__				
Nov.	28		J1	300	Nov.	29		J1	1,225
	30		CP1	1,600		30		P1	7,250

Capital Stock, $10 par   (30)

					19__				
					Nov.	1		CR1	25,000

Gain on Sale of Land   (40)

					19__				
					Nov.	10		CR1	2,000

Sales   (41)

					19__				
					Nov.	30		CR1	825
						30		S1	6,195

Sales Returns and Allowances   (42)

19__									
Nov.	25		J1	50					

General Ledger Accounts (Continued)

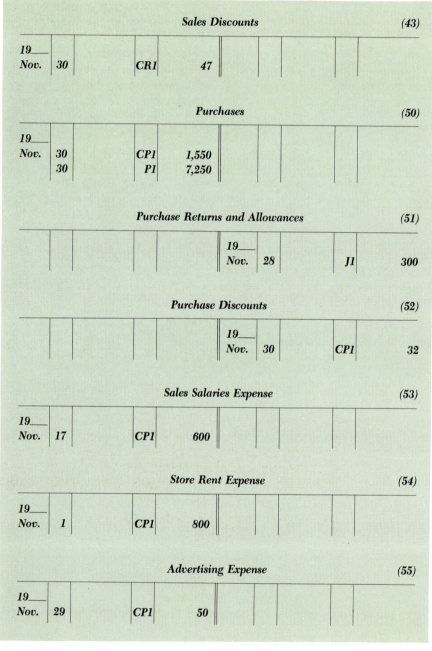

Sales Discounts (43)

19__								
Nov.	30		CR1	47				

Purchases (50)

19__								
Nov.	30		CP1	1,550				
	30		P1	7,250				

Purchase Returns and Allowances (51)

					19__				
					Nov.	28	J1	300

Purchase Discounts (52)

					19__				
					Nov.	30	CP1	32

Sales Salaries Expense (53)

19__								
Nov.	17		CP1	600				

Store Rent Expense (54)

19__								
Nov.	1		CP1	800				

Advertising Expense (55)

19__								
Nov.	29		CP1	50				

Accounts receivable ledger. The subsidiary ledger for accounts receivable appears as follows after the posting of the various journals has been completed.

Customers'
Accounts

John Adams

19__						
Nov.	2		S1	450		450
	8		CR1		450	0

Harold Black

19__						
Nov.	4		S1	1,000		1,000
	12		CR1		1,000	0

Robert Cross

19__						
Nov.	5		S1	975		975

H. R. Davis

19__						
Nov.	11		S1	620		620

C. D. Early

19__						
Nov.	18		S1	900		900
	20		CR1		900	0

John Frost

19__						
Nov.	23		S1	400		400
	25		J1		50	350

D. H. Gray

19__						
Nov.	29		S1	1,850		1,850

Accounts payable ledger. The accounts with creditors in the accounts payable subsidiary ledger are as follows:

Creditors'
Accounts

Alabama Supply Co.

19___					
Nov.	2		P1		3,325	3,325

Barker & Bright

19___						
Nov.	4		P1		700	700
	8		CP1	700		0

Canning & Sons

19___					
Nov.	10		P1		500	500

Davis Co.

19___						
Nov.	17		P1		900	900
	26		CP1	900		0

Excelsior, Inc.

19___						
Nov.	27		P1		1,825	1,825
	28		J1	300		1,525

XYZ Equipment Co.

19___					
Nov.	29		J1		1,225	1,225

*General
Ledger
Trial
Balance*

SEASIDE COMPANY
Trial Balance
November 30, 19___

Cash	$ 7,840	
Notes receivable	6,000	
Accounts receivable (see schedule below)	3,795	
Unexpired insurance	720	
Land	10,000	
Building	35,000	
Office equipment	1,225	
Notes payable		$34,000
Accounts payable (see schedule below)		6,575
Capital stock		25,000
Gain on sale of land		2,000
Sales		7,020
Sales returns and allowances	50	
Sales discounts	47	
Purchases	8,800	
Purchase returns and allowances		300
Purchase discounts		32
Sales salaries expense	600	
Store rent expense	800	
Advertising expense	50	
	$74,927	$74,927

*Subsidiary
Ledgers in
Balance
with
Control
Accounts*

Schedule of Accounts Receivable
November 30, 19___

Robert Cross	$ 975
H. R. Davis	620
John Frost	350
D. H. Gray	1,850
Total (per balance of controlling account)	$3,795

Schedule of Accounts Payable
November 30, 19___

Alabama Supply Co.	$3,325
Canning & Sons	500
Excelsior, Inc.	1,525
XYZ Equipment Co.	1,225
Total (per balance of controlling account)	$6,575

Proving the ledgers

At the end of each accounting period, proof of the equality of debits and credits in the general ledger is established by preparation of a trial balance, as illustrated in preceding chapters. When controlling accounts and subsidiary ledgers are in use, it is also necessary to prove that each subsidiary ledger is in agreement with its controlling account. This proof is accomplished by preparing a schedule of the balances of accounts in each subsidiary ledger and determining that the totals of these schedules agree with the balances of the corresponding control accounts.

Variations in special journals

The number of columns to be included in each special journal and the number of special journals to be used will depend upon the nature of the particular business and especially upon the volume of the various kinds of transactions. For example, the desirability of including a Sales Discount column in the cash receipts journal depends upon whether a business offers discounts to its customers for prompt payment and whether the customers frequently take advantage of such discounts.

A retail store may find that customers frequently return merchandise for credit. To record efficiently this large volume of sales returns, the store may establish a sales returns and allowances journal. A purchase returns and allowances journal may also be desirable if returns of goods to suppliers occur frequently.

Special journals should be regarded as laborsaving devices which may be designed with any number of columns appropriate to the needs of the particular business. A business will usually benefit by establishing a special journal for any type of transaction that occurs quite frequently.

Direct posting from invoices

In many business concerns the efficiency of data processing is increased by posting sales invoices directly to the customers' accounts in the accounts receivable ledger rather than copying sales invoices into a sales journal and then posting to accounts in the subsidiary ledger. If the sales invoices are serially numbered, a file or binder of duplicate sales invoices arranged in numerical order may take the place of a formal sales journal. By accounting for each serial number, it is possible to be certain that all sales invoices are included. At the end of the month, the invoices are totaled on an adding machine, and a general journal entry is made debiting the Accounts Receivable controlling account and crediting Sales for the total of the month's sales invoices.

Direct posting may also be used in recording purchase invoices. As soon as purchase invoices have been verified and approved, credits to the creditors' accounts in the accounts payable ledger may be posted directly from the purchase invoices.

The trend toward direct posting from invoices to subsidiary ledgers is mentioned here as further evidence that accounting records and procedures can be designed in a variety of ways to meet the individual needs of different business concerns.

MECHANICAL DATA PROCESSING

The processing of accounting data may be performed manually, mechanically, or electronically. The term *data processing* means preparing source documents (such as invoices and checks) and the flow of the data contained in these source media through the major accounting steps of recording, classifying, and summarizing. A well-designed system produces an uninterrupted flow of all essential data needed by management for planning and controlling business operations.

Unit record for each transaction

Our discussion has thus far been limited to a manual accounting system. One of the points we have emphasized is that an immediate record should be made of every financial transaction. The *medium* used to make this record is usually a document or form, such as an invoice or a check. This concept of a unit record for each transaction is an important one as we consider the alternatives of processing these media by accounting machines, by punched cards, or by a computer. Regardless of whether we use mechanical or electronic equipment, the source document representing a single transaction is a basic element of the accounting process.

Use of office equipment in a manual data-processing system

Manually kept records are a convenient means of demonstrating accounting principles, and they are also used by a great many small businesses. Strictly defined, a manual system of processing accounting data would call for handwritten journals, ledgers, and financial statements. Even in a small business with some handwritten records, however, the use of office machines and laborsaving devices such as cash registers, adding machines, desk calculators, and multicopy forms has become standard practice.

Simultaneous preparation of documents, journals, and ledgers

Traditionally, each business transaction was recorded, copied, and recopied. A transaction was first evidenced by a source document such as a sales invoice, then copied into a journal (book of original entry), and later posted to a ledger. This step-by-step sequence of creating accounting records is time-consuming and leaves room for the introduction of errors at each step. Whenever a figure, an account title, or an account number is copied, the danger of introducing errors exists. This is true regardless of whether the copying is done with pen and ink or by punching a machine keyboard. The copying process is subject to human errors. From this premise it follows that if several accounting records can be created by writing a transaction only once, the recording process will be not only faster but also more accurate.

Accounting machines

The development of accounting machines designed to create several accounting records with a single writing of a transaction has progressed at a fantastic rate. Machines with typewriter keyboards and computing mechanisms were early developments useful in preparing journals, invoices, payrolls, and other records requiring the typing of names and the computation of amounts. *Accounting machines* is a term usually applied to electromechanical equipment capable of performing arithmetic functions and used to produce a variety of accounting records and reports.

Punched cards and tabulating equipment

Punched cards are a widely used medium for recording accounting data. Information such as amounts, names, account numbers, and other details is recorded by punching holes in appropriate columns and rows of a standard-sized card, usually by means of a key-punch machine. The information punched on the cards can then be read and processed by machines.

Every business receives original documents such as invoices and checks in many shapes and sizes. By punching the information on each such document into a card, we create a document of standard size which machines and computers can use in creating records and reports. For example, once the information on sales invoices has been punched into cards, these cards can be run through machines to produce a schedule of accounts receivable, an analysis of sales by product, by territory, and by salesman, and a listing of commissions earned by salesmen.

Processing accounting data by means of punched cards may be viewed as three major steps, with specially designed machines for each step. The first step is that of recording data; a machine often used for this purpose is an electrically operated *key punch* with a keyboard similar to that of a typewriter.

The second major step is classifying or sorting the data into related groups or categories. For this step a machine called a *sorter* is used. The sorter reads the information on each punched card and then arranges the cards in a particular order, or sorts a deck of cards into groups based on the relationship of the data punched into the cards.

The third major step is summarizing the data. This step is performed by a *tabulating machine*, which has an *output* of printed information resulting from the classifying and totaling of the data on the cards.

Automated data processing

Automated data processing (ADP) and *integrated data processing* (IDP) are terms widely used to describe the processing of data by automatic equipment, either mechanical or electronic, with manual activities reduced to a minimum. The term *electronic data processing* (EDP) is restricted to systems which process data by use of electronic computers.

The integration of an accounting system signifies that forms and procedures are not designed for the needs of a single department but rather as part of a complete information system for the entire business. To create such an integrated system, the accounting systems specialist tries to coordinate all paper work and procedures in a manner that will provide a rapid and uninterrupted flow of all information needed in the conduct of the business as an entity.

ELECTRONIC DATA PROCESSING

EDP in the field of business

Although computers are vital to many complex scientific tasks such as directing the flight of space vehicles, their use is probably increasing most rapidly in the field of business. The first advantage of electronic data processing (EDP) is its incredible speed. The number of computations made by an electronic computer is measured in millions per second. In one minute an electronic printer can produce as much as the average clerk-typist in a day. A second advantage of EDP is its ability to produce more information useful in the control of business activities. The use of electronic data processing usually provides information not previously available—current information which gives management better control and a better basis for sound decisions.

Elements of an EDP system

An electronic data-processing system includes a computer and a number of related machines, which are often called *peripheral equipment.* The computer is the heart of the system; it performs the processing function which includes the storage of information, arithmetic computations, and control. The other two major elements are (1) *input* devices which prepare and insert information into the computer and (2) *output* devices which transfer information out of the computer to the accountant or other user. Both input and output devices perform the function of translation. The machines used to feed information into a computer translate the data into computer language; the output devices translate the processed data back into the language of written words, or of punched cards, paper tape, or magnetic tape.

Hardware and software. The machines and related equipment used in an EDP system are called the *hardware.* All the other materials utilized in selecting, installing, and operating the system (except the operating personnel) are called *software.* Software includes not only the *computer programs* (the sequence of instructions given to the computer), but also feasibility studies, training materials such as films and manuals, studies of equipment requirements, and everything about the EDP system other than the hardware.

Input devices

Among the input devices used to transfer instructions and accounting data into a computer are card readers, punched-paper-tape readers, magnetic-tape readers, character readers, and keyboards. The card-reading device will either transmit information from punched cards into the memory unit of the computer or convert the information to paper or magnetic tape. Punched cards will be read by the card-reading devices at rates of several hundred or even several thousand per minute.

Punched-paper tape can be created as part of the process of recording transactions on cash registers or adding machines. This type of input medium is inexpensive to create and easy to use, but it does not permit the insertion of additional data or the making of corrections after the tape has been punched. Punched-tape readers deliver the data to the computer at high speeds. Both punched-card readers and paper-tape readers are usually connected directly to the computer and are described as part of the "on-line" system. They offer the advantage of compatibility with nonelectronic equipment utilizing punched cards or tape.

Magnetic tape is a far faster means of feeding information into a computer and has the advantage of being easily stored. Corrections are also easily made on magnetic tape. Magnetic tape reels are, however, more expensive than paper tape.

Character-reading machines are perhaps best known in the banking field. They read the account numbers printed in magnetic ink on checks and deposit tickets and convert these data into codes acceptable to the computer. Another type of character-reading device is the optical scanner, with a photoelectric cell which can read a printed document and convert the characters into computer language. This device makes unnecessary the costly step of translating printed matter into punched-card form.

Keyboard devices make it possible to enter limited amounts of data into the EDP system without punching the information into cards or tape as a preliminary step. Keyboards are extremely slow in comparison with the operating capacity of the computer because they are manually operated. However, they may also be used separately from the computer to create punched cards or paper tape for later insertion into the computer.

Machine-sensible forms. Machines have long been able to read punched cards, paper tape, and documents marked or printed with magnetic ink. Nearly all large banks provide depositors with check blanks on which the depositor's account number is printed in magnetic ink. When the check is deposited, the machine reads the account number directly from the check, thus reducing errors in charging the wrong account and increasing the speed of processing. Many large companies now send their stockholders' dividend checks in the form of punched cards. When these checks have been deposited and returned to the company, the bank reconciliation can be quickly prepared by machine. Recent developments indicate that electronic equipment may soon be available which will be able to read written characters.

Output devices

The *printer* is the most important output device. It interprets the computer code and prints several hundred lines per minute, either at the computer center or at remote locations. The printer might be used to produce payroll checks, customers' statements, and many types of accounting reports.

Card-punching machines and paper-tape-punching machines transfer data from the computer into punch cards and paper tape which later may be used as input data for subsequent analysis or processing.

Processing operations in the computer

The processing operations performed by a computer include storage of information, arithmetic manipulation of data, and control. The computer receives and stores instructions and data; it calls this information from the memory or storage unit as required by the processing routine; it goes through arithmetic operations, makes comparisons of numbers, and takes the action necessary to produce the required output of information.

The term *control* describes the ability of the computer to guide itself through the processing operations utilizing detailed lists of instructions concerning the work to be done.

Program. A program is a series of steps planned to carry out a certain process, such as the preparation of a payroll. Each step in the program is a command or instruction to the computer. A program for payroll might be compared with a very detailed written set of instructions given to an inexperienced employee assigned to the payroll function in a manual accounting system. A most important attribute of the computer is its ability to receive and store a set of instructions which controls its behavior.

The preparation of a computer program is a complicated and costly task. A company may employ its own programmers or may rely on outside organizations which specialize in such services.

Differences between mechanical and electronic data-processing systems

Mechanical data-processing equipment such as electric calculators, bookkeeping machines, and key-punch machines is extremely slow when compared with electronic equipment. The processing of data in the electronic system is accomplished by electrical impulses traveling through electronic circuits. Such equipment functions hundreds of times faster than mechanical devices.

Another point of contrast is that the units of equipment comprising an EDP system are interconnected so that the processing of data is a continuous operation from the point of reading input data to the point of printing the report or other final result. On the other hand, a mechanical data-processing system employs separate machines which do not communicate directly with each other. After each machine, such as a key punch, has performed its function, the output media (punched cards or paper tape) must be transported manually to another machine.

Dependability of EDP equipment

A great deal of the data going into a computer is first transferred from source documents to punched cards or paper tape. This process of key punching to create a file of punched cards is comparable to the use of a typewriter, and the making of errors is quite possible. The additional step of transferring information from invoices or checks into the form of punched cards or tape creates new opportunities for error. The danger also exists that data may be omitted or may be processed twice. The computer program may contain errors, or the computer operator may make the mistake of using an obsolete program.

Despite these numerous possible sources of errors, electronic data processing makes possible a higher degree of accuracy and reliability than any other system of record keeping. One reason for this potential of accuracy is that the computer is extremely reliable in processing the data fed into it. If these input data are accurate and the computer program is free from error, we can have a high degree of confidence in the output of the computer. Furthermore, much progress is being made in developing techniques for detecting and correcting errors which enter the EDP system.

Earlier generations of computers were often designed to perform arithmetic operations twice and to compare the two sets of answers. This *double circuitry* has been eliminated from most later-model computers because experience has proved the reliability of electronic circuits. Many other types of controls, however, are built into the equipment. For example, the punched cards and paper tape which constitute the data being fed into the computer are read twice as they enter the equipment and any inconsistencies are automatically signaled. A similar control is the "read after write" technique in which the computer reads back the data immediately after they have been recorded. The "parity check" is another important built-in control which offers assurance as to the accuracy of data within the computer equipment.[1]

In summary, we can respect the high degree of reliability inherent in the computer yet recognize that the use of a computer entails the services of people and supporting mechanical equipment. The opportunity for error from these sources exists as it does in any type of manual or mechanical operation.

Accounting applications of the computer

The use of electronic data-processing equipment is possible for virtually every phase of accounting operations. Even the CPA, in conducting an annual audit, may use the computer as an audit tool. For this purpose he may employ

---

[1] The computer automatically places all characters of input on a par by making binary digit totals for all characters either all odd or all even, depending on the type of computer. To achieve this parity a digit is added to any totals that deviate from the odd or even pattern. In subsequent processing any variations from this parity will indicate an error. Thus the parity check serves as a safeguard against malfunction in the processing of data by the computer.

specially written computer programs to aid in his work of sampling and analyzing data to prove the fairness of the financial statements.

The most common application of the computer, however, is to process large masses of accounting data relating to routine repetitive operations such as accounts receivable, accounts payable, inventories, and payrolls.

Payrolls. In a manual accounting system the preparation of payroll checks is usually separate from the maintenance of records showing pay rates, positions, time worked, payroll deductions, and other personnel data. An EDP system, however, has the capability of maintaining all records relating to payroll as well as turning out the required paychecks. Payroll processing is usually one of the first accounting operations to be placed on the computer.

The payroll procedure consists of determining for each employee gross earnings, making deductions, computing net pay, preparing the payroll check, and maintaining a record of each individual's earnings. In addition, the company needs a payroll summary for each period and usually a distribution of payroll costs by department, by product, or classified by the various productive processes. The payroll function has become increasingly complex and time-consuming in recent years because of the advent of social security taxes, income tax withholding, and many other payroll deductions. Each employee must receive not only a payroll check but a statement showing the gross earnings, deductions, and net pay. The company's records must be designed to facilitate filing with the federal and state governments regular payroll reports such as income tax, unemployment insurance, disability, and social security. The time and the expense required to prepare payrolls has risen in proportion to the need for more information. The demands by governments, labor unions, credit unions, and other outside agencies have added to the problem.

An EDP payroll system will not only maintain the necessary records, print the checks, and print these reports, but it can also keep management informed of the costs of various functions within the business. For example, data can be produced showing the man-hours and labor costs on each job, labor cost by department for each salesclerk, or the time required by different employees to perform similar work. In other words, much current information can be developed without significant extra expense that will provide management with a detailed breakdown of labor costs.

EDP services offered by banks and by data-processing centers. A computer and related hardware are costly to buy or rent. The employment of personnel qualified to operate the equipment is also a major expense, especially for a small business. One way in which a small business can avoid investing large sums yet gain the operating efficiencies of EDP is to turn over its raw data to a bank, an accounting firm, or a computer center that offers EDP services on a fee basis.

The major banks all have modern electronic equipment, which they do not need 24 hours each day for their own work alone. In addition, some of these banks were pioneers in the field of electronic data processing and have had years of experience in developing effective systems. Similarly, some accounting firms have much experience in rendering accounting services for small businesses and have acquired EDP equipment to enable them to perform these services more effectively.

To illustrate the use of an outside EDP service by a small business, let us compare what must be done with respect to payroll if (1) the work is performed manually within the small business and (2) the work is performed by an outside agency offering EDP services.

Payroll May Be Prepared within the Company or by an EDP Service Center	*Function*	*Payroll Prepared Manually within the Company*	*Payroll Handled by an Outside Agency Offering EDP Services*
	1. Timekeeping	Employer fills in new set of records each period, making extensions manually.	Employer enters raw data on forms supplied by the agency.
	2. Computation of gross pay	Compute gross pay for each employee, perhaps with desk calculator, and enter manually in records.	Performed electronically.
	3. Calculation of deductions	For each employee, refer to charts and make computations; enter manually in records.	Performed electronically.
	4. Prepare checks, earnings statements, and payroll register	Write by hand or type checks. Proofread, and maintain controls.	Performed electronically.
	5. Bank reconciliation	Reconcile payroll bank account per books with monthly bank statement.	Performed electronically.
	6. Reports to government	Prepare quarterly reports showing for each employee and in total amounts earned, deducted, and paid. Reconcile individual data with controls.	Performed electronically.
	7. Managerial control data	Prepare distribution of hours and labor cost by department or by job. Other analyses may be needed.	Performed electronically.

In brief, the business which uses the EDP service offered by an outside agency is initially provided with forms on which to enter basic pay information such as employee names, pay rates, and deductions. The EDP service center incorporates these data into electronic records. Thereafter, the business need only report to the service center such variable information as hours worked and pay changes. The EDP center calculates wages and deductions, writes checks and payroll registers, and prepares tax reports for government and for individual employees. Personnel at the computer service center can be payroll specialists conversant with current reporting requirements and with the most efficient techniques of payroll processing.

Other accounting applications. Our emphasis on electronic data processing of payrolls is not intended to minimize the potential advantages in other areas. In the area of accounts payable, for example, the computer can prepare all the various accounts payable records with one handling of the data on purchase invoices. The computer output includes a remittance advice for the vendor, an invoice register and distribution journal, the check to the vendor, a check register, and a report summarizing the distribution of charges to various accounts. Equally attractive opportunities lie in the areas of accounts receivable and inventories.

Do computers make decisions?

Computers do not make decisions in the sense of exercising judgment. A computer can choose among alternatives by following specific rules for clearly defined situations. For example, if a dollar credit limit is set for a given customer, the computer can be programmed to reject (and refer for special consideration) any sales order from that customer which would cause his account to exceed the predetermined maximum. Such an approach illustrates the principle of "management by exception"; that is, management time is reserved for problem situations.

EDP advantages other than speed

Although computers are sometimes installed simply because they are the fastest means of record keeping, management can expect more than speed of processing. As we become more skilled in developing accounting applications for the computer, we will have the opportunity to obtain currently much more information about a business than has previously been possible. We will be able, for example, to obtain answers to questions on profit margins on individual products, to forecast the profit possibilities inherent in alternative courses of action, and to determine with reasonable accuracy our future financial requirements far in advance.

QUESTIONS

1. What advantages are offered by the use of special journals?

2. Flow Line Company uses a cash receipts journal, a cash payments journal, a sales journal, a purchases journal, and a general journal. Indicate which journal should be used to record each of the following transactions:

    a. Purchase of merchandise on account
    b. Purchase of delivery truck for cash
    c. Return of merchandise by a customer for credit to his account
    d. Payment of taxes
    e. Adjusting entry to record depreciation
    f. Purchase of typewriter on account
    g. Sale of merchandise on account
    h. Sale of merchandise for cash
    i. Refund to a customer who returned merchandise sold him for cash
    j. Return of merchandise to a supplier for credit

3. When accounts receivable and accounts payable are kept in subsidiary ledgers, will the general ledger continue to be a self-balancing ledger with equal debits and credits? Explain.

4. Explain how, why, and when the cash receipts journal and cash payments journal are crossfooted.

5. Pine Hill General Store makes about 500 sales on account each month, using only a two-column general journal to record these transactions. What would be the extent of the work saved by using a sales journal?

6. During November the sales on credit made by the Hardy Company actually amounted to $41,625, but an error of $1,000 was made in totaling the amount column of the sales journal. When and how will the error be discovered?

7. Considerable repetitious copying work may be entailed in the preparation of a sales invoice, a sales journal, and a receivables ledger. Is this step-by-step sequence with its attendant opportunity for errors a characteristic of all types of accounting systems? Explain.

8. What are the principal advantages of electronic data processing in the accounting division of a company?

9. In which phases or areas of accounting can EDP equipment be used to advantage? Which phases can most conveniently and advantageously be converted to electronic data processing?

10. What avenues are open to a small business, interested in gaining the efficiencies of electronic data processing, which lacks funds for purchase or rental of a computer and also does not have employees familiar with computer operations?

11. Distinguish between *hardware* and *software* as these terms are used in data-processing systems.

12. Evaluate the following quotation: "The computer will ultimately replace both bookkeepers and accountants and will be able to make many of the decisions now made by top management."

EXERCISES

1. Accounts receivable of the Early Co. on January 1, 1971, are shown below.

John Allen	$1,610	
Peter Brown	820	
James Crown	1,100	$3,530

The sales journal for the first week of January includes sales on account as follows:

Edward Davis	*$650*	
John Allen	*420*	
James Crown	*755*	
George Evans	*570*	*$2,395*

The cash receipts journal shows that Peter Brown paid $370 on January 4 and that James Crown paid $1,100 on January 5.

Prepare a schedule of accounts receivable at the end of the first week of January.

2. The after-closing trial balance of the Farley Co. on June 30 and the unadjusted trial balance on July 31 are shown below:

	After-closing Trial Balance, June 30		Trial Balance, July 31	
Cash	*$ 17,800*		*$ 13,400*	
Accounts receivable	*24,000*		*26,100*	
Inventory	*25,200*		*25,200*	
Equipment	*35,000*		*36,800*	
Accumulated depreciation: equipment		*$ 7,500*		*$ 7,500*
Accounts payable		*19,500*		*13,000*
Capital stock		*50,000*		*60,000*
Retained earnings		*25,000*		*25,000*
Sales				*17,000*
Purchases			*12,500*	
Salaries expense			*4,000*	
Advertising expense			*500*	
Supplies expense			*750*	
Property tax expense			*1,250*	
Miscellaneous expense			*2,000*	
	$102,000	*$102,000*	*$122,500*	*$122,500*

All purchases and sales are made on credit. During July all transactions were recorded in the special journals; no entries were made in the general journal.
a. What was the total amount of cash receipts from all sources in July?
b. What was the total amount of cash payments for all purposes in July?
c. Prepare one compound journal entry (general journal form) summarizing all July transactions involving the receipt of cash. The entry should include a debit to Cash for the amount computed in **a** and credits to other accounts.
d. Prepare one compound journal entry (general journal form) summarizing all July transactions involving the payment of cash. The entry should include a credit to Cash for the amount computed in **b** and debits to other accounts.

3. The balance in the Purchase Discounts account is $385.

a. List all possible ways that this figure can be erroneously picked up (by a transposition of digits) in the trial balance. (Do not consider the possible misplacing of the decimal point.)

b. What would be the magnitude of the error in the trial balance totals in each case?

c. Do the possible amounts of the error have a common characteristic?

4. Complete the following statements:

a. The X Co. pays $346.92 to a supplier after deducting a 2% cash discount. The gross amount of the invoice was $_____.

b. When special journals are used, debits to the Equipment account can originate either in the _____ journal or the _____ journal.

c. All accounts with customers are placed in alphabetical order in the

_____ .

d. All accounts with creditors are placed in alphabetical order in the _____

_____ .

e. On an adjusted trial balance for a law firm, the difference between all assets and the total of all liability and owners' equity accounts is equal to the _____ for the period.

PROBLEMS

6-1 The cash activities and certain selected other transactions of Jensen Company for the month of February are presented below. The company sells and also rents heavy-duty machinery to its customers.

Feb. 1 Received cash of $1,750 for machinery rented to Smith Construction Co. for the month of February.

Feb. 1 Received from Langley Company, in settlement of open account, a 6%, 90-day note for $5,000.

Feb. 3 Received $975 in payment of non-interest-bearing note.

Feb. 8 Purchased merchandise for cash, $5,700, from Adco Company.

Feb. 10 Cash sales today, $1,784.

Feb. 11 Returned merchandise purchased for cash on February 8. Credit of $210 was used to reduce previous account payable to Adco Company.

Feb. 14 Purchased office furniture at cost of $13,000, paying $4,000 cash to Faber Company and signing a 90-day non-interest-bearing note for balance.

Feb. 15 Received cash from Cross & Sons, $730, as rent for machinery during remainder of February.

Feb. 16 Purchased office supplies for cash, $75.

Feb. 18 Purchased merchandise for cash, $2,100.

Feb. 20 Received check from Baker Corporation in settlement of invoice, $1,900 less 2% cash discount.

Feb. 22 Cash sales today, $2,745.

Feb. 22 Paid Acker Co. invoice, $4,300 less 2% cash discount.

Feb. 24 Paid installment on mortgage, $852, including $208 interest.

Feb. 25 Received check from East Co. in payment of invoice, $1,500 less 2% cash discount.

Feb. 26 Sold land, with cost of $6,000, for $7,600 cash and a 6%, two-year note receivable for $8,000.

Feb. 28 Paid Royal Co. invoice, $3,300 less 2% cash discount.

Feb. 28 Paid monthly salaries, $4,200.

Instructions

a. Record the above transactions in the appropriate journals. (Use a six-column cash receipts journal, a six-column cash payments journal, and a two-column general journal.)

b. Foot and rule the journals.

6-2 The Sample Corporation began operations on November 1, 19___. The chart of accounts used by the Corporation included the following accounts, among others:

Cash	10
Marketable securities	15
Office supplies	18
Notes payable	30
Accounts payable	32
Purchases	60
Purchase returns & allowances	62
Purchase discounts	64
Salaries expense	70
Utilities expense	71

November transactions relating to the purchase of merchandise and to accounts payable are listed below, along with selected other transactions.

Nov. 1   Purchased merchandise from Moss Co. for $3,210. Invoice dated today; terms 2/10, n/30.

Nov. 3   Returned for credit to Moss Co. merchandise having a list price of $195.

Nov. 3   Received shipment of merchandise from Wilmer Co. and invoice dated November 2 for $7,600; terms 2/10, n/30.

Nov. 6   Purchased merchandise from Archer Company at cost of $5;600. Invoice dated November 5; terms 2/10, n/30.

Nov. 9   Purchased marketable securities, $1,200.

Nov. 10   Issued check to Moss Co. in settlement of balance resulting from purchase of November 1 and purchase return of November 3.

Nov. 12   Received shipment of merchandise from Cory Corporation and their invoice dated November 11 in amount of $7,100; terms net 30 days.

Nov. 14   Issued check to Archer Company in settlement of invoice of November 5.

Nov. 16   Paid cash for office supplies, $110.

Nov. 17   Purchased merchandise for cash, $950.

Nov. 19   Purchased merchandise from Klein Co. for $11,500. Invoice dated November 18; terms 2/10, n/30.

Nov. 21   Purchased merchandise from Belmont Company for $8,400. Invoice dated November 20; terms 1/10, n/30.

Nov. 24   Purchased merchandise for cash, $375.

Nov. 26   Purchased merchandise from Brooker Co. for $6,500. Invoice dated today; terms 1/10, n/30.

Nov. 28   Paid utilities, $150.

Nov. 30   Paid salaries for November, $2,900.

Nov. 30   Paid $2,600 cash to Wilmer Co. and issued 6%, 90-day promissory note for $5,000 in settlement of invoice dated November 2.

Instructions

a. Record the transactions in the appropriate journals. Use a single-column purchases journal, a six-column cash payments journal, and a two-column general journal.

b. Foot and rule the special journals. Make all postings to the proper general ledger accounts and to the accounts payable subsidiary ledger.

c. Prepare a schedule of accounts payable at November 30 to prove that the subsidiary ledger is in balance with the controlling account for accounts payable. (A trial balance of the general ledger is not required, because only a part of the general ledger accounts are utilized in this problem.)

6-3 The Bray Company began operations on July 1 using the chart of accounts shown.

Cash	10	*Sales*	50
Marketable securities	13	*Sales returns & allowances*	52
Notes receivable	14	*Sales discount*	54
Accounts receivable	15	*Purchases*	60
Merchandise inventory	17	*Purchase returns & allowances*	62
Unexpired insurance	19	*Purchase discounts*	64
Land	20	*Transportation-in*	66
Building	21	*Rent expense*	70
Furniture and fixtures	24	*Salaries expense*	72
Notes payable	30	*Taxes expense*	74
Accounts payable	32	*Supplies expense*	76
Mortgage payable	36	*Insurance expense*	78
Capital stock	40	*Interest earned*	80
Retained earnings	42	*Interest expense*	83
Income summary	45	*Loss on sale of securities*	84

The transactions for the month of July are listed below.

July 1   Sold stock for $100,000 and deposited this amount in the bank under the name of the Bray Company.

July 4   Purchasing land and building on contract, paying $40,000 cash and signing a mortgage note for the remaining balance of $55,000. Estimated value of the land was $25,000.

July 6   Sold merchandise to J. V. Thomas, $2,500. Invoice No. 1; terms 2/10, n/60.

July 7   Purchased merchandise from Drill Company, $5,100. Invoice dated today; terms 2/10, n/30.

July 7   Sold merchandise for cash, $740.

July 7   Paid $270 for a two-year fire insurance policy.

July 10   Paid freight charges of $205 on Drill Company purchase of July 7.

July 12   Sold merchandise to Everett Company, $4,900. Invoice No. 2; terms 2/10, n/60.

July 13   Purchased merchandise for cash, $1,420.

July 15   Received payment in full from J. V. Thomas. Invoice No. 1, less 2% discount.

July 15   Purchased securities, $1,600.

July 16   Issued credit memorandum No. 1 to Everett Company, $400, for goods returned today.

July 17   Paid Drill Company invoice of July 7, less discount on $5,100.

July 18   Purchased merchandise from Wyatt Corporation, $3,700. Invoice dated today; terms 2/10, n/30.

July 20   A portion of merchandise purchased from Wyatt Corporation was found to be substandard. After discussion with the vendor, a price reduction of $100 was agreed upon and debit memorandum No. 1 was issued in that amount.

July 22   Received payment in full from Everett Company; invoice No. 2, less returns and discount.

July 23   Purchased merchandise from Drill Company, $4,200. Invoice dated today; terms 2/10, n/60.

July 25   Sold for $1,420 the securities purchased on July 15.

July 27   Sold merchandise for cash, $515.

July 28   Borrowed $3,000 from the bank, issuing a 60-day, 5% note payable as evidence of indebtedness.

July 28   Paid Wyatt Corporation invoice dated July 18, less discount.

July 30   Paid first installment on mortgage, $500. This payment included interest of $90.

July 30   Purchased merchandise for cash, $920.

July 31   Paid monthly salaries of $2,115.

July 31   Sold merchandise to B. Frank, $2,750. Invoice No. 3; terms 2/10, n/60.

Instructions

a.   Journalize the July transactions in the following journals:
One-column sales journal
One-column purchases journal
Two-column general journal
Six-column cash receipts journal
Six-column cash payments journal

b.   Indicate how postings would be made by placing ledger account numbers in the journals.

6-4   Westport Company is in the business of selling and leasing machinery. The cash transactions for the month of April, plus some other selected transactions, are presented below.

Apr. 1   Sold merchandise to Rex Company for cash, $3,055.

Apr. 3   Received cash of $720 for machinery rented to Sims Company for the month of April.

Apr. 4   Paid cash for merchandise, $350.

Apr. 5   Issued a check for $10,000 in payment for dividend declared in March, at which time the Dividends Payable account was credited.

Apr. 6   Purchased office supplies for $48 cash.

Apr. 8   Cash sales today, $3,400.

Apr. 9   Received check from Brussels Company in payment of a $1,500 invoice, less 2% cash discount.

Apr. 11   Received $700 from Blue Company in payment of a past-due invoice.

Apr. 14   Returned for credit to a supplier, ABC Corporation, certain defective merchandise purchased in March in the amount of $600.

Apr. 14   Received check from Ryan, Inc., in settlement of invoice, $1,800 less 2% cash discount.

Apr. 15 Purchased office equipment at cost of $6,240, paying $2,240 cash and signing a 90-day non-interest-bearing note for the balance.

Apr. 16 Paid semimonthly salaries amounting to $2,850.

Apr. 17 Purchased merchandise for cash, $125.

Apr. 18 Paid bank $2,020 in settlement of a note payable for $2,000 and interest of $20. No previous entry had been made to record interest.

Apr. 20 Purchased office equipment at cost of $8,900, issuing a non-interest-bearing note payable for the full amount.

Apr. 21 Paid for advertising for April, $745.

Apr. 22 Collected $1,000 in full settlement of a non-interest-bearing note.

Apr. 23 Paid for accumulated gas and oil purchases for company cars, $148. No liability has previously been recorded.

Apr. 24 Paid Norman Co. invoice, $3,600 less 2% cash discount.

Apr. 25 Paid installment on mortgage, $765, including $240 interest.

Apr. 26 Cash sales today, $315.

Apr. 27 Sold land, originally acquired as a building site at cost of $8,000, for $10,000 cash plus a 6%, two-year note receivable for $5,000.

Apr. 30 Paid semimonthly salaries, $2,850.

Apr. 30 Purchased merchandise for cash, $130.

Apr. 30 Paid James Co. invoice $2,400 less 2% cash discount.

Instructions

a. Record the above transactions in the appropriate journals, making your choice from a six-column cash receipts journal, a six-column cash payments journal, or a two-column general journal.

b. Foot and rule the cash journals and post totals to general ledger accounts. Also make any necessary individual postings affecting general ledger accounts. Do not post to subsidiary ledger accounts. Assign account numbers to the general ledger accounts used, and cross-reference the journals and general ledger.

6-5 The schedules of accounts receivable and accounts payable as of August 31, 19___, for the General Hardware Corporation are shown below:

Schedule of Accounts Receivable *August 31, 19___*		*Schedule of Accounts Payable* *August 31, 19___*	
Fife Company	*$2,560*	*Clair Company*	*$4,000*
Slowe Paving Co.	*1,750*		

All transactions of the General Hardware Corporation for the month of September are presented below:

Sept. 2 Purchased merchandise on account from Clair Company, $5,175. Invoice was dated today with terms of 2/10, n/30.

Sept. 3 Sold merchandise to Fife Company, $4,600. Invoice No. 428; terms 2/10, n/30.

Sept. 4 Purchased supplies for cash, $175.

Sept. 5 Sold merchandise for cash, $1,120.

Sept. 7 Paid the Clair Company invoice for $4,000, representing August purchases. No discount is allowed by the Clair Company.

Sept. 10 Purchased merchandise from Axle Company, $6,500. Invoice dated September 9 with terms of 1/10, n/30.

Sept. 10 Collected from Fife Company for invoice No. 428 for $4,600, and for August sales of $2,560 on which the discount had lapsed.

Sept. 12 Sold merchandise to Martin Company, $4,350. Invoice No. 429; terms 2/10, n/30.

Sept. 14 Paid freight charges of $410 on goods purchased September 10 from Axle Company.

Sept. 14 Sold equipment for $1,800, receiving cash of $300 and a 30-day, 7% note receivable for the balance. Equipment cost $4,000 and accumulated depreciation was $2,600.

Sept. 15 Issued credit memorandum No. 38 in favor of Martin Company upon return of $200 of merchandise.

Sept. 18 Paid for one-year fire insurance policy, $285.

Sept. 18 Purchased merchandise for cash, $1,525.

Sept. 19 Paid the Axle Company invoice dated September 9, less the 1% discount.

Sept. 20 Sold merchandise on account to Evans Brothers, $2,730; invoice No. 430. Required customer to sign a 30-day, non-interest-bearing note. (Record this sale by a debit to Accounts Receivable, then transfer from Accounts Receivable to Notes Receivable by means of an entry in the general journal.)

Sept. 22 Purchased merchandise for cash, $810.

Sept. 22 Sold merchandise for cash, $935.

Sept. 22 Received payment from Martin Company for invoice No. 429. Customer made deduction for credit memorandum No. 38 issued September 15, and a 2% discount.

Sept. 23 Sold merchandise on account to Tracy Corp., $1,990. Invoice No. 431; terms 2/10, n/30.

Sept. 24 Declared a cash dividend of $7,500 on capital stock, payable October 20, 19____.

Sept. 25 Purchased merchandise from Davis Company, $5,300. Invoice dated September 24 with terms of 2/10, n/60.

Sept. 26 Issued debit memorandum No. 42 to Davis Company in connection with merchandise returned today amounting to $425.

Sept. 27 Purchased equipment having a list price of $12,000. Paid $2,000 down and signed a promissory note for the balance of $10,000.

Sept. 30 Paid monthly salaries of $2,960 for services rendered by employees during September.

Sept. 30 Paid monthly installment on mortgage, $700, of which $204 was interest.

The corporation has been using the following accounts in recording transactions:

Cash	10	Notes payable	30
Marketable securities	12	Accounts payable	32
Notes receivable	14	Accrued salaries payable	34
Accounts receivable	16	Accrued property taxes payable	36
Supplies	17	Dividends payable	38
Unexpired insurance	18	Mortgage payable	40
Land	20	Capital stock	50
Buildings	22	Retained earnings	52
Accumulated depreciation: buildings	24	Dividends	54
Equipment	26	Sales	60
Accumulated depreciation: equipment		Sales returns & allowances	62
ment	28	Sales discounts	64

Purchases.....................	70	Supplies expense	84
Purchases returns & allowances....	72	Insurance expense	86
Purchase discounts..............	74	Depreciation expense.............	88
Transportation-in...............	76	Gain on sale of equipment........	90
Salaries expense................	80	Interest expense.................	92
Property tax expense............	82		

Instructions

a. Record the September transactions in the general journal and special journals as required.

b. Foot and rule all special journals.

c. Prepare a schedule of accounts receivable and accounts payable as of September 30, 19___.

Chapter

7 Forms of business organization

Three forms of business organization are common to American industry: the single proprietorship, the partnership, and the corporation. When these forms of organization were introduced in Chapter 1, it was emphasized that most accounting principles apply to all three forms and that the main area of difference lies in the accounting for owners' equity. In this chapter we shall describe briefly some accounting processes peculiar to single proprietorships and partnerships, and then move to a discussion of corporations. Our consideration of accounting problems relating to corporations will be continued in Chapter 8.

SINGLE PROPRIETORSHIPS

Owner's equity accounts for a single proprietorship

The accounting records for a single proprietorship (or a partnership) do not include accounts for capital stock, retained earnings, or dividends. Instead of these accounts, a capital account and a drawing account are maintained for the owner.

Capital account (as, for example, John Jones, Capital). The capital account is credited with the amount of the proprietor's original investment in the business and also with any subsequent investments. When the books are closed at the end of each accounting period, the capital account is credited with the net income earned (or debited with the net loss incurred). Withdrawals by the proprietor during the period are debited to a Drawing account and later transferred to the Capital account at the time of closing the books. The total ownership equity in the business, therefore, appears as a single amount in the balance sheet.

Drawing account (as, for example, John Jones, Drawing). A withdrawal of cash or other assets by the owner reduces his equity in the business and could be recorded by debiting his Capital account. However, a clearer record is created if a separate Drawing account is maintained. The Drawing account is debited for any of the following transactions:

1. Withdrawals of cash or other assets. If the proprietor of a clothing store, for example, withdraws merchandise for his personal use, his Drawing account is debited for the cost of the goods withdrawn. The offsetting credit is to the Purchases account (or to Inventory if a perpetual inventory system in maintained).

2. Payment of the proprietor's personal bills out of the business bank account.

3. Collection of an account receivable of the business, with the cash collected being retained personally by the proprietor.

Withdrawals by the proprietor are not an expense of the business. Expenses are incurred for the purpose of generating revenue, and a withdrawal of cash or other assets by the proprietor does not have this purpose.

Closing the books

The revenue and expense accounts of a single proprietorship are closed into the Income Summary account in the same way as for a corporation. However, the net income or net loss is closed to the proprietor's Capital account rather than to a Retained Earnings account. To complete the closing of the books, the balance of the Drawing account is transferred into the proprietor's Capital account.

Financial statements and work sheet for a single proprietorship

The balance sheet of a single proprietorship differs from the balance sheet of a corporation only in the owner's equity section. An illustration of the ownership equity portion of the balance sheet for a proprietorship, a partnership, and a corporation was presented in Chapter 1 (page 19).

A statement of owner's equity may be prepared in a form similar to the statement of retained earnings used by a corporation. An illustration follows:

Net Income Exceeded Withdrawals by Owner

GREENHILL REAL ESTATE COMPANY
Statement of Owner's Equity
For the Month Ended November 30, 19___

James Greenhill, capital, Nov. 1, 19___	$30,257
Add: Net income for November	1,228
Total	$31,485
Less: Withdrawals	500
James Greenhill, capital, Nov. 30, 19___	$30,985

The income statement for a single proprietorship does not include any salary expense representing managerial services rendered by the owner. One reason for not including among the expenses a salary to the owner-manager is the fact that he would be able to set his own salary at any amount he chose. The use of an arbitrarily chosen, unrealistic salary to the proprietor would tend to destroy the significance of the income statement as a device for measuring the earning power of the business. Another reason may be that in the proprietor's own thinking he is not working for a salary when he manages his own business but is investing his time in order to make a profit. The net income of a single proprietorship must, therefore, be considered in part as the equivalent of a salary earned by the owner.

Another distinctive feature of the income statement for a single proprietorship is that income tax is not included. The proprietor reports on his individual tax return the taxable income from his business and from other sources such as personal investments. The rate of tax is determined by the total of his income; consequently, the tax applicable to the income from the business is influenced by factors unrelated to the business enterprise. As explained later in this chapter, the financial statements for a corporation will include income tax expense in the income statement, and income taxes payable among the current liabilities in the balance sheet.

The work sheet for a single proprietorship is similar to the work sheet for a corporation except that a pair of columns for Owner's Capital replaces the pair of columns for Retained Earnings.

PARTNERSHIPS

A *partnership* may be defined as "an association of two or more persons to carry on, as co-owners, a business for profit." In the professions and in businesses which stress the factor of personal service, the partnership form of organization is widely used. The laws of the state may even deny the incorporation privilege to persons engaged in such professions as law and public accounting, because the personal responsibility of the professional practitioner to his client might be lost behind the impersonal corporate entity. However, an increasing number of states are now affording professional men such as dentists and physicians the privilege of incorporating. In the fields of manufacturing, wholesaling, and retail trade, the partnership form is popular, because it affords a convenient means of combining the capital and abilities of two or more persons.

Features of a partnership

Before taking up the accounting problems of partnerships, it will be helpful to point out some of the distinctive characteristics of the partnership form of organization.

1. Ease of formation. A partnership can be created without any legal formalities. When two or more persons agree to become partners, a partnership is created. The voluntary aspect of a *partnership agreement* means that no one can be forced into a partnership or forced to continue as a partner.

2. Limited life. A partnership may be ended at any time by the death or withdrawal of any member of the firm. Other factors which may bring an end to a partnership include the bankruptcy or incapacity of a partner, or the completion of the project for which the partnership was formed. The admission of a new partner or the retirement of an existing member means an end to the old partnership, although the business may be continued by the formation of a new partnership.

3. *Mutual agency.* Each partner acts as an agent of the partnership, with authority to enter into contracts. The partnership is bound by the acts of any partner as long as these acts are within the scope of normal operations. The factor of mutual agency suggests the need for exercising great caution in the selection of a partner.

4. *Unlimited liability.* Each partner is personally responsible for all the debts of the firm. The lack of any ceiling on the liability of a partner may deter a wealthy person from entering a partnership.

5. *Co-ownership of partnership property and profits.* When a partner invests property other than cash in a partnership, he does not retain any personal right to such property. The property becomes jointly owned by all partners. Similarly, each partner has an ownership right in the profits earned by the partnership.

Advantages and disadvantages of a partnership

Perhaps the most important advantage and the principal reason for the formation of most partnerships is the opportunity to bring together sufficient capital to carry on a business. The opportunity to combine special skills, as, for example, the specialized talents of engineers, accountants, or lawyers may also induce individuals to join forces in a partnership. Members of a partnership enjoy more freedom and flexibility of action than do the owners of a corporation; the partners may withdraw funds and make business decisions of all types without the necessity of formal meetings or legalistic procedures. Finally, operating as a partnership may, in certain instances, result in significant income tax advantages.

Offsetting these advantages of a partnership are such serious disadvantages as limited life, unlimited liability, and mutual agency. Furthermore, if a business is to require a very large amount of capital, the partnership is a less effective device for raising the capital than is a corporation.

Partnership accounting

An adequate accounting system and an accurate measurement of net income are needed by every business, but they are especially important in a partnership because the net income is divided among two or more partners. Each partner needs current, accurate information on net income so that he can make intelligent decisions on such questions as additional investments, expansion of the business, or sale of his ownership interest.

To illustrate the significance to partners of accurate accounting data, consider the following case. Allen and Baker became partners, each investing $50,000. Allen maintained the accounting records and fraudulently contrived to make the financial statements show operating losses although the business was in fact quite profitable. Discouraged by these misleading financial statements, Baker sold his share of the business to Allen for $20,000, when in fact his equity was worth considerably more than his original investment of $50,000.

Partnership accounting requires the maintenance of a separate capital account for each partner; a separate drawing account for each partner is also desirable.

The accounting entries in these accounts parallel those discussed earlier in this chapter for a single proprietorship. The other distinctive feature of partnership accounting is the division of each year's net income or loss among the partners in the proportions specified by the partnership agreement. In the study of partnership accounting, the new concepts lie almost entirely in the owners' equity section; accounting for partnership assets and liabilities follows the same principles as for other forms of business organization.

Opening the books

When a partner contributes assets other than cash, a question always arises as to the value of such assets; the valuations assigned to noncash assets should be their *fair market values* at the date of transfer to the partnership. The valuations assigned must be agreed to by all the partners.

To illustrate the opening entries for a newly formed partnership, assume that on January 1 John Blair and Richard Cross, who operate competing retail stores, decide to form a partnership by consolidating their two businesses. A Capital account will be opened for each partner and credited with the agreed valuation of the *net assets* (total assets less total liabilities) he contributes. The journal entries to open the books of the partnership of Blair and Cross are as follows:

Formation of Partnership	*Cash*	*20,000*	
	Accounts Receivable	*30,000*	
	Inventory	*45,000*	
	Accounts Payable		*15,000*
	John Blair, Capital		*80,000*
	To record the investment by John Blair in the partnership of Blair and Cross.		
	Cash	*5,000*	
	Land	*30,000*	
	Building	*50,000*	
	Inventory	*30,000*	
	Accounts Payable		*35,000*
	Richard Cross, Capital		*80,000*
	To record the investment by Richard Cross in the partnership of Blair and Cross.		

The values assigned to assets on the books of the new partnership may be quite different from the amounts at which these assets were carried on the books of their previous owners. For example, the land contributed by Cross and now valued at $30,000 might have appeared on his books at a cost of $10,000. The building which he contributed was valued at $50,000 by the partnership, but it might have cost Cross only $40,000 some years ago and might have been depreciated on his records to a net value of $35,000. Assuming that market values of land and buildings had risen sharply while Cross owned this property, it is no more than fair to recognize the present market value of these assets at the time he transfers them to the partnership and to credit his capital account accordingly. Depreciation of the building will begin anew on the partnership books (except for income tax purposes) and will be based on the assigned value of $50,000 at date of acquisition by the partnership.

Additional investments

Assume that after six months of operation the firm is in need of more cash, and will be based on the assigned value of $50,000 at date of acquisition by the partnership.

Recording	*Cash* *10,000*	
Additional	*John Blair, Capital*	*5,000*
Investments	*Richard Cross, Capital*	*5,000*
	To record additional investments by Blair and Cross.	

Withdrawals by partners

In our example of the Blair and Cross partnership, we might assume that the partners made numerous withdrawals during the year. Such withdrawals are represented by the following summary entry:

Recording	*John Blair, Drawing* *6,000*	
Withdrawals	*Richard Cross, Drawing* *4,000*	
by Partners	*Cash*	*10,000*
	To record withdrawals of cash by partners.	

Closing the books of a partnership

The revenue and expense accounts of a partnership are closed into the Income Summary account in the same way as for a corporation. However, the net income or net loss shown by the Income Summary account is closed into the partners' Capital accounts rather than to a Retained Earnings account. Finally, the Drawing accounts are closed by transferring their balances into the partners' Capital accounts. The following entries illustrate these procedures:

Dividing	*Income Summary*		30,000	
the	*John Blair, Capital*		15,000
Net	*Richard Cross, Capital*		15,000
Income	*To transfer net income of $30,000 for the year from the Income Summary account to the partners' Capital accounts. Blair and Cross share income equally.*		

Closing	*John Blair, Capital*	6,000	
the	*Richard Cross, Capital*	4,000	
Drawing	*John Blair, Drawing*		6,000
Accounts	*Richard Cross, Drawing*		4,000
	To close the Drawing accounts by transferring their debit balances to the respective Capital accounts.		

Income statement and income distribution for a partnership

The income statement for a partnership may include a final section to show the division of the net income between the partners, as illustrated below for the firm of Blair and Cross.

Note Distribution of Net Income

BLAIR AND CROSS
Income Statement
For the Year Ended December 31, 19___

Sales		$300,000
Less: Cost of goods sold:		
Inventory, Jan. 1	$ 75,000	
Purchases.................................	155,000	
Cost of goods available for sale	$230,000	
Less: Inventory, Dec. 31	100,000	
Cost of goods sold		130,000
Gross profit on sales		$170,000
Less: Operating expenses:		
Selling expenses........................	$100,000	
General & administrative expenses.............	40,000	140,000
Net income		$ 30,000
Distribution of net income:		
To John Blair (50%)	$ 15,000	
To Richard Cross (50%)	15,000	$ 30,000

In our example, Blair and Cross divided net income equally. Partners can, however, share net income in any way they wish. Factors that partners might consider in arriving at an equitable plan to divide net income include

(1) the amount of time each partner devotes to the business, (2) the amount of capital invested by each partner, and (3) any other contribution by each partner to the success of the partnership. Net income, for example, may be shared in any agreed ratio such as 4 to 1, in the ratio of average capital invested, or in a fixed ratio after an allowance is made to each partner for salary and interest on capital invested.

Assume that the partnership of Adams and Barnes earned $24,000 (before interest and salary allowances to partners) in 1971, and that they had agreed to share net income as follows:

1. Salary allowances of $6,000 per year to Adams and $12,000 per year to Barnes. (Partners' salaries are merely a device for sharing net income and are not necessarily withdrawn from the business.)

2. Interest at 6% on average capitals to be allowed to each partner. Average capital balances for Adams and Barnes amounted to $40,000 and $10,000 respectively.

3. Any amount in excess of the foregoing salary and interest allowances to be divided equally.

Pursuant to this agreement, the net income of $24,000 would be divided between Adams and Barnes as follows:

Income Sharing; Salaries, Interest, and Fixed Ratio as Basis

Distribution of Net Income			
Net income to be divided			$24,000
Salaries to partners:			
Adams	$ 6,000		
Barnes	12,000	$18,000	
Interest on average capitals:			
Adams ($40,000 × 0.06)	$ 2,400		
Barnes ($10,000 × 0.06)	600	3,000	21,000
Remaining net income to be divided equally			$ 3,000
Adams	$ 1,500		
Barnes	1,500	3,000	

This three-step division of the year's net income of $24,000 has resulted in giving Adams a total of $9,900 and Barnes a total of $14,100. The amounts credited to each partner may be summarized as follows:

	Adams	Barnes	Total
Salaries	$6,000	$12,000	$18,000
Interest on average capitals	2,400	600	3,000
Remaining income divided equally	1,500	1,500	3,000
Totals	$9,900	$14,100	$24,000

The entry to close the Income Summary account will be:

Income Summary	*24,000*	
Adams, Capital		*9,900*
Barnes, Capital		*14,100*
To close the Income Summary account by crediting each partner with his authorized salary, with interest on his average capital at 6%, and by dividing the remaining income equally.		

Authorized salaries and interest in excess of net income. In the preceding example the total of the authorized salaries and interest was $21,000 and the net income to be divided was $24,000. Suppose that the net income had been only $15,000; how should the division have been made?

If the partnership contract provides for salaries and interest on invested capital, these provisions are to be followed even though the net income for the year is less than the total of the authorized salaries and interest. If the net income of the firm of Adams and Barnes amounted to only $15,000, this amount would be distributed as follows:

Authorized Salaries and Interest May Exceed Net Income	*Distribution of Net Income*			
	Net income to be divided			*$15,000*
	Salaries to partners:			
	Adams	*$ 6,000*		
	Barnes	*12,000*	*$18,000*	
	Interest on average capitals:			
	Adams ($40,000 × 0.06)	*$ 2,400*		
	Barnes ($10,000 × 0.06)	*600*	*3,000*	*21,000*
	Residual loss to be divided equally			*$ 6,000*
	Adams		*$ 3,000*	
	Barnes		*3,000*	*6,000*

The result of this distribution of the net income of $15,000 has been to give Adams a total of $5,400 and Barnes a total of $9,600.

Partnerships are not required to pay income taxes; however, a partnership is required to file an information tax return showing the amount of the partnership net income and the share of each partner in the net income. Each partner must include his share of the partnership net income (including interest and salary allowances) on his individual income tax return, regardless of the amount that he actually withdrew from the business. Partnership net income is thus taxable to the partners individually in the year in which it is earned.

Statement of partners' capitals

The partners will usually want an explanation of the change in their capital accounts from one year-end to the next. A supplementary schedule called a *statement of partners' capitals* is prepared to show this information and is illustrated below for Blair and Cross:

Changes in Partners' Capital Accounts during the Year

BLAIR AND CROSS			
Statement of Partners' Capitals			
For the Year Ended December 31, 19____			
	Blair	*Cross*	*Total*
Investment, Jan., 19____	$ 80,000	$ 80,000	$160,000
Add: Additional investment, July, 19____	5,000	5,000	10,000
Net income for the year	15,000	15,000	30,000
Totals	$100,000	$100,000	$200,000
Less: Withdrawals	6,000	4,000	10,000
Balances, Dec. 31, 19____	$ 94,000	$ 96,000	$190,000

The balance sheet for Blair and Cross would show the capital balance for each partner, as well as the total of $190,000.

Other aspects of partnership accounting

The foregoing discussion of partnership accounting is by no means exhaustive. The admission of a new partner to the partnership, the withdrawal of a partner, and the liquidation of a partnership, for example, may raise some very complex accounting issues. These issues are primarily of interest to advanced accounting students and for that reason are not included in this introductory text.

CORPORATIONS

The corporation has become the dominant form of business organization in America, largely because it can bring together vast amounts of capital more readily than single proprietorships or partnerships. Because of its ability to pool the savings of many individuals, the corporation is an ideal means of obtaining the capital necessary for large-scale operations.

The corporation has been defined as "an artificial being . . . existing only in contemplation of the law." The corporation is regarded as a legal person, having a continuous existence apart from that of its owners. By way of contrast, we have seen that a partnership is a relatively unstable type of organization which is dissolved by the death or retirement of any one of its members, whereas the continuous existence of a corporation is in no way threatened by the death of a stockholder.

Ownership in a corporation is evidenced by transferable shares of stock, and the owners are called *stockholders* or *shareholders*. To administer the affairs of the corporation, the stockholders elect a *board of directors*. The directors in turn select a president and other corporate officers to carry on active management of the corporation.

Advantages of the corporate form of organization

The corporation offers a number of advantages not available in other forms of organization. Among these advantages are the following:

1. Greater amounts of capital can be gathered together. Some corporations have a half million or more stockholders. The sale of stock is a means of obtaining funds from the general public; both small and large investors find stock ownership a convenient means of participating in ownership of business enterprise.

2. Limited liability. Creditors of a corporation have a claim against the assets of the corporation only, not against the personal property of the owners of the corporation. Since a stockholder has no personal liability for the debts of the corporation, he can never lose more than the amount of his investment.

3. Shares of stock in a corporation are readily transferable. The ease of disposing of all or part of one's stockholdings in a corporation makes this form of investment particularly attractive.

4. Continuous existence. A corporation is a separate legal entity with a perpetual existence. The continuous life of the corporation despite changes in ownership is made possible by the issuance of transferable shares of stock.

5. Centralized authority. The power to make all kinds of operating decisions is lodged in the president of a corporation. He may delegate to others limited authority for various phases of operations, but he retains final authority over the entire business.

6. Professional management. The person who owns a few shares of stock in a large corporation usually has neither the time nor the knowledge of the business necessary for intelligent participation in operating problems. Because of this the functions of management and of ownership are sharply separated in the corporate form of organization, and the corporation is free to employ as executives the best managerial talent available.

Disadvantages of the corporate form of organization

Among the disadvantages of the corporation are:

1. Heavy taxation. A corporation must pay a high rate of taxation on its income. If part of its net income is distributed to the owners in the form of dividends, the dividends are considered to be personal income to the stockholders and are subject to personal income tax. This practice of first taxing corporate income to the corporation and then dividends to the stockholder is referred to as *double taxation.*

2. Greater regulation. Corporations come into existence under the terms of state laws and these same laws may provide for considerable regulation of the corporation's activities. For example, the withdrawal of funds from a corporation is subject to certain limits set by law. Large corporations, especially those with securities listed on stock exchanges, have gradually come to accept the necessity for extensive public disclosure of their affairs.

3. *Separation of ownership and control.* The separation of the functions of ownership and management may be an advantage in some cases but a disadvantage in others. On the whole, the excellent record of growth and earnings in most large corporations indicates that the separation of ownership and control has benefited rather than injured stockholders. In a few instances, however, a management group has chosen to operate a corporation for the benefit of insiders (for example, paying excessive executive salaries and bonuses). The stockholders may find it difficult in such cases to take the concerted action necessary to oust the officers.

Formation of a corporation

To form a corporation, an application signed by at least three incorporators is submitted to the corporation commissioner (or other designated official) of the state in which the company is to be incorporated. The approved application contains the *articles of incorporation* and becomes the company *charter.* The incorporators (who have subscribed for capital stock and therefore are now stockholders) hold a meeting to elect *directors* and to pass *bylaws* as a guide to the company's affairs. The directors in turn hold a meeting at which officers of the corporation are appointed. Capital stock certificates are then issued and the formation of the corporation is complete.

Organization costs. The formation of a corporation is a much more costly step than the organization of a partnership. The necessary costs include the payment of an incorporation fee to the state, the payment of fees to attorneys for their services in drawing up the articles of incorporation, payments to promoters, and a variety of other outlays necessary to bring the corporation into existence. These costs are charged to an asset account called Organization Costs.

The result of organization costs is the existence of the corporate entity; consequently, the benefits derived from these costs may be regarded as extending over the entire life of the corporation. Since the life of a corporation is indefinite, organization costs may be carried at the full amount until the corporation is liquidated. Because present income tax law permits organization costs to be written off over a period of five years or more, most companies elect to write off organization costs over a period of five years.

The rights of stockholders. The ownership of stock in a corporation usually carries the following basic rights:

1. To vote for directors, and thereby to be represented in the management of the business. The approval of a majority of stockholders may also be required for such important corporate actions as mergers and acquisitions, the selection of auditors, the incurring of long-term debts, establishment of stock option plans, or the splitting of capital stock into a larger number of shares.

2. To share in profits by receiving dividends declared by the board of directors.

3. To share in the distribution of assets if the corporation is liquidated. When a corporation ends its existence, the creditors of the corporation must first be paid in full; any remaining assets are divided among stockholders in proportion to the number of shares owned.

4. To subscribe for additional shares in the event that the corporation decides to increase the amount of stock outstanding. This *preemptive right* entitles each stockholder to maintain his percentage of ownership in the company by subscribing, in proportion to his present stockholdings, to any additional shares issued. Corporations organized in certain states do not grant preemptive rights to their stockholders. In other cases stockholders sometimes agree to waive their preemptive rights in order to grant more flexibility to management in negotiating mergers.

The ownership of stock does not give a stockholder the right to intervene in the management of a corporation or to transact business in its behalf. Although the stockholders as a group own the corporation, they do not personally own the assets of the corporation; neither do they personally owe the debts of the corporation. The stockholders have no direct claim on income earned; income earned by a corporation does not become income to the stockholders unless the board of directors orders the distribution of the income to stockholders in the form of a cash dividend.

Stockholders' meetings are usually held once a year. Each share of stock is entitled to one vote. In large corporations, these annual meetings are usually attended by relatively few persons, often by less than 1% of the stockholders. Prior to the meeting, the management group will request stockholders who do not plan to attend in person to send in *proxy statements* assigning their votes to the existing management. Through this use of the proxy system, management may secure the right to vote as much as, perhaps, 90% or more of the total outstanding shares.

The role of the board of directors. The board of directors is elected by the stockholders; the primary functions of the board are to manage the corporation and to protect the interests of the stockholders. At this level, management may consist principally of formulating policies and reviewing acts of the officers. Specific duties of the directors include declaring dividends, setting the salaries of officers, authorizing officers to arrange loans from banks, and authorizing important contracts of various kinds.

The responsibilities of corporate officers. Corporate officers usually include a president, one or more vice-presidents, a controller, a treasurer, and a secretary. A vice-president is often made responsible for the sales function; other vice-presidents may be given responsibility for such important functions as personnel, finance, production, and research and development.

The responsibilities of the controller, treasurer, and secretary are most directly related to the accounting phase of business operation. The *controller* is the chief accounting officer. He is responsible for the maintenance of adequate internal control and for the preparation of accounting records and financial statements. Such specialized activities as budgeting, tax planning, and preparation of tax returns are usually placed under his jurisdiction. The *treasurer* has custody of the company's funds and is generally responsible for planning and controlling the company's cash position. The *secretary* maintains minutes of the meetings of directors and stockholders and represents the corporation in many contractual and legal matters. Another of his responsibilities is to coordinate the preparation of the *annual report,* which includes the financial statements and other information relating to corporate activities. In small corporations, one officer frequently acts as both secretary and treasurer.

Sources of corporate capital

Corporations may raise capital by borrowing money, by issuing capital stock, or by retaining the funds provided by profitable operations after payment of income taxes. Borrowing, for example, may be in the form of short-term notes in order to meet seasonal and temporary needs, or the corporation may issue long-term bonds in order to meet more or less permanent needs for capital. Notes and bonds payable will be discussed in Chapter 12; capital raised through issuance of stock and through profitable operations will be discussed in the remaining pages of this chapter.

Up to this point, we have assumed that the stockholders' equity of a corporation is carried in only two ledger accounts, Capital Stock and Retained Earnings. In this chapter we shall see that different classes of capital stock may be issued by a corporation and that capital stock may be issued at a price which differs from the par or stated value. At the end of each accounting period, the balance of the Income Summary account (after income taxes have been recognized) is closed into the Retained Earnings account; dividends distributed to stockholders serve to reduce the Retained Earnings account. Consequently, the balance of the Retained Earnings account at any balance sheet date represents the accumulated earnings of the company since the date of incorporation, minus any losses and minus all dividends distributed to stockholders. (Various types of dividends are discussed in Chapter 8.) Alternative names for the Retained Earnings account include Earned Surplus, Accumulated Earnings, and Reinvested Income.

Stockholders' equity in the balance sheet. For a corporation with $100,000 of capital stock and $40,000 of retained earnings, the stockholders' equity section of the balance sheet will appear as follows:

Paid-in Capital and Earned Capital	*Stockholders' equity:*		
	Capital stock	*$100,000*	
	Retained earnings	*40,000*	*$140,000*

If this same company had been unprofitable and had incurred losses aggregating $30,000 since its organization, the stockholders' equity section of the balance sheet would be as follows:

Paid-in Capital Reduced by Losses Incurred

Stockholders' equity:		
Capital stock....................................	$100,000	
Less: Deficit.....................................	30,000	$70,000

This second illustration tells us that $30,000 of the original $100,000 invested by stockholders has been lost. Note that the capital stock in both illustrations remains at the fixed amount of $100,000, the stockholders' original investment. The accumulated earnings or losses since the organization of the corporation are shown as retained earnings (or as a deficit) and are not intermingled with paid-in capital.

Income taxes in corporate financial statements. A corporation is a legal entity subject to corporation income tax; consequently, the ledger of a corporation should include accounts for recording income taxes. No such accounts are needed for a business organized as a single proprietorship or partnership.

Income taxes are based on a corporation's earnings. At year-end, before preparing financial statements, income taxes are recorded by an adjusting entry such as the following:

Recording Corporate Income Taxes

Income Taxes	45,650	
Income Taxes Payable.....................		45,650
To record the income taxes payable for the year ended Dec. 31, 19___.		

The account debited in this entry, Income Taxes, is an expense account and usually appears as the very last deduction in the income statement as follows:

Final Step in Income Statement

Income before income taxes........................	$100,000
Income taxes.......................................	45,650
Net income	$ 54,350

The liability account, Income Taxes Payable, will ordinarily be paid within a few months and should, therefore, appear in the current liability section of the balance sheet. More detailed discussion of corporation taxes is presented in Chapter 17.

AUTHORIZATION AND ISSUANCE OF CAPITAL STOCK

The articles of incorporation specify the number of shares of capital stock which a corporation is authorized to issue and the par value, if any, per share. The corporation may choose not to issue immediately all of the authorized shares; in fact, it is customary to secure authorization for a larger number of shares than presently needed. In future years, if more capital is needed, the previously authorized shares will be readily available for issue; otherwise, the corporation would be forced to apply to the state for permission to alter its charter by increasing the number of authorized shares.

Capital stock outstanding

The unit of stock ownership is the share, but the corporation may issue stock certificates in denominations of 10 shares, 100 shares, or any other number. The total capital stock outstanding at any given time represents 100% ownership of the corporation. Outstanding shares are those in the hands of stockholders. Assume, for example, that the Draper Corporation is organized with authorization to issue 100,000 shares of stock. However, only 50,000 shares are issued, because this amount of stock provides all the capital presently needed. The holders of the 50,000 shares of stock own the corporation in its entirety.

If we assume further that Thomas Draper acquires 5,000 shares of the 50,000 shares outstanding, we may say that he has a 10% interest in the corporation. Suppose that Draper now sells 2,000 shares to Evans. The total number of shares outstanding remains unchanged at 50,000, although Draper's percentage of ownership has declined to 6% and a new stockholder, Evans, has acquired a 4% interest in the corporation. The transfer of 2,000 shares from Draper to Evans had no effect upon the corporation's assets, liabilities, or amount of stock outstanding. The only way in which this transfer of stock affects the corporation is that the list of stockholders must be revised to show the number of shares held by each owner.

Preferred and common stock

In order to appeal to as many investors as possible, a corporation may issue more than one kind of stock, just as an automobile manufacturer may make sedans, convertibles, and station wagons in order to appeal to various groups of car buyers. When only one type of stock is issued, it must be *common stock*, although it is often referred to as *capital stock*. Common stock has the four basic rights previously mentioned. Whenever these rights are modified, the term *preferred stock* (or sometimes Class B Common) is used to describe this second type of stock. A few corporations issue two or three classes of preferred stock, each class having certain distinctive features designed to interest a particular type of investor. In summary, we may say that every business corporation has common stock; a good many corporations also issue preferred stock; and a few companies have two or more types of preferred stock.

Common stock may be regarded as the basic, residual element of ownership. It carries voting rights and, therefore is the means of exercising control over the business. Common stock has unlimited possibilities of increase in value; during the last decade the market prices of common stocks of some leading corporations rose to three or four times their former values. On the other hand, common stocks lose value more rapidly than other types of securities when corporations encounter periods of unprofitable business.

The following stockholders' equity section illustrates the balance sheet presentation for a corporation having both preferred and common stock; note that the item of retained earnings is not apportioned between the two groups of stockholders.

Balance Sheet Presentation of Stockholders' Equity	**Stockholders' equity:**

Stockholders' equity:

Preferred stock, 5% cumulative, $100 par value, authorized and issued 100,000 shares	$10,000,000
Common stock, $5 par value, authorized and issued 1 million shares	5,000,000
Total paid-in capital	$15,000,000
Retained earnings	3,500,000
Total stockholders' equity	$18,500,000

Characteristics of preferred stock. Most preferred stocks have the following distinctive features:

1. Preferred as to dividends
2. Preferred as to assets in event of the liquidation of the company
3. Callable at stated prices at the option of the corporation
4. No voting power

Another very important but less common feature is a clause permitting the conversion of preferred stock into common at the option of the holder. Preferred stocks vary widely with respect to the special rights and privileges granted. Careful study of the terms of the individual preferred stock contract is a necessary step in the evaluation of any preferred stock.

Stock preferred as to dividends. Stock preferred as to dividends is entitled to receive each year a dividend of specified amount before any dividend is paid on the common stock. The dividend is usually stated as a dollar amount per share. For example, the balance sheet of General Motors Corporation shows two types of preferred stock outstanding, one paying $5.00 a year and the other $3.75 a year, as shown on page 216.

Some preferred stocks state the dividend preference as a percentage of par value. For example, a 5% preferred stock with a par value of $100 per share would mean that $5 must be paid yearly on each share of preferred stock before any dividends are paid to the common.

The holder of a preferred stock has no assurance that he will always receive the indicated dividend. A corporation is obligated to pay dividends to stockholders only when the board of directors declares a dividend. Divi-

<table>
<tr><td>

Dividend
Stated as
Dollar
Amount

</td><td>

Capital stock:
  Preferred, without par value (authorized 6,000,000 shares):
    $5.00 series, stated value $100 per share, redeemable at $120
      per share (issued, 1,875,366 shares; in treasury 39,722 shares;
      outstanding, 1,835,644 shares) *$183,564,400*
    $3.75 series, stated value $100 per share, redeemable at $101
      per share (issued and outstanding, 1,000,000 shares) *100,000,000*

</td></tr>
</table>

dends must be paid on preferred stock before anything is paid to the common stockholders, but if the corporation is not prospering, it may decide not to pay dividends on either preferred or common stock. For a corporation to pay dividends, profits must be earned and cash must be available. However, preferred stocks in general offer more assurance of regular dividend payments than do common stocks.

Cumulative preferred stock. The dividend preference carried by most preferred stocks is a *cumulative* one. If all or any part of the regular dividend on the preferred stock is omitted in a given year, the amount in arrears must be paid in a subsequent year before any dividend can be paid on the common stock. Assume that a corporation was organized January 1, 1971, with 1,000 shares of $4 cumulative preferred stock and 1,000 shares of common stock. Dividends paid in 1971 were at the rate of $4 per share of preferred stock and $3 per share of common. In 1972, earnings declined sharply and the only dividend paid was $1 per share on the preferred stock. No dividends were paid in 1973. What is the status of the preferred stock as of December 31, 1973? Dividends are in arrears in the amount of $7 a share ($3 omitted during 1972 and $4 omitted in 1973). On the entire issue of 1,000 shares of preferred stock, the dividends in arrears amount to $7,000.

In 1974, we shall assume that the company earned large profits and wished to pay dividends on both the preferred and common stocks. Before paying a dividend on the common, the corporation must pay the $7,000 in arrears on the cumulative preferred stock plus the regular $4 a share applicable to the current year. The preferred stockholders would, therefore, receive a total of $11,000 in dividends in 1974; the board of directors would then be free to declare dividends on the common stock.

Dividends in arrears *are not listed among the liabilities of a corporation,* because no liability exists until a dividend is declared by the board of directors. Nevertheless, the amount of any dividends in arrears on preferred stock is an important factor to investors and should always be disclosed. This disclosure is usually made by a note accompanying the balance sheet such as the following:

"As of December 31, 1973, dividends on the $4 cumulative preferred stock were in arrears to the extent of $7 per share, and amounted in total to $7,000."

For a *noncumulative preferred stock,* any unpaid or omitted dividend is lost forever. Because of this factor, investors view the noncumulative feature as an unfavorable element, and very few noncumulative preferred stocks are issued.

Participating clauses in preferred stock. Since participating preferred stocks are very seldom issued, discussion of them will be brief. A fully participating preferred stock is one which, in addition to the regular specified dividend, is entitled to participate in some manner with the common stock in any additional dividends paid. For example, a $5 participating preferred stock would be entitled to receive $5 a share before the common stock received anything. After $5 a share had been paid to the preferred stockholders, a $5 dividend could be paid on the common stock. If the company desired to pay an additional dividend to the common, say, an extra $3 per share, the preferred stock would also be entitled to receive an extra $3 dividend. In brief, a fully participating preferred stock participates dollar for dollar with the common stock in any dividends paid in excess of the stated rate on the preferred.

Stock preferred as to assets. Most preferred stocks carry a preference as to assets in the event of liquidation of the corporation. If the business is terminated, the preferred stock is entitled to payment in full of a stated liquidation value (or par value) before any payment is made on the common stock. This priority also includes any dividends in arrears.

Callable preferred stock. Most preferred stocks are callable at the option of the corporation at a stipulated price, usually slightly above the issuance price. The *call price* or *redemption price* for a $100 par value preferred stock is often $103 or $104 per share.

In the financing of a new or expanding corporation, the organizers usually hold common stock, which assures them control of the company. However, it is often necessary to obtain outside capital. One way of doing this, without the loss of control or any serious reduction in possible future earnings on the common stock, is to issue a callable preferred stock.

It may be argued that the position of the holder of a callable preferred stock is more like that of a creditor than that of an owner. He supplies capital to the company for an agreed rate of return, has no voice in management, and may find his relationship with the company terminated at any time through the calling in of his certificate. If a company is so fortunate as to enter upon a period of unusually high earnings, it will probably increase the dividend payments on its common stock, but it will not consider increasing the income of the preferred stockholder. On the contrary, the corporation may decide that this era of prosperity is a good time to eliminate the preferred stock through exercise of the call provision.

Regardless of the fact that preferred stock lacks many of the traditional aspects of ownership, it is universal practice to include all types of preferred stock in the stockholders' equity section of the balance sheet.

Convertible preferred stock. In order to add to the attractiveness of preferred stock as an investment, corporations sometimes offer a conversion privilege which entitles the preferred stockholder to exchange his shares for common stock in a stipulated ratio. If the corporation prospers, its common stock will probably rise in market value, and dividends on the common stock will probably be increased. The investor who buys a convertible preferred stock rather than common stock has greater assurance of regular dividends. In addition, through the conversion privilege, he is assured of sharing in any substantial increase in value of the company's common stock.

As an example, assume that the Remington Corporation issued a 5%, $100 par, convertible preferred stock on January 1, at a price of $100 a share. Each share was convertible into four shares of the company's no-par value common stock at any time. The common stock has a market price of $20 a share on January 1, and an annual dividend of 60 cents a share was being paid. The yield on the preferred stock was 5% ($5 ÷ $100); the yield on the common stock was only 3% ($0.60 ÷ $20).

During the next few years, the Remington Corporation's earnings increased, the dividend on the common stock was raised to an annual rate of $1.50, and the market price of the common stock rose to $40 a share. At this point the preferred stock would have a market value of at least $160, since it could be converted at any time into four shares of common stock with a market value of $40 each. In other words, the market value of a convertible preferred stock will tend to move in accordance with the price of the common. When the dividend rate is increased on the common stock, many holders of the preferred stock will convert their holdings into common stock in order to obtain a higher return on their investments.

If the holder of 100 shares of the preferred stock presented these shares for conversion, the Remington Corporation would make the following entry:

Conversion of Pre-ferred Stock into Common	*5% Convertible Preferred Stock* 10,000	
	Common Stock	10,000
	To record the conversion of 100 shares of preferred stock, par $100, into 400 shares of no-par value common stock.	

The preceding illustration was based on the assumption that the Remington Corporation enjoyed larger earnings after the issuance of its convertible preferred. Let us now take a contrary assumption and say that shortly after issuance of the convertible preferred stock, the company's profits declined and the directors deemed it necessary to cut the annual dividend on the common stock from 60 cents a share to 20 cents a share. A stockholder who acquired common stock at a cost of $20 a share now finds that his dividend income has dropped to a rate of 1% ($.20 ÷ $20 cost). The dividend on the preferred stock remains at $5 a share.

These two illustrations indicate that the convertible preferred stock has two important advantages from the viewpoint of the investor: it increases in value along with the common stock when the company prospers, and it offers greater assurance of steady dividend income during a period of poor earnings.

Par value

In an earlier period of the history of American corporations, all capital stock had par value, but in more recent years state laws have permitted corporations to choose between par value stock and no-par value stock. The corporate charter always states the par value, if any, of the shares to be issued.

Par value may be $1 per share, $5, $100, or any other amount decided upon by the corporation. The par value of the stock is no indication of its market value; the par value merely indicates the amount per share to be entered in the Capital Stock account. The par value of most common stocks is relatively low. Polaroid Corporation common stock, for example, has a par value of $1; General Motors Corporation common stock has a par of $1⅔; Pan American World Airways, Inc., stock has a par value of 25 cents per share. The market value of all these securities is significantly above their par value.

The chief significance of par value is that it represents the *legal capital* per share; that is, the amount below which stockholders' equity cannot be reduced except by (1) losses from business operations, or (2) legal action taken by a majority vote of stockholders. A dividend cannot be declared by a corporation if such action would cause the stockholders' equity to fall below the par value of the outstanding shares. Par value, therefore, may be regarded as a minimum cushion of capital existing for the protection of creditors.

Issuance of capital stock

Mere authorization of a stock issue does not bring an asset into existence, nor does it give the corporation any capital. The obtaining of authorization from the state for a stock issue merely affords a legal opportunity to obtain assets through sale of stock.

When par value stock is issued, the Capital Stock account is credited with the par value of the shares issued, regardless of whether the issuance price is more or less than par. Assuming that 6,000 of the authorized 10,000 shares of $10 par value shares are issued at a price of $10 each, Cash would be debited and Capital Stock would be credited for $60,000. When stock is sold for more than par value, the Capital Stock account is credited with the par value of the shares issued, and a separate account, Paid-in Capital in Excess of Par Value, is credited for the excess of selling price over par. If, for example, the issuance price is $15, the entry is as follows:

Stockholders'	Cash 90,000
Invest-	*Capital Stock, $10 par* 60,000
ment in	*Paid-in Capital in Excess of Par Value* 30,000
Excess of	*Issued 6,000 shares of $10 par value stock at a price of $15 a*
Par Value	*share.*

An alternative title for the account Paid-In Capital in Excess of Par Value is Premium on Capital Stock. The premium or amount received in excess of par value does not represent a profit to the corporation. It is part of the invested capital and it will be added to the capital stock on the balance sheet to show the total paid-in capital. The stockholders' equity section of the balance sheet would be as follows (the existence of $10,000 in retained earnings is assumed in order to have a complete illustration):

Corporation's Capital Classified by Source	*Stockholders' equity:*	
	Capital stock, $10 par value, authorized 10,000 shares, issued and outstanding 6,000 shares	*$ 60,000*
	Paid-in capital in excess of par value	*30,000*
	Total paid-in capital	*$ 90,000*
	Retained earnings	*10,000*
	Total stockholders' equity	*$100,000*

If stock is issued by a corporation for less than par, the account Discount on Capital Stock should be debited for the difference between the issuance price and the par value. Sale of stock at a discount is seldom encountered; it is illegal in many states.

The underwriting of stock issues

When a large amount of stock is to be issued, the corporation will probably utilize the services of an investment banking firm, frequently referred to as an *underwriter.* The underwriter guarantees the issuing corporation a specific price for the stock and makes a profit by selling the stock to the investing public at a higher price. For example, an issue of 1,050,000 shares of $1 par value common stock might be sold to the public at a price of $21 a share, of which $1.20 a share is retained by the underwriter and $19.80 represents the net proceeds to the issuing corporation.[1] The corporation would enter on its books only the net amount received from the underwriter ($19.80) for each share issued. The use of an underwriter assures the corporation that the entire stock issue will be sold without delay, and the entire amount of funds to be raised will be available on a specific date.

Market price of common stock

The preceding sections concerning the issuance of stock at prices above and below par raise a question as to how the market price of stock is determined. The price which the corporation sets on a new issue of stock is based

---

[1] These figures are taken from a prospectus issued by the Western Gear Corporation covering the issuance of 375,000 shares by the corporation and 675,000 shares by stockholders in an initial public offering by the corporation. Figures taken from the face of the prospectus follow:

	Price to Public	Underwriting Discount	Proceeds to Company	Proceeds to Selling Stockholders°
Per share	$21.00	$1.20	$19.80	$19.80
Total	$22,050,000	$1,260,000	$7,425,000	$13,365,000

° Before deducting expenses estimated at $120,000.

on several factors including (1) an appraisal of the company's expected future earnings, (2) the probable dividend rate per share, (3) the present financial condition of the company, and (4) the current state of the investment market.

After the stock has been issued, the price at which it will be traded among investors will tend to reflect the progress of the company, with primary emphasis being placed on earnings and dividends per share. *Earnings per share* of common stock, for example, is computed by dividing the annual net income available to the common stock by the number of shares outstanding. At this point in our discussion, the significant fact to emphasize is that market price is not related to par value, and that it tends to reflect current and future earnings and dividends.

Stock issued for assets other than cash

Corporations generally sell their capital stock for cash and use the cash obtained in this way to buy the various types of assets needed in the business. Sometimes, however, a corporation may issue shares of its capital stock in a direct exchange for land, buildings, or other assets. Stock may also be issued in payment for services rendered by accountants, attorneys, and promoters.

When a corporation issues capital stock in exchange for services or for assets other than cash, a question arises as to the proper valuation of the property or services received. For example, assume that a corporation issues 1,000 shares of its $1 par value common stock in exchange for a tract of land. A problem may exist in determining the fair market value of the land, and consequently in determining the amount of paid-in capital. If there is no direct evidence of the value of the land, we may value it by using indirect evidence as to the alternative amount of cash for which the shares might have been sold. Assume that the company's stock is listed on a stock exchange and is presently selling at $90 a share. The 1,000 shares which the corporation exchanged for the land could have been sold for $90,000 cash, and the cash could have been used to pay for the land. The direct exchange of stock for land may be considered as the equivalent of selling the stock for cash and using the cash to buy the land. It is therefore logical to say that the cost of the land to the company was $90,000, the market value of the stock given in exchange for the land. *Note that the par value of the stock is not any indication of the fair value of the stock or of the land.*

Once the valuation question has been decided, the entry to record the issuance of stock in exchange for noncash assets can be made as follows:

How Were	Land	90,000	
Dollar	Common Stock, $1 par value		1,000
Amounts	Paid-in Capital in Excess of Par Value		89,000
Deter-	To record the issuance of 1,000 shares of $1 par value com-		
mined?	mon stock in exchange for land. Current market value of		
	stock ($90 a share) used as basis for valuing the land.		

Par value and no-par value stock

An understanding of no-par stock can best be gained by reviewing the reasons why par value was originally required in an earlier period of American corporate history. The use of the par value concept in state laws was intended for the protection of creditors and of public stockholders. In some states stock could not be issued at less than par value; in most states if stock *was* issued at less than par value the purchaser was contingently liable for the discount below par. A corporation was thus discouraged from selling its stock to the public at, say, $100 a share and concurrently to insiders or promoters at, say, $10 a share.

Protection was also afforded to creditors by laws prohibiting a corporation from paying any dividend which would "impair its capital" (reduce its capital to an amount less than the par value of the outstanding shares). Because of these statutes concerning par value, a creditor of a corporation could tell by inspection of the balance sheet the amount which owners had invested permanently in the corporation. This permanent investment of ownership capital (par value times the number of outstanding shares) represented a buffer which protected the corporation creditor from the impact of any losses sustained by the corporation. Such protection for creditors was considered necessary because stockholders have no personal liability for the debts of the corporation.

The par value device proved rather ineffective in achieving its avowed objective of protecting creditors and stockholders, and in 1912 New York State enacted legislation permitting corporations to issue stock without par value. Other states have since passed similar laws.

When all stock was of the par value type, the par value of the shares issued represented the stated (or legal) capital not available for dividends or withdrawal by stockholders. With the advent of no-par stock, state legislatures attempted to continue the protection of corporate creditors by designating all or part of the amount received by the corporation for its no-par shares as stated capital not subject to withdrawal.

Assume that a corporation is organized in a state which permits the board of directors to establish a stated value on the 100,000 shares authorized, and that the board passed a resolution setting the stated value per share at $5. If a total of 80,000 shares were issued at $12, the journal entry to record the issuance would be:

Note Stated Value per Share

Cash	*960,000*	
Common Stock, $5 stated value		*400,000*
Paid-in Capital in Excess of Stated Value		*560,000*
Issued 80,000 shares of no-par value common stock at $12 each. Stated value set by directors at $5 per share.		

If in the foregoing example the company reported a net income of $25,000 during the first month, the stockholders' equity section of the balance sheet would be as follows:

	Stockholders' equity:	
Only Part of Paid-in Capital in Common Stock Account	*Common stock, no par value, stated value $5 per share, authorized 100,000 shares, issued and outstanding 80,000 shares*	*$400,000*
	Paid-in capital in excess of stated value	*560,000*
	Total paid-in capital	*$960,000*
	Retained earnings	*25,000*
	Total stockholders' equity	*$985,000*

In the absence of a stated value, the entire proceeds on the sale of stock ($960,000) would be credited to the Common Stock account and would be viewed as legal capital.

Subscriptions to capital stock

Small corporations sometimes sell stock on a subscription plan, in which the investor agrees to pay the subscription price at a future date or in a series of installments. For example, Subscriptions Receivable would be debited and Common Stock Subscribed would be credited when the subscription contract was signed. Collections would be credited to Subscriptions Receivable; when the entire subscription price had been collected and the stock issued, Common Stock Subscribed would be debited and Common Stock would be credited.

Special records of corporations

When a corporation first issues its stock, the transaction is between the corporation and the investor; once the stock is outstanding, any further stock transactions are between individuals and do not affect the corporation which issued the stock. However, the corporation must be informed of each such stock transaction so that it can correct its records of stock ownership by eliminating the name of the former owner and adding the name of the new owner.

For a company with a large number of stockholders, it is not practicable to include in the general ledger an account with each stockholder. Instead, a single controlling account entitled Common Stock is carried in the general ledger, and a subsidiary stockholders' ledger with individual stockholders is maintained. (When a great many separate accounts must be maintained, a ledger is usually in the form of a file of cards rather than a book.) In this *stockholders' ledger,* each stockholder's account shows the number of shares which he owns, the certificate numbers, and the dates of acquisition and sale. Entries are not made in dollars but in number of shares.

The large corporation with thousands of stockholders and a steady flow of stock transfers usually turns over the function of maintaining capital stock records to an independent *stock transfer agent* and a *stock registrar.* A bank or trust company serves as stock transfer agent and another bank acts as the stock registrar. When certificates are to be transferred from one owner to another, the certificates are sent to the transfer agent, who cancels them, makes the necessary entries in the stockholders' ledger, and signs new certificates which are forwarded to the stock registrar. The function of the registrar is to prevent any improper issuance of stock certificates.

Another record kept by corporations is the **minutes book**, which consists of a narrative record of all actions taken at official meetings of the corporation's board of directors and of its stockholders. Typical of the actions described in the minutes book are the declaration of dividends by the board of directors, the authorization of important transactions such as mergers, sale of additional stock, bank loans, and the adoption of pension plans.

DEMONSTRATION PROBLEM

Milton Farr and John Garr started separate concrete pipe manufacturing businesses and operated successfully as single proprietorships for many years. In 1961, they agreed to form a partnership, each transferring the assets and liabilities of his business to the new partnership.

Their income-sharing plan has been altered several times since 1961 in order properly to recognize the changing contribution of each partner to the business. The current plan calls for the partnership net income (before deducting interest on capital and partners' salaries) to be distributed as follows:

1. Interest of 8% per year on beginning capital balances.
2. Salary allowances: Farr, $25,000; Garr, $20,000.
3. Balance of net income, if any, 60% to Farr and 40% to Garr.

The interest and salary allowances are to be made to partners regardless of the amount of net income earned by the partnership. Any excess of such allocation over the amount of net income available is to be charged to the two partners in their "residual" income-sharing ratio (60:40).

On December 31, 1970, the records of the partnership show the following information:

FARR AND GARR
Preliminary Balance Sheet
December 31, 1970

Assets			*Liabilities*	
Current assets:				
Cash	$ 180,000		Notes payable	$ 205,000
Notes receivable	60,000		Accounts payable	135,000
Accounts receivable	250,000		Mortgage payable	310,000
Less: Allowance for estimated			Misc. accrued liabilities	20,000
uncollectible accounts	(15,000)		Total liabilities	$ 670,000
Inventories	225,000			
Total current assets	$ 700,000			

Capital

Plant and equipment:			Farr, capital on			
Machinery (net of accum. depr.			Jan. 1, 1970	$500,000		
of $120,000)............		$ 250,000	Farr, drawing......	(36,000)	$ 464,000	
Buildings (net accum. depr. of			Garr, capital on			
$200,000)..............		500,000	Jan. 1, 1970	$400,000		
Land		150,000	Garr, drawing	(30,000)	370,000	
Total plant and equipment		$ 900,000	Net income for 1970..........		96,000	
			Total capital............		$ 930,000	
Total assets		$1,600,000	Total liabilities & capital		$1,600,000	

Incorporation of partnership

The net income of $96,000 was distributed per agreement, and the partners decided to incorporate as the F and G Concrete Corporation, effective January 1, 1971, as follows:

1. Each partner is to receive 25,000 shares of 5% cumulative convertible preferred stock with a stated value of $10 per share. Only 50,000 of these shares are authorized and each share is convertible into two shares of common stock.
2. A total of 100,000 shares of common stock with a stated value of $1 per share will be issued to the partners in proportion to their adjusted capital balance (Item 3 below) after issuance of the preferred stock. A total of 250,000 shares of common stock has been authorized.
3. Books of the partnership will be retained by the corporation; however, the following adjustments will be made to asset and liability balances:
   a. Prepayments of $10,000 consisting of rents, supplies, insurance, etc., have been charged to expense on the partnership's books. The partners wish to report these assets on the opening balance sheet for the corporation.
   b. Costs of organizing the corporation amounting to $12,500 have been inadvertently charged to general expenses by the partnership during 1970.
   c. The accrued liabilities on the partnership balance sheet do not include $3,000 of interest which has accrued on notes payable.

   The activities of the F and G Concrete Corporation during 1971 are summarized as follows:

4. Net income (after income taxes) amounted to $105,000.
5. Dividends of 50 cents per share were paid on the preferred stock and cash dividends of 35 cents per share were paid on the common stock.
6. After all cash dividends were paid, each partner converted one-half of his holdings of the 5% preferred stock into common stock at the contractual rate of two shares of common for each share of preferred stock.

Instructions

a. Distribute the partnership net income for 1970 ($96,000) to the partners pursuant to the income-sharing agreement and show the capital balance for each partner as of December 31, 1970.
b. Starting with the capital balances on December 31, 1970, as determined in part

(a), prepare a schedule adjusting the partners' capital accounts in accordance with the incorporation plan and determine the number of shares of common stock to be issued to each partner. Round shares to be issued to the nearest whole share.

c. Prepare compound entries required
  (1) To adjust the asset and liability balances
  (2) To change to the corporate form of business organization.

d. (1) Determine the balance in retained earnings as of December 31, 1971.
  (2) Prepare an entry to record the conversion of 25,000 shares of preferred stock for 50,000 shares of common stock.
  (3) Prepare the stockholders' equity section of the balance sheet for the F and G Concrete Corporation at December 31, 1971.

QUESTIONS

1. Stevens is the proprietor of a small manufacturing business. He is considering the possibility of joining in partnership with Thomas, whom he considers to be thoroughly competent and congenial. Prepare a brief statement outlining the advantages and disadvantages of the potential partnership to Stevens.

2. Vernon has land having a book value of $7,500 and a fair market value of $20,000, and a building having a book value of $60,000 and a fair market value of $54,500. The land and building represent Vernon's sole capital contribution to a partnership. What is Vernon's capital balance in the new partnership? Why?

3. State the effect of each of the transactions given below on a partner's capital and drawing accounts:
  a. Partner borrows cash from the business, and signs a promissory note.
  b. Partner collects a partnership account receivable while on vacation and uses the cash for personal purposes.
  c. Partner receives in cash the salary allowance provided in the partnership agreement.
  d. Partner takes home merchandise (cost $100; selling price $125) for his personal use.
  e. Partner has loaned money to the partnership. The principal together with interest at 8% is now repaid in cash.

4. Distinguish between corporations and partnerships in terms of the following characteristics:
  a. Owners' liability
  b. Transferability of ownership interest
  c. Continuity of existence
  d. Federal taxation of net income

5. The corporate form of organization is usually considered advantageous for large enterprises. Why do you suppose large firms of certified public accountants or attorneys do not incorporate?

6. Describe three kinds of costs that may be incurred in the process of organizing a corporation. How are such expenditures treated for accounting purposes? Why?

7. Distinguish between paid-in capital and retained earnings of a corporation. Why is such a distinction useful?

8. Describe the usual nature of the following features as they apply to a share of preferred stock:
   a. Cumulative
   b. Participating
   c. Convertible
   d. Callable

9. What is the purpose of assigning a par or stated value to common stock?

10. In 19___, Universal Airlines Company sold 300,000 shares of no-par common stock through underwriters at $21 per share. The company paid $408,000 in underwriting discounts and commissions, thus receiving only $5,892,000. In addition, the company paid other costs of $82,000 in connection with the underwriting.
   a. What benefits did the company receive from the $490,000 of costs and how should this cost be reported on the balance sheet?
   b. Is this a steep price to pay for new financing by an established company?

11. When stock is issued by a corporation in exchange for assets other than cash, the accountant faces the problem of determining the dollar amount at which to record the transaction. Discuss the factors he should consider and explain their significance.

12. State the classification (asset, liability, stockholders' equity, or expense) of each of the following items. If any item does not fit in this classification, explain.
   a. Accumulated earnings
   b. Common stock
   c. Deficit
   d. Organization costs
   e. Paid-in capital in excess of par value
   f. Preferred stock subscribed
   g. Dividends in arrears on preferred stock
   h. Subscriptions receivable on preferred stock

EXERCISES

1. Abrams and Baker open a shoe retailing business on January 3, 19___, and agree to share net income as follows:
   a. Interest at 8% of beginning capital balance. Abrams invested $15,000 in cash, and Baker invested $9,500 in merchandise.
   b. Salary allowances of $8,000 to Abrams and $6,000 to Baker.
   c. Any partnership earnings in excess of the amount required to cover the interest and salary allowances to be divided 45% to Abrams and 55% to Baker.

The partnership net income for the first year of operation amounted to $20,000 before interest and salary allowances. Show how this $20,000 should be divided between the two partners.

2. A and B decide to combine their single proprietorships into a partnership. The partnership is to take over all assets and assume all liabilities of A and B. The balance sheets for A and B are shown below:

	A's Business		B's Business	
	Book Value	Fair Value	Book Value	Fair Value
Cash	$ 1,500	$ 1,500	$ 3,800	$ 3,800
Accounts receivable.............	12,000	11,600	30,000	29,000
Merchandise....................	18,000	20,400	40,000	35,000
Equipment (net)................	23,000	23,500	62,000	76,200
	$54,500	$57,000	$135,800	$144,000
Accounts payable................	$19,500	$19,500	$ 38,500	$ 40,000
Accrued wages..................	600	600	1,000	1,000
A, capital	34,400	36,900		
B, capital			96,300	103,000
	$54,500	$57,000	$135,800	$144,000

Prepare a *classified* balance sheet in good form for A and B immediately following formation of the partnership. Show accounts receivable at $42,000 less an allowance for uncollectible accounts of $1,400.

3. Atlas Mineral Company has outstanding two classes of $100 par value stock: 1,000 shares of 6% cumulative preferred and 5,000 shares of common. The company had a $10,000 deficit at the beginning of the current year, and preferred dividends had not been paid for two years. During the current year, the company earns $50,000. What will be the balance in retained earnings at the end of the current year, if the company pays a dividend of $2 per share on common stock?

4. Clayton Tidyman owns 1,000 shares of convertible preferred stock of North Oil Company each of which is convertible into 1.5 shares of North's common stock. The preferred stock is currently selling at $80 per share and pays a dividend of $2.50 per year. The common stock sells for $50 and pays an annual dividend of $2 per share. Tidyman wants to convert the preferred stock in order to increase his total dividend income, but an accounting student suggests that he sell his preferred stock and then buy 1,500 shares of common on the open market. Tidyman objects to the student's suggestion on the grounds that he would have to pay income taxes at the rate of 25% on the gain from sale of preferred stock, which he had acquired at $68 per share a year ago. Prepare a schedule showing the results under the two alternatives.

5. The following is the stockholders' equity section of the balance sheet as it appeared in a recent annual report of the Continental Baking Company:

Stockholders' equity:
  Capital stock:
    $5.50 dividend cumulative preferred stock; without
        par value
      Authorized—274,425 shares
        Outstanding—128,000 shares, stated at . . . . $ 12,800,000
    Common stock, $2.50 par value
      Authorized—8,000,000 shares
        Issued—4,298,140 shares, stated at   37,955,240
  Retained earnings   72,748,347
        Total stockholders' equity $123,503,587

Complete the following statements from the information given above:

a. The annual dividend requirement on the preferred stock amounts to $_____.

b. Total dividends of $4,983,817 were declared on the preferred and common stock during the year, and the balance in retained earnings at the beginning of the year amounted to $63,770,512. The net income for the year amounted to $_____.

c. The stated value of preferred stock is $_____ per share.

d. The average issuance price of a share of common stock was $_____ per share.

e. Total legal capital amounts to $_____ and total paid-in capital amounts to $_____.

PROBLEMS

7-1 Ronald J. Patten owns a fashion shop. Because he needs additional working capital in the business and has an immediate personal need for $15,000 in cash, Patten agreed on July 31, 1971, to join in partnership with Joseph Gaston. It is agreed that Patten will contribute all noncash assets of his fashion shop to the partnership and will withdraw (from funds supplied by Gaston) $15,000 in cash. Gaston will invest $40,000 in the business. The partnership contract provides that income shall be divided 55% to Patten and 45% to Gaston.

Information as to the assets and liabilities of Patten's business on July 31, 1971, and their agreed valuation is shown below. None of the receivables has been identified as definitely uncollectible.

	Per Patten's Books	Agreed Valuation
Accounts receivable	$34,000	
Allowance for uncollectible accounts	3,200	$28,400
Merchandise	66,400	54,000
Store equipment	12,400	
Accumulated depreciation	4,200	9,000
7% note payable (dated May 1, 1971, due Apr. 30, 1972) . .	24,000	24,420
Accounts payable	14,000	14,000

It is agreed that the new partnership (to be called Latest Fashion Shop) will assume all present debts of Patten's business.

Instructions

a. Make the necessary journal entries to record the formation of the Latest Fashion Shop partnership at July 31, 1971. (Credit Allowance for Uncollectible Accounts $5,600.)

b. At the end of August, after all adjusting entries, the Income Summary account of the Latest Fashion Shop shows a credit balance of $4,500. The partners' drawing accounts have debit balances as follows: Patten, $2,000; Gaston, $1,000. Make the journal entries necessary to complete the closing of the partnership books at the end of August.

c. Prepare a statement of partners' capital for the month of August.

7-2 The information appearing on the trial balance of Felt-Hyde Company at the end of the current year is given below:

Accounts payable	$ 27,000
Accounts receivable	50,000
Accrued liabilities	2,400
Accumulated depreciation: equipment	13,000
Administrative expenses	76,350
Allowance for uncollectible accounts	2,500
Felt, capital (beginning of year)	62,000
Felt, drawing	8,400
Cash	31,000
Equipment	75,000
Hyde, capital (beginning of year)	50,050
Hyde, drawing	6,000
Merchandise inventory (beginning of year)	22,800
Merchandise purchases (including transportation-in)	326,500
Notes payable	10,000
Prepaid expenses	3,100
Sales	522,800
Selling expenses	90,600

There were no changes in partners' capital accounts during the year.

The inventory at the end of the year was $23,500. The partnership agreement provides that partners are to be allowed 10% interest on invested capital as of the beginning of the year and are to divide "residual" net income in the ratio of Felt 60%, Hyde 40%.

Instructions

a. Prepare an income statement for the current year, showing the distribution of net income as illustrated on page 205.

b. Prepare a statement of partners' capital accounts for the current year.

c. Prepare a balance sheet as of the end of the current year.

7-3 The three partners of Kleeman & Company agreed on December 31, 1970, to incorporate their business. The balance sheet of the partnership on this date is shown below:

Assets.....................	$500,000	Accounts payable..........	$125,000
		Kleeman, capital...........	187,500
		Lewis, capital.............	112,500
		Mars, capital.............	75,000
	$500,000		$500,000

The partners applied for and received a charter authorizing 100,000 shares of $10 par value common stock and 10,000 shares of $100 par value 6% cumulative preferred stock. Organization costs amounted to $8,200. On January 1, 1971, the corporation was formed, and each partner was issued, at par, common stock for one-half of his capital interest and preferred stock for the remaining half. The organization costs were paid on January 1 and were not amortized during the year.

During 1971, the corporation earned $125,000 before income taxes. Accounts payable increased by $24,800 during 1971; the only other liability at year-end was income taxes payable. The provision for income taxes is 40% of taxable income. Regular quarterly dividends were paid on preferred stock, and a dividend of $1.50 per share was paid on common stock.

Instructions
Prepare the balance sheet of Kleeman & Company as of December 31, 1971. Show in two separate supporting schedules how you arrive at:
a. The amounts of stock issued
b. The amount of retained earnings at December 31, 1971

7-4   The stockholders' equity section of the Catalina Corporation's balance sheet at the close of the current year is given below:

Stockholders' equity:		
$1.50 preferred stock, $25 par value, authorized		
500,000 shares:		
Issued	$3,600,000	
Subscribed......................	1,800,000	$ 5,400,000
Common stock, no par, $5 stated value,		
authorized 2,000,000 shares		4,100,000
Paid-in capital in excess of par or stated value:		
On preferred stock	$ 270,000	
On common stock	2,542,000	2,812,000
Retained earnings (deficit)		(200,000)
Total stockholders' equity......................		$12,112,000

Among the assets of the corporation appears the following item: subscriptions receivable, $374,400.

Instructions
On the basis of this information, write a brief answer to the following questions, showing any necessary supporting computations.
a. How many shares of preferred and common stock have been issued?
b. How many shares of preferred stock have been subscribed?

    c. What was the average price per share received (including stock subscribed) by the corporation on its preferred stock?

    d. What was the average price per share received by the corporation on its common stock?

    e. What is the average amount per share that subscribers of preferred stock have yet to pay on their subscriptions?

    f. What is the total paid-in capital of the Catalina Corporation?

    g. What is the total legal or stated value of its capital stock?

7-5 Western Oil Corporation has net assets of $3,000,000, represented by $1,000,000 of 6% preferred stock and $2,000,000 of common shares. A prospective investor, Martin Barrett, is interested in comparing the return that will accrue to preferred and common stockholders under five different assumptions as to the corporation's earnings before income taxes. (The following independent cases do *not* represent five successive years, but rather five separate assumptions about the operating results of a single year.)

Case No.	Assumed Rate of Earnings (before Income Taxes) on Net Assets, %	Earnings before Income Taxes
1	2.0	$ 60,000
2	5.0	150,000
3	7.5	225,000
4	10.0	300,000
5	20.0	600,000

The corporation is subject to income taxes at the rate of 22% on the first $25,000 of earnings and 48% on all earnings over $25,000.

Instructions

    a. Prepare a schedule for Barrett showing the relative amounts that would be received by preferred and common stockholders in each of these five cases, assuming that cash equal to 100% of net income after taxes is distributed to stockholders as dividends. Use the following headings:

Earnings before Taxes	Income Taxes	Net Income	Dividend Applicable to			
			Preferred Stock		Common Stock	
			Amount	Percent°	Amount	Percent°

° "Percent" in these columns refers to the return accruing to preferred and common stockholders as a percentage of their respective investment in net assets.

    b. From Case 5 in the above schedule it may be shown that the net income applicable to common stockholders is a larger percentage of their $2,000,000 investment than is the percentage of corporate net income after taxes to the $3,000,000 total net assets of the corporation. Write a statement explaining the reason for this result.

7-6 Each of the cases described below is independent of the others.

Case A. Corporation A was organized in 1970 and was authorized to issue 100,000 shares of $5 par value common. The stock was issued at par, and the corporation reported a net loss of $30,000 for 1970 and a net loss of $70,000 in 1971. In 1972, net income was $2.10 per share.

Case B. Corporation B was organized in 1968. The company was authorized to issue 125,000 shares of $10 par value common and 10,000 shares of cumulative preferred stock. All of the preferred and 120,000 shares of common were issued at par. The preferred stock was callable at 105% of its $100 par value and was entitled to dividends of 6% before any dividends were paid to common. During the first five years of its existence, the corporation earned a total of $720,000 and paid dividends of 25 cents per share each year on the common stock.

Case C. Corporation C was organized in 1969, issuing at par one-half of the 100,000 shares of $20 par common stock authorized. On January 1, 1970, the company sold at par the entire 5,000 authorized shares of $100 par value, 5%, cumulative preferred. On January 1, 1971, the company issued 8,000 shares of an authorized 10,000 shares of $6 no-par cumulative preferred, for $815,000. The $6 preferred cumulative provided that after common stockholders had received $3 per share, it participated in all additional dividends on a share-for-share basis up to $6 per share. The company suffered losses in 1969 and 1970, reporting a deficit of $150,000 at the end of 1970. Dividends of $1 per share of common were paid in 1971 and $4.25 in 1972. Thus in 1972, the $6 preferred stock participated to the extent of $1.25 per share with common stockholders in dividends. The company earned a total of $752,600 during 1971 and 1972.

Instructions
For each of the independent situations described, prepare in good form the stockholders' equity section of the balance sheet as of December 31, 1972. Include a supporting schedule for each case showing your determination of the balance of retained earnings that should appear in the balance sheet.

7-7 Each of the cases described below is independent of the others.

Case A. On May 31, 1972, the Realty Corporation had outstanding 175,000 of 300,000 authorized shares of $20 par value common stock, and 15,000 of 50,000 shares of $7 preferred stock, cumulative, par value $100. The preferred was entitled to liquidation preference of par, plus any dividends in arrears. The company had been in existence for three years and had lost money in each year, accumulating a deficit of $148,000 as of May 31, 1972. On that date all assets, other than cash on hand of $92,000, were sold for 80% of their book value, and liabilities of $800,000 were paid in full.

Instructions. Prepare a schedule showing the amount of assets available for distribution to stockholders, and the amount per share that would be received in liquidation on each of the two kinds of stock as of May 31, 1972.

Case B. Alaska Corporation was organized on January 1, 1971, and authorized to issue 200,000 shares of $10 par value common stock and 25,000 shares of $2 cumulative preferred stock, par value $40 per share. Promoters and attorneys were given 10,000 shares of common stock for their services in organizing the corporation, and 85,000 shares were sold at $12 in cash. During 1971. the company lost $100,000. At the beginning of 1972, the company needed funds, and in order to sell its preferred at par, the preferred stock was made convertible into four shares of common stock. On this basis, 12,000 shares of preferred were sold at par early in 1972. During 1972, Alaska Corporation earned $380,000 and declared a dividend of $1.50 per share on common stock after 10,000 of the preferred shares were converted into common stock. A $1 dividend was declared on these shares and was paid before they were converted. All of the 135,000 common shares outstanding on December 31, 1972, received the $1.50 dividend.

Instructions. Prepare in good form the stockholders' equity section of the balance sheet as of December 31, 1972. Show in a separate schedule how you arrived at the balance of retained earnings at that date.

Case C. After several years of profitable operation, Sandison Corporation had net assets of $2,700,000 as of January 1, 1972, represented by 270,000 shares of $5 par value common and 3,600 shares of 6%, $100 par value, cumulative preferred stock. All shares had been issued at par. The preferred stock is convertible into common at any time on the basis of one share of preferred for 15 shares of common. Operating income before income taxes is expected to be 20% of net assets during 1972. The company is subject to income taxes at an average rate of 45%.

Instructions. Assuming that earnings are as forecast:
a. Compute the amount of net income in 1972 that is allocable to each share of common stock, assuming that none of the preferred shares is converted during the year.
b. Compute the 1972 net income available per share of common stock, assuming that all preferred shares are converted at the beginning of 1972. Round off earnings per share to the nearest cent.
c. Determine the maximum legal dividend per share of common that could be paid at the end of 1972, assuming that all shares of preferred were converted at the beginning of 1972 and that no part of paid-in capital is available for dividends. Carry computations to the nearest cent.

8

Corporations: Retained earnings, dividends, and book value

REPORTING THE RESULTS OF CORPORATE OPERATIONS

The most important aspect of corporate financial reporting, in the view of most stockholders, is the determination of periodic net income. The level of dividends and the market price of common stock depend heavily on the company's operating performance. For this reason, the *earnings per share* figure is of particular interest to stockholders.

The determination of corporate income is also a key step leading to the retained earnings figure reported in the balance sheet. In other words, we are dealing at this point with the *source* of retained earnings; a discussion of *uses* of retained earnings for the payment of dividends will follow.

Extraordinary gains and losses

From time to time, most businesses will realize gains and incur losses which are not a part of the main activities of the business. Examples of such items include (1) gains and losses on the sale of plant assets; (2) uninsured losses from fires, theft, floods, and earthquakes; (3) gains and losses from the sale of investments; and (4) damages awarded in lawsuits. These gains and losses are shown in the income statement, usually under a separate caption such as Extraordinary Gains and Losses, Nonrecurring Gains and Losses, or Non-operating Gains and Losses. To warrant this separate reporting in the income statement, the item must be material in amount and not directly related to the regular activities of the business.

Until recently, two opposing views existed as to the proper presentation of extraordinary gains and losses in the income statement. One group of accountants believed that these gains and losses should be included in the income statement of the year in which they occur, but listed as separate items and clearly described. The extraordinary gain or loss would thus be reflected in the amount of net income reported for the year. Other accountants favored charging or crediting large extraordinary gains and losses directly to the Retained Earnings account and thus excluding them from the determination of the current year's net income. Under this approach, the extraordinary gain or loss appeared in the statement of retained earnings.

Both methods provided for full disclosure, but the key figure of net income often proved to be misleading to users of financial statements.

Recently, the Accounting Principles Board (APB) of the AICPA has taken the position that net income should include *all items of profit and loss recognized during the period with the sole exception of "prior period adjustments,"* which should be entered directly to retained earnings.[1] The APB requires that extraordinary gains and losses be reported separately (net of tax) in arriving at net income. Not all gains or losses, however large, should be treated as extraordinary items, because they may be "of a character typical of the customary business activity of the entity," and therefore should be reflected in the determination of income *before* extraordinary items.

As an example of an adjustment *which should be taken into account in arriving at income before extraordinary items,* consider the situation in which certain accounts receivable are determined to be uncollectible, and the uncollectible amount is much larger than the balance in Allowance for Uncollectible Accounts. The recognition of this greater collection loss should be shown as part of the current year's operations and not as an extraordinary loss.

What if a business discovers that the remaining useful life of its depreciable assets will be less than previously estimated? The increased amount of depreciation expense to be recognized during the remaining useful life of the asset should be treated as an element in the determination of operating income for the current and future periods, and not as a prior period adjustment or as an extraordinary loss.

Still another example of a correction which does not qualify either as a prior period adjustment or as an extraordinary item is a write-off to recognize inventory obsolescence. In other words, the normal recurring errors which inevitably come to light in any business are not to be treated as extraordinary items or as corrections to retained earnings, but should be treated as revenue or deductions from revenue *in arriving at income from operations.*

The use of estimates to deal with uncertainties is a necessary part of the accounting process. Since these estimates are seldom, if ever, entirely accurate, a number of errors will come to light which relate to some extent to prior fiscal periods. We have mentioned as examples the noncollectibility of receivables, the change in the estimated life of a depreciable asset, and inventory obsolescence. Financial reporting would not be improved by giving all these corrections special treatment in the income statement. Because of the inevitability of these corrections, the user of financial statements should be aware that the operating results reported each year may include the effects of some errors made in prior periods.

Income statement for a corporation illustrated

To illustrate the preparation of an income statement for a corporation with extraordinary items, assume that the Thorell Corporation has a net gain of

[1] "Reporting the Results of Operations," *Opinion No. 9 of the Accounting Principles Board,* AICPA (New York: 1966), pp. 112–113.

$1,300,000 after applicable income taxes from sale of plant assets in 1971 and a net loss of $800,000 from disposal of long-term investments in 1970. In 1971, the corporation paid $1,950,000 of additional income taxes applicable to fiscal year 1969 and also wrote off $600,000 of obsolete inventory accumulated during the past four years. A condensed income statement as it might appear in the annual report of the Thorell Corporation appears below:

How Is This Company Doing?

THORELL CORPORATION
Income Statement
For Years Ended June 30, 1971, and June 30, 1970

	1971	1970
Net sales and other revenues.................	$42,200,000	$37,200,000
Costs and expenses:		
Cost of goods sold (includes write-off of $600,000 of obsolete inventory in 1971)....	$28,000,000	$25,300,000
Operating expenses.......................	6,000,000	5,200,000
Other miscellaneous deductions	300,000	250,000
Income taxes, excluding tax on extraordinary items shown below....................	3,700,000	3,300,000
	$38,000,000	$34,050,000
Income before extraordinary items............	$ 4,200,000	$ 3,150,000
Extraordinary items, net of tax°.............	1,300,000	(800,000)
Net income	$ 5,500,000	$ 2,350,000
Per share of common stock:		
Income before extraordinary items...............	$4.20	$3.15
Extraordinary items, net of tax°	1.30	(.80)
Net income	$5.50	$2.35

° Gain on sale of plant assets in 1971 and loss on disposal of long-term investments in 1970.

Note that the income tax assessment of $1,950,000 for fiscal year 1969 is not shown in the income statement; this item is a "prior period adjustment" and will appear on the statement of retained earnings, which is illustrated on page 242. The write-off of obsolete inventory is included in the cost of goods sold for 1971 and is disclosed parenthetically. The extraordinary gain or loss is added to income before extraordinary items in arriving at total net income and also net income per share.

Companies whose stock is widely held or is listed on the major stock exchanges provide to their stockholders *interim* income statements (usually quarterly) in order to provide them with current earnings progress. A recent interim income statement issued by Alan Wood Steel Company is shown on page 238.

Interim
Earnings
Report
of
Publicly
Owned
Company

ALAN WOOD STEEL COMPANY
Consolidated Statement of Income

	3rd Quarter 1968	3rd Quarter 1967	Nine Months 1968	Nine Month. 1967
Net sales and operating revenues	$25,051,590	$19,897,392	$76,637,162	$61,915,031
Income before items shown below	$ 3,488,637	$ 1,411,234	$11,713,340	$ 5,013,839
Depreciation...............	$ 1,565,501	$ 1,342,471	$ 4,516,599	$ 4,304,820
Interest, bond discount, and debt expense..................	1,105,168	539,244	2,876,912	1,596,765
Federal and Pennsylvania income taxes (credit).............	114,000	(299,000)	1,333,000	(587,000
	$ 2,784,669	$ 1,582,715	$ 8,726,511	$ 5,314,585
Net income (loss)....	$ 703,968	$ (171,481)	$ 2,986,829	$ (300,746
Income (loss) per share of Common Stock after Preferred Stock dividend requirement........	$ .88	$ (.23)	$ 3.81	$ (.63
Dividends declared: Preferred—$1.25 per share each quarter	$ 53,944	$ 54,319	$ 162,582	$ 164,019
Common—$0.35 per share each quarter	$ 259,652	$ 256,710	$ 776,327	$ 770,130

The Company changed its depreciation method on certain assets from accelerated depreciation to straight-line depreciation in the third quarter of 1968. As a result of this change in depreciation and the relatec tax effects, net income was increased $335,000 ($0.46 per share) for the third quarter and $1,011,00C ($1.37 per share) for the nine months.

Retained earnings

In preceding chapters, the term *retained earnings* has been used to describe that portion of stockholders' equity derived from profitable operations. An older term for this part of stockholders' equity is *earned surplus.* Because of the misleading connotations of the word "surplus," accountants have recommended that use of the term be discontinued. In accordance with this recommendation, a strong trend has developed to use "retained earnings" or "accumulated earnings" in place of "earned surplus" in corporate balance sheets.

Retained earnings is a historical concept, representing the accumulated earnings (including prior period adjustments) minus dividends declared from the date of incorporation to the present. Each year the Income Summary account is closed by transferring the net income or net loss into the Retained Earnings account. If we assume that all extraordinary gains and losses are cleared through the Income Summary account and that there are no prior period adjustments, the only entries in the Retained Earnings account will be (1) the periodic transfer of net income (or loss) from the Income Summary account, (2) the debit entries for dividend declarations, and (3) transfers to or from reserve accounts representing appropriations of accumulated earnings.

In successful corporations the Retained Earnings account normally has a credit balance; but if total losses should exceed total net income, the Retained Earnings account will have a debit balance. This debit amount is listed in the balance sheet under the title Deficit, and is deducted from the total of the paid-in capital, as previously illustrated on page 213.

Prior period adjustments to Retained Earnings account

Earlier in this chapter, it was suggested that extraordinary items of gain or loss should be included in the income statement, and that prior period adjustments be reported as debits or credits directly to the Retained Earnings account. Such adjustments are rare since they must be material items which are directly related to the activities of a prior period and which were not susceptible to a reasonably accurate measurement in the prior period. Furthermore, such adjustments must not be attributable, in any sense, to an economic event of the current year. Examples of adjustments which should be recorded directly in the Retained Earnings account include (1) additional tax assessments for prior years, (2) settlement of litigation based on events of earlier periods, and (3) settlement of rate disputes by public utilities.

Going back to the Thorell Corporation example described on page 237, the entry in 1971 to record the income tax assessment of $1,950,000 for the fiscal year 1969, would be recorded as follows:

Recording a Prior Period Adjustment

Retained Earnings...........................	1,950,000	
Income Tax Assessment Payable—Prior Period		1,950,000
To record income tax assessment applicable to the year		
1969 as a prior period adjustment.		

The presentation of this prior period adjustment in the statement of retained earnings for the Thorell Corporation is illustrated on page 242.

Appropriations from retained earnings

Some corporations prefer to subdivide their retained earnings into two or more accounts. This subdivision is accomplished by journal entries which transfer a portion of the Retained Earnings account into various "reserve" accounts. A reserve account established in this manner is referred to as an *appropriation of retained earnings.*

Assume, for example, that a corporation is engaged in a highly speculative business in which operations may result in either large profits or large losses from one year to the next. The corporation has accumulated a balance of $1 million in the Retained Earnings account, and the board of directors decides to make a portion of this amount unavailable for dividends by transferring $250,000 from the Retained Earnings account to a Reserve for Contingencies. The journal entry to carry out the decision of the directors is as follows:

Retained Earnings...............................	250,000	
Reserve for Contingencies		250,000
To establish a reserve for contingencies.		

The point of this action is to make clear to readers of the financial statements that $250,000 of the retained earnings is not available for dividends. The Reserve for Contingencies appears in the stockholders' equity section of the balance sheet; the corporation still has a total of $1 million of retained earnings, but it shows this $1 million as two separate items, as follows:

Retained Earnings:		
Free and available for declaration of dividends.....	$750,000	
Reserve for contingencies....................	250,000	$1,000,000

Both the total stockholders' equity and the equity of each stockholder would be unchanged by this subdivision of retained earnings.

Contractual and voluntary appropriations of retained earnings

The reserve for contingencies described in the preceding section was created voluntarily by the board of directors. The board may bring an end to the existence of the reserve at any time merely by ordering it to be transferred back into the Retained Earnings account. The entry to dispose of the reserve would be as follows:

Reserve for Contingencies..........................	250,000	
Retained Earnings		250,000
To eliminate the reserve for contingencies.		

Another example of a voluntary appropriation is a Reserve for Plant Expansion. A company which plans to retain a considerable part of its profits as a means of financing the construction of additional plant facilities may wish to inform its stockholders of this plan by transferring a portion of the retained earnings to Reserve for Plant Expansion. Once the plant expansion program is complete, the board of directors may decide to transfer the Reserve for Plant Expansion account back to the Retained Earnings account.

Not all appropriations of retained earnings are voluntary. When a corporation borrows money through the issuance of long-term notes or bonds, the borrowing contract may place a limit on the cash dividends which the corporation can pay during the life of the indebtedness. One means of limiting cash dividends is to transfer a portion of the retained earnings into a reserve account with a title such as Reserve for Retirement of Long-term Debt, or Reserve for Bond Sinking Fund.

Reserves do not consist of assets

Some readers of financial statements erroneously assume that a Reserve for Plant Expansion, for example, consists of cash set aside to pay for a new building. This is completely untrue. A Reserve for Plant Expansion has a credit balance; it does not consist of cash or any other assets; it is merely a subdivision of retained earnings. This comment applies not only to Reserve for Plant Expansion but to all reserves created from retained earnings. If management wishes to set aside a fund of cash for a specific future use, this is done by transferring cash to a special bank account. This special bank account would be a *fund* and not a reserve. It would have a debit balance and would appear on the asset side of the balance sheet.

Are appropriations of retained earnings necessary?

The only purpose of appropriating retained earnings is to inform readers of the financial statements that a portion of the retained earnings is "reserved" for a specific purpose and is not available for dividends. This information could be conveyed more directly, with less danger of misunderstanding, by a note accompanying the balance sheet. Only the board of directors has the authority to declare dividends. If the board wishes to retain the earnings in the business for plant expansion or other purposes, it is free to do so without going through the procedure of dividing the Retained Earnings account into two or more portions. Similarly, creditors can limit the payment of dividends by requiring that dividend payments shall not exceed a specified percentage of net income during the period of indebtedness, or that dividends can be paid only if the current ratio and the amount of working capital are above specified levels.

Misuse of the term "reserve"

In present-day terminology, the term *reserve* is properly used in only one sense, that is, to describe appropriations of retained earnings. Therefore, "reserves" should appear only in the stockholders' equity section of the balance sheet. In past years, the word *reserve* was often applied to asset valuation accounts, such as Reserve for Doubtful Accounts and Reserve for Depreciation. It was also used to describe liabilities of estimated amount, such as Reserve for Income Taxes. Such overworking of the term caused confusion and misunderstanding among readers of financial statements. Some companies aggravated the situation by including in their balance sheets a separate section for reserves, located between the liabilities and the stockholders' equity sections. Some of these undesirable practices persist today in published balance sheets, although considerable progress has been made in improving the terminology used in financial statements.

Statement of retained earnings

In addition to the balance sheet and the income statement, most corporations include a statement of retained earnings in their annual reports to stockholders. The typical format of the statement of retained earnings is illustrated below for the Thorell Corporation, based on data given earlier in this chapter:

Statement of Retained Earnings Shows Prior Period Adjustments, Net Income, and Dividends

THORELL CORPORATION
Statement of Retained Earnings
For Years Ended June 30, 1971, and June 30, 1970

	1971	1970
Retained earnings at beginning of year:		
As originally reported...............	$15,400,000	$14,850,000
Prior period adjustment—additional income taxes for year ended June 30, 1969........	(1,950,000)	(1,950,000)
As restated.......................	$13,450,000	$12,900,000
Net income........................	5,500,000	2,350,000
	$18,950,000	$15,250,000
Less: Cash dividends on common stock:		
$2.40 per share in 1971...............	(2,400,000)	
$1.80 per share in 1970...............		(1,800,000)
Retained earnings at end of year...........	$16,550,000	$13,450,000

The additional income tax assessment for 1969 is shown as a correction to the balance in retained earnings for both years, since both beginning figures are overstated as originally reported. The statement of retained earnings thus provides a useful vehicle for the disclosure of prior period adjustments and for the reconciliation of changes in the Retained Earnings account resulting from net income (or net loss) and dividends.

An alternative presentation of net income and retained earnings is used by many companies. The reconciliation of retained earnings is shown in the body of the *combined statement of income and retained earnings,* as illustrated on page 243 for Swift & Company:

The Swift statement emphasizes the close relationship of operating results and accumulated earnings. Many readers of financial statements, however, object to the fact that net income (or loss) is "buried" in the body of the statement rather than being prominently displayed as the final figure before earnings per share are computed.

DIVIDENDS AND STOCK SPLITS

The term *dividend,* when used by itself, is generally understood to mean a distribution of cash by a corporation to its stockholders. Dividends are stated as a specific amount per share as, for example, a dividend of $1 per share.

*Combined
Statement
of Income
and
Retained
Earnings*

SWIFT & COMPANY
Consolidated Statement of Operations
and Accumulated Earnings

	52 Weeks Ended	
	Oct. 26, 1968	*Oct. 28, 1967*
Revenues	$2,832,022,624	$2,924,449,385
Cost and expenses.	2,805,300,329	2,872,228,093
Earnings before income taxes and extra- ordinary items	$ 26,722,295	$ 52,221,292
Income taxes, less investment tax credits of $2,342,093 ($2,017,958 in 1967).	11,289,562	22,108,317
Earnings before extraordinary items	$ 15,432,733	$ 30,112,975
Extraordinary credit (charge)	(57,000,000)	827,240
Net earnings (loss).	$ (41,567,267)	$ 30,940,215
Accumulated earnings at beginning of year	220,452,931	202,855,837
	$ 178,885,664	$ 233,796,052
Dividends on common stock $0.90 per share ($1.10 per share in 1967)	11,016,755	13,343,121
Accumulated earnings at end of year	$ 167,868,909	$ 220,452,931
Earnings (loss) per common share Earnings before extraordinary items.	$ 1.12	$2.32
Extraordinary credit (charge)	$(4.66)	$ .07
Net earnings (loss).	$(3.54)	$2.39

It follows that the amount received by each stockholder is in proportion to the number of shares owned.

Dividends are paid only through action by the board of directors. The board has full discretion to declare a dividend or to refrain from doing so. Once the declaration of a dividend has been announced, the obligation to pay the dividend is a current liability of the corporation and cannot be rescinded.

Dividends are occasionally paid in assets other than cash. When a corporation goes out of existence (particularly a small corporation with only a few stockholders), it may choose to distribute noncash assets to its owners rather than to convert all assets into cash.

A dividend may also be paid in the form of additional shares of a company's own stock. This type of distribution is called a *stock dividend.* Stock dividends are of great practical importance and also of much theoretical interest. They will be discussed at length later in this chapter.

A *liquidating* dividend occurs when a corporation returns to stockholders all or part of their paid-in capital investment. Liquidating dividends are usually paid only when a corporation is going out of existence or is making a permanent reduction in the size of its operations. Normally dividends are paid from the profits of a corporation, and the recipient of a dividend is entitled to assume that the dividend represents a distribution of profits unless he is specifically notified that the dividend is a return of invested capital.

Cash dividends

The prospect of receiving cash dividends is a principal reason for investing in the stocks of corporations. An increase or decrease in the established rate of dividends will usually cause an immediate rise or fall in the market price of the company's stock. Stockholders are keenly interested in prospects for future dividends and as a group are generally strongly in favor of more generous dividend payments. The board of directors, on the other hand, is primarily concerned with the long-run growth and financial strength of the corporation; it may prefer to restrict dividends to a minimum in order to conserve cash for purchase of plant and equipment or for other needs of the company. The so-called "growth companies" generally plow back into the business most of their earnings and pay little or nothing in cash dividends.

The preceding discussion suggests three requirements for the payment of a cash dividend. These are:

1. Retained earnings. Since dividends represent a distribution of earnings to stockholders, the theoretical maximum for dividends is the total net income (after income taxes) of the company. As a practical matter, most corporations limit dividends to somewhere near 50% of earnings, in the belief that a major portion of the profits must be retained in the business if the company is to grow and to keep pace with its competitors.

2. An adequate cash position. The fact that the company reports large earnings does not mean that it has a large amount of cash in the bank. Earnings may have been invested in new plant and equipment, or in paying off debts, or in stocking a larger inventory. There is no necessary relationship between the balance in the Retained Earnings account and the balance in the Cash account. The traditional expression of "paying dividends out of retained earnings" is misleading. Cash dividends can be paid only "out of" cash.

3. Dividend action by the board of directors. Even though the company's profits are substantial and its cash position seemingly satisfactory, dividends are not paid automatically. A positive action by the directors is necessary to declare a dividend.

Regular and special dividends

Many corporations establish a regular quarterly or annual dividend rate and pay this same amount for a period of years regardless of the year-to-year changes in earnings. Such a policy gives a higher investment quality to a company's stock. A strong cash position is necessary if a company is to be prepared to make regular dividend payments in the face of irregular earnings.

If earnings increase but the increase is regarded as a temporary condition, the corporation may decide to pay a "special dividend" in addition to the regular dividend. The implication of a special dividend is that the company is making no commitments as to a permanent increase in the amount of dividends to be paid. Of course, even a "regular" dividend may be reduced or discontinued at any time, but well-financed companies which have long-established regular dividend rates are not likely to omit or reduce dividend payments except in extreme emergencies.

Dividends on preferred stock

As indicated in Chapter 7, a preferred stock carries a stated annual dividend rate, such as $5 per share, or 5% of par value. Under no circumstances does a corporation pay more than the required dividend on preferred stock. This policy of not permitting the preferred stockholder to share in any unusually large profits suggests that the corporation views the preferred stockholder only as a supplier of capital rather than as a full-fledged owner in the traditional sense of the word.

Dividends on preferred stocks are not paid unless declared by the board of directors. Since most preferred stocks are of the cumulative variety, any omitted dividend must be made up before any payment can be made to the common. Dividends in arrears on preferred stock do not constitute a liability of the corporation but should be disclosed by a footnote to the balance sheet. Separate accounts are used to record the declaration of preferred and common dividends.

Dividend dates

Four significant dates are involved in the distribution of a dividend. These dates are:

1. Date of declaration. On the day on which the dividend is declared by the board of directors, a liability to make the payment comes into existence. A Dividends account is debited and a liability account, Dividends Payable, is credited.

2. Date of record. The date of record always follows the date of declaration, usually by a period of three or four weeks, and is always stated in the dividend declaration. In order to be eligible to receive the dividend, a person must be listed as the owner of the stock on the date of record.

3. Ex-dividend date. The ex-dividend date is significant for investors in companies with stocks traded on the stock exchanges. To permit the compilation of the list of stockholders as of the record date, it is customary for the stock to go "ex-dividend" three business days before the date of record. A stock is said to be selling ex-dividend on the day that it loses the right to receive the latest declared dividend. A person who buys the stock before the ex-dividend date is entitled to receive the dividend; conversely, a stockholder who sells his shares in the period between the date of declaration and the ex-dividend date does not receive the dividend.

4. Date of payment. The declaration of a dividend always includes announcement of the date of payment as well as the date of record. Usually the date of payment comes from two to four weeks after the date of record.

Stock dividends

Stock dividend is an important but confusing term which requires close attention. It is confusing because all dividends are distributions to stockholders and "stock dividend" may suggest to some people merely a dividend on capital stock. A stock dividend is a pro rata distribution of additional shares to a company's stockholders; in brief, the dividend consists of shares of stock rather than cash. Perhaps a better term for a stock dividend would be a "dividend payable in capital stock," but the expression "stock dividend" is too firmly entrenched to be easily replaced. Most stock dividends consist of common stock distributed to holders of common stock, and our discussion will be limited to this type of stock dividend.

What is the effect of a stock dividend on the company's financial position? Why does a corporation choose to pay a dividend in shares of stock rather than in cash? Would you as an investor prefer to receive a stock dividend or a cash dividend? These questions are closely related, and a careful analysis of the nature of a stock dividend should provide a basis for answering them.

A cash dividend reduces the assets of a corporation and reduces the stockholders' equity by the same amount. A stock dividend, on the other hand, causes no change in assets and no change in the *total* amount of the stockholders' equity. The only effect of a stock dividend on the accounts is to transfer a portion of the retained earnings into the Capital Stock and Additional Paid-in Capital accounts. In other words, a stock dividend merely "reshuffles" the stockholders' equity accounts, increasing the permanent capital accounts and decreasing the Retained Earnings account. A stockholder who receives a stock dividend will possess an increased number of shares, but his equity in the company will be no larger than before.

An example may make this fundamental point clear. Assume that a corporation with 800 shares of stock is owned equally by James Davis and Frank Miller, each owning 400 shares of stock. The corporation pays a stock dividend of 25% and distributes 200 additional shares (25% of 800 shares), with 100 shares going to each of the two stockholders. Davis and Miller now hold 500 shares apiece, but each still owns one-half of the business. The corporation has not changed; its assets and liabilities and its total capital are exactly the same as before the dividend. From the stockholder's viewpoint, the ownership of 500 shares out of a total of 1,000 outstanding shares represents no more than did the ownership of 400 shares out of a total of 800 shares previously outstanding.

Assume that the market value of this stock was $10 per share prior to the stock dividend. Total market value of all the outstanding shares was, therefore, 800 times $10, or $8,000. What would be the market value per share and in total after the additional 200 dividend shares were issued? The

1,000 shares now outstanding should have the same total market value as the previously outstanding 800 shares, because the "pie" has merely been divided into more but smaller pieces. The price per share should have dropped from $10 to $8, and the aggregate market value of outstanding shares would consequently be computed as 1,000 shares times $8, or $8,000. Whether the market price per share will, in actuality, decrease in proportion to the change in number of outstanding shares is another matter, for market prices are subject to many conflicting influences, some as unpredictable as the state of mind of investors.

Reasons for distribution of stock dividends. Many reasons have been given for the increasing popularity of stock dividends, for example:

1. To conserve cash. When the trend of profits is favorable but cash is needed for expansion, a stock dividend may be an appropriate device for "passing along the profits" to stockholders without weakening the corporation's cash position.[2]

2. To reduce the market price of a corporation's stock to a more convenient trading range by increasing the number of shares outstanding. This objective is usually present in large stock dividends (25 to 100% or more).

3. To avoid income tax on stockholders. Stock dividends are not considered as income to the recipients; therefore, no income tax is levied.

4. To mollify stockholders when poor operating results do not permit the payment of cash dividends. Since many stockholders do not understand the nature of stock dividends, they may be content to accept additional shares in lieu of cash.

5. To avoid giving the impression of excessive profits, which might result if earnings, cash dividends, and market price per share reached high levels.

Some critics of stock dividends argue that a stock dividend is not really a dividend at all. These critics say that a company which cannot afford to pay a cash dividend should pay no dividends, rather than trying to deceive stockholders by increasing the number of outstanding shares. The popularity of stock dividends, according to such critics, is based on a lack of understanding on the part of stockholders.

Regardless of the merit of the arguments for and against stock dividends, most stockholders welcome these distributions. In many cases a small stock dividend has not caused the market price per share to decline appreciably; consequently, the increase in the number of shares in the hands of each stockholder has, regardless of logic, resulted in an increase in the total market value of his holdings.

---

[2] For example, the Standard Oil Company of California, in a recent letter to stockholders, gave the following reason for the "payment" of a 5% stock dividend: "Payment of this stock dividend recognizes the continuing increase in your stockholder's equity in the Company's assets, resulting from reinvestment of part of the Company's earnings. Reinvestment of earnings has helped to sustain the Company's long-range program of capital and exploratory expenditures and investments aimed to increase future income and enhance further the value of your shareholding."

Entries to record stock dividends. Assume that a corporation had the following stockholders' equity accounts on December 15, 1971, just prior to declaring a 10% stock dividend:

Stock-holders' Equity before Stock Dividend	*Stockholders' Equity*

Stockholders' Equity

Common stock, $10 par value, authorized 30,000 shares, issued and outstanding 10,000 shares $100,000
Paid-in capital in excess of par 50,000
Retained earnings 200,000
Total stockholders' equity $350,000

Assume also that the closing market price of the stock on December 15, 1971, was $30 a share. The company declares and issues a 10% stock dividend, consisting of 1,000 shares (10% × 10,000 = 1,000). The entry to record the declaration of the dividend is as follows:

Stock Dividend Declared; Note Use of Market Price

1971			
Dec. 15	*Retained Earnings*	30,000	
	Stock Dividends to Be Distributed		10,000
	Paid-in Capital from Stock Dividends ...		20,000

To record declaration of a 10% stock dividend consisting of 1,000 shares of $10 par value common stock. To be distributed on February 9, 1972, to stockholders of record on January 15, 1972. Amount of retained earnings transferred to permanent capital is based on market price of $30 a share on December 15, 1971.

The entry to record distribution of the dividend shares is as follows:

Stock Dividend Distrib-uted

1972			
Feb. 9	*Stock Dividends to Be Distributed*	10,000	
	Common Stock		10,000

To record distribution of stock dividend of 1,000 shares.

Note that the amount of retained earnings transferred to permanent capital accounts by the above entries is not the par value of the new shares, but the *fair market value*, as indicated by the market price prevailing at the date of declaration. The reasoning behind this practice is simple: since stockholders tend to measure the "worth" of a small stock dividend (say,

20 to 25% or less) in terms of the market value of the additional shares issued, then Retained Earnings should be reduced by this amount. Stock dividends in excess of 20 to 25% should be recorded by transferring only the par or stated value of the dividend shares from the Retained Earnings account to the Common Stock account.

The Stock Dividends to Be Distributed account is not a liability, because there is no obligation to distribute cash or any other asset. If a balance sheet is prepared between the date of declaration of a stock dividend and the date of distribution of the shares, this account, as well as Paid-in Capital from Stock Dividends, should be presented in the stockholders' equity section of the balance sheet.

Stock splits

Most large corporations are interested in as wide as possible a distribution of their securities among the investing public. If the market price reaches very high levels as, for example, $150 per share, the corporation may feel that, by splitting the stock 5 to 1 and thereby reducing the price to $30 per share, the number of shareholders may be increased. The bulk of trading in securities occurs in 100-share lots and an extra commission is charged on smaller transactions. Many investors with limited funds prefer to make their investments in 100-share lots of lower-priced stocks. The majority of leading American corporations have split their stock; some have done so several times. Generally the number of shareholders has increased noticeably after the stock has been split.

A stock split consists of increasing the number of outstanding shares and reducing the par or stated value per share in proportion. For example, assume that a corporation has outstanding 1 million shares of $10 par value stock. The market value is $90 per share. The corporation now reduces the par value from $10 to $5 per share and increases the number of shares from 1 million to 2 million. This action would be called a 2 for 1 stock split. A stockholder who formerly owned 100 shares of the $10 par old stock would now own 200 shares of the $5 par new stock. Since the number of outstanding shares has been doubled without any change in the affairs of the corporation, the market price will probably drop from $90 to approximately $45 a share.

A stock split does not change the balance of any ledger account; consequently, the transaction may be recorded merely by a memorandum notation in the general journal and in the Common Stock account.

Distinction between stock splits and large stock dividends. What is the difference between a 2 for 1 stock split and a 100% stock dividend? Both will double the number of outstanding shares without changing total stockholders' equity, and both will serve to cut the market price of the stock in half. The stock dividend, however, will cause a transfer from the Retained Earnings account to the Common Stock account equal to the par or stated value of the dividend shares, whereas the stock split does not change the dollar balance of any account.

Paid-in capital as a basis for dividends

Among the several sources of paid-in capital in excess of par (or stated value) are: (1) premiums on par value stock, (2) excess of issuance price over stated value of no-par stock, (3) excess of proceeds from reissuance of treasury stock over the cost of these shares, (4) purchase and retirement of shares at a cost less than the issuance price, and (5) donation of property to the corporation.

A separate ledger account should be used for each specific type of paid-in capital in excess of par. Examples of the appropriate ledger titles are Premium on Capital Stock, Additional Paid-in Capital in Excess of Stated Value, Paid-in Capital from Treasury Stock Transactions, Paid-in Capital from Retirement of Stock, and Paid-in Capital from Donated Property. This last account usually arises when a city or a civic organization donates land or other property as a means of persuading a corporation to locate in the area. In a condensed balance sheet, two or more of these ledger accounts may be combined into a single amount and labeled as Additional Paid-in Capital.

Is paid-in capital available for dividends? Although the laws of many states make it legally possible to declare dividends from paid-in capital, this is rarely done. Whenever a corporation does declare a dividend from any source other than retained earnings, it is obligated to disclose to stockholders that the dividend is of a liquidating nature, representing a return of paid-in capital rather than a distribution of earnings. A liquidating dividend does not constitute taxable income to stockholders.

TREASURY STOCK

Corporations frequently reacquire shares of their own capital stock by purchase in the open market. The effect of reacquiring shares is to reduce the assets of the corporation and to reduce the stockholders' equity by the same amount. One reason for such purchases is to have stock available to reissue to officers and employees under some type of bonus plan. Other reasons may include a desire to increase the reported earnings per share, to support the market value of the stock, and to have shares available for use in acquisition of other companies.

Treasury stock may be defined as a corporation's own stock which has been issued, fully paid, and reacquired but not canceled. Treasury shares may be held indefinitely or may be issued again at any time. Treasury stock is not entitled to share in dividends. It has no voting rights, no preemptive right to share in new issues, and no right to share in assets in the event of dissolution of the company.

Recording purchases and sales of treasury stock

The procedures for recording treasury stock transactions are the same for both par value and no-par value stocks. Purchases of treasury stock should be recorded by debiting the Treasury Stock account with the cost of the stock.

For example, if a corporation reacquires 10 shares of its own $100 par stock at a price of $150 per share, the entry is as follows:

Treasury
Stock
Recorded
at Cost

Treasury Stock	*1,500*	
Cash		*1,500*
Purchased 10 shares of $100 par treasury stock at $150 per share.		

Treasury stock is customarily recorded *at cost* regardless of whether it is par value stock or no-par stock, and regardless of the price paid or of the price at which the shares were originally issued. In short, it is current practice to record all treasury stock at cost. When and if the treasury shares are reissued, the Treasury Stock account would be credited for *the cost* of the shares sold, and Paid-in Capital from Treasury Stock Transactions would be debited or credited for the difference between cost and resale price.

To illustrate the reissuance of treasury stock at a price above cost, assume that the 10 shares acquired at a cost of $1,500 are reissued for a higher price, $1,800. The entry is:

Reissued
above
Cost

Cash	*1,800*	
Treasury Stock		*1,500*
Paid-in Capital from Treasury Stock Transactions ...		*300*
Sold 10 shares of treasury stock, which cost $1,500, at a price of		
$180 each.		

If treasury stock is resold at a price below cost and a paid-in capital account exists as a result of previous treasury stock transactions, this account may be debited. If there is no paid-in capital as a result of previous treasury stock transactions, the excess of cost over reissuance price could be charged against any other paid-in capital account or against the Retained Earnings account.

Treasury stock not an asset

Corporations sometimes list treasury stock among the assets on the grounds that the shares could be sold for cash just as readily as shares owned in another corporation. The same argument could be made for treating unissued shares as assets. Treasury shares are basically the same as unissued shares, and an unissued share of stock is definitely not an asset.[3]

When treasury stock is purchased, the corporation is eliminating a part of the stockholders' equity by paying off one or more stockholders. It is, therefore, reasonable to think of the purchase of treasury stock not as the acquisition of an asset, but as the returning or refunding of capital to stock-

---

[3] Despite general agreement among accountants that treasury stock is not an asset, a few corporations in their published financial statements still list treasury stock among the assets. General Motors is a prominent example.

holders. For this reason treasury stock should appear in the balance sheet *as a deduction in the stockholders' equity section.*

Conversely, if the treasury shares are later reissued, this is a separate transaction in which the corporation is securing additional invested capital. Assume, for example, that a corporation pays $10 to acquire a share of treasury stock and later reissues this share for $15. Has the corporation made a $5 profit on this transaction with its owners? Definitely not; there is no profit or loss on treasury stock transactions. When the treasury share was reissued for $15, the corporation was merely receiving a larger amount of invested capital than was previously withdrawn when a stockholder surrendered the share to the company. A corporation earns profits by selling goods and services to outsiders at a price above cost, not by issuing or reissuing shares of its own stock.

Restriction of retained earnings by cost of treasury stock purchased

If a corporation is to maintain its contributed capital intact, it must not pay out to its stockholders any more than it earns. As previously stated in the section dealing with dividends, the amount of dividends to be paid must not exceed the corporation's earnings, or the corporation will be returning the stockholders' original investment to them.

The payment of cash dividends and the acquisition of treasury stock have a good deal in common. In both transactions, the corporation is handing out cash to its stockholders. Of course, the dividend payment is spread out among all the stockholders, whereas the payment to purchase treasury stock may go to only a few stockholders, but this does not alter the fact that the corporation is turning over some of its assets to its owners. The total amount which a corporation may pay to its stockholders without impairing its permanent capital is shown by the balance in the Retained Earnings account. Consequently, it is important that a corporation keep track of the total amount disbursed in payment for treasury stock and make sure that this amount plus any dividends paid does not exceed the company's earnings. This objective is conveniently accomplished by restricting the availability of retained earnings for dividends to the extent of the cost of treasury stock purchased. The restriction can be accomplished by debiting the Retained Earnings account and crediting a Reserve for Purchase of Treasury Stock account. A preferable way of disclosing the restriction on dividends is to insert an explanatory note opposite the item of Retained Earnings. The latter procedure is used in the illustration of the stockholders' equity section of the balance sheet at the end of this chapter.

BOOK VALUE PER SHARE OF CAPITAL STOCK

The word *value* is applied with various meanings to a share of stock. Par value, stated value, and market value per share have previously been discussed. Since there are several other types of value for a share of stock, to avoid confusion "value" should be used only with a qualifying adjective, as for example, book value, liquidation value, and redemption value.

The *book value* of a share of stock, as the name suggests, is determined by referring to the books of account, or more specifically to a balance sheet prepared from the books. Book value is equal to the net assets per share of stock. It is computed by dividing the paid-in capital and retained earnings applicable to a class of stock by the number of outstanding shares of that class.

For example, assume that a corporation has 4,000 shares of common stock outstanding and the stockholders' equity section of the balance sheet is as follows:

How Much Is Book Value per Share?

Common stock, $1 par value	*$ 4,000*
Paid-in capital in excess of par value	*40,000*
Retained earnings	*76,000*
Total stockholders' equity	*$120,000*

The book value per share is $30; it is computed by dividing the stockholders' equity of $120,000 by the 4,000 shares of outstanding stock. In computing book value, we are not concerned with the number of authorized shares but merely with the outstanding shares, because the total of the outstanding shares represents 100% of the stockholders' equity. In determining the number of outstanding shares, treasury shares are not to be included.

What is the significance of book value per share of stock? The stockholders' equity in total is equal to the book value of the assets minus the liabilities. Therefore, the stockholders' equity is equal to the *net assets* (assets minus liabilities), and the book value of each share of stock may be thought of as the net assets represented by a single share.

Book value does *not* indicate the amount which the holder of a share of stock would receive if the corporation were to be dissolved. In liquidation, the assets would probably be sold at prices quite different from their carrying values on the books, and the stockholders' equity would go up or down accordingly.

The concept of book value is of vital importance in many contracts. For example, a majority stockholder might obtain an option to purchase the shares of the minority stockholders at book value at a specified future date. Many court cases have hinged on definitions of book value.

Book value is occasionally used in judging the reasonableness of the market price of a stock. However, it must be used with great caution; the fact that a stock is selling at less than its book value does not necessarily indicate a bargain. The disparity between book value and market price per share is indicated by the following data currently available for three well-known corporations: Lockheed Aircraft Corporation, book value $33, market price $18; Polaroid Corporation, book value $11, market price $126; U.S. Steel Corporation, book value $63; market price $34. Earnings per share, dividends per share, and prospects for future earnings are usually more important factors affecting market price than is book value.

Book value when company has both preferred and common stock

When a company has two or more issues of stock outstanding, the book value for each class of stock may be computed by dividing the paid-in capital and retained income applicable to that class of stock by the number of shares outstanding. Book value is generally computed for common stock only, so the practical aspect of the question may be stated as follows: How is book value per common share computed when a company has both preferred and common stock?

Assuming that there are no dividends in arrears on the preferred stock, book value per common share is equal to the total stockholders' equity (exclusive of the redemption value of the preferred stock) divided by the number of common shares outstanding.

To illustrate, assume that the stockholders' equity is as follows:

Two	*5% preferred stock, $100 par, callable at $110* $1,000,000
Classes	*Common stock, no-par; $5 stated value; authorized 100,000 shares*
of Stock	*Issued and outstanding 80,000 shares* 400,000
	Paid-in capital in excess of par value 800,000
	Retained earnings 900,000
	Total stockholders' equity $3,100,000

All the capital belongs to the common stockholders, except the $1.1 million applicable to the preferred stock (and any dividends in arrears on the preferred stock). This reasoning is supported by the general practice of making the preferred stock callable at or near its issuance price, so that the eventual elimination of the preferred stock is not at all improbable. The calculation of book value per share of common stock can therefore be made as follows:

Compute	*Total stockholders' equity* $3,100,000
Book	*Less: Preferred stock (at call price of $110 per share)* 1,100,000
Value per	*Equity of common stockholders* $2,000,000
Share of	*Number of shares of common stock outstanding* 80,000
Common	
Stock	*Book value per share of common stock* $\dfrac{\$2,000,000}{80,000}$ $25

The computation of book value is made in the same way for par value and no-par value stock. The basic concept is the net assets per share.

Illustration of stockholders' equity section

The following illustration of a stockholders' equity section of a balance sheet shows a fairly detailed classification by source of the various elements of capital:

Compare with Published Financial Statements	*Stockholders' Equity*		
	Capital stock:		
	6% preferred stock, $100 par value, authorized and issued 1,000 shares	*$100,000*	
	Common stock, no-par, stated value $5 a share, authorized 100,000 shares, issued 60,000 shares, of which 1,000 are held in treasury	*300,000*	
	Common stock subscribed, 6,000 shares	*30,000*	*$430,000*
	Additional paid-in capital:		
	Premium on preferred stock	*$ 10,000*	
	Paid-in capital in excess of stated value: common stock	*330,000*	
	Paid-in capital from treasury stock transactions	*5,000*	*345,000*
	Total paid-in capital		*$775,000*
	Retained earnings (of which $12,000, an amount equal to the cost of treasury stock purchased, is unavailable for dividends)		*162,000*
			$937,000
	Less: Cost of 1,000 shares of treasury stock		*12,000*
	Total stockholders' equity		*$925,000*

The published financial statements of leading corporations indicate that there is no one standard arrangement for the various items making up the stockholders' equity section. Variations occur in the selection of titles, in the sequence of items, and in the extent of detailed classification. Many companies, in an effort to avoid excessive detail in the balance sheet, will combine several related ledger accounts into a single balance sheet item with a title such as Additional Paid-in Capital.

DEMONSTRATION PROBLEM

A comparative summary of the stockholders' equity of the Arnett Corporation, together with certain additional information, is given below:

	June 30, 1972		*June 30, 1971*
Stockholders' equity:			
Capital stock, authorized 100,000 shares; issued:			
As of June 30, 1972, 70,000 shares, $8 par value (1,000 held in treasury)	*$ 560,000*		
As of June 30, 1971, 40,000 shares, $10 par value			*$ 400,000*
Stock dividend to be distributed (6,900 shares)	*55,200*	*$ 615,200*	

	June 30, 1972		June 30, 1971	
Additional paid-in capital:				
From sale of capital stock, in excess of				
par value	$ 800,700			200,000
From stock dividends	276,000			
From treasury stock transactions	8,000	1,084,700		
Total paid-in capital		$1,699,900		$ 600,000
Retained earnings:				
Appropriated:				
Reserve for plant expansion			$ 100,000	
Reserve for acquisition of treasury stock	$ 37,000			
Unappropriated	1,198,100	1,235,100	1,280,000	1,380,000
Total paid-in capital and retained earnings		$2,935,000		
Less: Cost of 1,000 shares held in treasury		(37,000)		
Total stockholders' equity		$2,898,000		$1,980,000

In August of 1971, the board of directors voted a 5 for 4 stock split, which was approved by stockholders on September 1. On December 20 the company purchased 2,000 shares of its stock at $37 per share. On March 2, 1972, 1,000 shares of treasury stock were sold at $45 per share. On March 10, 20,000 previously unissued shares of $8 par value were issued in exchange for the net assets of another company. The total market value of the 20,000 shares was $760,700.

A cash dividend of $1 per share was declared on June 2, payable on June 29, to stockholders of record on June 15; a 10% stock dividend was declared on June 30, to be distributed on August 28. The market value of the stock on June 30 was $48 per share.

The net income for the year ended June 30, 1972, amounted to $255,300, which included a gain of $34,500 (net of applicable income taxes) on the sale of a plant site in Garden City. The Reserve for Plant Expansion was eliminated by vote of the board of directors on June 30, 1972.

Instructions
a. Prepare journal entries to record transactions relating to stockholders' equity that took place during the year ended June 30, 1972.
b. Prepare the lower section of the income statement for the year ended June 30, 1972, showing income from operations and the extraordinary gain. Also illustrate how the earnings per share should be presented in the income statement, assuming that earnings per share are determined on the basis of the number of shares actually outstanding at the end of the year.
c. Prepare a statement of retained earnings for the year ended June 30, 1972. Use three columnar headings: Unappropriated, Reserve for Plant Expansion, and Reserve for Acquisition of Treasury Stock.
d. Compute the book values per share of capital stock as of June 30, 1971, and as of June 30, 1972.

QUESTIONS

1. **a.** Briefly outline the recommendations of the Accounting Principles Board of the AICPA regarding the reporting of the results of operations by corporations.

   b. Distinguish between *extraordinary items* and *prior period adjustments.*

2. The accountant of W Company discovers during the current year that the Internal Revenue Service has determined that an additional $100,000 of income tax applicable to last year's operations is due. W Company agrees with the IRS finding. How should this tax deficiency be recorded in the accounts? How should it be shown in the financial statements? The amount is regarded as material.

3. What is the purpose of an appropriation of retained earnings? What are the arguments for and against the use of such appropriations?

4. Explain the nature of the following items appearing on a corporate balance sheet: Reserve for Depreciation, Reserve for Income Taxes Payable, and Reserve for Future Plant Expansion. What better titles can you suggest?

5. Explain the significance of the following dates relating to dividends: date of declaration, date of record, date of payment, ex-dividend date.

6. Jones purchased 100 shares of stock in X Corporation at the time it was organized. At the end of the first year's operations, the corporation reported earnings (after taxes) of $5 per share, and declared a dividend of $2.50 per share. Jones complains that he is entitled to the full distribution of the amount earned on his investment. Is there any reason why a corporation that earns $5 per share may not be able to pay a dividend of this amount? Are there any advantages to Jones in the retention by the company of one-half of its earnings.

7. Distinguish between a *stock split* and a *stock dividend.* Is there any reason for the difference in accounting treatment of these two events?

8. Precision Corporation has a total of 10,000 shares of common stock outstanding and no preferred stock. The net assets of the Precision Corporation at the end of the current year are $200,000, and the market value of the stock is $24 per share. At year-end, the company declares a stock dividend of one share for each five shares held. If all parties concerned clearly recognized the nature of the stock dividend, what would you expect the market value per share of Precision's common stock to be on the ex-dividend date?

9. What is treasury stock? Why do corporations purchase their own shares? Is treasury stock an asset? How should it be reported in the balance sheet?

10. In many states, the corporation law requires that retained earnings be restricted for dividend purposes to the extent of the cost of treasury shares. What is the reason for this legal rule?

11. How would the *book value* of a share of common stock be computed, assuming that preferred stock with dividends in arrears is also outstanding? List three events which increase the book value of a share of common stock, and three events which decrease the book value of a share of common stock.

12. International Machinery Corporation sold to the public 125,000 shares of common stock (*$1 par value*) at $21 per share. The *book value* of the 750,000

shares previously outstanding was approximately $4.50 per share and the *market price* a few weeks after this initial public offering was over $30 per share. The *earnings per share* of the company in the preceding four years had increased steadily and had averaged $0.90. Define each italicized per-share value mentioned above and suggest some factors which may have been important in determining the initial public offering price of $21 per share.

EXERCISES

1. The Forbes Corporation has 1 million shares of $1 par value capital stock outstanding. You are to prepare the journal entries to record the following transactions:

    Feb. 4   Declared a cash dividend of 5 cents per share.
    Mar. 1   Paid cash dividend to stockholders.
    June 14   Declares 2% stock dividend. Market value of stock is $18 per share.
    July 6   Issued 20,000 shares pursuant to 2% stock dividend.
    Dec. 20   Declared 50% stock dividend. Market value of stock is $30 per share.

2. The following data are taken from the records of the Sentinel Corporation:

7% preferred stock, cumulative (liquidation value, $105,000). . .	$100,000
Common stock, no par, 51,500 shares	640,000
Paid-in capital from treasury stock transactions	1,500
Dividends in arrears on preferred stock	21,000
Deficit	110,000
Organization costs	10,000
Treasury stock, 1,500 shares, at cost	19,500
Total liabilities	388,000

    a. Compute the amount of net assets (stockholders' equity).
    b. If all assets are sold for 80% of book value, how much would each share of common stock receive as a liquidating dividend?

3. Barron's Mining Company has 100,000 shares of $10 par value stock outstanding at the end of 1971. During 1971, the stock was split 2 for 1 and the company earned $320,000 from mining activities and $210,000 (net of taxes) from the sale of timberlands surrounding an abandoned mine. In 1970, the company had earned $4.10 per share from mining activities (based on shares then outstanding), and reported an extraordinary loss of $40,000 net of taxes. How should the foregoing information be presented on a per-share basis in reporting the company's earnings for the last two years in terms of the 100,000 shares now outstanding?

4. The balance sheet of the Fortune Printing Company is shown below:

Cash.	$ 10,000	Liabilities	$ 20,000
Other assets.	90,000	Capital stock, $5 par	50,000
		Retained earnings	30,000
	$100,000		$100,000

The other assets are sold for $150,000; all liabilities are paid (including income taxes of $15,000 on the gain from sale of other assets); and the cash remaining is distributed to stockholders.

a. Record the foregoing transactions on the books of the Fortune Printing Company. Assume that the gain (net of income taxes) is credited to Gain on Sale of Assets.

b. Assuming that this company had paid a total $115,000 in cash dividends since it was organized four years ago, and issued 2,500 shares of its stock as a 33⅓% stock dividend two years ago, what is the amount of income that it earned during its life?

5. The Chronicle Company has 10,000 shares of capital stock outstanding. The stock was originally issued at the par value of $10 per share. The book value per share of stock on January 1, 1971, is $30. During 1971, the following transactions were completed by the company:

Jan. 4   An additional 2,000 shares of stock were sold to investors at $45 per share.

Mar. 1   The company acquired 1,000 shares of its own stock for $38,000.

Nov. 30   A cash dividend of 60 cents per share was declared by the board of directors.

Dec. 31   A net income of $38,500 was reported for 1971.

Compute the successive book values per share of Chronicle Company stock after each transaction is consummated.

6. The treasurer for Business Weekly, Inc., has prepared a balance sheet at the end of the current year, which includes the following stockholders' equity accounts:

6% cumulative preferred stock, 20,000 shares	$1,000,000
Common stock, 30,000 shares	273,000
Surplus	807,000

The company is authorized to issue 25,000 shares of $50 par value preferred and 100,000 shares of $10 par value common. Of the 20,000 shares of preferred issued, 18,000 were issued at par and 2,000 were issued at $53 per share. A total of 33,000 shares of common have been issued at an average price of $22 per share. Of this total, 3,000 shares have been reacquired by the company at a cost of $57,000, which amount the treasurer has deducted from the Common Stock account. The preferred stock is callable at any time at $55 per share. The company plans to call 2,000 shares of preferred in the future, and the board of directors has authorized that, to this extent, retained income be earmarked as not available for dividends. The Surplus account contains the premiums on the sale of preferred and common stock and $405,000 of retained income. Prepare the stockholders' equity section for Business Weekly, Inc., in accordance with good accounting practices; include a full description of each stock issue with respect to par value, call provision, and number of shares authorized, issued, and held in the treasury.

8-1 The Lorin Company prepared the following income statement for 1971:

Net sales		$1,500,000
Gain on sale of treasury stock		25,000
Issuance of capital stock at a premium		160,000
Total revenues		$1,685,000
Less:		
Cost of goods sold	$825,000	
Operating expenses	340,000	
Loss on disposal of obsolete equipment	70,000	
Dividends declared on capital stock	50,000	
Addition to reserve for contingencies	100,000	
Income taxes (estimated at 40%)	80,000	1,465,000
Net income		$ 220,000

At the beginning of the current year, the audited financial statements of the company show unappropriated retained earnings of $322,000 and a balance in the Reserve for Contingencies account of $150,000. The gain on the sale of treasury stock is not taxable and the loss on the disposal of obsolete equipment is fully deductible in computing taxable income. Income taxes should be estimated at 40% of *income from operations,* and the loss on the sale of obsolete equipment should be reported *net of income taxes.*

Instructions

a. Prepare a revised income statement, assuming that the extraordinary gains and losses are reported in the income statement as recommended by the Accounting Principles Board of the AICPA. The company has 100,000 shares of capital stock outstanding. Show data for earnings per share at the end of the income statement.

b. Prepare a statement of retained earnings. The statement should have three columns as follows: Reserve for Contingencies, Unappropriated, and Total Retained Earnings.

8-2 The stockholders' equity of the O'Neil Corporation on January 1 of the current year is as follows:

Capital stock:		
6% preferred stock, $100 par value, 50,000 shares		
authorized, 7,500 shares issued		$ 750,000
Common stock, $5 par value, 500,000 shares		
authorized, 240,000 shares issued		1,200,000
Additional paid-in capital:		
Premium on preferred stock		75,000
Premium on common stock		960,000
Total paid-in capital		$2,985,000
Retained earnings:		
Reserve for plant expansion	$ 600,000	
Unappropriated	1,350,000	1,950,000
Total stockholders' equity		$4,935,000

The transactions relating to the stockholders' equity accounts during the current year are shown below:

Feb. 1 — Paid regular semiannual dividend on preferred stock, and 80 cents per share cash dividend on common. Both these dividends were declared in December of the past year and properly recorded at that time.

June 20 — Declared semiannual dividend on preferred stock to stockholders of record on July 15, payable on July 28.

Oct. 10 — Declared a 5% stock dividend on common to stockholders of record on October 24, to be distributed November 15; market value $12 a share.

Nov. 18 — Sold 20,000 shares of common stock for $13.50 per share.

Nov. 20 — The board of directors authorized the addition of $100,000 to the Reserve for Plant Expansion.

Dec. 20 — Declared regular semiannual dividend on preferred stock and a dividend of 80 cents per share on common shares of record at January 4, payable on January 20.

Dec. 31 — Net income for the current year amounted to $525,000 (debit Income Summary and credit Retained Earnings).

Instructions

a. Prepare in general journal form the entries necessary to record these transactions on the books of the O'Neil Corporation during the current year.

b. Did O'Neil Corporation increase or decrease the total amount of cash dividend *declared* on common shares during 1971 in comparison with the dividends declared in 1970? Explain.

c. Prepare a balance sheet for the O'Neil Corporation at the end of the current year, assuming that total assets amount to $7,500,000.

8-3 Bunker Bakeries Co. on January 1 of the current year had total retained earnings of $5,920,000. On July 31, the company declared and paid a cash dividend of 50 cents per share.

At November 30 of the current year, the stockholders' equity was as follows:

Capital stock, $10 par value, authorized	
1,000,000 shares, issued and outstanding 700,000 shares	$ 7,000,000
Paid-in capital in excess of par value	4,200,000
Retained earnings	6,790,000
Total stockholders' equity	$17,990,000

During December the company earned net income of $132,540, and on December 30 the board of directors declared a cash dividend of 60 cents per share. The stockholders' equity accounts were also affected during December by the company's action in reacquiring 10,000 shares of its own capital stock for $295,000. Later in the month (and prior to the December 30 dividend declaration), the company sold 6,000 shares of the treasury stock at $32 per share.

Instructions

a. Prepare the stockholders' equity section of the balance sheet at December 31.

b. Prepare a statement of retained earnings for the year.

c. Compute book value per share at November 30 and at December 31. [Net assets at November 30 − (cost of treasury stock acquired and dividends) + (proceeds from sale of treasury stock and December earnings) = net assets at December 31.]

8-4   The stockholders' equity of the Cameron Brick Corporation at December 31, 1972, includes the following accounts:

Stockholders' equity:

$6 noncumulative preferred stock, stated value $100; authorized	
10,000 shares, issued and outstanding 7,500 shares	$ 750,000
Common stock, no par, stated value $8 per share; authorized	
200,000 shares, issued and outstanding 100,000 shares	800,000
Additional paid-in capital: common stock	375,000
Retained earnings (deficit)	(89,150)
Total stockholders' equity, December 31, 1972	$1,835,850

The income statement for 1972, as prepared by the company's bookkeeper, is shown below:

Sales (net)		$1,240,000
Cost of goods sold		760,000
Gross profit on sales		$ 480,000
Operating expenses		404,150
Operating income (not subject to income tax because of flood loss		
and operating loss carry-over from 1971)		$ 75,850
Extraordinary items:		
Loss on resale of treasury stock	($30,000)	
Income tax refund applicable to 1970	24,000	
Uninsured flood loss	(44,000)	(50,000)
Net income		$ 25,850

The company paid no dividends during 1972. An audit at the end of 1972 disclosed the following: On July 1, 1972, the company had purchased equipment for $40,000 which was charged to an operating expense account by mistake. The equipment has an estimated service life of 10 years and an estimated salvage value of $4,000. On March 1, 1972, the company paid a three-year insurance premium in the amount of $2,700, which the bookkeeper charged to an expense account.

Instructions

a.   Prepare the necessary journal entries to correct the errors discovered in the audit. Include depreciation for one-half year on the equipment acquired July 1. Any adjustments of revenue or expense for the current year should be made through the Income Summary account.

b.   Prepare a revised income statement for 1972, showing extraordinary items and earnings per share as recommended by the Accounting Principles Board. The tax refund for 1970 is a prior period adjustment.

c.   Prepare a corrected statement of retained earnings for 1972. (Deficit of $89,150 combined with reported net income of $25,850 indicates reported deficit of $115,000 at January 1, 1972.)

8-5 The net assets of the McGregor Dredging Corporation on December 31, 1972, are represented by the following:

Common stock, $30 par value, issued 120,000 shares,	
of which 115,000 are outstanding	*$3,600,000*
Additional paid-in capital	*670,000*
Retained earnings	*1,200,000*
Total	*$5,470,000*
Less: Treasury stock (at cost: 5,000 shares)	*180,000*
Total stockholders' equity (net assets)	*$5,290,000*

On the basis of the number of shares outstanding at the end of prior years, the **book value** of the common stock was $85 per share on December 31, 1971, and $100 per share on December 31, 1970.

Early in 1972 the company split its shares 2 for 1 and repurchased 5,000 shares of stock shortly after the stock split. A 20% stock dividend had been declared in 1971, at a time when the **market value** of the stock was $77 per share.

The balance of retained earnings on January 1, 1970, was $1,400,000, and the changes in retained earnings throughout the three-year period resulted solely from net income and dividends.

Edward Sherer, a stockholder of McGregor Dredging Corporation, owned 1,000 shares of stock on December 31, 1970, and has neither sold any shares nor purchased additional shares. He received cash dividends from this investment at the end of each year as follows: 1970, $1,400; 1971, $1,800; and 1972, $2,400.

Instructions
a. Prepare a statement of stockholders' equity at December 31, 1971. (*Suggestion:* Compute the total stockholders' equity at December 31, 1971, by determining the number of shares outstanding at that date, and multiplying by the $85 per share book value stated in the problem.)
b. Prepare a statement of stockholders' equity at December 31, 1970.
c. Determine the net income of the McGregor Dredging Corporation for each of the three years, 1970–1972, inclusive. (*Suggestion:* The dividends paid each year can be determined by computing the dividend per share indicated by the information on Sherer's investment.)

8-6 The Miller Company reported retained earnings of $105,000 on December 31, 1971, after appropriating $62,650 for the acquisition of treasury stock. During 1972, the company paid quarterly dividends on its 6% preferred stock and declared a dividend of $1.20 per share on outstanding common shares at December 31, 1972.

Income taxes for the company amounted to $120,000, or 40% of taxable income, and gross profits amounted to 30% on net sales of $2,500,000.

The accounts listed alphabetically below appear in the general ledger of the Miller Company at December 31, 1972, after the books have been closed:

Accounts payable	*$ 53,340*
Accounts receivable	*101,000*
Accrued liabilities	*25,320*
Accumulated depreciation: buildings	*180,000*

Accumulated depreciation: equipment...................	$159,600
Allowance for uncollectible accounts	8,000
Buildings	597,070
Cash.......................................	57,690
Common stock, no par, stated value $10	320,000
Dividends payable	39,000
Equipment	506,300
Income taxes payable (balance due on 1972 income)	34,000
Inventories	145,000
Land.......................................	60,000
Long-term note payable, due July 1, 1976	226,000
Notes receivable...............................	48,400
Organization costs	15,300
Paid-in capital from treasury stock transactions	13,000
Paid-in capital in excess of stated value: common stock	32,000
Preferred stock, 6%............................	200,000
Premium on preferred stock	10,000
Prepaid expenses	6,500
Reserve for treasury stock	62,650
Retained earnings, as of Dec. 31	237,000
Treasury stock (at cost: 2,000 shares)	62,650

The company is authorized to issue 25,000 shares of 6%, $100 par value preferred stock and 50,000 shares of no-par common, stated value $10.

Instructions
a. Prepare a combined statement of income and retained earnings for the Miller Company similar to the statement illustrated for Swift & Company on page 243 of the text. Include the Reserve for Treasury Stock in beginning and ending balances of retained earnings.
b. Prepare a balance sheet suitable for publication for the Miller Company as of December 31, 1972.

9 Cash and investments in securities

CASH

Accountants use the word *cash* to include coin, paper money, checks, money orders, and money on deposit with banks. However, cash does not include postage stamps, IOU's, or postdated checks.

In deciding whether a particular item comes within the classification of cash, the following rule is a useful one: Any medium of exchange which a bank will accept for deposit and immediate credit to the depositor's account should be included in cash.

Balance sheet presentation of cash

Cash is a current asset. In fact, cash is the most current and most liquid of all assets. In judging whether other types of assets qualify for inclusion in the current assets section of the balance sheet, we consider the length of time required for the asset to be converted into cash.

Some bank accounts are restricted as to their use, so that they are not available for disbursement to meet normal operating needs of the business. An example is a bond sinking fund, consisting of cash being accumulated by a corporation for the specific purpose of paying bonded indebtedness at a future date. Such restricted bank deposits are not regarded as current assets because they are not available for use in paying current liabilities.

The banker, credit manager, or investor who studies a balance sheet critically will always be interested in the total amount of cash as compared with other balance sheet items, such as accounts payable. These outside users of a company's financial statements are not interested, however, in such details as the number of separate bank accounts, or in the distinction between cash on hand and cash in banks. A business concern that carries checking accounts with several banks will maintain a separate ledger account for each bank account. On the balance sheet, however, the entire amount of cash on hand and cash on deposit with the several banks will be shown as a single amount. One objective in preparing financial statements is to keep them short, concise, and easy to read.

Management responsibilities relating to cash

Efficient management of cash includes measures that will:

1. Prevent losses from fraud or theft.

2. Provide accurate accounting for cash receipts, cash payments, and cash balances.

3. Maintain a sufficient amount of cash at all times to make necessary payments, plus a reasonable balance for emergencies.

4. Prevent unnecessarily large amounts of cash from being held idle in bank accounts which produce no revenue.

Internal control over cash is sometimes regarded merely as a means of preventing fraud or theft. A good system of internal control, however, will also aid in achieving management's other objectives of accurate accounting and the maintenance of adequate but not excessive cash balances.

Basic requirements for internal control

To achieve internal control over cash, or any other group of assets, requires first of all that the custody of assets be clearly separated from the recording of transactions. Secondly, the recording function should be subdivided among employees, so that the work of one person is verified by that of another. This subdivision of duties discourages fraud, because collusion among employees would be necessary to conceal an irregularity. Internal control is more easily achieved in large companies than in small concerns, because extensive subdivision of duties is more feasible in the larger business.

Cash is more susceptible to theft than any other asset. Furthermore, a large portion of the total transactions of a business involve the receipt or disbursement of cash. For both these reasons, internal control over cash is of great importance to management and also to the employees of a business. If a cash shortage arises in a business in which internal controls are weak or nonexistent, every employee is under suspicion. Perhaps no one employee can be proved guilty of the theft, but neither can any employee prove his innocence.

On the other hand, if internal controls over cash are adequate, theft without detection is virtually impossible except through the collusion of two or more employees.

The major steps in establishing internal control over cash include the following:

1. Separate the function of handling cash from the maintenance of accounting records. The cashier should not maintain the accounting records and should not have access to the records. Accounting personnel should not have access to cash.

2. Separate the function of receiving cash from that of disbursing cash. The same person should not handle cash receipts and also make cash disbursements.

3. Require that all cash receipts be deposited daily in the bank, and that all cash payments be made by check. Keep cash on hand under lock.

The application of these principles in building an adequate system of internal control over cash can best be illustrated by considering separately the topics of cash receipts and cash disbursements.

Cash receipts

Cash receipts consist of two major types: cash received over the counter at the time of a sale, and cash received through the mail as collections on accounts receivable.

Use of cash registers. Cash received over the counter at the time of a sale should be rung up on a cash register, so located that the customer will see the amount recorded. If store operations can be so arranged that two employees must participate in each sales transaction, stronger internal control will be achieved than when one employee is permitted to handle a transaction in its entirety. In some stores this objective is accomplished by employing a central cashier who rings on a cash register the sales made by all clerks.

At the end of the day, the store manager or other supervisor should compare the cash register tape, showing the total sales for the day, with the total cash collected.

Use of prenumbered sales tickets. Internal control may be further strengthened by writing out a prenumbered sales ticket in duplicate at the time of each sale. The original is given to the customer and the carbon copy retained. At the end of the day an employee computes a total sales figure from these duplicate tickets, and also makes sure that no tickets are missing from the series. The total amount of sales as computed from the duplicate sales tickets is then compared with the total sales recorded on the cash register.

Cash received through the mail. The procedures for handling checks and currency received through the mail are also based on the internal control principle that two or more employees should participate in every transaction.

The employee who opens the mail should prepare a list of the amounts received. In order that this list shall represent the total receipts of the day, the totals recorded on the cash registers may be included in the list. One copy of the list is forwarded with the cash to the cashier, who will deposit the cash in the bank. Another copy of the list is sent with the customers' remittance letters to the bookkeeper, who will record the cash collections.

The total cash receipts each day by the bookkeeper should agree with the amount of the cashier's deposit, and also with the list of total cash receipts for the day.

Cash over and short. In handling over-the-counter cash receipts, a few errors in change making will inevitably occur. These errors will cause a cash shortage or overage at the end of the day, when the cash is counted and compared with the reading on the cash register.

For example, assume that the total cash sales for the day as recorded by the cash register amount to $500, but that the cash in the drawer when counted amounts to only $490. The following entry would be made to record the day's sales and the cash shortage of $10.

Recording	*Cash*	*490*	
Cash	*Cash Over and Short*	*10*	
Shortage	*Sales*		*500*

The account entitled Cash Over and Short is debited with shortages and credited with overages. If the cash shortages during an entire accounting period are in excess of the cash overages, the Cash Over and Short account will have a debit balance and will be shown as a miscellaneous expense in the income statement. On the other hand, if the overages exceed the shortages, the Cash Over and Short account will show a credit balance at the end of the period and should be treated as an item of miscellaneous revenue.

Cash disbursements

An adequate system of internal control requires that each day's cash receipts be deposited intact in the bank and that all disbursements be made by check. Checks should be prenumbered. Any spoiled checks should be marked "Void" and filed in sequence so that all numbers in the series can be accounted for.

The official designated to sign checks should not be given authority to approve invoices for payment or to make entries in the accounting records. When a check is presented to an official for signature, it should be accompanied by the approved invoice and voucher showing that the transaction has been fully verified and that payment is justified. When the check is signed, the supporting invoices and vouchers should be perforated or stamped "Paid" to eliminate any possibility of their later being presented in support of another check. If these rules are followed, it is almost impossible for a fraudulent cash disbursement to be concealed without the collusion of two or more persons.

BANK CHECKING ACCOUNTS

Opening a bank account

When a depositor first opens a bank account, he must sign his name and a signature card, exactly as he will sign checks. The signature card is kept on file by the bank, so that any check bearing a signature not familiar to bank employees may be compared with the depositor's signature card. When a corporation opens a bank account, the board of directors will pass a resolution designating the officers or employees authorized to sign checks. A copy of this resolution is given to the bank.

Making deposits

The depositor fills out a deposit ticket (usually in duplicate) for each deposit. The deposit ticket includes a listing of each check deposited and the code number of the bank on which it is drawn. Space is also provided for listing the amounts of coin and currency deposited.

The bank statement

Each month the bank will provide the depositor with a statement of his account, accompanied by the checks paid and charged to his account during the month. The bank statement illustrated below shows the balance on deposit at the beginning of the month, the deposits, the checks paid, any other debits and credits during the month, and the new balance at the end of the month.

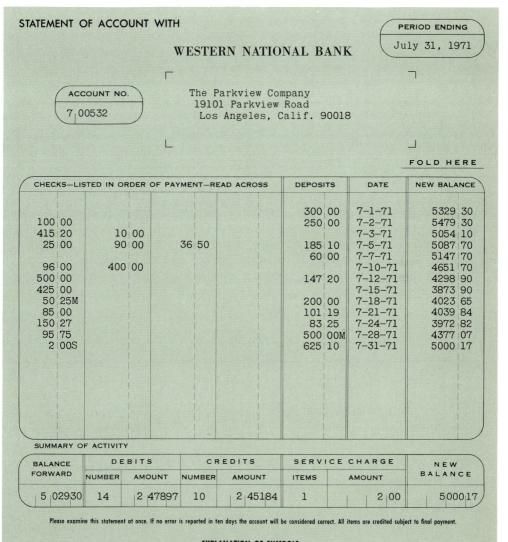

STATEMENT OF ACCOUNT WITH

WESTERN NATIONAL BANK

PERIOD ENDING
July 31, 1971

ACCOUNT NO.
7 00532

The Parkview Company
19101 Parkview Road
Los Angeles, Calif. 90018

FOLD HERE

CHECKS—LISTED IN ORDER OF PAYMENT—READ ACROSS					DEPOSITS	DATE	NEW BALANCE
					300 00	7-1-71	5329 30
100 00					250 00	7-2-71	5479 30
415 20	10 00					7-3-71	5054 10
25 00	90 00	36 50			185 10	7-5-71	5087 70
					60 00	7-7-71	5147 70
96 00	400 00					7-10-71	4651 70
500 00					147 20	7-12-71	4298 90
425 00						7-15-71	3873 90
50 25M					200 00	7-18-71	4023 65
85 00					101 19	7-21-71	4039 84
150 27					83 25	7-24-71	3972 82
95 75					500 00M	7-28-71	4377 07
2 00S					625 10	7-31-71	5000 17

SUMMARY OF ACTIVITY

BALANCE FORWARD	DEBITS		CREDITS		SERVICE CHARGE		NEW BALANCE
	NUMBER	AMOUNT	NUMBER	AMOUNT	ITEMS	AMOUNT	
5 02930	14	2 47897	10	2 45184	1	2 00	5000 17

Please examine this statement at once. If no error is reported in ten days the account will be considered correct. All items are credited subject to final payment.

EXPLANATION OF SYMBOLS

S SERVICE CHARGE   M MISCELLANEOUS ENTRY

Uncollected checks. Certain items in the bank statement of The Parkview Company illustrated above warrant explanation. On July 12 The Parkview Company received a check for $50.25 from J. B. Ball, and the check was included in the bank deposit made on that day. The Ball check was returned to Western National Bank by the bank on which it was drawn marked NSF (Not Sufficient Funds), indicating that Mr. Ball did not have a sufficient balance in his account to cover the check. Western National Bank therefore charged the NSF check against The Parkview Company's account as shown by the July 18 item of $50 25. (The letter M alongside this entry stands for Miscellaneous Entry.)

Upon receipt of the NSF check returned by the bank, The Parkview Company should remove this item from the cash classification by a journal entry debiting an account receivable from J. B. Ball and crediting Cash. The NSF check is thus regarded as a receivable until it is collected directly from the drawer and redeposited, or is determined to be worthless.

Bank service charges. Under the date of July 31 on the illustrated bank statement is a debit for $2 accompanied by the symbol S. This symbol means Service Charge, a charge made by the bank to cover the expense of handling the account. The amount of the service charge is based upon such considerations as the average balance of the account and the number of checks and deposits. (Most banks would probably not make a service charge on The Parkview Company's account because the balance is substantial and the activity is low. However, a service charge is shown here for the purpose of illustrating its use.) When the bank sends the monthly statement and paid checks to the depositor, it will include debit memoranda for service charges and any other charges not represented by checks.

Miscellaneous charges. Other charges which may appear on the bank statement include rental fees for safe deposit boxes, charges for printing checks, collection charges on notes left with the bank for collection, and interest charges on borrowing from the bank.

Reconciling the bank account

The balance shown on the monthly statement received from the bank will usually not agree with the balance of cash shown by the depositor's books. Certain transactions recorded by the depositor will not yet have been recorded by the bank. The most common examples are:

1. Outstanding checks. These are checks issued and recorded by the depositor but not yet presented to the bank for payment.

2. Deposits in transit. Deposits mailed to the bank are usually not entered on the bank's books until a day or two later than the entry on the depositor's books.

Transactions which may appear on the bank statement but which have not yet been recorded by the depositor include:

1. Service charges
2. Charges for NSF checks
3. Miscellaneous bank charges and credits

In some cases the bank reconciliation will be complete after such items as outstanding checks, deposits in transit, and miscellaneous bank charges have been taken into account. Other cases may require the correction of errors by the bank or by the depositor to complete the reconciliation. When a company maintains accounts in several banks, a common type of error is to record a check drawn on one bank as a payment from another bank account. Similar errors may occur in recording deposits.

Procedures for preparing a bank reconciliation

The term *reconciliation* means determining those items which make up the difference between the balance appearing on the bank statement and the balance of cash according to the depositor's records. By listing and studying these discrepancies, it is possible to determine the correct figure for cash to appear on the balance sheet. Specific steps to be taken in preparing a bank reconciliation are:

1. Compare the deposits listed on the bank statement with the deposits shown in the company's records. Place check marks in the company's cash records and on the bank statement beside the items which agree. Any unchecked item in the company's record of deposits will be deposits not yet recorded by the bank, and should be added to the balance reported by the bank. Determine that any deposits in transit listed in last month's bank reconciliation are included in the current month's bank statement.

2. Arrange the paid checks in numerical order and compare each check with the corresponding entry in the cash payments journal. (In the case of personal bank accounts for which the only record maintained is the checkbook, compare each paid check with the check stub.) Place a check mark in the depositor's cash payments journal opposite each entry for which a paid check has been returned by the bank. The unchecked entries should be listed in the bank reconciliation as outstanding checks to be deducted from the balance reported by the bank. Determine whether the checks listed as outstanding in the bank reconciliation for the preceding month have been returned by the bank this month. If not, such checks should be listed as outstanding in the current reconciliation.

3. Deduct from the balance per the books any debit memoranda issued by the bank which have not been recorded by the depositor. In the illustrated bank reconciliation on page 273, examples are the NSF check for $50.25 and the $2 service charge.

4. Add to the balance per books any credit memoranda issued by the bank which have not been recorded by the depositor. An example in the illustrated bank reconciliation on page 273 is the credit of $500 collected by the bank in behalf of The Parkview Company.

5. Prepare a bank reconciliation, reflecting the preceding steps, similar to the illustration on page 273.

6. Make journal entries for any items on the bank statement which have not yet been recorded in the depositor's accounts.

Illustration. The July bank statement prepared by the bank for The Parkview Company was illustrated on page 269. This statement shows a balance of cash on deposit at July 31 of $5,000.17. We shall assume that The Parkview Company's records at July 31 show a bank balance of $4,172.57. Our purpose in preparing the bank reconciliation is to identify the items that make up this difference and to determine the correct cash balance.

Assume that the specific steps to be taken in preparing a bank reconciliation have been carried out and that the following reconciling items have been discovered:

1. A deposit of $310.90 mailed to the bank on July 31 does not appear on the bank statement.

2. A credit memorandum issued by the bank on July 28 in the amount of $500 was returned with the July bank statement and appears in the Deposits column of that statement. This credit represents the proceeds of a note receivable left with the bank by The Parkview Company for the purpose of collection. The collection of the note has not yet been recorded by The Parkview Company.

3. Four checks issued in July or prior months have not yet been paid by the bank. These checks are:

Check No.	Date	Amount
801	June 15	$100.00
888	July 24	10.25
890	July 27	402.50
891	July 30	205.00

4. A debit memorandum issued by the bank on July 31 for a $2 service charge was enclosed with the July bank statement.

5. Check No. 875 was issued July 20 in the amount of $85 but was erroneously listed on the check stub and in the cash payments journal as $58. The check, in payment of telephone service, was paid by the bank, returned with the July bank statement, and correctly listed on the bank statement as an $85 charge to the account.

6. No entry has as yet been made in The Parkview Company's accounts to reflect the bank's action on July 18 of charging against the account the NSF check for $50.25 drawn by J. B. Ball.

The July 31 bank reconciliation for The Parkview Company follows:

Bank
Statement
and
Depositor's
Records
Must Be
Reconciled

THE PARKVIEW COMPANY
Bank Reconciliation
July 31, 19___

Balance per books, July 31		$4,172.57
Add: Note receivable collected for us by bank		500.00
		$4,672.57
Less: Service charge.	$ 2.00	
NSF check of J. B. Ball	50.25	
Error on check stub No. 875	27.00	79.25
Adjusted book balance		$4,593.32
Balance per bank statement, July 31.		$5,000.17
Add: Deposit of July 31 not recorded by bank.		310.90
		$5,311.07
Less: Outstanding checks		
No. 801.	$100.00	
No. 888. . . . . :	10.25	
No. 890.	402.50	
No. 891.	205.00	717.75
Adjusted balance (as above)		$4,593.32

The adjusted balance of $4,593.32 is the amount of cash owned by The Parkview Company and is, therefore, the amount which should appear as cash on the July 31 balance sheet.

Note that the adjusted balance of cash differs from both the bank statement and the depositor's records. This difference is explained by the fact that neither set of records is up to date as of July 31, and also by the existence of an error on The Parkview Company's records.

Adjusting the records after the reconciliation. To make The Parkview Company's records up-to-date and accurate, entries are necessary for

1. The note receivable collected by the bank. Debit Cash $500; credit Notes Receivable $500.

2. The service charge by the bank. Debit Miscellaneous Expense $2; credit Cash $2.

3. The NSF check of J. B. Ball. Debit Accounts Receivable—J. B. Ball $50.25; credit Cash $50.25

4. The error in recording the $85 check for telephone service as a $58 item. Debit Telephone Expense $27; credit Cash $27.

Petty cash

As previously emphasized, adequate internal control over cash requires that all receipts be deposited in the bank and all disbursements be made by check. However, every business finds it convenient to have a small amount of cash on hand with which to make some very small expenditures. Examples include payments for postage stamps, collect telegrams, and taxi fares. Internal control over these small cash payments can best be achieved through a petty cash fund.

Establishing the petty cash fund. To create a petty cash fund, also called an *imprest fund,* a check is written for a round amount such as $50 or $100, which will cover the small expenditures to be paid in cash for a period of two or three weeks. This check is cashed and the money kept on hand in a petty cash box or drawer in the office.

The entry for the issuance of the check is:

Creating the Petty Cash Fund	*Petty Cash*	*100*
	Cash	*100*

Making disbursements from the petty cash fund. As cash payments are made out of the petty cash box, the custodian of the fund is required to fill out a *petty cash voucher* for each expenditure. A petty cash voucher shows the amount paid, the purpose of the expenditure, the date, and the signature of the person receiving the money. A petty cash voucher should be prepared for every payment made from the fund. The petty cash box should, therefore, always contain cash and/or vouchers totaling the exact amount of the fund.

The petty cash custodian should be informed that occasional surprise counts of the fund will be made and that he is personally responsible for the fund being intact at all times. Careless handling of petty cash has often been a first step toward large defalcations; consequently, misuse of petty cash funds should not be tolerated.

Replenishing the petty cash fund. Assume that a petty cash fund of $100 was established on June 1 and that payments totaling $89.75 were made from the fund during the next two weeks. Since the $100 originally placed in the fund is nearly exhausted, it is necessary that the fund be replenished. A check is drawn payable to Petty Cash for the exact amount of the expenditures, $89.75. This check is cashed and the money placed in the petty cash box. The vouchers totaling that amount are perforated to prevent their reuse and filed in support of the replenishment check. The journal entry to record the issuance of the check will debit the expense accounts indicated by inspection of the vouchers, as follows:

Replenishment of Petty Cash Fund	*Postage Expense*	*60.60*
	Telephone & Telegraph Expense	*4.80*
	Freight-in	*6.00*
	Gasoline Expense	*5.25*
	Miscellaneous Expense	*13.10*
	Cash	*89.75*

In studying the procedures for operation of a petty cash fund, emphasis should be placed on the fact that the Petty Cash account *is debited only when the fund is first established. Expense accounts will be debited each time the fund is replenished.* There will be no further entries in the petty cash fund after it is established, unless the fund is discontinued or a decision is made to change the size of the fund from the original $100 amount.

The petty cash fund is usually replenished at the end of an accounting period, even though the fund is not running low, so that all vouchers in the fund are charged to expense accounts before these accounts are closed and financial statements prepared. If the petty cash fund were not replenished at the end of the period, expenditures from petty cash would not be reflected in the income statement for the period in which these expenditures occurred.

INVESTMENTS IN CORPORATE SECURITIES

Security transactions from the viewpoint of investors

The capital stocks and bonds of most large corporations are listed on the New York Stock Exchange or on other organized security exchanges. Among the investors in these securities are trust funds, pension funds, universities, banks, insurance companies, industrial corporations, and great numbers of individuals. The stocks and bonds of many smaller companies are not listed on an organized exchange but are bought and sold *over the counter.* At the time of issuance of bonds or stocks, the transaction is between the investor and the issuing corporation (or its underwriting agent). The great daily volume of security transactions, however, consists of the sale of stocks and bonds by investors to other investors. Virtually all these security transactions are made through a stockbroker acting as intermediary.

Listed corporations report to a million owners. When a corporation invites the public to purchase its stocks and bonds, it accepts an obligation to keep the public informed on its financial condition and the profitability of operations. This obligation of disclosure includes public distribution of financial statements. The Securities and Exchange Commission is a government agency responsible for seeing that corporations make full and fair disclosure of their affairs so that investors have a basis for intelligent investment decisions. The flow of corporate accounting data distributed through newspapers and financial advisory services to millions of investors is a vital force in the functioning of our economy; in fact, the successful working of a profit-motivated economy rests upon the quality and dependability of the accounting information being reported.

Listed corporations are audited by certified public accountants. Corporations with securities listed on organized stock exchanges are required to have regular audits of their accounts by independent public accountants. The financial statements distributed each year to stockholders are accompanied by a report by a firm of certified public accountants indicating that an audit has been made and expressing an opinion as to the fairness of the company's financial statements. It is the independent status of the auditing firm that enables investors to place confidence in audited financial statements.

Government bonds as current assets

A recent balance sheet of Zenith Radio Corporation shows the following items listed first in the current asset section:

Current assets:	
Cash..	*$17,370,826*
U.S. government securities, at cost, which approximates market	*92,066,509*

The action of Zenith Radio Corporation in investing in United States government bonds is in no way unusual. The published balance sheets of a great many corporations show holdings of such securities. These bonds differ from the Series E United States savings bonds owned by many individuals, in that they pay interest every six months and may be sold at any time in the securities market without any loss of interest. Government bonds are just as safe and almost as liquid as cash itself. In the event that cash is needed for any operating purpose, the bonds can be quickly converted into cash; in the meantime, bonds are preferable to cash because of the interest income which they produce. From the viewpoint of creditors as well as that of management, it is often said in appraising a company's financial strength that "cash and government securities" amount to so many dollars. This practice of lumping together cash and government securities reflects the general attitude that these two assets are essentially similar.

A security investment consisting of United States government bonds is a current asset, regardless of the maturity date of the bonds and regardless of how long the bonds have been held or how long the company expects to hold them. The important point is that these securities *can be converted into cash at any time without interfering with the normal operation of the business.* A principal purpose of the balance sheet classification of current assets and current liabilities is to aid in portraying short-run debt-paying ability. For this purpose government bonds deserve to be listed immediately after cash because they are even more liquid than accounts receivable or inventory. To a loan officer in a bank reviewing an application for a loan, there is no more impressive or reassuring asset on the balance sheet of a prospective borrower than a large amount of high-quality bonds.

Investments in other marketable securities

Some corporations choose to invest in bonds and stocks of other corporations as well as in United States government bonds. If these industrial securities are listed on a securities exchange and are not held for the purpose of exercising control over the issuing corporation, they should be classified as current assets. Some accounting writers have attempted to distinguish between "temporary" and "permanent" investments in marketable securities with the objective of excluding the latter type from current assets. In the opinion of the authors, such a distinction cannot be made consistently in practice and, furthermore, is quite unnecessary. For example, assume that a department store owns 500 shares of the common stock of American Telephone and Telegraph. The store has owned the stock for several years and has no intention of selling it in the near future, so this investment could reasonably be called a permanent one. Of course these shares are not held for the purpose of exercising control over the telephone company, or for any business reason other than that of sound investment. This security investment is a current asset of the highest quality; any analysis of the store's balance sheet for credit purposes would be facilitated by having the AT&T stock listed immediately after cash in the current asset section.

In summary, if security investments are limited to securities of unquestioned marketability (and are not owned for the purpose of bolstering business relations with the issuing corporation), these stocks and bonds may be converted into cash at any time without interfering with normal operations. An expressed *intention* by management as to near-term sale of the securities is *not* a requisite for classification as a current asset.

Investments for purpose of control. Some corporations buy stocks of other corporations in sufficient quantity that a degree of control may be exercised over the issuing corporation. Sometimes a substantial investment in stock of a customer company may be helpful in maintaining good business relations. Investments of this type cannot be sold without disturbing established policies; therefore, such investments are not current assets. They should be carried on the books at cost. On the balance sheet, they should be listed below the current asset section under a heading such as Investments.

Valuation of marketable securities

At cost. Investments in securities are usually carried at cost, and no gain or loss is recognized until the securities are sold. One of the basic concepts in accounting is that gains shall not be recognized until they are realized, and the usual test of realization is the sale of the asset in question. In current practice the market value of securities is often disclosed in a parenthetical note on the balance sheet, but the securities are nevertheless valued at cost.

Some accountants argue that investments in securities *should* be valued in the balance sheet at current market price regardless of whether this price is above or below cost. There appear to be at least three strong arguments for showing security investments at current market value: (1) the keen interest of creditors in the present market value of security holdings, (2) the availability of current market quotations, which definitely establish market value for this type of asset, and (3) the fact that the securities can be sold without interfering with the normal operation of the business. Despite these arguments, however, market price has not won acceptance in current practice as a basis for balance sheet valuation of security investments.

One argument against market price as a valuation basis is that in a rising market the writing up of the Investments account would involve the recording of an unrealized profit. However, accountants often recognize losses on the basis of objective evidence, even though the amount of the loss has not been established through sale of the property. Consequently, when the current value of marketable securities declines below cost, some accountants would favor writing down the Investment account and debiting an account such as Loss from Decline in Market Value of Securities.

At the lower of cost or market. The valuation of investment securities at cost is generally accepted, but accounting theory also treats as acceptable the lower-of-cost-or-market method. The objective of this method of valuation is to give effect to market declines without recognizing market increases, and the result is a most conservative statement of investments in the balance sheet. The lower-of-cost-or-market concept has two alternative interpretations. It may be applied by (1) taking the lower of cost or market for each security owned, or (2) comparing the cost of the total holdings of securities with the market value of the securities as a group. Application of the lower-of-cost-or-market rule to each security individually will produce the lowest possible balance sheet amount for security investments.

Once the carrying value of an investment in securities has been written down to reflect a decline in market price, it is not considered acceptable to restore the amount written off even though the market price afterward recovers to as much as or more than the original cost. To do so would be regarded as recording an unrealized profit. When the security is sold, the gain or loss to be recorded is the difference between the sale price and the adjusted carrying value of the security on the books.

In terms of the usefulness of the balance sheet to creditors and other readers, it seems probable that the lower-of-cost-or-market rule should be applied to the securities holdings as a group rather than on an individual basis. Assume, for example, that a company owned a dozen securities and 11 of them advanced strongly in price during the year while the price of the twelfth security declined below its cost. If the lower-of-cost-or-market rule were applied on an individual basis, the company's balance sheet at the end of the year would show a reduction in the carrying value of securities and the income statement would show a loss from decline in market value of securities. Such reporting seems to have no justification other than conservatism, and conservatism is surely not a virtue when it results in misleading financial statements.

Disclosing the basis of valuation in the balance sheet. Because of the variety of methods possible for valuation of investments in securities, the balance sheet should contain a notation as to the valuation method being used. It is also important that the method selected be used consistently from year to year. To illustrate the balance sheet presentation of marketable securities under different valuation methods, the following excerpts are taken from published statements of leading corporations:

United States Steel Corporation:
    U.S. government securities, at cost $317,659,464

Sears, Roebuck and Co.:
    Marketable securities, market value $29,647,804 . . . . $ 1,350,409

Standard Oil Company (New Jersey):
    Marketable securities, at lower of cost or market $904,189,000

Effect of income tax regulations upon security valuation. For tax purposes no gain or loss is recognized on an investment in securities until the time of sale. Many businesses which invest in securities prefer to follow this policy for general accounting purposes as well and therefore carry their security investments at cost, unless there is a substantial and apparently permanent decrease in the market value of securities owned.

Determining the cost of investments in stocks and bonds

The par value or face value of the security is not used in recording an investment; only the cost is entered in the Investments account.[1] Cost includes any commission paid to a broker.

The principal distinction between the recording of an investment in bonds and investment in stocks is that interest on bonds accrues from day to day. The interest accrued since the last semiannual interest payment date is paid for by the purchaser and should be recorded separately from the cost of the bond itself. Dividends on stock, however, do not accrue and the entire purchase price paid by the investor in stocks is recorded in the Investments account.

Income on investments in stocks. Dividends are usually not recorded as income until received. The entry upon receipt of a dividend check consists of a debit to Cash and a credit to Dividends Earned.

Dividends in the form of additional shares of stock are not income to the stockholder, and only a memorandum entry needs to be made to record the increase in number of shares owned. The *cost basis per share* is decreased, however, because of the larger number of shares comprising the investment after distribution of a stock dividend. As an example, assume that an investor paid $72 a share for 100 shares of stock, a total cost of $7,200. Later he received 20 additional shares as a stock dividend. His cost per share is thereby reduced to $60 a share, computed by dividing his total cost of $7,200 by the 120 shares owned after the 20% stock dividend.

Purchase of bonds between interest dates. When bonds are purchased between interest dates, the purchaser pays the agreed price for the bond

---

[1] The market price of a bond is stated as a percentage of its par value; thus a price of 92 means $920 market value for a bond of $1,000 par value. See Chap. 12 for a more complete explanation of bond prices.

plus the interest accrued since the last interest payment date. By this arrangement the new owner becomes entitled to receive in full the next semiannual interest payment. An account entitled Accrued Bond Interest Receivable should be debited for the amount of interest purchased. For example, assume the purchase of a 6%, $1,000 bond at a price of 100 (100% of par value) and accrued interest of $10. The entry is as follows:

Separate Account for Accrued Bond Interest Purchased

Investment in Bonds	*1,000*	
Accrued Bond Interest Receivable	*10*	
Cash		*1,010*
Purchased 6% bond of XYZ Co. at 100 and accrued interest.		

Four months later at the next semiannual interest payment date, the investor will receive an interest check for $30, which will be recorded as follows:

Note Portion of Interest Check Earned

Cash	*30*	
Accrued Bond Interest Receivable		*10*
Bond Interest Earned		*20*
Received semiannual interest on XYZ Co. bond.		

This $20 credit to Bond Interest Earned represents the amount actually earned during the four months the bond was owned.

Entries to record bond interest earned each period. If the investor in bonds is to determine bond interest earned each year on an accrual basis, an adjusting entry will be necessary at the balance sheet date for any interest earned but not yet received. This procedure is similar to that used in accounting for interest on notes receivable. The series of entries on page 281 illustrates the accounting for bond interest earned by a company on a calendar-year basis of accounting. The investment consists of $100,000 face value of 6% bonds with interest dates of February 28 and August 31.

Acquisition of bonds at premium or discount

In the discussion of bonds payable from the viewpoint of the issuing corporation (to be presented in Chapter 12) emphasis will be placed on the point that the issuing company *must* amortize the premium or discount over the life of the bonds. The position of the *investor in bonds,* however, is very different with respect to the significance of premium or discount. Many investors purchasing bonds above or below par do *not* amortize the premium or discount on these investments, because they do not expect to hold the bonds until maturity. Since bond issues often run for 25 years or more, it is the exception rather than the rule for an individual investor to hold the bond until it matures. If the investor sells the bond before it matures, the price he receives may be either above or below his cost, according to the current state of the bond market. Under these circumstances there is no

1971				
Dec. 31	*Accrued Bond Interest Receivable*	*2,000*		
	Bond Interest Earned			*2,000*
	To accrue four months' interest earned on $100,000			
	face value of 6% bonds.			
1972				
Feb. 28	*Cash*	*3,000*		
	Accrued Bond Interest Receivable.			*2,000*
	Bond Interest Earned			*1,000*
	Received semiannual bond interest.			
Aug. 31	*Cash*	*3,000*		
	Bond Interest Earned			*3,000*
	Received semiannual bond interest.			
Dec. 31	*Accrued Bond Interest Receivable*	*2,000*		
	Bond Interest Earned			*2,000*
	To accrue four months' interest earned on $100,000			
	face value of 6% bonds.			

assurance that amortization of premium or discount would give any more accurate measurement of investment income than would be obtained by carrying the bonds at cost.

Amortization of premium on bonds owned. Large institutional investors who purchase bonds at a premium or discount with the possibility of holding them until maturity may decide to follow a policy of amortizing or writing off the premium or discount over the remaining life of the bonds. When a bond reaches maturity, only the face value of $1,000 will be paid by the issuing corporation. The value of a bond purchased at a premium will, therefore, tend to decrease toward par as the maturity date approaches, and the carrying value of the bond in the balance sheet can logically be reduced in each successive year.

The income to an investor from a bond purchased at a premium and held until maturity *equals the total interest received minus the premium paid;* consequently, the interest earned in each year should be reduced by deducting a portion of the premium paid for the bond. As an example, assume that on January 1, 1972, an investor purchased $100,000 of 6% bonds of the Fox Corporation payable January 1, 1982. Interest is payable on July 1 and January 1. The purchase price was 104¾ and the broker's commission $250, making a total cost of $105,000. The $5,000 excess of cost over maturity value is to be written off against the interest received during the 10 years the bonds will be held. Since there are 20 interest periods of six months each, the premium to be amortized each six months is $5,000 ÷ 20, or $250. A check for $3,000 bond interest will be received each six months; of this amount $250 may be regarded as recovery of the premium paid and the remaining $2,750 as interest earned. The journal entries for the first year the bonds are owned will be as follows:

Investor's Entries Showing Amortization of Premium

```
1972
Jan.  1   Investment in Bonds .....................   105,000
              Cash .........................                   105,000
          Purchased 100 6% bonds of Fox Corporation at
          104¾ plus commission of $250. Bonds mature
          Jan. 1, 1982.

July  1   Cash..........................             3,000
              Bond Interest Earned ..............             3,000
          Received semiannual bond interest payment.

July  1   Bond Interest Earned.....................    250
              Investment in Bonds ................             250
          To amortize ½₀ of $5,000 premium.

Dec. 31   Accrued Bond Interest Receivable ...........   3,000
              Bond Interest Earned ..............             3,000
          To accrue bond interest earned to end of year.

Dec. 31   Bond Interest Earned.....................    250
              Investment in Bonds................             250
          To amortize ½₀ of $5,000 premium.

Dec. 31   Bond Interest Earned.....................  5,500
              Income Summary.................             5,500
          To close Bond Interest Earned account.
```

The accrued bond interest receivable of $3,000 at December 31 will appear in the balance sheet as a current asset, which will be collected January 1 upon receipt of the bond interest check. The bonds will also appear in the current asset section at $104,500, which represents the cost of $105,000 minus the $500 of premium amortized during the year.

The two essential ideas portrayed by this series of entries may be stated as follows: (1) The carrying value of the bonds is gradually being reduced to par by amortizing the premium; and (2) the net interest earned each year is equal to the interest received minus the amount of premium amortized.

Amortization of discount on bonds owned. The value of a bond purchased for *less than its face value* will tend to increase to par as the maturity date approaches. Amortization of the discount on an investment in bonds means writing up the carrying value of the bonds each year with an offsetting credit to the Bond Interest Earned account. The income from a bond purchased at a discount and held until maturity is equal to the total of the interest payments received plus the amount of the discount.

As an example of the periodic entries for amortization of discount on bond investments, assume that on January 1, 1972, an investor purchased

$200,000 face value of 6% bonds of the Bay Corporation payable January 1, 1982. Interest is payable July 1 and January 1. The purchase price was 94¾ and the broker's commission $500, making a total cost of $190,000. Since there are 20 interest periods of six months each, the discount to be amortized each six months is $10,000 ÷ 20, or $500. A check for $6,000 bond interest will be received each six months; in addition, the bond interest earned will be increased $500 by writing up the carrying value of the investment.

The journal entries for the first year the bonds are owned will be as follows:

Investor's
Entries
Showing
Amortiza-
tion of
Discount
	1972
	Jan. 1 Investment in Bonds ....
	    Cash............................
	    Purchased 200 6% bonds of Bay Corporation at
	    94¾ plus commission of $500. Bonds mature
	    Jan. 1, 1982.
		190,000
		
		190,000

	July 1 Cash ....
	    Bond Interest Earned............
	    Received semiannual bond interest payment.
		6,000
		
		6,000

	July 1 Investment in Bonds ....
	    Bond Interest Earned............
	    To amortize ¹⁄₂₀ of $10,000 discount.
		500
		
		500

	Dec. 31 Accrued Bond Interest Receivable...........
	    Bond Interest Earned..............
	    To accrue bond interest earned to end of year.
		6,000
		
		6,000

	Dec. 31 Investment in Bonds ....
	    Bond Interest Earned............
	    To amortize ¹⁄₂₀ of $10,000 discount.
		500
		
		500

	Dec. 31 Bond Interest Earned ....
	    Income Summary ....
	    To close Bond Interest Earned account.
		13,000
		
		13,000

The fact that a bond will be paid at par at a distant maturity date does not ensure that its price will move closer to par during each year of its life; bond prices fluctuate with changes in market rates of interest, business activity, and other elements of the economic environment.

Gains and losses from sale of investments in securities

The sale of an investment in stocks is recorded by debiting Cash for the amount received and crediting the Investment account for the carrying value of the stocks sold. Any difference between the proceeds of sale and the carrying value of the investment is recorded by a debit to Loss on Sale of Investments or by a credit to Gain on Sale of Investments.

At the date of sale of an investment in bonds, any interest accrued since the last interest payment date should be recorded. For example, assume that 10 bonds of the Elk Corporation carried on the books of an investor at $9,600 are sold at a price of 94 and accrued interest of $50. The commission on the sale is $25. The following entry should be made:

Investment	*Cash*	*9,425*	
in Bonds	*Loss on Sale of Investments*	*225*	
Sold at	*Investment in Bonds*		*9,600*
a Loss	*Bond Interest Earned*		*50*
	Sold 10 bonds of Elk Corporation at 94 and accrued interest of $50 less broker's commission of $25.		

Gains and losses on the sale of investments are extraordinary items and should be presented in the income statement below the figure representing income from operations.

Investments in mortgages and long-term notes

Mortgages are often acquired at less than face value. As an example, an investor purchases for $18,000 a mortgage of $20,000 face amount maturing in five years and paying interest quarterly at the rate of 6% a year. Two alternatives are open with regard to the recognition of income: (1) The mortgage may be carried at cost and only cash interest payments credited to income; or (2) the mortgage investment account may be written up by one-fifth of the discount in each of the five years and this amount credited to Interest Earned, in addition to the cash interest received. Under the first method, the yearly interest earned will be $1,200 (6% × $20,000), but when the mortgage is collected at the end of the fifth year an additional $2,000 of income (the excess of the face amount over cost) must be recognized. Under the second method calling for the yearly amortization of discount, the annual interest earned would be $1,600, consisting of $1,200 received in cash plus a $400 increase in the carrying value of the investment. The second method will usually give a more meaningful picture of periodic income and is preferable from the viewpoint of accounting theory. Both methods, however, are acceptable in the determination of taxable income.

DEMONSTRATION PROBLEM

The information listed below is available in reconciling the bank statement for the Glendale Company on November 30, 1971.

(1) The ledger account for Cash showed a balance at November 30 of $7,766.64, including a $100 petty cash fund which contains vouchers for miscellaneous

expense of $60. Petty cash should be transferred to a separate account. The bank statement at November 30 indicated a balance of $9,734.70.

(2) The November 30 cash receipts of $5,846.20 had been mailed to the bank on that date and did not appear among the deposits on the November bank statement. The receipts include a check for $4,000 from a brokerage house for the sale of 150 shares of stock of the Axe Co. which cost $6,270. Neither the proceeds on the sale of stock nor the collections on accounts receivable ($1,846.20) has been recorded on the books of the Glendale Company.

(3) Included with the November bank statement was an NSF check for $160 signed by a customer James Ruddock. This amount had been charged against the bank account on November 30.

(4) Of the checks issued in November, the following were not included among the paid checks returned by the bank:

Check No.	Amount	Check No.	Amount
924	$136.25	944	$ 95.00
940	105.00	945	716.15
941	11.46	946	60.00
943	826.70		

(5) A service charge for $340 by the bank had been made in error against the Glendale Company's account.

(6) A non-interest-bearing note receivable for $690 owned by the Glendale Company had been left with the bank for collection. On November 30 the company received a memorandum from the bank indicating that the note had been collected and credited to the company's account after deduction of a $5 collection charge. No entry has been made by the company to record collection of the note.

(7) A debit memorandum for $7.50 was enclosed with the paid checks at November 30. This charge covered the printing of checkbooks bearing the Glendale Company's name and address.

Instructions

a. Prepare a bank reconciliation at November 30, 1971. Check No. 946 for $60 was written on November 30 to replenish the petty cash fund.

b. Prepare journal entries required as of November 30, 1971, to bring the company's records up to date.

QUESTIONS

1. Mention some principles to be observed by a business in establishing strong internal control over cash receipts.

2. Explain how internal control over cash transactions is strengthened by compliance with the following rule: "Deposit each day's cash receipts, intact, in the bank, and make all disbursements by check."

3. List two items often encountered in reconciling a bank account which may cause cash per the bank statement to be larger than the balance of cash shown by the books.

4. In the reconciliation of a bank account, what reconciling items necessitate a journal entry on the depositor's books?

5. Pico Stationery Shop has for years maintained a petty cash fund of $100, which is replenished twice a month.
   a. How many debit entries would you expect to find in the Petty Cash account each year?
   b. When would expenditures from the petty cash fund be entered in the ledger accounts?

6. A check for $455 issued in payment of an account payable was erroneously listed in the cash payments journal as $545. The error was discovered early in the following month when the paid check was returned by the bank. What corrective action is needed?

7. In bidding for some surplus property offered at auction by a government agency, the Argus Company on December 28 drew a check for $3,000, and mailed it with the bid. The government agency on January 3 rejected the bid and returned the check. Should the $3,000 be included as cash in the December 31 balance sheet, which was prepared by the Argus Company on January 5 after the check had been returned? Explain.

8. Why are government securities commonly called *secondary cash reserves*?

9. To what extent should the maturity date or the intention of management as to the holding period of an investment in marketable securities influence its classification on the balance sheet?

10. Writing down securities to market value when market is below cost, but refusing to recognize an increase in valuation when market is above cost is inconsistent procedure. What arguments may be given *in favor* of this treatment?

11. "To substitute market value for cost as a basis for valuing marketable securities would represent a departure from traditional accounting practice." Discuss the case for and against using market value consistently as the basis of valuation in accounting for marketable securities.

12. An investor buys a $1,000, 6%, 10-year bond at 110 and a $1,000, 4%, 10-year bond at 90, both on the date of issue. Compute the average annual interest income that will be earned on these bonds if they are held to maturity.

13. If an investor buys a bond between interest dates he pays, as a part of the purchase price, the accrued interest since the last interest date. On the other hand, if he buys a share of common or preferred stock, no "accrued dividend" is added to the quoted price. Explain why this difference exists.

14. Z buys a $1,000, 5% bond for 106, five years from the maturity date. After holding the bond for four years, he sells it for 102. Z claims that he has a loss of $40 on the sale. A friend argues that Z has made a gain of $8 on the sale. Explain the difference in viewpoint. With whom do you agree? Why?

EXERCISES

1. On December 31, 1971, the petty cash drawer of the Mondo Company includes the following:

Cash on hand	*$ 39.41*
Expense vouchers:	
Flowers for funeral of deceased customer	*10.40*
Box of cigars for purchasing agent of the James Corporation . . .	*7.09*
Office supplies expense	*23.10*
Salary advance to employee	*20.00*
Total	*$100.00*

Prepare the entry required at the end of the fiscal year to replenish the petty cash fund.

2. From the information shown below for the Pattison Corporation, prepare a bank reconciliation as of September 30, 1971:

   (1) As of September 30, cash per books was $5,770; per bank statement, $4,782.
   (2) Cash receipts of $1,401 on September 30 were not deposited until October 1.
   (3) Among the paid checks returned by the bank was a stolen check for $210 paid in error by the bank after Pattison Corporation had issued a "stop payment" order to the bank.
   (4) The following memoranda accompanied the bank statement:
       a. A debit memo for service charges for the month of September, $3.
       b. A debit memo attached to a $62 check of Joseph Voss, marked NSF.
   (5) The following checks had been issued but were not included in the canceled checks returned by the bank: No. 921 for $326, No. 924 for $201, and No. 925 for $161.

3. In preparing the financial statements for the Papercraft Corporation, the accountant finds the following:

Cash on hand	*$ 150*
Cash in Manufacturers Bank	*10,144*
U.S. government bonds	*15,115*
Interest accrued on U.S. government bonds	*120*
Checks from customers by bank marked NSF	
(considered collectible)	*310*
Investment in stock of General Motors (held for short-term	
purposes).	*6,800*
Investment in stock of supplier (held to maintain good	
business relations)	*35,000*
Accounts receivable	*25,000*

The market value of the U.S. government bonds (excluding accrued interest) is $15,800; the market value of the General Motors stock is $6,650.

Show how the foregoing items would be reported in the balance sheet prepared for the Papercraft Corporation. Show total of current assets. Accrued interest may be combined with U.S. Government bonds into a single item on the balance sheet if a parenthetical note of explanation is used.

4. Peter Ellery acquires $10,000 par value 6% bonds of the Evers Co. on May 1, 1971, for a total cost of $9,700, including accrued interest of $200 from January 1, 1971. The bonds mature on June 30, 1975. Interest on the bonds is paid by the Evers Co. on June 30 and December 31 of each year. The discount on the bonds is amortized only at the end of Ellery's fiscal period, which ends on December 31.

    Prepare all entries (including the closing entry) required on the books of Peter Ellery for 1971 relating to the investment in Evers Co. bonds.

5. John Herman purchased 500 shares of Mason Company common stock at 42 plus brokerage fees of $200 on March 31. The company had declared a cash dividend of 60 cents per share on March 20, payable on April 15 to stockholders of record on April 6. On June 30 the company declared a 20% stock dividend. On December 15 the shares were split 2 for 1. On December 20 the company declared a cash dividend of 50 cents per share to stockholders of record on December 30, payable on January 10. On December 31 Herman sold 300 shares of the stock at $30 per share, net of commission.

    Prepare journal entries to account for this investment on Herman's books. Since Herman keeps accrual records, an entry to Dividends Receivable should be made on December 30.

6. Rex Corporation purchased $300,000 of 4%, 10-year state bonds at 94. The bonds mature eight years from the date of purchase. The bonds were sold for 96½ four years after the date of purchase.

    a. Assuming that the corporation had no intention of holding the bonds to maturity at the time of purchase, determine the total interest revenue during the four-year period and the gain or loss on disposal.

    b. Assuming that the corporation intended to hold the bonds until maturity at the time of purchase, determine the total interest revenue during the four-year period and the gain or loss on disposal.

PROBLEMS

9-1 Information for the General Cork Co. is given below:

(1) Cash balance per bank statement, as of September 30, was $8,564.55.

(2) Two debit memoranda accompanied the bank statement: one for $3 was for service charges for the month; the other for $50 was attached to an NSF check from Sally Hamer.

(3) The paid checks returned with the September bank statement disclosed two errors in the cash records. Check No. 723 for $231.50 had been erroneously recorded as $321.50 in the cash disbursements journal, and check No. 741 for $88.66 had been recorded as $66.88. Check No. 723 was issued in payment for a store display counter; check No. 741 was for telephone expense.

(4) A collection charge for $106.00 (not applicable to General Cork Co.) was erroneously deducted from the account by the bank.

(5) Cash receipts of September 30 amounting to $532.25 were mailed to the bank too late to be included in the September bank statement.

(6) Checks outstanding as of September 30 were as follows: No. 768 for $160, No. 771 for $141.10, and No. 774 for $52.

(7) The Cash account showed the following entries during September:

Cash   *(111)*

Sept.	*1*	*Balance*		5,068.20	*Sept.*	*30*		*CD7*	10,364.72
	30		*CR5*	14,131.00					

19,159.20   *10,364.72*

Instructions

a. Prepare a bank reconciliation as of September 30.

b. Prepare the necessary adjusting entries in general journal form.

9-2 Information for the Sill Corp. on March 31 is given below:

(1) The balance per books of the Sill Corp. is $16,289.26.

(2) The bank statement shows a balance of $18,377.61 as of March 31.

(3) Accompanying the bank statement was a check of Nathan Eddy for $142.00, which was marked NSF by the bank.

(4) Checks outstanding as of March 31 were as follows: No. 94 for $1,052.27; No. 98 for $1,232.00; No. 99 for $47.24.

(5) Also accompanying the bank statement was a debit memorandom for $44.50 for safe deposit box rent; the bank had erroneously charged this item to the account of the Sill Corp.

(6) On March 29, the bank collected a non-interest-bearing note for the Sill Corp. The note was for $2,254; the bank charged a fee of $4.80.

(7) A deposit of $2,409.40 was in transit; it had been mailed to the bank on March 31.

(8) In recording a $120 check received on account from a customer, Clark Company, the bookkeeper for the Sill Corp. erroneously listed the collection in the cash receipts journal as $12. The check appeared correctly among the deposits on the March bank statement.

(9) The service charge on the account for March amounted to $4.46; a debit memo in this amount was returned with the bank statement.

Instructions

a. Prepare a bank reconciliation as of March 31.

b. Prepare the necessary journal entries.

9-3 The internal control procedures over cash transactions in the Hycel Company were not adequate. James Cagey, the cashier-bookkeeper, handled cash receipts, made small disbursements from the cash receipts, maintained accounting records, and prepared the monthly reconciliations of the bank account. At November 30, the statement received from the bank showed a balance of $17,500. The outstanding checks were as follows: No. 7062 for $268.55; No. 7183 for $170; No. 7284 for $261.45; No. 8621 for $175.19; No. 8623 for $341; and No. 8632 for $172.80. The balance of cash as shown by the Hycel Company records was $20,258.31, which included the cash on hand. The bank statement for November showed a credit of $200 arising from the collection of a note left with the bank; the company's books did not include an entry to record this collection.

Recognizing the weakness existing in internal control over cash transactions, Cagey removed all the cash on hand in excess of $3,347.30, and then prepared the following reconciliation in an attempt to conceal his theft.

Balance per books, Nov. 30		$20,258.31
Add: Outstanding checks:		
No. 8621	$175.19	
No. 8623	341.00	
No. 8632	172.80	588.99
		$20,847.30
Less: Cash on hand		3,347.30
Balance per bank statement, Nov. 30		$17,500.00
Less: Unrecorded credit		200.00
True cash, Nov. 30		$17,300.00

Instructions

a. Determine how much the cashier took and explain how he attempted to conceal his theft. Prepare a correct bank reconciliation.

b. Suggest some specific control devices for the Hycel Company.

9-4 The investment portfolio of the Joyce Corporation on January 1, 1971, consists of the following four securities:

$100,000 par value Bay Resorts Corp. 6% bonds due Dec. 31, 1978. Interest is payable on June 30 and Dec. 31 of each year.	$97,600
$50,000 par value Copper Products Co. 7½% bonds due Apr. 30, 1982. Interest is payable on Apr. 30 and Oct. 31 of each year.	52,720
1,000 shares of no-par $4.50 cumulative preferred stock of Donner-Pass, Inc.	80,000

Transactions relating to investments that were completed during the first six months of 1971 follow.

Jan. 10   Acquired 500 shares of Evans Co. common stock at 72. Brokerage commissions paid amounted to $231.

Jan. 21   Received quarterly dividend of $1.12½ per share on 1,000 shares of Donner-Pass, Inc., preferred stock.

Mar. 5   Sold 200 shares of Donner-Pass, Inc., preferred stock at 84½, less commissions and transfer taxes amounting to $105.

Apr. 1   Received additional 1,000 shares of Evans Co. common stock as a result of a 3 for 1 split.

Apr. 20   Received quarterly dividend of $1.12½ per share on 800 shares of Donner-Pass, Inc., preferred stock.

Apr. 30   Received semiannual interest on Copper Products Co. 7½% bonds and amortized premium on these bonds from January 1 to April 30. Accrued interest of $625 had been recorded on December 31, 1970, in the Accrued Bond Interest Receivable account.

May 1   Sold entire holdings of Copper Products Co. bonds at 102½ net of commissions.

June 4   Received a cash dividend of 70 cents per share on Evans Co. common stock.

June 30   Received semiannual interest on Bay Resorts Corp. 6% bonds. Amortized the discount on the Bay Resorts Corp. bonds for six months.

Instructions

a. Prepare journal entries to record the foregoing transactions.

b. Prepare a schedule of the investment portfolio for the Joyce Corporation as of June 30, 1971. Show the name of the security, the number of shares (or par value), and the cost basis for financial reporting purposes.

9-5 Roger Golden keeps a detailed record of his investments and amortizes discounts and premiums in determining his investment earnings. He held the portfolio shown below throughout the current year:

4,000 shares of ADM Corporation common stock; cost $48½ per share, market value at December 31, $290,000. Received dividends of $1.20 per share on March 1, 10% stock dividend on June 1, and $1.50 per share on December 1 of current year.

$50,000 in 5% New Orleans school bonds, maturing eight years from the date of purchase. Purchased for $46,120, market value on December 31, 94½. Received two regular semiannual interest payments during the current year.

$100,000 in 7% Carl Corporation debenture bonds, due four years and two months from date of purchase. Purchased for $102,500; market value at end of current year, 101⅞. Received two regular semiannual interest payments during current year.

1,600 shares of Danube Corporation $4.50 convertible preferred stock, no par value. Purchased for $180,000, current market value at end of year, 130½. Received regular dividends on March 1 and September 1 of current year.

Instructions

a. Prepare a schedule showing the amount earned during the current year on each of these investments and the rate of return as a percentage of cost and of market value at the end of the year. This schedule may be in columnar form with the following column headings:

Name of Security	*Original Cost*	*End-of-year Market Value*	*Earnings This Year*	*Rate Earned on Cost*	*Rate Earned on Market Value*

b. In a friendly discussion with a business associate Golden commented on his average return for the year on the total cost of his investment. His friend retorted that return on market value was a better measure of earning performance. Discuss the merits of the percentage earned on cost and the percentage earned on market value as measures of investment success.

9-6 The Witter Trust Company has an opening for a promotion in its investment department. The qualifications of the two candidates for the job, Jim Bear and Robert Bull, appear equally good. As an aid in making the choice, each man was given $100,000 to invest in corporate bonds. It was understood, though not openly stated, that their performance in investing these funds would be the basis for the promotion decision.

The record of their performance for one full year, as prepared by the assistant to the president, is as follows:

		Interest
Cost	*Investment*	*received*
	Jim Bear's Portfolio	
$ 7,560	B & B Co. 4½% bonds, $10,000 face value, due in 10 years....	$ 450
77,200	Copper Corp. 5% bonds, face value $80,000, due in 4 years....	4,000
15,240	Sound Co. 4% bonds, $20,000 face value, due in 10 years	800
$100,000		$5,250

Return on investment for the year ($5,250 ÷ $100,000) = 5.3%

	Robert Bull's Portfolio	
$ 86,720	Sumatra Oil Company, 8% bonds, face value $80,000, due in 10 years	$6,400
13,280	Slope Drilling Co., 7% bonds, $12,000 face value, due in 4 years	840
$100,000		$7,240

Return on investment for the year ($7,240 ÷ $100,000) = 7.2%

On the basis of this record, the assistant to the president chose Bull for the position. Bull's promotion was announced in the company bulletin, where it was read by Edward Smart, a vice-president.

Instructions

a. Explain why Smart should (1) congratulate the assistant to the president for his choice or (2) complain to the president about the decision. Prepare a schedule in support of your conclusion.

The following column headings are suggested:

Name of Security	Cost	Maturity Value	Total Discount or Premium	Discount or Premium Amortized	Interest Received	Interest Earned

b. Assuming that interest rates in general and the financial positions of the companies have not changed since the beginning of the year, make an estimate of the market value, as of the end of the year, of the investment portfolios of Bear and Bull. Show the basis for your estimate.

10 Receivables

One of the key factors underlying the tremendous expansion of the American economy has been the trend toward selling all types of goods and services on credit. The automobile industry has long been the classic example of the use of retail credit to achieve the efficiencies of large-scale output. Today, however, in nearly every field of retail trade it appears that sales and profits can be increased by granting customers the privilege of making payment a month or more after the date of sale. The sales of manufacturers and wholesalers are made on credit to an even greater extent than in retail trade.

ACCOUNTS RECEIVABLE

The credit department

No business concern wants to sell on credit to a customer who will prove unable or unwilling to pay his account. Consequently, most business organizations include a credit department which must reach a decision on the credit worthiness of each prospective customer. The credit department investigates the debt-paying ability and credit record of each new customer and determines the maximum amount of credit to be extended.

If the prospective customer is a business concern as, for example, a retail store, the financial statements of the store will be obtained and analyzed to determine its financial condition and the trend of operating results. The credit department will always prefer to rely upon financial statements which have been audited by independent public accountants.

Regardless of whether the prospective customer is a business concern or an individual consumer, the investigation by the credit department will probably include the obtaining of a credit report from a local credit agency or from a national credit-rating institution such as Dun & Bradstreet, Inc. A credit agency compiles credit data on individuals and business concerns, and distributes this information to its clients. Most business concerns that make numerous sales on credit find it worthwhile to subscribe to the services of one or more credit agencies.

Uncollectible accounts

A business that sells its goods or services on credit will inevitably find that some of its accounts receivable are uncollectible. Regardless of how thoroughly the credit department investigates prospective customers, some uncollectible accounts will arise as a result of errors in judgment or because of unanticipated developments. As a matter of fact, a limited amount of uncollectible accounts is evidence of a sound credit policy. If the credit department should become too cautious and conservative in rating customers, it might avoid all credit losses, but in so doing, lose profitable business by rejecting many acceptable accounts.

Reflecting uncollectible accounts in the financial statements

One of the most fundamental principles of accounting is that *revenue must be matched with the expenses incurred in securing that revenue.*

Uncollectible accounts expense is caused by selling goods on credit to customers who fail to pay their bills; such expenses, therefore, are incurred in the year in which the sales are made, even though the accounts are not determined to be uncollectible until the following year. An account receivable which originates from a sale on credit in the year 1971 and is determined to be uncollectible sometime during 1972 represents an expense of the year 1971. Unless each year's uncollectible accounts expense is *estimated* and reflected in the year-end balance sheet and income statement, both of these financial statements will be seriously deficient.

To illustrate, let us assume that Arlington Corporation began business on January 1, 1971, and made most of its sales on credit throughout the year. At December 31, 1971, accounts receivable amounted to $200,000. On this date the management reviewed the status of the accounts receivable, giving particular study to accounts which were past due. This review indicated that the collectible portion of the $200,000 of accounts receivable amounted to approximately $190,000. In other words, management estimated that uncollectible accounts expense for the first year of operations amounted to $10,000. The following adjusting entry should be made at December 31, 1971:

Provision for Uncollectible Accounts	*Uncollectible Accounts Expense*..................... 10,000	
	Allowance for Uncollectible Accounts..........	*10,000*
	To record the estimated uncollectible account expense for the year 1971.	

The Uncollectible Accounts Expense account created by the debit part of this entry is closed into the Income Summary account in the same manner as any other expense account. The Allowance for Uncollectible Accounts which was credited in the above journal entry will appear in the balance sheet as a deduction from the face amount of the accounts receivable. It serves to reduce the accounts receivable to their realizable value in the balance sheet, as shown by the following illustration:

How Much Is the Estimated Realizable Value of the Accounts Receivable?

ARLINGTON CORPORATION
Partial Balance Sheet
December 31, 1971

Assets

Cash.		$ 75,000
Accounts receivable.	$200,000	
Less: Allowance for uncollectible accounts	10,000	190,000
Inventory.		100,000
Other assets.		175,000
		$540,000

The allowance for uncollectible accounts

There is no way of telling in advance which accounts receivable will be collected and which ones will prove to be worthless. It is therefore not possible to credit the account of any particular customer to reflect our overall estimate of the year's credit losses. Neither is it possible to credit the Accounts Receivable control account in the general ledger. If the Accounts Receivable control account were to be credited with the estimated amount of expense from uncollectible accounts, this control account would no longer be in balance with the total of the numerous customers' accounts in the subsidiary ledger. The only practicable alternative, therefore, is to credit a separate account called Allowance for Uncollectible Accounts with the amount estimated to be uncollectible. The credit balance of the Allowance for Uncollectible Accounts is shown on the balance sheet as a deduction from the total amount of accounts receivable. The resulting net figure is the estimated realizable value of the accounts receivable.

In the preceding chapters accounts have repeatedly been classified into five groups: (1) assets, (2) liabilities, (3) owners' equity, (4) revenue, and (5) expense. In which of these five groups of accounts does the Allowance for Uncollectible Accounts belong? The answer is indicated by the position of the Allowance for Uncollectible Accounts on the balance sheet. It appears among the assets and is used to reduce an asset (Accounts Receivable) from a gross value to a net realizable value. From the standpoint of account classification, the Allowance for Uncollectible Accounts is, therefore, included in the asset category.

The Allowance for Uncollectible Accounts is sometimes described as a *contra* account, an *offset* account, an *asset reduction* account, a *negative asset* account, and most frequently of all, a *valuation* account. All these terms are derived from the fact that the Allowance for Uncollectible Accounts is an account with a credit balance, which is offset against an asset account to produce the proper balance sheet value for an asset.

Alternative titles for the Allowance for Uncollectible Accounts are Allowance for Bad Debts, Allowance for Doubtful Accounts, or Reserve for Bad Debts. Bad Debts Expense is also commonly used as an alternative title for Uncollectible Accounts Expense.

Other valuation accounts

The Allowance for Uncollectible Accounts has a good deal in common with the Accumulated Depreciation (or Allowance for Depreciation) account, which appears on the balance sheet as a deduction from depreciable asset accounts such as buildings or office equipment. Both the Allowance for Uncollectible Accounts and the Accumulated Depreciation account are created by adjusting entries and are based on estimates rather than on precisely determined amounts. In each case the debit side of the adjusting entry affects an expense account (Uncollectible Accounts Expense or Depreciation Expense).

In some respects, however, these two valuation accounts perform quite different functions. The Allowance for Uncollectible Accounts serves to reduce the accounts receivable to net realizable value. The Accumulated Depreciation account is *not* intended to reduce the building to realizable value but merely to show what portion of the original cost has expired and has been recorded as expense. Realizable value is not a significant concept in accounting for plant and equipment, because these properties are not intended to be sold but are to be used in the operation of the business.

Estimating uncollectible accounts expense

Before the books are closed and financial statements are prepared at the end of the accounting period, an estimate of uncollectible accounts expense must be made. This estimate will usually be based upon past experience, perhaps modified in accordance with current business conditions.

Since the allowance for uncollectible accounts is necessarily an estimate and not a precise calculation, the factor of personal judgment may play a considerable part in determining the size of this valuation account. There is a fairly wide range of reasonableness within which the amount may be set. Most businessmen intend that the allowance shall be adequate to cover probable losses. The term *adequate,* when used in this context, suggests an amount somewhat larger than the minimum probable amount.

Conservatism as a factor in valuing accounts receivable. The larger the allowance established for uncollectible accounts, the lower the net valuation of accounts receivable will be. Some accountants and some businessmen tend to favor the most conservative valuation of assets that logically can be supported. Conservatism in the preparation of a balance sheet implies a tendency to state assets at their minimum values rather than to establish values in a purely objective manner. From a theoretical point of view, the doctrine of balance sheet conservatism is difficult to support, but from the viewpoint of bankers and others who use financial statements as a basis for granting loans, conservatism in valuing assets has long been regarded as a desirable policy.

Assume that the balance sheet of Company A presents optimistic, exaggerated values for the assets owned. Assume also that this "unconservative" balance sheet is submitted to a banker in support of an application for a loan. The banker studies the balance sheet and makes a loan to Company A in reliance upon the values listed. Later the banker finds it impossible to collect the loan and also finds that the assets upon which he had based the loan were greatly overstated in the balance sheet. The banker will undoubtedly consider the overly optimistic character of the balance sheet as partially responsible for his loss. Experiences of this type have led bankers as a group to stress the desirability of conservatism in the valuation of assets.

In considering the argument for balance sheet conservatism, it is important to recognize that the income statement is also affected by the estimates made of uncollectible accounts expense. The act of providing a relatively large allowance for uncollectible accounts involves a correspondingly heavy charge to expense. Setting asset values at a minimum in the balance sheet has the related effect of stating the current year's net income at a minimum amount.

Two methods of estimating uncollectible accounts expense

The provision for uncollectible accounts is an estimate of expense to be sustained. Two alternative approaches are widely used in making the annual estimate for uncollectible accounts. One method consists of adjusting the valuation account to a new balance equal to the estimated uncollectible portion of the existing accounts receivable. This method is referred to as the *balance sheet* approach and rests on an *aging of the accounts receivable.* The adjusting entry takes into consideration the existing balance in the Allowance for Uncollectible Accounts.

The alternative method requires an adjusting entry computed as a percentage of the year's net sales. This method may be regarded as the *income statement* approach to estimating uncollectible accounts. This *percentage of sales* method emphasizes the expense side of the adjustment and leaves out of consideration any existing balance in the valuation account. If any substantial balance should accumulate in the allowance account, however, a change in the percentage figure being applied to sales might be appropriate. These two methods are explained below.

Aging the accounts receivable. A past-due account is always viewed with some suspicion. The fact that an account is past due suggests that the customer is either unable or unwilling to pay. The analysis of accounts by age is known as aging the accounts, as illustrated by the schedule given on page 298.

This analysis of accounts receivable gives management a useful picture of the status of collections and the probabilities of credit losses. Almost half of the total accounts receivable are past due. The question "How long past due?" is pertinent, and is answered by the bottom line of the aging analysis. About 29% of the total receivables are past due from 1 to 30 days; another

Analysis of Accounts Receivable by Age, December 31, 19___

Customer	Total	Not Yet Due	1–30 Days Past Due	31–60 Days Past Due	61–90 Days Past Due	Over 90 Days Past Due
A. B. Adams .	$ 500	$ 500				
B. L. Baker ..	150			$ 150		
R. D. Carl...	800	800				
H. V. Davis..	900				$ 800	$ 100
R. M. Evans..	400	400				
Others	32,250	16,300	$10,000	4,200	200	1,550
	$35,000	$18,000	$10,000	$4,350	$1,000	$1,650
%	100	51	29	12	3	5

12% are past due from 31 to 60 days; about 3% are past due from 61 to 90 days; and 5% of the total receivables consist of accounts past due more than three months. If an analysis of this type is prepared at the end of each month, management will be continuously informed of the trend of collections and can take appropriate action to ease or tighten credit policy. Moreover, a yardstick is available to measure the effectiveness of the persons responsible for collection activities.

When a customer makes a partial payment on an account containing several invoices, he has the right to designate the invoice to which his payment applies. If he makes no designation, the creditor will usually consider the payment applicable to the oldest invoice.

The further past due an account receivable becomes, the greater the likelihood that it will not be collected in full. In recognition of this principle, the analysis of receivables by age groups can be used as a stepping-stone in determining a reasonable amount to add to the Allowance for Uncollectible Accounts. To make this determination it is desirable to estimate the percentage of probable expense for each age group of accounts receivable. This percentage, when applied to the dollar amount in each age group, gives a probable expense for each group. By adding together the probable expense for all the age groups, the required balance in the Allowance for Uncollectible Accounts is determined. The schedule on page 299 lists the group totals from the preceding illustration and shows how the total probable expense from uncollectible accounts is computed.

This summary indicates that an allowance for uncollectible accounts of $1,940 is required. Before making the adjusting entry, it is necessary to consider the existing balance in the allowance account. If the allowance for uncollectible accounts presently has a credit balance of, say, $500, the adjusting entry should be for $1,440 in order to bring the account up to the estimated probable expense of $1,940.

On the other hand, if the Allowance for Uncollectible Accounts contained

Estimate of Probable Uncollectible Accounts Expense

Accounts Receivable by Age Groups			
	Amount	% Considered Uncollectible	Allowance for Uncollectible Accounts
Not yet due................	$18,000	1	$ 180
1–30 days past due.........	10,000	3	300
31–60 days past due........	4,350	10	435
61–90 days past due........	1,000	20	200
Over 90 days past due.......	1,650	50	825
	$35,000		$1,940

Increasing Allowance for Uncollectible Accounts

Uncollectible Accounts Expense......................	1,440	
Allowance for Uncollectible Accounts............		1,440

To increase the valuation account to the estimated
probable expense of $1,940, computed as follows:

Present credit balance of account..............	$ 500
Current provision	1,440
New balance in valuation account	$1,940

a debit balance of $500 before adjustment, the adjusting entry would be made in the amount of $2,440 ($1,940 + $500) in order to create the desired credit balance of $1,940.

Estimating uncollectible accounts as a percentage of net sales. An alternative approach to providing for uncollectible accounts preferred by some companies consists of computing the charge to uncollectible accounts expense as a percentage of the net sales for the year. The question to be answered is not "How large a valuation allowance is needed to show our receivables at realizable value?" Instead, the question is stated as "How much uncollectible accounts expense is associated with this year's volume of sales?"

As an example, assume that for several years the expense of uncollectible accounts has averaged 1% of net sales (sales minus returns and allowances and sales discounts). At the end of the current year, before adjusting entries, the following account balances appear in the ledger:

	Dr	Cr
Sales..		$1,060,000
Sales Returns and Allowances	$40,000	
Sales Discounts...............................	20,000	
Allowance for Uncollectible Accounts		1,500

The net sales of the current year amount to $1,000,000; 1% of this amount is $10,000. The existing balance in the Allowance for Uncollectible Accounts should be ignored in computing the amount of the adjusting entry, because the percentage of net sales method stresses the relationship between uncollectible accounts expense and net sales rather than the current valuation of receivables at the balance sheet date. The entry is:

Provision	
for Un-	
collectible	*Uncollectible Accounts Expense* 10,000
Accounts	*Allowance for Uncollectible Accounts* 10,000
Based on	*To record uncollectible accounts expense of 1% of the year's*
Percentage	*net sales (0.01 × $1,000,000).*
of Net	
Sales	

If a concern makes both cash sales and credit sales, it may be desirable to exclude the cash sales from consideration and to compute the percentage relationship of uncollectible accounts expense to credit sales only.

Writing off an uncollectible account receivable

Whenever an account receivable from a customer is determined to be uncollectible, it no longer qualifies as an asset and should immediately be written off the books. To write off an account receivable is to reduce the balance of the customer's account to zero. The journal entry to accomplish this consists of a credit to the Accounts Receivable control account in the general ledger (and to the customer's account in the subsidiary ledger), and an offsetting debit to the Allowance for Uncollectible Accounts.

Referring again to the example of the Arlington Company as shown on page 295, the ledger accounts were as follows after the adjusting entry for estimated uncollectible accounts had been made on December 31, 1971.

Accounts receivable $200,000
Less: Allowance for uncollectible accounts   10,000

Next let us assume that on January 27, 1972, a customer by the name of William Benton became bankrupt and the account receivable from him in the amount of $1,000 was determined to be worthless. The following entry should be made by the Arlington Company:

Writing	
off an	*Allowance for Uncollectible Accounts* 1,000
Uncol-	*Accounts Receivable, William Benton* 1,000
lectible	*To write off the receivable from William Benton as uncollectible.*
Account	

The important thing to note in this entry is that the debit is made to the Allowance for Uncollectible Accounts and *not* to the Uncollectible Accounts Expense account. The estimated expense is charged to the Uncollectible

Accounts Expense account at the end of each accounting period. When a particular account receivable is later ascertained to be worthless and is written off, this action does not represent an additional expense but merely confirms our previous estimate of the loss. If the Uncollectible Accounts Expense account were first charged with estimated credit losses and then later charged with proved credit losses, we would be guilty of double counting of uncollectible accounts expense.

After the entry writing off William Benton's account has been posted, the Accounts Receivable control account and the Allowance for Uncollectible Accounts appear as follows:

Both Accounts Reduced by Write-off of Worthless Receivable

Accounts Receivable

1971		**1972**	
Dec. 31	200,000	Jan. 27 (Benton write-off)	1,000

Allowance for Uncollectible Accounts

1972		**1971**	
Jan. 27 (Benton write-off)	1,000	Dec. 31	10,000

Note that the *net* amount of the accounts receivable was unchanged by writing off William Benton's account against the Allowance for Uncollectible Accounts.

Net Value of Receivables Unchanged by Write-off

Before the Write-off		After the Write-off	
Accounts receivable......	$200,000	Accounts receivable......	$199,000
Less: Allowance for un-collectible accounts.....	10,000	Less: Allowance for un-collectible accounts.....	9,000
Net value of receivables...	$190,000	Net value of receivables...	$190,000

The fact that writing off an uncollectible receivable against the Allowance for Uncollectible Accounts does not change the net carrying value of accounts receivable shows that no expense is entered in the books when an account is written off. This example bears out the point stressed earlier in the chapter: Credit losses belong in the period in which the sale is made, not in a later period in which the account is discovered to be uncollectible.

Write-offs seldom agree with previous estimates. The total amount of accounts receivable written off in a given year will seldom, if ever, be exactly equal to the estimated amount previously credited to the Allowance for Un-collectible Accounts.

If the amounts written off as uncollectible turn out to be less than the estimated amount, the Allowance for Uncollectible Accounts will continue to show a credit balance. If the amounts written off as uncollectible are greater than the estimated amount, the Allowance for Uncollectible Accounts will acquire a debit balance, which will be eliminated by the adjustment at the end of the period.

Recovery of an account previously written off

Occasionally an account which has been written off as worthless will later be collected in full or in part. Such collections are often referred to as *recoveries* of bad debts. Collection of an account previously written off is evidence that the write-off was an error; the write-off entry should therefore be reversed.

Let us assume, for example, that a past-due account receivable in the amount of $400 from J. B. Barker was written off by the following entry:

Barker Account Considered Uncollectible	*Allowance for Uncollectible Accounts*	*400*	
	Accounts Receivable, J. B. Barker		*400*
	To write off the receivable from J. B. Barker as uncollectible.		

At some later date the customer, J. B. Barker, pays his account in full. The reversing entry to restore Barker's account will be:

Barker Account Reinstated	*Accounts Receivable, J. B. Barker*	*400*	
	Allowance for Uncollectible Accounts		*400*
	To reverse the entry writing off J. B. Barker's account.		

A separate entry will be made in the cash receipts book to record the collection from Barker. This entry will debit Cash and credit Accounts Receivable.

Direct charge-off method of recognizing uncollectible accounts expense

Instead of making adjusting entries to record uncollectible accounts expense on the basis of estimates, some concerns merely charge uncollectible accounts to expense at the time such receivables are determined to be uncollectible. This method makes no attempt to match revenue and related expenses. Uncollectible accounts expense is recorded in the period in which the individual accounts are determined to be worthless rather than in the period in which the sales were made.

When the direct charge-off method is in use, the accounts receivable will be listed in the balance sheet at their gross amount, and no valuation allowance will be used. The receivables, therefore, are not stated at their probable realizable value.

In the determination of taxable income under present federal income tax regulations, both the direct charge-off method and the allowance method of estimating uncollectible accounts expense are acceptable. From the standpoint of accounting theory, the allowance method is much the better, for it enables expenses to be matched with related revenues and thus aids in making a logical measurement of net income.

Analysis of accounts receivable

What dollar amount of accounts receivable would be reasonable for a business making annual credit sales of $1,200,000? Comparison of the average amount of accounts receivable with the sales made on credit during the period indicates how long it takes to convert receivables into cash. For example, if annual credit sales of $1,200,000 are made at a uniform rate throughout the year and the accounts receivable at year-end amount to $200,000, we can see at a glance that the receivables represent one-sixth of the year's sales, or about 60 days of uncollected sales. Management naturally wants to make efficient use of the available capital in the business, and therefore is interested in a rapid "turnover" of accounts receivable. If the credit terms offered by the business in the above example were, say, 30 days net, the existence of receivables equal to 60 days' sales would warrant investigation. The analysis of receivables is considered more fully in Chapter 16.

Receivables from installment sales

The importance of *installment sales* is emphasized by a recent annual report of Sears, Roebuck and Co., which shows over $3 billion of "customer installment accounts." Nearly all of the company's receivables call for collection in periodic installments.

An installment sale may or may not require a down payment; substantial interest charges are usually added to the "cash selling price" of the product in determining the total dollar amount to be collected in the series of installment payments. The seller usually has the right to repossess the merchandise if installments are not collected according to the terms of the installment contract. Repossessed merchandise is recorded at its current value rather than at its original cost or at the uncollected portion of the installment receivable.

Although the collection period for an installment sale often runs as long as 24 to 36 months, such installment receivables are regarded as current assets, if they correspond to customary terms of the industry.

Installment-basis accounting for income tax purposes

Current provisions of the federal income tax law permit a dealer in personal property to spread the profit from installment sales over the years in which collections are received. The result is to defer the recognition of taxable income and the payment of income tax.

Assume, for example, that Cross Company sells an article for $3,000 which cost $1,800. No down payment is received, but the buyer promises to make 30 monthly payments of $100 each. The gross profit on the sale is 40% of the $3,000 total price or $1,200; therefore 40% of each installment collected is regarded for tax purposes as profit realized. If three $100 monthly collections were received in the year in which the sale occurred, the profit reported for tax purposes would be only $120 (that is, 40% × $300). In following years the same 40% rate would be applied to all collections under the contract.

The installment basis of measuring income is acceptable for income tax purposes, but not for financial statements. The Accounting Principles Board of the AICPA in *Opinion No. 10* reaffirmed that "revenues should ordinarily be accounted for at the time a transaction is completed, with appropriate provision for uncollectible accounts." Thus in our example of a $3,000 sale on a 30-month installment plan, proper accounting (for all purposes other than tax returns) would require a $3,000 debit to Accounts Receivable and a $3,000 credit to Sales. The entire gross profit of $1,200 would be regarded as earned in the year of the sale.

The basic accounting principle of matching revenues with related expenses will usually best be accomplished by recognizing the entire gross profit in the period of sale, and by charges to expense to establish an adequate allowance for uncollectible accounts. There are a number of other more complex issues relating to installment sales; these are covered in *Advanced Accounting* by the authors.

NOTES RECEIVABLE

Definition of a promissory note

A promissory note is an unconditional promise in writing to pay on demand or at a future date a definite sum of money.

The person who signs the note and thereby promises to pay is called the *maker* of the note. The person to whom payment is to be made is called the *payee* of the note. In the illustration below G. L. Smith is the maker of the note and A. B. Davis is the payee.

From the viewpoint of the maker, G. L. Smith, the illustrated note is a

Simplified Form of Promissory Note

$1,000	Los Angeles, California	July 10, 19--

One month after date I promise to pay

to the order of A. B. Davis

-----One thousand and no/100------- dollars

payable at First National Bank of Los Angeles

for value received, with interest at 6%

G. L. Smith

liability and is recorded by crediting the Notes Payable account. However, from the viewpoint of the payee, A. B. Davis, this same note is an asset and is recorded by debiting the Notes Receivable account. The maker of a note expects to pay cash at the maturity date; the payee expects to receive cash at that date. Notes payable will be discussed in Chapter 12.

Nature of interest

Interest is a charge made for the use of money. To the borrower (maker of a note) interest is an expense; to the lender (payee of a note) interest is revenue.

Computing interest. A formula used in computing interest is as follows:

$$\textit{Principal} \times \textit{rate of interest} \times \textit{time} = \textit{interest}$$

Interest rates are usually stated on an annual basis. For example, the interest on a $1,000, one-year, 6% note is computed as follows:

$$\$1,000 \times 0.06 \times 1 = \$60$$

If the term of the note were only four months instead of a year, the interest charge would be $20, computed as follows:

$$\$1,000 \times 0.06 \times \tfrac{4}{12} = \$20$$

If the term of the note is expressed in days, the exact number of days must be used in computing the interest. As a matter of convenience, however, it is customary to assume that a year contains 360 days. Suppose, for example, that a 75-day, 6% note for $1,000 is drawn on June 10. The interest charge would be computed as follows:

$$\$1,000 \times 0.06 \times \tfrac{75}{360} = \$12.50$$

The principal of the note ($1,000) plus the interest ($12.50) equals $1,012.50, and this amount (the maturity value) will be payable on August 24. The computation of days to maturity is as follows:

Days remaining in June (30 − 10)	20
Days in July	31
Days in August to maturity date	24
Total days called for by note	75

Sixty-day, 6% method for computing interest. A considerable saving of time is often possible by using the 60-day, 6% method of computing interest. If the interest rate is 6% a year, the interest for 60 days on any amount of money may be determined merely by *moving the decimal point two places to the left.* For example,

> *The interest at 6% for 60 days on $1,111.00 is $11.11*
> *The interest at 6% for 60 days on $9,876.43 is $98.76*

The reasoning underlying the 60-day, 6% shortcut may be summarized as follows:

> *Since interest on $1.00 for one year is $0.06*
> *And 60 days is ⅙ of a year*
> *Interest on $1.00 for 60 days is $0.01 (⅙ of $0.06)*

If the interest on $1.00 at 6% for 60 days can be computed by moving the decimal point two places to the left, then the interest on any amount at 6% for 60 days can be computed in the same manner.

The 60-day, 6% method can be used for time periods other than 60 days. The time of the note can be stated as a fraction or a multiple of 60 days and the interest quickly computed. For example, assuming an annual interest rate of 6%, what is the interest on $8,844 for 15 days?

> *Interest for 60 days on $8,844 is $88.44*
> *Interest for 15 days on $8,844 is ¼ of $88.44, or $22.11*

The 60-day, 6% method can also be applied when the interest rate is higher or lower than 6%. If the interest rate is something other than 6%, the interest is first computed at 6%, and an adjustment is then made for the difference between 6% and the actual rate. For example, what is the interest at 8% on $963 for 60 days?

> *Interest at 6% on $963 for 60 days is $ 9.63*
> *Interest at 2% on $963 for 60 days is   3.21 (⅓ × $9.63)*
> *Interest at 8% on $963 for 60 days is $12.84*

Although this shortcut method of computing interest can be used for almost any rate and any time period, not much time is saved by using it in cases in which elaborate computations are required.

Accounting for notes receivable

In some lines of business, notes receivable are seldom encountered; in other fields they occur frequently and may constitute an important part of total assets. Business concerns that sell high-priced durable goods such as auto-mobiles and farm machinery often accept notes receivable from their customers. Many companies obtain notes receivable in settlement of past-due accounts.

All notes receivable are usually posted to a single account in the general ledger. A subsidiary ledger is not essential because the notes themselves, when filed by due dates, are the equivalent of a subsidiary ledger and provide any necessary information as to maturity, interest rates, collateral pledged, and other details. The amount debited to Notes Receivable is always the face amount of the note, regardless of whether or not the note bears interest. When an interest-bearing note is collected, the amount of cash received will be larger than the face amount of the note. The interest collected is credited to an Interest Earned account, and only the face amount of the note is credited to the Notes Receivable account.

Illustrative entries. Assume that a 6%, 90-day note receivable is acquired from a customer, Marvin White, in settlement of an existing account receivable of $2,000. The entry for acquisition of the note is as follows:

Note Received to Replace Account Receivable	*Notes Receivable* *2,000*	
	Accounts Receivable, Marvin White	*2,000*
	Accepted 6%, 90-day note in settlement of account receivable.	

The entry 90 days later to record collection of the note will be:

Collection of Principal and Interest	*Cash* *2,030*	
	Notes Receivable	*2,000*
	Interest Earned	*30*
	Collected 6%, 90-day note from Marvin White.	

When a note is received from a customer at the time of making a sale of merchandise, two entries should be made as follows:

Sale May Be Run through Accounts Receivable When Note Is Received from Customer	*Accounts Receivable, F. H. Russ* *1,500*	
	Sales	*1,500*
	To record sale of merchandise.	
	Notes Receivable *1,500*	
	Accounts Receivable, F. H. Russ	*1,500*
	To record acquisition of note from customer.	

When this procedure is employed, the customer's account in the subsidiary ledger for accounts receivable provides a complete record of all transactions with him, regardless of the fact that some sales may have been made on open account and others may have involved a note receivable. Having a complete history of all transactions with a customer on a single ledger card may be helpful in reaching decisions as to collection efforts or further extensions of credit.

When the maker of a note defaults. A note receivable which cannot be collected at maturity is said to have been *dishonored* by the maker. Failure by the maker to pay interest or principal of a note at the due date is also known as *defaulting* on the note. Immediately after the dishonor or default of a note, an entry should be made by the holder to transfer the amount due from the Notes Receivable account to an account receivable from the debtor.

Assuming that a 60-day, 6% note receivable from Robert Jones is not collected at maturity, the following entry would be made:

Default	*Accounts Receivable, Robert Jones* *1,010*	
of Note	*Notes Receivable*	*1,000*
Receivable	*Interest Earned*.............................	*10*
	To record dishonor by Robert Jones of a 6%, 60-day note.	

Note that the interest earned on the note is recorded as a credit to Interest Earned and is also included in the account receivable from the maker. The interest receivable on a defaulted note is just as valid a claim against the maker as is the principal of the note; if the principal is collectible, then presumably the interest too can be collected.

By transferring past-due notes receivable into Accounts Receivable, two things are accomplished. First, the Notes Receivable account is limited to current notes not yet matured and is, therefore, regarded as a highly liquid type of asset. Secondly, the account receivable ledger card will show that a note has been dishonored and will present a complete picture of all transactions with the customer.

Renewal of a note receivable. Sometimes the two parties to a note agree that the note shall be renewed rather than paid at the maturity date. If the old note does not bear interest, the entry could be made as follows:

Renewal	*Notes Receivable* *1,000*	
of Note	*Notes Receivable*.............................	*1,000*
Should Be	*A 60-day, non-interest-bearing note from Ray Bell renewed today*	
Recorded	*with new 60-day, 6% note.*	

Since the above entry causes no change in the balance of the Notes Receivable account, a question may arise as to whether the entry is necessary.

The renewal of a note is an important transaction requiring managerial attention; a general journal entry is needed to record the action taken by management and to provide a permanent record of the transaction. If journal entries were not made to record the renewal of notes, confusion might arise as to whether some of the notes included in the balance of the Notes Receivable account were current or dishonored.

Adjustments for interest at end of period. Notes receivable acquired in one accounting period often do not mature until a following period. Interest is being earned throughout the life of the note, and this revenue should be apportioned between the two accounting periods on a time basis. At the end of the accounting period, interest earned to date on notes receivable should be accrued by an adjusting entry debiting the asset account, Accrued Interest Receivable, and crediting the revenue account, Interest Earned. When the note matures and the interest is received in the following period, the entry to be made consists of a debit to Cash, a credit to Accrued Interest Receivable for the amount of the accrual, and a credit to Interest Earned for the remainder of the interest collected.

Discounting notes receivable

Many business concerns which obtain notes receivable from their customers prefer to sell the notes to a bank for cash rather than to hold them until maturity. Selling a note receivable to a bank or finance company is often called *discounting* a note receivable. The holder of the note signs his name on the back of the note (as in endorsing a check) and delivers the note to the bank. The bank expects to collect the *maturity value* (principal plus interest) from the maker of the note at the maturity date, but if the maker fails to pay, the bank can demand payment from the endorser.

The amount of cash received from discounting a note receivable is called the *proceeds* or *cash proceeds.* The term *carrying value* means the face amount of the note plus any accrued interest which has been recorded. Usually the cash proceeds will be less than the carrying value of the note; the difference is recorded by a debit to Interest Expense. If the cash proceeds were greater than the carrying value, the excess received would be credited to Interest Earned.

For example, assume that we own a note receivable for $10,000 on which we have recorded $100 of accrued interest receivable. We now discount the note receivable at the bank and receive cash of $10,020. The entry would be as follows:

Discounting a Note Receivable			
Cash	10,020	
Interest Expense	80	
Notes Receivable		10,000
Accrued Interest Receivable		100
To record discounting of a note receivable.		

When a businessman endorses a note and turns it over to a bank for cash, he is promising to pay the note if the maker fails to do so. The endorser is therefore contingently liable to the bank. A *contingent liability* may be regarded as a potential liability which either will develop into a full-fledged liability or will be eliminated entirely by a subsequent event. The subsequent event in the case of a discounted note receivable is the payment (or dishonoring) of the note by the maker. If the maker pays, the contingent liability of the endorser is thereby ended. If the maker fails to pay, the contingent liability of the endorser becomes a real liability. In either case the period of contingent liability ends at the maturity date of the note.

Contingent liabilities should be reflected in the balance sheet, because they have a considerable bearing on the credit rating of the person or firm contingently liable. The contingent liability arising from the discounting of notes receivable is usually disclosed by a footnote to the balance sheet. The following footnote is typical: "Note: At December 31, 19____, the company was contingently liable for notes receivable discounted in the amount of $250,000."

Classification of receivables in the balance sheet

Accounts receivable from customers will ordinarily be collected within the operating cycle; they are therefore listed among the current assets on the balance sheet. Receivables may also arise from miscellaneous transactions other than the sale of goods and services. These miscellaneous receivables, such as advances to officers and employees, and claims against insurance companies for losses sustained, should be listed separately on the balance sheet and should not be merged with trade accounts receivable. If an account receivable from an officer or employee originates as a favor to the officer or employee, efforts at collection may await the convenience of the debtor. Consequently, it is customary to exclude receivables of this type from the current asset category. An exception to this rule is found in the case of retail stores, which may sell merchandise to employees in accordance with regular credit policy and may enforce collection of employee accounts on the same basis as for other customers. Under these circumstances the receivables from employees may properly be intermingled with customers' accounts.

Notes receivable usually appear among the current assets; however, if the maturity date of a note is more than a year distant and beyond the operating cycle of the business, it should be listed as noncurrent under a heading such as Investments. Any accrued interest receivable at the balance sheet date is a current asset but may be combined on the balance sheet with other accrued items such as accrued rent or royalties receivable. Each of these accounts would be represented by a separate account in the ledger, but combination of like items of modest amount is desirable in the balance sheet to achieve a concise financial statement.

DEMONSTRATION PROBLEM

General Wire Company is short of working capital and attempts to minimize the funds tied up in receivables by discounting notes receivable obtained from customers. Banks apply a discount rate to the maturity value of the notes which varies depending on the quality of the note and the level of interest rates charged by banks. The company makes some sales on 30-day open account, but any customer who does not pay in full within 30 days is asked to substitute an interest-bearing note for the past-due account. Some customers are required to sign promissory notes at the time of sale.

The company uses the allowance method in accounting for uncollectible accounts.

A partial list of transactions for the six months ended December 31, 19___, is given below.

July 1   Sale of merchandise to P. Linn on account, $1,545. It was agreed that Linn would submit a 60-day, 8% note upon receipt of the merchandise, and should deduct any freight he paid on the goods.

July 3   Received from Linn a letter stating that he had paid $45 freight on the shipment of July 1. He enclosed a 60-day, 8% note dated July 3 for $1,500.

July 18   Sold merchandise on account, $2,200, to Baxter Company; terms 2/10, n/30.

July 27   Discounted Linn note at bank and received $1,508 in cash.

July 28   Baxter Company paid account in full.

Aug. 8   Sold merchandise to E. Jones on account, $1,200; terms 2/10, n/30.

Sept. 1   Received notice from the bank that Linn had dishonored this note due today. The bank charged the company's account for $1,520, the maturity value of the note.

Sept. 7   Received a 60-day, 7% note from E. Jones in settlement of open account.

Sept. 10   It was ascertained that an account receivable from K. L. Treff amounting to $120 cannot be collected and was written off.

Oct. 15   An account receivable of $300 from Allen Blaine had been written off in June; full payment was unexpectedly received from Blaine.

Oct. 25   Received cash from P. Linn in full settlement of his account due today, including interest of 8% on $1,520 from September 1, maturity date of note.

Nov. 6   E. Jones paid his note due today.

Dec. 31   As a result of substantial write-offs, the Allowance for Uncollectible Accounts has a *debit* balance of $200. Aging of the accounts receivable (which amount to $80,000) indicates that a credit balance of $1,200 in the Allowance for Uncollectible Accounts is required.

Instructions

Prepare journal entries (in general journal form) to record the transactions and adjustments listed above.

QUESTIONS

1.   Morgan Corporation has decided to write off the account receivable from Brill Company because the latter has entered bankruptcy. What general

ledger accounts should be debited and credited, assuming that the allowance method is in use? What general ledger accounts should be debited and credited if the direct charge-off method is in use?

2. Mill Company, which has accounts receivable of $309,600 and an allowance for uncollectible accounts of $3,600, decides to write off as worthless a past-due account receivable for $1,500 from J. D. North. What effect will the write-off have upon total current assets? Upon net income for the period? Explain.

3. Describe a procedure by which management could be informed each month of the status of collections and the overall quality of the accounts receivable on hand.

4. At the end of its first year in business, Baxter Laboratories had accounts receivable totaling $148,500. After careful analysis of the individual accounts, the credit manager estimated that $146,100 would ultimately be collected. Give the journal entry required to reflect this estimate in the accounts.

5. In February of its second year of operations, Baxter Laboratories (Question 4 above) learned of the failure of a customer, Sterling Corporation, which owed Baxter $800. Nothing could be collected. Give the journal entry to recognize the uncollectibility of the receivable from Sterling Corporation.

6. In making the annual adjusting entry for uncollectible accounts, a company may utilize a *balance sheet approach* to making the estimate or it may use an *income statement approach.* Explain these two alternative approaches.

7. What is the direct charge-off method of handling credit losses as opposed to the allowance method? What is its principal shortcoming?

8. The A Corporation has in its ledger an account entitled Allowance for Bad Debts; B Corporation uses an account entitled Allowance for Doubtful Accounts; and C Corporation maintains an account called Reserve for Uncollectible Accounts. Does this information indicate that the three companies follow different methods of accounting for the expense arising from uncollectible accounts? Into which of the five major groups of accounts would you classify the three accounts listed?

9. Magnum Corporation had accounts receivable of $100,000 and an Allowance for Uncollectible Accounts of $3,500 just prior to writing off as worthless an account receivable from Standard Company in the amount of $1,000. State the net realizable value of the accounts receivable before and after the write-off of this receivable from Standard Company.

10. Determine the maturity date of the following notes:
    a. A three-month note dated March 10
    b. A 30-day note dated August 15
    c. A 90-day note dated July 2

11. a. How would you report installment accounts receivable in the balance sheet when the collection period extends over 36 months?
    b. Briefly describe the installment basis of accounting which can be used in the determination of taxable income.
    c. Why is the installment basis of accounting not acceptable for financial reporting purposes?

EXERCISES

1. The unadjusted trial balance for the Intertherm Corporation at the end of the current year includes the following accounts:

	Debit	Credit
Accounts receivable	*$100,000*	
Allowance for uncollectible accounts		*$ 800*
Sales (25% represent cash sales)		*400,000*

Compute the uncollectible accounts expense for the current year, assuming that uncollectible accounts expense is determined as follows:
   a. 1% of total sales $_____.
   b. 1½% of credit sales $_____.
   c. Allowance for uncollectible accounts is increased to equal 3% of gross accounts receivable $_____.

2. The Thompson Corp. reports sales of $2 million and outstanding accounts receivable of $400,000 at the end of its first year of operations. Uncollectible accounts amounting to $2,000 have been written off during the year and an additional $6,000 of receivables arising from current year's sales may prove to be uncollectible.
   a. Uncollectible accounts expense in the income statement would amount to $_____ when the allowance for uncollectible accounts is used.
   b. Uncollectible accounts expense in the income statement would amount to $_____ when the direct charge-off method of accounting for uncollectible accounts is used.

3. Furni-Mat, Inc., reports the following balance on its balance sheet dated September 30, 1971:

Notes receivable from customers	*$10,000*	
Accrued interest on notes receivable	*200*	
Accounts receivable	*42,000*	
Less: Allowance for uncollectible accounts	*(1,000)*	*$51,200*

Record the following in journal entry form during the ensuing fiscal year:
   a. Accounts of $800 are written off as uncollectible.
   b. A customer's note for $125 on which interest of $5 has been accrued on the books is deemed uncollectible and both balances are written off against the Allowance for Uncollectible Accounts.
   c. An account for $100 previously written off is collected.
   d. Aging of accounts as of September 30, 1972, indicates a need for a $1,500 allowance to cover possible failure to collect accounts currently outstanding.

4. The General Dry Goods Corp. has been in business for three years and has charged off accounts receivable as they proved to be uncollectible. At the end of 1971, management decides to adopt the allowance method of accounting for uncollectible accounts and asks you to help them determine the proper

balance in the Allowance for Uncollectible Accounts. The following information is available for your consideration:

Year	Sales	Accounts Written Off	Year of Origin of Accounts Written Off			Net Income
			1969	*1970*	*1971*	
1969	$150,000	$1,200	$1,200			$10,000
1970	250,000	2,600	600	$2,000		20,000
1971	440,000	4,500		1,800	$2,700	25,000

Accounts receivables at the end of 1971 amount to $80,000, all from 1971 sales.

a. Based on the experience for 1969 and 1970, the *total* uncollectible accounts that can reasonably be anticipated on the sales for 1971 amount to $_____.

b. Since $2,700 of accounts originating in 1971 have already been written off, an allowance of $_____ should be established at the end of 1971 to cover estimated uncollectible accounts.

c. In comparison with the actual write-off of receivables originating in 1969 and 1970 and in comparison with the estimated uncollectibles for 1971, the use of the direct-charge-off method caused the income before taxes to be overstated by $_____ in 1969, $_____ in 1970, and $_____ in 1971.

5. Use the 60-day, 6% method to compute interest on the following notes:
   a. $2,167 at 6% for 60 days = $_____.
   b. $3,946 at 6% for 90 days = $_____.
   c. $7,124 at 6% for 30 days = $_____.
   d. $8,415 at 4% for 60 days = $_____.
   e. $12,636 at 7% for 120 days = $_____.
   f. $4,626 at 5% for 90 days = $_____.

6. Among the assets of the Barnes Company at December 31, 1971, was a 60-day, 6% note receivable for $8,000 dated November 16, 1971.
   a. Give the adjusting entry to record the interest accrued to December 31.
   b. Give the entry to record collection of the note at maturity.

PROBLEMS

10-1 The Kit Mfg. Company makes most of its sales on 30-day open account but requires customers who fail to pay invoices as agreed to substitute 6% promissory notes for their past-due accounts. A partial list of recent transactions relating to notes receivable is as follows:

Apr. 16   Sold merchandise to E. L. Clark on account, $4,000; terms 2/10, n/30.

Apr. 22   Sold merchandise on account to Conklin & Sons, $3,000; terms 2/10, n/30.

May 16   Received a 30-day, 6% note from E. L. Clark in settlement of his open account.

May 19   Received payment of cash from Conklin & Sons in settlement of open account.

May 31   Discounted the Clark note. The proceeds received from the bank amounted to $4,008.

June 15   Received notice from the bank that the Clark note was dishonored at maturity. The bank charged the company's account for $4,020, the maturity value of the note.

June 18   Loaned $9,000 to J. D. Black on a 60-day, 7% note.

Instructions

a.   Prepare in general journal form the entries necessary to record the above transactions.

b.   Prepare any adjusting journal entries needed at June 30, the end of the company's fiscal year. Do not accrue interest on the defaulted Clark note.

10-2   Among the receivables of the Rheem Corporation on January 1, 1971, the end of its fiscal year, were the following items:

Accounts receivable:

C. B. Altman	$1,512
M. E. Jackson	2,280
I. J. Wall	5,160
Total	$8,952

Notes receivable:

R. K. Rogers, 7%, 45-day note, dated Dec. 6, 1970	$6,000
P. J. King, 8%, 60-day note, dated Dec. 31, 1970	2,400
Total	$8,400

Installment contracts receivable:

K. P. Kerr (monthly payment $125)	$2,125

Unearned interest on installment contracts:

Applicable to K. P. Kerr contract	$ 170

During the month of January, 1971, the following additional transactions took place:

Jan. 3   Received a 30-day, 6% note from C. B. Altman in full settlement of his account.

Jan. 14   M. E. Jackson paid $780 on his account and gave a 60-day, 7% note to cover the balance.

Jan. 20   R. K. Rogers wrote that he would be unable to pay his note due today. He included a check to cover the interest due and a new 30-day, 8% note renewing the old note. No accrued interest has been recorded.

Jan. 27   Discounted the C. B. Altman note at the bank. The proceeds on the note amounted to $1,517.50.

Jan. 31   Received the monthly payment on the K. P. Kerr contract. The payment of $125 includes $10 of interest revenue which was originally recorded as unearned interest.

Instructions

a. Prepare journal entries (in general journal form) for January, including any adjusting entries relating to accrued interest at January 31.

b. Show how the accounts relating to notes receivable, accounts receivable, installment contracts receivable, and accrued interest receivable would appear in the balance sheet as of January 31. Show the actual balances.

10-3 At December 31, 1971, the balance sheet of the Pine Company included accounts receivable of $634,400, and an allowance for uncollectible accounts of $16,200. The company's sales volume in 1972 reached a new high of $4,270,000 and cash collections from customers amounted to $4,131,280. Among these collections was the recovery in full of a $7,800 receivable from James Walburn, a customer whose account had been written off as worthless late in 1971. During 1972 it was necessary to write off as uncollectible customers' accounts totaling $16,830.

On December 1, 1972, the Pine Company sold for $360,000 a tract of land acquired as a building site several years earlier at a cost of $240,000. The land was now considered unsuitable as a building site. Terms of sale were $100,000 cash and a 6%, six-month note for $260,000. The buyer was a large corporation and the note was regarded as fully collectible. Income taxes applicable to the sale of the land may be ignored.

At December 31, 1972, the accounts receivable included $100,290 of past-due accounts. After careful study of all past-due accounts, the management estimated that the probable loss contained therein was 10%, and that in addition, 2% of the current accounts receivable ($663,800) might prove uncollectible.

Instructions

a. Prepare journal entries, in general journal form, for all 1972 transactions relating to accounts and notes receivable.

b. Prepare the necessary adjusting entries at December 31, 1972.

c. What amount should appear in the income statement for 1972 as uncollectible accounts expense?

d. Prepare a partial balance sheet at December 31, 1972, showing the accounts indicated above.

10-4 The Keenan Furniture Co. has been engaged in the manufacture of furniture for years. Sales are made to furniture wholesalers and also to retail dealers. Although most sales are made on credit, there have been few credit losses of consequence. The company's experience has shown that an annual provision for uncollectible accounts expense of ½ of 1% of net sales is adequate.

In April, 1971, the company decided to develop a new sales territory and sales of $426,000 were achieved in this new territory during 1971, but some of the sales were made to customers of questionable credit standing. During the period of development of the new territory, it was decided that the provision for uncollectible accounts for sales made in this area should be 3% of net sales.

During the latter part of 1971, the anticipated credit losses became apparent. The Small Furniture Company, which owed $3,600, notified Keenan Furniture Co. that it had been forced to suspend operations and was unable to pay any of its existing debts. Further collection efforts proved futile, and on September 12 the account was written off as worthless.

Another new customer, E Z Furniture House, entered receivership. On October 10, the receiver sent Keenan Furniture Co. a check for $1,850 and stated that nothing further could be paid. The balance of the account prior to this compromise settlement had been $4,550. The balance of the account was worthless.

On October 15, receivables of $1,500 from the Moss Furniture Co. and $3,380 from the Oak Furniture Company were written off as uncollectible, after extensive collection efforts had failed. On November 2, however, both of these accounts were collected in full.

Total net sales during 1971 by the Keenan Furniture Co. amounted to $2,737,200, including sales in the new territory. At the beginning of the year, the credit balance in the Allowance for Uncollectible Accounts had amounted to $21,960. In addition to the credit losses in the new sales territory, accounts receivable aggregating $15,085 has been written off as worthless during 1971 in the company's old territory.

Instructions
a. Prepare journal entries (in general journal form) for all the indicated 1971 transactions including the sales, all of which were credit transactions.
b. Compute the uncollectible accounts expense for 1971, make the adjusting entry and closing entry needed at December 31, 1971, and post these entries to the ledger accounts required in (c).
c. Open general ledger accounts for Uncollectible Accounts Expense and for the Allowance for Uncollectible Accounts. Post the entries called for in (a) to these accounts and compute the balance in the allowance at December 31, 1971.

10-5 The Retail Supply Company sells paint and supplies to retail stores. Sales are made on credit and an accounts receivable subsidiary ledger is maintained. Credit terms to all customers are 1/10, n/30.

During July, you are employed by the company to substitute for an employee who is on vacation. The following transactions affecting accounts receivable are to be recorded.

Sales Journal

Date		Customer	Invoice No.	Amount
July	8	Roller Paint Stores	9184	2,622.00
	9	Cooper Hardware Co.	9185	2,193.00
	18	Psychedelic Paint Co.	9186	4,094.00
	24	Porter Paint Shop	9187	1,116.00
	31	Other sales transactions	9188–9760	190,723.00
		Total		200,748.00

Cash Receipts Journal

Date		Customer	Invoice No.	Amount
July	11	Cooper Hardware Co.	9185	2,171.07
	25	Porter Paint Shop	9187	1,116.00
	31	Other collections (all within discount period, and includes Invoice No. 9184)		187,166.43
		Total		190,453.50

Sales Returns & Allowances

Date		Customer	Invoice No.	Amount
July	28	Porter Paint Shop (credit memo No. 184)	9187	366.00

The balance in Accounts Receivable on July 1 was $145,000. On July 30, notice is received that the Psychedelic Paint Co. has become bankrupt. Invoice No. 9186 for $4,094 is therefore recorded as uncollectible. The cashier for the Porter Paint Shop had paid the entire amount due on invoice No. 9187 without taking the 1% discount. Subsequently, about one-third of the shipment was returned because it was of poor quality. On July 25, credit was given to the Porter Paint Shop for the invoice price of goods returned, $366, plus a discount on the $750 of goods found to be in satisfactory condition.

The Allowance for Uncollectible Accounts had a credit balance of $2,535 on July 1. On July 31, the owner instructs you to make the necessary entry to carry out the company's established policy of providing for uncollectible accounts at a rate of 2% of net sales (after deducting sales returns and allowances and sales discounts).

Instructions

a. Prepare an individual entry in general journal form for each July transaction affecting receivables or uncollectible accounts.

b. Draft the relevant sections of the balance sheet at July 31.

10-6 Given below is a balance sheet prepared by Doris Keller, part owner of J. & D. Keller, Incorporated:

J. & D. KELLER, INCORPORATED
Balance Sheet
April 30, 1971

Assets		*Equities*	
Cash....................	$ 22,500	Accounts payable.........	$ 18,750
Accounts and notes receivable	48,100	Notes payable............	25,000
Investments..............	28,000	Allowance for uncollectible	
Inventories..............	19,600	accounts	250
Equipment (net)	35,400	Capital stock $10 par.......	50,000
		Surplus.................	59,600
	$153,600		$153,600

Additional data relating to the amounts included on the balance sheet are presented below:

(1) **Cash** includes a check from a customer for $1,500 which has been returned by the bank because of insufficient funds and postage stamps amounting to $25. The check is considered to be fully collectible.

(2) **Accounts and notes receivable** balance includes a note receivable for $10,000

on which interest of $500 has accrued. The interest has not been recorded on the books. Of accounts receivable, $800 is considered uncollectible and should be written off. Of the remaining accounts receivable ($37,300), 2% may prove to be uncollectible, and an appropriate allowance for uncollectible accounts should be recorded.

(3) Analysis of the *Investments* account discloses the following:

11/1/70	*Acquired 500 shares of X Co. common stock*	$35,000
2/2/71	*Acquired as short-term investment $10,000 par value 4%*	
	U.S. Treasury bonds. Interest through Apr. 30, 1971,	
	has been received	8,200
4/25/71	*Sold 200 shares of X Co. common stock at $76 per share,*	
	net of commission	(15,200)
	Balance	$28,000

(4) *Inventories* include $350 of office supplies and damaged merchandise; the merchandise was valued at $400 by Donald Keller.

(5) *Equipment* cost $50,000 and depreciation has been properly recorded through April 30, 1971.

(6) Accrued interest on *notes payable* amounting to $750 has not been recorded.

(7) Analysis of the *Surplus* account is presented below:

2/9/65	*Proceeds from issuance of capital stock*	
	in excess of par value	$ 7,000
1965–1971	*Earnings*.	143,000
1965–1971	*Dividends declared*	(88,200)
3/10/71	*Acquisition of 100 shares of treasury stock*	(2,200)
	Balance in Surplus account.	$ 59,600

Instructions

a. Give a brief description of the correction required for each of the seven items listed above. Disregard income taxes.

b. Prepare a classified balance sheet for J. & D. Keller, Incorporated, as of April 30, 1971, in accordance with good accounting practices.

c. Prepare a reconciliation of the "Surplus" figure of $59,600 as determined by Doris Keller and the amount shown as Retained Earnings in the balance sheet prepared in part (*a*).

11 Chapter
inventories

Some basic questions relating to inventory

In earlier sections of this book the procedures for recording inventory at the end of the accounting period have been illustrated. The use of the inventory figure in both the balance sheet and the income statement has been demonstrated, and particular emphasis has been placed on the procedure for computing the cost of goods sold by deducting the ending inventory from the cost of goods available for sale during the period.

In all the previous illustrations, the dollar amount of the ending inventory has been given with only a brief explanation as to how this amount was determined. The valuation of inventory, as for most other types of assets, has been stated to be at cost, but the concept of cost as applied to inventories of merchandise has not been explored or defined.

In this chapter we shall consider some of the fundamental questions involved in accounting for inventories. Among the questions to be considered are these:

1. What goods are to be included in inventory?
2. How is the amount of the ending inventory determined?
3. What are the arguments for and against each of several alternative methods of inventory valuation?

Inventory valuation and the measurement of income

In measuring the gross profit on sales earned during an accounting period, we subtract the *cost of goods sold* from the total *sales* of the period. The figure for sales is easily accumulated from the daily record of sales transactions, but no day-to-day record is maintained showing the cost of goods sold.[1] The figure representing the cost of goods sold during an entire accounting period is computed at the end of the period by separating the cost of goods available for sale into two elements:

[1] As explained in Chap. 5, a company that maintains perpetual inventory records will have a day-to-day record of the cost of goods sold and of goods in inventory. Our present discussion, however, is based on the assumption that the periodic method of inventory is being used.

1. The cost of the goods sold

2. The cost of the goods not sold, which therefore comprise the ending inventory

This idea, with which you are already quite familiar, may be concisely stated in the form of an equation as follows:

Finding Cost of Goods Sold

$$\text{Cost of goods available for sale} - \text{ending inventory} = \text{cost of goods sold}$$

Determining the amount of the ending inventory is the key step in establishing the cost of goods sold. In separating the *cost of goods available for sale* into its components of *goods sold* and *goods not sold,* we are just as much interested in establishing the proper amount for cost of goods sold as in determining a proper figure for ending inventory. Throughout this chapter you should bear in mind that the procedures for determining the amount of the ending inventory are also the means for determining the cost of goods sold. The valuation of inventory and the determination of the cost of goods sold are in effect the two sides of a single coin.

The American Institute of Certified Public Accountants has summarized this relationship between inventory valuation and the measurement of income in the following words: "A major objective of accounting for inventories is the proper determination of income through the process of matching appropriate costs against revenues."[2] The expression "matching costs against revenues" means determining what portion of the cost of goods available for sale should be deducted from the revenues of the current period and what portion should be carried forward (as inventory) to be matched against the revenues of the following period.

Inventory defined

One of the largest assets of a retail store or of a wholesale business is the inventory of merchandise, and the sale of this merchandise at prices in excess of cost is the major source of revenue. The inventory of a merchandising concern consists of all goods owned and held for sale in the regular course of business. Merchandise held for sale will normally be converted into cash within less than a year's time and is therefore regarded as a current asset. In the balance sheet, inventory is listed immediately after accounts receivable, because it is just one step further removed from conversion into cash than are the accounts receivable.

In manufacturing businesses there are three major types of inventories: *raw materials, goods in process of manufacture,* and *finished goods.* All three classes of inventories are included in the current asset section of the balance sheet.

[2]American Institute of Certified Public Accountants, *Accounting Research and Terminology Bulletins,* Final Edition (New York: 1961), p. 28.

The term *inventory* has been defined to mean "the aggregate of those items of tangible personal property which (1) are held for sale in the ordinary course of business, (2) are in process of production for such sale, or (3) are to be currently consumed in the production of goods or services to be available for sale."[3]

Importance of an accurate valuation of inventory

The most important current assets in the balance sheets of most companies are cash, accounts receivable, and inventory. Of these three, the inventory of merchandise is usually much the largest. Because of the relatively large size of this asset, an error in the valuation of inventory may cause a material misstatement of financial condition. An error of 20% in valuing the inventory may have as much effect on the financial statements as would the complete omission of the asset cash.

An error in inventory will of course lead to other erroneous figures in the balance sheet, such as the total current assets, total assets, owners' equity, and the total of liabilities and owners' equity. The error will also affect key figures in the income statement, such as the cost of goods sold, the gross profit on sales, income taxes, and the net income for the period. Finally, it is important to recognize that the ending inventory of one year is also the beginning inventory of the following year. Consequently, the income statement of the second year will also be in error by the full amount of the original error in inventory valuation.

Illustration of the effects of an error in valuing inventory. Assume that on December 31, 1971, the inventory of the Hillside Company is actually $100,000 but, through an accidental error, it is recorded as $90,000. The current assets in the December 31, 1971, balance sheet will be understated $10,000, income taxes payable will be understated $4,000 (assuming a 40% income tax rate), and the retained earnings will be understated $6,000. For the moment, however, let us focus our attention on the income statement.

In the income statement for the year ended December 31, 1971, the "income before income taxes" will be understated $10,000. The several other effects of the $10,000 error on the income statement for the year 1971 are indicated in the first illustration on page 323. Two income statements are presented side by side. In the one on the left, the correct ending inventory of $100,000 is used; in the one on the right, the ending inventory is understated $10,000.

If we assume a 40% corporate income tax rate, the effect of the $10,000 understatement of ending inventory will be to reduce income taxes by $4,000 and net income by $6,000, as shown in the second illustration on page 323.

This illustration shows that an understatement of $10,000 in the ending inventory for the year 1971 caused an understatement of $10,000 in the income before taxes for 1971. Next, consider the effect of this error on the income statement of the following year. The ending inventory of 1971 is,

---

[3] *Ibid.*, p. 27.

*Effect of
Error in
Inventory*

HILLSIDE COMPANY
*Income Statement
For the Year Ended December 31, 1971*

	Statement with Correct Ending Inventory		Statement with Incorrect Ending Inventory	
Sales		$265,000		$265,000
Cost of goods sold:				
Beginning inventory, Dec. 31, 1970	$ 75,000		$ 75,000	
Purchases	210,000		210,000	
Cost of goods available for sale	$285,000		$285,000	
Less: Ending inventory, Dec. 31, 1971	100,000	185,000	90,000	195,000
Gross profit on sales		$ 80,000		$ 70,000
Operating expenses		30,000		30,000
Income before income taxes		$ 50,000		$ 40,000

Income Statement—Concluded

Income before income taxes	$50,000	$40,000
Income taxes	20,000	16,000
Net income	$30,000	$24,000

of course, the beginning inventory of 1972. The preceding illustration is now continued on page 324 to show side by side a correct statement and an incorrect statement for 1972. The ending inventory for 1972 is the same in both statements and is to be considered correct. Note that the $10,000 error in the beginning inventory of the right-hand statement causes an error in the cost of goods sold, in gross profit on sales, and in net income for the year 1972.

Counterbalancing errors. The illustrated income statements for the years 1971 and 1972 show than an understatement of the ending inventory in 1971 caused an understatement of net income in that year and an offsetting overstatement of net income for 1972. Over a period of two years the effects of an inventory error on net income will counterbalance, and the total income for the two years taken together is the same as if the error had not occurred. Since the error in reported net income for the first year is exactly offset by the error in reported net income for the second year, it might be argued that an inventory error has no serious consequences. Such an argument is not sound, for it disregards the fact that accurate yearly income figures are

Effect on Succeeding Year

HILLSIDE COMPANY
Income Statement
For the Year Ended December 31, 1972

	With Correct Beginning Inventory		With Incorrect Beginning Inventory	
Sales....................		$300,000		$300,000
Cost of goods sold:				
Beginning inventory, Dec. 31, 1971..................	$100,000		$ 90,000	
Purchases...............	230,000		230,000	
Cost of goods available for sale................	$330,000		$320,000	
Less: Ending inventory, Dec. 31, 1972..............	120,000	210,000	120,000	200,000
Gross profit on sales		$ 90,000		$100,000
Operating expenses		35,000		35,000
Income before income taxes....		$ 55,000		$ 65,000
Income taxes		22,000		26,000
Net income................		$ 33,000		$ 39,000

a primary objective of the accounting process. Moreover, many actions by management and many decisions by creditors and investors are based directly on the annual financial statements. To produce dependable financial statements, inventory must be accurately determined at the end of each accounting period. The counterbalancing effect of an inventory error is illustrated below:

Counterbalancing Effect on Net Income

	With Inventory Correctly Stated	With Inventory at Dec. 31, 1971, Understated	
		Reported Net Income Will Be	Reported Net Income Will Be Overstated (Understated)
Net income for 1971	$30,000	$24,000	($6,000)
Net income for 1972	33,000	39,000	6,000
Total net income for two years ...	$63,000	$63,000	-0-

Relation of inventory errors to net income. The effects of errors in inventory upon net income may be summarized as follows:

1. When the *ending* inventory is understated, the net income for the period will be understated.

2. When the *ending* inventory is overstated, the net income for the period will be overstated.

3. When the *beginning* inventory is understated, the net income for the period will be overstated.

4. When the *beginning* inventory is overstated, the net income for the period will be understated.

Taking a physical inventory

At the end of each accounting period up-to-date balances for most of the assets will be shown in the ledger accounts. For inventory, however, the balance in the ledger account represents the beginning inventory, because no entry has been made in the Inventory account since the end of the preceding year. All purchases of merchandise during the present year have been recorded in the Purchases account. The ending inventory does not appear anywhere in the ledger accounts; it must be determined by a physical count of merchandise.

Establishing a balance sheet valuation for the ending inventory requires two steps: (1) determining the quantity of each kind of merchandise on hand, and (2) multiplying the quantity by the cost per unit. The first step is called *taking the inventory;* the second is called *pricing the inventory.* Taking inventory, or more precisely, taking a physical inventory, means making a systematic count of all merchandise on hand.

In most merchandising businesses the taking of a physical inventory is a year-end event. In some lines of business an inventory may be taken at the close of each month. It is common practice to take inventory after regular business hours or on Sunday. By taking the inventory while business operations are suspended, it is possible to make a more accurate count than would be possible if goods were being sold or received while the count was in process.

Including all goods owned. All goods to which the company has title should be included in the inventory, regardless of their location. Title to merchandise ordinarily passes from seller to buyer at the time the goods are delivered. No question arises as to the ownership of merchandise on the shelves, in stock rooms, or in warehouses. A question of ownership does arise, however, for merchandise which has been ordered from suppliers but not yet received on the last day of the period. A similar question of ownership concerns goods in the process of shipment to customers at year-end.

Do goods in transit belong in the inventory of the seller or of the buyer? If the seller makes delivery of the merchandise in his own trucks, the merchandise remains his property while in transit. If the goods are shipped by rail, air, or other public carrier, the question of ownership of the goods while in transit depends upon whether the public carrier is acting as the agent of the seller or of the buyer. If the terms of the shipment are f.o.b. (free on board) shipping point, title passes at the point of shipment and the goods are the property of the buyer while in transit. If the terms of the shipment are f.o.b. destination, title does not pass until the shipment reaches the destination, and the goods belong to the seller while in transit. In deciding whether goods in transit at year-end should be included in inventory, it is therefore necessary to refer to the terms of the agreements with vendors and customers.

At the end of the year a company may have received numerous orders from customers, for which goods have been segregated and packed but not yet shipped. These goods should generally be included in inventory. An exception to this rule is found occasionally when the goods have been prepared for shipment but are being held for later delivery at the request of the customer.

The debit to the customer's account and the offsetting credit to the Sales account should be made when title to the goods passes to the customer. It would obviously be improper to set up an account receivable and at the same time to include the goods in question in inventory. Great care is necessary at year-end to ensure that all last-minute shipments to customers are recorded as sales of the current year and, on the other hand, that no customer's order is recorded as a sale until the date when the goods are shipped.

Merchandise in inventory is valued at *cost*, whereas accounts receivable are stated at the *sales price* of the merchandise sold. Consequently, the recording of a sale prior to delivery of the goods results in an unjustified increase in the total assets of the company. The increase will equal the difference between the cost and the selling price of the goods in question. The amount of the increase will also be reflected in the income statement, where it will show up as additional earnings. An unscrupulous company, which wanted to make its financial statements present a more favorable picture than actually existed, might do so by treating year-end orders from customers as sales even though the goods were not yet shipped.

Pricing the inventory

One of the most interesting and widely discussed problems in accounting is the pricing of inventory. Even those businessmen who have little knowledge of accounting are usually interested in the various methods of pricing inventory, because inventory valuation has a direct effect upon reported net income. Federal income taxes are based on income, and the choice of inventory method may have a considerable effect upon the amount of income taxes which a business is required to pay. Federal income tax authorities are therefore much interested in the problem of inventory valuation and have taken a definite position on the acceptability of various methods of pricing inventory.

In approaching our study of inventory valuation, however, it is important that we do not overemphasize the income tax aspects of the problem. It is true that in selected cases one method of inventory valuation may lead to a substantially lower income tax liability than would another method, but there are other important considerations in pricing inventory apart from the objective of minimizing the current income tax burden.

Proper valuation of inventory is one part of a larger undertaking, that is, to measure net income accurately and to provide all those persons interested in the financial condition and operating results of a business with accounting data which are dependable and of maximum usefulness as a basis for business decisions.

Although several acceptable methods are used in pricing the inventory, the most significant basis of accounting for inventories is *cost.* Another important method, which is acceptable for income tax purposes and is widely used, is known as the *lower of cost or market.* First we shall consider the cost basis of accounting for inventories, for an understanding of the meaning of the term *cost* as applied to inventories is a first essential in appreciating the complexity of the overall problem of inventory valuation.

Cost basis of inventory valuation

"The primary basis of accounting for inventory is cost, which has been defined generally as the price paid or consideration given to acquire an asset. As applied to inventories, cost means in principle the sum of the applicable expenditures and charges directly or indirectly incurred in bringing an article to its existing condition and location."[4]

Incidental expenditures relating to the acquisition of goods such as transportation-in, customs duties, insurance, and storage are necessary to place the goods in condition and location for sale. However, in pricing the year-end inventory, often there is no convenient method of determining how much transportation and other incidental costs may have been incurred on specific types of merchandise. This is particularly true when certain shipments have included various kinds of merchandise and the freight, insurance, and other charges were for the shipment as a whole. For reasons of convenience and economy, therefore, a merchandising business may choose to determine inventory cost at year-end by listing each item in stock at the purchase invoice price, and then adding to the inventory as a whole a reasonable proportion of the incidental inventory costs incurred on inbound shipments during the year.

In many lines of business it is customary to price the year-end inventory without giving any consideration to transportation and other incidental costs. This practice may be justified by the factors of convenience and economy, even though it is not theoretically sound. If freight charges, for example, are not material in amount, it may be advisable in terms of operating convenience to treat the entire amount as part of the cost of goods sold during the year. Accounting textbooks stress theoretical concepts of cost and of income determination; the student of accounting should be aware, however, that in many business situations an approximation of cost will serve the purpose at hand.

[4] *Ibid.,* p. 28.

In other words, the extra work involved in computing more precise cost data must be weighed against the benefits to be obtained.

Purchase discounts as a factor in inventory valuation. When a merchant purchases goods he often has the opportunity of saving 1 to 2% of the invoiced amount by making payment within a specified period, usually 10 days. Since purchase discounts are shown as a deduction from purchases in the income statement, they should logically be deducted from the invoice price of the items comprising the year-end inventory. Often, however, it is impracticable to compute the precise amount of discount applicable to each item in inventory. One reasonable alternative is to deduct from the invoice cost of the entire ending inventory an amount representing the estimated purchase discount applicable to these goods. If purchase discounts are not significant in amount, they may be ignored for the purpose of inventory pricing.

Determining cost when purchase prices vary

The price of many kinds of merchandise are subject to frequent change. When identical lots of merchandise are purchased at various dates during the year, each lot may be acquired at a different cost price.

To illustrate the several alternative methods in common use for determining which purchase prices apply to the units remaining in inventory at the end of the period, assume the data shown below.

	Number of Units	Cost per Unit	Total Cost
Beginning inventory.	10	$ 8	$ 80
First purchase (Mar. 1).	5	9	45
Second purchase (July 1).	5	10	50
Third purchase (Oct. 1).	5	12	60
Fourth purchase (Dec. 1).	5	13	65
Available for sale.	30		$300
Units sold	18		
Units in ending inventory.	12		

This schedule shows that 18 units were sold during the year and that 12 units are on hand at year-end to make up the ending inventory. In order to establish a dollar amount for cost of goods sold and for the ending inventory, we must make an assumption as to which units were sold and which units remain on hand at the end of the year. There are several acceptable assumptions on this point; four of the most common will be considered. Each assumption made as to the identity of the units in the ending inventory leads to a different method of pricing inventory and to different amounts in the financial statements. The four assumptions (and inventory valuation methods) to be considered are known as : (1) specific identification, (2) average cost, (3) first-in, first-out, and (4) last-in, first-out.

Although each of these four methods will produce a different answer as to the cost of goods sold and the cost of the ending inventory, the valuation of inventory in each case is said to be at "cost." In other words, these methods represent alternative definitions of cost.

Specific identification method. If the units in the ending inventory can be identified as coming from specific purchases, they may be priced at the amounts listed on the purchase invoices. Continuing the example already presented, if the ending inventory of 12 units can be identified as, say, five units from the purchase of March 1, four units from the purchase of July 1, and three units from the purchase of December 1, the cost of the ending inventory may be computed as follows:

Specific	*Five units from the purchase of Mar. 1 @ $9*	*$ 45*
Identifica-	*Four units from the purchase of July 1 @ $10*	*40*
tion	*Three units from the purchase of Dec. 1 @ $13*	*39*
Method	*Ending inventory (specific identification)*	*$124*
and . . .		

The cost of goods sold during the period is determined by subtracting the ending inventory from the cost of goods available for sale.

. . . Cost	*Cost of goods available for sale*	*$300*
of Goods	*Less: Ending inventory*	*124*
Sold Com-	*Cost of goods sold*	*$176*
putation		

A business may prefer not to use the specific identification method even though the cost of each unit sold could be identified with a specific purchase. The flow of cost factors may be more significant than the flow of specific physical units in measuring the income of the period.

As a simple example, assume that a coal dealer purchased 100 tons of coal at $18 a ton and a short time later made a second purchase of 100 tons of the same grade coal at $20 a ton. The two purchases are in separate piles and it is a matter of indifference as to which pile is used in making sales to customers. Assume that the dealer makes a retail sale of one ton of coal at a price of $25. In measuring the gross profit on the sale, which cost figure should be used, $18 or $20? To insist that the cost depended on which of the two identical piles of coal was used in filling the delivery truck is an argument of questionable logic.

A situation in which the specific identification method is more likely to give meaningful results is in the purchase and sale of such high-priced articles as boats, automobiles, and jewelry.

Average-cost method. Average cost is computed by dividing the total cost of goods available for sale by the number of units available for sale. This computation gives a *weighted average unit cost,* which is then applied to the units in the ending inventory.

Average-	*Cost of goods available for sale*	*$300*
Cost	*Number of units available for sale*	*30*
Method	*Average unit cost*	*$ 10*
and . . .	*Ending inventory (at average cost, 12 units @ $10)*	*$120*

Note that this method, when compared with the actual invoice price method, leads to a different amount for cost of goods sold as well as a different amount for the ending inventory.

. . . Cost	*Cost of goods available for sale*	*$300*
of Goods	*Less: Ending inventory*	*120*
Sold Com-	*Cost of goods sold*	*$180*
putation		

When the average-cost method is used, the cost figure determined for the ending inventory is influenced by all the various prices paid during the year. The price paid early in the year may carry as much weight in pricing the ending inventory as a price paid at the end of the year. A common criticism of the average-cost method of pricing inventory is that it attaches no more significance to current prices than to prices which prevailed several months earlier.

First-in, first-out method. The first-in, first-out method, which is often referred to as *fifo,* is based on the assumption that the first merchandise acquired is the first merchandise sold. In other words, each sale is made out of the oldest goods in stock; the ending inventory therefore consists of the most recently acquired goods. The fifo method of determining inventory cost may be adopted by any business regardless of whether or not the physical flow of merchandise actually corresponds to this assumption of selling the oldest units in stock. Using the same data as in the preceding illustrations, the 12 units in the ending inventory would be regarded as consisting of the most recently acquired goods, as follows:

First-in,	*Five units from the Dec. 1 purchase @ $13*	*$ 65*
First-out	*Five units from the Oct. 1 purchase @ $12*	*60*
Method	*Two units from the July 1 purchase @ $10*	*20*
and . . .	*Ending inventory (at fifo cost)*	*$145*

During a period of rising prices the first-in, first-out method will result in a larger amount being assigned as the cost of the ending inventory than would be assigned under the average-cost method. When a relatively large amount is allocated as cost of the ending inventory, a relatively small amount will remain as cost of goods sold, as indicated by the following calculation:

...Cost of Goods Sold Computation

Cost of goods available for sale	$300
Less: Ending inventory	145
Cost of goods sold	$155

It may be argued in support of the first-in, first-out method that the inventory valuation reflects recent costs and is therefore a realistic value in the light of conditions prevailing at the balance sheet date.

Last-in, first-out method. The title of this method of pricing suggests that the most recently acquired goods are sold first, and that the ending inventory consists of "old" merchandise acquired in the earliest purchases. Such an assumption is, of course, not in accord with the actual physical movement of goods in most businesses, but there is nevertheless a strong logical argument to support this method. As merchandise is sold, more goods must be purchased to replenish the stock on hand. Since the making of a sale necessitates a replacement purchase of goods, the cost of replacement should be offset against the sales price to determine the gross profit realized.

The supporters of last-in, first-out, or *lifo,* as it is commonly known, contend that the accurate determination of income requires that primary emphasis be placed on the matching of current costs of merchandise against current sales prices, regardless of which physical units of merchandise are being delivered to customers. Keeping in mind the point that the flow of costs may be more significant than the physical movement of merchandise, we can say that, under the lifo method, the cost of goods sold consists of the cost of the most recently acquired goods, and the ending inventory consists of the cost of the oldest goods which were available for sale during the period.

Using the same data as in the preceding illustrations, the 12 units in the ending inventory would be priced as if they were the oldest goods available for sale during the period, as follows:

Last-in, First-out Method and...

Ten units from the beginning inventory @ $8	$80
Two units from the purchase of Mar. 1 @ $9	18
Ending inventory (at lifo cost)	$98

Note that the lifo cost of the ending inventory ($98) is very much lower than the fifo cost ($145) of ending inventory in the preceding example. Since a relatively small part of the cost of goods available for sale is assigned to ending inventory, it follows that a relatively large portion must have been assigned to cost of goods sold, as shown by the following computation:

Cost of goods available for sale	$300
Less: Ending inventory	98
Cost of goods sold	$202

Comparison of the alternative methods of pricing inventory. We have now illustrated four common methods of pricing inventory at cost; the specific identification method, the average-cost method, first-in, first-out method, and the last-in, first-out method. By way of contrasting the results obtained from the four methods illustrated, especially during a period of rapid price increases, let us summarize the amounts computed for ending inventory, cost of goods sold, and gross profit on sales under each of the four methods. Assume that sales for the period amounted to $275.

	Specific Identification Method	Average-cost Method	First-in, First-out Method	Last-in, First-out Method
Sales	$275	$275	$275	$275
Cost of goods sold:				
Beginning inventory	$ 80	$ 80	$ 80	$ 80
Purchases	220	220	220	220
Cost of goods available for sale	$300	$300	$300	$300
Less: Ending inventory	124	120	145	98
Cost of goods sold	$176	$180	$155	$202
Gross profit on sales	$ 99	$ 95	$120	$ 73

This comparison of the four methods makes it apparent that during periods of *rising prices,* the use of lifo will result in lower profits being reported than would be the case under the other methods of inventory valuation. Perhaps for this reason many businesses have adopted lifo in recent years. Current income tax regulations permit virtually any business to use the last-in, first-out method in determining taxable income.

During a period of *declining prices,* the use of lifo will cause the reporting of relatively large profits as compared with fifo, which will hold reported profits to a minimum. Obviously, the choice of inventory method becomes of greatest significance during prolonged periods of drastic changes in price levels.

Which method of inventory valuation is best? All four of the inventory methods described are regarded as acceptable accounting practices and all four are acceptable in the determination of taxable income. No one method of inventory valuation can be considered as the "correct" or the "best" method. In the selection of a method, consideration should be given to the probable effect upon the balance sheet, upon the income statement, upon the amount of taxable income, and upon such business decisions as the establishment of selling prices for goods.

When prices are changing drastically, the most significant cost data to use as a guide to sales policies are probably the current replacement costs of the goods being sold. The lifo method of inventory valuation comes closer than any of the other methods described to measuring profits in the light of current selling prices and current replacement costs.

On the other hand, the use of lifo during a period of rising prices is apt to produce a balance sheet figure for inventory which is far below the current replacement cost of the goods on hand. The fifo method of inventory valuation will lead to a balance sheet valuation of inventory more in line with current replacement costs.

Some business concerns which adopted lifo 30 years ago now show a balance sheet figure for inventory which is less than half the present replacement cost of the goods in stock. An inventory valuation method which gives significant figures for the income statement may thus produce misleading amounts for the balance sheet, whereas a method which produces a realistic figure for inventory on the balance sheet may provide less realistic data for the income statement.

The search for the "best" method of inventory valuation is rendered difficult because the inventory figure is used in both the balance sheet and the income statement, and these two statements are intended for different purposes. In the income statement the function of the inventory figure is to permit a matching of costs and revenues. In the balance sheet the inventory and the other current assets are regarded as a measure of the company's ability to meet its current debts. For this purpose a valuation of inventory in line with current replacement cost would appear to be most significant.

The high rates of income tax in recent years have stimulated the interest of businessmen in the choice of inventory methods. No one can predict with certainty the course of future prices or income tax rates. Increasing numbers of businesses, however, have reacted to the experience of rising prices, large profits, and high income taxes by adopting lifo as a means of minimizing reported profits and required income tax payments. Many accountants believe that the use of average cost or of fifo during a period of rising prices results in the reporting of fictitious profits and consequently in the payment of excessive income taxes.

The lower-of-cost-or-market rule

Although cost is the primary basis for valuation of inventories, circumstances may arise under which inventory may properly be valued at less than its cost.

If the utility of the inventory has fallen below cost by reason of physical deterioration, obsolescence, or decline in the price level, a loss has occurred. This loss may appropriately be recognized as a loss of the current period by reducing the accounting value of the inventory from cost to a lower level designated as market. The word *market* as used in this context *means current replacement cost.* For a merchandising concern, *market* is the amount which the concern would have to pay at the present time for the goods in question, purchased in the customary quantities through the usual sources of supply and including transportation-in. To avoid misunderstanding, the rule might better read "lower of cost or replacement cost."

In the early days of accounting when the principal users of financial statements were creditors and attention was concentrated upon the balance sheet, conservatism was a dominant consideration in asset valuation. The lower-of-cost-or-market rule was then considered justifiable because it tended to produce a "safe" or minimum value for inventory. The rule was widely applied for a time without regard for the possibility that although replacement costs had declined, there might be no corresponding and immediate decline in selling prices.

As the significance of the income statement has increased, considerable dissatisfaction with the lower-of-cost-or-market rule has developed. If ending inventory is written down from cost to a lower market figure but the merchandise is sold during the next period at the usual selling prices, the effect of the write-down will have been to reflect a fictitious loss in the first period and an exaggerated profit in the second period. Arbitrary application of the lower-of-cost-or-market rule ignores the historical fact that selling prices do not always drop when replacement prices decline. Even if selling prices do follow replacement prices downward, they may not decline by a proportionate amount.

Because of these objections, the lower-of-cost-or-market rule has undergone some modification and is now qualified in the following respects. If the inventory can probably be sold at prices which will yield a *normal profit,* the inventory should be carried at cost even though current replacement cost is lower. Assume, for example, that merchandise is purchased for $1,000 with the intention of reselling it to customers for $1,500. The replacement cost then declines from $1,000 to $800, but it is believed that the merchandise can still be sold to customers for $1,450. In other words, the normal anticipated profit has shrunk by $50. The carrying value of the inventory could then be written down from $1,000 to $950. There is no justification for reducing the inventory to the replacement cost of $800 under these circumstances.

Another qualification of the lower-of-cost-or-market rule is that inventory should never be carried at an amount greater than *net realizable value,* which may be defined as prospective selling price minus anticipated selling expenses. Assume, for example, that because of disturbed market conditions, it is believed that goods acquired at a cost of $500 and having a current replacement cost of $450 will probably have to be sold for no more than $520 and that the selling expenses involved will amount to $120. The inventory should then be reduced to a carrying value of $400, which is less than current replacement cost.

Application of the lower-of-cost-or-market rule. The lower of cost or market for an inventory is most commonly computed by determining the cost and the market figures for each item in inventory and using the lower of the two amounts in every case. If, for example, item A cost $100 and market is $90, the item should be priced at $90. If item B cost $200 and market is $225, this item should be priced at $200. The total cost of the two items is $300 and total market is $315, but the total inventory value determined by applying the lower-of-cost-or-market rule to each item in inventory is only $290. This application of the lower-of-cost-or-market rule is illustrated by the tabulation shown below.

Pricing Inventory at Lower of Cost or Market

| | | Unit Price | | Lower of Cost or Market |
Item	Quantity	Cost	Market	
A	10	$100	$ 90	$ 900
B	8	200	225	1,600
C	50	50	60	2,500
D	80	90	70	5,600
Total				$10,600

Application of Lower-of-cost-or-market Rule, Item by Item Method

If the lower-of-cost-or-market rule is applied item by item, the carrying value of the above inventory would be $10,600. However, in some circumstances the lower-of-cost-or-market rule may be applied to the total of the entire inventory rather than to the individual items. If the above inventory is to be valued by applying the lower-of-cost-or-market rule to the total of the inventory, the balance sheet amount for inventory is determined merely by comparing the total cost of $12,300 with the total replacement cost of $11,300 and using the lower of the two figures. This application of the lower-of-cost-or-market rule is appropriate when no loss of income is anticipated, because the decline in cost prices of certain goods is fully offset by higher replacement costs for other items.

Gross profit method of estimating inventories

The taking of a physical inventory is a time-consuming and costly job in many lines of business; consequently, a physical inventory may be taken only once a year. Monthly financial statements are needed, however, for intelligent administration of the business, and the preparation of monthly statements requires a determination of the amount of inventory at the end of each month. This dilemma may be solved satisfactorily by estimating the inventory each month by using the *gross profit method.*

The gross profit method of estimating the inventory is based on the assumption that the rate of gross profit remains approximately the same from year to year. This assumption is a realistic one in many fields of business. The first step in using the gross profit method is to obtain from the ledger the figures for beginning inventory, purchases, and sales. Cost of goods sold is then computed by reducing the sales figure by the usual gross profit rate. The difference between the cost of goods sold and the cost of goods available for sale represents the ending inventory.

To illustrate, let us assume that the beginning inventory is $25,000, the purchases of the period $70,000, and the net sales $100,000. The gross profit rate is assumed to have approximated 40% of net sales for the past several years. This information is now assembled in the customary form of an income statement as follows:

Gross	Net sales	**$100,000 (100%)**
Profit	Beginning inventory $25,000	
Method	Purchases 70,000	
. . .	Cost of goods available for sale $95,000	
	Less: Ending inventory . . . . ?	
	Cost of goods sold	60,000 (60%)
	Gross profit (40% × $100,000)	$ 40,000 (40%)

Customarily, in preparing an income statement, the ending inventory is deducted from the cost of goods available for sale to determine the cost of goods sold. In this case our calculation to determine the ending inventory consists of deducting the estimated cost of goods sold from the cost of goods available for sale.

. . . to	Cost of goods available for sale	$95,000
Estimate	Less: Cost of goods sold (60% of $100,000)	60,000
Ending	Ending inventory (estimate)	$35,000
Inventory		

The gross profit method of estimating inventory has several uses apart from the preparation of monthly financial statements. This calculation may be used after the taking of a physical inventory to confirm the overall reasonableness of the amount determined by the counting and pricing process. In the event of a fire which destroys the inventory, the approximate amount of goods on hand at the date of the fire may also be computed by the gross profit method.

Consistency in the valuation of inventory

A business has considerable latitude in selecting a method of inventory valuation best suited to its needs; once a method has been selected, however, that method should be followed consistently from year to year. A change from one inventory method to another will ordinarily cause reported income to vary considerably in the year in which the change occurs. Frequent switching of methods would therefore make the income statements quite undependable as a means of portraying operating results.

The need for consistency in the valuation of inventory does not mean that a business should *never* make a change in inventory method. However, when a change is made, the approval of tax authorities must be obtained, and full disclosure of the nature of the change and of its effect upon the year's net income should be included in the financial statements or in a footnote to the statements. Even when the same method of inventory pricing is being followed consistently, the financial statements should include a disclosure of the pricing method in use.

Inventories for a manufacturing business

A typical manufacturing firm buys raw materials and converts them into a finished product. The raw materials purchased by an aircraft manufacturer, for example, include sheet aluminum, jet engines, and a variety of electronic gear and control instruments. The completed airplanes assembled from these components are the *finished goods* of the aircraft manufacturer. The terms *raw materials* and *finished goods*, as used in accounting, are defined from the viewpoint of each manufacturing firm. Sheet aluminum, for example, is a raw material from the viewpoint of an aircraft company, but it is a finished product of an aluminum company.

In converting raw materials into finished goods, the manufacturer employs factory labor, uses machinery, and incurs many other manufacturing costs, such as heat, light, and power, machinery repairs, and supervisory salaries. These production costs are added to the cost of raw materials to determine the cost of the finished goods manufactured during any given period. The accounting records of a manufacturing firm must be expanded to include ledger accounts for these various types of factory costs. Financial statements must also be changed to reflect the costs of manufacturing and several new classes of inventories. At any given moment, a manufacturer will have on hand a stock of raw materials, finished goods awaiting shipment and sale, and partially completed products in various stages of manufacture. Inventories of each of these classes of items must be taken at the beginning and end of each accounting period in order to measure the cost of goods that have been completed and the cost of goods sold during the period.

In place of the single inventory account found on the balance sheet of a retail or wholesale business, a manufacturing concern has three separate inventory accounts, all of which are current assets.

1. Raw materials inventory. This account represents the unused portion of the raw materials purchased. The amount is determined at year-end by taking a physical count of the raw materials which have not yet been placed in production. As a matter of convenience, factory supplies on hand (oil, grease, sweeping compounds) acquired for use in maintaining and servicing the factory building and machinery are often merged with raw materials.

2. *Goods in process inventory.* This inventory consists of the partially completed goods on hand in the factory at year-end, determined by a physical count. The cost of these partially manufactured goods is determined by estimating the costs of the raw materials, direct labor, and factory overhead associated with these units.

Comparison of Income Statements for a Merchandising Company and a Manufacturing Company

A MERCHANDISING COMPANY
Income Statement
For the Current Year

Sales		$1,000,000
Cost of goods sold:		
Beginning inventory of merchandise	$300,000	
PURCHASES	600,000	
Cost of goods available for sale	$900,000	
Less: Ending inventory of merchandise	250,000	
Cost of goods sold		650,000
Gross profit on sales		$ 350,000
Operating expenses:		
Selling expenses	$100,000	
General expenses	150,000	250,000
Income before income taxes		$ 100,000
Income taxes		41,000
Net income		$ 59,000

A MANUFACTURING COMPANY
Income Statement
For the Current Year

Sales		$1,000,000
Cost of goods sold:		
Beginning inventory of finished goods	$300,000	
COST OF GOODS MANUFACTURED (per Exhibit A)	600,000	
Cost of goods available for sale	$900,000	
Less: Ending inventory of finished goods	250,000	
Cost of goods sold		650,000
Gross profit on sales		$ 350,000
Operating expenses:		
Selling expenses	$100,000	
General expenses	150,000	250,000
Income before income taxes		$ 100,000
Income taxes		41,000
Net income		$ 59,000

3. Finished goods inventory. This account shows the cost of finished goods on hand and awaiting sale to customers as of the end of the year. The cost of these finished units is composed of the factory costs of raw material, direct labor, and factory overhead.

Comparison of income statements for manufacturing and merchandising concerns. The treatment of sales, selling expenses, general administrative expenses, and income taxes is the same on the income statement of a manufacturing company as for a merchandising concern. The only difference in the comparative income statements shown on page 338 lies in the cost of goods sold section. In the income statement of the manufacturing company, Cost of Goods Manufactured replaces the item labeled Purchases in the income statement of the merchandising company.

Statement of cost of goods manufactured. The principal new element in the illustrated income statement for a manufacturing company is the item: "Cost of goods manufactured. . . $600,000." This amount was determined from the Statement of Cost of Goods Manufactured, a financial statement prepared to accompany and support the income statement, as shown below:

A MANUFACTURING COMPANY			Exhibit A
Statement of Cost of Goods Manufactured			
For the Current Year			
Goods in process inventory, beginning of year			$ 70,000
Raw materials:			
Beginning raw materials inventory		$ 50,000	
Purchases of raw materials	$100,000		
Less: Purchase returns and allowances	3,000	97,000	
Transportation-in		5,000	
Cost of raw materials available for use		$152,000	
Less: Ending raw materials inventory		42,000	
Cost of raw materials used		$110,000	
Direct labor		230,000	
Factory overhead:			
Indirect labor	$ 60,000		
Supervisory salaries	100,000		
Heat, light, and power	18,000		
Repairs and maintenance	12,000		
Property taxes	18,000		
Insurance expired	15,000		
Depreciation on factory assets	19,000		
Miscellaneous factory costs	8,000		
Total factory overhead		250,000	
Total manufacturing costs			590,000
Total cost of goods in process during the year			$660,000
Less: Goods in process inventory, end of year			60,000
Cost of goods manufactured			$600,000

DEMONSTRATION PROBLEM

The operating results achieved by Olive Company for the years ended December 31, 1970 and 1971, are summarized as follows:

	1970	1971
Net sales	$710,000	$760,000
Cost of goods sold:		
Beginning inventory	$240,000	$253,040
Net purchases	409,326	426,960
Cost of goods available for sale	$649,326	$680,000
Ending inventory	253,040	260,000
Cost of goods sold	$396,286	$420,000
Gross profit on sales	$313,714	$340,000
Expenses	143,714	180,000
Net income	$170,000	$160,000

The balance sheets of the company showed retained earnings as follows: December 31, 1969, $300,000; December 31, 1970, $370,000, and December 31, 1971, $410,000.

Other data

In May, 1971, Jim Klein, chief accountant for the Olive Company, decided to make a careful review of the documents and procedures which had been used in taking the physical inventory at December 31, 1970. Klein felt that this review might disclose errors which still required correction or, at least, should be given consideration to assure maximum accuracy in the taking of the next annual physical inventory. Klein's investigation disclosed three questionable items which are described below. No adjustment or correction of any kind was made for these possible errors prior to preparing the 1971 income statement.

(1) Merchandise costing $9,840, which had been received on December 31, 1970, had been included in the inventory taken on that date, although the purchase was not recorded until January 4, when the vendor's invoice arrived. The invoice was then recorded in the purchases journal as a January transaction.

(2) Merchandise shipped to a customer on December 31, 1970, f.o.b. shipping point, was included in the physical inventory taken that day. The cost of the merchandise was $2,600 and the sales price was $3,600. Because of the press of year-end work, the sales invoice was not prepared until January 6, 1971. On that date the sale was recorded as a January transaction by entry in the sales journal, and the sales invoice was mailed to the customer.

(3) An error of $2,000 had been made in footing one of the inventory sheets at December 31, 1970. This clerical error had caused the inventory total to be overstated.

Instructions

a. Prepare corrected income statements for the years ended December 31, 1970 and 1971. It may be helpful to set up T accounts for Sales 1970 and Sales 1971; Purchases 1970 and Purchases 1971; and Inventory December 31, 1970.

Corrections may then be entered in these accounts. Ignore income taxes.

b. Compute corrected amounts for retained earnings at December 31, 1970 and 1971.

c. Prepare any correcting journal entries that you consider should have been made at May 12, 1971, the date that these items came to Klein's attention. Any items relating to the net income for 1970 may be entered in an account entitled Correction in Net Income for 1970.

d. Assume that the $9,840 worth of merchandise described in item 1 had not been included in inventory on December 31, 1970. Would this handling of the transaction have caused an error in the cost of goods sold for 1970?

QUESTIONS

1. Is the establishment of a proper valuation for the merchandise inventory at the end of the year important in producing a dependable income statement, or in producing a dependable balance sheet?

2. Explain the meaning of the terms *physical inventory* and *perpetual inventory.*

3. Through an accidental error in counting of merchandise at December 31, 1971, the Trophy Company overstated the amount of goods on hand by $8,000. Assuming that the error was not discovered, what was the effect upon net income for 1971? Upon the owners' equity at December 31, 1971? Upon the net income for 1972? Upon the owners' equity at December 31, 1972?

4. Near the end of December, Hadley Company received a large order from a major customer. The work of packing the goods for shipment was begun at once but could not be completed before the close of business on December 31. Since a written order from the customer was on hand and the goods were nearly all packed and ready for shipment, Hadley felt that this merchandise should not be included in the physical inventory taken on December 31. Do you agree? What is probably the reason behind Hadley's opinion?

5. During a prolonged period of rising prices, will the fifo or lifo method of inventory valuation result in higher reported net income?

6. Throughout several years of strongly rising prices, Company A used the lifo method of inventory valuation and Company B used the fifo method. In which company would the balance sheet figure for inventory be closer to current replacement cost of the merchandise on hand? Why?

7. Explain the usefulness of the gross profit method of estimating inventories.

8. Estimate the ending inventory by the gross profit method, given the following data: beginning inventory $40,000; purchases $100,000; net sales $106,667; average gross profit rate 25% of net sales.

9. One of the items in the inventory of Grayline Stores is marked for sale at $125. The purchase invoice shows the item cost $95, but a newly issued price list from the manufacturer shows the present replacement cost to be $90. What inventory valuation method should be assigned this item if Grayline Stores follows the lower-of-cost-or-market rule?

10. You are making a detailed analysis of the financial statements and accounting records of two companies in the same industry, Adams Corporation and Barry

Corporation. Price levels have been rising steadily for several years. In the course of your investigation, you observe that the inventory value shown on the Adams balance sheet is quite close to the current replacement cost of the merchandise on hand. However, for Barry Corporation, the carrying value of the inventory is far below current replacement cost. What method of inventory valuation is probably used by Adams Corporation? By Barry Corporation? If we assume that the two companies are identical except for the inventory valuation method used, which company has probably been reporting higher net income in recent years?

EXERCISES

1. Partial income statement data for the Perlman Corporation for a three-year period appear below:

	Year 3	Year 2	Year 1
Net sales.	$200,000	$125,000	$100,000
Cost of goods sold	134,000	85,000	70,000
Gross profit on sales.	$ 66,000	$ 40,000	$ 30,000
Gross profit percentage	33%	32%	30%

The inventory was understated by $2,500 at the end of Year 1 and overstated by $8,000 at the end of Year 3.

Prepare a revised statement of gross profit percentages for the three years. Comment on the trend of gross profit percentages before and after the revision.

2. The inventory card for Item X showed the following information:

Beginning balance, Jan. 1	100 units @ 80¢ =	$ 80
Purchases:		
Jan. 10	400 units @ 85¢ =	340
Jan. 15	200 units @ 88¢ =	176
Jan. 20	200 units @ 90¢ =	180
Jan. 30	100 units @ 98¢ =	98
Total goods available for sale	1,000	$874

The inventory on January 31 consists of 150 units. The cost of the ending inventory, based on each of the following methods of pricing inventory, is:

a. Average cost . . . . $_____
b. Fifo . . . . $_____
c. Lifo . . . . $_____

3. The inventory for Neighborhood Lumber Co. at the end of the latest accounting period includes the following items of a certain hardwood used in construction:

		Unit Price	
Stock No.	Quantity	Cost	Market
1120	100	$4.00	$4.10
1121	80	6.20	5.80
1122	130	2.50	2.20
1123	40	5.10	5.45
1123A	60	8.40	8.00

Cost for each item was determined on a first-in, first-out basis. You are to determine the following:

a. Total cost of the hardwood items . . . . $_____
b. Total market value of the hardwood items . . . . $_____
c. Inventory valuation using lower of cost or market
   (applied to each item) . . . . $_____
d. Inventory valuation using lower of cost or market
   (applied to entire inventory) . . . . $_____

4. On June 20, 1971, Littler arrived at his store to find it empty; thieves had broken in during the night and removed the entire inventory. Littler's books show that he had a $10,000 inventory on hand on June 1, and that he had made sales of $40,000 and purchases of $31,500 during the period June 1–20. Littler's gross profit had averaged 30% of sales during the past several years. In filing an insurance claim, Littler should estimate the *cost* of his inventory at the time of the theft at $_____.

5. The following information is available from the accounting records of Zee Sales Company:

Beginning inventory	$14,100	Ending inventory	$12,700
Operating expenses	16,100	Purchases	55,500
Income taxes	10,000	Net income	18,400
Miscellaneous revenue	2,000	Dividends declared	7,500

On the basis of the above information, total sales for the period were $_____.

6. The records of the Pure Mfg. Co. include the following information:

	July 1	July 31
Raw materials inventory	$10,000	$12,000
Goods in process inventory	8,000	6,500
Finished goods inventory, July 1 (1,000 units)	15,000	-0-
Purchases of raw materials		42,000
Direct labor cost for July		60,000
Factory overhead costs for July		58,500

During July 10,000 units were produced and 9,000 units were sold.

Instructions
a. Prepare a statement of cost of goods manufactured for July.
b. Compute the cost of producing a single unit during July.
c. Compute the cost of goods sold during July, assuming that the first-in, first-out method of inventory costing is used.

PROBLEMS

11-1 The Western Pulp Corporation deals in a single product of relatively low cost. The volume of sales in 1971 was $480,000, at a unit price of $6. The inventory at January 1, 1971, amounted to 14,500 units valued at cost of $43,500; purchases for the year were as follows: 20,500 units @ $3.10; 33,000 units @ $3.25; 23,000 units @ $3.40; and 9,000 units @ $3.50.

Instructions
a. Compute the December 31, 1971, inventory using

(1) The weighted average method
(2) The first-in, first-out method
(3) The last-in, first-out method

Compute average unit cost to the nearest cent.
b. Prepare an income statement for each of the above three methods of pricing inventory. The income statements are to be carried only to the determination of gross profit on sales.
c. Which of the three methods of pricing inventory would be most advantageous from an income tax standpoint during a period of rising prices? Comment on the significance of the inventory figure under the method you recommend with respect to current replacement cost.

11-2 Velocity & Co. stresses a rapid turnover of merchandise at a relatively low margin of profit. Emphasis is placed on holding expenses to a minimum. The company has regularly taken a physical inventory of merchandise each December 31, as a preliminary step toward preparing annual financial statements. Recently management has decided that monthly financial statements are needed as an aid to more efficient administration. However, the company is reluctant to interrupt operations and incur the expense of taking a physical inventory at the end of each month.

You are called upon to make an investigation of the company's records and to suggest a means by which monthly financial statements can be developed without the taking of a monthly physical inventory.

You find that the company has in recent years consistently priced its goods to sell at approximately 125% of cost. Management indicates that this pricing policy will continue unchanged during 1972.

At December 31, 1971, the physical inventory indicated goods on hand with a cost of $275,000. Purchases and sales during the first three months of 1972 were as follows:

	Purchases (Cost)	Sales (Selling Price)
January	$155,000	$202,000
February	200,000	280,000
March	305,000	375,000

Instructions

a. Compute the estimated inventories at cost at the end of each of the three months of 1972. State the rate of gross profit on sales.

b. Show how your computations in (a) would vary if the gross profit experiences in the past had been 25% of sales.

c. If the gross profit rate computed above had resulted from sales of a variety of products, would this have required any special consideration?

11-3 The following information was taken from the books of Adriatic Manufacturing Company:

	Sept. 1	Sept. 30
Inventories:		
Raw materials	$50,600	$39,200
Goods in process	23,400	37,000
Finished goods	43,400	54,200

	Month of September
Purchases of raw materials	$458,400
Transportation-in on raw materials	55,600
Factory overhead costs	169,000
Direct labor	203,600
Selling expenses	77,200
Raw material purchase discounts	4,600
Raw material purchase returns	4,800
General expenses	153,600
Income taxes	40,000

Instructions

a. Prepare a statement of cost of goods manufactured for the month of September.

b. Prepare a schedule showing the cost of goods sold for the month of September.

11-4 The management of the Oxnard Tile Company is considering the desirability of changing the method of pricing the year-end inventory in order to take full advantage of any tax savings which might be available. The company is presently using the last-in, first-out method of pricing the inventory and has requested your recommendation as to the method to be used. The inventory on December 31, 1971, consisted of 100,000 units at a cost of $1 per unit. During the year 1972, sales amounted to $421,500, and the following purchases took place.

Date	Units	Total Cost	Unit Cost
Jan. 10	60,000	$54,000	$0.90
March 3	80,000	64,000	0.80
July 14	100,000	70,000	0.70
Nov. 20	70,000	42,000	0.60
Dec. 18	90,000	45,000	0.50

The inventory on December 31, 1972 consists of 160,000 units.

Instructions

a. Compute the amount of the inventory at December 31, 1972, under:
The weighted average cost method
The first-in, first-out method
The last-in, first-out method

b. Prepare comparative income statements showing the effects of the three alternative inventory valuation methods on net income. Assume that selling and administrative expenses totaled $76,500 and that the income tax rate is 45%.

c. Prepare a brief memorandum recommending one of the three methods and explaining the reasons for your choice.

11-5 You have been employed by an insurance adjuster to examine the records of the Cash Register Company, which suffered the loss by fire of its entire inventory on June 1, 1972. Your investigation has produced the information shown below for the year ended December 31, 1971.

Net sales		$800,000
Cost of goods sold:		
Inventory, Jan. 1.	$160,000	
Purchases	740,000	
Cost of goods available for sale.	$900,000	
Less: Inventory, Dec. 31	260,000	640,000
Gross profit on sales		$160,000

Included in the purchases figure shown above was $25,000 of office equipment which the company has acquired late in December of 1971 for its own use from a competing concern which was quitting business. The bookkeeper had not understood the nature of this transaction and had recorded it by debiting the Purchases account. The office equipment, however, was not included in the inventory as of December 31, 1971.

The sales figure of $800,000 for 1971 did not include $20,000 of merchandise packaged and ready for shipment to a customer on December 31, 1971. The customer had originally ordered this merchandise for delivery on December 10; just prior to that date he had requested, because of overcrowded warehouses, that the goods be held by the Cash Register Company until January 10. It was agreed that the regular 30-day credit terms should run from December 10 per the original agreement. This merchandise had not been included in the Cash Register Company's year-end inventory; the goods were delivered to the customer on January 10, 1972 and payment was received the same day.

Records salvaged from the fire revealed the merchandise transactions from January 1, 1972, to the date of the fire to be: sales, $360,000; sales returns and allowances, $3,000; transportation-in, $2,000; purchases, $220,000; purchase returns and allowances, $4,000. The sales figure for 1972 includes the $20,000 described above.

Instructions

a. Prepare a report addressed to the insurance adjuster summarizing your findings. Include an estimate of the inventory value as of the date of the fire and a computation of the applicable gross profit rate.

b. Explain how the gross profit method of estimating inventories may be used other than in case of a fire loss.

11-6 John Tracy, controller for the Leather Products Corporation, prepared the income statement shown below from the accounting records at December 31, 1971. This statement indicated a significant improvement over the preceding year; the net income had been $362,500 for the year ended December 31, 1970. The corporation's income has not been subject to income taxes because of operating loss carry-overs from the years 1965–1969.

LEATHER PRODUCTS CORPORATION
Income Statement
For the Year Ended December 31, 1971

Sales			$4,142,000
Less: Sales returns & allowances		$ 29,000	
Sales discounts		73,000	102,000
Net sales			$4,040,000
Cost of goods sold:			
Inventory, Jan. 1		$ 650,000	
Purchases	$2,588,000		
Less: Purchase returns &			
allowances	$11,000		
Purchase discounts . . .	17,000	28,000	
		$2,560,000	
Transportation-in		27,000	2,587,000
Cost of goods available for sale		$3,237,000	
Less: Inventory, Dec. 31		302,000	
Cost of goods sold			2,935,000
Gross profit on sales			$1,105,000
Selling and administrative expenses			702,500
Net income			$ 402,500

Other data

On March 3, 1972, while reviewing inventory records, Tracy noted that incoming shipments of merchandise received near the annual closing dates had been handled as follows:

(1) Purchases in transit amounting to $28,000 on December 31, 1970, had not been included in the closing inventory of that year, although the invoice had been entered in the purchases journal on December 29, 1970, and the goods had been shipped f.o.b. shipping point on December 28, 1970.

(2) Goods on hand on December 31, 1971, in the amount of $15,500 were not included in the inventory as of that date. The reason for this omission was that the purchase invoice for this $15,500 shipment had not yet been received and the employee supervising the physical count was of the opinion that the goods were not the property of the company until the purchase invoice was recorded. The purchase invoice in question arrived in the afternoon mail on December 31, 1971, but no entry was made for it before closing the books for 1971. The invoice was recorded on January 8, 1972, in the purchases journal as a January transaction.

Instructions

a. Compute the corrected net income for the years 1970 and 1971. State the effect of the errors on the net income for the year 1972.

b. Indicate which items, if any, were incorrectly stated in the income statement for 1971, and in the balance sheet prepared at December 31, 1971. Consider particularly whether the figures for total assets, total liabilities, and stockholders' equity were correctly stated. For any items you list as incorrect, indicate whether the item was understated or overstated, and the dollar amount of the error.

c. Prepare any correcting journal entries you consider necessary as of March 3, 1972, the date of discovery of the errors.

Chapter
12 Liabilities

One of the most difficult problems facing business managers is finding sources of capital. Several alternatives are generally available in meeting the temporary and the more permanent capital needs of a business. Management evaluates the cost and availability of each form of financing and selects the type most advantageous to the firm and to its stockholders.

Some of the funds needed to meet seasonal peaks of activity may be obtained from trade creditors. Accounts payable, however, seldom constitute a sufficient source. Short-term capital needed for seasonal peaks of activity may also be obtained through borrowing from banks. For example, a six-month bank loan might be arranged in order to buy merchandise for the peak selling season. The sale of the merchandise would provide cash with which to repay the bank loan.

If funds are needed for long-term purposes such as the construction of a new factory building, the borrowing may take the form of long-term mortgage notes or bonds. This will allow time for the increased earnings from the new plant facilities to be used in retiring the debt. A small business in need of permanent financing will often issue a long-term note secured by a mortgage on its plant assets; a large corporation in need of permanent capital will probably consider the issuance of bonds or additional shares of capital stock.

CURRENT LIABILITIES

Current liabilities are obligations that must be paid within the operating cycle or one year (whichever is longer). Comparison of the amount of current liabilities with the amount of current assets is one means of appraising the financial position of a business. In other words, a comparison of the amount of current liabilities with the amount of current assets available for paying these debts helps us in judging a company's short-run debt-paying ability.

In accounting for current liabilities, we are especially interested in making certain that all such obligations are included in the balance sheet. The omission or understatement of a current liability can easily occur and will usually be accompanied by an overstatement of stockholders' equity, or by an understatement of assets. Depending on the nature of the error, the net income of the business may also be overstated.

Among the more common current liabilities are notes payable, accounts payable, dividends payable, accrued liabilities such as wages, interest, and taxes, and finally deferred revenues. The accounting problems relating to some current liabilities (accounts payable and dividends payable, for example) have been covered in earlier chapters. We shall now consider notes payable, payrolls, and other current liabilities.

NOTES PAYABLE

Notes payable are issued whenever bank loans are obtained. Other transactions which may give rise to notes payable include the purchase of real estate or costly equipment, the purchase of merchandise, and the substitution of a note for a past-due open account. The use of notes payable in each of these situations is illustrated in the following pages.

Notes payable issued to banks

Assume that John Caldwell, the sole proprietor of a retail business, applies to his bank for a 90-day, unsecured loan of $10,000. In support of the loan application Caldwell submits a balance sheet and income statement. The business has recently been audited by a certified public accountant, whose audit report is attached to the financial statements. This report indicates that the balance sheet and income statement have been prepared in conformity with generally accepted accounting principles and present fairly the financial condition of the business and the results of operations.

After studying the financial statements, reading the auditor's report, and making inquiries about Caldwell's credit rating, the bank indicates its willingness to lend the $10,000 requested, at an interest rate of 8%. The note which Caldwell signs will read as shown below, if we omit some of the minor details.

Interest Stated Separately

Los Angeles, California   June 15, 19--

.... Ninety days .... after date I promise to pay to Security National Bank the sum of $............ 10,000 .... with interest at the rate of 8% per annum.

John Caldwell

The journal entry on Caldwell's books to record this borrowing from the bank is:

Face	Cash	10,000	
Amount	*Notes Payable*.		10,000
of Note	*Borrowed $10,000 for 90 days at 8%.*		

No interest expense is recorded at the time of issuing the note. When the note is paid on September 13, the entry to be made is:

Payment of	*Notes Payable*.	10,000	
Principal	*Interest Expense*	200	
and	*Cash*.		10,200
Interest	*Paid bank at maturity date of loan.*		

Alternative form of notes for bank loans. Instead of stating the interest separately as in the preceding illustration, the note payable to the bank could have been so drawn as to include the interest charge in the face amount of the note, as shown below:

Interest	Los Angeles, California		June 15, 19—
Included			
in Face			
Amount	On September 13, 19— the undersigned promises to pay to		
of Note	Security National Bank or order the sum of $10,200		
	John Caldwell		

When the note is drawn in this manner the entry on Caldwell's books is:

Notes			
Payable	Cash	10,000	
Credited	*Discount on Notes Payable*.	200	
for Face	*Notes Payable*.		10,200
Amount	*Borrowed $10,000 for 90 days at 8%.*		
of Note			

Note that the amount of money borrowed ($10,000) was less than the face amount of the note ($10,200). However, as in all previous illustrations, the amount of the credit to the Notes Payable account was the face amount of the note. The liability to the bank at this time is equal to the amount of money borrowed, or $10,000. In order to show the proper measurement of the liability on the balance sheet, the Discount on Notes Payable account should be listed as a deduction from the Notes Payable account. The result is $10,200 − $200, or a net liability of $10,000.

On September 13, the maturity date of the note, Caldwell will hand the bank a check for $10,200 in payment of the note and will make the following journal entries:

Payment	*Notes Payable*	*10,200*	
of Note	*Cash*		*10,200*
and	*Paid bank at maturity date of loan.*		
Interest			
Expense	*Interest Expense*	*200*	
	Discount on Notes Payable		*200*
	To record interest expense on matured note.		

Adjustments for interest at end of period

When a note is issued in one accounting period and matures in a later period, the interest expense must be apportioned. Adjusting entries for interest-bearing notes were illustrated in Chapter 4.

A different type of adjustment is necessary at the end of the period for notes payable to banks in which the interest has been included in the face amount of the note. For example, assume that Baker Company borrows $20,000 from its bank on November 1 on a 6%, six-month note with interest of $600 included in the face of the note. The entry for the borrowing on November 1 would be:

Interest	*Cash*	*20,000*	
Included	*Discount on Notes Payable*	*600*	
in Face	*Notes Payable*		*20,600*
of Note	*Issued to bank a 6%, six-month note payable with interest*		
and . . .	*included in face amount of note.*		

At December 31, the adjusting entry required is:

. . . Related	*Interest Expense*	*200*	
Adjusting	*Discount on Notes Payable*		*200*
Entry	*To record interest expense incurred to end of year on 6%, six-month*		
	note dated Nov. 1.		

On May 1, when the six-month note matures and the Baker Company pays the bank, the entry is as shown on page 353.

Discount on Notes Payable should be classified as a contra-liability account and deducted from the face value of notes payable in the current liability section of the balance sheet. This treatment results in showing as

Two-thirds of Interest Applicable to Second Year	Notes Payable..............................	20,600	
	Interest Expense	400	
	Cash..................................		20,600
	Discount on Notes Payable		400
	To record payment to bank of 6%, six-month note dated Nov. 1, with interest included in face of note.		

a liability at statement date the principal of the debt plus the accrued interest payable at that time.

Prepaid interest

Discount on notes payable is sometimes called *prepaid interest* and classified as a current asset, a practice which has little theoretical justification. To prepay interest on a loan has the effect of reducing the amount of money borrowed and increasing the effective rate of interest. Assume that on January 2 you borrow $1,000 from a bank for a period of two years at an annual interest rate of 8%. Assume also that you pay the bank the full two years' interest ($1,000 × 8% × 2) of $160 at the date of borrowing the $1,000. Under this procedure you have increased your cash position by only $840. A more realistic view of the transaction is to say you have incurred a liability of $840 which will increase to $1,000 during the next two years.

Current income tax regulations recognize the concept of prepaid interest. A taxpayer on the cash basis (and this includes most individuals) may deduct interest when it is paid, even though paid in advance. Thus, in the example of borrowing $1,000 and concurrently paying two years' interest in advance, you could deduct the entire interest charge of $160 for income tax purposes in the year paid. At present, however, tax regulations do not permit the deduction of interest for more than one year beyond the year in which the payment occurs.

Other transactions involving notes payable

Notes payable are often issued for the acquisition of real estate or expensive equipment. In recording such a transaction, the debit to the asset account (such as Land or Office Equipment) should be for the amount which would be paid if the asset were being purchased for cash. Any additional charge because of the delay in payment is interest, and is an expense applicable to the period of credit extension. In other words, we do not conceal interest expense by inflating the cost of assets acquired through issuance of notes payable.

If an account payable becomes past due, the debtor may be asked to sign a note payable to replace the open account. The issuance of the note payable is recorded by a debit to Accounts Payable and a credit to Notes Payable. When the debtor pays the note at maturity, his accounting entry will be a debit to Notes Payable and to Interest Expense, offset by a credit to Cash.

Next, let us assume the issuance of a note in payment for a $2,000 purchase of merchandise from National Supply Co. A note issued for the purchase of merchandise could be recorded by debiting Purchases and crediting Notes Payable. However, a more informative record will be available if the following pair of entries is made at the time of the purchase. (In practice, the first of these two entries would be made in the purchases journal.)

Purchase May Be Run through Accounts Payable When Note Is Issued to Supplier

Purchases	2,000	
Accounts Payable, National Supply Co.		2,000
To record purchase of merchandise.		
Accounts Payable, National Supply Co.	2,000	
Notes Payable		2,000
Issued a 60-day, 8% note to National Supply Co. for merchandise.		

Under this method, information on the total volume of purchases from a particular supplier will be readily available by reference to the supplier's account in the subsidiary ledger for accounts payable.

PAYROLL ACCOUNTING

Accurate detailed payroll records are essential for several reasons. These records provide a basis for maintaining satisfactory relations with employees; they provide significant information as to operating costs; and they enable employers to meet their obligations under federal and state laws concerning payroll taxes. Social security legislation requiring payroll deductions and taxes on payrolls has had a considerable effect on payroll records and procedures. Employers are also required to withhold a portion of employees' earnings for payment of federal income taxes. In addition, specific sums may be withheld from employees' earnings for a variety of purposes such as union dues and insurance premiums.

A distinction must be drawn between *employees* and *independent contractors.* Public accountants, architects, attorneys, and other persons who render services to a business for a fee but are not controlled or directed by the client are not employees but independent contractors, and the amounts paid to them are not subject to payroll taxes.

Deductions from earnings of employees

The take-home pay of most employees is considerably less than the gross earnings. Major factors explaining this difference between the amount earned and the amount received are social security taxes, federal income taxes withheld, and other deductions discussed below.

Social security taxes (FICA). Under the terms of the Social Security Act, qualified workers in covered industries who retire after reaching a specified age, receive monthly retirement payments and Medicare benefits. Benefits are also provided for the family of a worker who dies before or after reaching this retirement age. Funds for the operation of this program are obtained through taxes levied under the Federal Insurance Contributions Act, often referred to as FICA taxes, or simply as *social security taxes.*

Employers are required by the Federal Insurance Contributions Act to withhold a portion of each employee's earnings as a contribution to the social security program. A tax at the same rate is levied against the employer. For illustrative purposes, we shall assume the rate of tax to be 5% on both the employee and the employer of the first $7,800 of wages received in each calendar year. The rates have been increased many times in recent years and probably will continue to be changed in future years. However, these changes in rates do not affect the accounting principles or procedures involved. Consequently, our assumption of a 5% rate and a $7,800 ceiling on the amount subject to tax is a convenient one, regardless of frequent changes in the actual rates.

Income tax withholding. The pay-as-you-go system of federal income tax requires employers to withhold a portion of the earnings of their employees. The amount withheld depends upon the amount of the earnings and upon the number of exemptions allowed the employee. The employee is entitled to one exemption for himself, and an additional exemption for each person qualifying as a dependent. (More extensive consideration of exemptions and of other aspects of federal income taxes will be found in Chapter 17.) The government provides withholding tax tables which indicate the amount to withhold for any amount of earnings and any number of exemptions.

The graduated system of withholding is designed to make the amount of tax withheld closely approximate the rates used in computing the individual's tax liability at the end of the year. Since persons in higher income brackets are subject to higher rates of taxation, the withholding rates are correspondingly higher for them.

States or cities which levy income taxes may also require the employer to withhold the tax from employees' earnings; since such situations are not common, they will not be discussed here.

Other deductions from employees' earnings. Programs of unemployment compensation insurance are found in every state, but they are generally financed by taxes on employers rather than on employees. In a few states unemployment insurance taxes are levied on employees and such taxes are withheld by employers from employees' earnings.

In addition to the compulsory deductions for taxes, many other deductions are voluntarily authorized by employees. Union dues and insurance premiums have already been mentioned as examples of payroll deductions. Others include charitable contributions, supplementary retirement programs and pension plans, and repayments of salary advances or other loans.

Employer's responsibility for amounts withheld. When an employer withholds a portion of an employee's earnings for any reason, he must maintain accounting records which will enable him to file required reports and make designated payments of the amounts withheld. From the employer's viewpoint, most amounts withheld from employees' earnings represent current liabilities. In other words, the employer must pay to the government or some other agency the amounts which he withholds from the employee's earnings. A statement of earnings and deductions is usually prepared by the employer and presented to the employee with each paycheck or pay envelope to explain how the net pay was determined.

Payroll records and procedures

Although payroll records and procedures vary greatly according to the number of employees and the extent of automation in processing payroll data, there are fundamental steps common to payroll work in most organizations. One of these steps taken at the end of each pay period is the preparation of a *payroll* showing the names, earnings, and the net amount payable to each employee. When the computation of the payroll sheet has been completed, the next step is to reflect the expense and the related liability in the ledger accounts. A general journal entry, such as shown below, may be made to bring into the accounts the data summarized on the payroll.

Recording Payroll	*Sales Salaries Expense*	*1,200*	
	Office Salaries Expense	*800*	
	FICA Taxes Payable (5% of $2,000)		*100*
	Liability for Income Tax Withheld		*320*
	Group Insurance Payments Withheld		*10*
	Accrued Payroll		*1,570*
	To record the payroll for the pay period ended January 15.		

The two debits to expense accounts indicate that the business has incurred a total salary expense of $2,000; however, only $1,570 of this amount will be paid to the employees on payday. Payment can be made in cash or by check. The payment will be recorded by a debit to Accrued Payroll and a credit to Cash. The remaining $430 (consisting of deductions for taxes and insurance premiums withheld) is lodged in liability accounts. Payment of these liabilities will be made at various later dates.

Withholding statement. By January 31 each year, employers are required to furnish every employee with a withholding statement (Form W-2). This form shows the gross earnings for the preceding calendar year, and the amounts withheld for FICA tax and income tax. The employer sends one copy of this form to the Director of Internal Revenue and also gives two copies to the employee. When the employee files his federal income tax return, he must attach a copy of the withholding statement.

To facilitate preparation of the withholding statements and to determine the amount of FICA tax to be withheld for each employee, the employer is required to maintain an individual record of earnings and deductions for each employee.

Payroll taxes on the employer

The discussion of payroll taxes up to this point has dealt with taxes levied on the employee and withheld from his pay. From the viewpoint of the employer, such taxes are significant because he must account for and remit the amounts withheld to the appropriate government offices. Payroll taxes are also levied on the *employer;* these taxes are expenses of the business and are recorded by debits to expense accounts, just as in the case of property taxes or license fees for doing business.

Social security (FICA) taxes. The employer is taxed to help finance the social security program. The tax is figured at the same rate and on the same amount of earnings used to compute FICA tax on employees. (In all problems and illustrations in this book, the tax is assumed to be 5% on the first $7,800 of gross earnings by each employee in each calendar year.)

Federal unemployment insurance tax. Unemployment insurance is a separate element of the national social security program designed to offer temporary relief to unemployed persons. The federal unemployment tax is levied on employers only and is not deducted from the wages of employees. The tax (presently 3.1%) applies to approximately the same classes of employment as the FICA tax except that an employer of fewer than four persons is excluded. The federal unemployment tax applies to the first $3,000 of wages paid to each covered employee during the calendar year.

The federal law provides that the employer may take a credit against his federal tax (not in excess of 2.7% of the wages) for amounts paid by him into state unemployment funds. As a result, an employer may be subject to a federal tax of only 0.4% on wages up to $3,000 per employee.

State unemployment compensation taxes. All the states participate in the federal-state unemployment insurance program. Although the state laws vary somewhat as to types of covered employment, the usual rate of tax is 2.7% of the first $3,000 of earnings by each employee during a calendar year. Most states have a merit-rating plan which permits a reduction in the tax rate for employers who establish a record of stable employment.

Accounting entry for employer's payroll taxes. The entry to record the employer's payroll taxes is usually made at the same time the payroll is recorded. For the payroll illustrated on page 356, the entry for all three of the payroll taxes on the employer is as follows:

Payroll Taxes on Employer	*Payroll Taxes Expense*	*162*	
	FICA Taxes Payable (5% of $2,000)		*100*
	State Unemployment Taxes Payable (2.7% of $2,000)		*54*
	Federal Unemployment Taxes Payable (0.4% of $2,000) ..		*8*
	To record payroll taxes on employer for pay period ended January 15.		

Statement presentation and payment of payroll taxes. The payroll taxes levied on the employer and the taxes withheld from employees are current liabilities of the business until payment to the government is made. The following accounts are, therefore, classified in the balance sheet as current liabilities: FICA Taxes Payable, Federal Unemployment Taxes Payable, State Unemployment Taxes Payable, and Liability for Income Tax Withheld.

Payroll taxes expense appears in the income statement. It may be apportioned among selling expenses, and general expenses on the basis of the amount of payroll originating in each functional division. Thus, payroll taxes on factory wages are classified as a manufacturing cost; payroll taxes on salaries of salesmen are classified as selling expense; and payroll taxes on office salaries are classified as general expense.

Four times a year the employer is required to file a tax form showing amounts of income taxes withheld and FICA taxes payable to the government. The FICA tax on the employer is also reported on the same tax form. These tax forms are due at the end of the month following the close of each calendar quarter of the year. If the totals of the amounts withheld from employees plus the FICA tax on the employer exceeds certain amounts, the taxes must be deposited by the employer at a bank on a current basis. Such deposits are made either monthly or semimonthly, depending on the amount of taxes involved.

A business must use the calendar year in accounting for payroll taxes even though it uses a fiscal year for its financial statements and its income tax return. The employer must file his federal unemployment tax return by January 31 of each year for the preceding calendar year. Most states require employers to file tax returns and make payment of the state unemployment compensation tax on a quarterly basis.

Other current liabilities

In addition to the current liabilities discussed in this chapter, a wide variety of short-term obligations may be found on the balance sheet of a typical business unit. Some of these, such as accounts payable, dividends payable, and deferred revenues were discussed in earlier chapters. Other examples of current liabilities include advances from customers, income taxes payable, liabilities for services received by the business before the end of the period but not billed until the following period, and *estimated liabilities.*

An estimated liability is one known to exist, but for which the dollar amount is uncertain. A common example is that of a company which issues coupons redeemable in merchandise. The company's experience may show that only a portion of the coupons will ever be redeemed. The liability represented by the outstanding coupons must be estimated at the balance sheet date by use of a percentage based on prior experience as to the portion of outstanding coupons which will eventually be presented for redemption.

A distinction should be made between an estimated liability and a *contingent liability.* A contingent liability may or may not exist, depending on the outcome of some future event, such as a pending lawsuit or possible additional income tax assessments. Contingent liabilities should be fully disclosed by footnotes or other means in the balance sheet.

THE VOUCHER SYSTEM

Control over expenditures

Closely related to our discussion of current liabilities is the problem of ensuring that expenditures are properly authorized and that payments to liquidate liabilities are legitimate. In every business, large or small, a considerable number of expenditures must be made each month for goods and services. Handling these transactions requires such steps as the following:

1. Purchase orders or other authorization for expenditures must be given.

2. Goods and services received must be inspected and approved.

3. Invoices from suppliers must be examined for correctness of prices, extensions, shipping costs, and credit terms.

4. Checks must be issued in payment.

In a very small business it may be possible for the owner or manager to perform all these steps for every transaction. By doing this work personally, he may be assured that the business is getting what it pays for, and that funds are not being disbursed carelessly or fraudulently. As a business grows and the volume of daily transactions increases, it becomes impossible for the owner or manager to give personal attention to each expenditure. When this work is assigned to various employees, a well-designed accounting system is needed to guard against waste and fraud.

Some businesses take great pains to safeguard cash receipts and cash on hand, but quite inconsistently permit a number of employees to incur liabilities by ordering goods or services without any record being made of their actions. When an invoice is received, the absence of any record of the purchase makes it difficult to determine whether the invoice is a proper statement of an amount owed. In this confused situation, invoices are apt to be paid without adequate verification. The opportunity exists for a dishonest employee to collaborate with an outsider to arrange for duplicate payments of invoices, for payment of excessive prices, or for payment for goods and services never received. Fraud is particularly likely when an employee has authority to incur expenses and to issue checks in payment as well. In larger organizations, the work of placing orders, verifying invoices, recording liabilities, and issuing checks should be divided among several employees in such a manner that the work of each person serves to prove that of the others. A chain of documentary evidence should be created for each transaction, consisting of written approvals by key employees for the phases of the transaction for which each is responsible.

One method of establishing control over the making of expenditures and the payment of liabilities is the *voucher system.* This system requires that every liability be recorded as soon as it is incurred, and that checks be issued only in payment of approved liabilities. A written authorization called a *voucher* is prepared for each expenditure, regardless of whether the expenditure covers services, merchandise for resale, or assets for use in the business. The voucher system is widely used, and it is particularly common in large organizations which have given serious study to the problem of internal control. Perhaps the greatest single advantage of the voucher system is the assurance that every expenditure of the business is systematically reviewed and verified before payment is made.

BONDS PAYABLE

A corporation may obtain funds for a long-term purpose, such as construction of a new plant, by issuing a long-term mortgage note payable or by issuing corporation bonds. Usually the amount of money needed is greater than any single lender can supply. In this case the corporation may sell bonds to the investing public, thus splitting the loan into a great many units, usually of $1,000 each. An example of corporation bonds is the 4% general mortgage bonds of the Atchison, Topeka and Santa Fe Railway Company due October 1, 1995, by which the Santa Fe borrowed approximately $156 million. These bonds are listed on the New York Stock Exchange and are bought and sold by investors daily.

Characteristics of a bond

A bondholder is a creditor of the corporation; a stockholder is an owner. From the viewpoint of the issuing corporation, bonds payable constitute a long-term liability. Throughout the life of this liability the corporation makes semiannual payments of interest to the bondholder for the use of his money. These interest payments constitute an expense to the corporation and are deducted from each year's revenues in arriving at net income for the year.

Formal approval of the board of directors and of the stockholders is usually required before bonds can be issued. The contract between the corporation and the trustee representing the bondholders may place some limitation on the payment of dividends to stockholders during the life of the bonds. For example, dividends may be permitted only when cash or total current assets are above specified amounts. This type of restriction protects the bondholder more effectively than does the creation of a reserve by appropriation of retained earnings.

Of course, in the event that the corporation encounters financial difficulties and is unable to make the required payments of interest or principal, the bondholders may foreclose on the pledged assets, but this is a slow and complicated procedure which bondholders look upon only as a last-ditch alternative. When investing in a bond, the bondholder hopes and expects to receive all payments promptly without the need for taking any legal action.

Not all bonds are secured by the pledge of specific assets. An unsecured bond is called a *debenture bond;* its value rests upon the general credit of the corporation. A debenture bond issued by a very large and strong corporation may have a higher investment rating than a secured bond issued by a corporation in less satisfactory financial condition.

Some bonds have a single fixed maturity date for the entire issue. Other bond issues, called *serial bonds,* provide for varying maturity dates to lessen the problem of accumulating cash for payment. For example, serial bonds in the amount of $10 million issued in 1967 might call for $1 million of bonds to mature in 1977, and an additional $1 million to become due in each of the succeeding nine years. Almost all bonds are *callable,* which means that the corporation reserves the right to pay off the bonds in advance of the scheduled maturity date. The call price is usually somewhat higher than the face value of the bonds.

As an additional attraction to investors, corporations sometimes include a conversion privilege in the bond indenture. A *convertible bond* is one which may be exchanged for common stock at the option of the bondholder. The advantages to the investor of the conversion feature in the event of increased earnings for the company have already been described in Chapter 8 with regard to convertible preferred stock.

Registered bonds and coupon bonds. Nearly all corporation bonds issued in recent years have been *registered* bonds; that is, the name of the owner is registered with the issuing corporation. Payment of interest is made by semiannual checks mailed to the registered owner.

Coupon bonds were popular some years ago and many are still outstanding. Coupon bonds have interest coupons attached; each six months during the life of the bond one of these coupons becomes due. The bondholder detaches the coupon and deposits it with his bank for collection.

Transferability of bonds. Corporation bonds, like capital stocks, are traded daily on organized security exchanges. The holder of a 25-year bond need not wait 25 years to convert his investment into cash. By placing a telephone call to a broker, he may sell his bond within a matter of minutes at the going market price. This quality of liquidity is one of the most attractive features of an investment in corporation bonds.

Quotations for bonds. Corporate bond prices are quoted at a given amount per $100 of face value. For example, assume that a bond of $1,000 face amount (par value) is quoted at 106. The total price for the bond is 10 times 106, or $1,060. Market quotations for corporate bonds use an eighth of a dollar as the minimum variation. The following line from the financial page of a daily newspaper summarizes the day's trading in the bonds of Sears, Roebuck and Co.

	Bonds	Sales	High	Low	Close	Net Change
What Is Market Value of This Bond?	Sears R 4¾s 83	66	80	79½	79½	−1

This line of condensed information indicates that 66 of Sears, Roebuck and Co.'s 4¾%, $1,000 bonds maturing in 1983 were traded today. The highest price is reported as 80, or $800 for a bond of $1,000 face value. The lowest price was 79½, or $795 for a $1,000 bond. The closing price (last sale of the day) was also 79½ or $795. This was one point below the closing price of the previous day, a decrease of $10 in the price of a $1,000 bond.

Effect of bond financing on holders of common stock

Interest payments on bonds payable are deductible as an expense in determining net income subject to corporation income tax, but dividends paid on common and preferred stock are not. High tax rates on corporate earnings thus encourage the use of bonds to obtain long-term capital.

Assume that a growing and profitable corporation with 100,000 shares of common stock outstanding is in need of $10 million cash to finance a new plant. The management is considering whether to issue 6½% preferred stock, issue an additional 100,000 shares of common stock, or sell 6% bonds. Assume also that after acquisition of the new plant, the annual earnings of the corporation, before deducting interest expense or income taxes, will amount to $2 million. From the viewpoint of the common stockholders, which financing plan is preferable? The following schedule shows the net earnings available to the common stockholder under the three alternative methods of financing:

Which Financing Plan Is Best?

	If 6½% Pre-ferred Stock Is Issued	If Common Stock Is Issued	If 6% Bonds Are Issued
Annual earnings before bond interest or income taxes.	$2,000,000	$2,000,000	$2,000,000
Less: Interest on bonds, 6% of $10,000,000.			600,000
Earnings before income taxes	$2,000,000	$2,000,000	$1,400,000
Less: Income taxes (assume 50% rate). .	1,000,000	1,000,000	700,000
Net income.	$1,000,000	$1,000,000	$ 700,000
Less: Preferred stock dividends	650,000		
Net income available for common stock	$ 350,000	$1,000,000	$ 700,000
Number of shares of common stock outstanding.	100,000	200,000	100,000
Net income per share of common stock.	$3.50	$5.00	$7.00

The use of 6% bonds rather than 6½% preferred stock under these circumstances offers a yearly saving to common stockholders of $350,000, or $3.50 per share of common stock. The saving arises from two factors: (1) the deductibility of bond interest and (2) the fact that the bonds were marketed at an interest rate lower than the dividend rate on the preferred stock. Financing through issuance of additional common stock rather than sale of bonds saves $300,000 (after taxes) but results in *lower earnings per share* because of the *dilution* caused by doubling the number of common shares outstanding.

The principal argument for the 6½% preferred stock as opposed to the 6% bond issue is that if the company's earnings should fall drastically, the operation of the business might be disrupted by inability to meet the fixed bond interest payments, whereas a preferred dividend could be postponed for a year or longer without serious repercussions.

The use of stockholders' equity as a basis for borrowing is referred to as *trading on the equity;* this is discussed further in Chapter 16.

Management planning of the bond issue

A corporation wishing to borrow money by issuing bonds faces months of preliminary work. Decisions must be made on such points as the amount to be borrowed, the interest rate to be offered, the conversion privilege, if any, the maturity date, and the property to be pledged, if any. Answers must be found for such questions as the following: How much debt can the company safely handle in the event of adverse business conditions? What volume of sales will be necessary for the company to "break even" in the future after the fixed expenses have been increased by agreeing to make regular interest payments?

In forecasting the company's cash position for future periods, consideration must be given to the new requirement of semiannual bond interest payments as well as to the long-range problem of accumulating the cash required to pay the bonds at maturity. If the borrowed funds are to be invested in new plant facilities, will this expansion produce an increase in the cash inflow sufficient to meet the interest payments? If the bond issue includes a call provision, the company may plan to call in bonds in small amounts each year as cash becomes available. Perhaps the bond issue should be of the convertible variety; this feature might attract investors even though the interest rate were set at a relatively low level. In addition, if the bonds are convertible, the company may not have to accumulate cash for repayment of the entire issue. Effective long-range planning of the company's financial needs will greatly reduce the cost of securing capital and will leave the door open to issuing additional securities in the future on advantageous terms.

Authorization of a bond issue. After the board of directors has decided upon the details of a bond issue, the proposal is presented to stockholders for their approval. Once this approval has been gained, the deed of trust is drawn and the bonds are printed. If the company's present financial requirements are for less than the amount of bonds authorized, only a portion of the bonds may be issued at this time. As each bond is issued it must be signed or "authenticated" by the trustee.

No formal entry in the accounts is required for the act of authorization; however, a memorandum notation may be made in the Bonds Payable ledger account indicating the total amount of bonds authorized. The total authorized amount of a bond issue should always be disclosed in the balance sheet.

Recording the issuance of bonds. To illustrate the entries for issuance of bonds, assume that Bidwell Corporation was authorized on June 1, 1971, to issue $1 million of 20-year, 6% debenture bonds. All the bonds in the issue bear the June 1, 1971, date, and interest is computed from this date. 80% of the bonds were issued on June 1 at face value, and the following entry was made:

Issuance of Bonds	*Cash* *800,000*	
	6% Debenture Bonds Payable	*800,000*
	To record sale of 800 6%, 20-year bonds at par.	

The balance sheet should disclose all significant features of each bond issue, including exact title, interest rate, maturity date, and amounts authorized and issued. Thus, in our example, the fact that only 80% of the authorized bonds have been issued is significant; issuance of the remaining 20% would materially change the ratio of debt to stockholders' equity and also the relationship between bond interest expense and the company's earnings.

Recording the issuance of bonds between interest dates. The semiannual interest dates (such as January 15 and July 15, or April 1 and October 1) are printed on the bond certificates. However, bonds are often issued between the specified interest dates. The investor is then required to pay the interest accrued to date of issuance in addition to the stated price of the bond. This practice enables the corporation to pay a full six month's interest on all bonds outstanding at the semiannual interest payment date. The accrued interest collected from an investor purchasing a bond between interest payment dates is thus returned to him on the next interest payment date. To illustrate, let us modify our previous example of Bidwell Corporation and assume that the $800,000 face value of 6% bonds were issued at par and accrued interest, *two months after the interest date printed on the bonds.* The entry will be:

Bonds	*Cash* *808,000*		
Issued	*6% Debenture Bonds Payable*		*800,000*
between	*Bond Interest Payable*		*8,000*
Interest	*Issued $800,000 face value of 6%, 20-year bonds at 100*		
Dates	*plus accrued interest for two months.*		

Four months later on the regular semiannual interest payment date, a full six months' interest ($30 per bond) will be paid to all bondholders, regardless of when they purchased their bonds. The entry for the semiannual interest payment is illustrated on page 365.

Now consider these interest transactions from the standpoint of the investor. He paid for two months' accrued interest at the time of purchasing

Bond Interest Payable	*8,000*	
Bond Interest Expense	*16,000*	
Cash..........................		*24,000*
Paid semiannual interest on $800,000 face value of 6% bonds.		

the bonds, and he received a check for six months' interest after holding the bonds for only four months. He has, therefore, been reimbursed properly for the use of his money for four months.

Bond discount

A corporation wishing to borrow money by issuing bonds must pay the going market rate of interest. On any given date, the going market rate of interest is in reality a whole schedule of rates corresponding to the financial strength of different borrowers. Since market rates of interest are constantly fluctuating, it must be expected that the contract rate of interest printed on the bonds will seldom agree with the market rate of interest at the date the bonds are issued.

If the interest rate carried by an issue of bonds is lower than the market rate for bonds of this grade, the bonds can be sold only at a discount. For example, assume that a corporation issues $1 million face value of 7%, 10-year bonds. Each bond will pay the holder $70 interest (7% × $1,000) each year, consisting of two semiannual payments of $35 each. If the market rate of interest were exactly 7%, the bonds would sell at par, but if the market rate of interest is higher than 7%, no one will be willing to pay $1,000 for a bond which will return only $70 a year. The price at which the bonds can be sold will, therefore, be less than par. Assume that the best price obtainable is 98 ($980 for each $1,000 bond). The issuance of the bonds will be recorded by the following entry:

Cash........................	*980,000*	
Discount on Bonds Payable.......................	*20,000*	
Bonds Payable.......................		*1,000,000*
Issued $1,000,000 face value of 7%, 10-year bonds at 98.		

Bond discount as part of the cost of borrowing. Whenever bonds are issued at a discount, *the total interest cost over the life of the issue is equal to the amount of the discount plus the regular cash interest payments.*

For the $1 million bond issue in our example, the total interest cost over the life of the bonds is $720,000, of which $700,000 represents 20 semiannual cash payments of interest and $20,000 represents the discount on the issue. On a yearly basis, total interest expense is $72,000, consisting of $70,000 paid in cash and $2,000 of the bond discount. This analysis is illustrated by the following tabulation of the total amounts of cash received and paid out by the corporation in connection with the bond issue.

<table>
<tr><td>Cash
Received
and Paid
over Life
of Bond
Issue</td><td>

Cash to be paid by the borrowing corporation:

Face value of bonds at maturity	$1,000,000	
Interest ($70,000 a year for 10 years)	700,000	
Total cash to be paid		$1,700,000
Cash received:		
From issuance of bonds at a discount		980,000
Excess of cash to be paid over cash received (total interest expense)		$ 720,000
Yearly interest expense ($720,000 ÷ 10)		$ 72,000

</td></tr>
</table>

In our example the Bond Discount account has an initial debit balance of $20,000; each year one-tenth of this amount, or $2,000, will be amortized or written off to Bond Interest Expense. Amortizing bond discount means transferring a portion of the discount to Bond Interest Expense each accounting period during the life of the bonds. Assuming that the interest payment dates are June 30 and December 31, the entries to be made each six months to record bond interest expense are as follows:

<table>
<tr><td>Payment
of Bond
Interest
and Amor-
tization
of Bond
Discount</td><td>

Bond Interest Expense	35,000	
Cash		35,000
Paid semiannual interest on $1,000,000 of 7% 10-year bonds.		
Bond Interest Expense	1,000	
Discount on Bonds Payable		1,000
Amortized ¹⁄₂₀ of discount on 10-year bond issue.		

</td></tr>
</table>

The above entries serve to charge Bond Interest Expense with $36,000 each six months, or a total of $72,000 a year. Bond interest expense will be uniform throughout the 10-year life of the bond issue, and the Discount on Bonds Payable account will be completely written off by the end of the tenth year. As an alternative, some companies choose to record amortization of bond discount or premium only at the end of the year rather than at each interest-payment date.

Bond premium

Bonds will sell above par if the contract rate of interest specified on the bonds is higher than the current market rate for bonds of this grade. Let us now change our basic illustration by assuming that the $1 million issue of 7%, 10-year bonds is sold at a price of 102 ($1,020 for each $1,000 bond). The entry is shown at the top of page 367.

The amount received from issuance of the bonds is $20,000 greater than the amount which must be repaid at maturity. This $20,000 premium is not a gain but is to be offset against the regular cash interest payments in determining the net cost of borrowing. Whenever bonds are issued at a pre-

Issuing *Bonds at* *Premium*	Cash 1,020,000	
	Bonds Payable	1,000,000
	Premium on Bonds Payable	20,000
	Issued $1,000,000 face value of 7% 10-year bonds at *price of 102.*	

mium, *the total interest cost over the life of the issue is equal to the regular cash interest payments minus the amount of the premium.* In our example, the total interest cost over the life of the bonds is computed as $700,000 of cash interest payments minus $20,000 of premium amortized, or a net borrowing cost of $680,000. The annual interest expense will be $68,000, consisting of $70,000 paid in cash less an offsetting $2,000 transferred from the Premium on Bonds Payable account to the credit side of the Bond Interest Expense account. The semiannual entries on June 30 and December 31 to record payment of bond interest and amortization of bond premium are as follows:

Payment *of Bond* *Interest* *and Amor-* *tization* *of Bond* *Premium*	Bond Interest Expense............................. 35,000	
	Cash..	35,000
	Paid semiannual bond interest on $1,000,000 of 7%, 10-year *bonds.*	
	Premium on Bonds Payable 1,000	
	Bond Interest Expense	1,000
	Amortized ½₀ of premium on 10-year bond issue.	

Year-end adjustments for bond interest expense

In the preceding illustration, it was assumed that one of the semiannual dates for payment of bond interest coincided with the end of the company's accounting year. In most cases, however, the semiannual interest payment dates will fall during an accounting period rather than on the last day of the year.

For purposes of illustration, assume that $1 million of 6%, 10-year bonds are issued at a price of 98 on October 1, 1972. Interest payment dates are April 1 and October 1. The total discount to be amortized amounts to $20,000, or $1,000 in each six-month interest period. The company keeps its accounts on a calendar-year basis; consequently, adjusting entries will be necessary as of December 31 for the accrued interest and the amortization of discount applicable to the three-month period since the bonds were issued.

The effect of these year-end adjusting entries is to make the Bond Interest Expense account show the proper interest expense ($15,500) for the three months that the bonds were outstanding (October 1 to December 31) during 1972. The Bond Interest Expense account will be closed to the Income Summary account; the Bond Interest Payable account will remain

Bond Interest Expense	*15,000*	
Bond Interest Payable......................		*15,000*
To record bond interest accrued for three-month period from Oct. 1 to Dec. 31.		
Bond Interest Expense	*500*	
Discount on Bonds Payable..................		*500*
To record amortization of bond discount for three-month period from Oct. 1 to Dec. 31.		

on the books as a liability until the next regular interest payment date, at which time $15,000 of the interest payment will be charged to Bond Interest Payable and the other $15,000 to Bond Interest Expense.

If the above bonds had been issued at a premium, similar entries would be made at the end of the period for any accrued interest and for amortization of premium for the fractional period from October 1 to December 31.

Bond discount and bond premium in the balance sheet

In the preceding example a 6%, 10-year bond issue of $1 million was issued for $980,000, and bond discount of $20,000 was recorded. One year later, on October 1, 1973, the bond discount would have been amortized to the extent of $2,000 and the net liability would have risen accordingly in the balance sheet.

Long-term liabilities:		
6% bonds payable, due Oct. 1, 1982	*$1,000,000*	
Less: Discount on bonds payable	*18,000*	*$982,000*

At the maturity of the bond issue 10 years after issuance, the corporation must pay $1 million, but at the time of issuing bonds, the "present value" of this debt is $980,000. As the bond discount is amortized, the *net amount* of the liability shown on each succeeding balance sheet will be $2,000 greater than for the preceding year. At the maturity date of the bonds, the valuation account, Discount on Bonds Payable, will have been reduced to zero and the liability will have risen to $1 million.

Parallel reasoning applies to bond premium, which is logically shown on the balance sheet as an addition to bonds payable. As the premium is amortized, the net amount of the liability is reduced year by year, until, at the maturity date of the bonds, the premium will have been completely written off and the liability will stand at the face amount of the bond issue.

Although the above-described treatment of bond discount and bond premium is regarded as theoretically sound by most accountants, some corporation balance sheets show bond discount among the assets, under the group caption of Deferred Charges. Under this method of balance sheet presentation, bond discount is regarded as deferred interest that will become interest expense over the life of the bonds. Similarly, premium on bonds is sometimes listed under the heading of Deferred Credits on the liability side of the balance sheet.

The role of the underwriter in marketing a bond issue

An investment banker or underwriter is usually employed to market a bond issue, just as in the case of capital stock. The corporation turns the entire bond issue over to the underwriter at a specified price (say, 98); the underwriter sells the bonds to the public at a slightly higher price (say, 100). By this arrangement the corporation is assured of receiving the entire amount of funds on a specified date. The calculation of the bond discount or bond premium is based on the net amount which the issuing corporation receives from the underwriter, not on the price paid by the public for the bonds.

Retirement of bond before maturity

Bonds are sometimes retired before the scheduled maturity date. Most bond issues contain a call provision, permitting the corporation to redeem the bonds by paying a specified price, usually a few points above par. Even without a call provision, the corporation may retire its bonds before maturity by purchasing them in the open market. If the bonds can be purchased by the issuing corporation at less than their book value, a gain is realized on the retirement of the debt. If the bonds are reacquired by the issuing corporation at a price in excess of their book value, a loss must be recognized. By *book value* is meant the face value of the bonds plus any unamortized premium or minus any unamortized discount.

Retirement of bonds at maturity

On the maturity date of the bonds, the discount or premium will be completely amortized and the accounting entry to retire the bonds (assuming that interest is paid separately) will consist of a debit to Bonds Payable and a credit to Cash.

One year before the maturity date, the bonds payable may be reclassified from long-term debt to a current liability in the balance sheet if payment is to be made from current assets rather than from a sinking fund.

Bond sinking fund

To make a bond issue attractive to investors, the corporation may agree in the bond indenture to create a sinking fund, exclusively for use in paying the bonds at maturity. A bond sinking fund is created by setting aside a specified amount of cash at regular intervals. The cash is usually deposited with a trustee, who invests it in conservative securities and adds the interest earned on these securities to the amount of the sinking fund. The periodic deposits of cash plus the interest earned on the sinking fund securities should cause the fund to approximately equal the amount of the bond issue by the maturity date. When the bond issue approaches maturity, the trustee sells all the securities in the fund and uses the cash proceeds to pay the holders of the bonds. Any excess cash remaining in the fund will be returned to the corporation.

Bond sinking fund and sinking fund income in the financial statements. A bond sinking fund is not included in current assets because it is not available for payment of current liabilities. The cash and securities comprising the fund are usually shown as a single amount under the group heading *Investments*, placed just below the current asset section. Interest earned on sinking fund securities constitutes earnings of the corporation.

Mortgages and other long-term liabilities

Mortgages are usually payable in equal monthly installments. A portion of each payment represents interest on the unpaid balance of the loan and the remainder of the payment reduces the amount of the unpaid balance (principal). This process is illustrated by the following schedule of payments for a three-month period on a 6.6% mortgage note with an unpaid balance of $100,000 as of September 11, 19___.

Monthly Payments on a Mortgage		*Monthly Payment*	*Interest for One Month at 6.6% on Unpaid Balance*	*Reduction in Principal*	*Unpaid Principal Balance*
Sept. 11, 19___					*$100,000.00*
Oct. 11		*$1,000.00*	*$550.00*	*$450.00*	*99,550.00*
Nov. 11		*1,000.00*	*547.53*	*452.47*	*99,097.53*
Dec. 11		*1,000.00*	*545.04*	*454.96*	*98,642.57*

On December 31, 19___, the portion of the unpaid principal of $98,642.57, due within one year, should be classified as a current liability and the remainder as a long-term liability. In addition, accrued interest for 20 days amounting to $361.69 ($98,642.57 × 6.6% × 20/360) should be shown as a current liability.

Other long-term liabilities often appearing in published balance sheets of corporations include pension obligations, amounts payable under deferred compensation plans, deferred income taxes, and unearned revenues.

DEMONSTRATION PROBLEM

The statement of financial position for the Bateman Corporation on December 31, 1971, includes the following liabilities:

Current liabilities:
Note payable, due June 30, 1972 . . . . $ 100,000
Less: Discount on note payable . . . .   3,750 $ 96,250

Accounts payable—merchandise creditors		$ 141,000
Income taxes payable, due March 15, 1972		85,000
Accrued liabilities relating to payroll:		
FICA taxes	$ 1,500	
Income taxes withheld	4,200	
State unemployment taxes	360	
Federal unemployment taxes	1,400	7,460
Total current liabilities		$ 329,710
Long-term liabilities:		
5% bonds payable, due Jan. 1, 1976	$5,000,000	
Less: Discount on bonds payable	72,000	4,928,000
Total liabilities		$5,257,710

During January of 1972, the corporation completed the following transactions relating to liabilities:

(1) Borrowed $50,000 from the National City Bank on January 11, 1972; issued a 6½%, 6-month promissory note for $50,000 to the bank.
(2) Cash disbursements during January include payments to merchandise creditors, $128,000, and to liquidate the accrued liabilities relating to payroll, $7,460.
(3) Purchases of merchandise on account during January amounted to $112,500.
(4) The payroll for January is summarized below:

Gross Wages	FICA Withheld	Income Taxes Withheld	Take-home Pay	Payroll Taxes on Employer
$65,000	$3,250	$5,050	$56,700	$5,265

Payroll taxes on the employer consist of FICA, 5%; state unemployment, 2.7%; federal unemployment, 0.4%. Employees were paid on January 31; however, none of the taxes relating to the January payroll has been remitted to governmental agencies.

(5) On January 1, 1972, the 5% bonds were redeemed at a call price of 102 and new 10-year bonds were issued on January 10 as follows:

6% bonds—$10,000,000 @ 101½	$10,150,000
Add: Interest from Jan. 1 to Jan. 10 (nine days)	15,000
Proceeds	$10,165,000

The face value of the new bonds ($10,000,000), the premium on bonds payable ($150,000), and the bond interest payable ($15,000) should be recorded in three separate liability accounts.

(6) The corporation has 250,000 shares of $10 par value capital stock outstanding. On January 5, 1972, a cash dividend of 15 cents a share and a 2% stock dividend were declared payable on February 10, 1972, to holders of record on January 28, 1972. The market value of the capital stock on the date of dividend declaration was $32 a share.

Instructions
a.   Prepare the journal entries to record the foregoing transactions.
b.   Prepare the adjusting entries required to bring the books up to date as of January 31, 1972. Assume that the premium on bonds payable is amortized to January 31, 1972 as an adjustment to Bond Interest Expense. Compute accrued interest on bonds payable to nearest dollar.
c.   Prepare the liabilities section of the statement of financial position as of January 31, 1972.

QUESTIONS

1.   Distinguish between
     a.   Current and long-term liabilities
     b.   Estimated and contingent liabilities

2.   Howard Benson applied to the City Bank for a loan of $20,000 for a period of three months. The loan was granted at an annual interest rate of 7½%. Show how the note would be drawn if
     a.   Interest is stated separately in the note.
     b.   Interest is included in the face amount of the note.

3.   With reference to Question 2 above, give the journal entry required on the books of Howard Benson for issuance of each of the two types of notes.

4.   Far West Company on October 31 borrowed $50,000 by issuing its note for six months, with interest at 6% on this sum included in the face amount of the note. Assuming that proper adjusting entries were made at year-end, what information relating to the borrowing would appear in the December 31 balance sheet? Where in the balance sheet would this information be placed?

5.   Explain how a purchase order, receiving report, voucher, and check constitute a chain of documentary evidence that facilitates control over business expenditures.

6.   Explain which of the following taxes relating to an employee's wages are borne by the employee and which by the employer:
     a.   FICA taxes
     b.   Federal unemployment taxes
     c.   State unemployment taxes
     d.   Federal income taxes

7.   Distinguish between the two terms in each of the following pairs:
     a.   Long-term notes; bonds
     b.   Mortgage bonds; debenture bonds
     c.   Fixed-maturity bonds; serial bonds
     d.   Coupon bonds; registered bonds

8.   The Dynamics Corporation has decided to finance expansion by issuing $10 million of 20-year debenture bonds and will ask a number of underwriters to bid on the bond issue. Discuss the factors that will determine the amount bid by the underwriters for these bonds.

9. What are *convertible* bonds? Discuss the advantages and disadvantages of convertible bonds from the standpoint of
   a. The investor
   b. The issuing corporation

10. The Computer Sharing Co. has paid-in capital of $10 million and retained earnings of $3 million. The company has just issued $1 million in 20-year, 8% bonds. It is proposed that a policy be established of appropriating $50,000 of retained earnings each year to enable the company to retire the bonds at maturity. Evaluate the merits of this proposal in accomplishing the desired result.

11. The following excerpt is taken from an article in a leading business periodical: "In the bond market high interest rates mean low prices. Bonds pay out a fixed percentage of their face value, usually $1,000; a 5% bond, for instance. will pay $50 a year. In order for its yield to rise to $6\frac{1}{4}$%, its price would have to drop to $800." Give a critical evaluation of this quotation.

12. A recent annual report of Lear Siegler, Inc., contained the following note accompanying the financial statements: "The loan agreements . . . contain provisions as to working capital requirements and payment of cash dividends. At June 30, retained earnings of approximately $13,400,000 were available for payment of cash dividends." What is the meaning of this note and why is it considered necessary to attach such a note to financial statements? (The total retained earnings of Lear Siegler, Inc., at this date amounted to $77.5 million; working capital amounted to $100 million; and total liabilities amounted to $142 million.)

EXERCISES

1. Dan McLain borrows $10,000 at a bank and signs two notes for $5,531 each. The first note is due at the end of the first year and the other note at the end of the second year. The interest rate quoted by the bank was "approximately 7% per annum."
   a. Give the journal entries to record the borrowing and the repayments. *Hint:* Record $1,062 as Discount on Notes Payable. Payment at the end of the first year consists of $700 interest and $4,831 repayment of principal.
   b. Show how McLain's liability would appear on his balance sheet immediately following the repayment of the first note.

2. Nolan earns a salary of $12,000 a year from Hull Corporation. FICA taxes are 5% of wages up to $7,800 a year. Federal unemployment taxes are 3.1% of wages up to $3,000 a year, but a credit against this FUTA tax is permitted for payment to the state of 2.7% of wages up to $3,000 a year. Federal income tax of $2,400 was withheld from Nolan's paychecks during the year.
   a. Prepare in general journal form a compound entry summarizing the payroll transactions for employee Nolan for the full year. (In drafting this entry, ignore any payments of tax during the year and let the liability accounts show the totals for the year.)
   b. What is the total yearly cost (including taxes) to Hull Corporation of having Nolan on the payroll at an annual salary of $12,000?

3. Companies A and B have the same amount of operating income. Determine the amount earned per share of common stock for each company and explain the source of any difference in the earnings per share for each company.

	Company A	Company B
5% debenture bonds	$500,000	$ 200,000
6% cumulative preferred stock, $100 par	500,000	300,000
Common stock, $25 stated value	500,000	1,000,000
Retained earnings	250,000	250,000
Operating income, before interest and income taxes (assume a 40% tax rate)	300,000	300,000

4. The following liability appears on the balance sheet of the Smiddy Company on December 31, 1971:

Bonds payable, 6%, due 12/31/85	$1,000,000	
Premium on bonds payable	42,000	$1,042,000

On January 1, 1972, 20% of the bonds are retired at 98. Interest was paid on December 31, 1971.
a. Record the retirement of $200,000 of bonds on January 1, 1972.
b. Record the interest payment for the six months ending December 31, 1972, and the amortization of the premium on December 31, 1972, assuming that amortization is recorded only at the end of each year.

5. Determine the average annual interest cost of the following bond issues:

	Company C	Company D
Maturity value of bonds	$1,000,000	$4,000,000
Contract interest rate	5%	4%
Price received for bonds on issue date	103	96
Length of time from issue date to maturity	10 years	10 years

6. Ex-Mar Company issued $100,000 par value 6% bonds on July 1, 1971 at 97½. Interest is due on June 30 and December 31 of each year and the discount is amortized only at the end of the fiscal year, which is the calendar year. The bonds mature on June 30, 1981. Prepare the required journal entries on
a. July 1, 1971, to record the sale of the bonds
b. December 31, 1971, to pay interest and to amortize the discount
c. June 30, 1981, to pay interest, amortize the discount, and retire the bonds

PROBLEMS

12-1 In the fiscal year ended September 30, the Green Corporation engaged in the following transactions involving notes payable:

May 6 Borrowed $4,000 from A. B. Clawson and issued a 45-day, 8% note payable as evidence of the debt.

June 12 Purchased office equipment from G-D Company. The invoice amount was $6,000 and the G-D Company agreed to accept as full payment a 6%, three-month note for the invoiced amount.

June 20 Paid the note made out to A. B. Clawson plus accrued interest.

Aug. 1 Borrowed $80,000 from Security Bank at an interest rate of 7% per annum; signed a 90-day note with interest included in the face amount of the note.

Aug. 31 Purchased merchandise in the amount of $3,000 from Erdmore Company. Gave in settlement a 90-day note bearing interest at 8%.

Sept. 12 The $6,000 note payable to G-D Company matured today. Paid in cash the interest accrued and issued a new 30-day note bearing interest at 7% to replace the maturing note.

Instructions

a. Prepare journal entries (in general journal form) to record the above transactions.

b. Prepare the adjusting entries needed at September 30, prior to closing the books.

12-2 The transactions listed below represent a small portion of the business transacted by the firm of Haas and Inman, a partnership, during the three months ended December 31.

Oct. 2 Purchased fixtures from Axel Company for $7,200, paying $1,200 as a cash down payment and signing a one-year, 8% installment contract for the balance. The interest charges were included in the face amount of the contract and are recorded as Discount on Notes Payable. The contract required 12 monthly payments of $540, the first payment due on November 1.

Oct. 21 Gave $4,000 cash and a 90-day, 7½% note to Lees Company in settlement of open account due today in the amount of $12,000.

Oct. 27 Purchased factory machinery from ELB Company for $24,000, giving a 60-day, 6% note in settlement thereof.

Oct. 31 Borrowed $72,000 from Manufacturers Bank, giving a 90-day note as evidence of indebtedness. Interest at 6% per annum was included in the face of the note.

Nov. 1 Paid the first installment due on the Axel Company contract.

Nov. 23 Purchased merchandise from Herman Morris, $44,000.

Nov. 26 Issued a 60-day note bearing interest at 6% in settlement of the Morris account.

Dec. 1 Made the second installment payment on Axel Company contract.

Dec. 26 Paid the 60-day, 6% note due to ELB Company.

Instructions

a. Prepare journal entries (in general journal form) to record the listed transactions for the three months ended December 31.

b. Prepare adjusting entries for interest at December 31.

c. Prepare a partial balance sheet as of December 31 reflecting the above transactions.

12-3 Precision Machine Company has five employees; two are employed on a monthly salary, and three are paid an hourly rate with provision for time and one-half for overtime. The basic data for the July 31 payroll are given below:

Employee	Hours Regular	Hours Over-time	Pay Rate	Com-pensation to June 30	Gross Pay for July	Federal Income Tax Withheld
Adams..........	160	15	$ 4.00/hr	$4,800	$ 730	$ 82
Bell	160		3.50/hr	3,400	560	62
Carr...........	160	10	2.00/hr	2,450	350	20
Drake	Salary		720.00/mo	4,320	720	98
Ewart	Salary		1,200.00/mo	7,200	1,200	95
Totals					$3,560	$357

Compensation of Drake and Ewart is recorded in Administrative Salaries; the balance of the earnings is chargeable to Shop Wages. Payroll taxes apply as follows: FICA, 5% up to a maximum of $7,800; state unemployment, 2.7% up to a maximum of $3,800; federal unemployment, 0.4% up to a maximum of $3,000. Precision Machine Company has group insurance and a supplementary retirement plan under which each employee contributes 6% of his gross pay, with the company matching this contribution. Both employees' and employer's contributions are deposited with the Prudent Insurance Company at the end of each month.

Instructions
a. Prepare a payroll record for July using the following columns:

Employee	Gross Pay	Amount Subject to State Unemploy-ment Taxes	Amount Subject to FICA Taxes	Federal Income Tax Withheld	FICA Tax Withheld	Retire-ment Deduc-tion	Net Pay Due

b. Explain how the gross pay for Carr was computed for the month of July.
c. Explain why the federal income taxes withheld for Ewart are less than those withheld for Drake despite the fact that Ewart received a higher gross compensation.
d. Prepare in general journal form the entry to record the payroll for the month of July.
e. Prepare in general journal form the entry to record the employer's payroll taxes and insurance plan contributions for the month of July, also an entry for payment of these liabilities.

12-4 First Company issued $5 million of 7%, 10-year bonds on January 1, 1971. Interest is payable semiannually on June 30 and December 31. The bonds were sold to an underwriting group at 110.

Second Company issued $5 million of 5%, 10-year bonds on January 1, 1971. Interest is payable semiannually on June 30 and December 31. The bonds were sold to an underwriting group at 90% of par value.

Instructions
a. Prepare journal entries, omitting explanations, to record all transactions relating to the bond issues of these two companies during the year 1971.
b. Explain why the average bond interest cost per year is the same for the two companies, despite the difference in the terms of the two bond contracts.

12-5 Emerging Industries, Inc., reported the balances given below at the end of the current year:

Total assets	$7,000,000
Current liabilities	1,400,000
Stockholders' equity:	
Common stock, par $20	2,000,000
Paid-in capital in excess of par value	1,500,000
Retained earnings	1,900,000

The company is planning an expansion of its plant facilities, and a study shows that $6 million of new funds will be required to finance the expansion. Two proposals are under consideration:
Proposal A. Issue 120,000 shares of common stock at a price of $50 per share.
Proposal B. Borrow $6 million on a 20-year bond issue, with interest at 7%.
The assets and liabilities of Emerging Industries, Inc., have remained relatively constant over the past five years, and during this period the earnings *after* income taxes have averaged 10% of the stockholders' equity as reported at the end of the current year. The company expects that its earnings *before* income taxes will increase by an amount equal to 12% of the new investment in plant facilities.
Past and future income taxes for the company may be estimated at 40% of taxable income.

Instructions
a. Prove that the company's average income *before* income taxes during the past five years was $900,000.
b. Prepare a schedule showing the expected net income per share of common stock during the first year of operations following the completion of the $6 million expansion, under each of the two proposed means of financing.
c. Evaluate the two methods of financing from the viewpoint of a major stockholder of Emerging Industries, Inc.

12-6 The items shown below appear on the balance sheet of the Betty-Ron Corporation as of December 31, 1971.

Current liabilities:		
Accrued interest on bonds payable (3 months)		$ 121,875
Long-term debt:		
Bonds payable, 6½% due Apr. 1, 1982	$7,500,000	
Discount on bonds payable	147,600	7,352,400

The bonds are callable on any interest date; on October 1, 1972, the Betty-Ron Corporation called $1 million of its bonds at 103½.

Instructions

a.   Prepare journal entries to record the semiannual interest payment on April 1, 1972. Discount was amortized to December 31, 1971, and is amortized at each interest payment date. Base the amortization on the 123-month period from December 31, 1971 to April 1, 1982.

b.   Prepare journal entries to record the amortization of bond discount and payment of bond interest at October 1, 1972, and also to record the calling of the bonds at this date.

c.   Make a journal entry to record the accrual of interest expense as of December 31, 1972. Include the amortization of bond discount to the year-end.

12-7   The following information is taken from the trial balance of the Marauder Ferry Company:

	Adjusted 12/31		Unadjusted 12/31
	Year 1	Year 2	Year 3
Bonds payable, due Oct. 1, Year 11	$1,000,000	$1,000,000	$800,000
Discount on bonds payable	23,400	21,000	19,200
Bond interest expense (include amortization)	10,400	62,400	46,800
Bond interest payable..................	15,000	15,000	
Gain on retirement of bonds............			6,000

The bonds were issued on November 1, Year 1, with one month's accrued interest at 6%. On October 1 of Year 3, $200,000 of bonds were retired at a price of 97. No discount on bonds payable was written off at the time of the retirement. *The company adjusts its books at the end of every calendar quarter.* (Notice the $1,200 decrease in Discount on Bonds Payable during the 12 months between the first two trial balances.)

Instructions

a.   Prepare the entry that was made to record the issuance of bonds on November 1, Year 1. (First, compute the discount at date of issuance.)

b.   Prepare a correcting entry required to measure properly the gain on retirement of bonds. (Compute the book value of the bonds retired.)

c.   Prepare the adjusting entry required at the end of Year 3 to record the accrued interest and to amortize the discount for the period October 1 to December 31.

d.   What will be the adjusted interest expense for Year 4 if $800,000 bonds remain outstanding? Why does it differ from the interest expense in Year 2 and Year 3?

Chapter

13 Plant and equipment, depreciation, natural resources, and intangibles

PLANT AND EQUIPMENT

The term *plant and equipment* is used to describe long-lived assets acquired for use in the operation of the business and not intended for resale to customers. Among the more common examples are land, buildings, machinery, furniture and fixtures, office equipment, and automobiles. A delivery truck in the showroom of an automobile dealer is inventory; when this same truck is sold to a corporation for use in making deliveries to customers it becomes a unit of plant and equipment.

The term *fixed assets* has long been used in accounting literature to describe all types of plant and equipment. This term, however, has virtually disappeared from the published financial statements of large corporations. *Plant and equipment* appears to be a more descriptive term. Another alternative title used on many corporation balance sheets is *Property, plant, and equipment.*

Plant and equipment represent bundles of services to be received

It is convenient to think of a plant asset as a bundle of services to be received by the owner over a period of years. Ownership of a delivery truck, for example, may provide about 100,000 miles of transportation. The cost of the delivery truck is customarily entered in an account entitled Delivery Truck, which in essence represents payment in advance for several years of transportation service. Similarly, a building may be regarded as several years' supply of housing services. As the years go by, these services are utilized by the business and the cost of the plant asset is gradually transferred into depreciation expense. An awareness of the similarity between plant assets and prepaid expenses is essential to an understanding of the accounting process by which the cost of plant assets is allocated to the years in which the benefits of ownership are received.

Major categories of plant and equipment

Plant and equipment items are often classified into one of the following categories:

1. *Tangible plant assets.* The term *tangible* denotes bodily substance, as exemplified by land, a building, or a machine. This category may be subdivided into two groups.
   a. *Plant property subject to depreciation.* Included are plant assets of limited useful life such as buildings and equipment.
   b. *Land.* The only plant asset not subject to depreciation is land; which has an unlimited term of existence.
2. *Intangible assets.* Examples are patents, copyrights, trademarks, franchises, organization costs, leaseholds, leasehold improvements, and goodwill. Current assets such as accounts receivable or prepaid rent are not included in the intangible classification, even though they are lacking in physical substance. The term *intangible assets* is used to describe a noncurrent asset, which is lacking in physical substance.

Natural resources

Natural resources are subject to depletion rather than to depreciation. Examples are mines, oil and gas wells, and tracts of timber. The term *depletion* means the exhaustion of a natural resource through mining, pumping, cutting, or otherwise using up the deposit or growth.

Accounting problems relating to plant and equipment

Some major accounting problems relating to plant and equipment are indicated by the following questions:

1. How is the cost of plant and equipment determined?
2. How should the costs of plant and equipment be allocated against revenues?
3. How should charges for repairs, maintenance, and replacements be treated?
4. How should disposals of plant assets be recorded?

We are presently concerned with answering the first of these questions; an understanding of how the cost of plant and equipment is determined will be helpful in subsequent study of the problem of depreciation.

Determining the cost of plant and equipment. The cost of plant and equipment includes all expenditures reasonable and necessary in acquiring the asset and placing it in a position and condition for use in the operations of the business. Only *reasonable* and *necessary* expenditures should be included. For example, if the company's truck driver receives a traffic ticket while hauling a new machine to the plant, the traffic fine is *not* part of the cost of the new machine. If the machine is dropped and damaged while being unloaded, the expense of repairing the damage should *not* be added to the cost of the asset.

Cost is most easily determined when an asset is purchased for cash. The cost of the asset is then equal to the cash outlay necessary in acquiring the asset plus any expenditures for freight, insurance while in transit, installation, trial runs, and any other costs necessary to make the asset ready for use. If plant assets are purchased on the installment plan or by issuance of notes payable, the interest element or carrying charge should be recorded as interest expense and not as part of the cost of the plant assets.

This principle of including in the cost of a plant asset all the incidental charges necessary to put the asset in use is illustrated by the following example. A factory in Los Angeles orders a machine from a San Francisco tool manufacturer at a list price of $10,000, with terms of 2/10, n/30. A sales tax of 4% must be paid, also freight charges of $1,250. Transportation from the railroad station to the factory costs $150 and installation labor amounts to $400. The cost of the machine and the amount to be entered in the Machinery account are computed as follows:

Items	List price of machine.	*$10,000*
Included	Less: Cash discount (2% × $10,000).	*200*
in Cost of	Net cash price.	*$ 9,800*
Machine	Sales tax (4% × $9,800)	*392*
	Freight	*1,250*
	Transportation from railroad station to factory.	*150*
	Installation labor	*400*
	Cost of machine	*$11,992*

Why should all the incidental charges relating to the acquisition of a machine be included in its cost? Why not treat these incidental charges as expenses of the period in which the machine is acquired?

The answer is to be found in the basic accounting principle of *matching costs and revenues.* The benefits of owning the machine will be received over a span of years, 10 years, for example. During those 10 years the operation of the machine will contribute to revenues. Consequently, the total costs of the machine should be recorded in the accounts as an asset and allocated against the revenues of the 10 years. All costs incurred in acquiring the machine are costs of the services to be received from using the machine.

Land. When land is purchased, various incidental charges are generally incurred, in addition to the purchase price. These additional costs may include commissions to real estate brokers, escrow fees, legal fees for examining and insuring the title, delinquent taxes paid by the purchaser, and fees for surveying, draining, clearing, grading, and landscaping the property. All these expenditures are part of the cost of the land. Special assessments for local improvements such as the paving of a street or the installation of sewers may also be charged to the Land account, for the reason that a more or less permanent value is being added to the land.

Separate ledger accounts are necessary for land and buildings, because buildings are subject to depreciation and land is not. The treatment of land as a nondepreciable asset is based on the premise that land used as a building site has an unlimited life. When land and building are purchased for a lump sum, the purchase price must be apportioned between the land and the building. An appraisal may be necessary for this purpose. Assume, for example, that land and a building are purchased for a total price of $100,000. The apportionment of this cost on the basis of an appraisal may be made as follows:

	Value per Appraisal	Percent of Total	Apportionment of Cost
Land...................	$ 48,000	40%	$ 40,000
Building	72,000	60%	60,000
Total	$120,000	100%	$100,000

Sometimes a tract of land purchased as a building site has on it an old building which is not suitable for the buyer's use. The Land account should be charged with the entire purchase price plus any costs incurred in tearing down or removing the building. Salvage proceeds received from sale of the building are recorded as a credit in the Land account.

Land acquired as a future building site should be reported under Other Assets, rather than as part of Plant and Equipment, since it is not currently used in operations.

Land improvements. Improvements to real estate such as driveways, fences, parking lots, and sprinkler systems have a limited life and are therefore subject to depreciation. For this reason they should be recorded not in the Land account but in a separate account entitled Land Improvements. On the other hand, any improvements which will last indefinitely and are not to be depreciated are entered in the Land account.

Buildings. Old buildings are sometimes purchased with the intention of repairing them prior to placing them in use. Repairs made under these circumstances are charged to the Building account. After the building has been placed in use, ordinary repairs are considered as maintenance expense when incurred.

When a building is constructed by the business itself, rather than being purchased, cost includes the materials and labor used plus an equitable portion of overhead or indirect expenses, such as executive salaries. Any other outlays specifically relating to the construction such as architectural fees, insurance during the construction period, and building permits should also be included in the cost of the building. A building or machine constructed by a company for its own use should be recorded in the accounts at cost, not at the price which might have been paid to outsiders if the asset had been acquired through purchase.

Depreciation

Allocating the cost of plant and equipment. Plant assets, with the exception of land, are of use to a company for only a limited number of years, and the cost of each plant asset is allocated as an expense of the years in which it is used. Accountants use the term *depreciation* to describe this gradual conversion of the cost of a plant asset into expense.

Depreciation, as the term is used in accounting, does not mean the physical deterioration of an asset. Neither does depreciation mean the decrease in market value of a plant asset over a period of time. *Depreciation means the allocation of the cost of a plant asset to the periods in which services are received from the asset.*

When a delivery truck is purchased, its cost is first recorded as an asset. This cost becomes expense over a period of years through the accounting process of depreciation. When gasoline is purchased for the truck, the price paid for each tankful is immediately recorded as expense. In theory, both outlays (for the truck and for a tank of gas) lead to the acquisition of assets, but since it is reasonable to assume that a tankful of gasoline will be consumed in the accounting period in which it is purchased, we record the outlay for gasoline as an expense immediately. It is important to recognize, however, that both the outlay for the truck and the payment for the gasoline become expense in the period or periods in which each is assumed to render services.

A separate Depreciation Expense account and a separate Accumulated Depreciation account are generally maintained for each group of depreciable assets such as factory buildings, delivery equipment, and office equipment so that a proper allocation of depreciation expense can be made between functional areas of activity such as sales and manufacturing. Depreciation on manufacturing facilities is not necessarily an expense of the period in which it is recorded; the depreciation charge is first embodied in the inventory of goods manufactured, and the cost of this inventory is later deducted from revenue as an expense of the period when the goods are sold.

Because of the noncash nature of depreciation expense and because the dollar amount is materially affected by the depreciation method selected, it is generally desirable that the total amount of depreciation be disclosed in the income statement.

Depreciation not a process of valuation. Accounting records and financial statements do not purport to show the constantly fluctuating market values of plant and equipment. Occasionally the market value of a building may rise substantially over a period of years because of a change in the price level, or for other reasons. Depreciation is continued, however, regardless of the increase in market value. The accountant recognizes that the building will render useful services for only a limited number of years, and that its full cost must be allocated as expense of those years regardless of fluctuations in market value.

Causes of depreciation. There are two major causes of depreciation, physical deterioration and obsolescence.

Physical deterioration. Physical deterioration of a plant asset results from use, and also from exposure to sun, wind, and other climatic factors. When a plant asset has been carefully maintained, it is not uncommon for the owner to claim that the asset is as "good as new." Such statements are not literally true. Although a good repair policy may greatly lengthen the useful life of a machine, every machine eventually reaches the point at which it must be discarded. In brief, the making of repairs does not lessen the need for recognition of depreciation.

Obsolescence. The term *obsolescence* means the process of becoming out of date or obsolete. An airplane, for example, may become obsolete even though it is in excellent physical condition; it becomes obsolete because better planes of superior design and performance have become available. Obsolescence relates to the capacity of a plant asset to render services to a particular company for a particular purpose.

The usefulness of plant assets may also be reduced because the rapid growth of a company renders such assets inadequate. Inadequacy of a plant asset may necessitate replacement with a larger unit even though the asset is in good physical condition and is not obsolete. Obsolescence and inadequacy are often closely associated; both relate to the opportunity for economical and efficient use of an asset rather than to its physical condition. Obsolescence is probably a more significant factor than physical deterioration in putting an end to the usefulness of most depreciable assets. Current accounting practice, however, does not usually attempt to separate the effects of physical deterioration and obsolescence.

Methods of computing depreciation

Straight-line method. The simplest and most widely used method of computing depreciation is the straight-line method. This method was described in Chapter 3 and has been used repeatedly in problems throughout the book. Under the straight-line method, an equal portion of the cost of the asset is allocated to each period of use; consequently, this method is most appropriate when usage of an asset is fairly uniform from year to year.

In theory, the computation of the periodic charge for depreciation is made by deducting the estimated residual or salvage value from the cost of the asset and dividing the remaining depreciable cost by the years of estimated useful life, as shown in the following example:

Computing	*Cost of the depreciable asset*	*$5,200*
Deprecia-	*Less: Estimated residual value (amount to be realized by sale of asset*	
tion by	*when it is retired from use)*	*400*
Straight-	*Total amount to be depreciated.*	*$4,800*
line	*Estimated useful life*	*4 years*
Method	*Depreciation expense each year ($4,800 ÷ 4).*	*$1,200*

The following schedule summarizes the accumulation of depreciation over the useful life of the asset. The amount to be depreciated is $4,800 (cost of $5,200 minus residual value of $400).

Constant Annual Depreciation Expense

	Depreciation Schedule: Straight-line Method				
Year	*Computation*	*Depreciation Expense*	*Accumulated Depreciation*	*Book Value*
				$5,200
First	(¼ × $4,800)	$1,200	$1,200	4,000
Second	(¼ × $4,800)	1,200	2,400	2,800
Third.	(¼ × $4,800)	1,200	3,600	1,600
Fourth.	(¼ × $4,800)	1,200	4,800	400
		$4,800		

In practice, the possibility of residual value is often ignored and the annual depreciation charge computed merely by dividing the total cost of the asset by the number of years of estimated useful life. This practice is justified in many cases in which residual value is not material and is difficult to estimate accurately. Under this approach the yearly depreciation expense in the above example would be $5,200 ÷ 4, or $1,300.

Units-of-output method. A more equitable distribution of the cost of some plant assets can be obtained by dividing the cost by the estimated units of output rather than by the estimated years of useful life. A truck line or bus company, for example, might compute depreciation on its vehicles by a mileage basis. If a truck costs $10,000 and is estimated to have a useful life of 200,000 miles, the depreciation rate per mile of operation is 5 cents ($10,000 ÷ 200,000). At the end of each year, the amount of depreciation to be recorded would be determined by multiplying the 5-cent rate by the number of miles the truck had operated during the year. This method is not very suitable to situations in which obsolescence is an important factor.

Accelerated depreciation methods. The term *accelerated depreciation* means recognition of relatively large amounts of depreciation in the early years of use and correspondingly reduced amounts in the later years.

One reason for adoption of accelerated methods of depreciation is that the increasingly rapid pace of invention of new products is making obsolescence a factor of greater significance than physical deterioration. When an industry is in a period of rapid technological change, plant and equipment may have to be replaced within shorter periods than would be necessary in a less dynamic economy. Businessmen may, therefore, reason that the acquisition of a new plant facility is justified only if most of the cost can be recovered within a comparatively short period of years. Also significant is the pleasing prospect of reducing the current year's income tax burden by recognizing a relatively large amount of depreciation expense.

Another argument for allocating a comparatively large share of the cost of a depreciable asset to the early years of use is that repair expenses tend to increase as assets grow older. The combined expense of depreciation and repairs may be more uniform from year to year under an accelerated method of depreciation than when straight-line depreciation is followed.

Fixed-percentage-on-declining-balance method. For income tax purposes, one of the acceptable methods of "rapid write-off" of depreciable assets consists of doubling the normal rate of depreciation and applying this doubled rate each year to the undepreciated cost (book value) of the asset.

Assume, for example, that an automobile is acquired for business use at a cost of $4,000. Estimated useful life is four years; therefore, the normal depreciation rate under the straight-line method would be 25%. To depreciate the automobile by the fixed-percentage-on-declining-balance method, we double the normal rate of 25% and apply the doubled rate of 50% to the book value. Depreciation expense in the first year would then amount to $2,000. In the second year the depreciation expense would drop to $1,000, computed at 50% of the remaining book value of $2,000. In the third year depreciation would be $500, and in the fourth year only $250. The following table shows the allocation of cost under this method of depreciation:

Accelerated Depreciation: Fixed Percentage on Declining Balance

	Depreciation Schedule: Fixed-percentage-on-declining-balance Method				
Year	Computation		Depreciation Expense	Accumulated Depreciation	Book Value
					$4,000
First...........	(50% × $4,000)		$2,000	$2,000	2,000
Second.........	(50% × $2,000)		1,000	3,000	1,000
Third.........	(50% × $1,000)		500	3,500	500
Fourth.........	(50% × $500)		250	3,750	250

If the automobile is continued in use beyond the estimated life of four years, depreciation will be continued at the 50% rate on the book value. In the fifth year, for example, the depreciation expense will be $125 (50% × $250), and in the sixth year $62.50 (50% × $125).

Sum-of-the-years'-digits method. This is another method of allocating a large portion of the cost of an asset to the early years of its use. The depreciation rate to be used is a fraction, of which the numerator is the remaining years of useful life and the denominator is the sum of the years of useful life. Consider again the example of an automobile costing $4,000 and having an estimated life of four years, but in this instance assume an estimated residual value of $400. (Present income tax regulations require that residual value be taken into account when either the straight-line method or the sum-of-the-years'-digits method of depreciation is used.) Since the automobile has an estimated life of four years, the denominator of the fraction will be 10, computed as follows (1 + 2 + 3 + 4 = 10). For the first year, the depreciation will be $\frac{4}{10}$ × $3,600, or $1,440. For the second year, the depreciation will be $\frac{3}{10}$ × $3,600, or $1,080; in the third year $\frac{2}{10}$ × $3,600, or $720; and in the fourth year, $\frac{1}{10}$ × $3,600, or $360. In tabular form this depreciation program will appear as follows:

Accelerated Depreciation: Sum of the Years' Digits

Year	Computation	Depreciation Expense	Accumulated Depreciation	Book Value
				$4,000
First	($\frac{4}{10}$ × $3,600)	$1,440	$1,440	2,560
Second	($\frac{3}{10}$ × $3,600)	1,080	2,520	1,480
Third	($\frac{2}{10}$ × $3,600)	720	3,240	760
Fourth	($\frac{1}{10}$ × $3,600)	360	3,600	400

Depreciation Schedule: Sum-of-the-years'-digits Method

Depreciation for fractional periods. In the case of depreciable assets acquired sometime during the year, it is customary to figure depreciation to the nearest month. For example, if an asset is acquired on July 12, depreciation would be computed from July 1; if the asset had been acquired on July 18 (or any other date in the latter half of July, depreciation would be recorded for only five months (August through December) for the current calendar year.

Some businesses prefer to begin depreciation on the first of the month following the acquisition of a depreciable asset. This method, or any one of many similar variations, is acceptable so long as it is followed consistently by the business.

Revision of depreciation rates

Depreciation rates are based on estimates of the useful life of assets. These estimates of useful life are seldom precisely correct and sometimes are grossly in error. Consequently, the annual depreciation expense based on the estimated useful life may be either excessive or inadequate. What action should be taken when, after a few years of using a plant asset, it is decided that the asset is actually going to last for a considerably longer or shorter period than was originally estimated? When either of these situations arises, a revised estimate of useful life should be made and the periodic depreciation expense decreased or increased accordingly.

The procedure for correcting the depreciation program may be stated in a very few words: *spread the undepreciated cost of the asset over the years of remaining useful life.* The annual depreciation expense is increased or decreased sufficiently so that the depreciation program will be completed in accordance with the revised estimate of remaining useful life. The following data illustrate a revision which increases the estimate of useful life and thereby decreases the annual depreciation expense.

Data	
Prior to	*Cost of asset* $10,000
Revision	*Estimated useful life (no residual value)* .... 10 years
of Depre-	*Annual depreciation expense (prior to revision)* .... $ 1,000
ciation	*Accumulated depreciation at end of six years ($1,000 × 6)* .... $ 6,000
Rate	

At the beginning of the seventh year, it is decided that the asset will last for eight more years. The revised estimate of useful life is, therefore, a total of 14 years. The depreciation expense to be recognized for the seventh year and for each of the remaining years is $500, computed as follows:

Revision	
of Depre-	*Undepreciated cost at end of sixth year ($10,000 − $6,000)* $4,000
ciation	*Revised estimate of remaining years of useful life* .... 8 years
Program	*Revised amount of annual depreciation expense ($4,000 ÷ 8)* .... $ 500

The method described above for the revision of a depreciation program is generally used and is acceptable in the determination of taxable income. The Accounting Principles Board of the AICPA also supports this approach for financial reporting purposes.[1]

Depreciation and income taxes

Accelerated methods of depreciation became quite popular some years ago when the federal government approved their use for income tax purposes. By offering businessmen the opportunity of writing off as depreciation expense a large portion of the cost of a new asset during its early years of use, the government has provided a powerful incentive for investment in new productive facilities. Since an increased charge for depreciation expense will reduce taxable income, the businessman may feel that by purchasing new assets and writing off a large part of the cost in the early years of use, he is in effect paying for the new assets with dollars that otherwise would have been used to pay income taxes.

In theory, the ideal depreciation policy is one that allocates the cost of a depreciable asset to the several periods of its use in proportion to the services received each period. Accelerated methods of depreciation sometimes fail to allocate the cost of an asset in proportion to the flow of services from the property and therefore prevent the determination of annual net income on a realistic basis. If annual net income figures are misleading, stockholders, creditors, management, and others who use financial statements as a basis for business decisions may be seriously injured. For income

[1] Opinions of the Accounting Principles Board, No. 9. AICPA (New York: 1966), p. 116. The Board considers changes in estimated useful life of assets as "prospective" rather than retroactive. Such changes, therefore, do not require a correction in retained earnings for past errors in recording depreciation. See Chapter 8 for a more extensive discussion of "prior period adjustments" which are recorded directly in the Retained Earnings account.

tax purposes, however, accelerated methods of depreciation may be effective in encouraging businessmen to invest in new productive facilities and thereby to raise the level of business activity.

In recent years a number of corporations have changed back from accelerated depreciation to straight-line depreciation, possibly motivated in part by a desire to report higher earnings per share of stock. (A reduction in depreciation expense causes an increase in net income.) Management in general is anxious to report rising earnings per share of stock in order to attract more investors and to enhance the company's reputation. The following footnote from the financial statements of a steel company indicates how significant a change in accounting method may be on reported earnings per share.

The above earnings reflect a change from accelerated to straight-line depreciation for book purposes on certain of the company's properties. . . . The change has the effect of increasing the company's earnings by 46 cents for the third quarter and by $1.37 per share of common stock for the first nine months. . . .

In the above example, the change in depreciation policy caused the company's reported earnings to rise by 110% for the third quarter of the year and by 56% for the first nine months of the year. The change from accelerated depreciation to straight-line depreciation for financial reporting does not prevent the continued use of accelerated depreciation for the determination of taxable income.

Depreciation and inflation

The valuation of plant and equipment on a cost basis and the computation of depreciation in terms of cost work very well during periods of stable price levels. However, the substantial rise in the price level in recent years has led many businessmen to suggest that a more realistic measurement of net income could be achieved by basing depreciation on the estimated replacement cost of plant assets rather than on the original cost of the assets presently in use. An alternative proposal is to adjust each year's depreciation expense by a price index measuring changes in the purchasing power of the dollar. This price-level adjustment would cause depreciation expense to be stated in *current dollars,* as are such expenses as wages and taxes.

As a specific illustration, assume that a manufacturing company purchased machinery in 1960 at a cost of $100,000. Estimated useful life was 15 years and straight-line depreciation was used. Throughout this 15-year period the price level rose sharply. By 1975 the machinery purchased in 1960 was fully depreciated; it was scrapped and replaced by new machinery in 1975. Although the new machines were not significantly different from the old, they cost $300,000, or three times as much as the depreciation expense which has been recorded during the life of the old machinery. Many businessmen would argue that the depreciation expense for the 15 years was in reality $300,000, because this was the outlay required for new machinery if the company was merely to "stay even" in its productive facilities. It is also argued that reported profits will be overstated during a period of rising prices if depreciation is based on the lower plant costs of some years ago. An overstatement of profits causes higher income taxes and perhaps larger demands for wage increases than are justified by the company's financial position and earnings.

As yet there has been no general acceptance of the suggestion for basing depreciation on replacement cost. Replacement cost is difficult to determine on any objective basis. Who can say how much it will cost to buy a new machine 15 years from now? The proposal to use a general price index to adjust each year's depreciation expense appears more promising, and is illustrated in Chapter 15.

Depreciation and the problem of asset replacement

Many readers of financial statements who have not studied accounting mistakenly believe that accumulated depreciation accounts (depreciation reserves) represent funds accumulated for the purpose of buying new equipment when the present facilities wear out. Perhaps the best way to combat such mistaken notions is to emphasize that the credit balance in an accumulated depreciation account represents the expired cost of assets acquired in the past. The amounts credited to the accumulated depreciation account could, as an alternative, have been credited directly to the plant and equipment account. An accumulated depreciation account has a *credit* balance; it does not represent an asset; and it cannot be used in any way to pay for new equipment. To buy a new plant asset requires cash; the total amount of cash owned by a company is shown by the asset account for cash.

Capital expenditures and revenue expenditures

The term *expenditure* means making a payment or incurring an obligation to make a future payment for an asset or service received. The acquisition of an asset (such as an automobile) or of a service (such as repairs to the automobile) may be for cash or on credit. In either situation the transaction is properly referred to as an expenditure.

Expenditures for the purchase or expansion of plant assets are called *capital expenditures* and are recorded in asset accounts. Expenditures for repairs, maintenance, fuel, and other items necessary to the ownership and use of plant and equipment are called *revenue expenditures* and are recorded by debits to expense accounts. The charge to an expense account is based on the assumption that the benefits from the expenditure will be used up in the current period, and the payment should therefore be deducted from the revenues of the current period in determining the net income. In brief, *any expenditure that will benefit several accounting periods is considered a capital expenditure; any expenditure that will benefit only the current accounting period is referred to as a revenue expenditure.* Careful distinction between capital and revenue expenditures is important in the determination of net income. If the cost of constructing a new building, for example, is recorded as ordinary repairs expense (a revenue expenditure), the net income of the current period will be understated. The net income of future periods will be overstated because of the absence of depreciation expenses applicable to the unrecorded asset.

Extraordinary repairs

The term *extraordinary repairs* has a specific meaning in accounting terminology; it means a thorough reconditioning that will extend the useful life of a plant asset beyond the original estimate. For example, a new automobile may be depreciated on the basis of an estimated useful life of four years. Assume that after three years of use, a decision is made to install a new engine in the automobile and thereby to extend its overall useful life from the original estimate of four years to a total of six years.

An extraordinary repair of this type may be recorded by debiting the Accumulated Depreciation account. This entry is sometimes explained by the argument that the extraordinary repair cancels out some of the depreciation previously recorded. The effect of this reduction (debit entry) in the Accumulated Depreciation account is to *increase* the book value of the asset by the cost of the extraordinary repair. Since an extraordinary repair causes an increase in the book value of the asset and has no immediate direct effect upon income, it may be regarded as a form of capital expenditure.

Disposal of plant and equipment

When depreciable assets are disposed of at any date other than the end of the year, an entry should be made to record depreciation for the fraction of the year ending with the date of disposal. In the following illustrations of the disposal of items of plant and equipment, it is assumed that any necessary entries for fractional-period depreciation have been recorded. When units of plant and equipment wear out or become obsolete, they must be discarded, sold, or traded in on new equipment. Upon the disposal or retirement of a depreciable asset, the cost of the property is removed from the asset account, and the accumulated depreciation is removed from the related valuation account. Assume, for example, that office equipment purchased 10 years ago at a cost of $500 has been fully depreciated and is no longer useful. The entry to record the discarding of the worthless equipment is as follows:

Scrapping Fully De- preciated Asset	*Accumulated Depreciation: Office Equipment* *500*	
	Office Equipment	*500*
	To remove from the accounts the cost and the accumulated depreciation on fully depreciated office equipment now being discarded. No salvage value.	

When an asset has been fully depreciated, no more depreciation should be recorded on it, even though the property is in good condition and is continued in use. The objective of depreciation is to spread the *cost* of an asset over the periods of its usefulness; in no case can depreciation expense be greater than the amount paid for the asset. When a fully depreciated asset is continued in use beyond the original estimate of useful life, the asset account and the Accumulated Depreciation account should remain on the books without further entries until the asset is retired.

Gains and losses on disposal of plant and equipment. The book value of a plant asset is its cost minus the total recorded depreciation, as shown by the Accumulated Depreciation account. When a depreciable asset is sold, the loss or gain on the disposal is computed by comparing the book value with the amount received from the sale. A sales price in excess of the book value produces a gain; a sales price below the book value produces a loss. If these gains or losses are material in amount, they should be shown separately in the income statement under Extraordinary Items, as illustrated in Chapter 8.

Disposal at a price above book value. Assume that a machine which cost $10,000 and has a book value of $2,000 is sold for $3,000. The journal entry to record this disposal is as follows:

Gain on Plant Asset Disposed of	*Cash*	*3,000*	
	Accumulated Depreciation: Machinery	*8,000*	
	Machinery		*10,000*
	Gain on Disposal of Plant Assets		*1,000*
	To record sale of machinery at a price above book value.		

Disposal at a price below book value. Now assume that the same machine were sold for $500. The journal entry in this case would be as follows:

Loss on Plant Asset Disposed of	*Cash*	*500*	
	Accumulated Depreciation: Machinery	*8,000*	
	Loss on Disposal of Plant Assets	*1,500*	
	Machinery		*10,000*
	To record sale of machinery at a price below book value.		

The disposal of a depreciable asset at a price equal to book value would result in neither a gain nor a loss. The entry for such a transaction would consist of a debit to Cash for the amount received, a debit to Accumulated Depreciation for the balance accumulated, and a credit to the asset account for the original cost.

Trading in used assets on new

Certain types of depreciable assets, such as automobiles and office equipment, are customarily traded in on new assets of the same kind. The trade-in allowance granted by the dealer may differ materially from the book value of the old asset. If the dealer grants a trade-in allowance in excess of the book value of the asset being traded in, there is the suggestion of a gain being realized on the exchange. The evidence of a gain is not conclusive, however, because the list price of the new asset may purposely have been set higher than a realistic cash price to permit the offering of inflated trade-in allowances.

For the purpose of determining taxable income, no gain or loss is recognized when a depreciable asset is traded in on another similar asset. The tax regulations provide that the cost of the new asset shall be the sum of the book value of the old asset traded in plus the additional amount paid or to be paid in acquiring the new asset.

To illustrate the handling of an exchange transaction in the manner required for tax purposes (and followed for general accounting purposes by most companies), assume that a truck is acquired at a cost of $3,200. The truck is depreciated on the straight-line basis with the assumption of a four-year life. After three years of use, the truck is traded in on a new model having a list price of $4,000. The dealer grants a trade-in allowance of $1,200 for the old truck; the additional amount to be paid to acquire the new truck is, therefore, $2,800 ($4,000 list price minus $1,200 trade-in allowance). The cost basis of the new truck is computed as follows:

Trade-in:	*Cost of old truck*	*$3,200*
Cost Basis	*Less: Accumulated depreciation*	*2,400*
of New	*Book value of old truck*	*$ 800*
Truck	*Add: Cash payment for new truck (list price, $4,000 — $1,200 trade-in*	
	allowance)	*2,800*
	Cost basis of new truck	*$3,600*

The trade-in allowance and the list price of the new truck are not recorded in the accounts; their only function lies in determining the amount which the purchaser must pay in addition to turning in the old truck. The journal entry for this exchange transaction is as follows:

Trade-in:	*Truck (new)*	*3,600*	
Income	*Accumulated Depreciation: Truck*	*2,400*	
Tax	*Truck (old)*		*3,200*
Method	*Cash*		*2,800*
	To remove from the accounts the cost of the old truck and		
	accumulated depreciation thereon, and to record the new truck		
	at cost equal to the book value of the old truck traded in plus		
	cash paid.		

An alternative method of recording trade-ins (not acceptable for income tax purposes but having strong theoretical support) calls for recognizing a gain or loss on the exchange in an amount equal to the difference between the book value of the old asset and its estimated fair market value at the time of the trade-in. The validity of this alternative method rests upon the assumption that the trade-in allowance represents the fair market value of the old asset being traded in. If we make that assumption for the preceding example of the trading-in of a truck, the journal entry would be as follows:

Trade-in:	*Truck (new)*... **4,000**	
Alternative	*Accumulated Depreciation: Trucks*....................... **2,400**	
Method	*Truck (old)*.................................	*3,200*
	Cash...	*2,800*
	Gain on Disposal of Plant Assets	*400*
	To remove from the accounts the cost of the old truck and accumulated depreciation thereon, and to record the new truck at its list price.	

NATURAL RESOURCES

Accounting for natural resources

Mining properties, oil and gas wells, and tracts of standing timber are leading examples of natural resources or "wasting assets." The distinguishing characteristics of these assets are that they are physically consumed and converted into inventory. In a theoretical sense, a coal mine might even be regarded as an "underground inventory of coal"; however, such an inventory is certainly not a current asset. In the balance sheet, mining property and other natural resources are usually listed as a separate topic.

Natural resources should be recorded in the accounts at cost. As the resource is removed through the process of mining, cutting, or drilling, the asset account must be proportionately reduced. The carrying value (book value) of a coal mine, for example, is reduced by a small amount for each ton of coal mined. The original cost of the mine is thus gradually transferred out of the asset account and becomes part of the cost of the coal mined and sold.

Depletion. The term *depletion* is used to describe the pro rata allocation of cost of a natural resource to the units removed. Depletion is computed by dividing the cost of the natural resource by the estimated available number of units, such as barrels of oil or tons of coal. The depletion charge per unit is then multiplied by the number of units actually removed during the year to determine the total depletion charge for that period.

To illustrate the computation of depletion expense, assume that the sum of $500,000 is paid for a coal mine believed to contain 1 million tons of coal. The depletion charge per unit is $500,000 ÷ 1,000,000, or 50 cents a ton.

If we assume that 200,000 tons of coal were mined and sold during the first year of operation, the depletion charge for the year would be 50 cents × 200,000, or $100,000. The journal entry necessary at the end of the year to record depletion of the mine would be as follows:

Recording *Depletion*	*Depletion Expense* *100,000*	
	Accumulated Depletion	*100,000*
	To record depletion expense for the year; 200,000 tons *mined @ 50 cents per ton.*	

In reporting natural resources in the balance sheet, accumulated depletion should be deducted from the cost of the property. A recent balance sheet of Anaconda Company, for example, reports its natural resources as follows:

Natural *Resources* *in the* *Balance* *Sheet*	*Mines and mining claims, water rights and lands, less accumulated* *depletion of $149,874,000*	*$138,410,000*
	Timberlands and phosphate and gravel deposits, less accumulated *depletion of $5,602,000*	*2,111,000*

Development costs. The cost of a natural resource may include not only the purchase price of the property, but also expenditures for recording fees, surveying, and a variety of exploratory and developmental charges. If such expenditures are included in the cost of the natural resource, they will be allocated to production costs as a part of the depletion charge. Buildings erected at a mine site or drilling site may be useful only at that particular location; consequently, such assets should be depreciated over their normal useful lives, or over the useful life of the natural resource, whichever is shorter. Often it is convenient to compute depreciation on such assets by the units-of-output method, thus relating the depreciation expense to the rate of exploitation of the natural resource.

Some exploratory and developmental expenditures will prove to be unproductive; these expenditures should be recognized as losses or expenses of the current period and not carried forward as assets. Most natural resource companies engage in a continuous program of exploration and development of new areas. Since outlays for exploration and development thus become normal and continuous, they are usually charged to expense in the period in which incurred. This method of accounting is allowed for income tax purposes and is condoned by accountants more on the grounds of expediency and conservatism than on theoretical considerations.

INTANGIBLE ASSETS

As the word *intangible* suggests, assets in this classification have no physical substance. Leading examples are goodwill, leaseholds, copyrights, franchises, licenses, and trademarks. Intangible assets are classified on the balance sheet as a subgroup of plant assets. However, not all assets which lack physical substance are regarded as intangible assets; an account receivable, for example, or a prepaid expense, is of nonphysical nature but is classified as a current asset and is never regarded as an intangible. In brief, intangible assets are noncurrent and nonphysical.

The basis of valuation for intangible assets is cost. In some companies, certain intangible assets such as trademarks may be of great importance but may have been acquired without the incurring of any cost. An intangible asset should appear on the balance sheet *only* if a cost of acquisition or development has been incurred.

Since a variety of items is included in the intangible asset category, it will be helpful to emphasize some of the characteristics common to most intangible assets. Many types of intangible assets are not transferable, and therefore have no liquidation value or realizable value. Goodwill, for example, is so closely related to the business as a whole that it cannot be sold without disrupting operations. Because of this lack of realizable value, many companies choose to carry their intangible assets on the balance sheet at a nominal valuation of $1; International Business Machines Corporation and the Polaroid Corporation are prominent examples.

There is little doubt, however, that in some companies the intangible assets, such as goodwill or trademarks, may be vitally important to profitable operations. The carrying of intangible assets on the balance sheet is justified only when there is good evidence that future earnings will be derived from these assets.

Classification

Intangible assets have traditionally been classified for discussion purposes into two broad groups, as follows:

1. Those with limited useful lives, such as patents and copyrights

2. Those with an unlimited term of existence, such as a perpetual franchise granted to a public utility

This classification emphasizes that the cost of an intangible asset with a limited useful life must be written off to expense during its years of usefulness, whereas a "permanent" intangible asset need not be written off. Even though an intangible asset may have an unlimited legal life, the probability of an unending economic usefulness may well be open to question.

Amortization

The term *amortization* is used to describe the systematic write-off to expense of the cost of an intangible asset over the periods of its economic usefulness. The usual accounting entry for amortization consists of a debit to an expense account and a credit to the intangible asset account. There is no theoretical objection to crediting an accumulated amortization account rather than the intangible asset, but this method is seldom encountered in current practice.

Although it is difficult to estimate the useful life of an intangible such as goodwill, it is highly probable that such an asset will not contribute to future earnings on a permanent basis. The cost of the intangible asset should, therefore, be deducted from revenues during the years in which it may be expected to aid in producing revenues.[1]

Arbitrary write-off of intangibles. Arbitrary, lump-sum write-off of intangibles (leaving a nominal balance of $1 in the accounts) is a practice sometimes found in companies which have not adopted a systematic amortization program. Arguments for this practice emphasize the element of conservatism, the practical difficulty of estimating an appropriate period for amortization, and the absence of any realizable value for intangibles. Accountants generally agree that whenever any event occurs which indicates that an intangible has lost all value, immediate write-off of the entire cost is warranted regardless of whether an amortization program has previously been followed. Lump-sum write-offs of intangible assets should be reported as extraordinary items in the income statement.

On the other hand, arbitrary write-offs of valuable, revenue-producing intangible assets are no more in accordance with accounting theory than would be the arbitrary write-off of land or buildings.

Goodwill

Businessmen and lawyers used the term *goodwill* in a variety of meanings before it became a part of accounting terminology. One of the more common meanings of goodwill in a nonaccounting sense concerns the benefits derived from a favorable reputation among customers. To accountants, however, goodwill has a very specific meaning not necessarily limited to customer relationships. It means the *present value of future earnings in excess of the earnings normally realized in the industry.* Above-average earnings may arise, not only from favorable customer relations, but also from such factors as location, monopoly, manufacturing efficiency, and superior management.

The existence of the intangible asset of goodwill is indicated when an entire business is sold for a price in excess of the fair market value of the other assets. The willingness of the purchaser of a going business to pay a price greater than the sum of the values of the tangible assets indicates that he is paying for intangible assets as well. If the business does not include such specific intangibles as patents or franchises, the extra amount paid is presumably for goodwill. Superior earnings in past years are of significance to a prospective purchaser of an enterprise only to the extent that he believes such earnings may continue after he acquires the business. If the prospective purchaser believes that by purchasing a particular company with a record of superior earnings in the past, he will receive these above-average earnings in the future, he may reasonably be expected to pay a premium price for the business. The premium which he pays represents the cost of purchased goodwill and may properly be recorded in the accounting records of the new owner in a Goodwill account.

Assume that two businesses in the same line of trade are for sale and

---

[1] Present tax regulations do not permit the amortization of goodwill in computing taxable income.

that the normal rate of earnings on capital invested in this industry is 10% a year. The relative earning power of the two companies during the past five years is indicated by the following schedule.

	Company X	Company Y
Net assets other than goodwill	*$1,000,000*	*$1,000,000*
Normal rate of earnings on invested capital.	*10%*	*10%*
Average net income for past five years.	*$ 100,000*	*$ 140,000*
Net income computed at normal rate (10%) on net assets other than goodwill	*100,000*	*100,000*
Annual earnings in excess of average for the industry	*$ 000*	*$ 40,000*

A prospective investor would be willing to pay more for Company Y than for Company X because Y has a record of superior earnings which will presumably continue for some time in the future. Company Y has goodwill; Company X does not. Very few concerns are able to maintain above-average earnings for more than a few years. Consequently, the purchaser of a business will usually limit his payment for goodwill to not more than four or five times the excess annual earnings.

Estimating the amount of goodwill. Goodwill is to be recorded in the accounts only when paid for; this situation usually occurs only when a going business is purchased in its entirety. When ownership of a business changes hands, any amount paid for goodwill rests on the assumption that earnings in excess of normal will continue under the new ownership. The following are methods of estimating a value for goodwill:

1. Arbitrary agreement between buyer and seller of the business may be reached on the amount of goodwill. For example, it might be agreed that the fair market value of the net tangible assets is $1,000,000 and that the total purchase price for the business will be $1,100,000, thus providing a $100,000 payment for goodwill. The term *net tangible assets* may require explanation. *Net assets* means assets minus liabilities; *net tangible assets* therefore means all assets (except the intangibles) minus liabilities. Another way of computing the amount of net tangible assets is merely to deduct the intangible assets from the stockholders' equity.

2. Goodwill may be determined as a multiple of the average profits of past years. For example, assume that a business has earned an average annual net income of $25,000 during the past five years. The business is sold for the book value of the net tangible assets, plus two years' average net income. The payment for goodwill is, therefore, $50,000. This method may be criticized because it ignores completely the concept of *excess* earnings as a basis for estimating goodwill.

3. Goodwill may be determined as a multiple of the amount by which the average annual earnings exceed normal earnings. To illustrate, assume the following data:

Goodwill as Multiple of Excess Earnings

Average investment in the business	*$100,000*
Average annual earnings (rate of 14%)	*$ 14,000*
Normal earnings for this industry (rate of 10%)	*10,000*
Average earnings in excess of normal.	*$ 4,000*
Multiple of excess annual earnings	*4*
Goodwill.	*$ 16,000*

The multiple applied to the excess annual earnings may vary widely from perhaps 1 to 10, depending on the nature of the industry and the reliance placed on the earnings projections. This method is more in accord with the concept of goodwill as earning power in *excess* of normal, whereas method 2 relates goodwill to the *total* profits.

4. Goodwill may be determined as the capitalized value of excess earning power, using a capitalization rate considered normal in the industry. Assume that the normal rate of earnings in a given line of business is 10% and that a particular company presents the following picture:

Goodwill Based on Capitalization of Excess Earnings

Average investment in the business	*$100,000*
Average annual earnings (rate of 14%).	*$ 14,000*
Normal earnings for this industry (rate of 10%).	*10,000*
Average earnings in excess of normal	*$ 4,000*
Goodwill, computed by capitalizing excess earnings of 10% *($4,000 ÷ 0.10)*	*$ 40,000*

Patents

A patent is an exclusive right granted by the federal government for manufacture, use, and sale of a particular product. Patents, like other intangible assets, should be recorded in the accounts at cost. Since patents may be acquired by purchase or may be obtained directly from the government by the inventor, the cost may consist of the purchase price or of the expenditures for research and development leading to the application for the patent. In addition, cost may include legal fees for obtaining the patent and for infringement suits. Companies which carry on extensive research and development programs on a permanent basis often treat the costs of such work as expense when incurred, on the grounds that constant research iş necessary merely to maintain a competitive position in the industry.

Patents are granted for a period of 17 years, and the period of amortization must not exceed that period. However, if the patent is likely to lose its usefulness in less than 17 years, amortization should be based on the shorter period of estimated useful life. Assume that a patent is purchased from the inventor at a cost of $30,000, after five years of the legal life have expired. The remaining *legal* life is, therefore, 12 years, but if the estimated *useful* life is only five years, amortization should be based on this shorter period. The entry to be made to record the annual amortization expense would be:

Amortiza-
tion of
Patent

Amortization Expense: Patents	**6,000**	
Patents		**6,000**
To amortize cost of patent on a straight-line basis and estimated		
life of five years.		

Copyrights

A copyright is an exclusive right granted to protect the production and sale of literary or artistic materials for a period of 28 years. The cost of obtaining a copyright is minor and therefore chargeable to expense when paid. Only when a copyright is purchased will the expenditure be material enough to warrant capitalization and spreading over the useful life. The revenues from copyrights are usually limited to only a few years, and the purchase cost should, of course, be amortized over the years in which the revenues are expected.

Trademarks

A permanent exclusive right to the use of a trademark, brand name, or commercial symbol may be obtained by registering it. Because of the unlimited legal life, a trademark may be carried without amortization at the original cost. If the use of the trademark is abandoned or if its contribution to earnings becomes doubtful, immediate write-off of the cost is called for. The outlay for securing a trademark is often not consequential, and it is treated as expense when incurred.

Leasehold improvements

When buildings or other improvements are constructed on leased property by the lessee, the costs should be recorded in a Leasehold Improvements account, and written off as expense during the remaining life of the lease or of the estimated useful life of the building, whichever is shorter. This procedure is usually followed even though the lessee has an option to renew the lease, because there is no assurance in advance that conditions will warrant the exercise of the renewal clause.

Other intangibles and deferred charges

Many other types of intangible assets are found in the published balance sheets of large corporations. Some examples are oil exploration costs, formulas, processes, designs, research and development costs, franchises, name lists, and film rights.

Intangibles, particularly those with limited lives, are sometimes classified as "deferred charges" in the balance sheet. A *deferred charge* is an expenditure that is expected to yield benefits for several accounting periods, and should be amortized over its estimated useful life. Included in this category are such items as bond issuance costs, plant rearrangement and moving costs, start-up costs, and organization costs. The distinction between intangibles and deferred charges is not an important one; both represent "bundles of services" in the form of long-term prepayments awaiting allocation to those accounting periods in which the services will be consumed.

DEMONSTRATION PROBLEM

After several years of managerial experience in the retailing of sporting goods, Arthur Barr decided to buy an established business in this field. He is now attempting to make a choice among three similar companies which are available for purchase. All three companies have been in business for exactly five years. The balance sheets presented by the three companies are summarized as follows:

	Company A	Company B	Company C
Assets			
Cash	$ 45,000	$ 18,000	$ 25,000
Accounts receivable................	95,000	119,000	85,000
Inventories	212,500	140,000	180,000
Plant and equipment (net)	90,000	120,000	100,000
Intangible assets	7,500	3,000	
Total assets......................	$450,000	$400,000	$390,000
Liabilities & Stockholders' Equity			
Current liabilities...................	$208,000	$185,000	$200,000
Capital stock	150,000	100,000	25,000
Retained earnings	92,000	115,000	165,000
Total liabilities & stockholders' equity	$450,000	$400,000	$390,000

The average net income of the three companies during the past five years had been as follows: Company A, $35,600; Company B, $29,300; Company C, $38,200.

With the permission of the owners of the three companies, Barr arranged for a certified public accountant to examine the accounting records of the companies. This investigation disclosed the following information:

Accounts receivable. In Company A, no provision for uncollectible accounts had been made at any time, and no accounts receivable had been written off. Numerous past-due receivables were on the books, and the estimated uncollectible items which had accumulated during the past five years amounted to $6,000. In both Company B and Company C, the receivables appeared to be carried at net realizable value.

Inventories. Company B had adopted the first-in, first-out method of inventory valuation when first organized but had changed to the last-in, first-out method after one year. As a result of this change in method of accounting for inventories, the present balance sheet figure for inventories was approximately $13,500 less than replacement cost. The other two companies had used the first-in, first-out method continuously, and their present inventories were approximately equal to replacement cost.

Plant and equipment. Each of the companies owns a building, acquired at the beginning of Year 1 at a cost of $52,500, which had an estimated useful life of 20 years with no residual value. Company A had taken no depreciation on its building; Company B had used straight-line depreciation at 5% annually; and Company C had depreciated its building by using the sum-of-the-years'-digits method. All plant assets other than buildings had been depreciated on a straight-line basis by the three companies. Barr believed that the book value of the plant assets of all three companies would approximate fair market value if depreciation were uniformly computed on a straight-line basis.

In addition to the foregoing, the following items relate to plant and equipment: A fully depreciated machine for which Company A paid $3,500 is no longer in use but has not been formally retired. Company B sold an asset in Year 4 and recorded the transaction by a debit to Cash and a credit to Machinery for $4,000. The cost of the machine was $10,000 and the book value was $5,400. No depreciation was recorded on this machine in Year 5. Installation costs on another machine amounting to $2,400 were charged to expense by Company C at the beginning of Year 3. The machine is being depreciated on a straight-line basis over a five-year life.

Intangible assets. The $7,500 reported as an intangible asset by Company A represents the cost of a patent acquired two years ago. The patent has not been amortized, although its useful life will probably not extend beyond four more years. The $3,000 item in the balance sheet of Company B is the cost of a nonrecurring advertising campaign conducted during the first year of operation.

Current liabilities. The following accrued liabilities have not been recorded by Companies A and C:

	Company A	Company C
End of Year 4	$600	$360
End of Year 5	420	800

Barr is willing to pay for net assets (excluding cash but including the patent) at book value, plus an amount for goodwill equal to three times the average annual net income for the past five years in excess of 10% on current stockholders' equity, as adjusted (excluding goodwill). Cash will not be included in the transfer of assets.

Instructions
a. Prepare a revised summary of balance sheet data after correcting all errors made by the companies. In addition to correcting errors, make the necessary changes to apply straight-line depreciation and first-in, first-out inventory methods in all three companies.
b. Determine revised amounts for average net income of the three companies after taking into consideration the correction of errors and changes in accounting methods called for in (a) above.

c. Determine the price which Barr should offer for each of the three companies. Compute all amounts to the nearest dollar.

QUESTIONS

1. Company A's balance sheet shows accumulated depreciation on machinery and equipment of $100,000 and Company B shows accumulated depreciation of $50,000. Both companies are considering the acquisition of new equipment costing $60,000. From the information given, can you determine which company is in a better position to purchase the new equipment for cash? Explain.

2. The Damon Company purchased machinery with a list price of $36,000 and credit terms of 2/10, n/30. Payment was made immediately. Freight charges on the machinery amounted to $1,200 and the labor cost of installing the machines in the plant was $2,000. During the unloading and installation work a part of the machinery fell off the loading platform and was damaged. Replacement of the damaged parts cost $1,800. After the machinery had been in use for three months it was thoroughly cleaned and lubricated at a cost of $400. State the total amount which should be capitalized by charge to the Machinery account.

3. Factory machinery owned by the Dodge Company is considered physically capable of being used for 15 years, but management believes that the development of new, more efficient types of machines will make it necessary to replace the present equipment within 10 years. After using the machines for two years, the company changed from its customary one shift per day to operating three shifts per day. The new three-shift operation was considered necessary for about a year to meet a temporary increase in demand resulting from a strike affecting competing plants.

    Assuming that the company employs straight-line depreciation, what period of useful life should be used? Should the company increase its depreciation charges proportionately during the year when operations were increased from one to three shifts daily?

4. Identify the following expenditures as capital expenditures or revenue expenditures:
    a. Purchased new spark plugs at a cost of $9.20 for two-year-old delivery truck.
    b. Installed an escalator at a cost of $3,800 in a three-story building which had previously been used for some years without elevators or escalators.
    c. Purchased an electric pencil sharpener at a cost of $3.95.
    d. Immediately after acquiring new delivery truck at a cost of $3,800, paid $75 to have the name of the store and other advertising material painted on the truck.
    e. Painted delivery truck at a cost of $82 after two years of use.

5. Criticize the following quotation:
    "We shall have no difficulty in paying for new plant assets needed during the coming year because our estimated outlays for new equipment amount

to only $20,000, and we have more than twice that amount in our depreciation reserves at present."

6. Two businessmen were discussing the accounting issues involved in distinguishing between capital expenditures and revenue expenditures. Jones made the following statement: "A good example of a revenue expenditure is the cost of painting our factory building and of replacing broken window glass all the time. Certainly all costs of this nature should always be charged to expense."

Smith replied as follows: "Your examples are good but on the other hand we recently had a rather special situation in which we capitalized the cost of repainting a building and of replacing a large number of window panes."

"You were way off base," said Jones. "The Internal Revenue Service won't allow it and your CPA won't approve your financial statements."

Evaluate these statements. What kind of special situation might Smith be referring to?

7. Under what circumstances does good accounting call for a mining company to depreciate a plant asset over a period shorter than the normal useful life?

8. Lead Hill Corporation recognizes $1 of depletion for each ton of ore mined. During the current year the company mined 600,000 tons but sold only 500,000 tons, as it was attempting to build up inventories in anticipation of a possible strike by employees. How much depletion should be deducted from revenues of the current year?

9. Under what circumstances should goodwill be recorded in the accounts?

10. In reviewing the financial statements of Digital Products Co., with a view to investing in the company's stock, you notice that net tangible assets total $1 million, that goodwill is listed as $100,000, and that average earnings for the past five years have been $20,000 a year. How would these relationships influence your thinking about the company?

11. Space Research Company paid $500,000 cash to acquire the entire business of Saturn Company, a strong competitor. In negotiating this lump-sum price for the business, a valuation of $60,000 was assigned to goodwill, representing four times the amount by which Saturn Company's annual earnings had exceeded normal earnings in the industry. Assuming that the goodwill is recorded on the books of Space Research Company, should it remain there permanently or be amortized? What basis of amortization might be used?

12. After four years of using a machine acquired at a cost of $15,000, Kral Construction Company determined that the original estimated life of 10 years had been too short and that a total useful life of 12 years was a more reasonable estimate. Explain briefly the method that should be used to revise the depreciation program, assuming that straight-line depreciation has been used.

13. **a.** Give some reasons why a company may change its depreciation policy for financial reporting purposes from an accelerated-depreciation method to the straight-line method.
   b. Is it possible for a corporation to use accelerated depreciation for income tax purposes and straight-line depreciation for financial reporting purposes?

14. A change in depreciation accounting by the United States Steel Corporation in 1968 resulted in the following operating results:

	1968 Income (Millions)	
	Before Adjustment	*As Adjusted*
First quarter	$ 50.8	$ 69.7
Second quarter	77.7	102.9
Third quarter	11.0	33.0
Nine months	$139.5	$205.6
Fourth quarter	19.8	47.7
Year	$159.3	$253.3

The effect of this change was to increase reported income for the year by $94 million, or $1.74 per share of common stock.

a. Determine the approximate number of shares of common stock that United States Steel Corporation has outstanding. What were the approximate earnings per share before the adjustment for depreciation?

b. The change in depreciation accounting resulted in an increase of 32% in the income of the second quarter and an increase of 200% in the income of the third quarter. Explain why the effect on the income of the third quarter was so much larger.

EXERCISES

1. John Allen acquired three machines at an auction for $11,300. He paid $700 to deliver the machines to his place of business and $800 interest on money borrowed to pay for the machines. The estimated fair market value of the machines and the costs in preparing the machines for use are approximately as follows:

	Machine No. 1	*Machine No. 2*	*Machine No. 3*
Fair market value	$5,000	$8,000	$2,000
Installation costs	300	650	150
Costs of trial runs	100	120	*None*

Determine the cost of each machine for accounting purposes, assuming that the auction and delivery cost is apportioned to the three machines on the basis of relative market value.

2. A machine acquired at a cost of $45,800 had an estimated life of five years. Residual salvage value was estimated to be $800. Compute the annual depreciation charges during the useful life of the machine under each of the following methods of depreciation:

    a. Straight-line
    b. Sum-of-the-years'-digits
    c. Double-declining-balance

3. A truck with a book value of $800 is traded in on a new truck with a list price of $8,000. The trade-in allowance on the old truck is $1,200.
    a. How much cash must be paid for the new truck?
    b. What is the cost basis of the new truck for income tax purposes?
    c. How much depreciation should be recorded on the new truck for the first year of use, assuming a four-year life, a residual value of $1,000, and the use of straight-line depreciation?

4. A tractor which cost $4,800 had an estimated useful life of five years and an estimated salvage value of $800. Straight-line depreciation was used. Give the entry to record the disposal of the tractor under each of the following alternative assumptions:
    a. The tractor was sold for cash of $3,000 after two years' use.
    b. After three years the tractor was traded in on another tractor with a list price of $6,000. Trade-in allowance was $2,700. The trade-in was recorded in a manner acceptable for income tax purposes.
    c. The tractor was scrapped after four years' use. Since scrap dealers were unwilling to pay anything for the tractor, it was given to a scrap dealer for his services in removing it.

5. Platt River Mining Company started mining activities early in 1971. At the end of the year its accountant prepared the following summary of its mining costs:

Labor	$1,700,000
Materials	175,000
Miscellaneous	385,200

These costs do not include any charges for depletion or depreciation. Data relating to assets used in mining the ore follow:

Cost of mine (estimated deposit, 10 million tons; residual value of the mine estimated at $300,000)	$1,500,000
Buildings (estimated life, 15 years; no residual value).	132,000
Equipment (useful life, six years regardless of number of tons mined; residual value $30,000)	240,000

During the year 800,000 tons (8%) of ore were mined, of which 600,000 tons were sold. It is estimated that it will take at least 15 years to extract the ore.

Determine the cost that should be assigned to the inventory of unsold ore at the end of 1971.

6. The Fremont Company has net assets (total assets less all liabilities) of $200,000 and has earned an average return of 5% on average sales of $650,000 per year for the past several years. An investor is negotiating to purchase the company. He offers to pay an amount equal to the book value for the net assets (assets minus liabilities) and to assume all liabilities. In addition, he is willing to pay for goodwill an amount equal to net earnings in excess of 12% on net assets, capitalized at a rate of 20%.

On the basis of this agreement, what price should the investor offer for the Fremont Company?

PROBLEMS

13-1 Crosby Media Company purchased equipment on July 1, 1968, at a cost of $99,500. Useful life was estimated to be 10 years and scrap value $4,500. Crosby Media Company depreciates its plant assets by the straight-line method and closes its books annually on June 30.

In June, 1971, after considerable experience with the equipment, the company decided that the estimated total life should be revised from 10 years to 6 years and the residual scrap value lowered from $4,500 to $3,000. This revised estimate was made prior to recording depreciation for the fiscal year ended June 30, 1971.

On December 31, 1972, the equipment was sold for $17,125 cash.

Instructions

Prepare journal entries to record all the above transactions and the depreciation expense from July 1, 1968 to December 31, 1972. Do not prepare closing entries.

13-2 Madison Mouldings, Inc., is engaged in a high technology industry, in which products and methods of producing them change very rapidly. Because of the significance of the obsolescence factor, the company is interested in depreciating some newly acquired equipment by allocating most of the cost to the early years of estimated useful life. The president of Madison Mouldings, Inc., has asked that comparative figures be developed showing the annual depreciation charges under (a) the straight-line method and (b) the sum-of-the-years'-digits method.

The equipment was acquired on January 1, 1969, at a cost of $312,000. Estimated useful life is five years, and residual value is estimated as $12,000.

Instructions

Using column headings as shown below, prepare *separate* five-year depreciation schedules for
a. The straight-line method
b. The sum-of-the-years'-digits method

Year Ending Dec. 31	*Cost of Equipment*	*Residual Value*	*Amount to Be Depreciated*	*Annual Depreciation Expense*	*Accumulated Depreciation*	*Book Value*

13-3 The Kansas Steel Corporation has acquired four machines in recent years, but management has given little consideration to depreciation policies. At the time of acquisition of each machine, a different bookkeeper was employed; consequently, various methods of depreciation have been adopted for the several machines. Information concerning the four machines appears below:

Machine	Date Acquired	Cost	Estimated Useful Life, Years	Estimated Residual Value	Method of Depreciation
A	Jan. 1, 1970	$ 81,000	6	None	Fixed-percentage-on-declining-balance
B	June 30, 1970	168,000	8	10%	Straight-line
C	Jan. 1, 1971	56,000	10	$1,000	Sum-of-the-years'-digits
D	Jan. 1, 1972	66,000	12	None	Fixed-percentage-on-declining-balance

Instructions

a. Compute the amount of accumulated depreciation, if any, on each machine at December 31, 1971. For machines A and D, assume that the depreciation rate was double the rate which would be applicable under the straight-line method.

b. Prepare a depreciation schedule for use in the computation of the 1972 depreciation expense. Use the following column headings:

Machine	Method of Depreciation	Date of Acquisition	Cost	Estimated Residual Value	Amount to Be Depreciated	Useful Life, Years	Accumulated Depreciation, Dec. 31, 1971	Depreciation Expense, 1972

c. Prepare a journal entry to record the depreciation expense for 1972.

13-4 On July 1, 1971, Louisiana Milling Company purchased a new machine at the advertised price of $36,000. The terms of payment were 2/10, n/30 and payment was made immediately, including a 4% state sales tax. On July 3, the machine was delivered; Louisiana Milling Company paid freight charges of $788.80 and assigned its own employees to the task of installation. The labor costs for installing the machine amounted to $2,520. During the process of installation, carelessness by a workman caused damage to an adjacent machine, with resulting repairs of $320.

On November 10, 1971, after more than four months of satisfactory operations, the machine was thoroughly inspected, cleaned, and oiled at a cost of $420.

The useful life of the machine was estimated to be 10 years and the scrap value to be zero. The policy of the Louisiana Milling Company is to use straight-line depreciation and to begin depreciation as of the first of the month in which a plant asset is acquired. During 1971 and 1972, however, numerous changes in the company's accounting personnel were responsible for a number of errors and deviations from policy.

At December 31, 1972, the unaudited financial statements of the Louisiana

Milling Company showed the machine to be carried at a cost of $35,280 and the accumulated depreciation as $5,292. Net income reported for 1971 was $99,200 and for 1972 it was $110,600.

Instructions
a. Prepare correct journal entries for all the above transactions from July 1 to December 31, 1972. Include the year-end entry for depreciation and the related closing entry.
b. Compute the correct balances for the Machinery account and for the Accumulated Depreciation account at December 31, 1972.
c. Compute revised figures for net income for 1971 and 1972. Disregard income taxes.

13-5 On January 1, 1971, Cal-Crude Company, as established concern, borrowed $4.5 million from the Bank of Tulsa, issuing a note payable in five years with interest at 8% payable annually, on December 31. Also on January 1, the company purchased for $2.4 million the Black Sands East oil field estimated to contain at least 6 million barrels of crude oil. Movable oil-field equipment having an estimated useful life of five years and no residual value was acquired at a cost of $78,000 on January 1.
  During January the company spent $375,000 in developing the oil field and several shallow wells were brought into production. The established accounting policy of the company was to treat drilling and development costs of this type as expense of the period in which the work was done.
  Construction of a pipeline was completed on May 1, 1971, at a cost of $720,000. Although this pipeline was physically capable of being used for 10 years or more, its economic usefulness was limited to the productive life of the wells; therefore, the depreciation method employed was based on the estimated number of barrels of crude oil to be produced.
  Operating costs incurred during 1971 (other than depreciation and depletion) amounted to $480,000; 690,000 barrels of oil were produced and sold.
  In January, 1972, additional drilling costs were incurred in the amount of $300,000, and the estimated total capacity of the oil field was raised from the original 6 million barrels to 7,770,000 barrels, including the oil produced to date.
  Cash operating costs for 1972 amounted to $750,000, in addition to the $300,000 of drilling cost mentioned above. Oil production totaled 2.4 million barrels, of which all but 240,000 barrels were sold during the year.

Instructions
Prepare journal entries to record the transactions of 1971 and 1972, including the setting up of the inventory at December 31, 1972. The inventory valuation should include an appropriate portion of the operating costs of the year, including depreciation and depletion (debit Inventory of Oil and credit respective expense accounts for costs allocable to ending inventory).

13-6 On January 2, 1972, the Goodsen Company is considering purchase of the assets, exclusive of cash, of Trader's Paradise, a single proprietorship owned by John Martin. Trader's Paradise has been a going business for six years and has had average net income of $25,000 (excluding income taxes) during this period.
  The purchase plan calls for a cash payment of $100,000 and a 7½% note payable, due January 2, 1974, with interest payable annually, as payment for the

assets, including goodwill but excluding the cash of $12,500, after any necessary adjustments have been made. The Goodsen Company has agreed to assume all the liabilities of the single proprietorship. The goodwill is to be determined as four times the average excess earnings over a normal rate of return of 12½% (excluding income taxes) on the present *net tangible assets* (capital less patents and goodwill).

The balance sheet for Trader's Paradise on December 31, 1971, follows:

Assets

Cash			$ 12,500
Other current assets			60,000
Plant and equipment:			
Land		$35,000	
Buildings	$122,000		
Less: Accumulated depreciation	31,500	90,500	
Machinery	$ 95,000		
Less: Accumulated depreciation	64,500	30,500	
Equipment	$ 60,000		
Less: Accumulated depreciation	33,500	26,500	182,500
Patents			52,500
Goodwill			10,000
Total assets			$317,500

Liabilities & Owner's Equity

Current liabilities	$ 51,250
Long-term liabilities:	
Mortgage note payable, 6½%	91,750
John Martin, capital	174,500
Total liabilities & owner's equity	$317,500

The goodwill was recorded on the books three years ago when Martin decided that the increasing profitability of the company should be recognized. The patent appears at original cost; it was acquired by purchase six years ago from a competitor who had recorded amortization for two years on the basis of its legal life. The patent is considered to be very valuable to the business and should have a useful life equal to its legal life (15 years from date Martin acquired it).

Instructions

a. Prepare any adjusting entries needed on the books of Trader's Paradise as a preliminary step toward carrying out the sale agreement.

b. Determine the amount to be paid by Goodsen Company for goodwill after considering the effects of the entries in (a).

c. Prepare the entries on the books of Trader's Paradise to record the sale to Goodsen Company.

d. Prepare the entries on Goodsen Company's books to record the purchase of assets (including the goodwill as determined above) and the assumption of liabilities of the Trader's Paradise. The Goodsen Company records the assets acquired net of depreciation.

13-7 On January 1, 1971, the Sullivan Manufacturing Co. purchased a tract of land on which two old buildings were located. The old buildings were torn down and construction of a new plant was begun at once. All expenditures relating to the new plant were charged to a single account entitled Land and Buildings.

Construction of the new plant was completed on November 30, 1971, and regular production operations were begun in the new facilities on December 1, 1971. The balance in the Land and Buildings account at the end of the year was $910,000, determined as follows:

Debit entries:

Cost of land and old buildings purchased as site for construction of new plant (appraised value of old buildings, $40,000)	*$169,500*
Legal fees involved in securing title to property	*300*
Cost of demolishing old buildings	*12,700*
Surveying and grading costs	*14,000*
Contract price of new building, $465,000, paid for by delivery to contractor of $480,000 par value of United States government bonds, which had cost the Sullivan Manufacturing Co. $490,000 and had a market value at date of delivery to contractor of $465,000	*490,000*
Salary paid R. Brown, plant engineer, assigned to supervise construction of new plant (Jan. 1 to Nov. 30)	*12,000*
Paving of plant parking lot	*7,000*
Cost of machinery badly damaged by fire while awaiting installation in new building. Sold as scrap. Not insured	*40,000*
Machinery for new plant, including units to replace those damaged by fire	*120,000*
Cost of installing machinery in new plant	*6,000*
Landscaping of grounds	*4,000*
Office equipment	*24,000*
Rent for December on old plant. Vacated on Nov. 30; lease expired Dec. 12	*2,000*
Retaining walls and fences	*14,000*
Payment to architect for plans and for services during construction	*19,000*
Insurance on building during construction	*2,000*
Repairs to building damaged by earthquake on Dec. 20 (not insured)	*3,500*
Total debits	*$940,000*

Credit entries:

Proceeds from sale of materials from old buildings demolished	*$10,000*	
Proceeds from sale of machinery damaged by fire	*20,000*	
Total credits		*30,000*
Balance, Dec. 31, 1971		*$910,000*

Information for use in computing depreciation follows:

Asset	Useful Life, Years	Residual Value, %
Building...............................	20	10
Land improvements	20	
Machinery	15	10
Office equipment	10	10

Instructions

a. Reclassify the items in the Land and Buildings account to the proper ledger accounts. This reclassification may conveniently be made on an analytical work sheet with the following column headings:

Entries to account	Land Buildings	Land	Building	Other Accounts	
				Title	Amount

b. Prepare a depreciation schedule showing the fractional-year depreciation for 1971 (straight-line method) for each type of depreciable asset.

Asset	Date of Completion	Cost	Residual Value 10%	Amount to be Depreciated	Useful Life, Months	Depreciation Expense for 1971 (1 mo.)

14

Consolidated financial statements

Since corporations are usually granted the power to hold title to any form of property, one corporation may own shares of stock in another. When one corporation controls another corporation through the ownership of a majority of its capital stock, the controlling corporation is called a *parent* company, and the company whose stock is owned is called a *subsidiary* company. Because both the parent and subsidiary companies are legal entities, separate financial statements may be prepared for each company. However, it may also be useful to prepare financial statements for the affiliated companies as if they were a single unified business. Such statements are called *consolidated financial statements.*

Nature and advantages of corporate affiliation

If Corporation A owns a majority of the voting shares of Corporation B, A is said to own a *controlling* interest in B. If A Company owns 80% of the outstanding common shares of B Company, for example, note how the inter-company power structure will operate: The stockholders of A Company will elect the board of directors of A Company, who will in turn appoint the officers of A Company. The managers of A Company will manage and control all property owned by A Company. Included in A Company's property is 80% of the common stock of B Company. Therefore when the time comes to vote these shares, A Company's directors can determine how these votes should be cast and can elect the board of directors of B Company. Through B Company's board of directors the officers and directors of A Company can control B Company's property and actions. In effect A and B Companies are operating under the unified control of the officers of A Company, control which is exercised through stock ownership. For this reason, it may be useful to develop financial statements for the economic entity formed by the affiliated companies. Consolidated financial statements provide this kind of financial perspective.

There are a number of economic, technical, and legal advantages which encourage businessmen to operate through separate parent and subsidiaries rather than one single corporate entity. As a result corporate affiliations are common in this country. A majority of the companies whose stock is listed on the New York Stock Exchange have one or more subsidiaries and publish *consolidated* financial statements. Anyone who uses corporate financial information will find it useful to know something about the basic principles of consolidation, as an aid in interpreting the data contained in consolidated statements. In this chapter these basic principles of consolidation will be described and illustrated.

Consolidation at date of acquisition

A consolidated balance sheet is prepared by combining the elements that appear in the individual statements of the parent and subsidiary companies. In the combining process, certain adjustments are made to eliminate duplication and to reflect the assets, liabilities, and stockholders' equity from the viewpoint of a single economic entity.

To illustrate, suppose P Company acquired all the outstanding common shares of S Company at the beginning of Year 1. S Company owned property which P Company had occupied under a lease arrangement for several years. For its investment in S Company, P Company paid $60,000 in cash, the book value of S Company's net assets. The separate balance sheets of the two companies immediately following P Company's stock purchase are shown in the first two columns of the following schedule. The third column shows a *combined* balance sheet and the final column a *consolidated* balance sheet.

P AND S COMPANIES
Balance Sheets—Separate, Combined, and Consolidated
At Beginning of Year 1 (date of acquisition)

	P Company	S Company	Combined	Consolidated
Assets				
Cash	$ 38,000	$ 22,500	$ 60,500	$ 60,500
Receivables	45,000		45,000	45,000
Inventories	47,000		47,000	47,000
Land		24,000	24,000	24,000
Building		180,000	180,000	180,000
Accumulated depreciation		(49,000)	(49,000)	(49,000)
Investment in S Company	60,000		60,000	
Total assets	$190,000	$177,500	$367,500	$307,500
Liabilities and Stockholders' Equity				
Accounts payable	$ 58,000	$ 17,500	$ 75,500	$ 75,500
Notes payable		100,000	100,000	100,000
Capital stock.............	100,000	50,000	150,000	100,000
Retained earnings, beginning of Year 1 (date of acquisition)	32,000	10,000	42,000	32,000
Total liabilities and stockholders' equity	$190,000	$177,500	$367,500	$307,500

The balances in the "Combined" column were formed simply by adding the items in the separate balance sheets of P and S Companies. *These combined balances do not constitute a consolidated balance sheet* for the two affiliated companies, because there is a double counting of both assets and stockholders' equity. The $60,000 investment in S Company common stock, which appears as an asset on P Company's statement, represents an interest in the net assets of S Company. To include as an asset of the consolidated entity both this stock investment *and* the underlying net assets of S Company is to count the same economic resources twice. Similarly there is double counting in the owners' equity. From a consolidated viewpoint, the $60,000 total ownership equity of S Company ($50,000 in capital stock and $10,000 in retained earnings) is represented by the capital stock and retained earnings of P Company, since P Company's stockholders own all of P Company's net assets, including all the outstanding shares of S Company.

The duplication of assets and equities in the combined balance sheet provides the essential clue to the adjustment that is necessary to prepare a consolidated balance sheet for P Company and its subsidiary at the date of acquisition. If we simply eliminate the investment account of P Company against the ownership equity accounts of S Company, we will have removed the double counting and will have a consolidated statement of assets, liabilities, and stockholders' equity which reflects the financial position of the economic entity represented by the two affiliated corporations. This process is illustrated in the consolidating working papers shown on page 416, and the result is presented in the "Consolidated" column of the schedule shown above.

The consolidated balance sheet is prepared using the figures in the far right-hand column of the working papers on page 416. The consolidated statement for P Company and subsidiary shows $307,500 total assets and $175,500 liabilities, or net assets of $132,000. The ownership interest in these net assets is represented by P Company's capital stock of $100,000 and retained earnings of $32,000, since the stockholders of P Company own all the stock in the two affiliated corporations.

Less than 100% control

If a parent company owns a controlling interest in a subsidiary but less than 100% of the outstanding shares, a new kind of ownership equity known as the *minority interest* will appear in the consolidated balance sheet. The consolidated balance sheet will include all the assets and liabilities of the affiliated companies (other than the parent's investment in subsidiary, which is eliminated). Only a portion of the ownership equity in these net assets is represented by the equity of the parent company stockholders because some of the equity interest in the subsidiary's net assets is held by the minority stockholders of S Company. We might conceivably prepare a consolidated balance sheet which included only the parent company's share of the assets of S Company. A more complete and useful financial picture of the consolidated entity results, however, if we include all of S Company's assets, and allocate the ownership equity in these assets between the controlling and minority interests.

P AND S COMPANIES
Working Papers—Consolidated Balance Sheet
At Beginning of Year 1 (date of acquisition)

	P Company	S Company	Intercompany Eliminations Dr	Intercompany Eliminations Cr	Consolidated Balance Sheet
Cash	38,000	22,500			60,500
Receivables	45,000				45,000
Inventories	47,000				47,000
Land		24,000			24,000
Building		180,000			180,000
Accumulated depreciation		(49,000)			(49,000)
Investment in S Company	60,000			(1) 60,000	
Totals	190,000	177,500			307,500
Accounts payable	58,000	17,500			75,500
Notes payable		100,000			100,000
Capital stock—P	100,000				100,000
Capital stock—S		50,000	(1) 50,000		
Beginning retained earnings—P	32,000				32,000
Beginning retained earnings—S		10,000	(1) 10,000		
Totals	190,000	177,500	60,000	60,000	307,500

(1) To eliminate investment in subsidiary against the appropriate stockholders' equity accounts.

To illustrate, consider the previously discussed case of P and S companies, and assume that P Company acquired from outsiders only an 80% interest in S Company, paying $48,000 (book value) for 80% of S Company's outstanding shares. In this situation the working papers to prepare a consolidated balance sheet would appear as on page 417.

The consolidated balance sheet in this case will show total assets of $319,500, liabilities of $175,500, and an equity interest in consolidated net assets of $144,000. This equity interest is composed of two elements, the controlling interest and the minority interest. The controlling interest of $132,000 is owned by the stockholders of P Company and is represented by P Company's outstanding capital stock ($100,000) and retained earnings ($32,000). The minority interest amounts to $12,000 and belongs to the outside stockholders of S Company. The $12,000 minority interest is 20% of the $60,000 total stockholders' equity in S Company.

In the consolidating entry on the working papers, the entire $60,000

P AND S COMPANIES
Working Papers—Consolidated Balance Sheet
At Beginning of Year 1 (date of acquisition)

	P Company	S Company	Intercompany Eliminations		Consolidated Balance Sheet
			Dr	Cr	
Cash	50,000	22,500			72,500
Accounts receivable	45,000				45,000
Inventories	47,000				47,000
Land		24,000			24,000
Building		180,000			180,000
Accumulated depreciation		(49,000)			(49,000)
Investment in S Company	48,000			(1) 48,000	
Totals	190,000	177,500			319,500
Accounts payable	58,000	17,500			75,500
Notes payable		100,000			100,000
Capital stock—P	100,000				100,000
Capital stock—S		50,000	(1) 50,000		
Beginning retained earnings—P	32,000				32,000
Beginning retained earnings—S		10,000	(1) 10,000		
Minority interest				(1) 12,000	12,000
Totals	190,000	177,500	60,000	60,000	319,500

(1) To eliminate P's investment in S against 80% of S Company's stockholders' equity, and to establish the 20% minority interest in S Company.

stockholders' equity of S Company (capital stock and retained earnings) is eliminated. Of this stockholders' equity, 20% is established as the $12,000 minority interest, and the remaining 80% is eliminated against the $48,000 investment account on P Company's statement. As an alternative, we might have eliminated only 80% of S Company's capital stock and retained earnings, leaving 20% of each to be carried into the consolidated balance sheet column to reflect the $12,000 minority interest. The reader of consolidated financial statements is primarily concerned with the total amount of the minority interest and not with its composition. Therefore no significant information is lost if we eliminate completely the stockholders' equity accounts of the subsidiary and establish the minority interest in consolidated net assets as a single amount.

Intercompany debt

If one affiliated company (either a parent or subsidiary) owes money to another there will be an asset (receivable) on the individual balance sheet of the creditor firm and a liability (payable) on the statement of the debtor company. When the financial statements of the two companies are consolidated, however, both the asset and liability should be eliminated. Neither a receivable nor a liability exists from the viewpoint of the consolidated entity. The situation is analogous to that of a student who has saved $500 to pay his fall semester tuition and who then borrows $10 from this fund for a date. In his internal financial thinking the student will consider that he owes $10 from his recreational funds to his tuition fund, but if he were to prepare a personal balance sheet he would not show this $10 receivable and payable as an asset and liability.

On consolidating working papers an eliminating entry is made to cancel out any intercompany debt between affiliated companies. Suppose, for example, that a parent company has borrowed $10,000 from its subsidiary and at the balance sheet date owes this amount plus $500 accrued interest. On consolidating working papers the following elimination entry would be made:

To Cancel Inter-company Debt	*Notes Payable—(Parent's balance sheet)*	*10,000*	
	Interest Payable—(Parent's balance sheet)	*500*	
	Notes Receivable—(Subsidiary's balance sheet) . . .		*10,000*
	Interest Receivable—(Subsidiary's balance sheet) . .		*500*
	To eliminate intercompany payables and receivables.		

The elimination entry shown above appears *only* on consolidating working papers; it would *not appear on the accounting records* of either the parent company or the subsidiary.

Consolidation after date of acquisition

If a parent company and subsidiary operate profitably after affiliation, the net assets of both companies will grow as a result of earnings after the date on which the parent acquires a controlling interest in the subsidiary. Some of this growth may be distributed to stockholders in the form of dividends. Dividends paid by a subsidiary will go to the parent company and to minority stockholders in proportion to their stockholdings. Assuming that the parent company carries its investment in the subsidiary at cost, any dividends received from the subsidiary will be added to the parent's assets and included in its earnings. Any undistributed growth (earnings less dividends) in the net asset of the parent and subsidiary will be reflected in the retained earnings accounts of each company.

In preparing consolidated financial statements after the date of acquisition, the net assets of the parent and subsidiary at statement date are combined. Our problem is to allocate the stockholders' equity in these net assets between the controlling and minority interests. The entire retained earnings balance of the parent company belongs to the parent's stockholders. The retained earnings balance of the subsidiary belongs to the parent company and the minority interest in proportion to their stockholdings. In developing consolidated financial statement data, however, we treat separately the subsidiary's retained earnings balance at date of acquisition, and the change in retained earnings from the date of acquisition to the date of the consolidated statement.

To illustrate, assume that X Company buys 75% of the stock of Y Company at a time when Y's retained earnings balance is $10,000. During the first year after acquisition Y Company earned $40,000 and paid no dividends. The $50,000 balance of Y Company's retained earnings at the end of the first year would be treated as follows on the consolidated balance sheet:

Who Owns Subsidiary's Retained Earnings?	$ 7,500	*This is 75% of the subsidiary's retained earnings at date of acquisition ($10,000). It is offset against the parent's investment account, since it is a part of the ownership equity purchased by the parent.*
	30,000	*This is 75% of the $40,000 growth in the subsidiary's retained earnings since date of acquisition. It is a part of consolidated net income and therefore is ultimately added to the parent's retained earnings balance, since it is an element of the controlling interest in the earnings of the consolidated entity.*
	12,500	*This is the 25% of the subsidiary's retained earnings (both the balance at date of acquisition and subsequent additions) that belongs to the minority stockholders; it is thus included in the minority interest balance.*
	$50,000	*Total retained earnings of Y Company (subsidiary) at statement date.*

When the parent purchased its controlling interest, it acquired an equity in the subsidiary's retained earnings balance at the date of acquisition. Therefore, in consolidation, the parent's share of the subsidiary's retained earnings at date of acquisition is offset against the parent's investment account; the minority share is credited to the minority interest. Any *change in the subsidiary's retained earnings after date of acquisition* is also allocated between the controlling and minority interests. In this latter case, however, the parent's share of any growth in the subsidiary's retained earnings becomes a part of the consolidated net income each year and ultimately is included in the retained earnings of the consolidated entity.

If a subsidiary declares dividends just before a balance sheet date, an intercompany asset (dividends receivable) will appear on the parent's statement, and an intercompany liability (dividends payable) will appear on the subsidiary's balance sheet. In the consolidated balance sheet, this intercompany payable and receivable representing the parent's share of the declared but unpaid dividend should be eliminated, since from a consolidated viewpoint neither an asset nor a liability exists. Only the portion of dividends payable to the minority stockholders represents a debt of the consolidated entity.

Balance sheet working papers. To illustrate the process of consolidation after date of acquisition, we shall carry forward the example of P and S Companies to the end of Year 1. Assume that during Year 1, P Company earned $23,000 and declared $14,000 in dividends near the end of the year. During Year 1, S Company earned $15,000 and declared $10,000 in dividends, of which $5,000 remained unpaid at the end of Year 1. P Company included its share of S Company's dividends (80% of $10,000 = $8,000) in its Year 1 net income, and reported dividends receivable from S of $4,000 (80% of $5,000) as an asset at the end of Year 1. On the books of both companies, dividends declared were charged to a Dividends account, a contra account that will be closed into Retained Earnings after financial statements are prepared.

The working papers to develop the necessary data for a consolidated balance sheet and statement of consolidated retained earnings appear on page 421.

Comments on working paper entries. Entry (1). This is the same eliminating entry that appears in the working papers to consolidate the balance sheets of these two companies at the *beginning* of Year 1. The stockholders' equity of S Company as of the beginning of Year 1 ($60,000) is eliminated against the 80% investment ($48,000) on P Company's statement, and the residual minority interest of $12,000 is established in a separate item.

Entry (2). This entry eliminates the Dividends Receivable account on P Company's statement against the Dividends Payable account on S Company's statement. Since P Company owns 80% of S Company's stock, its dividend receivable is 80% of the total $5,000 of S Company's dividends declared but unpaid at the balance sheet date.

Entry (3). This entry allocates S Company's dividends declared between the controlling and minority interests. The total $10,000 Dividends account is eliminated from S Company's statement. Of this amount, 80%, or $8,000, is eliminated from P Company's net income, and the minority interest in S Company is reduced by its share (20%) of the dividend. The elimination

P AND S COMPANIES
Working Papers—Consolidated Balance Sheet
End of Year 1 (one year after acquisition)

	P Company	S Company	Intercompany Eliminations Dr	Intercompany Eliminations Cr	Consolidated Balance Sheet
Cash	53,000	45,000			98,000
Accounts receivable	39,000				39,000
Dividends receivable	4,000			(2) 4,000	
Inventories	62,000				62,000
Land		24,000			24,000
Building		180,000			180,000
Accumulated depreciation		(58,000)			(58,000)
Investment in S Company	48,000			(1) 48,000	
Totals	206,000	191,000			345,000
Accounts payable	51,000	31,000			82,000
Dividends payable	14,000	5,000	(2) 4,000		15,000
Notes payable		90,000			90,000
Capital stock—P	100,000				100,000
Capital stock—S		50,000	(1) 50,000		
Beginning retained earnings—P	32,000				32,000
Beginning retained earnings—S		10,000	(1) 10,000		
Net income—P	23,000		(3) 8,000	(4) 12,000	27,000
Net income—S		15,000	(4) 15,000		
Dividends—P	(14,000)				(14,000)
Dividends—S		(10,000)		(3) 10,000	
Minority interest			(3) 2,000	(1) 12,000	
				(4) 3,000	13,000
Totals	206,000	191,000	89,000	89,000	345,000

(1) To eliminate investment in S against 80% of S Company's stockholders' equity accounts, and to establish 20% minority interest as of the beginning of Year 1.
(2) To eliminate intercompany dividends receivable and payable (80% of $5,000 = $4,000).
(3) To allocate S Company dividends declared of $10,000 between controlling (80%) and minority interest (20%). To eliminate $8,000 from P's income, because P Company recorded dividends from S Company as dividend revenues and included this $8,000 in net income.
(4) To allocate S Company's $15,000 net income between controlling interest (80%) and minority interest (20%).

of $8,000 from P Company's net income in effect cancels P Company's recording of dividend revenue in this amount. We do this because P Company's share of S Company's growth through operations is not limited to its share of S Company's dividends but is equal to its share of S Company's net income. In entry (4), we shall allocate to P Company 80% of S Company's entire net income, which will include the $8,000 portion distributed to P Company as dividends.

Entry (4). This entry apportions S Company's Year 1 net income between the controlling and minority interests. Of the total income of $15,000, the parent company's share is $12,000 (80%) and the minority interest share is $3,000 (20%). Note that the effect of entries (3) and (4) is to add to the parent's retained earnings, and to the minority interest the $5,000 growth in S Company's capital during Year 1 represented by the subsidiary's $15,000 net income, less dividends of $10,000. In the consolidated balance sheet, this $5,000 increase in S's stockholders' equity is divided between the controlling and minority interests in proportion to their stock ownership, that is, in a ratio of 80 to 20. By eliminating $8,000 from P Company's net income [entry (3)] and adding $12,000 [entry (4)] we have in effect increased P's retained earnings by 80% of $5,000, the growth in S Company during Year 1. Similarly, the addition of $3,000 to the minority interest [entry (4)] and the reduction of $2,000 [entry (3)] results in adding $1,000 (20% of $5,000) to the minority interest, which reflects the minority share of the growth in S Company's retained earnings during Year 1.

Consolidated balance sheet and statement of retained earnings. The data appearing in the consolidated balance sheet column of the working papers become the basis for both the consolidated balance sheet and retained earnings statements. These statements are illustrated on page 423.

The statement of consolidated retained earnings explains the change in the controlling interest in retained earnings from $32,000 at the beginning of Year 1 to $45,000 at the end. The $27,000 controlling interest in net income represents P Company's net income of $15,000 (P's reported income of $23,000 less $8,000 of intercompany dividend revenues from S Company) plus P Company's share of S Company's income (80% of $15,000 = $12,000).

On the statement of consolidated retained earnings, only the $14,000 dividend of P Company is shown, since this represents the distribution of earnings to the controlling stockholders during the year. The portion of S Company's dividends flowing to P Company was eliminated since this dividend represents simply a transfer of assets within the affiliated entity and is thus not a distribution from a consolidated viewpoint. The $2,000 S Company dividends applicable to minority stockholders are not reported separately but are deducted in computing the minority interest to be reported on the consolidated balance sheet.

The consolidated balance sheet as of the end of Year 1 shows the total assets ($345,000) and total liabilities ($187,000) of the consolidated entity,

Financial
Position
of the
Consoli-
dated
Entity

P AND S COMPANIES
Consolidated Balance Sheet
End of Year 1

Assets

Current assets:

Cash		$ 98,000
Accounts receivable		39,000
Inventories		62,000
Total current assets		$199,000
Plant and equipment:		
Land		24,000
Building	$180,000	
Less: Accumulated depreciation	58,000	122,000
Total assets		$345,000

Liabilities and Stockholders' Equity

Liabilities:

Notes payable, current portion		$ 10,000
Accounts payable		82,000
Dividends payable		15,000
Total current liabilities		$107,000
Notes payable, due after one year		80,000
Total liabilities		$187,000
Stockholders' equity:		
Capital stock	$100,000	
Retained earnings	45,000	
Minority interest	13,000	
Total stockholders' equity		158,000
Total liabilities and stockholders' equity		$345,000

Controlling
Interest in
Retained
Earnings
Has
Increased

P AND S COMPANIES
Statement of Consolidated Retained Earnings
Year 1

Balance at beginning of Year 1	$32,000
Net income	27,000
Dividends declared	(14,000)
Balance at end of Year 1	$45,000

leaving a stockholders' equity of $158,000. This stockholders' equity is composed of a controlling interest of $145,000 (capital stock plus retained earnings) and a minority interest of $13,000.

Consolidated income statement. A consolidated income statement is prepared by combining revenue and expenses of the parent and subsidiary. Revenues and expenses arising from intercompany transactions (for example, intercompany rent or interest revenues and expenses) are eliminated because they simply reflect transfers of assets from one affiliated company to another and do not change the net assets from a consolidated viewpoint.

To illustrate the procedure, consider the following Year 1 income statements for P Company and S Company, continuing our previous illustration:

This Doesn't Show Consolidated Income— Why?

P AND S COMPANIES
Year 1 Income Statements—Separate and Combined

	P Company	S Company	Combined
Sales revenues	$193,000		$193,000
Rental revenues		$35,000	35,000
Dividend revenues	8,000		8,000
Total revenues	$201,000	$35,000	$236,000
Cost of goods sold	$120,000		$120,000
Operating expenses	52,500	$16,000	68,500
Income taxes	5,500	4,000	9,500
Total expenses	$178,000	$20,000	$198,000
Net income	$ 23,000	$15,000	$ 38,000

Again it is apparent that we cannot simply combine the items on the two income statements to arrive at a consolidated statement of net income. The $8,000 of dividend revenues reported by P Company are not revenues from a consolidated viewpoint. P Company owns 80% of S Company's net income, and this $8,000 dividend represents merely a shift of that amount of assets from one unit of the consolidated entity to another. Similarly, the rental revenues of S Company represent rent paid by P Company to S Company and included in P Company's operating expense. This is neither a revenue nor an expense from a consolidated viewpoint.

The intercompany adjustments and eliminations necessary to arrive at a consolidated income statement are demonstrated in the working papers appearing on page 425.

Note that the income statements of P and S Companies in the working papers have been arranged in balancing form; that is, so that total debits and credits in each statement are equal. The self-balancing income statement is accomplished by adding the net income of each company to the expense items, and treating net income as if it were a debit balance item. (If revenues − expenses = net income, then revenues = expenses + net income.) This may seem a bit strange at first, but as a working paper technique this arrangement of income statement elements makes it possible to treat the income statement alone as if it were a balancing accounting schedule, and to prepare eliminating entries on the working papers in the familiar balancing debit and credit form. For example, an eliminating entry which reduces revenues, and thus net income, will be shown on the working papers as a debit to a revenue account and as a credit to the net income figure of the company whose revenue is being eliminated [see entry (2) on the working papers].

Comments on working paper eliminations. Entry (1). This entry eliminates

P AND S COMPANIES
Working Papers—Consolidated Income Statement
Year 1

	P Company	S Company	Intercompany Eliminations Dr	Intercompany Eliminations Cr	Consolidated Income Statement
Credit items:					
Sales revenues	193,000				193,000
Rental revenues		35,000	(1) 35,000		
Dividend revenues	8,000		(2) 8,000		
Total revenues	201,000	35,000			193,000
Debit items:					
Cost of goods sold	120,000				120,000
Operating expenses	52,500	16,000		(1) 35,000	33,500
Income taxes	5,500	4,000			9,500
Net income—P	23,000		(3) 12,000	(2) 8,000	27,000
Net income—S		15,000		(3) 15,000	
Minority interest in net income			(3) 3,000		3,000
Total expenses and net income	201,000	35,000	58,000	58,000	193,000

(1) To eliminate intercompany rental revenues and expense.
(2) To eliminate dividends declared by S Company on stock owned by P Company.
(3) To allocate S Company's net income between controlling (80%) and minority (20%) interests.

the intercompany rental revenue and expense accounts. Rent paid by P Company to S Company was included in P's operating expenses and in S Company's revenues. This eliminating entry has no effect on consolidated net income, because we are simply offsetting an item recorded as an expense by one company in the affiliated structure against the revenue recorded by the other affiliated company.

Entry (2). This entry cancels the dividend revenues which P Company recorded as a result of dividends received from S Company. Eliminating $8,000 from P Company's revenues results in reducing P Company's net income, which is the other half of the eliminating entry. (The student will recall that on the consolidated balance sheet working papers on page 421, the counterpart to this entry was a debit to P Company's net income and a credit to S Company's Dividend account.) Let us arrange these two working paper entries in this form:

	Entry on balance sheet working papers:		*Entry on income statement working papers:*	
Two Related Eliminating Entries	*Net Income—P* 8,000		*Dividend Revenues—P* 8,000	
	Dividends—S	8,000	*Net income—P*	8,000

We see that the net effect of the two working paper entries is to reduce S Company's dividend account by the amount of the intercompany dividends, and to reduce P Company's revenue (and net income) by a similar amount.

Entry (3). The purpose of this entry is to apportion S Company's net income of $15,000 between the parent company and the minority interest. Since P Company owns 80% of the stock of S Company, its share of S Company's earnings is $12,000 ($15,000 × 80% = $12,000). The 20% share of the minority stockholders amounts to $3,000 ($15,000 × 20% = $3,000). When P Company's interest in S Company's net income ($12,000) is added to the income earned by P Company other than dividends received from S [$23,000 less the $8,000 in entry (2)] we arrive at the controlling interest in consolidated net income of $27,000, which is the same result we derived previously on the consolidated balance sheet working papers on page 421.

When the various income statement items are combined, taking into account the effect of adjusting and eliminating entries on the working papers, the figures in the income statement column of the working papers provide the basis for the preparation of a consolidated income statement. The consolidated income statement of P Company and its subsidiary S Company is shown at the top of page 427.

Observe that the total Year 1 net income of the consolidated entity is $30,000, of which $27,000 is allocated to the controlling interest, and $3,000 to the minority interest. On the statement of consolidated retained earnings (see page 423) the figure described as consolidated net income is the

Who Owns
Total Con-
solidated
Net Income
of $30,000?

P AND S COMPANIES
Consolidated Income Statement
For Year 1

Sales revenues		$193,000
Cost of goods sold		120,000
Gross profit on sales		$ 73,000
Operating expenses	$33,500	
Income taxes	9,500	43,000
Total consolidated net income		$ 30,000
Less: Minority interest in net income		(3,000)
Controlling interest in net income, transferred to statement of con-		
solidated retained earnings		$ 27,000

$27,000 controlling interest in net income. The $3,000 share of the minority interest in the net income of the consolidated entity is simply combined with the minority interest at the beginning of Year 1 and the minority interest in dividends, and reported as a single figure ($13,000), representing the equity interest of minority stockholders at the end of Year 1.

The three consolidated statements we have discussed—the balance sheet, income statement, and statement of retained earnings—provide an integrated financial picture of the combined position and operating results of companies affiliated through controlling stock ownership.

Acquisition of subsidiary stock at more than book value

When a parent corporation purchases a controlling interest in a subsidiary it will probably pay a price for the shares that differs from their underlying book value. In consolidating the financial statements of two affiliated corporations, we cannot ignore a discrepancy between the cost of the parent company's investment in subsidiary shares and the book value of these shares on the statements of the subsidiary company. In consolidation, the parent's investment is offset against the appropriate stockholders' equity accounts of the subsidiary, and if the two amounts are not equal, we must consider what the difference between them represents.

To illustrate, suppose that at the end of the current year, C Company purchased all the outstanding shares of D Company for $120,000. At the date of acquisition, D Company reported on its balance sheet total assets of $300,000, total liabilities of $205,000, and total stockholders' equity of $95,000, consisting of capital stock of $50,000 and retained earnings of $45,000. If we were to attempt to prepare a consolidated balance sheet as of the date of acquisition, we would find difficulty in completing the eliminating entry. This is illustrated at the top of page 428.

Our problem is what to do with the $25,000 discrepancy between the price paid by C Company for all the capital stock of D Company, and the

<table>
<tr><td rowspan="3">What Does
the $25,000
Represent?</td><td>Capital Stock—D Company ....</td><td>50,000</td><td></td></tr>
<tr><td>Retained Earnings—D Company ....</td><td>45,000</td><td></td></tr>
<tr><td>? ....</td><td>25,000</td><td></td></tr>
<tr><td></td><td>Investment in D Company (on C's books) ....</td><td></td><td>120,000</td></tr>
<tr><td></td><td colspan="3">To eliminate the cost of C Company's 100% interest in
D Company against the appropriate stockholders' equity
accounts of D Company.</td></tr>
</table>

book value of D Company's stockholders' equity at the date of acquisition. If we ask ourselves why C Company paid $120,000 for its interest in D, the answer must be that the management of C Company considered the net assets of D Company to be worth $120,000 rather than their book value of $95,000. C's management may believe that the fair market value of certain specific assets of D Company are in excess of book value, or they may believe that D Company's future earnings prospects are so favorable as to justify paying $25,000 for D Company's unrecorded goodwill. Since C Company paid $120,000 for a 100% interest in D Company in an arm's length market transaction, the accountant has objective evidence that certain assets of D Company are undervalued, or that unrecorded goodwill of $25,000 exists. This evidence provides a basis for making the following eliminating entry on working papers:

<table>
<tr><td rowspan="6">D Company's
Assets
Were
Under-
stated</td><td>Capital Stock—D Company ....</td><td>50,000</td><td></td></tr>
<tr><td>Retained Earnings—D Company ....</td><td>45,000</td><td></td></tr>
<tr><td>Specific Assets (or Goodwill)—D Company ....</td><td>25,000</td><td></td></tr>
<tr><td>Investment in D Company (on C's books) ....</td><td></td><td>120,000</td></tr>
<tr><td colspan="3">To eliminate C Company's investment in D Company against
the appropriate stockholders' equity accounts and establish
unrecorded goodwill of D Company (or restate undervalued
assets of D Company).</td></tr>
</table>

The $25,000 in goodwill, or in increased valuation assigned to specific assets of D Company, will be carried over as an asset on the consolidated balance sheet. In practice this amount is often described on the consolidated balance sheet as "Excess of cost over book value of investment in subsidiary."

Acquisition of subsidiary stock at less than book value

If the parent company pays less than book value for its interest in a subsidiary, a similar problem of interpretation exists. For example, suppose in the previous case that C Company had paid $75,000 for all the outstanding shares of D Company, having a book value of $95,000. In this case we may assume that the management of C Company considered that D Company's assets were overvalued by $20,000 in terms of the future earnings prospects of the subsidiary company. The appropriate eliminating entry on the working papers to consolidate the financial statements of the two companies would be:

D Com-	*Capital Stock—D Company*	*50,000*	
pany's	*Retained Earnings—D Company*	*45,000*	
Assets	*Investment in D Company Stock*		*75,000*
Were Over-	*Specific Assets*		*20,000*
stated	*To eliminate investment in D Company against appropriate stockholders' equity accounts, and to record the indicated overvaluation of D Company's assets.*		

The credit balance of $20,000 would be reported in the consolidated balance sheet by reducing the value of specific assets of D Company by this amount, or as a deferred credit entitled "Excess of book value over cost of investment in subsidiary."

Intercompany sales and profits

Assume that Subsidiary Company sells to Parent Company for $1,000 merchandise which cost Subsidiary Company $700. From the viewpoint of Subsidiary Company as a legal entity, a gross profit of $300 has been realized on this transaction. From the viewpoint of the consolidation, goods have been transferred from one division of the economic entity to another, and no gain or loss will be realized until there has been a sale to someone outside the consolidated entity.

If this merchandise is in Parent Company's inventory at the time a consolidated balance sheet is prepared, the goods should be valued at $700, the cost to the consolidated entity. Therefore in the process of consolidation it would be necessary to remove $300 from the inventory account of Parent Company, and $300 from the net income (and retained earnings) of Subsidiary Company. In the next accounting period, if Parent Company sold the merchandise to outsiders for $1,200, both the $200 profit of Parent Company and the $300 profit of Subsidiary Company would be realized and reported in the consolidated income statement.

The problem of eliminating unrealized increases in inventory valuation as a result of intercompany sales of merchandise should be distinguished from that of eliminating the dollar amount of intercompany sales and purchases. When one affiliated company sells merchandise to another, and the second affiliate in turn sells all this merchandise to outsiders, there is no *unrealized* intercompany profit. The profit recognized by each affiliate on the sale of this merchandise has been fully substantiated by the sale of the goods to outsiders. For example, suppose a subsidiary sells merchandise which cost $40,000 to its parent for $50,000, and the parent in turn sells all this merchandise to outsiders for $65,000. Both the $10,000 gross profit recognized by the subsidiary and the $15,000 gross profit recognized by the parent are fully realized, since none of the merchandise remains in inventory within the consolidated entity. In preparing a consolidated income statement for these companies, however, it would be necessary to make an eliminating entry removing $50,000 from the sales of the subsidiary and $50,000 from the purchases (or cost of goods sold) of the parent. This eliminating entry would have no effect on consolidated assets or net income since its purpose is simply to remove the double counting of revenues and expenses resulting from the transfer of goods from one affiliate to another.

Since the accounting procedures necessary to remove intercompany profits in transactions between affiliated firms are somewhat complicated, they are beyond the scope of an introductory discussion. However, familiarity with the technical procedure is not necessary to understand consolidated financial statements. The reader of such statements may assume that profits on transfers of assets between affiliates are not reflected either in asset valuations on the consolidated balance sheet or in the consolidated income statement.

Consolidated statements on a pooling-of-interests basis

In recent years the acquisition of a subsidiary corporation has often been carried out by an exchange of stock, and the preparation of consolidated statements has followed a "pooling-of-interests" method. A key aspect of such acquisitions is that the stockholders of the subsidiary company being acquired become stockholders of the parent corporation. The stockholders of the two companies are said to have *pooled their interests,* rather than one ownership group having sold its equity to the other.

If we accept the view that no ownership interests have been severed (in other words no purchase or sale occurred), then there is no reason to revalue the assets of the acquired company, regardless of the market value of the securities exchanged. When the acquisition is treated as a pooling of interests, the Investment account on the books of the parent can be established at the par or stated value of the shares issued by the parent regardless of their current market price. Furthermore, if the parent acquired 100% of the stock of the subsidiary late in the year, the earnings (revenue and expenses) of the subsidiary *for the entire year* can be included in consolidated earnings.

To illustrate, let us assume that P Company acquired 100% of S Company stock on December 1, 1971, and that each company earned $60,000 during 1971. The consolidated net income for the two companies would be $120,000 even though $55,000 (11/12 of $60,000) of the earnings of S Company were earned before the two companies became affiliated.

The following brief summary emphasizes some of the points of contrast between treating a corporate acquisition as a *purchase* or as a *pooling of interests.*

Purchase Method	*Pooling-of-interests Method*
1. Parent records its investment in subsidiary at amount of cash paid or at market value of shares issued by parent in exchange for shares of subsidiary.	Parent records its investment in subsidiary at par value of shares issued.
2. Retained earnings of subsidiary at date of acquisition do not become part of consolidated retained earnings.	Retained earnings of subsidiary at date of acquisition become part of consolidated retained earnings.
3. Earnings of subsidiary are combined with the earnings of the parent *only* from the date of the affiliation.	Earnings of subsidiary for the entire year in which the affiliation occurred are included in the consolidated income statement.

The popularity of the pooling concept in recent years can be attributed largely to two factors. The first is the opportunity for the parent company to acquire valuable assets and to record these assets at relatively low values as shown on the books of the subsidiary company. As a result the consolidated earnings will not be penalized through amortization of higher (current) asset values against revenues. A second reason for the popularity of the pooling concept is that it permits a company whose stock sells at a high price-earnings multiple to show an *instant increase* in its earnings per share by issuing stock to acquire companies whose stock customarily sells at a low price-earnings multiple. A "growth" company may thus be able to maintain its reputation for reporting higher per-share earnings each year by continually acquiring other companies and accounting for such acquisitions on a pooling-of-interests basis. The effect of purchase procedures versus pooling procedures on consolidated financial statements is illustrated in the demonstration problem at the end of this chapter.

Who uses consolidated statements?

As noted at the beginning of this chapter, consolidated financial statements are designed to set aside the legal boundaries between affiliated companies and present a financial picture of the resources and operations of an economic entity. Persons looking to their *legal* rights will not find pertinent information in consolidated statements.

Consolidated statements are not significant to the minority stockholders or creditors of the subsidiary company. A strong financial position shown in a consolidated balance sheet may conceal a very weak situation in the particular subsidiary company in which a creditor or minority stockholder has an interest. These groups should rely on the individual financial statements of the affiliate in which they have a legal claim.

Long-term creditors of the parent company may find consolidated statements of some interest in assessing the general strength or weakness of the economic entity. In the long run, earning power is the primary source of creditor safety. The operating performance of the affiliated group may be a significant safety index for creditors of the controlling company.

The stockholders, managers, and members of the board of directors of the parent company have the primary interest in consolidated statements. The managers and directors are responsible for the entire resources under their control and for managing these resources profitably. Similarly, the stockholders of the parent company will prosper as the consolidated entity prospers. Their ownership interest is controlling, and they thus stand to benefit from strength anywhere in the entity and to suffer from weakness.

DEMONSTRATION PROBLEM

Presented below are the separate balance sheets, income statements, and other data for the Parent Company and the Subsidiary Company:

Balance Sheets—December 31, 1971

	Parent Company	Subsidiary Company
Cash	$ 80,000	$ 60,000
Accounts receivable	220,000	110,000
Merchandise	175,000	130,000
Plant and equipment (net)	1,200,000	560,000
Intangibles	125,000	40,000
Investment in Subsidiary Company (50,000 shares @ $20)	1,000,000	
	$2,800,000	$ 900,000
Accounts payable	$ 150,000	$ 75,000
Bonds payable	500,000	100,000
6% Preferred stock, $100 par	200,000	
Common stock, $1 par	100,000	50,000
Capital in excess of par value	1,300,000	500,000
Retained earnings	550,000	175,000
	$2,800,000	$ 900,000

Income Statements—Year Ended December 31, 1971

	Parent Company	Subsidiary Company
Sales	$2,000,000	$1,000,000
Cost of goods sold	1,200,000	660,000
Gross profit on sales	$ 800,000	$ 340,000
Operating expenses	$ 468,000	$ 200,000
Income taxes	120,000	40,000
Total expenses	$ 588,000	$ 240,000
Net income	$ 212,000	$ 100,000

	Parent Company	Subsidiary Company
Other data		
Earnings per share of common stock	$2.00	$2.00
Price of common stock, Oct. 1	$80	$20
Price-earnings ratio	40 times	10 times

On October 1, 1971, the Parent Company issued 12,500 shares of its common stock in exchange for all 50,000 shares of Subsidiary Company common stock. The Parent Company recorded the investment on the basis of the market value of its stock as follows:

Investment in Subsidiary Company (50,000 shares at
  $20 per share) 1,000,000
        Common Stock, $1 par value 12,500
        Capital in Excess of Par Value 987,500
To record acquisition of all outstanding stock of Subsidiary
Company in exchange for 12,500 shares of $1 par value com-
mon stock having a market value of $80 per share.

The Subsidiary Company sales and expenses through September 30, 1971, amounted to 75% of the total sales and expenses for the year. Thus, net income of $75,000 was earned by Subsidiary Company before Parent Company acquired control, and the stockholders' equity of Subsidiary Company on October 1, 1971, amounted to $700,000. Neither company declared any dividends on common stock during 1971. The dividends on preferred stock were paid by the Parent Company.

Early in December, the Parent Company sold merchandise costing $5,000 to the Subsidiary Company for $7,000. The Subsidiary Company sold all of this merchandise to its customers; however, it had not made payment to the Parent Company as of December 31, 1971.

Instructions

a. Prepare a consolidated balance sheet and a consolidated income statement as of December 31, 1971, assuming that the merger of the Parent Company and the Subsidiary Company is treated as a **purchase.** Sales and expenses of Subsidiary Company for the period October 1 to December 31, 1971, are combined with sales and expenses of the Parent Company. The excess of cost over book value of subsidiary interest acquired, $300,000 ($1,000,000 less $700,000), is assigned to intangible assets and is amortized (as an addition to operating expenses) over a five-year period starting October 1, 1971.

b. Prepare a consolidated balance sheet and a consolidated income statement as of December 31, 1971, assuming that the merger of the Parent Company and the Subsidiary Company is treated as a **pooling of interests.** Sales and expenses of the Subsidiary Company for the entire year 1971 are combined with the sales and expenses of the Parent Company. In **pooling** the balance sheets of the two companies, the Investment account is first reduced to $12,500 (the par value of the Parent Company shares issued in exchange for the shares of Subsidiary Company). This is accomplished by reducing Capital in Excess of Par Value by $987,500. The Investment account is then eliminated against the Common Stock account of the Subsidiary Company, and the excess of par value of Subsidiary Company common stock over the Investment account balance, $37,500 ($50,000 − $12,500), is added to consolidated Capital in

Excess of Par Value. The other stockholders' equity accounts are then combined in preparing a consolidated balance sheet on a pooling-of-interests basis.

c. Compute the earnings and the book value per share of common stock on a consolidated basis, assuming that the merger is recorded (1) as a purchase, and (2) as a pooling of interests.

QUESTIONS

1. Alexander Corporation owns 80% of the outstanding common stock of Benton Company. Explain the basis for the assumption that these two companies constitute a single economic entity operating under unified control.

2. The following item appears on a consolidated balance sheet: "Minority interest in subsidiary . . . $620,000." Explain the nature of this item, and where you would expect to find it on the consolidated balance sheet.

3. Cone Company is an 80%-owned subsidiary of Dodson Company. Dodson Company carries its investment in Cone Company at cost. During the first year after Dodson Company acquired its interest, Cone Company earned $50,000 and paid $20,000 in dividends. Dodson Company reported net income of $120,000.
   a. Assuming that no consolidating adjustments are necessary, what is the amount of total consolidated net income for Year 1?
   b. If Dodson Company had not had an interest in Cone Company, what income would it have reported for Year 1?
   c. What is the minority interest in Year 1 consolidated net income?
   d. What is the controlling interest in consolidated net income for Year 1?
   e. If only three-fourths of Cone Company's dividend had been paid at balance sheet date, what elimination of intercompany debt would be necessary?

4. In looking at a set of consolidated financial statements, you note that the total consolidated net income reported on the income statement is $360,000 but the net income added to consolidated retained earnings is only $295,000. What is the likely source of this discrepancy?

5. Explain why intercompany sales, rents, interest, etc., should be eliminated in preparing consolidated income statements in order to avoid double counting of revenues and expenses. Do these eliminations have any effect on consolidated net income? Why?

6. Q Company has purchased all the outstanding shares of X Company for $900,000. At the date of acquisition, an X Company balance sheet showed total assets of $1,300,000 and total liabilities of $500,000. Assuming that X Company's retained earnings at date of acquisition are one-third the amount of its stated capital, prepare, in journal entry form, the eliminating entry necessary to consolidate the balance sheets of these two corporations. Explain your treatment of any difference between the cost of Q's investment and the book value of Q's interest in X on X Company's financial records or on consolidated working papers.

7. Briefly explain the differences found in consolidated financial statements when the merger of two companies is reviewed as a *pooling of interests* rather than as a *purchase.*

8. What classes of persons are likely to be primarily interested in consolidated financial statements? Why?

9. A creditor of Great Mining Company is concerned because the company is in financial difficulty and has reported increasingly large losses in the past three years. Great Mining Company is a 75%-owned subsidiary of Hannah Company. When the creditor examines the consolidated statements of the two companies he finds that the earnings are satisfactory and that the consolidated entity is in sound financial condition. To what extent should the creditor be reassured by the consolidated statements, assuming that the information contained in them fairly presents the financial condition of the consolidated entity?

10. The 19__ annual report of the Fedders Corporation stated that its consolidated statement of income for the year ended August 31, 19__, included sales of $19,500,000 and net income of $120,000 from the Norge Division purchased on July 1, 19__. The division was acquired for approximately $45 million in cash, notes, and common stock. The balance sheet reported total assets of $129 million compared to only $61 million for the previous year. Would any of the foregoing amounts be reported differently if only common stock was issued in acquiring the Norge Division and the transaction was treated as a pooling of interests?

EXERCISES

1. On April 1, 1970, the Parent Co. acquired 90% of the stock of the Subsidiary Co. for $240,000 in cash. On this date, the subsidiary had $200,000 in capital stock outstanding and $55,000 in retained earnings. On December 31, 1972, the Parent Co. reports retained earnings of $1,500,000 and the Subsidiary Co. reports retained earnings of $130,000.
   Compute the amounts to be reported in the consolidated balance sheet as of December 31, 1972, for each of the following:
   a. Excess of cost of investment in Subsidiary Co. over book value
   b. Minority interest
   c. Retained earnings

2. Indiana Company owns an 85% interest in Jin Company. During Year 1, Jin Company sold to Indiana Company for $300,000 merchandise which cost Jin Company $210,000. At the end of Year 1, Indiana Company has in its ending inventory goods purchased from Jin Company at a cost of $75,000. What amount of intercompany profit should be eliminated in preparing consolidated statements? When will this profit be realized by the consolidated entity? At what value will the goods on hand purchased from Jin Company be shown on the consolidated balance sheet at the end of Year 1?

3. Keller Company paid $350,000 for all the capital stock of Lewis Company. At the date of acquisition, Keller Company's total stockholders' equity of

$1 million is composed of $800,000 in capital stock and $200,000 of retained earnings. Lewis Company has $400,000 in capital stock and a deficit of $20,000 at the date of acquisition. What is the total amount of stockholders' equity that will appear on a consolidated balance sheet prepared for these two affiliated companies at date of acquisition?

4. The Excelsior Corporation "purchased" 80% of the stock of the Acme Co. on July 1, 1960, when the retained earnings of the Acme Co. amounted to $100,000. The retained earnings of the Acme Co. now amount to $750,000. Show how much of the retained earnings of the Acme Co. would be reported on the latest consolidated balance sheet and what disposition would be made of any portion of Acme's retained earnings not reported on the con- solidated balance sheet.

5. Anderson Co. and Butler Corp. are planning to pool their activities into a single company. Data relating to the two companies follow:

	Anderson Co.	Butler Corp.
Total net assets (stockholders' equity).	$1,000,000	$2,000,000
Capital stock, $5 par (80,000 shares)	400,000	400,000
Retained earnings	600,000	1,600,000
Annual earnings per share	$3.00	$3.00
Price per share of stock	$60	$30
Price-earnings ratio	20 times	10 times

a. If Anderson Co. issues 40,000 additional shares in exchange for all the stock of Butler Corp. and aggregate earnings for the two companies remain unchanged, compute the earnings per share on Anderson Co. stock following the merger. The merger is treated as a pooling of interests.

b. Assuming that Anderson Co. stock continues to sell at 20 times earn- ings, what would be the price of Anderson Co. stock following the merger (pooling) of the two companies?

PROBLEMS

14-1 X Company owns 100% of the stock of Y Company. The income statements for each company for Year 1 appear below.

	X Company	Y Company
Sales	$600,000	$200,000
Cost of goods sold	400,000	130,000
Gross profit on sales	$200,000	$ 70,000
Operating expenses	(83,000)	(20,000)
Interest expense	(5,000)	(8,000)
Interest income	8,000	
Income taxes	(50,000)	(12,000)
Net income	$ 70,000	$ 30,000

Y Company sold merchandise to X Company for $30,000 which cost $24,000. One- half of this merchandise has not been sold by X Company to its customers and is included in its ending inventory at $15,000. Y Company paid $8,000 interest to X Company on a long-term loan.

Instructions
a. Prepare a consolidated income statement for X Company and its subsidiary, Y Company. You need not use working papers.
b. Prepare a consolidated income statement for the two companies, assuming the same facts as above except that X Company owns only 75% of the stock of Y Company and that all the merchandise acquired by X Company from Y Company has been sold by X Company. You need not use working papers.

14-2 The following data relate to P Company and S Company, several years after P Company acquired control of S Company.

	P Company	*S Company*	*Consolidated*
Investment in S Company stock	$ 300,000		
Other assets	1,700,000	$1,000,000	$2,470,000
	$2,000,000	$1,000,000	$2,470,000
Bonds payable.................	$ 500,000		$ 350,000
Other liabilities	280,000	$ 300,000	500,000
Capital stock	600,000	200,000	600,000
Retained earnings	620,000	500,000	890,000
Minority interest			70,000
Excess of book value over cost of invest-			
ment in subsidiary			60,000
	$2,000,000	$1,000,000	$2,470,000

The excess of book value over cost has not been amortized since acquisition. Additional stock has not been issued by either company.

Instructions
a. Compute the percentage of stock in S Company owned by P Company.
b. Compute the par value of bonds issued by P Company now held by S Company.
c. If S Company owes P Company $50,000 on open account, how much does P Company apparently owe to S Company?
d. How much of the retained earnings of $500,000 currently reported by S Company is included in the $890,000 retained earnings figure appearing on the consolidated balance sheet?
e. Compute S Company's retained earnings balance on the date that P Company acquired control of S Company.

14-3 Condensed balance sheets of Majestic Company and Northern Company at the end of Year 1 are shown below:

	Majestic Company	*Northern Company*
Assets:		
Current assets	$1,350,000	$250,000
Other assets	1,500,000	600,000
Total assets	$2,850,000	$850,000

	Majestic Company	Northern Company
Liabilities & stockholders' equity:		
Liabilities	$ 550,000	$270,000
Capital stock	1,500,000	300,000
Retained earnings	800,000	280,000
Total liabilities and stockholders' equity	$2,850,000	$850,000

Instructions
a. Assume that at the end of Year 1, Majestic Company purchased (using current assets) all the outstanding capital stock of Northern Company for $675,000. Prepare a consolidated balance sheet for Majestic and Northern Companies at the date of acquisition.
b. Assume that at the end of Year 1, Majestic Company purchased (using current assets) 80% of the outstanding common shares of Northern Company for $450,000. Prepare a consolidated balance sheet for Majestic and Northern Companies at the date of acquisition.
c. Explain any differences between the consolidated balance sheet prepared under assumption (**a**) and that prepared under assumption (**b**).

14-4 Income statement data for the current year for the Golden West Company and its 90% owned subsidiary, Sacramento Water Company, are shown below:

	Golden West Company	Sacramento Water Company
Revenues:		
Sales revenues	$ 980,000	$805,000
Rental revenues		95,000
Interest revenues	25,000	
Dividend revenues	81,000	
Total revenues	$1,086,000	$900,000
Expenses:		
Cost of goods sold	$ 465,000	$390,000
Operating expenses (including rent expense) . . .	280,000	230,000
Interest expense	15,000	32,000
Income taxes	120,000	93,000
Total expenses	$ 880,000	$745,000
Net income	$ 206,000	$155,000
Dividends declared	75,000	90,000
Increase in retained earnings during current year	$ 131,000	$ 65,000

The Sacramento Water Company leases land to the Golden West Company and received $5,000 per month in rent during the current year. Golden West Company holds Sacramento Water Company's $300,000, 7% note on which interest is payable annually. During the current year Golden West Company sold goods to Sacramento Company for $120,000, all of which had been sold by Sacramento Water Company to outsiders by the end of the current year.

Instructions

a. Prepare working papers for a consolidated income statement for the current year.

b. If you had not been told that the Golden West Company owned 90% of Sacramento Water Company, how could you have deduced this fact from the income and dividend data given in the problem?

c. Suppose that all goods sold by the Golden West Company to the Sacramento Water Company during the current year had not been resold by Sacramento Water Company, and an intercompany profit of $5,500 had been recorded by the Golden West Company on the sale of goods held in Sacramento Water Company's inventory at the close of the current year. How would this change the consolidated net income for the current year?

14-5 Given below are the liabilities and stockholders' equity sections of the balance sheets of General Cement Co. and Concrete Block, Inc., at the end of the current year:

	General Cement Co.	*Concrete Block, Inc.*
Liabilities	$ 720,000	$ 360,000
Capital stock	1,600,000	800,000
Retained earnings	740,000	320,000
Total liabilities and stockholders' equity	$3,060,000	$1,480,000

Instructions

For each of the following independent fact situations, prepare the liabilities and stockholders' equity section of the consolidated balance sheet as of the end of the current year:

a. General Cement Co. purchased all the outstanding capital stock of Concrete Block, Inc., just prior to the date of the above statements.

b. General Cement Co. purchased all the outstanding capital stock of Concrete Block, Inc., at the time of the latter's organization.

c. General Cement Co. purchased 90% of the outstanding capital stock of Concrete Block, Inc., just prior to the date of the above statements.

d. General Cement Co. purchased 75% of the outstanding capital stock of Concrete Block, Inc., at the date of the latter's organization.

e. General Cement Co. purchased 80% of the outstanding capital stock of Concrete Block, Inc., at the end of the previous year, at which time the retained earnings of Concrete Block, Inc., had a balance of $200,000.

14-6 Condensed balance sheets for Controls Company and its subsidiary, Research Data Company, as of December 31, Year 1, are shown below:

	Controls Company	Research Data Company
Assets:		
Current assets	$121,500	$255,000
Other assets	363,000	285,000
Investment in Research Data Company	324,000	
Total assets	$808,500	$540,000
Liabilities & stockholders' equity:		
Current liabilities	$153,750	$ 78,000
Capital stock	450,000	300,000
Retained earnings, Jan. 1, Year 1	172,500	132,000
Net income, Year 1	60,000	54,000
Dividends, Year 1	(27,750)	(24,000)
Total liabilities & stockholders' equity	$808,500	$540,000

Controls Company acquired 75% of the outstanding capital stock of Research Data Company at the beginning of Year 1 at a cost equal to the book value of the shares on that date. At December 31, Year 1, Controls Company owes Research Data Company $41,250 on open account.

Instructions
a. Prepare working papers for a consolidated balance sheet for the two affiliated companies as of December 31, Year 1.
b. Prepare a statement of consolidated retained earnings for Year 1.
c. Comment on the relationship between current assets and current liabilities as shown on the consolidated balance sheet, and that shown on the individual statements of the two companies. To what extent will creditors of Controls Company find the information on the consolidated balance sheet significant?

14-7 The latest balance sheets of Growth Corporation and Family Co., which Herman Hillman started over 30 years ago, are shown below.

	Growth Corporation	Family Co.
Assets:		
Current assets	$ 650,000	$200,000
Other assets	550,000	400,000
Total assets	$1,200,000	$600,000
Liabilities & stockholders' equity:		
Liabilities	$ 250,000	$ 50,000
Capital stock ($10 par value)	500,000	250,000
Retained earnings	450,000	300,000
Total liabilities & stockholders' equity	$1,200,000	$600,000

Each of the cases described below involves a situation in which Family Co. becomes a subsidiary of Growth Corporation.

Case A. Growth Corporation buys 20,000 shares of Family Co. capital stock on the open market, paying $650,000 ($250,000 in cash and $400,000 in long-term notes). The management of Growth Corporation paid more than book value because it believes that Family Co. has unrecorded goodwill of $262,500. This entire goodwill is reported in the consolidated balance sheet and the minority interest is increased accordingly.

Case B. Growth Corporation buys 20,000 shares of Family Co. capital stock on the open market for $400,000 ($100,000 in cash and $300,000 in long-term notes). Management of Growth Corporation believes that Other Assets of Family Co. are overvalued by $50,000. Other Assets are reduced by $50,000 in the consolidated balance sheet and the minority interest is reduced accordingly.

Case C. Growth Corporation acquires all 25,000 shares of capital stock in the Family Co. from the Hillman family in exchange for 25,000 unissued shares of the Growth Corporation. The shares of the Growth Corporation have a market value of $25 per share. The merger of these two companies is to be treated as a *purchase* and the excess of cost over book value of subsidiary interest is to be allocated to Other Assets.

Case D. Same facts as in Case **C,** except that the merger of the two companies is to be treated as a *pooling of interests.* Assets and retained earnings of Family Co. are combined with the assets and retained earnings of Growth Corporation at their book values.

Instructions
Using four money columns and a single list of statement titles, prepare comparative consolidated balance sheets for Growth Corporation and Family Co. under each of the four independent situations described above, as of the date at which Growth Corporation acquired its interest in Family Co. Head the four money columns Case A, Case B, Case C, and Case D. You need not prepare consolidating working papers, unless you find them necessary to arrive at your answer.

15 Accounting principles and the publicly owned corporation

Throughout this book we have tried to explain the theoretical roots of each new accounting procedure as it came under consideration. Anyone who travels through new territory, however, finds it useful to pause at some intermediate stage in his trip to consider what he has seen and to sort out his observations into some meaningful overall impression. This seems an appropriate point in our excursion through the territory of accounting for such a pause. The student, who now has an overview of the accounting process, is better prepared to understand how accounting procedures and rules are shaped by theoretical concepts. Our objective in this chapter is to reinforce and enhance the student's grasp of what he has learned about accounting thus far.

The need to establish principles

The need for medicine arrived with the first sickness and for engineering when man first tried to transport an object too heavy for him to lift. The roots of accounting do not lie in such primitive soil. Society had to develop a number system, the use of money as a medium of exchange, and commercial organizations before the need for accounting could be felt. Accounting was originated by the Italians in the 1400s when the first printed description of double-entry bookkeeping was published by Luca Paciolo, an Italian mathematician.

The art of accounting developed at an accelerating pace during and after the industrial revolution to meet the demands for quantitative information about business enterprises. Early accounting records were used primarily by the owner-managers of enterprises as an aid in running their businesses. Creditors were interested in financial reports, but they often knew the business owner well and relied more heavily on their personal knowledge of his financial status and integrity than on accounting information. Paciolo's double-entry record-keeping system was gradually refined and improved, but until the advent of the large publicly owned corporation there was little need to examine critically the theoretical implications of this system.

The emergence of the publicly owned corporation transformed accounting from a system of historical record keeping into a measurement process based on a cohesive set of measurement principles. Large accumulations of economic resources were gathered under the corporate wing. The legal concept of limited liability focused attention on the corporate entity and its financial position. Both these factors made relations between managers, stockholders, and creditors generally more remote and impersonal.

Corporate managers needed more sophisticated information systems to cope effectively with the resources under their control. More important to the development of accounting theory, outsiders—large credit grantors, stockholders, potential investors, and governmental agencies—demanded reliable information about the financial affairs of corporations. The need for accepted standards and a body of principles to govern accounting measurements reported to the public by corporations was apparent. A new profession, public accounting, emerged in the latter half of the 1800s and gradually gained recognition. The independent certified public accountant, rendering services to clients for a fee, filled the need for an outside expert to review the accounting records and financial statements of corporations and to attest to the fairness of the reports of corporate managers. Later the CPA enlarged the scope of his services by engaging in income tax work and management consulting.

Corporate managers are interested in having financial data that will aid them in making business decisions. In this area accounting theory is not a major issue, since any quantitative information that aids in making rational choices among alternative courses of action is relevant and useful. Such information may be based on rough estimates and projections of future events. Measurement methods may be inconsistent; one method may be used for one managerial purpose and other methods for different purposes. Accounting measurements of past operating results and current financial position are useful to management, but it is not necessary that internal information be developed in accordance with any particular set of measurement principles.

In reporting to outsiders, different considerations come into play. Corporate managers, even in small companies, have always been accountable to the stockholders who employ them. But the responsibility for managing a large corporation carries with it a great deal of economic and social power and requires a more extensive accountability. In most large corporations stock ownership is widely diffused. The owner of even several thousand of the nearly 300 million shares of General Motors common stock can scarcely expect to exert much influence on managerial policy. As stockholder power has diminished, managerial power and responsibility have broadened. Modern corporate managers are accountable not only to stockholders, but also to employees, customers, creditors, potential investors, and the public at large. Published financial statements are the primary means by which management reports on its accountability. The accounting data contained in such statements are used to evaluate management's overall performance, to guide investment decisions, and to support arguments on important public policy issues. It is necessary to the functioning of our economy that such financial information be widely disseminated and clearly understood. It is also important that there be general confidence in the reliability of corporate reports. In short, we need standards of disclosure and a well-defined body of accounting principles to govern managers in preparing financial reports and to guide the CPA in attesting to the fairness of such reports.

The CPA's opinion on financial statements

When a certified public accountant has audited the accounting records of a business, he attests to the reasonableness of the financial report of management by issuing an *audit opinion* (sometimes called a *certificate*). This opinion is published as a part of the company's annual report to stockholders. Because of its importance, the wording of the CPA's opinion has been carefully considered and a standard form has been developed. Considering the extensive investigation that precedes it, the auditor's certificate is surprisingly short. It usually consists of two brief paragraphs unless the CPA comments on unusual features of the financial picture. The first paragraph describes the *scope* of the auditor's examination; the second states his *opinion* of the financial statements. A recent report of the independent accountants of Procter & Gamble Company reads as follows:

To the Board of Directors and Shareholders of
The Procter & Gamble Company

We have examined the consolidated balance sheet of The Procter & Gamble Company and subsidiary companies as of June 30, 19___ and the related statement of earnings for the year then ended. Our examination was made in accordance with generally accepted auditing standards, and accordingly included such tests of the accounting records and such other auditing procedures as we considered necessary in the circumstances.

In our opinion, such statements present fairly the financial position of the companies at June 30, 19___ and the results of their operations for the year then ended, in conformity with generally accepted accounting principles applied on a basis consistent with that of the preceding year.

Observe that the CPA does not guarantee the accuracy of these financial statements. The report to stockholders and the public is made by management; the CPA renders a professional opinion as to the "fairness" of the presentation.

The phrase "in conformity with generally accepted accounting principles" in the second paragraph is particularly relevant to our discussion. __An authoritative exhaustive list of generally accepted accounting principles does not exist.__ Yet the widespread reliance upon this phrase implies that there is general consensus as to what these principles are. In making his audit and arriving at the basis for his opinion, the independent CPA must exercise considerable judgment based on a broad and thorough knowledge of accounting and business practices.

Nature of accounting principles

Accounting is a man-made information system. It rests not on a body of natural laws but on a set of basic assumptions and working rules that govern the measurement of economic events in accounting terms. The phrase "generally accepted accounting principles" as used in practice encompasses a broad set of basic assumptions, measurement methods, and reporting procedures followed by accountants. For many years accounting theorists have been arguing about the precise nature of accounting principles. Even today the subject generates heated controversy and precise terminology has yet to be established. There is a growing consensus that accounting principles are statements of the major objectives sought by accountants and the guidelines to be followed in making accounting measurements. There is also agreement that these principles rest on a few basic assumptions (called *postulates* by some) which establish the boundaries of the accounting process.

The *basic principles* of accounting have remained relatively unchanged for a long time; the *procedures* of accounting are subject to more frequent changes. Procedures are modified in response to improvements in the art of accounting, to changes in the laws governing business operations and income taxation, and at times in response to pressures from various groups who want to shape financial results to attain particular ends. Accounting is an endeavor of human beings to measure certain events in their economic environment. It is shaped by the clash of ideas, improves through human ingenuity, and suffers from human frailties.

Accounting authority

To qualify as "generally accepted," an accounting principle must usually receive substantial authoritative support. The most influential authoritative groups in this country are: (1) The American Institute of Certified Public Accountants (AICPA), the professional association of licensed CPAs; (2) the American Accounting Association (AAA), an academic organization composed primarily of accounting professors; and (3) the Securities and Exchange Commission (SEC), an agency of the federal government established in the Securities and Exchange Act of 1934 to administer the provisions of that act relating to the publication of financial information by corporations whose stock is widely held.

The AICPA has long been concerned with stating and defining accounting principles because its members face the problem of making decisions every day about generally accepted principles in their professional work. From 1939 to 1959 a series of *Accounting Research Bulletins* published by the AICPA was considered the most authoritative of accounting principles. In 1959, the AICPA created an Accounting Principles Board, composed of practitioners, educators, and industry representatives. This Board was authorized to issue pronouncements which are officially regarded by members of the AICPA as authoritative written expressions of generally accepted accounting principles.

At the same time the AICPA strengthened its research efforts and commissioned a series of Accounting Research Studies to aid the Accounting Principles Board in its work. Thus far the Accounting Principles Board has issued a number of formal *opinions* on particular controversial areas in accounting but has not yet put its stamp of approval on an overall statement of accounting principles.

The American Accounting Association has sponsored a number of research studies and monographs in which individual authors and Association committees attempt to summarize accounting principles.[1] These statements have no doubt had considerable influence on the thinking of accounting theorists and practitioners. However, the AAA lacks the power of the AICPA to impose its collective view on accounting practice, and therefore exercises its influence through the prestige of its authors and the persuasiveness of their views.

The SEC has considerable power to exercise its authority since it may reject corporate financial statements that do not, in the opinion of the Commission, meet acceptable standards. The views of the Commission on various accounting issues are published in the SEC's *Accounting Series Releases.*

The accounting environment

The principles of accounting are to a considerable extent shaped by the environment in which the accounting process is employed. Accounting is concerned with economic activity, that is, the ownership and exchange of goods and services. Accounting systems developed in response to the need for quantitative information about business activity as an aid both to outsiders and insiders in making rational economic decisions. Money is a common denominator in which diverse goods and services may be measured. Quantification in accounting is thus in terms of a monetary unit, whether it be dollars, francs, or lira. Most goods and services produced in our economy are distributed through exchange rather than being directly consumed by producers. It is logical, therefore, to base accounting measurements on exchange (market) prices generated by past, present, and future transactions and events.

For example, when the accountant reports the original cost of a plant site acquired some years ago, he is reflecting a past exchange. When he states inventory at market under the lower-of-cost-or-market rule, he is using a present exchange price as the basis for his measurement. When he accrues a liability for income taxes, he is measuring the present effect of a future cash outflow to the government.

Since present decisions can affect only current and future outcomes, current and future exchange prices are in general more relevant for decision making than past exchange prices. This factor has led some people to suggest that the accountant should make his measurements solely in terms of current

---

[1] The latest of these is *A Statement of Basic Accounting Theory,* American Accounting Association (Evanston, Ill.: 1966).

and future prices. These people would say, for example, that a plant site should be accounted for in terms of its current market value, not its original cost. We live in a world of uncertainty, however, and estimates of future, and even current, exchange prices are often subject to wide margins of error. Where to draw the line of acceptability in the trade-off between *reliability* and *relevance* is one of the crucial issues in accounting theory. The need for reliable and verifiable data is an important constraint, particularly with respect to information reported to outsiders. This factor has led the accountant to rely heavily on past exchange prices as the basis for his measurements.

In the remaining sections of this chapter we shall summarize briefly the major principles that govern the accounting process, and comment on some areas of controversy. We have noted the need for accepted principles to foster confidence in the published statements of widely held corporations. Most accounting principles are equally applicable to profit-making organizations of any size or form.

Accounting entities

Economic activity is carried on through a variety of entities. A basic principle of accounting is that information is compiled in terms of a specifiable accounting entity. An individual person is an accounting entity. So is a business enterprise, whether conducted as a proprietorship, partnership, or corporation. The estate of a deceased person is an accounting entity, as are nonprofit clubs and organizations. The basic accounting equation: Assets — Liabilities = Owners' Equity, reflects the *accounting entity concept,* since the elements of the equation relate to the particular entity whose economic activity is being metered in accounting statements.

We should distinguish between accounting and legal entities. In some cases the two coincide. For example, corporations, estates, trusts, and governmental agencies are both accounting and legal entities. In other cases accounting entities differ from legal entities. For example, an individual proprietorship is an accounting entity but the individual proprietor is a legal entity. He is legally liable both for his personal obligations and for those incurred in connection with his business operations, and the assets of his business may be called upon to satisfy the claims of his personal creditors. For accounting purposes the proprietor as an individual and his business enterprise are separate entities. Furthermore, a proprietor may own several businesses, each of which is treated as a separate entity for accounting purposes.

There are other cases where it is useful to compile financial reports for an accounting entity composed of two or more legal entities. For example, consolidated statements, as we saw in the previous chapter, are prepared for an economic entity composed of two or more legal corporate entities operated under common control exercised through stock ownership.

The choice of an accounting entity is somewhat flexible and should be based on informational needs. Any legal or economic unit which controls economic resources is a possible accounting entity.

The going-concern assumption

In making accounting measurements, it is often necessary to make some assumption about the length of life of the entity. For example, suppose that a company has just purchased a five-year insurance policy for $5,000. If we assume that the business is likely to terminate at any time, this policy should be recorded at its cancellation value, the amount of cash the insurance company will refund on immediate cancellation of the policy, which may be, say, $4,200. On the other hand, if we assume that the company will continue in operation for five years or more, it is appropriate to consider the $5,000 paid for the insurance as an asset whose services (freedom from risk) will be enjoyed by the accounting entity over a five-year period.

An underlying assumption in accounting is that an accounting entity will continue in operation for an indefinite period of time sufficient to carry out its existing commitments. This assumption is sometimes called the *going-concern assumption.* Since most accounting entities have indefinite lives, the assumption of continuity is in accord with experience in our economic system. In general, the going-concern assumption justifies our ignoring immediate liquidating values in presenting assets and liabilities in the balance sheet.

The continuity assumption does *not,* as is sometimes claimed, represent the accountant's justification for reporting assets at cost. To illustrate, suppose a firm paid $10,000 for land that subsequently proved to contain valuable minerals and to be worth $10 million. The assumption that the business owning this land is a going concern that will continue in operation and make use of these mineral rights does *not* make the $10 million valuation irrelevant. Similarly, if the firm paid $10 million for land which was thought to contain valuable natural resources but which was later proved to be barren and worth only $10,000, the going-concern assumption cannot be called upon to justify reporting the asset at the $10 million cost figure. We *can* say that the assumption of continuity removes the liquidation complex from the accountant's measuring process. We shall have to look elsewhere for the primary justification of the cost basis of reporting assets.

It is interesting to note that the going-concern assumption may be removed when it is not in accord with the facts. Accountants are sometimes asked to prepare financial statements for enterprises that are about to liquidate. In this case the assumption of continuity is no longer valid. In preparing a position statement (known as a statement of affairs) under these circumstances, the accountant drops his going-concern assumption and reports assets at their current liquidating value and liabilities at the amount required to settle the debts immediately.

Periodic financial reports

We assume an indefinite life for most accounting entities. But accountants are asked to measure operating progress and changes in economic position at relatively short time intervals during this indefinite life. Users of accounting data want periodic measurements for decision-making purposes. Dividing the life of an enterprise into time segments and trying to measure changes in financial position periodically is a difficult process. A precise measure of net income and financial position can be made only when a business has been liquidated and its resources have been fully converted into cash. At any time prior to liquidation, the worth of the assets and the amount of liabilities of a business entity are to some extent a matter of speculation. Thus periodic measures of net income and financial position are at best only informed estimates.

Periodic measurements are always *tentative.* This fact should be clearly understood by those who use and rely on periodic accounting information. The need for periodic measurements creates many of accounting's most serious problems. For example, the attempt to measure income over short time periods requires the selection of inventory flow assumptions and depreciation methods. The end-of-period adjustment procedures discussed in Chapter 4 stem directly from the need to update accounting information to a particular point in time.

Objectivity

A basic principle of accounting is that changes in the valuations assigned to assets and liabilities, and their resultant effect on net income and owners' equity, should not be recognized until they can be measured objectively.

The term *objective* refers to measurements that are unbiased and subject to verification by independent experts. For example, the price established in an arm's-length transaction is an objective measure of exchange value at the time of the transaction. It is not surprising, therefore, that exchange prices established in business transactions constitute much of the raw material from which accounting information is generated.

If a measurement is objective, 10 competent investigators who make the same measurement will come up with substantially identical results. It is probably true, however, that 10 competent accountants who set out independently to measure the net income of a given business would not arrive at an identical result. In the light of the objectivity principle, why is this so? The variation would probably arise because of the existence of alternative accounting measurement methods, rather than the lack of objectivity in any given measurement method. To illustrate, in measuring the cost of goods sold one accountant might use the lifo method, another the fifo method, and another the weighted average method. These choices could produce significant variations in the cost of goods sold figure and in net income. If a particular inventory flow assumption were specified, however, the 10 accountants should arrive at an identical cost of goods sold figure.

The accountant relies on various kinds of evidence to support his financial measurements, but he seeks always the most objective evidence he can get. Invoices, contracts, canceled checks, physical counts of inventory are examples of objective evidence used by accountants.

Despite the goal of objectivity, it is not possible to insulate all accounting data from opinion and personal judgment. The cost of a depreciable asset can be objectively determined but not the periodic depreciation charge. To measure the cost of the asset services that have expired during a given period requires estimates of the salvage value and service life of the asset and judgment as to the depreciation method that is appropriate in the circumstances.

Furthermore, objectivity is a relative term which allows for some reasonable latitude in the quality of the evidence. A past exchange price is more objective than a current market price because the accountant can observe an actual exchange transaction. Both are more objective than an estimated future exchange price. All three, however, may be independently verified within a range of accuracy that permits their use as accounting inputs. The allowance for uncollectible accounts, for example, is an estimate of probable future economic events based on an analysis of current receivables and past collection experience.

The principle of objectivity in accounting has its roots in the quest for reliability. Estimates of what might happen are often very useful for decision making. But differences in estimates of both current and future economic values are notorious in a free economy. The highly efficient market for the common stocks of publicly held corporations thrives on such differences. For every stockholder who sells his shares because he sniffs the winds of adversity on the corporate horizon there must be a buyer whose nose is tickled by the fragrance of prosperity. For every shrewd financial analyst who advises his clients to buy Stock A, there is an investment advisor with an equal reputation for investment sagacity who considers Stock A highly overvalued.

The accountant obviously wants to make his economic measurements reliable, and at the same time as relevant to decision makers as possible. Because the goals of reliability and relevance often pull in opposite directions, the accountant is faced with a dilemma. For example, the current fair market value of a business plant may be useful information to an investor trying to decide whether to purchase the stock of a corporation. But in the absence of a firm offer to buy the plant and acceptance by the seller, this current fair market value cannot be determined with a high degree of objectivity. Different expert appraisers arrive at widely varying estimates of the worth of complex industrial properties. On the other hand, the original cost of the plant, less estimated depreciation, is a more objective (and thus more reliable) figure which reflects the firm's unrecovered investment in these resources. It is, however, a less useful measurement for some purposes.

The accountant is constantly faced with the necessity of compromising between what his public would like to know and what it is possible to measure with a reasonable degree of reliability. Some authorities believe the accountant is too conservative and waits too long to measure and recognize in his accounts changes in assets and liabilities, and that he could measure some changes sooner than he does. Those who support present measurement principles argue that it is important that the public have confidence in financial statements, and that this confidence can best be maintained if the accountant recognizes changes in assets and liabilities only on the basis of objective evidence.

Consistency

We have seen that alternative accounting methods may affect the measurement of assets, liabilities, and net income. The standard phrase in the CPA's opinion (see page 444) "in conformity with generally accepted accounting principles *applied on a basis consistent with that of the preceding year,*" implies that a particular accounting method, once adopted, will not be changed from period to period. This principle of consistency is important because it enables the user of accounting data to interpret changes in net income or financial position from period to period.

The principle of consistency does not prevent the accountant from changing accounting methods when in his judgment a different method is advisable. When a material change in accounting methods occurs, however, the accountant is obliged to report both the fact that a change in method has been made and the dollar effect of the change. In published statements this disclosure is incorporated in the CPA's report. A typical disclosure might be as follows: "During the current year the company changed from the fifo to the lifo method of accounting for inventory flows. If this change in method had not been made, both ending inventories and income before taxes for the year would be $500,000 greater."

The principle of consistency applies to a single accounting entity and promotes the comparability of financial data from period to period. It is not a principle of accounting that *different* companies, even those in the same industry, will follow the same accounting methods. When comparing the financial results of two companies, it is important to look for and determine the effect of any differences in accounting methods.

Measurement and accounting

Accounting is basically a measurement process. Within the framework of the principles previously discussed, the accountant attempts to:

1. Measure the resources controlled by the accounting entity.
2. Measure the creditors' claims against these resources and the resultant ownership equity in the accounting entity.
3. Measure the changes that occur in these resources, claims, and equity interests.
4. Assign the changes to specifiable periods of time.
5. Express the measurements in terms of a monetary unit as the common denominator.

The measurement of resources, claims against resources, and ownership equity is expressed in the basic accounting equation: Assets − Liabilities = Owners' Equity. If we examine the elements of this equation, we see that assets and liabilities are the independent variables. The ownership equity in any accounting entity is a residual amount which can be determined only when the assets and liabilities have been measured.

Assets are expected future economic benefits, the rights to which have been acquired by the entity as a result of current or past transactions. For measurement purposes assets may be classified in two categories: (1) cash and claims to cash, and (2) all other assets. The first category includes cash, investments in marketable securities, notes receivable, and accounts receivable. These assets represent present holdings of cash or cash equivalents and future claims against cash. They are measured (with the exception of marketable securities) at their present monetary value. Cash, for example, is automatically stated at its monetary value. Receivables are stated at the present value of the future expected cash inflow, taking into account estimates of uncollectible amounts.

Assets other than cash and claims to cash are ultimately converted into cash through operations. The major classes of assets falling into this category are inventories, prepaid expenses, plant and equipment, and intangibles. At the original date of acquisition these assets are measured in terms of the cost of acquiring them and bringing them to the desired condition and location.

Liabilities, the claims against assets, are obligations to convey assets or perform services which result from past or current transactions, and which require settlement in the future. Liabilities are typically measured in terms of the value of assets or services that will be given up by the accounting entity to settle the obligation.

Measuring changes in assets and liabilities

A primary objective of the accounting process is the measurement of changes in assets and liabilities. Transactions involving an equal increase in assets and liabilities (for example, the acquisition of an asset on credit) create few accounting problems. Similarly, transactions involving an identical decrease in both assets and liabilities (for example, the payment of a debt) cause little difficulty. The central measurement problem is to determine when an increase in *net assets* (and thus owners' equity) has occurred, and to measure this change.

Increases in net assets. Changes which increase net assets (and owners' equity) are of three basic types:

1. Additional investments of capital by owners

2. Revenues—the gross increase in net assets resulting from the production or delivery of goods and the rendering of services

3. Gains—any increase in net assets other than those resulting from revenues or additional investment of capital

Decreases in net assets. Changes which decrease net assets (and owners' equity) may also be divided into three classes:

1. Distribution to owners, for example, dividends

2. Expenses—decreases in net assets resulting from the use of economic goods and services to create revenues or from the imposition of taxes by governmental bodies

3. Losses—decreases in net assets other than those resulting from expenses or distributions of capital to owners

If we ignore the cases of increased capital investment and distributions of capital to owners, the resultant of increases and decreases in net assets is the quantity we call net income. It is clear, therefore, that the accountant's measurement of net income is in essence the direct result of his measurement of the continuous recurring changes in net assets as a result of operations.   → SALE Completed when title is taken

Recognizing revenues. Revenues relate to the firm's output of goods and services, expenses to the input of goods and services. Net income arises when the value of output exceeds the cost of input. In theory it would be possible to measure the value of the output of an enterprise at a number of different times: (1) during production; (2) when production is completed; (3) when sale or delivery of the product is made or the services are rendered; (4) when the firm collects cash from customers.

In most cases the accountant chooses to measure the increase in net assets which he calls revenue at the time of the sale of goods or the rendering of services. Measuring revenues at this point is logical because the firm has essentially completed the earning process and the realized value of the goods or services sold can be objectively measured in terms of the billed price. At any time prior to sale the ultimate realizable value of the goods or services can only be estimated. After the sale the only step that remains is to collect from the customer, and this is usually a relatively certain event.

There are some circumstances in which the accountant finds it appropriate to measure revenue during production or when production is completed. An example arises in the case of long-term construction contracts, such as the building of a dam under a contract over a three-year period. In this case the ultimate selling price is known when the construction job is begun, and the ultimate "sale" of the dam is an anticlimax. Furthermore, it would be unreasonable to assume that the entire increase in the value of the output (in this case the dam) occurred in the accounting period in which the project happened to be completed. The accountant therefore estimates the sales value of the portion of the work completed during each accounting period, and recognizes revenues in proportion to completed production. Any error in estimates is corrected in the final period of the contract.

If at the end of any accounting period it appears that a loss will be incurred on an uncompleted contract (that is, the costs to date are larger than the proportion of the selling price earned), the loss is recognized at once by reducing the book value of the asset to its net realizable value.

An accounting procedure also exists for delaying the measurement of revenues until cash is finally collected. This measurement method is sometimes used when collections extend over relatively long periods of time and there is a strong possibility that full collection will not be made. As customers make installment payments, the seller recognizes the gross profit on sales in proportion to the cash collected. This method of revenue recognition exists largely because it is allowed for income tax purposes; it postpones the payment of income taxes until cash is collected from customers. From an accounting viewpoint, there is little theoretical justification for delaying the measurement of revenues beyond the point of sale, because few if any cases exist where the value of the receivable cannot be objectively measured at that time.

Measuring expenses. Revenues, the gross increase in net assets resulting from the production or sale of goods and services, are offset by expenses incurred in bringing the firm's output to the point of sale. The cost of merchandise sold, the expiration of asset services, and out-of-pocket expenditures for operating costs are examples of expenses relating to revenues. The measurement of expenses occurs in two stages: (1) measuring the cost of goods and services that constitute the firm's input in generating revenues, and (2) determining when the goods and services acquired have contributed to revenues and their cost thus becomes an expense. The second aspect of the measurement process is often referred to as *matching costs and revenues.*

Costs are associated with revenues (and thus become expenses) in two major ways:

1. In relation to the product sold or services rendered. If a good or service can be related to the product or service which constitutes the output of the enterprise, its cost becomes an expense when the product is sold or the service rendered to customers. The cost of goods sold in a merchandising firm is a good example of this type of expense. Similarly, a commission paid to a real estate salesman by a real estate brokerage office is an expense directly related to the revenues generated by the salesman.

2. In relation to the time period during which revenues are earned. Some costs incurred by businesses cannot be directly related to the product or service output of the firm. Expired fire insurance, property taxes, depreciation on a retail store building, the salary of the president of the company—all are examples of costs incurred in generating revenues which cannot be related to specific transactions. The accountant refers to this class of costs as *period costs,* and charges them to expense by associating them with the period of time during which they are incurred and presumably contribute to revenues, rather than by associating them with specific products or services of the firm.

Recognition of gains and losses. The same standards applied in recognizing revenues are applicable to the measurement of gains and losses on assets other than inventories. In general an increase in the value of a productive asset, such as machinery or buildings, is not recognized until the asset in question is sold, in which case the amount of the gain is objectively determinable.

If a productive asset increases in value while it is in service, the accountant ordinarily does not record this gain because it has not been realized. "Not realized" means that the gain in value has not been substantiated by a transaction in which an exchange price has been established. Actually an increase in the value of a productive asset may be reflected in net income indirectly prior to sale or disposal. To illustrate, suppose that a firm developed a new product and obtained a patent on it at a total cost of $100,000. The product was a strong success, and the firm turned down an offer of $5 million for the patent rights. Although the firm would carry the patent on its books at the $100,000 cost and charge this cost to expense over the useful life of the patent, the increased value of the patent would no doubt be reflected in the price the firm could command for its product. Thus revenues earned, particularly during the early years when the firm had an advantage over its competition, would be high and would be matched against the low costs of product development. The firm's net income would reflect indirectly the increased patent value, even though the gain in the value of the patent was not recognized directly as an increase in the value of net assets.

For many years accounting theorists have debated the question whether it would be desirable to attempt to recognize gains in the value of productive assets prior to their sale or disposal. This debate becomes particularly vigorous during periods of rising prices when it is likely that assets carried at cost less accumulated depreciation will be stated at figures considerably less than their current market value. The majority of accountants and businessmen have rejected proposals for measuring unexpired asset services at a figure other than cost because of the difficulty of obtaining objective measures of the current market value of assets and because *realization* had not taken place.

Accountants are not so insistent on following the rules of *realization* in measuring losses. We have seen in Chapter 11, for example, that the lower-of-cost-or-market valuation of inventories results in the recognition of losses in inventory investment prior to the sale of the goods in question. Recognizing losses when inventories appear to be worth less than their cost but refusing to recognize gains when inventories appear to be worth more than their cost is logically inconsistent. This inconsistency is justified by an accounting presumption that assets should not be measured at cost valuations in excess of the amount which can be expected to be recovered through revenues. The accountant takes a different attitude with respect to losses because of a belief that errors involving an overstatement of net assets are likely to have more serious consequences for readers of financial statements than errors involving understatement. Thus the accountant tends to resolve uncertainties in the direction of understatement. This attitude is sometimes referred to as the accounting convention of *conservatism.* Conservatism in dealing with cases when the evidence is uncertain does not, of course, justify deliberate understatement of net assets.

Money—a measuring unit

Money is the common denominator in which accounting measurements are made and summarized. The dollar, or any other monetary unit, represents a unit of value; that is, it reflects the ability to command all goods and services in the economy. Implicit in the use of money as a measuring unit is the assumption that the dollar is a stable unit of value, just as the mile is a stable unit of distance, and an acre is a stable unit of area.

Having accepted money as his measuring unit, the accountant freely combines dollar measures of economic transactions that occur at various times during the life of an accounting entity. He combines, for example, a $5,000 cost of equipment purchased in 1960 and the $10,000 cost of equipment purchased in 1970 and reports the total as a $15,000 investment in equipment. Similarly, the sale of a product in 1971 for $100 is measured and compared with the $75 cost of acquiring the goods in 1970, to determine gross profit. The proceeds of the sale of capital stock in 1930 is combined with the proceeds of the sale of stock in 1971 to arrive at the total paid-in capital as of the end of 1971.

Unlike the mile and the acre, which are stable units of distance and area, respectively, the dollar, unfortunately, is not a stable unit of value. The prices of goods and services (that is, the exchange rate between money and goods and services) in our economy change over time. When the *general price level* (a phrase used to describe the average of all prices) changes from period to period, the value of money (that is, its ability to command goods and services) also changes. For example, the consumer price index in the United States increased by approximately 50% from 1950 to 1970. We might thus say that the value of the dollar fell from 100 cents in 1950 to approximately 67 cents in 1970 (100% ÷ 150% = .67).

The effect of changing price levels. What effect do material changes in general price levels, and thus changes in the value of money, have on accounting measurements? By combining transactions measured in dollars of varying years, the accountant in effect ignores changes in the size of his measuring unit. For example, suppose that a company purchased land early in Year 1 for $50,000 and sold this land for $100,000 late in Year 10. If prices roughly doubled during that 10-year period and the value of money was cut in half, we might say that the company was no better off as a result of these two transactions; the $100,000 received for the land in Year 10 represented approximately the same command over goods and services as $50,000 did when invested in the land in Year 1. In terms of the *dollar* as a measuring unit, however, the accountant would record a gain of $50,000 ($100,000 − $50,000) at the time the land was sold in Year 10. Thus, by combining the Year 1 and Year 10 transactions in dollar terms to measure gains and losses, *the accountant assumes that a firm is as well off when it has recovered its original dollar investment, and that it is better off whenever it recovers more than the original number of dollars invested in any given asset.*

The assumption that the dollar is a stable measuring unit can hardly be defended on factual grounds. The issue is not whether money *is* a stable measuring unit; we know it is not. The question is whether measurements made using historical dollars as the measuring unit are more useful than measurements which might be made by using some other measuring unit.

This issue has received a great deal of attention among both accounting theorists and practitioners in the last 50 years. Immediately following World War I, in response to a runaway inflation in Germany, methods were devised for making accounting measurements and presenting financial statements in terms of current dollars rather than historical dollars. Such statements have come to be known as *common dollar* financial statements, because all historical dollar measurements are converted to their equivalent in terms of the dollar in existence at the date of the statement.

An extended discussion of the procedures used to prepare common dollar statements is beyond the scope of this book, but the process may be visualized through brief discussion of a simplified example.

Illustration: common dollar statements. To introduce a dramatic change in the general price level, we shall assume a situation in which all prices double within a short period of time. Suppose that at the end of Year 1, when an index of the general price level stood at 100, Flation Company's financial position was as follows:

How Will Inflation Affect This Company?

FLATION COMPANY
Balance Sheet
End of Year 1

Assets		Liabilities & Stockholders' Equity	
Cash.................	$20,000	Current liabilities	$15,000
Inventories.............	30,000	Capital stock	35,000
	$50,000		$50,000

By the middle of Year 2 all prices in the economy doubled and the index of the general price level rose to 200. After the price doubling, Flation Company completed only two transactions: (1) It sold one-half its inventory for $28,000 in cash; (2) it paid $10,000 to its current creditors. Income taxes are ignored for purposes of this illustration. A comparative balance sheet of the company in Year 2, immediately after these transactions, in historical dollars and in common dollars, appears on page 458.

An explanation of the differences between the historical dollar balances and the common dollar balances in the comparative balance sheet on page 458 will make clear the nature of the conversion process.

First, note that the balances of two items, cash and current liabilities, are exactly the same when stated either in historical or common (Year 2) dollars. The reason for this is that cash and obligations to pay cash represent monetary resources and monetary obligations that are fixed in terms of dollars. If we have $38,000 in cash and prices double, we still have $38,000 even though these dollars have only one-half the command over goods and services. Similarly if we owe $5,000 and prices double, we still have a fixed obligation to pay $5,000 even though settlement of the debt may be made in dollars that are only one-half as valuable. In general, cash, receivables,

Conventional
Income of
$13,000 Is
Offset by
Loss of
$20,000
Because of
Inflation

FLATION COMPANY
Comparative Balance Sheet
Middle of Year 2

	Historical Dollars	Common Dollars
Assets:		
Cash	$38,000	$38,000
Inventories......................	15,000	30,000
Total assets	$53,000	$68,000
Liabilities & Stockholders' Equity:		
Current liabilities	$ 5,000	$ 5,000
Capital stock....................	35,000	70,000
Retained earnings (deficit)	13,000	(7,000)
Total liabilities & stockholders' equity	$53,000	$68,000

and obligations to pay cash fall in this class of assets and liabilities, which may be called *monetary items.*

Changes in price levels produce gains and losses as a result of holding monetary assets, or as a result of owing monetary liabilities. We can compute these gains and losses by analyzing transactions that affect cash and liabilities and comparing the amount of these transactions measured in historical dollars with the amount measured in common dollars. In our Flation Company example, the common dollars are Year 2 dollars immediately after the doubling of all prices. In the schedule on the next page, actual cash and liability transactions are shown, first in historical dollars, and then in terms of their equivalent in Year 2 dollars. The difference between the cash and liability balances in the two columns represents the loss or gain to the Flation Company as a result of holding cash during rising prices, or as a result of owing money during rising prices.

In our very simple example, all transactions occurred after the major jump in prices. Therefore only the original balances of cash and current liabilities change when stated in common dollars. In a more realistic situation, prices might change gradually during the year and some transactions would occur when the price level was 110, others when the price level stood at 120, etc. In this case we would convert the amounts of these transactions to common dollars as of the date of the financial statements by multiplying the historical dollar amount by 200 (the price index at statement date) and dividing by the price index at the time of the transaction. For example, if we had incurred an obligation of $15,000 at a time when the price index stood at 150, we would convert this liability to $20,000 in terms of common dollars ($15,000 \times {}^{200}/_{150}$ = $20,000).

In the Flation Company case, our analysis shows that we would have

*Does It
Pay to
Hold Cash
during
Inflation?*

Analysis of Cash Transactions in Historical and Common Dollars

	Historical Dollars	Common Dollars
Original cash balance.....................	$20,000	
Equivalent amount of Year 2 dollars ($20,000 × 200/100 = $40,000)		$40,000
Sale of merchandise for cash in Year 2............	28,000	
Equivalent in Year 2 dollars is the same.........		28,000
Payment of debt in Year 2	(10,000)	
Equivalent in Year 2 dollars is the same.........		(10,000)
Cash balance......................	$38,000	
Cash balance that would be required to represent the equivalent of Year 2 dollars		$58,000
Loss in purchasing power as a result of holding cash during a period of rising price levels............		(20,000)
Cash balance to be reported in both historical and common dollars........................	$38,000	$38,000

*. . . or
to Owe
Money?*

Analysis of Current Liability Transactions in Historical and Common Dollars

	Historical Dollars	Common Dollars
Original balance of current liabilities.............	$15,000	
Equivalent amount in Year 2 dollars ($15,000 × 200/100 = $30,000)		$30,000
Payment on debt in Year 2....................	(10,000)	
Equivalent in Year 2 dollars is the same.........		(10,000)
Current liability balance......................	$ 5,000	
Current liabilities as they would be if company were required to pay an equivalent amount in Year 2 dollars................................		$20,000
Gain in purchasing power as a result of owing money during a period of rising price levels............		(15,000)
Balance of current liabilities to be reported in both historical and common dollars	$ 5,000	$ 5,000

to have $58,000 in cash to be as well off in Year 2 dollars as we were in terms of historical dollars at the time we either received or paid out cash. Since we have only $38,000 in cash, the company has suffered a loss in purchasing power of $20,000, which will be shown on the common dollar income statement, as we shall see later. Similarly, if we were forced to pay our creditors an amount of money which would put them in the same purchasing power position as they were in at the time they extended credit, Flation Company would owe $20,000 at the date of the balance sheet. Since the company owes only $5,000, it has gained $15,000 by being a debtor during a period in which the value of money fell in half and the real burden of owing a given number of dollars fell proportionately.

We can now demonstrate the reason for the difference in the historical dollar and common dollar retained earnings balances by the following comparative income statement:

FLATION COMPANY
Comparative Income Statement
Part of Year 2

	Historical Dollars	*Common Dollars*
Sales (Year 2 dollars in both cases)	*$28,000*	*$28,000*
Cost of goods sold:		
Historical dollars (½ of $30,000)	*15,000*	
Common dollars (200/100 × $15,000)		*30,000*
Net operating income (loss)	*$13,000*	*$ (2,000)*
Less: Purchasing power loss from holding monetary assets during rising price levels		*(20,000)*
Add: Purchasing power gain from owing money during rising price levels		*15,000*
Net operating loss and purchasing power loss		*$ (7,000)*

We can now see why the Flation Company is considered to be $7,000 worse off in common dollar terms, when they reported a $13,000 income in historical dollars. In Year 2 after the doubling of prices, the company sold for $28,000 goods which had cost $15,000 in the previous year before the general price rise. Since prices doubled, the investment in goods sold in Year 2 dollars is twice their $15,000 cost, or $30,000. When the $28,000 of realized revenues in Year 2 dollars is compared with the $30,000 of cost of goods sold in Year 2 dollars, the result is a $2,000 loss to the Flation Company in terms of its command over goods and services in general. Added to this operating loss is the net $5,000 purchasing power loss ($20,000 − $15,000) resulting from the company's monetary asset and liability position during a period in which prices doubled.

Inventory is not a monetary asset because it represents an investment in goods, and not a claim on a fixed number of dollars. On a balance sheet measured in common dollars we want to state the investment in inventory in terms of dollars at the statement date, that is, Year 2 dollars. The Year 1 investment of $15,000 in inventory is thus converted to its equivalent in Year 2 dollars ($15,000 × $200/100$ = $30,000), and reported as a $30,000 investment on the common dollar statement.

Similarly capital stock is not a monetary item, since it represents an amount invested by stockholders for an equity interest in net assets. Stockholders invested $35,000 in Year 1. This amount is converted to $70,000 ($35,000 $\times$ $200/_{100}$), to reflect the amount of the stockholders' investment in equivalent Year 2 dollars.

Implication of common dollar measurements. If we reexamine the Flation Company balance sheet stated in common (Year 2) dollars (see page 458), we can see four major implications of financial data measured in common dollars:

1. The firm is assumed to be better off (that is, to have earned income) only after it has recovered the equivalent general purchasing power represented by the dollars originally invested in productive resources. This is implied by the matching of $30,000 of cost of goods sold with the $28,000 of sales revenues, since the $30,000 cost of goods sold figure represents the Year 2 equivalent of the original $15,000 invested in the goods sold. Also the valuation of the remaining inventory at $30,000 on the balance sheet implies that the firm will have to sell these goods for more than this amount to earn a profit measured in common dollars, assuming no further change in the value of money.

2. Holding monetary assets (cash or receivables) during a period of rising prices results in a loss of purchasing power, since the value of money falls in periods of rising prices. This is illustrated by the $20,000 loss that resulted from carrying a $20,000 cash balance during a period when prices doubled.

3. Owing money during a period of rising prices results in a gain in purchasing power, which is reported in common dollar statements. This purchasing power gain results because the debtor company may settle its obligation in a fixed number of dollars which have a lesser value than the dollars which represented the original proceeds of the debt.

4. In periods of rising general price levels, net income reported in common dollar terms may be smaller or larger than conventional accounting net income, depending on each company's individual circumstances. The common dollar income of a company that has large amounts of monetary assets and a small amount of debt will be smaller than its conventional accounting income. On the other hand, the common dollar income of a company that has little in the way of monetary assets and has large amounts of debt is likely to be larger than its conventional accounting income because of its purchasing power gains as a debtor.

Common dollar statements in practice. Common dollar financial statements are not generally accepted as primary reports to stockholders. A few companies have published some version of common dollar financial statements in supplementary schedules included in their annual reports.[2] Thus far, however, the idea has received more attention from accounting theorists than from practitioners and businessmen.

[2] See Accounting Research Study No. 6, *Reporting the Financial Effects of Price Level Changes,* AICPA (New York: 1963), pp. 169–219. See also "Statement of the Accounting Principles Board No. 3: Financial Statements Restated for General Price-Level Changes," AICPA (New York: 1969).

The effort required to make accounting measurements in common dollar terms and to prepare financial statements on this basis is considerable. In an age of electronic computers, however, this additional data-processing effort is not a practical barrier to the preparation of common dollar statements.

The conversion of accounting data into common dollars is not widely used in the United States because thus far the business community is apparently not convinced of the increased usefulness of this information. The concept of using common dollars as a measuring unit is not easy to grasp. There is some feeling that readers of financial statements are likely to be confused by complex measurement processes that attempt to adjust for changes in the value of money. Some businessmen believe that statistical measures of changes in the general price level are not sufficiently precise to warrant the use of index numbers as the basis for common dollar accounting. Others argue that the average rate of rise in the general price level in this country in recent years has not been large enough to destroy the usefulness of historical dollars as an accounting measuring unit.

This issue will continue to be debated as long as price level changes occur. It is particularly important in relation to publicly held corporations because the financial affairs of such companies have an impact on a number of public policy issues. Continued experimentation with financial measurement in common dollar terms will be needed to test the usefulness of this potential modification of present accounting principles.

Replacement costs distinguished from common dollar accounting

We have used the expression *common dollar accounting* to describe financial statements in which historical costs have been adjusted to reflect changes in the general price level since the original cost was incurred. Common dollar accounting does not abandon historical cost as the basis of measurement but simply expresses cost in terms of a current monetary unit. Common dollar accounting also does not mean that *replacement costs* (which may be assumed to approximate fair market value) are used in the preparation of financial statements.

For example, a tract of land which cost $100,000 many years ago would be stated at $150,000 in common dollars if the general price level had risen by 50%. However, the replacement cost of the land might be a quite different amount because land prices might have risen much more or much less than the general price level. Furthermore, replacement of the land might be impossible, because no tract of land with identical characteristics could be found.

If accountants were to use current replacement costs in financial statements, the unit of measurement would be current dollars since replacement costs are naturally stated in these terms. But this approach would also change the basis of measurement to reflect the ability of the firm to command particular assets and services rather than goods and services in general. The use of replacement costs in preparing financial statements would clearly be a departure from the historical cost concept, and would require that account-ants develop reliable techniques for measuring the current cost of replacing various types of assets.

Some accountants have recommended that supplementary financial statements showing appraisal values of assets be prepared and submitted along with conventional statements. Although such statements are some-times prepared in connection with a loan application or the proposed sale of a business, accountants for the most part do not favor the use of replace-ment cost, because such appraisals lack the objectivity desired by most users of financial statements.

In cases of extreme increases in asset values as, for example, when land increases tenfold in market value over a period of years, it is difficult to argue that historical costs provide investors with more useful information than replacement costs, even though the estimates of replacement costs are sub-ject to some lack of precision and objectivity. In dealing with the measure-ment problem, the accountant is faced with a fundamental issue: Can the usefulness of accounting data be improved by providing more relevant data at the price of some significant loss in measurement objectivity? Professional accountants have for some time been seeking a satisfactory answer to this question.

Illustration of corporation balance sheet

In this chapter and the preceding chapters on corporations, sections of balance sheets have been shown in several illustrations. A complete and fairly detailed consolidated balance sheet of the Crenshaw Corporation is presented on pages 464 and 465 to bring together many of the individual features which have been discussed. In studying this corporation balance sheet, however, the student should bear in mind that current practice includes many varia-tions and alternatives in the choice of terminology and the arrangement of items in financial statements.

QUESTIONS

1. What developments were primarily responsible for the transformation of double-entry bookkeeping into the measurement process we now know as accounting?

2. The CPA's standard audit opinion consists of two major paragraphs. Describe the essential content of each paragraph.

3. In the phrase "generally accepted accounting principles," what determines general acceptability? Name three authoritative bodies that exercise consider-able influence over the development of accounting principles.

4. Accounting measurements are based on past, present, and future exchange transactions. Give an example of accounting measurement based on each kind of transaction.

Detailed
Balance
Sheet
for Cor-
poration

CRENSHAW CORPORATION
Consolidated Balance Sheet
December 31, 1971

Assets

Current assets:

Cash		$ 855,612
U.S. government securities, at cost (market value $312,800)		310,000
Accounts receivable	$1,180,200	
Less: Allowance for uncollectible accounts	15,000	1,165,200
Inventories (at lower of average cost or market)		1,300,800
Prepaid expenses		125,900
Total current assets		$3,757,512

Investments:

Bond sinking fund	$ 364,938	
Real estate not used in business	80,000	444,938

Plant and equipment:

Land		$ 500,000	
Buildings	$3,482,100		
Less: Accumulated depreciation	400,000	3,082,100	3,582,100

Other assets:

Organization costs	$ 60,000	
Deferred research and development costs	50,000	110,000

Total assets	$7,894,550

5. If the going-concern assumption were dropped, there would be no point in having current asset and current liability classifications in the balance sheet. Explain.

6. Barker Company has at the end of the current period an inventory of merchandise which cost $500,000. It would cost $600,000 to replace this inventory, and it is estimated that the goods will probably be sold for a total of $700,000. If the firm were to terminate operations immediately, the inventory could probably be sold to liquidators for $480,000. Discuss the relative reliability and relevance of each of these dollar measurements of the ending inventory.

Liabilities & Stockholders' Equity

Current liabilities:
Accounts payable.	$1,058,340	
Estimated income taxes payable	184,310	
Dividends payable.	10,000	
Bond interest payable	17,500	
Total current liabilities.		$1,270,150

Long-term liabilities:
Bonds payable, 7%, due Oct. 1, 1985	$1,000,000	
Less: Discount on bonds payable.	18,000	982,000
Total liabilities		$2,252,150

Stockholders' equity:
Cumulative 5% preferred stock, $100 par, 8,000 shares authorized and issued . .	$ 800,000	
Common stock, $1 par, authorized 1,000,000 shares, issued 600,000 shares of which 1,000 shares are held in the treasury	600,000	
Paid-in capital in excess of par value . .	2,400,000	
Total paid-in capital.		$3,800,000

Retained earnings:
Reserve for contingencies.	$ 400,000	
Unappropriated retained earnings, of which $8,000 is restricted by reason of treasury stock purchased.	1,250,400	1,650,400
Total paid-in capital and retained earnings . .		$5,450,400
Less: Treasury stock 1,000 shares (at cost).		8,000
		$5,442,400
Minority interest in subsidiary companies		200,000
Total stockholders' equity.		5,642,400
Total liabilities & stockholders' equity.		$7,894,550

7. Describe four stages of the productive process which might become the accountant's basis for recognizing changes in the value of a firm's output. Which stage is most commonly used as a basis for revenue recognition? Why?

8. **a.** Why is it important that any change in accounting procedures from one period to the next be disclosed in corporate reports?

   b. Does the concept of consistency mean that all companies in a given industry follow similar accounting methods?

9. A story in a prominent financial magazine stated that "One major newspaper recently reported earnings for a well-known corporation as 81¢ for the first nine months. Another paper, equally respected, interpreted the *same* earnings for the *same* period as 29¢." Give a possible explanation for this apparent disparity in reported earnings per share.

10. What is meant by the statement that accounting measurements are based on the assumption that the dollar is a stable measuring unit?

11. In presenting financial information to their stockholders and the public, it is not generally acceptable practice for corporations to report in common dollar terms, although such statements are occasionally presented in addition to regular financial statements as supplementary information. Why has the use of common dollars in financial reporting not gained general acceptance?

12. An increasing number of companies include in their annual report a description of the accounting "policies" or "principles" followed in the preparation of their financial statements. What advantages do you see in this practice?

EXERCISES

1. The following information relating to the latest fiscal year is available for the General Trading Company:

	Jan. 1	Cash Receipts or (Payments)	Dec. 31
Customers' accounts.	$12,500	$180,000	$19,200
Creditors' accounts	9,750	(88,200)	7,200
Prepaid supplies balance (or paid)	1,360	(4,900)	800
Merchandise inventories	20,000		23,600
Operating expenses, excluding supplies, accrued (or paid)	2,500	(39,000)	4,500

Prepare a comparative income statement (up to income before income taxes) as follows:
a. On a cash basis, showing only cash receipts and disbursements
b. As allowed for income tax purposes, that is, showing sales and cost of goods sold on the accrual basis and operating expenses on the cash basis
c. On a complete accrual basis, as required by generally accepted accounting principles

2. The Roberto Boat Company builds cabin cruisers for resale and on special order for wealthy boat enthusiasts. During its first year of operations, the company built and sold eight boats on the installment basis for a total consideration of $120,000. The eight boats cost approximately $87,000 to build. Cash collections from customers on these eight boats during the first year amounted to only $40,000. In addition, work is in progress on six custom cruisers which are on the average 60% completed. The total contract price on these six cruisers is $220,000 and the direct costs incurred on these boats during the year amount to $96,000 (60% of total estimated cost of $160,000).

Compute the gross profit for the company under each of the following assumptions:

a. Entire profit is recognized on the eight boats completed and profit on the six cruisers in progress is to be recognized in proportion to completed production.

b. Profit on the eight boats completed is to be recognized on the *installment basis* (in proportion to cash collected) and no portion of the profit on the six cruisers in progress is to be recognized until the boats are fully completed, delivered to customers, and cash is collected.

3. During a given five-year period, the general price index rose from 100 to 150. During the same period, the Brown Company had long-term debt of $10 million. At what figure would Brown's debt be reported in a common dollar balance sheet at the end of Year 5? What is Brown's purchasing power gain as a result of being a debtor during the five-year period? Where would this gain be reported in common dollar financial statements?

4. In Year 1, the New Company was started with a total capitalization of $5 million in order to acquire land for long-term investment. At this time, the general price index was 100. In Year 5, the general price index stands at 140 but the price of all land in the area in which the New Company invested has doubled in value. Rental receipts for grazing and farming during the five-year period were sufficient to pay all carrying charges on the land.

a. What is the purchasing power gain or loss for the New Company during the five-year period?

b. What is the "economic" gain or loss during this period?

PROBLEMS

15-1 In each of the situations described below, the question is whether generally accepted accounting principles have been violated. In each case state the accounting principle or concept, if any, that has been violated and explain briefly the nature of the violation. If you believe the treatment *is in accord with generally accepted accounting principles,* state this as your position and briefly defend it.

a. Merchandise inventory which cost $500,000 is reported in the balance sheet at $750,000, the expected sales price less estimated direct selling expenses.

b. New World Mining Company reports net income for the current year of $11,895,379. In the audit report the auditors stated: "We certify that the results of operations shown in the income statement are a true and accurate portrayal of the company's operations for the current year."

c. The Multiproduct Company has purchased a computer for $1.5 million. The company expects to use the computer for five years, at which time it will acquire a larger and faster computer. The new computer is expected to cost $3.5 million. During the current year the company debited $700,000 to the Depreciation Expense account to "provide for one-fifth of the estimated cost of the new computer."

d. X Corporation formed a partnership with Y Corporation to explore and develop certain mining properties. Each company furnishes one-half the total $10 million capital and has a one-half interest in both the net assets and the net income of the partnership, the XY Mining Company. Because X Corporation, as a partner, is ultimately liable for the debts of the mining partnership, the accountant included one-half of the partnership liabilities on the balance sheet of X Corporation, reducing the Retained Earnings account.

e. Dockson Corporation issued $50 million in 6% bonds, receiving proceeds of $48 million. The corporation reported the liability as $50 million on the balance sheet and debited $2 million to Bond Issue Expense, which was reported as an operating expense in the income statement.

f. Kearney Company has grown steadily since its founding in 1946 and has acquired its present plant assets at various dates. During the current year the board of directors authorized the controller to restate the cost of all properties acquired prior to 1960 in terms of current dollars and to restate accumulated depreciation accordingly.

g. The Edgington Oil Company reported on its balance sheet the total of all wages, supplies, depreciation on equipment, and other costs related to the drilling of a producing oil well as an intangible asset, and then amortized this asset as oil was produced from the well.

15-2 In each of the situations described below, the question is whether generally accepted accounting principles have been properly observed. In each case state the accounting principle or concept, if any, that has been violated and explain briefly the nature of the violation. If you believe the treatment *is in accord with generally accepted accounting principles,* state this as your position and defend it.

a. For a number of years the Armco Metals Company used the declining-balance method of depreciation both on its financial accounting records and in its income tax returns. During the current year the company decided to employ the straight-line method of depreciation in its accounting records but to continue to use the declining-balance method for income tax purposes.

b. During the current year the Beamer Company adopted a policy of charging purchases of small tools (unit cost less than $100) to expense as soon as they were acquired. In prior years the company had carried an asset account Small Tools which it had depreciated at the rate of 10% of the book value at the beginning of each year. The balance in the Small Tools account represented about 1% of the company's total plant and equipment, and depreciation on small tools was 0.4% of sales revenues. It is expected that purchases of small tools each year will run about the same as the depreciation that would be taken on these small tools.

c. Aracata Company had a large amount of cash and a large balance in its Retained Earnings account, but its net income during the past year was barely large enough to cover the regular $1 per share annual dividend on 1 million outstanding shares of common stock. Because the company had no immediate use for its excess cash, one of the directors suggested that an "extra" dividend of an additional $2 per share be declared and that of the total $3 million dividend, $1 million be debited to Retained Earnings and $2 million be recorded as an asset representing the advanced payment of the next two years' cash dividend on common stock. "This will make our stockholders happy and will save us money over the next two years when we will need funds for the construction of our Tacoma facility," argued the director.

d. Modern Foods Company acquired the plant, equipment, and inventories of Hamm & Rye Company, which was having financial difficulty. Modern Foods paid for its purchase by issuing 100,000 shares of its capital stock and agreed to pay $175,000 of unpaid property taxes owed by Hamm & Rye Company.

Modern Foods' controller charged the $175,000 to Property Tax Expense, recording the inventories and plant and equipment at an amount equal to the market value of the Modern Foods Company shares given in exchange.

e.   Idaho Company printed a large mail-order catalog in July of each year, at a cost of $1.8 million. Customers ordered from this catalog throughout the year and the company agreed to maintain the catalog prices for 12 months after the date of issue. The controller charged the entire cost of the catalog to Advertising Expense in August when it was issued. The Idaho Company's fiscal year ends on January 31 of each year. In defending his policy, the controller stated, "Once those catalogs are mailed they are gone. We could never get a nickel out of them."

f.   The Oregon Products Company owns a large acreage of filbert trees, the nuts from which are harvested in the fall of each year. The company in its financial statement on June 30 of the current year included among the current assets an account: Inventory in Process of Ripening—$120,000. This amount was computed by estimating the tonnage of nuts expected to be harvested during the current year, multiplying this tonnage by the anticipated selling price, and reducing the total dollar amount by 50%.

15-3   Dr. E. J. Lopay, a professor of business administration at Longview Beach State College, resigned at the beginning of Year 1 to form Lopay Associates, with the object of furnishing research services to private companies and governmental agencies for a fee. He rented a small building near the college for $900 per month and invested $45,000 of his savings in the company, issuing 4,500 shares of $10 par value common stock to himself and his wife. Dr. Lopay had done consulting on his own for a number of years and had several projects lined up. He hired four associates and a number of graduate students. At the end of Year 1, having kept only cash receipts and disbursements records during the year, Dr. Lopay drew up the following financial statements:

LOPAY ASSOCIATES
Income Statement
Year 1

Cash received for research services		$ 225,000
Salaries & payroll taxes paid	$154,500	
Building occupancy expense	14,700	
Travel expense	33,000	
Office supplies & expense	27,000	
Miscellaneous expense	15,300	244,500
Net loss		$(19,500)

LOPAY ASSOCIATES
Balance Sheet
December 31, Year 1

Cash	$	3,000
Office equipment		22,500
Total assets	$	25,500

Capital stock, $10 par value	$ 45,000
Less: Deficit	(19,500)
Total stockholders' equity	$ 25,500

Dr. Lopay was understandably discouraged by his first year's results. Before deciding whether to disband his operations, he asked Talmadge Tillman, a friend who was an accountant, to go over his records and review the situation with him. Tillman made the following notes as a result of his investigation:

(1) Office equipment was purchased on January 2, Year 1. Paid cash of $22,500 and signed a $15,000, 5% note due in 18 months. Equipment has average service life of 10 years and a salvage value of about 20% of original cost.

(2) Accounts receivable from clients at end of Year 1 total $28,415, of which $450 is in dispute and is probably not collectible. Dr. Lopay would like to show the uncollectible accounts expense as a deduction from research revenues in the income statement.

(3) Three research projects are in progress, on which no billings have yet been made to clients. Memorandum records indicate that the following direct charges relate to these projects: Salaries and payroll taxes, $12,000; travel expenses, $3,115; miscellaneous expense, $1,425.

(4) Rent on the building for one month ($900) has been prepaid at December 31.

(5) At December 31 the company owed the Ace Travel Bureau $1,460, and various creditors who furnished office supplies $375.

(6) Office supplies on hand at December 31, $3,510. Insurance premiums paid during Year 1, $1,950, of which $720 are applicable to Year 2. Premiums paid were recorded in Miscellaneous Expense account.

(7) Accrued but unpaid salaries and payroll taxes at December 31, $14,550.

(8) Income taxes should be estimated at 22% of any income before taxes earned by the company during the year.

Instructions

a. On the basis of the information developed by Tillman, prepare a revised balance sheet as of the end of Year 1 and an income statement for the year. It is suggested that you use a 10-column work sheet to revise Dr. Lopay's figures and compile the necessary data for the statements.

b. Write a letter to Dr. Lopay commenting on the results of his first year of operations.

15-4 The Hong Kong Trading Company was organized at the beginning of Year 1. Its opening balance sheet is presented below:

HONG KONG TRADING COMPANY
Balance Sheet
Beginning of Year 1

Cash	$150,000	*Accounts payable*	$100,000
Inventories	200,000	*Capital stock*	250,000
		Total liabilities &	
Total assets	$350,000	*stockholders' equity.*	$350,000

At the date of the above balance sheet, the index of general prices was 100; by July 1 of Year 1 the price index had risen to 125. On July 1 the Hong Kong Trading Company completed two transactions: Merchandise inventory costing $125,000 was sold for cash of $187,500; and cash of $37,500 was paid on accounts payable. At the end of Year 1 the general price index was 150. On December 31 the Hong Kong Trading Company paid $47,500 in cash for operating expenses.

Instructions
a. Prepare an analysis of cash transactions in terms of historical dollars and common (end-of-year) dollars.
b. Prepare an analysis of accounts payable transactions in terms of historical dollars and common (end-of-year) dollars.
c. Prepare a comparative balance sheet as of the end of Year 1 in historical and common (end-of-year) dollars.
d. Prepare a comparative income statement for Year 1 in historical and common (end-of-year) dollars.
e. Write a brief statement comparing the results as shown in the financial statements prepared in historical and common dollars.

15-5 Included among the assets of the Shirley Morgan Company, both at the beginning and the end of Year 1, is a time deposit of $600,000, which is held as a short-term investment.

An index of the general price level stood at 150 at the beginning of Year 1 and at 200 at the end of Year 1. In a presentation to the board of directors, the controller of the company wishes to demonstrate the loss of purchasing power that has resulted from holding this investment during a period of inflation. He is uncertain whether to measure the purchasing power loss in terms of end-of-year dollars, beginning-of-year dollars, or base-year dollars. The controller's assistant has made the following comparative calculations:

	End-of-year Dollars *(Index = 200)*	*Beginning-of-year Dollars* *(Index = 150)*	*Base-year Dollars* *(Index = 100)*
Balance of time deposit at beginning of Year 1	$800,000 (D)	$600,000	$400,000 (A)
Balance of time deposit at the end of Year 1	600,000	450,000 (C)	300,000 (B)
Loss of purchasing power	$200,000	$150,000	$100,000

Instructions
a. Explain how the figures labeled A, B, C, D, in the assistant's schedule were computed, and why.
b. Which measuring unit would you suggest that the controller use in making his presentation to the board of directors? Explain your reasoning.
c. On a common dollar balance sheet prepared at the end of Year 1, at what figure would the time deposit be reported? Why? What would be the amount of purchasing power loss reported on common dollar financial statements, relating to the ownership of this time deposit?

d. If, instead of a time deposit, the $600,000 were a note payable by the Shirley Morgan Company, due two years after the beginning of Year 1, how would this affect the assistant's analysis of the effect of the decline in the purchasing power of money during the period?

15-6 The balance sheet accounts listed alphabetically below appear, with normal balances, in the ledger of Mary Blackwell, Inc., at the end of 1971.

Accounts payable.	$ 884,000
Accounts receivable	1,134,100
Accumulated depreciation: buildings	1,410,000
Accumulated depreciation: equipment.	2,815,000
Allowance for uncollectible accounts	30,000
Bond interest payable	115,000
Bond sinking fund	1,100,000
Buildings	4,750,000
Capital in excess of par or stated value	1,600,000
Cash	490,000
Common stock, no par, $5 stated value 500,000 shares authorized . .	1,216,800
Debenture bonds payable, 7%, due Dec. 31, 1980	3,500,000
Deferred income taxes payable	500,000
Dividends payable	304,200
Earnings retained in business	3,987,500
Equipment	?
Income taxes payable—current	491,000
Inventories (lower of cost or market).	1,593,200
Land.	815,000
Long-term advance to supplier	275,000
Marketable securities (at cost; market $370,000)	360,000
Organization costs	90,000
Patents and licenses	470,000
Preferred stock, 6%, cumulative, $50 par, 10,000 shares authorized .	350,000
Premium on debenture bonds payable	59,200
Prepaid expenses	29,700
Research and development in progress	218,300
Tools	25,000
Treasury stock, 5,200 shares of common (at cost)	37,400

The premium on debenture bonds payable was not amortized for 1971, and miscellaneous accrued liabilities amounting to $10,920 were not recorded by the bookkeeper in the process of adjusting the accounts.

Instructions
Prepare, in a form suitable for publication, a statement of financial position as of the end of 1971. Determine the appropriate amount to insert in place of the question mark for Equipment, in order to complete the statement.

16

Analysis of financial statements; funds statement and cash flows

Financial statements are the instrument panel of a business enterprise. They constitute a report on managerial performance, attesting to managerial success or failure and flashing warning signals of impending difficulties. In reading a complex instrument panel, one must understand the gauges and their calibration to make sense out of the array of data they convey. Similarly, one must understand the inner workings of the accounting system and the significance of various financial relationships to interpret the data appearing in financial statements. To an astute reader, a set of financial statements tells a great deal about a business enterprise.

The financial affairs of any business are of interest to a number of different groups: management, creditors, investors, union officials, and government agencies. Each of these groups has somewhat different needs, and accordingly each tends to concentrate on particular aspects of a company's financial picture.

Sources of financial data

For the most part, the discussion in this chapter will be limited to the kind of analysis that can be made by "outsiders" who do not have access to internal accounting records. Investors must rely to a considerable extent on financial statements in published annual reports. In the case of large publicly owned corporations, certain statements that must be filed with public agencies, such as the Securities and Exchange Commission, are available. Financial information for most corporations is also published by Moody's Investors Service, Standard & Poor's Corporation, and stock brokerage firms.

Bankers are usually able to secure more detailed information by requesting it as a condition for granting a loan. Trade creditors may obtain financial information for businesses of almost any size from credit-rating agencies such as Dun & Bradstreet, Inc.

Tools of analysis

Few figures in a financial statement are highly significant in and of themselves. It is their relationship to other quantities, or the amount and direction of change since a previous date, that is important. Analysis is largely a matter of establishing significant relationships and pointing up changes and trends. There are three widely used analytical techniques: (1) dollar and percentage changes, (2) component percentages, and (3) ratios.

Dollar and percentage changes. The change in financial data over time is best exhibited in statements showing data for a series of years in adjacent columns. Such statements are called *comparative* financial statements. A highly condensed comparative balance sheet is shown below:

Condensed Three-year Balance Sheet

X CORPORATION
Comparative Balance Sheet
As of December 31
(in thousands of dollars)

	Year 3	Year 2	Year 1
Assets:			
Current assets	$180	$150	$120
Plant and equipment	450	300	345
Total assets	$630	$450	$465
Liabilities & Stockholders' Equity:			
Current liabilities	$ 60	$ 80	$120
Long-term liabilities	200	100	
Capital stock	300	300	300
Retained earnings (deficit)	70	(30)	45
Total liabilities & stockholders' equity	$630	$450	$465

The usefulness of comparative financial statements covering two or more years is well recognized. Published annual reports often contain comparative financial statements covering a period as long as 10 years. By observing the change in various items period by period, the analyst may gain valuable clues as to growth and other important trends affecting the business.

The dollar amount of change from year to year is of some interest; reducing this to percentage terms adds perspective. For example, if sales this year have increased by $100,000, the fact that this is an increase of 10% over last year's sales of $1 million puts it in a different perspective than if it represented a 1% increase over sales of $10 million for the prior year.

The dollar amount of any change is the difference between the amount for a *base* year and for a *comparison* year. The percentage change is computed by dividing the amount of the change between years by the amount for the base year. This is illustrated in the tabulation on page 475, using data from the comparative balance sheet above.

Although current assets increased $30,000 in both Year 2 and Year 3, the percentage of change differs because of the shift in the base year from Year 1 to Year 2.

Component percentages. The phrase "a piece of pie" is subject to varying

Dollar and Percentage Changes

	In Thousands			Increase or (Decrease)			
				Year 3 over Year 2		Year 2 over Year 1	
	Year 3	Year 2	Year 1	Amount	%	Amount	%
Current assets..........	$180	$150	$120	$30	20%	$30	25%
Current liabilities.......	$ 60	$ 80	$120	($20)	(25%)	($40)	(33.3%)

interpretations until it is known whether the piece represents one-sixth or one-half of the total pie. The percentage relationship between any particular financial item and a significant total that includes this item is known as a *component percentage;* this is often a useful means of showing relationships or the relative importance of the item in question. Thus if inventories are 50% of total current assets, they are a far more significant factor in the current position of a company than if they are only 10% of current assets.

One application of component percentages is to express each asset group on the balance sheet as a percentage of total assets. This shows quickly the relative importance of current and noncurrent assets, and the relative amount of financing obtained from current creditors, long-term creditors, and stockholders.

Another application is to express all items on an income statement as a percentage of net sales. Such a statement is sometimes called a *common size* income statement. A highly condensed income statement in dollars and in common size form is illustrated below:

How Successful Was Year 2?

Income Statement

	Dollars		Component Percentages	
	Year 2	Year 1	Year 2	Year 1
Net sales..................	$500,000	$200,000	100.0%	100.0%
Cost of goods sold............	350,000	120,000	70.0	60.0
Gross profit on sales........	$150,000	$ 80,000	30.0%	40.0%
Expenses (including income taxes)	100,000	50,000	20.0	25.0
Net income.................	$ 50,000	$ 30,000	10.0%	15.0%

Looking only at the component percentages, we see that the decline in the gross profit rate from 40 to 30% was only partially offset by the decrease in expenses as a percentage of net sales, causing net income to decrease from 15 to 10% of net sales. The dollar amounts in the first pair of columns, however, present an entirely different picture. It is true that net sales increased faster than net income, but net income improved significantly in Year 2, a fact not apparent from a review of component percentages alone. This points up an important limitation in the use of component percentages. Changes in the component percentage may result from a change in the component, in the total, or in both. Reverting to our previous analogy, it is important to know not only the relative size of a piece of pie, but also the size of the pie; 10% of a large pie may be a bigger piece than 15% of a smaller pie.

Ratios. A ratio is a simple mathematical expression of the relationship of one item to another. Ratios may be expressed in a number of ways. For example, if we wish to clarify the relationship between sales of $800,000 and net income of $40,000, we may state: (1) The ratio of sales to net income is 20 to 1 (or 20:1); (2) for every $1 of sales, the company has an average net income of 5 cents; (3) net income is ½₀ of sales. In each case the ratio is merely a means of describing the relationship between sales and net income in a simple form.

In order to compute a meaningful ratio, there must be a significant relationship between the two figures. A ratio focuses attention on a relationship which is significant, but a full interpretation of the ratio usually requires further investigation of the underlying data. Ratios are an aid to analysis and interpretation; they do not substitute for sound thinking in the analytical process.

Standards of comparison

In using dollar and percentage changes, component percentages, and ratios, the analyst constantly seeks some standard of comparison against which to judge whether the relationships that he has found are favorable or unfavorable. Two such standards are (1) the past performance of the company and (2) the performance of other companies in the same industry.

Past performance of the company. Comparing analytical data for a current period with similar computations for prior years affords some basis for judging whether the position of the business is improving or worsening. This comparison of data over time is sometimes called *horizontal* or *dynamic* analysis, to express the idea of reviewing data for a number of periods. It is distinguished from *vertical* or *static* analysis, which refers to the review of the financial information for only one accounting period.

In addition to determining whether the situation is improving or becoming worse, horizontal analysis may aid in making estimates of future prospects. Since changes may reverse their direction at any time, however, projecting past trends into the future is always a somewhat risky statistical pastime.

A weakness of horizontal analysis is that comparison with the past does not afford any basis for evaluation in absolute terms. The fact that net income was 2% of sales last year and is 3% of sales this year indicates improvement, but if there is evidence that net income *should be* 5% of sales, the record for both years is unfavorable.

Industry standards. The limitations of horizontal analysis may be overcome to some extent by finding some other standard of performance as a yardstick against which to measure the record of any particular firm. The yardstick may be a comparable company, the average record of several companies in the same industry, or an arbitrary standard based upon the past experience of the analyst.

Suppose that Y Company suffers a 5% drop in its sales during the current year. The discovery that the sales of all companies in the same industry fell an average of 20% would indicate that this was a favorable rather than an unfavorable performance. Assume further that Y Company's net income is 2% of net sales. Based on comparison with other companies in the industry, this would be grossly substandard performance if Y Company were an automobile manufacturer; but it would be a satisfactory record if Y Company were a grocery chain.

When we compare a given company with its competitors or with industry averages, our conclusions will be valid only if the companies in question are reasonably comparable. Because of the large number of *conglomerate* companies formed in recent years, the term *industry* is difficult to define, and companies that fall roughly within the same industry may not be comparable in many respects. One company may engage only in the marketing of oil products; another may be a fully integrated producer from the well to the gas pump, yet both are in the "oil industry."

Differences in accounting procedures may lessen the comparability of financial data for two companies. For example, the understatement of inventories on the balance sheet of a company using lifo may be so serious as to destroy the significance of comparisons with companies whose inventories are valued on a fifo basis.

Despite these limitations, studying comparative performances is a useful method of analysis if carefully and intelligently done.

Illustrative analysis

Keep in mind the above discussion of analytical principles as you study the illustrative financial analysis which follows. The basic data for our discussion are contained in a set of condensed two-year comparative financial statements for the Weaver Company shown on the following pages. Summarized statement data, together with computations of dollar increases and decreases, and component percentages where applicable, have been compiled.

Using the data in these statements, let us consider the kind of analysis that might be of particular interest to: (1) common stockholders, (2) long-term creditors, (3) preferred stockholders, and (4) short-term creditors. Organizing our discussion in this way emphasizes the differences in the viewpoint of

WEAVER COMPANY
Condensed Comparative Balance Sheet°
December 31

	Year 2	Year 1	Increase or (Decrease)		Percentage of Total Assets	
			Dollars	%	Year 2	Year 1
Assets						
Current assets	$390,000	$288,000	$102,000	35.4	41.1	33.5
Plant and equipment (net)	500,000	467,000	33,000	7.1	52.6	54.3
Other assets (loans to officers) . .	60,000	105,000	(45,000)	(42.8)	6.3	12.2
Total assets	$950,000	$860,000	$ 90,000	10.5	100.0	100.0
Liabilities & Stockholders' Equity						
Liabilities:						
Current liabilities	$147,400	$ 94,000	$ 53,400	56.8	15.5	10.9
Long-term liabilities	200,000	250,000	(50,000)	(20.0)	21.1	29.1
Total liabilities	$347,400	$344,000	$ 3,400	1.0	36.6	40.0
Stockholders' equity:						
6% preferred stock	$100,000	$100,000			10.5	11.6
Common stock ($50 par)	250,000	200,000	$ 50,000	25.0	26.3	23.2
Capital in excess of par	70,000	40,000	30,000	75.0	7.4	4.7
Retained earnings	182,600	176,000	6,600	3.8	19.2	20.5
Total stockholders' equity . .	$602,600	$516,000	$ 86,600	16.8	63.4	60.0
Total liabilities & stockholders' equity	$950,000	$860,000	$ 90,000	10.5	100.0	100.0

° In order to focus attention on important subtotals, this statement is highly condensed and does not show individual asset and liability items. These details will be introduced as needed in the text discussion. For example, a list of the Weaver Company's current assets and current liabilities appears on page 487.

these groups; all of them have of course, a considerable common interest in the performance of the company as a whole.

Analysis by common stockholders

Common stockholders and potential investors in common stock look first at a company's earnings record. Their investment is in shares of stock, so *earnings per share* are of particular interest.

Earnings per share of stock. As indicated in Chapter 8, earnings per share of stock are computed by dividing the income available to common stockholders by the number of shares of common stock outstanding. Any preferred dividend requirements must be subtracted from net income to determine

WEAVER COMPANY
Comparative Income Statement
Years Ended December 31

	Year 2	Year 1	Increase or (Decrease) Dollars	Increase or (Decrease) %	Percentage of Net Sales Year 2	Percentage of Net Sales Year 1
Net sales.................	$900,000	$750,000	$150,000	20.0	100.0	100.0
Cost of goods sold	585,000	468,800	116,200	24.9	65.0	62.5
Gross profit on sales.........	$315,000	$281,200	$ 33,800	12.0	35.0	37.5
Operating expenses:						
Selling expenses	$117,000	$ 75,000	$ 42,000	56.0	13.0	10.0
Administrative expenses.....	126,000	94,500	31,500	33.3	14.0	12.6
Total operating expenses...	$243,000	$169,500	$ 73,500	43.4	27.0	22.6
Operating income	$ 72,000	$111,700	$ (39,700)	(35.6)	8.0	14.9
Interest expense	12,000	15,000	(3,000)	(20.0)	1.3	2.0
Income before income taxes....	$ 60,000	$ 96,700	$ (36,700)	(38.0)	6.7	12.9
Income taxes	23,400	44,200	(20,800)	(47.1)	2.6	5.9
Net income................	$ 36,600	$ 52,500	$(15,900)	(30.3)	4.1	7.0

WEAVER COMPANY
Statement of Retained Earnings
Years Ended December 31

	Year 2	Year 1	Increase or (Decrease) Dollars	Increase or (Decrease) %
Balance, beginning of year.............	$176,000	$149,500	$26,500	14.0
Net income	36,600	52,500	(15,900)	(30.3)
	$212,600	$202,000	$10,600	4.4
Less: Dividends on common stock	$ 24,000	$ 20,000	$ 4,000	20.0
Dividends on preferred stock.......	6,000	6,000		
	$ 30,000	$ 26,000	$ 4,000	15.4
Balance, end of year.................	$182,600	$176,000	$ 6,600	3.0

income available for common stock, as shown in the following computations for Weaver Company:

Earnings per Share of Common Stock		
	Year 2	Year 1
Net income	$36,600	$52,500
Less: Preferred dividend requirements	6,000	6,000
Net income available for common .... (a)	$30,600	$46,500
Shares of common outstanding, end of year......... (b)	5,000	4,000
Earned per share (a ÷ b)	$ 6.12	$ 11.63

The importance of dividends varies among stockholders. Earnings reinvested in the business should produce an increase in the net income of the firm and thus tend to make each share of stock more valuable. Because the federal income tax rates applicable to dividend income are at least double the rate of tax on capital gains from the sale of shares of stock, some stockholders may prefer that the company reinvest most of its earnings. Others may be more interested in dividend income despite the tax disadvantage.

If we compare the merits of alternative investment opportunities, we should relate earnings and dividends per share to market value of stock. Dividends per share divided by market price per share determines the *yield* rate of a company's stock. Net income per share divided by market price per share determines the *earnings rate* of a company's stock. In financial circles the earning rate is often expressed as a *price-earnings ratio* by reversing the computation and dividing the price per share by the net income per share. Thus, a stock selling for $60 per share and earning $3 per share may be said to have an earning rate of 5% ($3 ÷ $60), or a price-earnings ratio of 20 times earnings ($60 ÷ $3).

Assume that the 1,000 additional shares of common stock issued by Weaver Company in Year 2 received the full annual dividend of $4.80 paid in Year 2. When these new shares were issued, Weaver Company announced that it planned to continue indefinitely the $4.80 dividend per common share currently being paid. With this assumption and the use of assumed market prices of the common stock at December 31, Year 1 and Year 2, the earnings rates and yields per share may be summarized as follows for the two years:

Rates of Earnings and Dividends per Share on Common Stock						
Date	Assumed Market Value per Share	Earnings per Share	Price-earnings Ratio	Dividends per Share	Rates per Share	
					Earnings, %	Dividend Yield, %
Dec. 31, Year 1	$125	$11.63	11	$5.00	9.3	4.0
Dec. 31, Year 2	$100	$ 6.12	16	$4.80	6.1	4.8

The decline in market value during Year 2 presumably reflects the decrease in earnings per share. An investor appraising this stock at December 31, Year 2, would consider whether an earning rate of 6.1% and a dividend yield of 4.8% represented a satisfactory return in the light of alternative investment opportunities open to him. Obviously he would also place considerable weight on his estimates of the company's prospective future earnings and their probable effect on the future market value of the stock.

Book value per share of common stock. The procedures for computing book value per share were fully described in Chapter 8 and will not be repeated here. We will, however, determine the book value per share of common stock for the Weaver Company:

Why Did Book Value per Share Decrease?

Book Value per Share of Common Stock		Year 2	Year 1
Common stockholders' equity:			
Common stock.		$250,000	$200,000
Capital in excess of par value		70,000	40,000
Retained earnings		182,600	176,000
Total common stockholders' equity . . . . (a)		$502,600	$416,000
Shares of common stock outstanding . . . . (b)		5,000	4,000
Book value per share of common stock (a ÷ b)		$ 100.52	$ 104.00

During Year 2, book value of common stock was increased as a result of earnings: book value was reduced as a result of dividend payments and the sale of 1,000 additional shares of stock at $80 per share, a figure significantly below per-share book value.

Revenue and expense analysis. The trend of earnings of the Weaver Company is unfavorable and stockholders would want to know the reasons for the decline in net income. The comparative income statement shows that despite a 20% increase in net sales, net income fell from $52,500 in Year 1 to $36,600 in Year 2, a decline of 30.3%. The primary causes of this decline were the increases in selling expenses (56.0%), in administrative expenses (33.3%), and in the cost of goods sold (24.9%), all exceeding the 20% increase in net sales.

These observations suggest the need for further investigation. Suppose we find that the Weaver Company cut its selling prices in Year 2. This fact would explain the decrease in gross profit rate and would also show that sales volume in physical units rose more than 20%, since it takes proportionally more sales at lower prices to produce a given increase in dollar sales. If reduced sales prices and increased volume had been accomplished with little change in expense, the effect on net income would have been favorable. Operating expenses, however, rose by $73,500, resulting in a $39,700 decrease in operating income.

The next step would be to find which expenses increased and why. An investor may be handicapped here, because detailed operating expenses are not usually shown in published statements. Some conclusions, however, can be reached on the basis of even the condensed information available in the comparative income statement for the Weaver Company shown on page 479.

The $42,000 increase in selling expenses presumably reflects greater selling effort during Year 2 in an attempt to improve sales volume. However, the growth in selling expenses from 10 to 13% of net sales indicates that the cost of this increased sales effort was not justified in terms of results. Even more disturbing is the change in administrative expenses. Some growth in administrative expenses might be expected to accompany increased sales volume, but because some of the expenses are fixed, the growth should be less than proportional to any increase in sales. The increase in administrative expenses from 12.6 to 14% of sales would be of serious concern to astute investors.

Return on total assets. An important test of management's ability to earn a return on funds supplied from all sources is the rate of return on total assets.

The income figure used in computing this ratio should be net income before deducting interest expense, since interest is a payment to creditors for the use of borrowed funds. Net income before interest reflects earnings throughout the year and therefore should be related to the average investment in assets during the year. The computation of this ratio for the Weaver Company is shown below.

Earnings Related to Investment in Assets	*Percentage Return on Total Assets*		
		Year 2	*Year 1*
Net income...........................		$ 36,600	$ 52,500
Add back: Interest expense....................		12,000	15,000
Income before interest expense.............. (a)		$ 48,600	$ 67,500
Total assets, beginning of year................		$860,000	$820,000
Total assets, end of year.....................		950,000	860,000
Average investment in assets................. (b)		$905,000	$840,000
Return on total assets (a ÷ b)................		5.4%	8.0%

This ratio shows that earnings per dollar of assets invested have fallen off in Year 2. If the same ratios were available for other companies of similar kind and size, the significance of this decline could be better appraised.

Return on common stockholders' equity. Because interest and dividends paid to creditors and preferred stockholders are fixed in amount, a company may earn a greater or smaller return on the common stockholders' equity than on its total assets. The computation of return on stockholders' equity for the Weaver Company is shown on page 483.

Does
Trading on
the Equity
Benefit
Common
Stock-
holders?

Return on Common Stockholders' Equity

		Year 2	Year 1
Net income		$ 36,600	$ 52,500
Less: Preferred dividend requirements		6,000	6,000
Net income available for common stock	(a)	$ 30,600	$ 46,500
Common stockholders' equity, beginning of year		$416,000	$389,500
Common stockholders' equity, end of year		502,600	416,000
Average common stockholders' equity	(b)	$459,300	$402,750
Rate of return (a ÷ b)		6.7%	11.6%
Rate of return on total assets (see page 482)		5.4%	8.0%

In both years the rate of return to common stockholders was higher than the return on total assets, because the average combined rate of interest paid to creditors and dividends to preferred stockholders was less than the rate earned on each dollar of assets used in the business.

Financing with fixed-return securities is often called *trading on the equity.* Results may be favorable or unfavorable to holders of common stock:

1. If the rate of return on total assets is *greater* than the average rate of payment to creditors and preferred stockholders, the common stockholders will *gain* from trading on the equity. This was the case in the Weaver Company.

2. If the rate of return on total assets is *smaller* than the average rate of payments to creditors and preferred stockholders, the common stockholders will *lose* from trading on the equity.

Equity ratio. The equity ratio measures the proportion of the total assets financed by stockholders, as distinguished from creditors. It is computed by dividing total stockholders' equity by total assets (or the sum of liabilities and stockholders' equity, which is the same). The equity ratio for the Weaver Company is determined as follows:

Proportion
of Assets
Financed
by Stock-
holders

Equity Ratio

		Year 2	Year 1
Total assets	(a)	$950,000	$860,000
Total stockholders' equity	(b)	602,600	516,000
Equity ratio (b ÷ a)		63.4%	60.0%

The Weaver Company has a higher equity ratio in Year 2 than in Year 1. Is this favorable or unfavorable?

From the common stockholder's viewpoint, a low equity ratio (that is, a large proportion of financing supplied by creditors) will produce maximum benefits from trading on the equity if management is able to earn a rate of return on assets greater than the rate of interest paid to creditors. However, a low equity ratio can be very unfavorable if the rate of return on total assets falls below the rate of interest paid to creditors. Furthermore, if a business incurs so much debt that it is unable to meet the required interest or principal payments, creditors may force liquidation or reorganization of the business, to the detriment of stockholders.

Because of these factors, the equity ratio is usually judged by stockholders in the light of the probable stability of the company's earnings, as well as the rate of earnings in relation to the rate of interest to creditors.

As we saw earlier in our analysis, trading on the equity from the common stockholder's viewpoint can also be accomplished through the issuance of preferred stock. Since preferred stock dividends are not deductible for income tax purposes, however, the advantage gained in this respect will usually be much smaller than in the case of debt financing.

Analysis by long-term creditors

Bondholders and other long-term creditors are primarily interested in three factors: (1) the rate of return on their investment, (2) the firm's ability to meet its interest requirements, and (3) the firm's ability to repay the principal of the debt when it falls due.

Yield rate on bonds. The yield rate on bonds or other long-term indebtedness cannot be computed in the same manner as the yield rate on shares of stock, because bonds, unlike stocks, have a definite maturity date and amount. The ownership of a 6%, 10-year bond represents the right to receive $1,000 at the end of 10 years and the right to receive $60 per year during each of the next 10 years. If the market price of this bond is $950, the yield rate on an investment in the bond is the rate of interest that will make the present value of these two contractual rights equal to $950. Determining the effective interest rate on such an investment requires the use of compound interest tables, a discussion of which is reserved to a more advanced coverage of this subject. We can, however, generalize the relation between yield rate and bond price as follows: the yield rate varies inversely with changes in the market price of the bond. If the price of a bond is above maturity value, the yield rate is less than the bond interest rate; if the price of a bond is below maturity value, the yield rate is higher than the bond interest rate.

Number of times interest earned. Long-term creditors have learned from experience that one of the best indications of the safety of their investment is the fact that, over the life of the debt, the company has sufficient income to cover its interest requirements by a wide margin. A failure to cover interest requirements may have serious repercussions on the stability and solvency of the firm.

A common measure of debt safety is the ratio of net income available for the payment of interest to the annual interest expense, called *times interest earned.* This computation for the Weaver Company would be:

Number of Times Interest Earned		
	Year 2	*Year 1*
Operating income (before interest and income taxes) . . *(a)*	*$72,000*	*$111,700*
Annual interest expense . . . . *(b)*	*12,000*	*15,000*
Times interest earned (a ÷ b)	*6.0*	*7.4*

The decline in the ratio during Year 2 is unfavorable, but a ratio of 6.0 times interest earned for that year would still be considered quite adequate.

Since businessmen and investors are strongly conditioned to an after-tax view of corporate affairs, the times interest earned ratio is often computed by a more conservative method of taking net income (after taxes) plus interest expense and dividing this total by the annual interest expense.

Debt ratio. Long-term creditors are interested in the amount of debt outstanding in relation to the amount of capital contributed by stockholders. The *debt ratio* is computed by dividing total liabilities by total assets, shown below for the Weaver Company.

Debt Ratio		
	Year 2	*Year 1*
Total liabilities . . . . *(a)*	*$347,400*	*$344,000*
Total assets (or total liabilities & stockholders'		
equity) . . . . *(b)*	*950,000*	*860,000*
Debt ratio (a ÷ b)	*36.6%*	*40.0*

From a creditor's viewpoint, the lower the debt ratio (or the higher the equity ratio) the better, since this means that stockholders have contributed the bulk of the funds to the business, and therefore the margin of protection to creditors against a shrinkage of the assets is high. When large amounts of debt fall due, repayment in some form must be made. On the other hand, payments to preferred and common stockholders are contingent upon the profitability of the business.

Analysis by preferred stockholders

If preferred stock is convertible, the interests of preferred stockholders are similar to those of common stockholders, previously discussed. If preferred stock is not convertible, the interests of preferred stockholders are more closely comparable to those of long-term creditors. (In this discussion we shall ignore participating preferred stock because such issues are extremely rare.)

Preferred stockholders are interested in the yield on their investment. The yield is computed by dividing the dividend per share by the market value per share. The dividend per share of Weaver Company preferred stock is $6. If we assume that the market value at December 31, Year 2, is $80 per share, the yield rate at that time would be 7.5% ($6 ÷ $80).

The primary measure of the safety of an investment in preferred stock is the ability of the firm to meet its preferred dividend requirements. The best test of this factor is the ratio of the net income available to pay the preferred dividend to the amount of the annual dividend, as shown below:

Is the Preferred Dividend Safe?	*Times Preferred Dividends Earned*		
		Year 2	*Year 1*
	Net income available to pay preferred dividends ......*(a)*	*$36,600*	*$52,500*
	Annual preferred dividend requirements ....*(b)*	*6,000*	*6,000*
	Times dividends earned (a ÷ b)	*6.1*	*8.8*

Although the margin of protection declined in Year 2, the annual preferred dividend requirement appears well protected.

Analysis by short-term creditors

Bankers and other short-term creditors share the interest of stockholders and bondholders in the profitability and long-run stability of a business. Their primary interest, however, is in the current position of the firm—its ability to generate sufficient funds to meet current operating needs and to pay current debts promptly. Thus the analysis of financial statements by a banker considering a short-term loan, or by a trade creditor investigating the credit position of a customer, is likely to center on the working capital position of the prospective debtor.

Amount of working capital. The amount of working capital is measured by the *excess of current assets over current liabilities.* The details of the working capital of the Weaver Company are shown on page 487.

This schedule shows that current assets increased $102,000, while current liabilities rose by only $53,400, with the result that working capital increased $48,600. There was a shift in the composition of the current assets and current liabilities.

The current ratio. One means of further evaluating these changes in working capital is to observe the relationship between current assets and current liabilities, a test known as the *current ratio.* The current ratio for the Weaver Company is computed at the bottom of page 487.

Despite the increase of $48,600 in the amount of working capital in Year 2, current assets per dollar of current liabilities declined. The margin of safety, however, still appears satisfactory.

In interpreting the current ratio, a number of factors should be kept in mind:

1. Creditors tend to feel that the larger the current ratio the better; however, from a managerial view there is an upper limit. Too high a current ratio may indicate that capital is not productively used in the business.

2. Because creditors tend to stress the current ratio as an indication of short-term solvency, some firms may take conscious steps to improve this ratio just before statements are prepared for submission to bankers or other creditors. This may be done by postponing purchases, allowing inventories to fall, pressing collections on accounts receivable, and using all available cash to pay off current liabilities.

WEAVER COMPANY
Comparative Schedule of Working Capital
As of December 31

	Year 2	Year 1	Increase or (Decrease) Dollars	%	Percentage of Total Current Items Year 2	Year 1
Current assets:						
Cash	$ 38,000	$ 40,000	$ (2,000)	(5.0)	9.8	13.9
Receivables (net).........	117,000	86,000	31,000	36.0	30.0	29.9
Inventories..............	180,000	120,000	60,000	50.0	46.1	41.6
Prepaid expenses	55,000	42,000	13,000	31.0	14.1	14.6
Total current assets	$390,000	$288,000	$102,000	35.4	100.0	100.0
Current liabilities:						
Notes payable to creditors..	$ 50,000	$ 10,000	$ 40,000	400.0	33.9	10.7
Accounts payable	66,000	30,000	36,000	120.0	44.8	31.9
Accrued liabilities	31,400	54,000	(22,600)	(42.0)	21.3	57.4
Total current liabilities ..	$147,400	$ 94,000	$ 53,400	56.8	100.0	100.0
Working capital............	$242,600	$194,000	$ 48,600	25.0		

Does This Current Ratio Indicate Satisfactory Debt-paying Ability?

Current Ratio

		Year 2	Year 1
Total current assets............................(a)		$390,000	$288,000
Total current liabilities ....(b)		147,400	94,000
Current ratio (a ÷ b)		2.6	3.1

3. The current ratio computed at the end of a fiscal year may not be representative of the current position of the company throughout the year. Since many firms arrange their fiscal year to end during an ebb in the seasonal swing of business activity, the current ratio at year-end is likely to be more favorable than at any other time during the year.

Use of both the current ratio and the amount of working capital help to place debt-paying ability in its proper perspective. For example, if Company X has current assets of $20,000 and current liabilities of $10,000 and Company Y has current assets of $2,000,000 and current liabilities of $1,990,000, both companies would have $10,000 of working capital, but the current position of Company X is clearly superior to that of Company Y. If the current ratio were computed for both companies, the difference would be clearly revealed.

As another example, assume that Company A and Company B both have current ratios of 3 to 1. However, Company A has working capital of $20,000 and Company B has working capital of $200,000. Although both companies appear to be good credit risks, Company B would no doubt be able to qualify for a much *larger* bank loan than would Company A.

A widely used rule of thumb is that a current ratio of 2 to 1 or better is satisfactory. Like all rules of thumb this is an arbitrary standard, subject to numerous exceptions and qualifications.

Quick ratio. Because inventories and prepaid expenses are further removed from conversion into cash than other current assets, a ratio known as the *quick ratio* or *acid-test ratio* is sometimes computed as a supplement to the current ratio. This ratio compares the highly liquid current assets (cash, marketable securities, and receivables) with current liabilities. The Weaver Company has no marketable securities; its quick ratio would be computed as follows:

A Measure of Liquidity	*Quick Ratio*		
		Year 2	*Year 1*
Quick assets (cash and receivables) .... *(a)*		*$155,000*	*$126,000*
Current liabilities .... *(b)*		*147,400*	*94,000*
Quick ratio (a ÷ b)		*1.1*	*1.3*

Here, again, the analysis reveals an unfavorable trend. Whether the quick ratio is adequate depends on the amount of receivables included among quick assets, and the average time required to collect receivables as compared to the credit period extended by suppliers. If the credit periods extended to customers and granted by creditors are roughly equal, a quick ratio of 1.0 or better would be considered satisfactory.

Inventory turnover. The cost of goods sold figure on the income statement represents the total cost of all goods that have been transferred out of inventories during any given period. Therefore the relationship between cost of goods sold and the average balance of inventories maintained throughout the year indicates the number of times that inventories "turn over" and are replaced each year.

Ideally we should total the inventories at the end of each month and divide by 12 to obtain an average inventory. This information is not always available, however, and the nearest substitute is a simple average of the inventory at the beginning and at the end of the year. This tends to overstate the turnover rate, since many companies choose an accounting year that ends when inventories are at a minimum.

Assuming that only beginning and ending inventories are available, the computation of inventory turnover for the Weaver Company may be illustrated as follows:

What Does Inventory Turnover Mean?

Inventory Turnover		
	Year 2	*Year 1*
Cost of goods sold . . . . *(a)*	*$585,000*	*$468,800*
Inventory, beginning of year	*$120,000*	*$100,000*
Inventory, end of year	*180,000*	*120,000*
Average inventory . . . . *(b)*	*$150,000*	*$110,000*
Average inventory turnover per year (a ÷ b)	*3.9 times*	*4.3 times*
Average days to turn over (divide 365 days by inventory turnover)	*94 days*	*85 days*

The trend indicated by this analysis is unfavorable, since the average investment in inventories in relation to the cost of goods sold is rising. Stating this another way, the company required on the average 9 days more during Year 2 to turn over its inventories than during Year 1.

The relation between inventory turnover and gross profits per dollar of sales may be significant. A high inventory turnover and a low gross profit rate frequently go hand in hand. This, however, is merely another way of saying that if the gross profit rate is low, a high volume of business is necessary to produce a satisfactory return on investment. Although a high inventory turnover is usually regarded as a good sign, a rate that is high in relation to that of similar firms may indicate that the company is losing sales by a failure to maintain an adequate stock of goods to serve its customers promptly.

Average age of receivables. The "turnover" of accounts receivable is computed in a manner comparable to that just described for inventories. The ratio between the net sales for the period and the average balance in accounts receivable is a rough indication of the average time required to convert receivables into cash. Ideally, a monthly average of receivables should be used, and only sales on credit should be included in the sales figure. For illustrative purposes, we shall assume that Weaver Company sells entirely on credit and that only the beginning and ending balances of receivables are available:

Average Age of Receivables		
	Year 2	*Year 1*
Net sales .... *(a)*	*$900,000*	*$750,000*
Receivables, beginning of year	*$ 86,000*	*$ 80,000*
Receivables, end of year	*117,000*	*86,000*
Average receivables .... *(b)*	*$101,500*	*$ 83,000*
Receivable turnover per year (a ÷ b)	*8.9 times*	*9.0 times*
Average age of receivables (divide 365 days by		
receivable turnover)	*41 days*	*41 days*

There has been no significant change in the average time required to collect receivables. The interpretation of the absolute figures would depend upon the company's credit terms and policies. If the company grants credit on normal 30-day open account, for example, the above analysis indicates that accounts receivable collections are reasonably good. If the terms were net 15 days, however, there is evidence that collections are lagging.

The *operating cycle* in Year 2 was approximately 135 days (computed by adding the 94 days required to turn over inventory and the average 41 days to collect receivables).

FUNDS STATEMENT

A funds statement shows the sources and uses of working capital during an accounting period. In published annual reports of corporations, the funds statement is often more formally labeled as a *statement of sources and uses of working capital,* or as a *statement of sources and disposition of funds.* A funds statement is useful to management and to financial analysts because it pictures the flow of net liquid resources in and out of a business.

Why are "funds" defined as working capital?

In ordinary usage, the term *funds* usually means cash. Businessmen and financial analysts, however, think of funds in a broader sense. Short-term credit is often used as a substitute for cash; notes and accounts payable as well as accrued liabilities are used to meet the short-term financing needs of a business. Current assets are constantly being converted into cash, which is used to pay current liabilities. The net amount of short-term liquid resources available to a firm at any given time, therefore, is represented by its working capital—the difference between current assets and current liabilities. This explains why it is natural to think of working capital as the quantity of "funds" on hand at any given time.

If working capital increases during a given fiscal period, this means that more working capital was generated than was used for various business purposes; if a decrease in working capital occurs, the reverse is true. The purpose of the funds statement is to explain fully the increase or decrease in working capital during a given fiscal period. This is done by showing where working capital originated and how it was used.

Sources and uses of funds

Any transaction that increases the amount of working capital is a *source of funds.* For example, the sale of merchandise for an amount greater than its cost is a source of funds, because the increase in cash or receivables is greater than the decrease in inventories.

Any transaction that decreases working capital is an *application of funds.* For example, either incurring a current liability to acquire a noncurrent asset or paying expenses in cash represents a use of funds, because the result is a decrease in working capital.

On the other hand, any transaction that affects current assets or current liabilities but does not result in a change in working capital is not a source or use of funds. For example, the collection of an account receivable (which increases cash and decreases accounts receivable by an equal amount) is not a source of funds. Similarly, the payment of an account payable (which decreases cash and decreases an account payable by an equal amount) does not change the amount of working capital, and therefore is not a use of funds.

The principal sources and uses of funds are listed below:

Sources of funds:
Operations (revenues minus expenses that require the use of funds)
Sale of noncurrent assets
Borrowing through the use of long-term debt contracts
Issuing additional shares of capital stock

Uses of funds:
Declaration of cash dividends
Repayment of long-term debt
Purchase of noncurrent assets
Repurchase of outstanding capital stock

The fund effect of transactions

In preparing a funds statement, it is convenient to view all business transactions as falling into three categories:

1. Transactions which affect only current asset or liability accounts but which do not change the amount of working capital. These transactions produce changes in individual working capital accounts but are not a factor in explaining any change in the amount of working capital. For example, the purchase of merchandise increases inventories and accounts payable but has no effect on working capital; it may therefore be ignored for funds statement purposes.

2. Transactions which affect a current asset or current liability account *and* a non-working capital account. These transactions bring about either an increase or a decrease in the amount of working capital. The issuance of long-term bonds, for example, increases current assets and increases bonds payable, a non-working capital account; therefore, this is a source of funds. Similarly, when the bonds approach maturity the amount of the debt is transferred to the current liability classification on the balance sheet. This causes a reduction of working capital, which represents an application of funds. If changes in non-working capital accounts are analyzed, these events are brought to light, and their effect on working capital will be reported in the funds statement.

3. Transactions which affect *only* noncurrent accounts and therefore have no effect on the amount of working capital. An entry to record depreciation is an example of such a transaction.

Transactions affecting only noncurrent accounts. Transactions of this type will be brought to light by an analysis of the changes in noncurrent accounts, but they are not relevant for funds statements purposes. To illustrate the procedures for handling such items, consider the following two examples: a nonfund exchange and depreciation.

Suppose that a building worth $105,000 is acquired in exchange for $100,000 par value of bonds payable. The entry to record this purchase would be:

A Nonfund Trans-action	*Building*.....................................	*105,000*	
	Bonds Payable		*100,000*
	Premium on Bonds Payable		*5,000*
	Exchange of $100,000 par value of bonds payable for building worth $105,000.		

It is quite clear that this transaction did not directly increase or decrease any current asset or current liability and for that reason had no effect on funds (working capital). Many accountants, however, argue that an exchange transaction of this type should be viewed as consisting of two transactions: (1) the sale of bonds for $105,000, and (2) the application of the proceeds to purchase a building for $105,000. Instead of ignoring an exchange transaction of this type in analyzing the flow of funds, it is possible for us to view the exchange as providing funds (the sale of bonds), and applying funds (the purchase of the building). This treatment, it is argued, is more informative since it shows more completely the movement of the company's *financial resources* during the year.

Either of these two approaches to handling nonfund exchanges is satisfactory and will fully reconcile the change in working capital that took place during the fiscal period.

Other examples of nonfund transactions that have no direct effect on working capital are declaration of stock dividend, retirement of a fully depreciated asset, and the conversion of bonds payable into capital stock.

Some expenses, such as depreciation, amortization of intangibles, and amortization of discount on bonds payable, reduce net income but have no immediate effect on the amount of working capital provided from operations. Such expenses should be added back to net income in measuring the increase in working capital as a result of current operations. To illustrate the reason for this, assume the following: Paul Rey starts a delivery service on January 2, 1971, with a truck that cost $10,000; he has no other assets or liabilities at this time. He does business on a cash basis and during 1971 collects $12,500 in billings and pays out $4,500 in expenses, thus showing an $8,000 improvement in cash, which is his only working capital account. He records depreciation of $3,000 on the truck, resulting in a net income of $5,000. The recording of depreciation did not change any current account, and the increase in working capital remains at $8,000. Thus, in order to measure this increase in working capital from current operations when the details of revenues and expenses are not given, we can either take the income figure before depreciation ($8,000) or the net income of $5,000 and add back depreciation of $3,000.

Obviously, depreciation itself is not a source of funds. The net income figure, however, understates the amount of funds provided by operations because it is net of the nonfund depreciation charge. The depreciation recorded during the period, is therefore shown as an addition to net income in measuring the working capital actually provided by operations. The effect of the depreciation deduction on net income is thus canceled out.

Illustration: Funds statement for the Weaver Company

To illustrate the points just discussed, we shall prepare a funds statement for the Weaver Company from the comparative financial statements appearing on pages 478 and 479 in this chapter.

Assume that the $33,000 increase in *net* plant and equipment during Year 2 reflects (1) the purchase of new equipment for $48,000 in cash, (2) the acquisition of land valued at $25,000 which is to be used for a parking lot, and (3) depreciation of $40,000 recorded during the year. For the sake of clarity, the changes in the Plant and Equipment account and the Accumulated Depreciation account are shown separately on the working papers on page 495. The land was turned over to the company by an officer, along with $20,000 in cash, in settlement of a $45,000 loan to him by the company. During Year 2, the company sold 1,000 additional shares of stock at $80 per share. The student will recall that the Weaver Company earned $36,600 during Year 2 and declared $30,000 in dividends, including $6,000 on preferred stock.

Working paper analysis of changes in noncurrent accounts. To account for the increase of $48,600 in Weaver Company's working capital, the first step is to analyze the changes in noncurrent accounts. Working papers showing this analysis appear on page 495. When these working papers are prepared, each change in noncurrent accounts is analyzed and the effect on working capital of such change is determined. When more than one transaction caused the change in a noncurrent account, the effect of each transaction must be analyzed separately. This is illustrated by the increase of $73,000 in the Plant and Equipment account during Year 2, which resulted from a purchase of new equipment for $48,000 in cash and the acquisition of land valued at $25,000 from an officer who owed money to the company. In some cases two or more changes may be conveniently combined, as in the case of the decrease of $45,000 in Other Assets, which reflects a source of funds of $20,000 and an acquisition of land of $25,000.

In our analysis on the working papers we have treated the acquisition of $25,000 in land received in settlement of an officer's loan as having no effect on working capital. As stated earlier, some accountants would prefer to treat a transaction of this type as if it had produced $25,000 of working capital, which was then used to acquire land. In such a case, the $25,000 repayment of the loan by the officer would be reported as a source of funds and the $25,000 acquisition of land would be reported as an application of funds.

Explanation of working papers adjustments and eliminations

By investigating the changes in the noncurrent accounts, we are able to find the reasons for the $48,600 increase in working capital. The "Adjustments and Eliminations" pair of columns is used as a vehicle to account for all transactions affecting noncurrent accounts. It is these changes that represent sources and uses of working capital. The eliminations and adjustments required on the working papers for funds statement for the Weaver Company are explained below:

(1) Net income of $36,600, which was closed to the Retained Earnings account, is shown under the caption "Operations" as a source of funds. Since revenues increase current assets and *most* expenses either decrease current assets or increase current liabilities, the net income is shown as a *tentative* measure of the increase in working capital as a result of current operations.

(2) Depreciation expense does not reduce a current asset or increase a current liability. The credit change in Accumulated Depreciation resulting from the entry which was made to record depreciation is offset on the working papers by a debit entry and "Operations" is credited by $40,000 to show that funds of $76,600 were generated by operations.

(3) The sale of additional capital stock for $80,000 increased the Common Stock account by $50,000 and the Paid-in Capital in Excess of Par account by $30,000. These credit changes are offset by debit entries on the working papers, and $80,000 is entered as a credit showing a source of funds from the sale of common stock.

(4) Equipment was purchased during the year for $48,000 in cash, resulting in a debit increase to the Plant and Equipment account. This debit increase is offset by a credit entry and $48,000 is entered as a debit showing an application of funds.

WEAVER COMPANY
Working Papers for Funds Statement
Year Ended December 31, Year 2

| | Net Changes in Noncurrent Accounts during Year 2 | | Adjustments and Eliminations | | Working Capital Flows | |
	Dr	Cr	Dr	Cr	Applications	Sources
Increase in working capital	48,600				48,600	
Plant and equipment	73,000			(4) 48,000 (5) 25,000		
Accumulated depreciation		40,000	(2) 40,000			
Other assets (loans to officers)		45,000	(5) 45,000			
Long-term liabilities	50,000			(6) 50,000		
Common stock ($50 par)		50,000	(3) 50,000			
Paid-in capital in excess of par		30,000	(3) 30,000			
Retained earnings		6,600	(1) 36,600	(7) 30,000		
	171,600	171,600				
Operations:						
Net income				(1) 36,600		
Add: Nonfund expenses:						
Depreciation				(2) 40,000		
Working capital from operations						76,600
Sale of common stock				(3) 80,000		80,000
Purchase of equipment			(4) 48,000		48,000	
Settlement of loan by officer				(5) 20,000		20,000
Payment of long-term liabilities			(6) 50,000		50,000	
Payment of cash dividends			(7) 30,000		30,000	
			329,600	329,600	176,600	176,600

Explanation of adjustments and eliminations:

(1) To recognize net income which was closed to Retained Earnings account.

(2) To eliminate depreciation, an expense not requiring the use of working capital.

(3) To recognize sale of 1,000 shares of $50 par value common stock for $80,000.

(4) To recognize purchase of equipment for cash.

(5) To recognize effect of loan settlement of $45,000 by officer; received land valued at $25,000, which does not affect working capital, and cash of $20,000, which represents a source of working capital.

(6) To recognize payment of long-term liabilities.

(7) To recognize payment of cash dividends.

(5) Other Assets representing loans to officers were reduced by $45,000 as a result of a transaction in which one of the officers transferred land worth $25,000 to the Weaver Company and, in addition, paid back $20,000 in cash. The acquisition of land had no direct effect on funds; the receipt of cash represents a source of funds.

(6) The reduction of $50,000 long-term liabilities represents a use of funds and is recognized as such on the working papers by a debit to Long-term Liabilities and a credit to Payments of Long-term Liabilities.

(7) The payment of cash dividends of $30,000 represents an application of funds and is reported as a debit entry to Payments of Cash Dividends on the working papers. The offsetting credit to Retained Earnings, when combined with the debit entry in (1) to account for the net income of $36,600, fully explains the net credit change of $6,600 in Retained Earnings.

The foregoing adjustments and eliminations accounted for all changes in noncurrent accounts and reported separately individual sources and applications of funds in the lower section of the working papers. All applications and sources are now transferred to the last pair of columns in the working papers, in order to confirm the $48,600 increase in working capital. The formal funds statement can now be prepared for the Weaver Company, as follows:

Funds Statement: Shows Sources and Uses of Working Capital

WEAVER COMPANY
Funds Statement
Year 2

Funds were provided by:
Operations:
Net income for Year 2 .... $ 36,600
Add: Expenses not requiring the use of current funds:
Depreciation 40,000
Total funds provided by operations .... $ 76,600
Sale of common stock 80,000
Collection on officer's loan 20,000
Total funds provided $176,600

Funds were applied:
To acquire plant and equipment $48,000
To retire long-term liabilities 50,000
To pay dividends on preferred and common stock 30,000
Total funds applied 128,000
Net increase in working capital .... $ 48,600

We can see that the $76,600 of funds provided by operations is more than double the net income for Year 2 because of the nonfund expense, depreciation. We can also see that the remaining $100,000 of funds came from nonoperating sources. Available funds were used to acquire plant assets, retire long-term liabilities, pay dividends, and add to the company's working capital. The funds statement thus provides a concise view of the way in which working capital was generated and used during Year 2.

CASH FLOWS

In recent years such terms as *cash earnings* or *cash generated per share* have appeared with increasing frequency in financial magazines and annual reports of corporations. The cash earnings referred to in these reports are usually computed by adding back to net income such nonfund expenses as depreciation and amortization of intangibles. The term *cash earnings* used in this context is ambiguous, and the implication that the resulting figure reflects the cash flow from operations is erroneous. To interpret such statements, it is important to understand the relation between net income and cash flows from operations.

Income statements, as we have shown in prior chapters, are prepared on an accrual basis. Accrual accounting was developed to overcome the limitations of cash movements as indicators of business performance. Cash outlays simply represent investments which may or may not prove sound. Cash receipts represent disinvestment and, taken by themselves, tell nothing about whether the inflow is beneficial or not. The accountant's measurement of net income is designed to tell something about the fate of a company's overall investment and disinvestment activities during a given period of time. Granting its imperfections, the income statement is still the best means we have for reporting operating performance of business enterprises.

There are good reasons why one may wish to reverse the accrual process and determine the amount of cash generated by operations. Reports of past cash flow may reveal a good deal about the financial problems and policies of a company. Forecasts of cash flows and cash budgets are useful managerial planning tools. The measurement of past and future cash flows from all sources, including operations, provides valuable information. But cash flow data are in no way a substitute for an income statement nor is the "cash earnings" figure in any sense a better indication of a company's operating performance.

Cash flow from operations

Suppose we wished to convert a company's income statement into a report of its cash flow from operations. How should we go about adjusting the data on the income statement to convert it into cash flow information?

To answer this question, we must consider the relation between accrual-basis income statement data and cash movements within the firm. For illustrative purposes, consider the income statement of the Weaver Company for Year 2, which was presented earlier in this chapter (page 479):

Condensed Income Statement: Accrual Basis

WEAVER COMPANY
Income Statement
Year 2

Net sales...	$900,000
Cost of goods sold.................................	585,000
Gross profit on sales.............................	$315,000
Expenses:	
Operating expenses (selling and administrative)........ $243,000	
Interest expense................................ 12,000	
Income taxes.................................... 23,400	
Total expenses..............................	278,400
Net income.......................................	$ 36,600

From the funds statement presented on page 496, we already know that cash was received from the sale of common stock ($80,000) and from collection of an officer's loan ($20,000); we also know that cash was paid to acquire plant and equipment ($48,000), to retire long-term liabilities ($50,000), and to pay dividends ($30,000). The remaining cash movements must consist of cash generated from customers and cash outlays to pay for merchandise purchases and other expenses.

Cash inflow from customers. Sales on account are an important factor in most companies. The relation between the amount of cash generated from customers and the net sales reported on the income statement depends on the change in receivables between the beginning and end of any period. The relationship may be stated as follows:

$$\text{Net sales} \begin{cases} - \text{ increase in receivables} \\ \qquad\qquad \text{or} \\ + \text{ decrease in receivables} \end{cases} = \text{cash receipts from customers}$$

In the Weaver Company example, a glance at the comparative schedule of working capital on page 487 tells us that net receivables increased from $86,000 to $117,000 during Year 2, an increase of $31,000. The amount of cash received from customers during Year 2 can be determined as follows:

Sales on Cash Basis

Net sales..	$900,000
Less: Increase in receivables during Year 2.................	31,000
Cash receipts from customers........................	$869,000

Cash disbursements for merchandise purchases. The relation between the cost of goods sold for a period and the cash outlays for the purchase of merchandise depends both on the change in inventories and the change in notes and accounts payable to merchandise creditors during the period. The relationship may be stated, in two stages, as follows:

Cash Paid to Merchandise Creditors

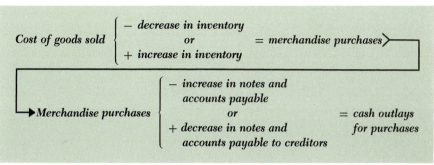

Again referring to the Weaver Company example, we can see that the company increased its inventory by $60,000 and that notes and accounts payable to merchandise creditors increased by $76,000 during Year 2. The cash outlays for the merchandise purchases during Year 2 would be computed as follows:

Purchases on Cash Basis

Cost of goods sold...	$585,000
Add: Increase in inventory....................................	60,000
Merchandise purchases..	$645,000
Less: Increase in notes and accounts payable to creditors...........	76,000
Cash outlays for merchandise purchases......................	$569,000

The result of this computation makes sense. If a company is increasing its inventory, it will be buying more merchandise than it sells during the period; furthermore, if the company is increasing its notes and accounts payable to merchandise creditors, it is not paying for all of its current purchases.

Cash outlays for expenses. Expenses on the income statement arise from three major sources: cash expenditures, the write-off of prepayments, and incurring obligations for accrued expenses. The relation between operating expenses and cash outlays, therefore, depends on changes in asset accounts representing the prepayment of expenses, and on changes in accrued liability accounts. These relationships may be stated as follows:

Converting Expense on Accrual Basis to Cash Basis

$$\text{Expense} \begin{cases} - \text{ increase in related accrued liability} \\ \quad\quad\quad or \\ + \text{ decrease in related accrued liability} \\ - \text{ decrease in related prepayment} \\ \quad\quad\quad or \\ + \text{ increase in related prepayment} \end{cases} = \text{cash outlay for expense}$$

In the case of a nonfund expense such as depreciation, the decrease in the book value of a depreciable asset is exactly equal to the expense recorded, and the resultant cash outlay is zero.

Using the data for the Weaver Company, we can summarize the relation between expenses reported in the income statement and cash outlays for expenses as follows:

Expenses	*Total expenses*	*$278,400*
on Cash	*Add: Decrease in accrued expenses*	*22,600*
Basis	*Increase in prepaid expenses*	*13,000*
	Less: Depreciation	*(40,000)*
	Cash outlays for expenses	*$274,000*

Cash earnings. The conversion of the income statement of the Weaver Company from an accrual to a cash basis is summarized below. Note that this schedule incorporates the adjustments discussed in the preceding paragraphs.

How Much Is "Cash Flow" for Year 2?

WEAVER COMPANY
Conversion of Income Statement from Accrual to Cash Basis
Year 2

	Income Statement (Accrual Basis)	*Add (Deduct)*	*Cash Basis*
Net sales	*$900,000*		
Less: Increase in receivables		*$(31,000)*	*$869,000*
Cost of goods sold	*(585,000)*		
Add: Increase in inventory		*60,000*	
Less: Increase in notes and accounts payable to merchandise creditors		*(76,000)*	*(569,000)*
Gross profit on sales	*$315,000*		*$300,000*
Total expenses	*(278,400)*		
Add: Decrease in accrued expenses		*22,600*	
Increase in prepaid expenses		*13,000*	
Less: Depreciation		*(40,000)*	*(274,000)*
Net income (accrual basis)	*$ 36,600*		
Cash flow from operations			*$ 26,000*

The cash flow from operations for the Weaver Company, $26,000, is lower than the amount of net income, $36,600, during Year 2. This difference is caused by a series of variations between revenues and expense transactions on the accrual basis and cash inflows and outflows during the year.

Some financial analysts add back depreciation to net income and refer to the total as "cash flow from operations." In our example such an approach would lead to the figure of $76,600, that is, $36,600 net income plus depreciation of $40,000. However, the cash flow from operations for the Weaver Company is only $26,000, and not $76,600. It would be misleading to say that the *cash earnings* of the Weaver Company for Year 2 were $14.12 per share of common stock ($76,600 less dividends on preferred stock, $6,000, divided by 5,000 shares of common stock), and to suggest that this is a better measure of the company's performance than the *earnings per share* figure of $6.12 (net income, $36,600, less dividends on preferred stock, $6,000, divided by 5,000 shares of common stock).

Complete cash flow statement. The cash flow from operations illustrated above does not tell the complete story of cash movements during the period. Let us now combine the $26,000 cash flow from operations with the information on cash receipts and payments gleaned from the comparative balance sheet by way of the funds statement. The result will be a statement that explains in full the $2,000 decrease in the cash balance during Year 2. Such a statement of cash flows for the Weaver Company is shown below:

Summary of Cash Movements for Year 2

WEAVER COMPANY
Statement of Cash Flows
Year 2

Cash payments:		
To acquire plant and equipment.		$ 48,000
To retire long-term liabilities.		50,000
To pay dividends		30,000
Total cash payments		$128,000
Cash receipts:		
Cash generated from operations (see schedule on p. 500)	$26,000	
Sale of common stock	80,000	
Collection of officer's loan.	20,000	
Total cash receipts		126,000
Decrease in cash during Year 2 ($40,000 − $38,000)		$ 2,000

The Weaver Company example was sufficiently simple that we could develop cash flow information from a direct inspection of the income statement and comparative balance sheets. In more complex situations, the accountant will usually use some form of working papers to convert the accounting data from an accrual to a cash basis in a systematic fashion. Familiarity with these working-paper procedures is not necessary in order to be able to understand and interpret cash flow information; therefore, discussion of this process is reserved for the *Intermediate Accounting* text by the authors.

DEMONSTRATION PROBLEM

Given below are the balance sheets and income statements for the Dexter Corporation for 1971 and 1972, accompanied by miscellaneous additional information. From these statements and additional information, certain ratios and other measurements can be computed in the process of evaluating the financial position and results of operations for the company.

	1972	1971
Cash	$ 35,000	$ 25,000
Accounts receivable (net)	91,000	90,000
Merchandise inventory	160,000	140,000
Prepaid expenses	4,000	5,000
Investments in subsidiaries	90,000	100,000
Equipment	880,000	640,000
Less: Accumulated depreciation	(260,000)	(200,000)
	$1,000,000	$ 800,000
Accounts payable	$ 105,000	$ 56,000
Taxes payable and other accrued liabilities	40,000	25,000
Bonds payable—6%	280,000	250,000
Premium on bonds payable	3,600	4,000
Common stock, $5 par	165,000	110,000
Retained earnings	406,400	355,000
	$1,000,000	$ 800,000
Sales (net of discounts and allowances)	$2,200,000	$1,600,000
Cost of goods sold	1,606,000	1,120,000
Gross profit on sales	$ 594,000	$ 480,000
Operating expenses	(330,000)	(352,000)
Income taxes	(110,000)	(48,000)
Loss on sale of equipment	(20,000)	
Gain on sale of investments in subsidiaries	12,400	
Net income	$ 146,400	$ 80,000

Equipment costing $60,000, with a book value of $35,000, was sold for $15,000 during 1972. Dividends of $40,000 were paid in cash and a 50% stock dividend was distributed. Additional bonds payable were issued at par during 1972 in exchange for equipment.

All sales are made on credit at a relatively uniform rate during the year. Inventories and receivables did not fluctuate materially during the year. The market value of the company's stock on December 31, 1972, was $68 per share; on December 31, 1971, it was $43.50 (before the 50% stock dividend).

Instructions
a. Compute the following for 1972 and 1971:
   (1) Quick ratio
   (2) Current ratio
   (3) Equity ratio

    (4) Debt ratio
    (5) Book value per share of stock (based on shares outstanding after 50% stock dividend)
    (6) Earnings per share (including extraordinary items) after stock dividend
    (7) Price-earnings ratio
    (8) Gross profit rate
    (9) Operating expenses as a percentage of net sales
    (10) Income before extraordinary items as a percentage of net sales
    (11) Inventory turnover (assume an average inventory of $150,000 for both years)
    (12) Age of receivables at year-end

b. Prepare a funds statement for 1972. Working papers are not required.

c. Prepare a cash flow statement for 1972 which will fully explain the reasons for the $10,000 increase in cash during the year.

QUESTIONS

1. In financial statement analysis, what is the basic objective of observing trends in data and ratios? What is an alternative standard of comparison?

2. In financial analysis, what information is produced by computing a ratio that is not available in a simple observation of the underlying data?

3. What single ratio do you think should be of greatest interest to:
    a. A banker considering a short-term loan
    b. A common stockholder
    c. An insurance company considering a long-term mortgage loan

4. Tilman Company earned (after taxes) a 5.3% return on its total assets. Current liabilities are 10% of total assets and long-term bonds carrying a 5% coupon are equal to 20% of total assets. There is no preferred stock. Would you expect the rate of return on common stockholders' equity to be greater or less than 5.3%? Explain.

5. Company A has a current ratio of 5 to 1. Company B has a current ratio of 3 to 1. Does this mean that A's working capital is larger than B's? Explain.

6. Company H experiences a considerable seasonal variation in its business. The high point in the year's activities comes in November, the low point in July. During which month would you expect the company's current ratio to be higher? If the company were choosing a fiscal year for accounting purposes, how would you advise them?

7. In a statement of sources and applications of funds, what is the meaning of the term *funds?* Why is this a useful definition?

8. What are the primary ways in which a firm generates working capital and the primary ways in which a firm uses working capital?

9. What information can a reader gain from a funds statement that is not apparent from reading an income statement?

10. **a.** Give an example of a transaction, other than the recording of depreciation, which reduces net income but which does not result in the use of working capital during the period.

b. Explain why the statement, "Depreciation is an important source of funds," is not accurate.

11. What is the major difference between a funds statement and a cash flow statement?

12. Criticize the following statement: "Although earnings fell from $3.60 per share in the previous year to $2.97 per share in the current year, cash earnings increased from $4 to $4.80 per share, a 20% increase that testifies to the continuing strength in the company's profitability."

13. An outside member of the board of directors of a small corporation made the following comment after studying the comparative financial statements for the past two years: "I have trouble understanding why our cash has increased steadily during the past two years, yet our profits have been negligible: we have paid no dividends; and inventories, receivables, payables, long-term debt, and capital stock have remained essentially unchanged." Write a brief statement to the director explaining how this situation might occur.

EXERCISES

1. The data below related to the activities of a hardware store:

	Year 2	Year 1
Sales (terms 2/10, n/30)	$400,000	$300,000
Cost of goods sold	260,000	210,000
Merchandise inventory at end of year	47,500	52,500
Accounts receivable at end of year	30,000	25,000

a. Complete the following for Year 2:
   (1) Gross profit percentage_____
   (2) Merchandise turnover_____
   (3) Turnover of accounts receivable_____
b. Briefly comment on the changes in the operating data during Year 2.

2. The following information is available for the Adams Company:

	Year 2	Year 1
Total assets (40% of which are current)	$800,000	$650,000
Current liabilities	$160,000	$200,000
Bonds payable, 7%	200,000	100,000
Capital stock, $10 stated value	300,000	300,000
Retained earnings	140,000	50,000
Total liabilities & stockholders' equity	$800,000	$650,000

The income tax rate is 50% and dividends of $12,000 were declared in Year 2.
a. Compute the following:
   (1) Current ratio for Year 2_____ and Year 1_____
   (2) Debt ratio for Year 2_____ and Year 1_____

      (3) Earnings per share for Year 2 _____

      (4) Book value per share at end of Year 2 _____

  b. Comment on the profitability of trading on the equity for the Adams Company by computing the rate earned on average assets (before taxes and interest).

3. The following information is taken from a recent annual report of E. Corman Company:

	Year 2	Year 1
Current assets	$175,000	$120,000
Equipment	300,000	210,000
Less: Accumulated depreciation	(100,000)	(60,000)
Investments	40,000	50,000
Current liabilities	75,000	40,000
Capital stock	100,000	100,000
Retained earnings	240,000	180,000

Cash dividends declared amounted to $25,000, no equipment items were sold, and investments were sold at a gain of $5,000.

    Prepare a funds statement for Year 2, without using working papers.

4. The information below is available from the records of the Tanner Dredging Company (a single proprietorship) for the current year:

	End of Year	Beginning of Year
Accounts receivable	$ 15,000	$12,000
Inventories	32,000	40,000
Prepaid expenses	2,300	1,500
Accounts payable (merchandise)	20,000	25,000
Accrued expenses	1,000	1,200
Net sales	200,000	
Cost of goods sold	120,000	
Operating expenses (includes depreciation of $13,800)	45,000	

Instructions

Compute the following:

  a. Cash collected from customers _____

  b. Cash paid to merchandise creditors _____

  c. Cash paid for operating expenses _____

  d. Working capital generated from operations _____

5. Figures for 1971 for two companies engaged in the same line of business are presented below:

	Safe Co.	Borrow Co.
Sales (all on credit)	$1,600,000	$1,200,000
Total assets	800,000	400,000
Total liabilities	100,000	100,000
Average receivables during 1971	200,000	100,000

	Safe Co.	Borrow Co.
Average inventory during 1971	$240,000	$140,000
Gross profit as a percentage of sales	40%	30%
Operating expenses as a percentage of sales . .	30%	18%
Net income as a percentage of sales	6%	8%

Instructions
a. Compute the following for each company:
   (1) Net income
   (2) Net income as a percentage of total assets
   (3) Net income as a percentage of stockholders' equity
   (4) Accounts receivable turnover
   (5) Inventory turnover
b. Comment briefly on the operating, financing, and pricing policies of each company based on the limited information given.

PROBLEMS

16-1 The following information is taken from the records of the Hercules Twine Corporation at the end of Year 1:

Sales (all on credit).	$200,000
Cost of goods sold	120,000
Average inventory (fifo method)	30,000
Average accounts receivable	40,000
Net income	20,000
Total assets	250,000
Total liabilities.	140,000

The corporation did not declare dividends during the year and capital stock was neither issued nor retired.

Instructions
From the information given, compute the following for Year 1:
a. Inventory turnover
b. Accounts receivable turnover
c. Total operating expenses, assuming that income taxes amounted to $7,500
d. Gross profit percentage
e. Rate earned on average stockholders' equity

16-2 The data shown below were taken from the financial records of the Merz Company at the close of the current year:

Accounts and notes payable	$ 69,300
Accrued liabilities (including income taxes payable).	30,700
Cash	54,000

Inventories, beginning of year.	$ 42,300
Inventories, end of year.	66,900
Marketable securities.	21,000
Operating expenses.	107,000
Prepaid expenses	27,500
Income taxes (expense).	39,400
Purchases (net)	351,600
Receivables, beginning of year	85,400
Receivables, end of year	70,600
Retained earnings, end of year	204,000
Sales	546,000
Sales returns & allowances.	20,000

Instructions

On the basis of this information, determine the following:

a. Amount of working capital
b. Current ratio
c. Quick ratio
d. Inventory turnover
e. Turnover of receivables
f. Rate of gross profit on net sales
g. Rate of net income on net sales

16-3 Condensed comparative financial statements for the Specialty Mfg. Co. appear below:

SPECIALTY MFG. CO.
Comparative Balance Sheets
As of May 31
(in thousands of dollars)

	Year 3	Year 2	Year 1
Assets:			
Current assets	$1,320	$ 870	$1,200
Plant and equipment (net of depreciation)	6,300	6,090	4,200
Intangible assets	780	540	600
Total assets	$8,400	$7,500	$6,000
Liabilities & Stockholders' Equity:			
Current liabilities	$ 738	$ 684	$ 600
Long-term liabilities (net of discount)	1,572	1,236	1,200
Capital stock ($25 par)	3,600	3,600	2,400
Capital in excess of par value	600	600	300
Retained earnings	1,890	1,380	1,500
Total liabilities & stockholders' equity.	$8,400	$7,500	$6,000

SPECIALTY MFG. CO.
Comparative Income Statements
For Years Ended May 31
(in thousands of dollars)

	Year 3	Year 2	Year 1
Net sales	$30,000	$25,000	$20,000
Cost of goods sold	19,500	15,500	12,000
Gross profit on sales	$10,500	$ 9,500	$ 8,000
Selling expenses	$ 6,000	$ 5,100	$ 4,000
Administrative expenses	3,300	3,250	3,000
Interest expense	90	75	80
Total expenses	$ 9,390	$ 8,425	$ 7,080
Income before income taxes	$ 1,110	$ 1,075	$ 920
Income taxes	510	500	420
Net income	$ 600	$ 575	$ 500

Instructions

a. Compute the trend percentages for all balance sheet items, using Year 1 as the base year.

b. Prepare common size comparative income statements for the three-year period, expressing all items as percentage components of net sales.

c. Comment on the significant trends and relationships revealed by the analytical computations in (a) and (b).

16-4 In the schedule below, certain items taken from the income statements of the Ace Window Company for two fiscal years ending January 31 have been expressed as a percentage of net sales:

	Percentage of Net Sales	
	Year 2	Year 1
Net sales	100%	100%
Beginning inventory	10	16
Net purchases	68	60
Ending inventory	8	12
Selling expenses (20% of which is depreciation)	13	15
Administrative expenses (10% of which is depreciation)	8	9
Income taxes	4	5

Net sales were $1 million in Year 1 and increased by 20% in Year 2. Average accounts receivable were $80,000 in Year 1 and $120,000 in Year 2. Credit sales were 80% of total net sales in both years.

Instructions

a. Did the net income increase or decrease in Year 2 as compared with Year 1? By how much? Prepare a comparative income statement to support your answer.

b. Approximately how many days did it take the Ace Window Company to convert its merchandise into cash during Year 2? In answering this question, compute the number of days' sales in average inventory and the number of days' sales in average accounts receivable.

c. What were the funds provided by operations in each year?

16-5 Allen and Baker are two companies operating in the same industry and are generally comparable in terms of product lines and scope of operations. The financial information given below for these two companies is stated in thousands of dollars and figures are as of the end of the current year:

	(Thousands of Dollars)	
	Allen Co.	Baker Co.
Current assets	$ 97,450	$132,320
Plant and equipment	397,550	495,680
Less: Accumulated depreciation	(60,000)	(80,000)
Patents		2,000
Goodwill	5,000	
	$440,000	$550,000
Current liabilities	$ 34,000	$ 65,000
Bonds payable, 6%, due in 12 years	120,000	100,000
7% preferred stock, par $100	80,000	120,000
Common stock, par $25	150,000	200,000
Capital in excess of par value	26,000	
Retained earnings	30,000	65,000
	$440,000	$550,000
Analysis of retained earnings:		
Balance, beginning of the year	$ 24,800	$ 45,600
Net income for the year	19,800	37,400
Dividends: preferred	(5,600)	(8,400)
Dividends: common	(9,000)	(9,600)
Balance, end of the year	$ 30,000	$ 65,000
Market price of common stock, per share	$30	$54½
Market price of preferred stock, per share	$102	$105

Instructions

Write a brief answer to each of the following questions. Use whatever analytical computations you feel will best support your conclusion and explain your reasoning. Show the amounts used in computing all ratios and percentages and carry computations to one place beyond the decimal, for example, 6.2%.

a. Although market prices for the bonds are not stated, which company's bonds do you think will sell at the higher price per $1,000 bond? Which company's bonds will probably yield the higher rate of return? (You may assume that the safer the bonds, according to your analysis, the lower the yield rate.)

b. Which company's preferred stock is the safer investment?
c. What are the dividend yield and the price-earnings ratios for the common stock of each company?

16-6 Comparative post-closing trial balances for the Farmer Company as of the end of Years 1 and 2 are shown below:

	Year 2	Year 1
Debits		
Cash	$ 63,000	$160,000
Marketable securities.		80,000
Accounts receivable	100,000	190,000
Inventories	110,000	150,000
Prepaid expenses	27,000	20,000
Land	100,000	
Buildings	500,000	
	$900,000	$600,000
Credits		
Allowance for uncollectible accounts	$ 5,000	$ 10,000
Accounts payable.	115,000	85,000
Accrued liabilities	85,000	65,000
Long-term note payable.	250,000	50,000
Capital stock, $1 par value.	330,000	300,000
Retained earnings	115,000	90,000
	$900,000	$600,000

During Year 1 the Farmer Company operated in rented space. Early in Year 2 the company acquired suitable land and made arrangements to borrow funds from a local bank on long-term notes to finance the construction of a building. The company also sold additional stock at par to existing stockholders and all of its marketable securities at book value. Construction was completed near the end of Year 2. The only entries in the company's Retained Earnings account during the two-year period were the closing of the annual net income and the dividend payments of $30,000 in Year 1 and $40,000 in Year 2.

Instructions
a. Prepare a schedule of changes in working capital similar to the one illustrated on page 487 (without showing the percentage changes).
b. Prepare working papers for a funds statement, as illustrated on page 495.
c. Prepare a funds statement for Year 2.
d. Prepare a statement of cash flows for Year 2 by converting the net income figure to a cash basis in a separate schedule and then listing the cash generated from operations with other receipts and disbursements of cash.

16-7 When Robert Hill, the controller of the Tracy Company, presented the following condensed comparative financial statements to the board of directors at the close of Year 2, the reaction of the board members was very favorable.

TRACY COMPANY
Comparative Income Statements
(in thousands of dollars)

	Year 2	Year 1
Net sales	$990	$700
Cost of goods sold	610	480
Gross profit on sales	$380	$220
Operating expenses	(190)	(160)
Income taxes	(80)	(25)
Net income	$110	$ 35

TRACY COMPANY
Comparative Financial Position
as of December 31
(in thousands of dollars)

Current assets	$ 380	$365
Less: Current liabilities	200	205
Net working capital	$ 180	$160
Plant and equipment (net)	1,000	660
Total assets minus current liabilities	$1,180	$820
Financed by:		
Long-term liabilities	$ 250	$ -0-
Capital stock ($50 par value)	500	500
Retained earnings	430	320
Total sources of long-term capital	$1,180	$820

Noting that net income rose from $3.50 per share of common stock to $11 per share, one member of the board proposed that a substantial cash dividend be paid on the company's stock. "Our working capital is up by $20,000; we should be able to make a distribution to stockholders," he commented. To which the controller replied that the company's cash position was precarious. "At the end of Year 2 we have a cash balance of only $15,000, a decline from $147,000 at the end of Year 1," Hill stated. "Remember that we bought $364,000 of new equipment during Year 2." When the board member asked for an explanation of the increase of $20,000 in working capital, Hill presented the following schedule (in thousands of dollars):

	Effect on Working Capital
Increases in working capital:	
Accounts receivable increased by	$ 85
Inventories increased by	45
Prepaid expenses increased by	17
Accounts payable were reduced by	32
Accrued expenses were reduced by	28
Total increases	$207

Decreases in working capital:
Cash decreased by. *$132*
Income tax liability increased by *55*   *$187*
Net increase in working capital during Year 2 . . . . *$ 20*

After examining this schedule, the board member shook his head and said, "I still don't understand how our cash position can be so tight in the face of an almost tripling of net income and a substantial increase in working capital!"

Instructions
a. Prepare a statement converting the Tracy Company's income statement to a cash basis, determining the cash generated by operations during Year 2.
b. From the information in (*a*) and an inspection of the comparative balance sheet, prepare a statement of cash flows during Year 2, explaining the $132,000 decrease in the cash balance.
c. Prepare a funds statement for the Tracy Company in a more acceptable form.
d. Write a brief note of explanation to the board member.

16-8 Below is given a comparative statement of the Astro-Space Company's working capital as of the end of two recent years and a condensed income statement for the second of the two years.

ASTRO-SPACE COMPANY
Comparative Statement of Working Capital
as of December 31

	Year 2	Year 1
Cash	$ 50,600	$ 10,000
Receivables (net)	78,000	85,000
Inventories	161,000	150,000
Prepaid expenses	10,400	15,000
Total current assets	$300,000	$260,000
Notes payable	$ 54,000	$ 70,000
Accounts payable.	44,000	32,000
Accrued liabilities	14,500	17,500
Income taxes payable	32,000	20,500
Total current liabilities	$144,500	$140,000
Working capital	$155,500	$120,000

ASTRO-SPACE COMPANY
Income Statement
Year 2

Net sales	$880,000
Cost of goods sold	650,000
Gross profit on sales	$230,000
Various expenses (details omitted)	$123,500
Depreciation expense.	21,000

Interest expense	$ 3,500
Income taxes	32,000
Total expenses	$180,000
Net income	$ 50,000

During Year 2 the company paid $19,500, including the interest listed above, on a note payable given in connection with a bank loan at the beginning of Year 1. The bank loan was due six months after issue, and has been repeatedly renewed since then. Accounts payable were all incurred in connection with the purchase of merchandise.

Instructions

a. Prepare a schedule showing the conversion of the income statement from an accrual to a cash basis, and determining the cash flow generated by operations for Year 2.

b. Assume that Astro-Space Company paid dividends of $25,000 during Year 2, purchased new equipment for $40,500, and sold treasury stock for $30,000. There were no other changes in noncurrent accounts. Prepare a statement explaining the increase in the cash balance during Year 2.

c. Without preparing a formal funds statement, give an explanation of the $35,500 increase in working capital during Year 2.

16-9   Comparative financial data as of the close of Years 1 and 2 for the Jackson Company are shown below:

	As of December 31	
	Year 2	Year 1
Debits		
Cash	$ 34,220	$ 15,800
Receivables (net)	41,400	24,000
Inventories	27,600	36,800
Prepaid expenses	4,180	4,400
Land	19,000	19,000
Buildings	255,000	250,000
Equipment	381,600	360,000
Patents and development costs	32,000	40,000
Total debits	$795,000	$750,000
Credits		
Accumulated depreciation: buildings	$ 95,000	$ 80,000
Accumulated depreciation: equipment	153,000	120,000
Accounts payable	36,000	30,000
Accrued liabilities	20,000	10,000
Long-term debt	60,000	90,000
Preferred stock ($100 par)	100,000	100,000
Common stock ($25 par)	210,000	200,000
Capital in excess of par	46,000	40,000
Retained earnings	75,000	80,000
Total credits	$795,000	$750,000

During Year 2 the board of directors of the company ordered that $16,000 be transferred from retained earnings to reflect a stock dividend on its common stock. In addition cash dividends of $6,000 were paid on the preferred stock, and cash dividends of $12,000 were paid on the common stock. The only entries recorded in the Retained Earnings account were for dividends and to close the Income Summary account. There were no sales or retirements of buildings and equipment during the year, and no new expenditures were made for patents and development costs.

Instructions
a. Compute the change in working capital during Year 2. You need not prepare a formal schedule.
b. Prepare working papers for a funds statement for Year 2. (See page 495.)
c. Prepare a formal funds statement for Year 2.

17

Taxes and their effect on business decisions

Nature and importance of taxes

Taxes levied by federal, state, and local governmental units are a significant part of the cost of operating a business enterprise. In terms of revenue generated, the three most important kinds of taxes in the United States are income taxes, sales taxes, and property taxes. The income tax is the major source of revenue for the federal government. Most states rely heavily on sales taxes, although a few depend strongly on both income and property taxes. The property tax is the mainstay of local governmental units such as counties, cities, and school districts.

The amount of tax due is usually determined from information contained in accounting records. Income taxes are levied on taxable income which, although not necessarily the same as accounting income, is computed from accounting data. Sales and various excise taxes are based on sales revenue. Property taxes are based on assessed value, determined by appraisal but influenced to some extent by accounting valuations, particularly in the case of inventories and equipment.

Most business costs are incurred because there is a direct relation between the expenditure and expected benefits. An important characteristic of taxes, however, is that the amount of taxes paid is not necessarily related to the amount and value of governmental services received.

Although involuntary and often unrelated to benefits, taxes are not entirely uncontrollable. Businessmen may legally alter their tax costs by their choice of plant location, form of business organization, methods of financing, and alternative accounting procedures. Thus taxes inevitably become an important factor in business decisions.

The knowledge required to be expert in taxation has made it a field of specialty among professional accountants. Tax practice is an important element of the services furnished to clients by CPAs. This service includes not only computing of taxes and preparation of tax returns, but also tax planning.

Tax planning

To minimize income taxes is the goal of tax planning. Almost every business decision is a choice among alternative actions: for example, should we lease or buy business automobiles; should we obtain needed capital by issuing bonds or preferred stock; should we use straight-line depreciation or an accelerated method? Some of these alternatives will lead to much lower income taxes than others. Tax planning, therefore, means determining in advance the income tax effect of every proposed business action, and then making business decisions which will minimize the income tax burden. If the tax rate is 50%, then every dollar of tax legally avoided is worth two dollars of pretax income.

A general understanding of our tax laws and the way in which they operate is essential to an understanding of accounting and the use of accounting data by businessmen. The remainder of this chapter will be devoted to a brief, and necessarily general discussion of income taxes, property taxes, sales taxes, and excise taxes.

THE FEDERAL INCOME TAX

The present federal income tax dates from the passage of the Sixteenth Amendment to the Constitution in 1913. This amendment removed all questions of the constitutionality of income taxes and paved the way for the more than 50 revenue acts passed by Congress since that date. In 1939 these tax laws were first combined into what is known as the Internal Revenue Code. The administration and enforcement of the tax laws are duties of the Treasury Department, operating through a division known as the Internal Revenue Service. The Treasury Department publishes its interpretation of the tax laws in Treasury regulations; the final word in interpretation lies with the federal courts.

Classes of taxpayers

In the eyes of the income tax law, there are four major classes of taxpayers: individuals, corporations, estates, and trusts. Proprietorships and partnerships are not taxed as business units; their income is taxed directly to the individual proprietor or partners, whether or not actually withdrawn from the business. A proprietor reports his business income on his personal tax return. A partner includes on his personal tax return his share of partnership net income. However, the partnership must file an information return showing the computation of total partnership net income and the net income allocated to each partner.

A corporation is a separate taxable entity; it must file a tax return and pay a tax on its annual taxable income. In addition, individual stockholders must report dividends received as part of their personal taxable income. The taxing of corporate dividends has led to the charge that there is "double taxation" of corporate income—once to the corporation and again when it is distributed to stockholders.

Special and complex rules apply to the determination of taxable income for estates and trusts. These rules will not be discussed in this chapter.

Cash basis of accounting for individual tax returns

Almost all individual tax returns are prepared on the cash basis of measuring income. Revenue is recognized when collected; expenses are recognized when paid. The cash basis is advantageous for the individual taxpayer because it is simple, requires a minimum of record keeping, and often permits tax saving by deliberately shifting the timing of revenue and expense transactions from one year to another. For example, a dentist whose taxable income is higher than usual in the current year may decide in December to delay billing patients until January 1, and thus postpone the receipt of gross income to the next year. The timing of expense payments near the year-end is also controllable by a taxpayer using the cash basis. If he has received a bill for a deductible expense item in December, he may choose to pay it before or after December 31 and thereby influence the amount of taxable income in each year. Further comparison of the cash basis with the accrual basis of income measurement is presented later in this chapter.

Tax rates

All taxes may be characterized as proportional, regressive, or progressive with respect to any given base. A *proportional* tax remains a constant percentage of the base no matter how that base changes. For example, a 4% sales tax remains a constant percentage of sales regardless of changes in the sales figure. A *regressive* tax becomes a smaller percentage of the base as the base increases. A business license tax of $500, for example, is regressive with respect to income, since the larger the income the smaller the tax as a percentage of income. A *progressive* tax becomes a larger portion of the base as that base increases. Federal income taxes are *progressive* with respect to income, since a higher tax rate applies as the amount of taxable income increases.

Individual tax rates. Few generalizations can be made about individual income tax rates since they are frequently changed by legislation. Different rate schedules apply to individual taxpayers, married taxpayers who file joint returns, and single taxpayers who qualify as the "head of a household." In computing the amount of the tax, the tax rates are applied to taxable income, the computation of which is discussed in a later section of this chapter. The rate schedule appearing on pages 518 and 519 shows the personal income tax rates in effect at the time this was written.[1]

Note that different and lower tax rates are applicable to the taxable income of married taxpayers who combine their income and deductions on a joint return. Certain persons who qualify as the *head of a household* are entitled to use still another schedule of tax rates. This schedule is not illustrated in this chapter.

Corporation tax rates. The corporate tax rate schedule is much simpler than the schedule for individuals. Corporations pay a normal tax on their

---

[1] The tax rate schedule illustrated here was in effect for calendar year 1969. The Tax Reform Act of 1969 reduced the rate of tax (starting mostly in 1971) for certain groups of taxpayers, such as single persons and those with large "earned" incomes.

entire net taxable income, and a surtax on all taxable income in excess of $25,000. These rates are also frequently changed by Congress. The corporate rates in effect at the time this was written are shown on page 519.

Personal Income Tax Rates

Tax Rate Schedule for Individuals

Single Taxpayers and Married Persons Filing Separate Returns

Taxable Income		Income Tax	
Not over $500		**14% of taxable income**	
Over—	**But not over—**		**of excess over—**
$ 500	$ 1,000	$ 70, plus 15%	$ 500
1,000	1,500	145, plus 16%	1,000
1,500	2,000	225, plus 17%	1,500
2,000	4,000	310, plus 19%	2,000
4,000	6,000	690, plus 22%	4,000
6,000	8,000	1,130, plus 25%	6,000
8,000	10,000	1,630, plus 28%	8,000
10,000	12,000	2,190, plus 32%	10,000
12,000	14,000	2,830, plus 36%	12,000
14,000	16,000	3,550, plus 39%	14,000
16,000	18,000	4,330, plus 42%	16,000
18,000	20,000	5,170, plus 45%	18,000
20,000	22,000	6,070, plus 48%	20,000
22,000	26,000	7,030, plus 50%	22,000
26,000	32,000	9,030, plus 53%	26,000
32,000	38,000	12,210, plus 55%	32,000
38,000	44,000	15,510, plus 58%	38,000
44,000	50,000	18,990, plus 60%	44,000
50,000	60,000	22,590, plus 62%	50,000
60,000	70,000	28,790, plus 64%	60,000
70,000	80,000	35,190, plus 66%	70,000
80,000	90,000	41,790, plus 68%	80,000
90,000	100,000	48,590, plus 69%	90,000
100,000		55,490, plus 70%	100,000

How to compute tax. To compute the amount of tax on any given taxable income:

(1) Use the appropriate schedule to find the taxable income that includes your income figure.
(2) Read the dollar tax on the taxable income column from the rate schedule.
(3) Using the percentages given in the table, compute the tax on the "excess."
(4) Add the results in (2) and (3).

Example. Find the tax for a *married couple filing a joint return* and having a taxable income of $35,000.

Answer. Tax on $32,000 (read from table) $8,660
Tax on   3,000 excess at 42% 1,260

Tax on $35,000 . . . . $9,920

| *Corporation Tax Rates* | Normal tax: 22% of all net taxable income |
| | Surtax: 26% of all net taxable income in excess of $25,000 |

Married Taxpayers Filing Joint Returns

Taxable Income		Income Tax	
Not over $1,000		14% of taxable income	
Over—	But not over—		of excess over—
$ 1,000	$ 2,000	$ 140, plus 15%	$ 1,000
2,000	3,000	290, plus 16%	2,000
3,000	4,000	450, plus 17%	3,000
4,000	8,000	620, plus 19%	4,000
8,000	12,000	1,380, plus 22%	8,000
12,000	16,000	2,260, plus 25%	12,000
16,000	20,000	3,260, plus 28%	16,000
20,000	24,000	4,380, plus 32%	20,000
24,000	28,000	5,660, plus 36%	24,000
28,000	32,000	7,100, plus 39%	28,000
32,000	36,000	8,660, plus 42%	32,000
36,000	40,000	10,340, plus 45%	36,000
40,000	44,000	12,140, plus 48%	40,000
44,000	52,000	14,060, plus 50%	44,000
52,000	64,000	18,060, plus 53%	52,000
64,000	76,000	24,420, plus 55%	64,000
76,000	88,000	31,020, plus 58%	76,000
88,000	100,000	37,980, plus 60%	88,000
100,000	120,000	45,180, plus 62%	100,000
120,000	140,000	57,580, plus 64%	120,000
140,000	160,000	70,380, plus 66%	140,000
160,000	180,000	83,580, plus 68%	160,000
180,000	200,000	97,180, plus 69%	180,000
200,000		110,980, plus 70%	200,000

This rate schedule may be stated alternatively as 22% on taxable income up to $25,000, and 48% on all taxable income in excess of $25,000. In computing the tax, it is often convenient to multiply the entire taxable income by 48% and then deduct $6,500 (26% of the first $25,000 of taxable income not subject to surtax).

Because of the progressive nature of the tax rates, taxpayers whose incomes fluctuate widely from year to year are taxed more heavily than those who receive the same total income in a relatively stable pattern. To illustrate, suppose that two *single taxpayers* receive a total of $32,000 of taxable income during a two-year period. A receives $4,000 the first year and $28,000 the second, while B receives $16,000 in each year. Over the two-year period A would pay $10,780 in federal income taxes while B would pay $8,660. To alleviate the inequities inherent in uneven flows of taxable income, Congress some years ago added to the tax law a five-year *income-averaging* provision.

Surcharge on individuals and corporations

In 1968 a "temporary" tax *surcharge* was levied by Congress on the amount of income tax as determined by using the tax rate schedules illustrated above. The surcharge rate was 10% for corporations; the rate for individuals varied, depending on the amount of income taxes due (before the surcharge). For individuals (filing either a separate or a joint return) whose income tax amounted to $734 or more, the surcharge rate was 7½% for 1968, 10% for 1969, and 5% for the first six months of 1970. It is likely that the surcharge will either expire in 1970 or will undergo frequent changes in response to changes in the status of the U.S. economy.

Marginal versus average tax rates. In any analysis of tax costs, it is important to distinguish the *marginal* rate of tax from the *average* rate. This distinction may be illustrated as follows: If a corporation has a taxable income of $50,000, its income tax will be $17,500 ($25,000 × 22% + $25,000 × 48%), an average tax rate of 35% of taxable income. On the last dollar of income, however, the tax is 48 cents, since the corporation is subject to a marginal tax rate of 48% on all income over $25,000.

Note from the tax rate schedules on pages 518 and 519 that even a wider discrepancy between marginal and average tax rates may exist in the case of individual taxpayers.

Income tax formula for individuals

The federal government supplies standard income tax forms on which taxpayers are guided to a proper computation of their taxable income and the amount of the tax. It is helpful to visualize the computation in terms of an income tax formula. The general formula for the determination of taxable income for all taxpayers (other than corporations, estates, and trusts) is outlined on page 521.

The actual sequence and presentation of material on income tax forms differs somewhat from the arrangement in the formula. However, it is easier to understand the structure and logic of the federal income tax and to analyze tax rules and their effect by referring to the tax formula.

Use this Formula to Compute Taxable Income

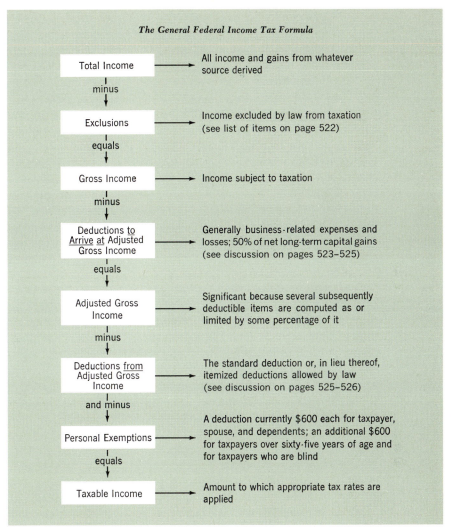

The General Federal Income Tax Formula

Total Income — All income and gains from whatever source derived

minus

Exclusions — Income excluded by law from taxation (see list of items on page 522)

equals

Gross Income — Income subject to taxation

minus

Deductions <u>to</u> <u>Arrive at</u> Adjusted Gross Income — Generally business-related expenses and losses; 50% of net long-term capital gains (see discussion on pages 523–525)

equals

Adjusted Gross Income — Significant because several subsequently deductible items are computed as or limited by some percentage of it

minus

Deductions <u>from</u> Adjusted Gross Income — The standard deduction or, in lieu thereof, itemized deductions allowed by law (see discussion on pages 525–526)

and minus

Personal Exemptions — A deduction currently $600 each for taxpayer, spouse, and dependents; an additional $600 for taxpayers over sixty-five years of age and for taxpayers who are blind

equals

Taxable Income — Amount to which appropriate tax rates are applied

Total and gross income. Total income is an economic concept; gross income is a tax concept. *Total income* includes, in the words of the law, "all income from whatever source derived." To determine whether an item is included in total income one need only ask, "Is it income?" (as distinguished, for example, from a return of capital).

Gross income for tax purposes is all income not excluded by law. To determine whether any given income item is included in taxable gross income, one must ask, "Is there a provision in the tax law excluding this item of income from gross income?" To identify legal exclusions from gross income, it is necessary to refer to the law and sometimes to Treasury regulations and court decisions.

Among the items presently excluded from gross income by statute are interest on state and municipal bonds, gifts and inheritances, life insurance proceeds, workmens' compensation and sick pay, social security benefits and the portion of receipts from annuities that represent return of cost, military bonuses, pensions to veterans, certain military pay in combat zones, compensation for damages, income earned outside the U.S. after 18 months abroad for employees other than of the U.S. government, and the first $100 of dividends from corporations ($200 on a joint tax return).

Capital gains and losses. Certain kinds of property are defined under the tax law as *capital assets.*[2] Gains or losses from the sale or exchange of such assets are granted special treatment for income tax purposes. Because long-term capital gains generally are taxed at one-half or less than the rates applicable to ordinary income, there is a strong incentive for taxpayers to arrange their business and personal affairs so that income will be realized in the form of capital gains. The government's efforts to keep such arrangements within bounds have been exceeded only by the collective ingenuity of taxpayers and tax advisers in making income appear in the form of capital gains. In a brief summary, we can only outline the general features of this phase of income taxation.

Amount of gain or loss. The tax gain (or loss) from the sale or exchange of capital assets is the difference between the selling price and the *basis* of property sold. Basis rules are complicated; tax basis depends, among other things, on how the property was acquired, whether it is personal or business property, and in some cases whether it is sold at a gain or at a loss. In general, the basis of purchased property is its cost, reduced by any depreciation that has been allowed for tax purposes.

Long-term versus short-term. Long and short are relative terms; in income taxation the dividing line is six months. Long-term capital gains or losses result from the sale or exchange of capital assets held for more than six months; short-term from those held six months or less.

Short-term gains must be reported in full and are taxed as ordinary income. Only one-half of long-term gains are included in adjusted gross income, and the maximum rate of tax on the total gain is generally 25% (ignoring the surcharge). For example, suppose that a taxpayer subject to a marginal tax rate of 30% has a $1,000 net long-term capital gain. He would include only $500 in adjusted gross income and pay a $150 (30% × $500) tax on the gain. The tax rate applicable to his $1,000 long-term gain is only 15%, one-half of his marginal rate. On the other hand, suppose that the same taxpayer has a marginal tax rate of 70%. If he were to include $500 (one-half of the $1,000 long-term gain) in adjusted gross income and apply the 70% marginal rate, his tax would be $350, or 35% of the total $1,000 gain. Through 1969 the maximum rate on capital gains was 25%. Therefore the taxpayer would have been entitled to compute his tax at $250 (25% of

[2]Capital assets are actually defined in the law by "exclusion"; that is, the law (IRC 1221) states that capital assets are all items of property *except* (*a*) inventories in a trade or business; (*b*) trade accounts and notes receivable; (*c*) copyrights, literary, musical, or artistic compositions in the hands of their creator; (*d*) any government obligations due within one year and issued at a discount; and (*e*) real or depreciable property in a trade or business.

$1,000). In this case the rate of tax applicable to the long-term capital gain was *less* than one-half the taxpayer's marginal rate of tax on other income. The 1969 Revenue Act, however, changed the effective rate on long-term capital gains for certain high-bracket taxpayers so that the rates may reach 35% in 1972.

In general, capital *losses,* either long-term or short-term, are deductible only against capital gains. If total capital losses exceed gains, however, individual taxpayers (but not corporations) may deduct capital losses against other gross income up to a maximum of $1,000 in any one year. Starting in 1970, only 50% of a net long-term capital loss can be used in arriving at this $1,000 maximum. Capital losses not deductible in any given year may be carried forward and treated as long- or short-term capital losses in future tax years.

Long- and short-term capital gains and losses must be combined in a certain way in arriving at adjusted gross income. First, all long-term gains and losses must be offset against each other to produce the *net* long-term gain or loss. Short-term gains and losses must be similarly combined into a *net* short-term gain or loss. The following possible situations may result:

1. Both a net long-term gain and a net short-term gain. In this case the two items are treated separately: The short-term gain is included in gross income and treated as ordinary income; only one-half of the long-term gain is included in adjusted gross income.

2. Net losses (of either type) greater than net gains (of either type); or both net long-term and net short-term losses. In this case the capital losses are combined into one figure and, up to $1,000, may be deducted to arrive at adjusted gross income. The amount of any net capital loss not deducted in a given year may be carried over and deducted in future years, following the same tax rules.

3. Gains (of either type) greater than losses (of either type). Long- and short-term gains and losses must be offset to produce a net capital gain that is either long- or short-term in nature, depending on the characteristic of the dominant gain.

The foregoing situations are illustrated in the tabulation on page 524.

Business plant and equipment. Real or depreciable property used in a trade or business is not a capital asset under the tax law. This means that any loss realized on the sale or disposal of such property is fully deductible. Prior to 1964, however, gains on such property were granted capital gains treatment. This provision encouraged business taxpayers to depreciate such property below fair market value as rapidly as possible and then sell it at a capital gain. In 1964 Congress closed this tax loophole by instituting a "recapture provision" providing that gains on the sale of such assets would be taxed as ordinary income to the extent of "excess depreciation deductions." The intent of the law is to remove much of the incentive toward overdepreciation as a means of converting ordinary income into capital gains.

Deductions to arrive at adjusted gross income. The deductions from gross income allowed in computing adjusted gross income are discussed below.

Case 1		Case 2(a)		Case 2(b)	
Net LTCG	*$2,000*	*Net LTCG*	*$2,000*	*Net LTCL*	*$2,000*
Net STCG	*800*	*Net STCL*	*2,900*	*Net STCL*	*3,000*
		Total capital loss	*$ 900*	*Total capital loss*	*$5,000*

Case 1	Case 2(a)	Case 2(b)
Result: Reported separately. All of STCG included in adjusted gross income; one-half of LTCG included in adjusted gross income.	*Result: All deductible to arrive at adjusted gross income.*	*Result: $1,000 (50% of LTCL, for example) deductible to arrive at adjusted gross income. Balance ($3,000 STCL) carried over to future years.*

Case 3(a)		Case 3(b)	
Net LTCG	*$3,000*	*Net LTCL*	*$2,600*
Net STCL	*1,800*	*Net STCG*	*3,000*
Total capital gain (long-term)	*$1,200*	*Total capital gain (short-term)*	*$ 400*

Case 3(a)	Case 3(b)
Result: $600 included in adjusted gross income.	*Result: Included in adjusted gross income in full and taxed as ordinary income.*

1. **Business expenses.** These include all ordinary and necessary expenses of carrying on a trade, business, or profession (other than as an employee). In the actual tax computation, business expenses are deducted from business revenues, and net business income is then included in adjusted gross income.

2. **Employees' expenses.** Certain limited expenses incurred by employees in connection with their employment are allowed as a deduction. These include reimbursed expenses, travel expenses, expenses of "outside salesmen," and moving expenses.

3. **Expenses attributable to rents and royalties.** Expenses, such as depreciation, property taxes, repairs, maintenance, interest on indebtedness related to property, and any other expense incurred in connection with the earning of rental or royalty income, are allowed as a deduction. This means that only the *net income* derived from rents and royalties is included in adjusted gross income.

4. **Losses from the sale of property used in a trade or business.** The loss resulting from the sale of property used in business may be deducted against other items of gross income.[3]

5. **Net capital losses.** Up to $1,000 in any one year, as discussed on pages 522 to 524, may be deducted to arrive at adjusted gross income.

6. **Long-term capital gain deduction.** One-half of the net long-term capital gains is a deduction to arrive at adjusted gross income.

---

[3] Losses arising from the sale of personal property, such as a home or personal automobile, are not deductible. On the other hand, gains from the sale of personal property are taxable. This appears inconsistent, until one realizes that a loss on the sale of personal property usually reflects depreciation through use, which is a personal expense.

7. Net operating loss carry-over. Taxable income may be either positive or negative. If positive income were taxed and no allowance made for operating losses, a taxpayer whose business income fluctuated between income and loss would pay a relatively higher tax than one having a steady income averaging the same amount. Therefore, the tax law allows the carry-over of net operating losses as an offset against the income of other years. At the present time a loss must be carried back against the income of the three preceding years, and then forward against the income of five years.

Deductions from adjusted gross income. The individual taxpayer has an option with respect to deductions *from* adjusted gross income. He may choose to take a lump-sum standard deduction, or he may choose to itemize his deductions, in which case he may deduct a number of expenses specified in the law as itemized deductions.

The standard deduction. The standard deduction has been equal to 10% of adjusted gross income, with a maximum deduction of $1,000.[4] For example, if a taxpayer has adjusted gross income of $8,000, his standard deduction is $800. If he has adjusted gross income of $25,000, his standard deduction is $1,000, the legal limit.

There is a *minimum standard deduction* of $200 plus $100 for each exemption allowable to the taxpayer. This provision may be advantageous to low-income taxpayers having large families, and is subject to certain limits.

Deductions *to arrive at* adjusted gross income do not affect the decision to elect the standard deduction. However, itemized deductions (discussed below) are relinquished if the standard deduction is taken. This explains why it is important to know whether a given deduction comes before or after adjusted gross income in the tax formula.

Itemized deductions. Instead of taking a standard deduction, a taxpayer may elect to itemize his personal deductions. The six major categories of itemized deductions allowable under the law are described below:

1. Interest. Interest on any indebtedness, within certain limits.

2. Taxes. State and local real and personal property taxes; state income taxes, all sales taxes, and gasoline taxes are deductible by the person on whom they are imposed. No federal taxes are deductible.

3. Contributions. Contributions by individuals to charitable, religious, educational, and certain other nonprofit organizations are deductible, within certain limits.

4. Medical expenses. Medical and dental expenses of the taxpayer and his family are deductible to the extent that they exceed 3% of adjusted gross income, subject to certain maximum limits, and limits on the deductibility of drugs and medicines.

5. Casualty losses. Losses in excess of $100 from any fire, storm, shipwreck, theft, or other unexpected or unusual causes are deductible.

6. Expenses related to the production of income. In this category are included any necessary expenses in producing income or for the management

[4] This is the rule applicable through 1970. From 1971 through 1973 the rule is subject to change gradually to 15% of adjusted gross income with a maximum of $2,000.

of income-producing property, other than those deductible to arrive at adjusted gross income. Some examples of miscellaneous *deductible* expenses are union dues, work clothes, professional dues, subscriptions to professional periodicals, investment advisors' fees, legal fees relating to investments, and fees for income tax advice and for preparation of tax return. Examples of *nondeductible* items are the cost of going to and from work, campaign expenses of candidates seeking election, and gifts to needy friends.

Personal exemptions. In addition to itemized deductions, a deduction from adjusted gross income is allowed for personal exemptions. One exemption each is allowed for the taxpayer, his spouse, and each person who qualifies as a dependent of the taxpayer. In recent years the amount of each personal exemption has been $600. Although this amount is scheduled to increase gradually to $750 by 1973, we will assume in all illustrations and problems in this book that the personal exemption is $600.

The term *dependent* has a particular meaning under the law. Briefly but incompletely stated, a dependent is a person who (1) receives over one-half of his support from the taxpayer, (2) is either closely related to the taxpayer or lives in his home, and (3) has gross income during the year of less than $600, unless he or she is a child of the taxpayer who is under nineteen years of age or a full-time student.[5]

A taxpayer and his spouse may each claim an additional exemption if he or she is blind, and another exemption if either is sixty-five years of age or over. These additional exemptions do not apply to dependents.

Tax returns and payment of the tax. Every individual who has gross income in excess of the amount of his own personal exemption (or two exemptions in the case of persons over sixty-five) must file an income tax return within 3½ months after the close of the taxable year. On the calendar-year basis, applicable to most taxpayers, the due date is thus April 15. If a set of accounting records is kept, a taxpayer may elect to report and pay income taxes on the basis of any 12-month fiscal year.

Currently, the payment of federal income taxes is on a "pay as you go" basis. The procedure by which employers withhold income taxes from the wages of employees has been discussed in a previous chapter. To equalize the treatment of employees and self-employed persons, the tax law requires persons who have income in excess of a given amount, from which no withholdings have been made, to file a Declaration of Estimated Income Tax and to pay estimated taxes in quarterly installments. Any under- or overpayment is adjusted when the tax return is filed at the regular time.

Tax credits. When the tax liability on taxable income has been computed, the final step in computing the amount of tax due is to deduct any allowable credits against the tax. Examples of tax credits are:

---

[5] A child under nineteen or a full-time student who qualifies as a dependent in all other respects but who earns over $600 in any one year has, in effect, two personal exemptions. One may be taken by the taxpayer who claims him as a dependent. The other he will claim for himself on his own personal tax return.

1. *Taxes withheld or paid on declared estimates.* The taxpayer takes credit for all taxes withheld from his salary and for any quarterly payments made on the basis of his declaration of estimated income tax.

2. *Retirement income credit.* A taxpayer aged sixty-five or over who receives retirement income is entitled to a tax credit of 15% of retirement income up to a certain amount. Retirement income in general is income from pensions, interest, rents, and dividends.

3. *Miscellaneous.* Certain other tax credits are allowed in special circumstances. For example, credit is allowed for taxes paid to foreign countries on income also taxed by the United States. Another credit against income tax allowed in certain years is the *investment tax credit* as a result of purchase of certain depreciable assets for business purposes.

Illustrative individual income tax computation. The computation of the federal income tax for a hypothetical taxpayer is illustrated below:

Compare with Tax Formula on Page 521	**MR. AND MRS. M. J. BRICKER** *Illustrative Federal Income Tax Computation*		
	Gross income (excluding $700 interest revenue from municipal bonds):		
	Gross fees from Mr. Bricker's law practice	$50,000	
	Dividends ($1,800 less $200 exclusion).............	1,600	
	Mrs. Bricker's salary	4,400	
	Interest revenue on savings account...............	320	
	Long-term capital gain (on stock held more than six months)	800	$57,120
	Deductions to arrive at adjusted gross income:		
	Operating expenses of Mr. Bricker's law practice......	$30,000	
	Travel expenses by Mrs. Bricker in connection with employer's business.........................	280	
	Long-term capital gain deduction (50% of $800).......	400	30,680
	Adjusted gross income		$26,440
	Deductions from adjusted gross income:		
	Itemized deductions..........................	$ 5,640	
	Personal exemptions (4 × $600, for example)........	2,400	8,040
	Taxable income...............................		$18,400
	Computation of tax: (using rates shown on page 519)		
	Tax on $16,000 (joint return)...................	$ 3,260	
	Tax on $2,400 × 28%........................	672	$ 3,932 °
	Less: Tax credits:		
	Withheld from Mrs. Bricker's salary...............	$ 460	
	Payments by Mr. Bricker on declaration of estimated tax	3,000	3,460
	Amount of tax remaining to be paid.................		$ 472

° *Exclusive of any surtax that may be applicable in certain years.*

In this example it is assumed that the taxpayer, M. J. Bricker, is married and provides over one-half the support of his son and daughter. Bricker is a practicing attorney who realized $50,000 in gross fees from his law practice, and incurred $30,000 of business expenses. Mrs. Bricker, who works as a secretary for an insurance company, earned $4,400 during the year, from which was withheld $460 in federal income taxes. The Brickers have interest revenue from municipal bonds of $700, and from savings accounts of $320. Dividends received on stock jointly held amounted to $1,800 during the year. During the year, stock purchased several years ago by Bricker for $1,600 was sold for $2,400, net of brokerage fees, thus producing an $800 long-term capital gain.

Mrs. Bricker incurred $280 of nonreimbursed travel expenses in connection with her employer's business. The Brickers have allowable itemized expenses (contributions, interest expense, taxes, medical costs, etc.) of $5,640. Bricker paid $3,000 in quarterly payments on his declaration of estimated income tax during the year.

On the basis of these facts, the taxable income of the Brickers is shown to be $18,400. Since they file a joint return, the tax on this amount of taxable income may be computed from the rate table for married couples, and is $3,932, ignoring the surcharge. Taking withholdings and payments on declared estimates into account, the Brickers have already paid $3,460 in taxes, and thus owe $472 at the time of the filing of their tax return. If their credits had amounted to $4,500, for example, they would be entitled to a refund of $568.

Partnerships

Under the federal income tax law partnerships are treated as a conduit through which taxable income flows to the partners. An information return must be filed by all partnerships showing the determination of net income and the share of each partner. However, certain items of partnership income and deductions are segregated, and each partner is required to treat his share of each of these items as if he had received or paid them personally. In general, segregated items are those granted special tax treatment; they include tax-exempt interest, capital gains and losses, charitable contributions, and dividends received. Any salaries actually paid to partners may be deducted in arriving at partnership income, but they must be reported as salaries by the individual partners on their personal tax returns.

Corporations

A corporation is a separate taxable entity and is subject to a tax at special rates on its net taxable income. Every corporation, unless expressly exempt from taxation, must file a return whether or not it has taxable income or any tax is due.

Corporate taxable income is computed in much the same manner as for individuals, with the following major differences:

1. The concept of adjusted gross income is not applicable to a corporation, since there is no standard deduction or itemized personal deductions.

2. Corporations are not entitled to the dividend exclusion of $100 allowed to individual taxpayers. Instead a corporation may deduct 85% of any dividends received from other domestic corporations. This means in effect that only 15% of dividends is taxed to the receiving corporation.

3. Corporations may deduct capital losses only to the extent of capital gains. If capital losses exceed gains, losses may be carried back three years and then forward five years and offset against capital gains.

4. Corporations are subject to a maximum tax rate of 30% (25% through 1969) on net long-term capital gains. A corporation is not entitled to the 50% long-term capital gain deduction. If corporate taxable income (including any long-term capital gain) is below $25,000, the corporation is better off to pay the 22% normal tax on the long-term capital gain, rather than to elect the 30% maximum capital gain tax rate.

5. Corporations may deduct charitable contributions only to the extent of 5% of taxable income, computed before the deduction of any contributions. Contributions in excess of the limit may be carried forward for five succeeding years if contributions (including those carried forward) in those years are within the 5% limit.

To illustrate some of the features of the income tax law as it applies to corporations, a tax computation for the Optics Corporation is shown below:

Note Difference between Accounting Income ($42,000) and Taxable Income ($37,700)

OPTICS CORPORATION
Illustrative Tax Computation

Revenues:

Sales		$200,000
Dividends received from domestic corporations		10,000
		$210,000
Expenses:		
Cost of goods sold	$118,000	
Other expenses (includes capital loss of $3,000)	50,000	168,000
Net income per books		$ 42,000
Add back (items not deductible for tax purposes):		
Capital loss deducted as part of operating expenses		3,000
Charitable contributions in excess of 5% limit		1,200
		$ 46,200
Special deductions:		
Dividends received credit (85% of $10,000)		8,500
Taxable income		$ 37,700
Tax computation:		
Tax on first $25,000 of income at 22%		$ 5,500
Tax on income over $25,000 ($12,700 × 48%)		6,096
Total tax°		$ 11,596

° Excludes 10% surcharge which was in effect in 1968 and certain years thereafter.

Accounting income versus taxable income

The accountant's objective in determining accounting income is to measure business operating results as accurately as possible, in accordance with the generally accepted principles summarized in Chapter 15. Taxable income, on the other hand, is a legal concept governed by statute. In setting the rules for determining taxable income, Congress is interested not only in meeting the revenue needs of government but in achieving certain public policy objectives. Since accounting and taxable income are determined with different purposes in mind, it is not surprising that they often differ by material amounts.

Cash versus accrual basis of income measurement. The *accrual method* of measuring income has been discussed throughout the preceding chapters of this book, because it is the method used by most business enterprises. Revenue is recognized when it is realized, and expenses are recorded when they are incurred, without regard to the timing of receipt or payment. Any taxpayer who maintains a set of accounting records *may* elect to use the accrual basis for tax purposes. When the production, purchase, or sale of merchandise is a significant factor in a business, the accrual method is mandatory.

The *cash basis* of measuring income does not reflect income in the accounting sense. Revenues are recognized when cash is received, and expenses are recorded when they are paid. This method is allowed for tax purposes because it is simple, requires a minimum of records, and produces reasonably satisfactory results for individuals not engaged in business and for businesses in which receivables, payables, and inventories are not a major factor.

The cash basis allowed for tax purposes and used on nearly all tax returns by individuals varies in two important ways from a simple offsetting of cash receipts and disbursements.

1. On the expenditure side, the cost of acquiring depreciable property having a service life of more than one year is not deductible in the year of purchase. The taxpayer must treat such a purchase as an asset and deduct depreciation in appropriate years. A similar treatment must be given to major items of prepaid expenses, such as rent paid in advance or insurance premiums which cover more than one year. Thus most expenses paid *in advance* are deductible only when they are incurred, but expenses paid *after* they are incurred are deductible in the year of payment.

2. On the revenue side, a cash basis taxpayer must report revenue when it has been *constructively received,* even though the cash is not yet in his possession. Constructive receipt means that the revenue is so much within the control of the taxpayer as to be equivalent to receipt. For example, if a taxpayer has a savings account, for income tax purposes the interest on that account is constructively received even though he does not draw it out. Similarly, a check received on December 31 is constructively received even though it is not cashed until January 2.

The choice between the cash and accrual method, where permitted, rests on the question of tax timing. Taxpayers are motivated to elect the cash basis because it permits postponing the recognition of taxable income and the payment of the tax. In this way they have the interest-free use of funds that would otherwise be paid in taxes.

Special tax treatment of revenues and expenses. Even when the accrual method is used for tax purposes, differences between taxable and accounting income may occur. Some differences result from special tax rules which are unrelated to accounting principles.

1. Some items included in accounting income are not taxable. For example, interest on state or municipal bonds is excluded from taxable income.

2. Some business expenses are not deductible. For example, donations to political candidates or parties are not deductible.

3. Special deductions in excess of actual business expenses are allowed some taxpayers. For example, depletion deductions in excess of actual cost are allowed taxpayers in the oil and mining industries. This "statutory depletion" allowance has been as high as 27½%, for oil and gas. Starting in 1970 the maximum rate was reduced to 22%.

4. Some business expenses must be treated as capital expenditures for tax purposes. For example, goodwill is sometimes amortized for accounting purposes; for tax purposes goodwill is a permanent asset and amortization is not a deductible expense.

Differences in timing of revenues and expenses. The timing of the recognition of certain revenues and expenses under tax rules differs from that under accounting principles. Two examples are the following:

Generally, income received in advance is taxed in the year of receipt. For example, rent revenue received for several years in advance is taxable in the year of receipt, even though for accounting purposes it would be prorated over the rental period.

Certain estimated expenses are not deductible for tax purposes until the cost is actually incurred. For example, the accountant may estimate the future costs of meeting warranty, guarantee, and service agreements on the sales of merchandise and treat them as current expenses. For tax purposes these costs are not deductible until they are actually incurred.

Alternative accounting methods. The student who has progressed this far in his study of accounting is aware that business income is not a precise calculation. Various accounting methods result in different net income figures, largely because of difference in the timing of revenue and expense recognition.

The tax law permits taxpayers, in some cases, to adopt for income tax purposes accounting methods which differ from those used for financial reporting. Businessmen are therefore faced with the option of choosing an accounting method for tax purposes that will result in minimizing their tax burdens—usually by postponing the tax.

The choice of inventory pricing methods will affect the timing of net income recognition, as we have seen in Chapter 11. One of the reasons for the popularity of the lifo pricing method is that it results in a minimal inventory figure and thus lowers gross profit and net income during periods of rising prices. In the long run, of course, lifo simply shifts recognition of income into future years, but so long as lifo inventories are carried at a cost below that of alternative methods, some tax postponement is permanent. A peculiarity of the *lifo* tax rules is that *this method must be used in published financial statements if it is elected for income tax purposes.*

The tax law allows the adoption of a variety of depreciation methods in computing taxable income. In general it will be advantageous for a taxpayer to adopt the depreciation method for tax purposes which results in the largest amount of cumulative depreciation over the shortest period of time. This will result in minimizing current taxable income and postponing the payment of income taxes.

There are a number of other less common examples of elective methods which postpone taxes. Taxpayers who sell merchandise on the installment basis may elect to report income in proportion to the cash received on the installment contract, rather than at the time of sale. The cost of drilling oil wells and preparing wells for production may be charged off as incurred, rather than capitalized and depreciated. Most research and development expenditures are accorded a similar elective treatment.

Taxes and financial reporting. When there are differences between accounting principles and tax rules, many businesses choose to keep their accounting records on a tax basis as a matter of bookkeeping convenience. In other words, accounting principles give way to tax laws. If the differences are not material, there is no objection to this practice as a means of simplifying the keeping of tax records. Where the differences between tax rules and accounting principles are material, however, the result of following the tax law is to distort financial statements. It is clearly preferable to maintain accounting records to meet the need for relevant information about business operations, and to adjust such data to arrive at taxable income annually.

When a corporation follows different accounting methods for book and tax purposes, a financial reporting problem may arise. The difference in procedure will usually have the effect of postponing the recognition of income (either because an expense deduction is accelerated or because revenue recognition is postponed). The question is whether the income tax expense should be accrued when the income is recognized on the accounting records, or when it is subject to taxation.

To illustrate the problem, let us consider a very simple case. Suppose the Pryor Company has before-tax accounting income of $200,000 in each of two years. However, the company takes as a tax deduction in Year 1 an expense of $100,000 which is reported for accounting purposes in Year 2. The company's accounting and taxable income, and the actual income taxes due (assuming a tax rate of 40%) are shown at the top of page 533.

Following one approach, the Pryor Company might simply report in its income statement in each year the amount of income taxes due for that year

	Year 1	Year 2
Accounting income (before income taxes)	$200,000	$200,000
Taxable income	100,000	300,000
Actual income taxes due each year, at assumed rate of 40% of taxable income	40,000	120,000

as computed on the company's tax returns. The effect on reported net income would be as follows:

Company Reports Actual Taxes

	Year 1	Year 2
Accounting income (before income taxes)	$200,000	$200,000
Income taxes	40,000	120,000
Net income	$160,000	$ 80,000

The reader of the Pryor Company's income statement might well wonder why the same accounting income before taxes in the two years produced such a widely variant tax load and after-tax income figure.

To deal with this distortion between pre- and after-tax income, an accounting policy known as *income tax allocation* has been devised, which is widely used in practice. Briefly, the objective of the tax allocation procedure is to accrue income taxes in relation to accounting income, whenever differences between accounting and taxable income are caused by differences in the *timing* of revenues or expenses. In the Pryor Company example, this means we would report on the Year 1 income statement a provision for the future income taxes on the $100,000 of income which was reported for accounting purposes in Year 1 but which will be taxed in Year 2. The effect of this accounting procedure is demonstrated by the journal entries that would be made to record the income tax expense in each of the two years:

Entries to Record Income Tax Allocation

Year 1	Income Taxes	80,000	
	Current Income Tax Liability		40,000
	Deferred Income Tax Liability		40,000
	To record current and deferred income taxes at 40% of accounting income of $200,000.		

Year 2	Income Taxes	80,000	
	Deferred Income Tax Liability	40,000	
	Current Income Tax Liability		120,000
	To record income taxes at 40% of accounting income of $200,000.		

Using tax allocation procedures, the Pryor Company would report its net income during the two-year period as follows:

	Year 1	Year 2
Income before income taxes	$200,000	$200,000
Income taxes (tax allocation basis)	80,000	80,000
Net income	$120,000	$120,000

Company Uses Tax Allocation Procedure

In this simple example, the difference between taxable and accounting income (caused by the accelerated deduction of an expense) was fully offset in a period of two years. In practice, differences between accounting and taxable income may persist over extended time periods and deferred tax liabilities may accumulate to significant amounts. For example, in a recent balance sheet of Sears, Roebuck and Co., deferred taxes of $598 million were reported as a result of the use of the installment sales method for tax purposes while reporting net income in financial statements on the usual accrual method.

Income taxes as a factor in business decisions

Federal income tax laws have become so complex that detailed tax planning has become a way of life for most business firms. Almost all businesses today engage professional tax specialists to review the tax aspects of major business decisions and to develop plans for legally minimizing income tax costs. Because it is important for even the nonspecialist to recognize areas in which tax factors may be of consequence, a few of the major opportunities for tax planning are discussed briefly below.

Effect of taxes on form of business organization. Tax factors should be carefully considered at the time a business is organized. As a sole proprietor or partner, a businessman will pay taxes at individual rates, ranging currently from 14 to 70%,[6] on his share of the business income earned in any year *whether or not he withdraws it from the business.* Corporations, on the other hand, are taxed on earnings at average rates varying from 22 to 48% (plus a surcharge in some years). Corporations may deduct salaries paid to owners for services but may not deduct dividends paid to stockholders. Both salaries and dividends are taxed to their recipients.

These factors must be weighed in deciding in any given situation whether the corporate or noncorporate form of business organization is preferable. There is no simple rule of thumb, even considering only these basic differences. To illustrate, suppose that Able, a married man, starts a business which is expected to produce an average of $50,000 annual net income before any remuneration to him either for services or capital contribution. Able plans

---

[6]Effective in 1971, the maximum rate on earned income of individuals is set at 60% and for 1972 and later years at 50%.

to withdraw $20,000 per year from the business. The combined corporate and individual taxes under the corporate and single proprietorship form of business organization are summarized below:

			Form of Organization	
			Corporate	*Single Proprietorship*
Business income............................			*$50,000*	*$50,000*
┌*Salary to Able*...........................			*20,000*	
│┌*Taxable income*			*$30,000*	*$50,000*
││*Corporate tax:*				
││ *22% of $25,000*	*$5,500*			
││ *48% of $ 5,000*	*2,400*	*7,900*		
││*Net income*.........................			*$22,100*	*$50,000*
││*Combined corporate and individual tax:*				
│└→*Corporate tax on $30,000 income (above)*....			*$ 7,900*	
│ *Individual tax:* °				
└──→*On Able's $20,000 salary*			*4,380*	
On Able's $50,000 share of business income				*$17,060*
Total tax on business income.............			*$12,280*	*$17,060*

° *Able's personal exemptions and deductions have been ignored, on the assumption that his other income equals personal exemptions and deductions.*

At first glance this comparison suggests that the corporate form of organization is favorable from an income tax viewpoint. It must be noted, however, that the $22,100 of earnings retained in the corporation will be taxed to Able as ordinary income when and if they are distributed as dividends. On the other hand, if Able later sells his business and realizes these earnings in the form of the increased value of his capital stock, any gain may be taxed at a maximum of, say, 25%. In either case Able can postpone the payment of tax on retained earnings so long as they remain reinvested in the business.

If Able decided to withdraw from his business each year all net income, the total tax on corporate net income and on the $22,100 that he would receive in dividends would amount to $21,048 ($7,900 corporate tax plus tax on personal income of $42,100, or $13,148) compared to only $17,060 tax paid on the $50,000 of earnings from the single proprietorship.

Under this assumption the income tax results under the single proprietorship form of organization are preferable. It is clear that both the marginal rate of tax to which individual business owners are subject and the extent to which profits are to be withdrawn from the business must be considered in assessing the relative advantages of one form of business organization over another.

In an attempt to alleviate the effect of income taxes on the choice of the form of business organization for small businesses, Congress added an elective provision to the tax laws. Under certain conditions, partnerships may choose to be taxed as corporations and small, closely held corporations may choose to be taxed as partnerships.

Effect of taxes on business transactions. Business transactions may often be arranged in such a way as to produce favorable tax treatment. For example, when property is sold under an installment contract, the taxable gain may be prorated over the period during which installment payments are received by the seller. To qualify for this treatment, payments received during the first year must not exceed 30% of the selling price. By arranging the transaction to meet these conditions, a substantial postponement of tax payments may be secured.

Sometimes a seller tries to arrange a transaction one way to his tax benefit and the buyer tries to shape it another way to produce tax savings for him. Income tax effects thus become a part of price negotiations. For example, in buying business property, the purchaser will try to allocate as much of the cost of the property to the building and as little to the land as possible, since building costs can be depreciated for tax purposes. Similarly, in selling a business the seller will try to allocate as much of the selling price as possible to goodwill, since this is a capital asset. The buyer of the business, however, will want the purchase price to be attributable to the purchase of inventories or depreciable assets, which are ultimately deductible against ordinary income. Goodwill cannot be amortized for tax purposes. The point is, the failure to consider the tax consequences of major business transactions can be costly.

Some examples of provisions of the federal tax laws clearly designed to affect business decisions include (1) accelerated depreciation; (2) additional first-year depreciation of 20% on assets of tangible personal property costing up to $10,000; and (3) rapid depreciation on assets "critical to the public interest" such as pollution-control facilities and coal-mine safety equipment.

Taxes and financial planning. Different forms of business financing produce different tax costs. Interest on debt, for example, is fully deductible while dividends on preferred or common stocks are not. This factor operates as a strong incentive to finance expansion by borrowing. Suppose that a company needs $100,000 to invest in productive assets on which it can expect to earn a 12% annual return. If the company issues $100,000 in 6% preferred stock, it will earn after taxes, assuming a 48% marginal tax rate, $6,240 ($12,000 less taxes at 48% of $12,000). This is barely enough to cover the $6,000 preferred dividend. If, on the other hand, the company borrowed the $100,000 at 6% interest, its taxable income would be $6,000 ($12,000 earnings less $6,000 interest expense). The tax on this amount at 48% would be $2,880, leaving income of $3,120 available for common stockholders or for reinvestment in the business. A similar analysis should be made in choosing between debt and common stock financing.

Taxable income computed on the accrual basis is not necessarily matched by an inflow of cash. A healthy profit picture accompanied by a tight cash position is not unusual for a rapidly growing company. Income taxes are a substantial cash drain and an important factor in planning business cash requirements.

PROPERTY TAXES

The property tax is an *ad valorem* tax, that is, it is based on the assessed value of property. Property falls into two classes, *real* and *personal,* and different rates of tax may be levied on each class. Real property includes land and all growth or structures attached to the land; all property other than real property is personal property.

The amount of property taxes levied by a governmental unit is a product of the assessed value of all property within its jurisdiction and the tax rate. Most local governments establish assessed value at some fraction of fair market value and the tax rate is determined after revenue needs and total assessed value are known.

Property taxes do not accrue in the same way that interest accrues; rather they attach to property as of a particular moment in time, the *lien date.* Economically, however, property taxes are a payment for the right to use and enjoy property throughout the fiscal year of the taxing authority. Since the tax comes into existence at the lien date, the appropriate entry at this time (assuming that the lien date is July 1 and that the tax is known to be $1,200 for the year) is as follows:

Entry	*July 1* *Deferred Property Taxes* *1,200*	
Reflects	*Property Taxes Payable*	*1,200*
Legal	*To recognize the liability for property taxes for the*	
Position	*period July 1 to June 30.*	

The tax should be prorated and charged against revenues over the fiscal year of the taxing unit, in this case July 1 to June 30. Property Tax Expense would be debited and Deferred Property Taxes would be credited, either monthly or whenever statements are prepared. When the tax is paid, the Property Taxes Payable account is debited.

In certain instances taxes on real property may represent an addition to the cost of the property rather than an expense. Delinquent taxes paid on newly acquired property and *special assessments* for improvements to real property, for example, would fall in this category.

SALES AND EXCISE TAXES

A *sales tax* based on retail sales is levied by many state and local governments. Typically certain classes of sales are exempt, notably food and some commodities, such as gasoline and cigarettes, already subject to special *excise taxes.* To restrict the practice of purchasing outside the state to avoid the tax, some states levy a supplementary *use tax,* applicable to goods purchased outside the state and brought in.

Typically a sales tax is imposed on the consumer, but the seller collects the tax, files tax returns at times specified by law, and remits a percentage of his reported sales. Since the seller acts as an agent in collecting the sales tax, he logically should record a liability at the time of the sale as follows:

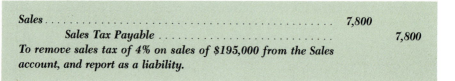

Sales Tax Recorded at Time of Sale

Accounts Receivable (or Cash)............................	1,040	
Sales Tax Payable		40
Sales....................................		1,000
To record the sale of $1,000 subject to 4% sales tax.		

When it is not convenient to set up the sales tax liability at the time of sale, an alternative procedure is to credit the Sales account with the entire amount to be collected, including the sales tax, and to make an adjustment at the end of each period to record the sales tax payable. To illustrate this, suppose that the total recorded sales for the period under this method were $202,800. Since the Sales account includes both the sale price and the 4% sales tax, it is apparent that $202,800 amounts to 104% of the actual sales figure. Actual sales are $195,000 ($202,800 ÷ 1.04) and the amount of sales tax due is $7,800 (4% of $195,000). The entry to record the liability for the sales tax would be:

Sales Tax Recorded as Adjustment of Sales

Sales..	7,800	
Sales Tax Payable		7,800
To remove sales tax of 4% on sales of $195,000 from the Sales account, and report as a liability.		

Any discrepancy between the tax due and the amount actually collected from customers, under this method, would be automatically absorbed in the sales figure.

The federal government levies a series of excise taxes on the sale, manufacture, or consumption of certain goods and services. Among the excise taxes currently in effect are those on the sale of automobiles, air travel, telephone service, gasoline, tires, alcohol, and tobacco products.

Sales and use taxes (and also excise taxes) paid in acquiring depreciable assets used in business should be included in the cost of the assets. This treatment is in accord with the general rule that all costs incurred in acquiring and placing long-lived assets in condition for use should be capitalized, and the total cost depreciated during the periods receiving benefits from the use of the assets. An individual taxpayer can deduct sales and use taxes on personal assets such as home furnishings and automobiles in the year such taxes are paid; he cannot, however, deduct any federal excise taxes paid on the purchase of property for personal use.

DEMONSTRATION PROBLEM

Robert Sandison has been engaged in various businesses for many years and has always prepared his own income tax return. His returns have been regularly audited by the Internal Revenue Service, and some material errors have been discovered. The errors generally understated taxable income. In 1971, Sandison decided to ask a certified public accountant to prepare his income tax returns.

Early in February of 1972, Sandison presented the following tax information for 1971 to his CPA:

Personal revenues:

Salary from Sandi Construction Company, after withholding of $3,168 and social security taxes of $382	$ 15,450
Dividends from Sandi Construction Company (jointly owned)	16,875
Drawings from Northwest Lumber Company	6,000
Drawings from S & S Business Advisers	9,600
Interest income—City of Norwalk bonds	800
Interest income—savings account.	950
Proceeds on sale of stock:	
Sale of stock acquired two years ago for $6,200	14,200
Sale of stock held for three months, cost $4,100	3,400
Sale of stock held for over six years, cost $3,500	1,800

Personal expenses:

Contribution to St. Jerome's Church	$ 610
Contribution to candidate for city mayor	250
Interest on mortgage, $3,820; on personal note, $900	4,720
Property taxes, including $400 on vacant land in Arizona and a special assessment of $500 on residence for street widening	3,980
Sales taxes, including $380 paid on purchase of new Cadillac for personal use	850
Income taxes paid to state of California	1,900
Medical expenses	1,100
Subscription to investment advisory service	165

Single proprietorship—wholesale lumber, doing business as Northwest Lumber Company:

Sales	$118,000
Cost of goods sold	82,000
Operating expenses	38,800
Drawings by Sandison	6,000

Partnership—business consulting under the name of S & S Business Advisers:

Fees earned	$ 76,300
Gain on sale of vacant lot acquired four years ago	4,400
Professional salaries and other wages paid	32,400
Supplies used	3,500
Contributions to Long Beach Opera Association	1,000

Rent expense.	$ 4,800
Miscellaneous business expenses	7,100
Drawings (Sandison, $9,600 and Sims, $6,400)	16,000

Corporation—engaged in construction under the
name of Sandi Construction Company:

Customer billings	$230,000
Materials used	70,000
Construction labor	60,000
Officers' salaries expense	25,000
Legal and professional fees paid	3,500
Advertising expense	2,000
Other business expenses.	19,800
Loss on sale surplus equipment.	4,200
Cash dividends paid	22,500

Sandison has a 60% equity in the profits of S & S Business Advisers and John Sims has a 40% interest. Sandison owns 75% of the stock of Sandi Construction Company. Because of his controlling interest, he is responsible for the preparation of the income tax returns for these organizations.

Sandison is married, has four children, and supports his seventy-nine-year-old mother. He is fifty-five years old and his wife is younger but will not give her date of birth. The oldest child, Bill, is twenty years old and attends school full time. Sandison provides all of his son's support, even though Bill earns approximately $1,500 per year from odd jobs and from investments inherited from his grandfather.

In April of 1971, Sandison paid $3,100 balance due on his 1970 federal income tax return. His total tax for the previous year amounted to $16,340; however, he received a refund of $1,700 as a result of errors made in preparing the return. In addition to the income taxes withheld by the Sandi Construction Company, Sandison made four equal payments of $2,000 each on his estimated tax for 1971.

Instructions
Using the income tax table on page 519, prepare the joint return for Mr. and Mrs. Sandison for last year, showing the amount of tax due (or refund coming). You should also prepare in summary form the information on the partnership tax return for S & S Business Advisers and the corporation income tax return for the Sandi Construction Company. Assume a personal exemption is $600, that the corporate tax rate is 30% on all taxable income, and that the Sandi Construction Company has not paid any part of its income tax for 1971.

QUESTIONS

1. What are the four major classes of taxpayers under federal income tax law?

2. It has been claimed that corporate income is subject to "double taxation." Explain the meaning of this statement.

3. Taxes are characterized as proportional, regressive, or progressive with respect to any given base. Describe an income tax rate structure that would fit each of these characterizations.

4. During the current year Davis, a bachelor, expects a taxable income of $15,000.

Using the tables on pages 518 and 519, determine how much federal income tax Davis would save were he to get married before the end of the year, assuming that his bride had no taxable income. Personal exemption, $600.

5. Doctor Black files his income tax return on a cash basis. During the current year he collected $6,300 from patients for medical services rendered in prior years, and billed patients $38,500 for services rendered this year. He has accounts receivable of $8,200 relating to this year's billings at the end of the year. What amount of gross income from his practice should he report on his tax return?

6. Jacobs files his income tax return on a cash basis. During the current year $300 of interest was credited to him on his savings account; he withdrew this interest on January 18 of the following year. Jacobs purchased a piece of business equipment having an estimated service life of five years in December of the current year. He also paid a year's rent in advance on certain business property on December 29 of the current year. Explain how these items would be treated on Jacob's current year's income tax return.

7. State in equation form the federal income tax formula, beginning with total income, and ending with taxable income.

8. Why does it make any difference in computing income taxes whether a given deduction may be taken *before* or *after* computing adjusted gross income?

9. From a taxpayer's viewpoint it is better to have a $10,000 net long-term capital gain than $10,000 of ordinary income; however, ordinary losses are usually more advantageous than net capital losses. Explain.

10. Even when a taxpayer uses the accrual method of accounting, his taxable income may differ from his accounting income. Give four examples of differences between the tax and accounting treatment of items that are included in the determination of income.

11. Under what circumstances is the accounting procedure known as *income tax allocation* appropriate? Explain the purpose of this procedure.

12. Explain how the corporate income tax makes debt financing in general more attractive than financing through the issuance of preferred stock.

EXERCISES

1. Malcolm Livermore is in the 70% income tax bracket because he refuses to see a tax advisor in order to seek out some income tax "shelters." He has $25,000 of long-term capital gains this year and expects to have only short-term capital gains next year. He purchased stock of X Co. seven months ago that he can sell at a loss of $10,000. Should he sell the stock this year or next year? Prepare a schedule in support of your answer, assuming that the maximum tax on net long-term capital gains is 30% for federal and state taxes and that Livermore's short-term gains next year are $10,000 or more.

2. Warren Bray is in the 80% income tax bracket (counting both state and federal taxes) for ordinary income and 30% for long-term capital gains. He owns 100

shares of Lucky Mining Co. stock which cost him $50 in total thirty years ago. The stock is now worth $6,050 and he wants to know whether he should sell the stock or give it to Atlantic State University, his alma mater. Prepare a schedule showing the income tax impact of the two alternatives, assuming that he can deduct the $6,050 value of the stock as a charitable contribution.

3. Complete the following statements by inserting the appropriate word(s) or number(s) in the space provided:
   a. Gains on sale or exchange of capital assets held for more than _____ months by an individual are taxed generally at a maximum rate of _____% (exclusive of any surtax). For a taxpayer in a 28% income tax bracket, a net long-term capital gain of $100 would be taxed at the marginal rate of _____%.
   b. Married taxpayers with five young children provide more than 50% of the support for each of their parents. Each of the four parents is over sixty-five years old. The taxpayers would be entitled to _____ exemptions for dependents on a joint return.
   c. Corporations pay income taxes on _____% of the dividends received from another domestic corporation and can deduct charitable contributions not to exceed _____% of taxable income (before the deduction for contributions).
   d. A corporation may deduct capital losses on its income tax return only to the extent of _____ _____.

4. a. The total assessed valuation in a certain city is $72,000,000. The city budget shows that $2,188,800 in revenues are needed during the coming year. What will be the tax rate, in mills, for the coming fiscal year? What amount of city tax will be paid by a person who owns property assessed at $20,000?
   b. A company reports a balance of $198,325 in Sales. This amount, however, includes $5,000 collected on a note receivable, credited to Sales in error, and 4½% sales tax on $193,325. Prepare an entry correcting the accounts and recognizing the sales tax liability.

5. A man over sixty-five had adjusted gross income of $5,200 last year. He has a young wife, four dependent children, and nominal personal deductions. Compute his income tax for last year using the minimum standard deduction and the tax rate table on page 519. Disregard any surcharge, and assume that personal exemption is $600.

6. The Barker Company uses accelerated depreciation and charges off currently all research and development costs for income tax purposes. On its financial statements it uses straight-line depreciation and amortizes research and development costs over a five-year period. Its taxable and accounting income for the last five years are shown below:

	1971	1970	1969	1968	1967
Taxable income . . .	$350,000	$300,000	$200,000	$150,000	$100,000
Accounting income	200,000	250,000	300,000	280,000	250,000

Assuming that corporate income is taxable at a flat rate of 45%, compute the net income for the company for financial reporting purposes

a. Based on *actual taxes paid.*
b. Based on *taxes that would be paid on the net income reported for accounting purposes.*
Comment on the results.

PROBLEMS

17-1 **a.** You are to consider the income tax status of each of the items listed below. List the numbers 1 to 15 on your answer sheet. For each item state whether it is included in gross income or excluded from gross income for federal income tax purposes.
   (1) Cash dividends received on stock of Thiokol Chemical Company.
   (2) Value of a color TV set won as a prize in a quiz contest.
   (3) Gain on the sale of an original painting.
   (4) Inheritance received on death of a rich uncle.
   (5) Interest received on Jersey City municipal bonds.
   (6) Proceeds of life insurance policy received on death of husband.
   (7) Tips received by a waitress.
   (8) Value of U. S. Treasury bonds received as a gift.
   (9) Rent received on personal residence while on extended vacation trip.
   (10) Share of income from partnership in excess of drawings from the business.
   (11) Amount received as damages for injury in automobile accident.
   (12) Salary received from a corporation by a stockholder who owns directly or indirectly all the shares of the company's outstanding stock.
   (13) Gain on sale of Commonwealth United capital stock, held for five months.
   (14) Taxpayer owed $1,000 on a note payable. During the current year the taxpayer painted a building owned by the creditor, and in return the creditor canceled the note.
   (15) Trip to Hawaii given by employer as reward for performance as a salesman.

 b. You are to determine the deductibility status, for federal tax purposes, of each of the items listed below. List the numbers 1 to 10 on your answer sheet. For each item state whether the item is deducted to arrive at adjusted gross income; deducted from adjusted gross income; or not deductible.
   (1) Interest paid on mortgage covering personal residence.
   (2) Carry-forward of an unused operating loss from previous year.
   (3) Capital loss on the sale of securities.
   (4) Damage in storm to motorboat used for pleasure.
   (5) State sales tax paid on purchase of family automobile.
   (6) Expenses incurred in moving from Chicago to Portland to accept a new position with a different company, not reimbursed by employer.
   (7) Travel expenses incurred by employee in connection with his job, not reimbursed.
   (8) Cost of traveling to and from home to place of employment.
   (9) Fee paid to accountant for assistance in contesting additional personal

income taxes assessed by Internal Revenue Service; contest was successful.

(10) Taxpayer does maintenance work on rental property which he owns. This
work would cost $500 if the taxpayer hired someone to do it.

17-2 *Case A.* During the current year Hutton has total income of $76,000. He has personal
exemptions of $4,800, deductions to arrive at adjusted gross income of $6,400,
itemized deductions of $8,200, and exclusions from gross income of $1,600.

Case B. Healy, who is an attorney, uses the cash basis of reporting income for federal
income tax purposes. During the current year his business net income (computed
on an accrual basis) was $86,400. Between the beginning and end of the current
year receivables from clients increased by $12,000, and payables relating to oper-
ating expenses decreased by $6,800. Included in reported business income is $1,200
of interest received on municipal bonds. Healy has a personal savings account to
which $720 in interest was credited during the year, none of which was withdrawn.
In addition to business expenses taken into account in computing the net income
of his business, Healy has $1,360 in deductions to arrive at adjusted gross income.
His personal exemptions amount to $4,200, and his itemized deductions are $960.

Instructions
For each of the situations described above, determine the amount of the taxpayer's
adjusted gross income and his taxable income for the year. Assume that the maximum limit for the standard deduction is $1,000.

17-3 Saul Short is a professor of finance with a wife and two children. His income and
expenses for the latest year are as follows:

Salary from State College	$22,000
Consulting fees (net of applicable expenses)	3,000
Dividends (jointly owned)	600
Interest on bonds of State of Texas	180
Casualty loss, interest, taxes and other expenditures (see list below)	13,390
Long-term capital gains	4,800
Short-term capital losses	2,000
Unused long-term capital loss from previous year	1,500
Proceeds on insurance policy on life of uncle	5,000
Prize won in Stock Selection Contest	2,500
Casualty loss, interest, taxes, and other expenditures:	
Theft of furniture on July 20 while on vacation	$ 2,000
Interest paid on loans to buy growth stocks	1,800
Medical expenses	500
Insurance on home	180
Income taxes withheld	4,500
Miscellaneous deductible expenses	150
Sales taxes	240
Property taxes	520
State income taxes	400
Clothes, food, and other living expenses	3,100
Total (as listed above)	$13,390

Instructions

Prepare a joint return for Professor and Mrs. Short. Use the tax table on page 519. Assume that the personal exemption is $600 and that the maximum standard deduction is $1,000.

17-4 The Helen Corporation reported an income before income taxes of $37,500 for 19___, its first year of operations. In computing the income, the following facts were taken into consideration:

(1) Accounts receivable of $400 were written off and charged to expense.

(2) Depreciation of $2,500 was recorded using the straight-line method.

(3) Inventories were reported on a fifo basis at $25,000.

(4) Research and development costs of $12,000 will be amortized over a five-year period; amortization of $2,400 was recorded in the current year.

Officers of the corporation are concerned over the large amount of income taxes they must pay and decide to restate taxable income as follows:

(1) An acceptable allowance for uncollectible accounts, after the write-off of $400, would be $1,600.

(2) Use of accelerated methods of depreciation would result in depreciation expense of $4,200.

(3) Inventories on a lifo basis would amount to $20,000.

(4) Research and development costs are to be charged off in full for income tax purposes as incurred.

Instructions

a. Determine the taxable income of the Helen Corporation on the revised basis.

b. If the tax rates for corporations are 20% on the first $25,000 of taxable income and 50% on any taxable income in excess of $25,000, compute the reduction in the current year's income tax liability for the Helen Corporation resulting from the accounting changes.

17-5 Frank and Eileen Dunne have three dependent children. In preparing their income tax return for the latest year you obtain the following information:

Gross income:

Salary *(including bonus of $1,000)*	$15,000
Dividends *(assume joint ownership)*	800
Proceeds on life insurance policy upon death of brother	10,000
Interest on City of Pasadena bonds	100
Interest on savings account	275
Gain on stock held over six months	2,000
Loss on stock held two months	(3,400)
Inheritance from uncle's estate	1,100
Oil royalty, net of statutory depletion allowance	725

Personal expenses paid:

Income tax withheld by employer	$ 2,000
Social security taxes withheld by employer	300
Grocery bills	2,800
Sales taxes	320
State income taxes	180
Contributions to church and other charities	210

Property taxes	$ 720
Federal excise taxes	130
Gifts to needy friends	150
Interest on mortgage	1,760
School tuition for children	600
Baby-sitting fees.	150
Medical expenses	700
Union dues	80
Preparation of tax returns	25
Gasoline taxes	73
Legal fees relating to slander suit.	110

Instructions
Compute the tax due (or refund) on a joint return filed for Frank and Eileen Dunne, both of whom are under sixty-five years old. Assume the personal exemption to be $600 each and the maximum standard deduction to be $1,000. Use the tax table on page 519.

17-6 Albert Wright files a joint federal income tax return with his wife. Wright owns and operates a small business. Mrs. Wright manages an apartment house which she received as a gift from her mother. Mr. and Mrs. Wright furnish over one-half the support of their son, Robert, who attends college and who earned $1,490 in part time jobs and summer work, and of Mrs. Wright's mother, who lives with the Wrights and who has no income of her own.

During the current year the Wrights had the following cash receipts and expenditures pertinent to the preparation of their income tax return:

From Mr. Wright's records:
Cash receipts:

Cash withdrawn from business (sales, $224,350; cost of goods sold, $150,100; operating expenses, $48,600)	$20,685
Cash dividends on stock owned.	1,480
Interest on Phoenix County bonds	610
Received from sale of stock purchased two years ago for $6,120 . .	8,420
Received from sale of stock purchased four months previously for $4,160	3,020
Received from sale of motorboat purchased three years ago for $2,995 and used entirely for pleasure	1,695

Cash expenditures:

Interest on mortgage on residence	$ 1,162
Property taxes on residence	983
Insurance on residence	140
State income tax paid	1,080
State sales and gasoline taxes	410
Repair windstorm damage to residence, $910; less insurance recovery of $610	300
Charitable contributions	1,415
Medical expenses	860
Contribution to governor's political campaign	250
Payments on declaration of estimated tax	8,420

From Mrs. Wright's records:

Cash receipts:

Gross rentals from apartment building	*$14,300*
Dividends on stocks owned	*410*
Received from sale of stock purchased five months previously for	
$3,100	*3,800*

Cash disbursements (all relating to apartment building):
(Depreciation basis is $95,000; depreciation rate is 4% on a
straight-line basis)

Interest on mortgage	*$ 1,390*
Property taxes	*2,200*
Insurance (one year)	*240*
Heat, light, and water	*1,990*
Repairs and maintenance	*1,560*
Pool maintenance	*500*

Instructions

a. Determine the amount of taxable income Mr. and Mrs. Wright would report on their federal income tax return for the current year. Personal exemption, $600.

b. Compute the Wright's income tax liability, using the rate schedule on page 519. Round all computations to the nearest dollar.

17-7 The following information appears in the accounting records of the Walters Corporation for the current year:

Net sales	*$2,040,000*
Cost of goods sold	*1,489,000*
Dividend revenues (on stock of domestic subsidiary corporation) . . .	*42,000*
Dividends declared on common stock	*80,000*
Selling expenses	*240,000*
Administrative expenses	*198,000*
Gain on sale of capital asset acquired five years ago	*104,200*
Loss on sale of capital asset acquired three months prior to sale . . .	*12,100*

During the current year the Walters Corporation incurred $60,000 of sales promotion expenses which were deducted in computing taxable income, but which the company has chosen to defer on its accounting records and charge against revenues during the two subsequent years when the benefits of the sales promotion are reflected in revenues. The controller will follow tax allocation procedures in reporting income taxes on the income statement during the current year. The company reports gains and losses net of taxes on the sale of capital assets on its income statement as extraordinary items.

Instructions

a. Prepare an income statement for the Walters Corporation for the current year. In a separate schedule show your computation of federal income taxes for the year, using the corporation rate schedule on page 519. The net gain on sale of capital assets is subject to a tax of 25%.

b. Prepare the journal entry which should be made to record the company's provision for income taxes and income tax liability as of the end of the year.

17-8 Roy Reeves is in the process of organizing a business which he expects will produce, before any compensation to himself, a net income of $50,000 per year. In deciding whether to operate as a corporation or as a proprietorship, Reeves is willing to make the choice on the basis of the relative income tax advantage under either form of organization.

Reeves is married, files a joint return with his wife, has no other dependents, and has itemized deductions that average $3,400 per year. If the business is operated as a proprietorship, Reeves expects to withdraw the entire $50,000 business income each year. If the business is operated as a corporation, Reeves and his wife will own all the shares; he will pay himself a salary of $30,000, and will withdraw as dividends the entire amount of the corporations' net income. It may be assumed that corporate accounting income and taxable income will be the same. Mr. and Mrs. Reeves have only minor amounts of nonbusiness income, which may be ignored. Assume that the personal exemption is $600.

Instructions
a. Determine the relative income tax advantage to Reeves of operating either as a proprietorship or as a corporation, and make a recommendation as to the form of organization he should adopt. Use the individual and corporate rate schedules given on page 519.
b. Suppose that Reeves planned to withdraw only $30,000 per year from his business, as drawings from a proprietorship or as salary from a corporation. Would this affect your recommendation? Explain.

Solutions to
Demonstration Problems

SOLUTION TO DEMONSTRATION PROBLEM

CHAPTER 1 CROWN AUTO WASH

a.

CROWN AUTO WASH
Balance Sheet
August 31, 19___

Assets		Liabilities & Stockholders' Equity		
Cash	$ 4,200	Liabilities:		
Accounts receivable	800	Notes payable .	$32,000	
Supplies	400	Accounts		
Land	40,000	payable. . . .	9,000	$41,000
Building	60,000	Stockholders' equity:		
Machinery & equipment . . .	85,000	Capital stock . .	$50,000	
		Retained		
		earnings. . . .	99,400	149,400
	$190,400			$190,400

b.

CROWN AUTO WASH
Balance Sheet
September 1, 19___

Assets		Liabilities & Stockholders' Equity		
Cash	$ 9,600	Liabilities:		
Accounts receivable	800	Notes payable .	$32,000	
Notes receivable	10,000	Accounts		
Supplies	3,000	payable. . . .	2,000	$ 34,000
Land	30,000	Stockholders' equity:		
Building	60,000	Capital stock . .	$65,000	
Machinery & equipment . . .	85,000	Retained		
		earnings . . .	99,400	164,400
	$198,400			$198,400

SOLUTION TO DEMONSTRATION PROBLEM

CHAPTER 2   AUTO PARKS, INC.

a.

Journal			*(Page 1)*

19__				
Oct. 1	Cash......................................	1	90,000	
	Capital Stock.....................	50		90,000
	Issued 9,000 shares of $10 par value capital stock for cash.			
2	Land......................................	21	24,000	
	Cash...........................	1		4,000
	Notes Payable	45		20,000
	Purchased land. Paid part cash and issued note payable for balance.			
3	Building.................................	23	3,600	
	Cash...........................	1		3,600
	Purchased a small portable building for cash.			
4	Office Equipment	25	1,600	
	Accounts Payable.................	43		1,600
	Purchased cash register from Bar & Co. on account.			
24	Accounts Payable........................	43	700	
	Cash...........................	1		700
	Paid part of account payable to Bar & Co.			

b. *To conserve space, the ledger accounts comprising part **b** of the demonstration problem are not shown here. However, the student can readily verify the accuracy of his work on part **b** by referring to the month-end account balances appearing in part **c** on page 552.*

c.

AUTO PARKS, INC.
Trial Balance
October 31, 19____

Cash	$ 81,700	
Land	24,000	
Building	3,600	
Office equipment	1,600	
Accounts payable		$ 900
Notes payable		20,000
Capital stock		90,000
	$110,900	$110,900

SOLUTION TO DEMONSTRATION PROBLEM

CHAPTER 3   REX INSURANCE AGENCY, INC.

a.   *Adjusting journal entry:*

Depreciation Expense: Office Equipment	40	
Accumulated Depreciation: Office Equipment		40

To record depreciation for November ($4,800 ÷ 120).

b.

REX INSURANCE AGENCY, INC.
Adjusted Trial Balance
November 30, 19___

Cash	$ 3,750	
Accounts receivable	1,210	
Office equipment	4,800	
Accumulated depreciation: office equipment		$ 120
Accounts payable		1,640
Capital stock		6,000
Retained earnings		1,490
Dividends	500	
Commissions earned		4,720
Advertising expense	800	
Salaries expense	2,600	
Rent expense	270	
Depreciation expense: office equipment	40	
	$13,970	$13,970

c.

REX INSURANCE AGENCY, INC.
Income Statement
For the Month Ended November 30, 19___

Commissions earned		$4,720
Expenses:		
Advertising expense	$ 800	
Salaries expense	2,600	
Rent expense	270	
Depreciation expense: office equipment	40	3,710
Net income		$1,010

REX INSURANCE AGENCY, INC.
Statement of Retained Earnings
For the Month Ended November 30, 19___

Retained earnings, Oct. 31, 19___	$1,490
Add: Net income for the month	1,010
Total	$2,500
Less: Dividends	500
Retained earnings, Nov. 30, 19___	$2,000

REX INSURANCE AGENCY, INC.
Balance Sheet
November 30, 19___

Assets

Cash		$3,750
Accounts receivable		1,210
Office equipment	$4,800	
Less: Accumulated depreciation	120	4,680
		$9,640

Liabilities & Stockholders' Equity

Liabilities:		
Accounts payable		$1,640
Stockholders' equity:		
Capital stock	$6,000	
Retained earnings	2,000	8,000
		$9,640

CHAPTER 4   CREATIVE ART & DESIGN COMPANY

a.   *Journal*   (*Page 1*)

1972	(1)			
Jan. ___	Prepaid Rent...............................	4	700	
	Cash...............................	1		700
	Paid rent for January and February.			
	(2)			
Jan. ___	Equipment...............................	5	1,500	
	Cash...............................	1		1,500
	Purchased equipment.			
	(3)			
Jan. ___	Dividends...............................	32	5,000	
	Dividends Payable...............	22		5,000
	Declared a cash dividend payable Feb. 26.			
	(4)			
Jan. ___	Accounts Receivable.......................	2	20,800	
	Fees Earned.....................	40		20,800
	Billed customers for work performed.			
	(5)			
Jan. ___	Cash...............................	1	24,100	
	Accounts Receivable...............	2		24,100
	Collections from customers.			
	(6)			
Jan. ___	Salaries Expense	50	9,250	
	Salaries Payable	21	1,950	
	Cash...............................	1		11,200
	Paid salaries, including $1,950 accrued on Dec. 31, 1971.			
	(7)			
Jan. ___	Art Supplies...............................	3	2,900	
	Accounts Payable...................	20		2,900
	Purchased art supplies on credit.			
	(8)			
Jan. ___	Accounts Payable	20	3,300	
	Cash...............................	1		3,300
	Paid creditors.			
	(9)			
Jan. ___	Miscellaneous Expense.....................	52	1,200	
	Cash...............................	1		1,200
	Paid miscellaneous expenses.			

d.

Adjusting Entries

1972		(1)			
Jan. 31		Art Supplies Expense	51	3,700	
		Art Supplies	3		3,700
		To adjust art supplies inventory.			
		(2)			
	31	Salaries Expense	50	600	
		Salaries Payable	21		600
		To recognize accrued salaries.			
		(3)			
	31	Depreciation Expense: Equipment	54	450	
		Accumulated Depreciation: Equipment	6		450
		To record depreciation for January.			
		(4)			
	31	Accounts Receivable	2	2,200	
		Fees Earned	40		2,200
		To recognize as accounts receivable the work performed, not yet billed.			
		(5)			
	31	Fees Earned	40	1,040	
		Unearned Fees	23		1,040
		To record unearned fees billed to clients, 5% of $20,800.			
		(6)			
	31	Rent Expense	53	350	
		Prepaid Rent	4		350
		To record rent expense for January.			

Closing Entries *(Page 3)*

1972				
Jan. 31	Fees Earned..............................	40	21,960	
	Income Summary	60		21,960
	To close revenue account.			
31	Income Summary	60	15,550	
	Salaries Expense	50		9,850
	Miscellaneous Expense..............	52		1,200
	Art Supplies Expense	51		3,700
	Depreciation Expense: Equipment	54		450
	Rent Expense	53		350
	To close expense accounts.			
31	Income Summary	60	6,410	
	Retained Earnings	31		6,410
	To close Income Summary.			
31	Retained Earnings.........................	31	5,000	
	Dividends	32		5,000
	To close Dividends account.			

b.

CREATIVE ART & DESIGN COMPANY
Work Sheet
For Month Ended January 31, 1972

	Trial Balance		Adjustments°	
Cash	26,650			
Accounts receivable	15,450		(4) 2,200	
Art supplies	6,700			(1) 3,700
Prepaid rent	700			(6) 350
Equipment	61,500			
Accum. depr.: equipment		10,000		(3) 450
Accounts payable		850		
Dividends payable		5,000		
Capital stock		50,000		
Retained earnings, Jan. 1, 1972		39,800		
Dividends	5,000			
Fees earned		20,800	(5) 1,040	(4) 2,200
Salaries expense	9,250		(2) 600	
Miscellaneous expense	1,200			
	126,450	126,450		
Art supplies expense			(1) 3,700	
Salaries payable				(2) 600
Depreciation expense: equipment			(3) 450	
Unearned fees				(5) 1,040
Rent expense			(6) 350	
			8,340	8,340
Net income				
Retained earnings, Jan. 31, 1972				

° (1) To adjust art supplies inventory.
  (2) To recognize accrued salaries.
  (3) To record depreciation for January.
  (4) To recognize as accounts receivable the work performed but not yet billed.
  (5) To record unearned fees billed to clients.
  (6) To record expired rent.

	Adjusted Trial Balance		Income Statement		Statement of Retained Earnings		Balance Sheet	
	26,650						26,650	
	17,650						17,650	
	3,000						3,000	
	350						350	
	61,500						61,500	
		10,450						10,450
		850						850
		5,000						5,000
		50,000						50,000
		39,800				39,800		
	5,000				5,000			
		21,960		21,960				
	9,850		9,850					
	1,200		1,200					
	3,700		3,700					
		600						600
	450		450					
		1,040						1,040
	350		350					
	129,700	129,700	15,550	21,960				
			6,410			6,410		
			21,960	21,960	5,000	46,210		
					41,210			41,210
					46,210	46,210	109,150	109,150

a. and **d.**

Cash (1)

1972					1972				
Jan.	1	Balance	✓	20,450	Jan.	—		1	700
	—	*Bal 26,650*	1	24,100		—		1	1,500
				44,550		—		1	11,200
						—		1	3,300
						—		1	1,200
						31	Balance		*17,900* 26,650
				44,550					44,550
Feb.	1	Balance	✓	26,650					

Accounts Receivable (2)

1972					1972				
Jan.	1	Balance	✓	18,750	Jan.	—		1	24,100
	—	*Bal 15,450*	1	20,800		31	Balance	31	17,650
	31		2	*39,550* 2,200					
				41,750					41,750
Feb.	1	Balance	✓	17,650					

Art Supplies (3)

1972					1972				
Jan.	1	Balance	✓	3,800	Jan.	31		2	3,700
	—		1	2,900		31	Balance		3,000
				6,700 6,700					6,700
Feb.	1	Balance	✓	3,000					

Prepaid Rent (4)

1972					1972				
Jan.	—		1	700	Jan.	31		2	350
						31	Balance	✓	350
				700					700
Feb.	1	Balance	✓	350					

Equipment (5)

1972					1972				
Jan.	1	Balance	✓	60,000	Jan.	31	Balance	✓	61,500
	—		1	1,500					
				61,500					
				61,500					61,500
Feb.	1	Balance	✓	61,500					

Accumulated Depreciation: Equipment (6)

1972					1972				
Jan.	31	Balance	✓	10,450	Jan.	1	Balance	✓	10,000
						31		2	450
				10,450					10,450
					Feb.	1	Balance	✓	10,450

Accounts Payable (20)

1972					1972				
Jan.	—		1	3,300	Jan.	1	Balance	✓	1,250
	31	Balance	✓	850		—	*Bal 850*	1	2,900
									4,150
				4,150					4,150
					Feb.	1	Balance	✓	850

Salaries Payable (21)

1972					1972				
Jan.	—		1	1,950	Jan.	1	Balance	✓	1,950
	31	Balance	✓	600		31		2	600
				2,550					2,550
					Feb.	1	Balance	✓	600

Dividends Payable (22)

					1972				
					Jan.	—		1	5,000

Unearned Fees (23)

					1972				
					Jan.	31		2	1,040

Capital Stock (30)

						1972				
						Jan.	1	Balance	✓	50,000

Retained Earnings (31)

1972						1972				
Jan.	31		3	5,000		Jan.	1	Balance	✓	39,800
	31	Balance		41,210			31		3	6,410
				46,210						46,210
						Feb.	1	Balance	✓	41,210

Dividends (32)

1972						1972				
Jan.	—		1	5,000		Jan.	31		3	5,000

Fees Earned (40)

1972						1972				
Jan.	31		2	1,040		Jan.	—		1	20,800
	31		3	21,960			31		2	2,200
				23,000						23,000

Salaries Expense (50)

1972						1972				
Jan.	—		1	9,250		Jan.	31		3	9,850
	31		2	600						
				9,850						9,850

Art Supplies Expense (51)

1972						1972				
Jan.	31		2	3,700		Jan.	31		3	3,700

Miscellaneous Expense (52)

1972						1972				
Jan.	—		1	1,200		Jan.	31		3	1,200

Rent Expense (53)

1972					1972				
Jan.	31		2	350	Jan.	31		3	350

Depreciation Expense: Equipment (54)

1972					1972				
Jan.	31		2	450	Jan.	31		3	450

Income Summary (60)

1972					1972				
Jan.	31		3	15,550	Jan.	31		3	21,960
	31		3	6,410					
				21,960					21,960

c.

CREATIVE ART & DESIGN COMPANY
Income Statement
For the Month Ended January 31, 1972

Fees earned		$21,960
Expenses:		
Salaries expense	$ 9,850	
Miscellaneous expense	1,200	
Art supplies expense	3,700	
Depreciation expense: equipment	450	
Rent expense	350	
Total expenses		15,550
Net income		$ 6,410

CREATIVE ART & DESIGN COMPANY
Balance Sheet
January 31, 1972

Assets

Cash		$26,650
Accounts receivable		17,650
Art supplies		3,000
Prepaid rent		350
Equipment	$61,500	
Less: Accumulated depreciation	10,450	51,050
		$98,700

Liabilities & Stockholders' Equity

Liabilities:		
Accounts payable		$ 850
Dividends payable		5,000
Salaries payable		600
Unearned fees		1,040
Total liabilities		$ 7,490
Stockholders' equity:		
Capital stock	$50,000	
Retained earnings	41,210	91,210
		$98,700

CREATIVE ART & DESIGN COMPANY
Statement of Retained Earnings
For the Month Ended January 31, 1972

Balance, Jan. 1, 1972	$39,800
Add: Net income for month	6,410
Total	$46,210
Less: Dividends	5,000
Balance, Jan. 31, 1972	$41,210

e.

CREATIVE ART & DESIGN COMPANY
After-closing Trial Balance
January 31, 1972

Cash	$ 26,650	
Accounts receivable	17,650	
Art supplies	3,000	
Prepaid rent	350	
Equipment	61,500	
Accumulated depreciation: equipment		$ 10,450
Accounts payable		850
Salaries payable		600
Dividends payable		5,000
Unearned fees		1,040
Capital stock		50,000
Retained earnings		41,210
	$109,150	$109,150

SOLUTION TO DEMONSTRATION PROBLEM

Chapter 5   N. B. TRADING COMPANY

a.

19__		(1)		
Dec.	31	Depreciation Expense: Building..............	3,600	
		Accumulated Depreciation: Building ..		3,600
		To record depreciation for the year, 4% of $90,000.		
		(2)		
	31	Unexpired Insurance.......................	400	
		Insurance Expense		400
		To record unexpired insurance.		
		(3)		
	31	Office Supplies...........................	200	
		Office Supplies Expense.............		200
		To record unused office supplies.		

b.

N. B. TRADING COMPANY
Income Statement
For the Year Ended December 31, 19___

Gross sales		$380,100	
Sales returns & allowances	$ 1,860		
Sales discounts	630	2,490	
Net sales			$377,610
Cost of goods sold:			
Inventory, Jan. 1, 19___		$ 70,865	
Purchases	$232,775		
Transportation-in	6,465		
Delivered cost of purchases	$239,240		
Less: Purchases returns &			
allowances	$1,940		
Purchase discounts	1,470	3,410	
Net purchases		235,830	
Cost of goods available for sale		$306,695	
Less: Inventory, Dec. 31, 19___		54,930	
Cost of goods sold			251,765
Gross profit on sales			$125,845
Operating expenses:			
Selling expenses:			
Salesmen's salaries	$ 39,650		
Advertising expense	7,245		
Depreciation exp: bldg.	900		
Depreciation exp: store			
equipment	600		
Miscellaneous selling exp.	1,480		
Total selling expense		$ 49,875	
General expenses:			
Office salaries	$ 5,520		
Depreciation exp: bldg.	2,700		
Office supplies expense	640		
Uncollectible accounts exp.	1,170		
Insurance expense	365		
Miscellaneous general exp.	835		
Total general expense		11,230	
Total operating expenses			61,105
Income from operations			$ 64,740
Interest expense			4,500
Net income			$ 60,240

c.

N. B. TRADING COMPANY
Balance Sheet
December 31, 19___

Assets

Current assets:

Cash		$15,655
Accounts receivable	$21,170	
Less: Allowance for uncollectible accounts	2,355	18,815
Inventory		54,930
Unexpired insurance		400
Office supplies		200
Total current assets		$ 90,000

Plant and equipment:

Land		$74,000
Building	$90,000	
Less: Accumulated depreciation	36,000	54,000
Store equipment	$15,400	
Less: Accumulated depreciation	6,400	9,000
Total plant and equipment		137,000

Other assets:

Land held for future expansion	17,000
Total assets	$244,000

Liabilities & Stockholders' Equity

Current liabilities:

Notes payable	$ 5,325
Accounts payable	19,260
Bank loans	19,600
Deferred revenue	2,270
Total current liabilities	$ 46,455

Long-term liabilities:

6% first-mortgage bonds payable	55,000
Total liabilities	$101,455

Stockholders' equity:

Capital stock	$50,000
Retained earnings	92,545*
Total stockholders' equity	142,545
Total liabilities & stockholders' equity	$244,000

* Explanation of retained earnings figure appears on page 569.

*Retained earnings as reported $118,045
Add: Unexpired insurance, $400, and
       unused office supplies, $200   600
                                  $118,645

Less: Depreciation on building
       not recorded . . . . $ 3,600
       Dividends paid (errone-
       ously reported as asset) .   22,500   26,100
Retained earnings as corrected . . . . . . $ 92,545

d.

N. B. TRADING COMPANY
Statement of Retained Earnings
For the Year Ended December 31, 19___

Retained earnings Jan. 1, 19___ . . . . $ 54,805**
Add: Net income 60,240
                                                    $115,045
Less: Dividends paid 22,500
Retained earnings, Dec. 31, 19___ . . . . $ 92,545

** *Retained earnings as reported, $118,045, less net income as computed by the assistant bookkeeper,*
$63,240, or $54,805.

SOLUTION TO DEMONSTRATION PROBLEM

CHAPTER 7   MILTON FARR AND JOHN GARR

a.   *Distribution of partnership net income for 1970:*

	Farr	Garr	Total
Interest on average capitals:			
Farr—8% of $500,000	$ 40,000		$ 40,000
Garr—8% of $400,000.		$ 32,000	32,000
Salary allowances	25,000	20,000	45,000
Total	$ 65,000	$ 52,000	$117,000
Deficiency of $21,000 ($117,000 − $96,000)			
charged to Farr and Garr in 60:40 ratio	(12,600)	(8,400)	(21,000)
Share of partnership net income	$ 52,400	$ 43,600	$ 96,000
Partners' capitals (net of drawings) before			
distribution of net income	464,000	370,000	834,000
Partners' capital balances on Dec. 31, 1970. . . .	$516,400	$413,600	$930,000

b.   *Determination of number of shares of common stock to be issued based on adjusted capital balances:*

	Farr	Garr	Total
Partners' capital balances on Dec. 31, 1970,			
see part (**a**)	$516,400	$413,600	$930,000
Adjustments:			
(1) *To increase capital accounts by $10,000 in*			
60:40 ratio, representing prepayments of			
$10,000 erroneously charged to expense . . .	6,000	4,000	10,000
(2) *To increase capital accounts by $12,500 in*			
60:40 ratio, representing organization costs			
which were erroneously charged to expense	7,500	5,000	12,500
(3) *To decrease capital accounts by $3,000 in*			
60:40 ratio as a result of increase in			
accrued liabilities (unrecorded interest			
expense)	(1,800)	(1,200)	(3,000)
Adjusted capital accounts	$528,100	$421,400	$949,500
Less: Issuance of 25,000 shares of 5% cumula-			
tive convertible preferred stock (with			
stated value of $10 per share) to each			
partner	(250,000)	(250,000)	(500,000)
Balance—to be used as the basis for the			
issuance of 100,000 shares of common			
stock (stated value $1 per share)	$278,100	$171,400	$449,500

Number of shares to be issued:
Farr: 278,100/449,500 × 100,000 shares . . . .   *61,869 shares*
Garr: 171,400/449,500 × 100,000 shares . . . .   *38,131 shares*

c. *Entries required (1) to adjust account balances and (2) to change to the corporate form of business organization:*

(1) Miscellaneous Prepayments 10,000
    Organization Costs 12,500
        Miscellaneous Accrued Liabilities   3,000
        Farr, Capital   11,700
        Garr, Capital   7,800
    To correct partnership accounts prior to incorporation.

(2) Farr, Capital 528,100
    Garr, Capital 421,400
        5% Cumulative Convertible Preferred Stock . .   500,000
        Common Stock   100,000
        Paid-in Capital in Excess of Stated Value . . .   349,500
    To record issuance of 50,000 shares of preferred stock
    with a stated value of $10 per share and 100,000 shares
    of common stock with a stated value of $1 per share.

d. (1) *Balance in retained earnings on December 31, 1971:*
       Net income for 1971 (first year of operations) $105,000
       Less: Dividends for 1971:
          Preferred: 5% of $500,000 . . . . $ 25,000
          Common: 100,000 shares @ $0.35 per share   35,000   60,000
       Balance in retained earnings on December 31, 1971 . . . . $ 45,000

(2) *Entry to record conversion of preferred stock into com-*
    mon stock:
    5% Cumulative Convertible Preferred Stock 250,000
        Common Stock   50,000
        Paid-in Capital in Excess of Stated Value   200,000
    To record conversion of 25,000 shares of preferred stock,
    stated value $10 per share, into 50,000 shares of
    common stock, stated value $1 per share.

(3) *Stockholders' equity section of the balance sheet at December 31, 1971:*
    5% cumulative convertible preferred stock, stated value
      $10 per share, 50,000 shares authorized and issued, of
      which 25,000 shares have been converted into
      common stock, leaving 25,000 outstanding $250,000
    Common stock, $1 stated value, authorized 250,000
      shares, issued and outstanding 150,000 shares   150,000
    Paid-in capital in excess of stated value.   549,500
        Total paid-in capital $949,500
    Retained earnings   45,000
        Total stockholders' equity $994,500

SOLUTION TO DEMONSTRATION PROBLEM

CHAPTER 8   ARNETT CORPORATION

a.   *Journal*

1971

Sept. 1   Memorandum: Stockholders approved a 5 for 4 stock
          split. This action increased the number of shares of
          capital stock outstanding from 40,000 to 50,000 and
          reduced the par value from $10 to $8 per share.

Dec. 20   Treasury Stock   74,000
              Cash   74,000
          Acquired 2,000 shares of treasury stock at $37 per
          share.

      20 Retained Earnings   74,000
              Reserve for Acquisition of Treasury Stock . .   74,000
          To record appropriation of retained earnings as a
          result of acquisition of treasury stock.

1972

Mar. 2   Cash   45,000
              Treasury Stock   37,000
              Paid-in Capital from Treasury Stock
                  Transactions   8,000
          Sold 1,000 shares of treasury stock at $45 per share.

      2   Reserve for Acquisition of Treasury Stock   37,000
              Retained Earnings   37,000
          To release the appropriation of retained earnings
          relating to the 1,000 shares of treasury stock sold.

      10 Net Assets   760,700
              Capital Stock   160,000
              Paid-in Capital in Excess of Par Value   600,700
          Issued 20,000 shares of previously unissued $8 par
          value stock (total market value $760,700) in
          exchange for the net assets of another company.

June 2   Dividends   69,000
              Dividends Payable   69,000
          To record declaration of cash dividend of $1 per
          share on 69,000 shares of capital stock outstanding
          (1,000 shares in treasury are not entitled
          to receive dividends).

          Note: Entry to record the payment of the cash
          dividend is not shown here since the action does
          not affect the stockholders' equity.

Journal

1972

June 30   Retained Earnings   331,200
                Stock Dividends to Be Distributed   55,200
                Paid-in Capital from Stock Dividends   276,000
        To record declaration of 10% stock dividend con-
        sisting of 6,900 shares of $8 par value common stock
        to be distributed on August 28, 1972. Excess of
        market value of stock over par value, $40 ($48 − $8),
        is credited to Paid-in Capital from Stock
        Dividends.

     30   Reserve for Plant Expansion   100,000
                Retained Earnings   100,000
        To eliminate the Reserve for Plant Expansion
        account.

     30   Income Summary   255,300
                Retained Earnings   255,300
        To close Income Summary account.

     30   Retained Earnings   69,000
                Dividends   69,000
        To close Dividends account.

b.

ARNETT CORPORATION
Partial Income Statement
For the Year Ended June 30, 1972

Income before extraordinary item $220,800
Extraordinary item: gain on sale of plant site, net of tax   34,500
Net income $255,300

Per share of capital stock°:
   Income before extraordinary item $3.20
   Extraordinary item, net of tax 50
   Net income $3.70

° On 69,000 shares of capital stock outstanding on June 30, 1972.

c.

ARNETT CORPORATION
Statement of Retained Earnings
For the Year Ended June 30, 1972

	Unappropriated	Reserve for Plant Expansion	Reserve for Acquisition of Treasury Stock
Balance, June 30, 1971	$1,280,000	$ 100,000	
Appropriation for acquisition of treasury stock	(74,000)		$ 74,000
Release of appropriations	137,000	(100,000)	(37,000)
Net income	255,300		
Dividends:			
Cash, $1 per share	(69,000)		
Stock, 10%	(331,200)		
Balance, June 30, 1972	$1,198,100	0	$ 37,000

d. *Computation of book value per share of capital stock:*

	June 30, 1972	June 30, 1971
Total stockholders' equity	$2,898,000	$1,980,000
Number of shares of capital stock outstanding	69,000	40,000
Book value per share of capital stock	$42.00	$49.50

SOLUTION TO DEMONSTRATION PROBLEM

CHAPTER 9 GLENDALE COMPANY

a.

GLENDALE COMPANY
Bank Reconciliation
November 30, 1971

Balance per books, Nov. 30		$ 7,766.64
Add: Proceeds on sale of stock	$4,000.00	
Collection on accounts receivable	1,846.20	
Note receivable collected by bank, $690, less		
collection charge, $5	685.00	6,531.20
		$14,297.84
Less: Petty cash fund reported separately	$ 100.00	
Petty cash fund replenishment	60.00	
NSF check, James Ruddock	160.00	
Charge by bank for printing checks	7.50	327.50
Adjusted balance		$13,970.34
Balance per bank statement, Nov. 30		$ 9,734.70
Add: Deposit of Nov. 30 not recorded by bank	$5,846.20	
Service charge made by bank in error	340.00	6,186.20
		$15,920.90
Less: Outstanding checks on Nov. 30:		
No. 924	$ 136.25	
940	105.00	
941	11.46	
943	826.70	
944	95.00	
945	716.15	
946	60.00	1,950.56
Adjusted balance (as above)		$13,970.34

b. *Journal*

1971

Nov. 30 *Cash* 6,531.20
　　　　Loss on Sale of Axe Co. Stock 2,270.00
　　　　Miscellaneous Expense 5.00
　　　　　　　　Investment in Axe Co. Stock . . . . 　　　　　6,270.00
　　　　　　　　Notes Receivable . . . . 　　　　　690.00
　　　　　　　　Accounts Receivable . . . . 　　　　　1,846.20
　　　　To record increase in Cash account as indicated
　　　　by bank reconciliation.

　　　30 *Petty Cash* 100.00
　　　　Miscellaneous Expense ($7.50 + $60.00) 67.50
　　　　Accounts Receivable, James Ruddock 160.00
　　　　　　　　Cash . . . . 　　　　　327.50
　　　　To record cash disbursements as indicated by bank
　　　　reconciliation and to record petty cash
　　　　in a separate account.

SOLUTION TO DEMONSTRATION PROBLEM

CHAPTER 10   GENERAL WIRE COMPANY

Journal

19___

July 1	Accounts Receivable, P. Linn	1,545.00	
	Sales		1,545.00
	Sale of merchandise on account.		
3	Notes Receivable	1,500.00	
	Freight-out	45.00	
	Accounts Receivable, P. Linn		1,545.00
	To record credit to P. Linn for freight paid by him and receipt of 60-day, 8% note for balance of account owed.		
18	Accounts Receivable, Baxter Company	2,200.00	
	Sales		2,200.00
	Sale of merchandise on account, terms 2/10, n/30.		
27	Cash	1,508.00	
	Interest Earned		8.00
	Notes Receivable		1,500.00
	Discounted note from P. Linn at bank		
28	Cash	2,156.00	
	Sales Discounts	44.00	
	Accounts Receivable, Baxter Company . . .		2,200.00
	Received payment from Baxter Company within discount period.		
Aug. 8	Accounts Receivable, E. Jones	1,200.00	
	Sales		1,200.00
	Sale of merchandise on account, terms 2/10, n/30.		
Sept. 1	Accounts Receivable, P. Linn	1,520.00	
	Cash		1,520.00
	To record payment to bank on dishonored note, and to charge this amount to maker of note.		
7	Notes Receivable	1,200.00	
	Accounts Receivable, E. Jones		1,200.00
	Received 60-day, 7% note in settlement of open account.		
10	Allowance for Uncollectible Accounts	120.00	
	Accounts Receivable, K. L. Treff		120.00
	Wrote off uncollectible account from K. L. Treff.		
Oct. 15	Accounts Receivable, Allen Blaine	300.00	
	Allowance for Uncollectible Accounts		300.00
	To reverse the entry writing off Blaine's account.		

Journal

Oct. 15 Cash 300.00
     Accounts Receivable, Allen Blaine 300.00
    To record collection of Blaine's account which was
    written off in June.

  25 Cash 1,538.24
     Accounts Receivable, P. Linn 1,520.00
     Interest Earned 18.24
    Collected Linn account in full plus interest @ 8% for
    54 days as follows: $1,520 $\times$ 8% $\times$ $^{54}/_{360}$, or $18.24.

Nov. 6 Cash 1,214.00
     Notes Receivable 1,200.00
     Interest Earned 14.00
    Received payment on note from E. Jones, including
    interest on $1,200 @ 7% for 60 days.

Dec. 31 Uncollectible Accounts Expense. 1,400.00
     Allowance for Uncollectible Accounts 1,400.00
    To provide for estimated uncollectibles as follows:
    Balance required. *$1,200*
    Present balance (debit) *200*
    Required increase in allowance *$1,400*

SOLUTION TO DEMONSTRATION PROBLEM

CHAPTER 11 OLIVE COMPANY

a.

OLIVE COMPANY
Income Statement
For the Years Ended December 31, 1970 and 1971

	1970	1971
Net sales ($3,600 represents sales of 1970, not 1971)	$713,600	$756,400
Cost of goods sold:		
Beginning inventory	$240,000	$248,440 (2)
Net purchases	419,166 (1)	417,120 (3)
Cost of goods available for sale	$659,166	$665,560
Ending inventory	248,440 (2)	260,000
Cost of goods sold	$410,726	$405,560
Gross profit on sales	$302,874	$350,840
Expenses	143,714	180,000
Net income	$159,160	$170,840

(1) $409,326 + $9,840 = $419,166
(2) $253,040 − $2,600 − $2,000 = $248,440
(3) $426,960 − $9,840 = $417,120

b.

Retained earnings, Dec. 31, 1969	$300,000
Add: Corrected net income for 1970	159,160
Less: Dividends for 1970 (See note below)	(100,000)
Retained earnings as corrected, Dec. 31, 1970	$359,160
Add: Corrected net income for 1971	170,840
Less: Dividends for 1971 ($370,000 + $160,000 − $410,000)	(120,000)
Retained earnings as corrected, Dec. 31, 1971	$410,000

The errors counterbalanced between the years 1970 and 1971; therefore, the amount of retained earnings reported at Dec. 31, 1971, $410,000, was correct.

Note: *The amount of dividends declared in 1970 is determined as follows: Retained earnings on December 31, 1969, $300,000 plus net income for 1970 as reported, $170,000, less retained earnings at the end of 1970, $370,000. The difference, $100,000, represents dividends declared. Similar calculations for 1971 indicate dividends declared of $120,000.*

c.   *Correcting journal entry:*

1971

May 12   Sales *3,600*

         Correction in Net Income for 1970 . . . .   *10,840*

               Purchases *9,840*

               Inventory, Jan. 1, 1971 ($2,600 + $2,000)   *4,600*

         To correct errors in cutoff of sales and purchases

       at Dec. 31, 1970, and to correct clerical error in

     compiling physical inventory on that date.

d.   *No. If the $9,840 worth of merchandise described in item 1 had not been included in inventory on December 31, 1970, the error of not including the goods in inventory would have offset the error of failing to record the purchase, with no net effect on cost of goods sold for 1970. However, the current ratio and other balance sheet relationships would have been slightly distorted through understatement of $9,840, both in inventory and accounts payable.*

SOLUTION TO DEMONSTRATION PROBLEM

CHAPTER 12   BATEMAN CORPORATION

a. (1) Cash   50,000

                 Notes Payable   50,000

        Borrowed $50,000 from National City Bank on Jan. 11, 1972. Issued a 6-month, 6½% note to the bank.

    (2) Accounts Payable—Merchandise Creditors   128,000

        FICA Taxes Payable   1,500

        Income Taxes Withheld   4,200

        State Unemployment Taxes Payable   360

        Federal Unemployment Taxes Payable   1,400

                 Cash   135,460

        To record cash disbursements during January in payment for current liabilities.

    (3) Purchases   112,500

                 Accounts Payable—Merchandise Creditors . .   112,500

        To record purchase of merchandise on account during January.

    (4) Wages Expense   65,000

                 FICA Taxes Payable   3,250

                 Income Taxes Withheld   5,050

                 Accrued Payroll   56,700

        To record payroll for January.

        Accrued Payroll   56,700

                 Cash   56,700

        To record payment of wages for January.

        Payroll Taxes Expense   5,265

                 FICA Taxes Payable   3,250

                 State Unemployment Taxes Payable   1,755

                 Federal Unemployment Taxes Payable   260

        To record payroll taxes on employer for January.

    (5) 5% Bonds Payable   5,000,000

        Loss on Redemption of Bonds   172,000

                 Discount on Bonds Payable   72,000

                 Cash   5,100,000

        To record redemption of bonds at 102 on January 1, 1972.

Cash 10,165,000

      6% Bonds Payable   10,000,000

      Premium on Bonds Payable   150,000

      Bond Interest Payable   15,000

To record issuance of bonds on Jan. 10, 1972, at $101\frac{1}{2}$
plus accrued interest for nine days.

(6)   Dividends.   37,500

      Dividends Payable   37,500

To record declaration of a cash dividend of 15 cents
a share on 250,000 shares of capital stock. The
dividend is payable on Feb. 10, 1972 to holders of
record on Jan. 28, 1972.

Retained Earnings   160,000

      Stock Dividend to Be Distributed   50,000

      Paid in Capital from Stock Dividends   110,000

To record declaration of a 2% stock dividend consisting of 5,000 shares of $10 par value. The dividend
is to be distributed on Feb. 10, 1972 to holders of
record on Jan. 28, 1972. Amount of retained earnings
capitalized is based on market price of $32 a share on
date of declaration.

b.   *Adjusting entries:*

Interest Expense   625

      Discount on Note Payable.   625

To record interest expense for Jan. on $100,000 note payable
maturing on June 30, 1972: $3,750 \times \frac{1}{6}$, or $625.

Interest Expense   181

      Accrued Interest on Notes Payable   181

To record accrued interest on $50,000, $6\frac{1}{2}$% note from
Jan. 11 to Jan. 31: $50,000 \times \frac{20}{360} \times 6\frac{1}{2}$%, or $181.

Bond Interest Expense   33,750

Premium on Bonds Payable ($150,000 \times \frac{1}{120}$)   1,250

      Bond Interest Payable   35,000

To record accrued interest and amortization on bonds
payable for January, $50,000 ($10,000,000 \times 6% for one
month less $15,000 recorded on January 10 when bonds
were issued.)

c. *Liabilities section of statement of financial position, Jan. 31, 1972:*
   Current liabilities:

Notes payable	$ 150,000	
Less: Discount on note payable...............	3,125	$ 146,875
Accounts payable—merchandise creditors		125,500
Income taxes payable, due March 15, 1972		85,000
Dividends payable on capital stock		37,500
Accrued liabilities:		
Income taxes withheld and payroll taxes	$ 13,565	
Interest on notes and bonds...............	50,181	63,746
Total current liabilities................................		$ 458,621
Long-term liabilities:		
6% bonds payable, due Jan. 1, 1982............	$10,000,000	
Add: Premium on bonds payable.............	148,750	10,148,750
Total liabilities		$10,607,371

SOLUTION TO DEMONSTRATION PROBLEM

CHAPTER 13   ARTHUR BARR

a.

Assets	Company A	Company B	Company C
Cash	$ 45,000	$ 18,000	$ 25,000
Accounts receivable (net)	89,000	119,000	85,000
Inventories	212,500	153,500	180,000
Plant and equipment (net)	76,875 (1)	118,600 (2)	110,335 (3)
Intangible assets	5,000 (4)		
Total assets	$428,375	$409,100	$400,335

Liabilities & Stockholders' Equity			
Current liabilities	$208,420	$185,000	$200,800
Capital stock	150,000	100,000	25,000
Retained earnings	69,955	124,100	174,535
Total liabilities & stockholders' equity . .	$428,375	$409,100	$400,335

(1) $90,000, less depreciation at 5% per year for five years on building costing $52,500, or $13,125. Plant and equipment = $90,000 − $13,125, or $76,875.

(2) $120,000, less loss of $1,400 not recognized in Year 4 = $118,600.

(3) $100,000 + 40% of $2,400 (undepreciated portion of installation costs) + $9,375, which is determined as follows:

Depreciation recorded last five years, $^{90}/_{210} \times \$52,500$	$22,500
Depreciation for five years using straight-line method, see (1)	13,125
Increase in book value of plant and equipment	$ 9,375

Plant and equipment = $100,000 + $960 + $9,375, or $110,335.

(4) $7,500 less amortization to date, $2,500 ($7,500 × ²⁄₆) = $5,000.

b. *Revised amounts of average net income:*

	Company A	Company B	Company C
Total net income for last five years (before corrections average net income × 5)	*$178,000*	*$146,500*	*$191,000*
Corrections:			
Estimated uncollectible accounts	*(6,000)*		
Inventory understated		*13,500*	
Depreciation restated—see part (**a**)	*(13,125)*		*9,375*
Loss on disposal of asset		*(1,400)*	
Installation costs, $2,400, less depreciation of 60% to date			*960*
Intangible assets amortized	*(2,500)*	*(3,000)*	
Accrued liabilities at end of Year 5 (understatement of net income at end of Year 4 counterbalanced in Year 5)	*(420)*		*(800)*
Revised total net income for five years	*$155,955*	*$155,600*	*$200,535*
Average net income	*$ 31,191*	*$ 31,120*	*$ 40,107*

c. *Price to be offered for each business:*

	Company A	Company B	Company C
Average net income (*b*).	*$ 31,191*	*$ 31,120*	*$ 40,107*
Less: 10% of adjusted stockholders' equity (*a*) . .	*21,996*	*22,410*	*19,954*
Average superior earnings	*$ 9,195*	*$ 8,710*	*$ 20,153*
Multiplied by 3 years	*×3*	*×3*	*×3*
Estimated amount of goodwill	*$ 27,585*	*$ 26,130*	*$ 60,459*
Add: Net tangible assets, excluding cash	*174,955*	*206,100*	*174,535*
Price to be offered	*$202,540*	*$232,230*	*$234,994*

SOLUTION TO DEMONSTRATION PROBLEM

CHAPTER 14   PARENT AND SUBSIDIARY COMPANIES

a.

PARENT AND SUBSIDIARY COMPANIES
Consolidated Balance Sheet (Purchase Basis)
December 31, 1971

Assets		Liabilities & Stockholders' Equity	
Cash	$ 140,000	Accounts payable	$ 218,000
Accounts receivable	323,000	Bonds payable	600,000
Merchandise	305,000	6% preferred stock	200,000
Plant and equipment (net)	1,760,000	Common stock, $1 par	100,000
Intangibles (1)	450,000	Capital in excess of par value	1,300,000
		Retained earnings (2)	560,000
		Total liabilities &	
Total assets	$2,978,000	stockholders' equity	$2,978,000

(1) $125,000 + $40,000 + $300,000 excess of cost over book value, reduced by $15,000 amortization since acquisition.

(2) $550,000 + $25,000 earnings of Subsidiary Company following acquisition, less $15,000 amortization of excess of cost over book value.

PARENT AND SUBSIDIARY COMPANIES
Consolidated Income Statement (Purchase Basis)
For Year Ended December 31, 1971

Sales ($2,000,000 + $250,000 − $7,000 intercompany sales)		$2,243,000
Cost of goods sold ($1,200,000 + $165,000 − $7,000 intercompany purchase)		1,358,000
Gross profit on sales		$ 885,000
Operating expenses ($468,000 + $50,000 + $15,000 amortization of excess of cost over book value, $300,000 × 3/60)	$533,000	
Income taxes ($120,000 + $10,000)	130,000	663,000
Net income		$ 222,000

b.

PARENT AND SUBSIDIARY COMPANIES
Consolidated Balance Sheet (Pooling Basis)
December 31, 1971

Assets		*Liabilities & Stockholders' Equity*	
Cash	$ 140,000	Accounts payable	$ 218,000
Accounts receivable	323,000	Bonds payable	600,000
Merchandise	305,000	6% preferred stock.	200,000
Plant and equipment (net) .	1,760,000	Common stock, $1 par . . .	100,000
Intangibles	165,000	Capital in excess of par	
		value (1).	850,000
		Retained earnings	725,000
		Total liabilities &	
Total assets	$2,693,000	stockholders' equity . . .	$2,693,000

(1) $1,300,000 − $987,500 + $37,500 + $500,000

PARENT AND SUBSIDIARY COMPANIES
Consolidated Income Statement (Pooling basis)
For Year Ended December 31, 1971

Sales ($2,000,000 + $1,000,000 − $7,000).		$2,993,000
Cost of goods sold ($1,200,000 + $660,000 − $7,000)		1,853,000
Gross profit on sales		$1,140,000
Operating expenses ($468,000 + $200,000)	$668,000	
Income taxes ($120,000 + $40,000)	160,000	828,000
Net income		$ 312,000

c.

	(1) Purchase	(2) Pooling
Earnings per share:		
Net income.	$222,000	$312,000
Less: Dividends on preferred stock	12,000	12,000
Earnings available to common stock	$210,000	$300,000
Earnings per share (100,000 shares of common stock		
outstanding).	$2.10	$3.00
Book value per share:		
Total stockholders' equity	$2,160,000	$1,875,000
Less: Equity of preferred stockholders	200,000	200,000
Common stockholders' equity	$1,960,000	$1,675,000
Book value per share (100,000 shares of common stock		
outstanding).	$19.60	$16.75

Note: The student should recognize the major differences between the purchase and pooling treatment of a corporate merger as illustrated in this problem. These are:

(1) In a pooling, the full year's earnings of the acquired company are included in the consolidated income statement, regardless of the date on which the acquisition was completed; in a purchase, only the postacquisition earnings of the acquired company are included in the consolidated income statement.

(2) In a purchase, the market value of assets acquired is reported on a consolidated balance sheet; in a pooling, assets of the acquired company are included in the consolidated balance sheet at the values as reflected by the acquired company's books.

(3) The excess of cost over book value of acquired assets may be assigned to depreciable or amortizable assets when the merger is treated as a purchase, thus diluting consolidated earnings. In this problem, the excess of cost over book value amounted to $300,000, which was assigned to intangible assets and is being amortized over a five-year life. Since the merger took place on October 1, 1971, amortization of $15,000 for three months was included in the consolidated income statement.

(4) In a pooling, the entire retained earnings of the acquired company may be combined with the retained earnings of the acquiring company in computing consolidated retained earnings.

(5) The earnings per share will be larger on a pooling basis when the price-earnings ratio of the acquiring company is higher than the price-earnings ratio of the acquired company and the merger is consummated on the basis of the fair market value of stock.

SOLUTION TO DEMONSTRATION PROBLEM

CHAPTER 16   DEXTER CORPORATION

			1972	1971
a.	*(1)*	*Quick ratio:*		
		$126,000 ÷ $145,000	0.9 to 1	
		$115,000 ÷ $ 81,000		1.4 to 1
	(2)	*Current ratio:*		
		$290,000 ÷ $145,000	2 to 1	
		$260,000 ÷ $ 81,000		3.2 to 1
	(3)	*Equity ratio:*		
		$571,400 ÷ $1,000,000	57%	
		$465,000 ÷ $800,000		58%
	(4)	*Debt ratio:*		
		$428,600 ÷ $1,000,000	43%	
		$335,000 ÷ $800,000		42%
	(5)	*Book value per share of stock:*		
		$571,400 ÷ 33,000 shares	$17.32	
		$465,000 ÷ 33,000 shares		$14.09
	(6)	*Earnings per share:*		
		$146,400 ÷ 33,000 shares	$ 4.44	
		$80,000 ÷ 33,000° shares		$ 2.42
	(7)	*Price-earnings ratio:*		
		$68 ÷ $4.44	15 times	
		$43.50 ÷ 1.5° = $29, adjusted price. $29 ÷ $2.42		12 times
	(8)	*Gross profit rate:*		
		$594,000 ÷ $2,200,000	27%	
		$480,000 ÷ $1,600,000		30%
	(9)	*Operating expenses as a percentage of net sales:*		
		$330,000 ÷ $2,200,000	15%	
		$352,000 ÷ $1,600,000		22%
	(10)	*Income before extraordinary items as a percentage of net sales:*		
		$154,000 ÷ $2,200,000	7%	
		$ 80,000 ÷ $1,600,000		5%
	(11)	*Inventory turnover:*		
		$1,606,000 ÷ $150,000	10.7 times	
		$1,120,000 ÷ $150,000		7.5 times
	(12)	*Age of receivables at year-end:*		
		$91,000/$2,200,000 × 365	15 days	
		$90,000/$1,600,000 × 365		21 days

° *Adjusted for 50% stock dividend.*

b.

DEXTER CORPORATION
Funds Statement
For Year Ended December 31, 1972

Funds were applied to:
Purchase of equipment [$880,000 − ($640,000 − $60,000)] $300,000
Payment of cash dividends.   40,000

     Total funds applied $340,000

Funds were provided by:
Operations
     Net income (before extraordinary items) $154,000
     Add: Expenses not requiring the use of funds:
         Depreciation [$260,000 − ($200,000 − $25,000)]. .   85,000
     Less: Increase in net income not representing
     a source of funds:
         Amortization of premium on bonds payable . . . .   (400)
     Total funds provided by operations $238,600
Sale of investment in subsidiaries ($10,000 +
   $12,400)   22,400
Sale of equipment   15,000
Issuance of bonds   30,000

     Total funds provided   306,000
Net decrease in working capital ($179,000 − $145,000) . . . . $ 34,000

c.

DEXTER CORPORATION
Statement of Cash Flows
For Year Ended December 31, 1972

Cash receipts:
Sales ($2,200,000 − $1,000 increase in accounts receivable) $2,199,000
Sale of investments in subsidiaries ($10,000 + $12,400)   22,400
Sale of equipment   15,000

     Total cash receipts. $2,236,400

Cash payments:
Purchase of merchandise ($1,606,000 + $20,000 increase
   in inventory − $49,000 increase in accounts payable) $1,577,000
Purchase of equipment   270,000
Cash dividends   40,000
Operating expenses and income taxes°   339,400

     Total cash payments   2,226,400
Increase in cash during 1972 . . . . $ 10,000

°Operating expenses and income taxes			$ 440,000
Add: Amortization of premium on bonds payable			400
			$ 440,400
Less: Decrease in prepaid expenses	$	1,000	
Increase in taxes payable and other accrued liabilities		15,000	
Depreciation expense [$260,000 − ($200,000 − $25,000)]		85,000	101,000
Cash paid for operating expenses and income taxes			$ 339,400

592

SOLUTION TO DEMONSTRATION PROBLEM

CHAPTER 17   MR. AND MRS. SANDISON

S & S BUSINESS ADVISERS (*a partnership*)
Computation of Ordinary Income
For Year Ended December 31, 1971

Fees earned		$76,300
Operating expenses:		
Professional salaries and other wages	$32,400	
Supplies used	3,500	
Rent expense	4,800	
Miscellaneous business expenses	7,100	47,800
Ordinary income		$28,500

*Ordinary income and other items are to be included
in partners' individual tax returns as follows:*

	Sandison (60%)	Sims (40%)
Ordinary income, $28,500	$17,100	$11,400
Gain on sale of vacant lot, long-term capital gain, $4,400	2,640	1,760
Contributions to Long Beach Opera Association, $1,000	600	400

Income tax return for Sandi Construction Company:

Customer billings		$230,000
Operating expenses:		
Materials used	$70,000	
Construction labor	60,000	
Officers' salaries expense	25,000	
Legal and professional fees	3,500	
Advertising expense	2,000	
Other business expenses	19,800	
Loss on sale of surplus equipment	4,200	184,500
Taxable income		$ 45,500
Income tax due, 30% of $45,500		$ 13,650

MR. AND MRS. SANDISON
Joint Income Tax Return
For 1971

Gross income:

Salary from Sandi Construction Company ($15,450 + $3,168 + $382)			$19,000
Dividends from Sandi Construction Company ($16,875, less $200 exclusion)			16,675
Interest on savings account			950
Income from S & S Business Advisers, a partnership			17,100
Net long-term capital gain:			
Stock acquired two years ago		$8,000	
Stock held over six years		(1,700)	
Gain on sale of vacant lot—from partnership return		2,640	
Total long-term		$8,940	
Less: Short-term loss on stock held for three months		700	8,240	$61,965

Deductions to arrive at adjusted gross income:

Loss incurred by Northwest Lumber Company, a single proprietorship ($118,000 − $82,000 − $38,800)		$ 2,800	
Long-term capital gain deduction (50% of $8,240)		4,120	6,920
Adjusted gross income			$55,045

Deductions from adjusted gross income:

Itemized deductions:

Contributions ($600 from partnership return and $610 to St. Jerome's Church)		$ 1,210	
Interest paid		4,720	
Property taxes ($3,980 − $500)		3,480	
Sales taxes		850	
Income taxes paid to state of California		1,900	
Subscription to investment advisory service		165	
		$12,325	
Personal exemptions (7 × $600)		4,200	16,525
Taxable income			$38,520

Computation of tax

Tax on $36,000 on joint return (See page 519 of text)		$10,340	
Tax on $2,520 excess at 45%		1,134	$11,474
Less: Tax credits:			
Withheld from Mr. Sandison's salary		$ 3,168	
Payments on declaration of estimated tax		8,000	11,168
Amount of tax remaining to be paid			$ 306

Notes:

(1) The loss from single proprietorship is properly deducted in arriving at adjusted gross income despite the fact that Sandison withdrew $6,000 from the business.

(2) Sandison's share of ordinary income from the partnership (S & S Business Advisers), $17,100, is fully taxable despite the fact that Sandison withdrew only $9,600 from the partnership.

(3) Sandison's salary from the Sandi Construction Company is included in gross income as $19,000, the gross salary before any deductions.

(4) The ordinary income for the partnership is determined without taking into account the contribution to the Long Beach Opera Association of $1,000 or the long-term capital gain of $4,400. These items are reported by the partners on their personal income tax return on the basis of the profit and loss sharing ratio agreed upon by the partners.

(5) The following two items of expense are not deductible in arriving at taxable income: contribution to candidate for city mayor, $250, and the special assessment on residence for street widening, $500.

(6) Medical expenses are less than 3% of adjusted gross income, and therefore none is deductible.

(7) Sandison's son, Bill, qualifies as a dependent even though he earned $1,500 because he is a full-time student.

(8) Interest on City of Norwalk bonds, $800, is not taxable.

Index

$$\begin{array}{r} 30 \\ 160\overline{\smash{\big)}\,51,300} \\ 480 \\ \hline 330 \\ 320 \\ \hline 100 \end{array}$$